D0002995

Capital in the Twenty-First Century

Winner of the *Financial Times* and McKinsey Business Book of the Year Award
Winner of the British Academy Medal
Finalist, National Book Critics Circle Award

A *Washington Post* Best Book of 2014
A *Financial Times* Best Book of 2014
A *Wall Street Journal* Favorite Read of 2014
An *Economist* Book of the Year, 2014
A *Fortune* Favorite Book of 2014
A *Globe and Mail* Best Book of 2014
An *Observer* Book of the Year, 2014
An *Independent* Economics Book of the Year, 2014
A *Sunday Times* Book That Best Explained the World in 2014
A *BBC News Magazine* "Big Ideas of 2014" Selection
An *Inc.* Top 7 Thought-Provoking Books of 2014
A *Foreign Affairs* Best Book of 2014
A *Mother Jones* Best Book of 2014
An Amazon Best Book of the Year in Business & Investing
A *Times Higher Education* Best Book of 2014
A Bloomberg News Favorite Read of 2014
A *Bloomberg View* Best Book of 2014
A *Publishers Weekly* Best Book of 2014
A *Kirkus Reviews* Best Book of 2014
A *strategy + business* Best Business Book of 2014
A *Library Journal* Best Book of 2014
A Hudson Booksellers Best Business Book, 2014
A *History Today* Book of the Year, 2014
A *Flavorwire* Best Book by Academic Publishers, 2014
An *Esquire* (UK) Best Book of 2014
A *Business Insider* Best Business Book of 2014
A *Daily Beast* Best Big Idea Book of 2014
An *Australian Financial Review* Top Page-Turner of 2014
A *Moyers & Co.* Recommended Book, 2014
A Google Trends Top Book Search of 2014

A *Choice* Outstanding Academic Title of 2014
A *Gates Notes* Top Read of 2014
A *PopMatters* Best Book of 2014
A *Scotsman* Best Book of 2014

A *New York Times* #1 Bestseller
A *Wall Street Journal* #1 Bestseller
A *USA Today* Bestseller
A *Sunday Times* Bestseller
An Amazon #1 Bestseller

"It seems safe to say that *Capital in the Twenty-First Century,* the magnum opus of the French economist Thomas Piketty, will be the most important economics book of the year—and maybe of the decade."
—Paul Krugman, *New York Times*

"The book aims to revolutionize the way people think about the economic history of the past two centuries. It may well manage the feat."
— *The Economist*

"Piketty's *Capital in the Twenty-First Century* is an intellectual tour de force, a triumph of economic history over the theoretical, mathematical modeling that has come to dominate the economics profession in recent years."
—Stephen Pearlstein, *Washington Post*

"Piketty has written an extraordinarily important book. . . . In its scale and sweep it brings us back to the founders of political economy."
—Martin Wolf, *Financial Times*

"A sweeping account of rising inequality. . . . Piketty has written a book that nobody interested in a defining issue of our era can afford to ignore."
—John Cassidy, *New Yorker*

"Stands a fair chance of becoming the most influential work of economics yet published in our young century. It is the most important study of inequality in over fifty years."
—Timothy Shenk, *The Nation*

"Piketty has transformed our economic discourse; we'll never talk about wealth and inequality the same way we used to."
—Paul Krugman, *New York Review of Books*

"The most remarkable work of economics in recent years, if not decades."
—Nick Pearce, *New Statesman*

"Its ambition is to shape debates about the next two centuries, not the past two. And in that it may succeed."
—Christopher Croke, *The Australian*

"Piketty's ground-breaking work on the historical evolution of income distribution is impressive . . . One of the best economic books in decades."
—Paul Sweeney, *Irish Times*

"[Piketty] is just about to emerge as the most important thinker of his generation . . . Unlike many economists he insists that economic thinking cannot be separated from history or politics."
—Andrew Hussey, *The Observer*

"Piketty's book is a timely intervention in the current debate about inequality and its causes."
—Robert Skidelsky, *Prospect*

"Thomas Piketty's *Capital in the Twenty-First Century* is a monumental book that will influence economic analysis (and perhaps policymaking) in the years to come. In the way it is written and the importance of the questions it asks, it is a book the classic authors of economics could have written if they lived today and had access to the vast empirical material Piketty and his colleagues collected."
—Branko Milanovic, *American Prospect*

"This book has all the makings of a classic. It has already changed the way economists think about inequality. One hopes that these ideas will percolate into the chambers of policy-makers in governments and lending institutions."
—K. Subramanian, *The Hindu*

"Piketty's book is revolutionary. It rewrites the mission of economics . . . Piketty's multi-century portrait of wealth and income obliterates economists' complacent narratives."
—Jedediah Purdy, *Los Angeles Review of Books*

"Piketty demonstrates in terrifying detail, with painstaking statistical research, that free-market capitalism, in the absence of major state redistribution, produces profound economic inequalities."
—Michael Robbins, *Chicago Tribune*

"An extraordinary sweep of history backed by remarkably detailed data and analysis . . . Piketty's economic analysis and historical proofs are breathtaking."
—Robert B. Reich, *The Guardian*

"Piketty's treatment of inequality is perfectly matched to its moment. Like [Paul] Kennedy a generation ago, Piketty has emerged as a rock star of the policy-intellectual world . . . But make no mistake, his work richly deserves all the attention it is receiving."
—Lawrence H. Summers, *Democracy*

"What makes Thomas Piketty's *Capital in the Twenty-First Century* such a triumph is that it seems to have been written specifically to demolish the great economic shibboleths of our time . . . Piketty's magnum opus."
—Thomas Frank, *Salon*

"The book is an attempt to ground the debate over inequality in strong empirical data, put the question of distribution back into economics, and open the debate not just to the entirety of the social sciences but to people themselves."
—Mike Konczal, *Boston Review*

"[A] 700-page punch in the plutocracy's pampered gut . . . It's been half a century since a book of economic history broke out of its academic silo with such fireworks."
—Giles Whittell, *The Times*

"Thomas Piketty of the Paris School of Economics has done the definitive comparative historical research on income inequality in his *Capital in the Twenty-First Century*."
—Paul Starr, *New York Review of Books*

"Piketty provides a fresh and sweeping analysis of the world's economic history that puts into question many of our core beliefs about the organization of market economies."
—Eduardo Porter, *New York Times*

"About as close to a blockbuster as there is in the world of economic literature—easily the most discussed book of its genre in years . . . Piketty challenges one of the underpinnings of modern democracies—namely, that growth and productivity make each generation better off than the previous one."
—Barrie McKenna, *Globe and Mail*

"Piketty gives us the most important work of economics since John Maynard Keynes's *General Theory*."
—Harold Meyerson, *Washington Post*

"The strength of [Piketty's] thesis is that it is founded on evidence rather than ideology."
—Oliver Kamm, *The Times*

"Defies left and right orthodoxy by arguing that worsening inequality is an inevitable outcome of free market capitalism."
—Thomas B. Edsall, *New York Times*

"Piketty's magnum opus . . . A lucid tale of why inequality in the world is increasing, and what we should be doing about it. The right leaning crowd may be dismayed with his prescriptions of stiff global wealth taxes, but neither leftists nor rightists can dispute the data that he presents."
—Ajit Ranade, *Business Today*

"Anyone remotely interested in economics needs to read Thomas Piketty's *Capital in the 21st Century*."
—Matthew Yglesias, *Slate*

"[A] timely, important book."
—Joseph E. Stiglitz, *New York Times*

"Piketty has written a trenchant critique of our current economic system."
—Michael Washburn, *Boston Globe*

"*Capital in the Twenty-First Century* is already being hailed as a seminal work of economic thought, and with very good reason."
—Thomas Flynn, *Daily Beast*

"Piketty solidifies and gives an intellectual edge to the view that something is wrong here, and something new and bold and radical has got to be done."
—Len McCluskey, *The Guardian*

"The book is a terrific achievement."
—Alan Ryan, *Literary Review*

"One of the strengths of Piketty's book is the depth and rigor of his historical analysis. Yet it is changes taking place now that make his concerns especially urgent."
—Andrew Neather, *London Evening Standard*

"There are books that you read and there are books that hit the nail on the head so hard that you want to get your teeth into them. Thomas Piketty's *Capital in the Twenty-First Century* . . . clearly belongs to the second category."
—Perry Lam, *South China Morning Post*

"[Piketty] has demolished the Western myth that all who work hard can expect success."
—Mary Riddell, *The Telegraph*

"It's going to be remembered as the economic tome of our era. Basically, Piketty has finally put to death, with data, the fallacies of trickle down economics . . . We can only hope that the politicians crafting today's economic programs will take this book to heart."
—Rana Foroohar, *Time*

"Magisterial . . . This book is economics at its best."
—Philip Roscoe, *Times Higher Education*

"[A] seminal work on capitalism."
—Madan Sabnavis, *Financial Express*

"Piketty has shown that we are living in a Second Gilded Age . . . Piketty's book is a call to citizenship, not as a series of fatalistic poses, but as a political responsibility."
—Stephen Marche, *Los Angeles Review of Books*

"Piketty hits bullseye after bullseye about the exacerbating inequalities that disfigure society . . . For [those] who suffer from the relentless blather about why the minimum wage cannot be raised; why 'job creators' cannot be taxed; and why American society remains the most open in the world, Piketty is what the doctor ordered."
—Russell Jacoby, *New Republic*

"Capital inequality has dispossessed us of our 'democratic sovereignty,' and that's something we should all really worry about . . . [Piketty's] book is as much a story about the limits of modern democratic politics as it is about the structures of inequality."
—Duncan Kelly, *Times Literary Supplement*

"[Piketty] argues that the degree of inequality is not just the product of economic forces; it is also the product of politics."
—George Fallis, *Literary Review of Canada*

"Thomas Piketty's *Capital in the Twenty-First Century* delivered a well placed kick up the backside to complacent mainstream economics."
—Paul Mason, *The Observer*

"This book is the key to understanding how the automatic accumulation and concentration of wealth poses a threat to the peaceful economies in which entrepreneurs prosper."
—Geoffrey James, *Inc.*

"One has to admire the way Piketty marshals the data to create a sweeping historical narrative, in a style reminiscent of the great thinkers of the 19th century."
—Ben Chu, *The Independent*

"*Capital in the Twenty-First Century* shows how privateers use privatization, debt creation and capital inflation as a mechanism for rent extraction, with catastrophic consequences for public services."
—Allyson Pollock, *Times Higher Education*

"Piketty's great achievement, and one possible reason for the enthusiastic reception of his book, is his effective empirical demonstration of a fact long denied by neoclassical economics and its champions throughout the world: markets, when left to their own devices, do not provide individuals with rewards that are proportional to their efforts."
—Hassan Javid, *Dawn*

CAPITAL IN THE TWENTY-FIRST CENTURY

Thomas Piketty

Translated by Arthur Goldhammer

The Belknap Press of Harvard University Press

CAMBRIDGE, MASSACHUSETTS
LONDON, ENGLAND
2017

First published as *Le capital au XXI siècle,*
copyright © 2013 Éditions du Seuil

First Harvard University Press paperback edition, 2017
Eighth printing

Design by Dean Bornstein

Library of Congress Cataloging-in-Publication Data
Piketty, Thomas, 1971–
[Capital au XXIe siècle. English]
Capital in the twenty-first century / Thomas Piketty ;
translated by Arthur Goldhammer.
pages cm
Translation of the author's Le capital au XXIe siècle.
Includes bibliographical references and index.
ISBN 978-0-674-43000-6 (alk. paper)
ISBN 978-0-674-97985-7 (pbk.)
1. Capital.   2. Income distribution.   3. Wealth.   4. Labor economics.
I. Goldhammer, Arthur, translator.   II. Title.
HB501.P43613 2014
332′.041—dc23
2013036024

Contents

Acknowledgments

This book is based on fifteen years of research (1998–2013) devoted essentially to understanding the historical dynamics of wealth and income. Much of this research was done in collaboration with other scholars.

My earlier work on high-income earners in France, *Les hauts revenus en France au 20e siècle* (2001), had the extremely good fortune to win the enthusiastic support of Anthony Atkinson and Emmanuel Saez. Without them, my modest Francocentric project would surely never have achieved the international scope it has today. Tony, who was a model for me during my graduate school days, was the first reader of my historical work on inequality in France and immediately took up the British case as well as a number of other countries. Together, we edited two thick volumes that came out in 2007 and 2010, covering twenty countries in all and constituting the most extensive database available in regard to the historical evolution of income inequality. Emmanuel and I dealt with the US case. We discovered the vertiginous growth of income of the top 1 percent since the 1970s and 1980s, and our work enjoyed a certain influence in US political debate. We also worked together on a number of theoretical papers dealing with the optimal taxation of capital and income. This book owes a great deal to these collaborative efforts.

The book was also deeply influenced by my historical work with Gilles Postel-Vinay and Jean-Laurent Rosenthal on Parisian estate records from the French Revolution to the present. This work helped me to understand in a more intimate and vivid way the significance of wealth and capital and the problems associated with measuring them. Above all, Gilles and Jean-Laurent taught me to appreciate the many similarities, as well as differences, between the structure of property around 1900–1910 and the structure of property now.

All of this work is deeply indebted to the doctoral students and young scholars with whom I have been privileged to work over the past fifteen years. Beyond their direct contribution to the research on which this book draws, their enthusiasm and energy fueled the climate of intellectual excitement in which the work matured. I am thinking in particular of Facundo Alvaredo, Laurent Bach, Antoine Bozio, Clément Carbonnier, Fabien Dell, Gabrielle Fack, Nicolas Frémeaux, Lucie Gadenne, Julien Grenet, Elise Huilery, Camille Landais, Ioana Marinescu, Elodie Morival, Nancy Qian, Dorothée Rouzet, Stefanie Stantcheva, Juliana Londono Velez, Guillaume Saint-Jacques, Christoph Schinke, Aurélie Sotura, Mathieu Valdenaire, and Gabriel Zucman. More specifically, without the efficiency, rigor, and talents of Facundo Alvaredo, the World Top Incomes Database, to which I frequently refer in these pages, would not exist. Without the enthusiasm and insistence of Camille Landais, our collaborative project on "the fiscal revolution" would never have been written. Without the careful attention to detail and impressive capacity for work of Gabriel Zucman, I would never have completed the work on the historical evolution of the capital/income ratio in wealthy countries, which plays a key role in this book.

I also want to thank the institutions that made this project possible, starting with the École des Hautes Études en Sciences Sociales, where I have served on the faculty since 2000, as well as the École Normale Supérieure and all the other institutions that contributed to the creation of the Paris School of Economics, where I have been a professor since it was founded, and of which I served as founding director from 2005 to 2007. By agreeing to join forces and become minority partners in a project that transcended the sum of their private interests, these institutions helped to create a modest public good, which I hope will continue to contribute to the development of a multipolar political economy in the twenty-first century.

Finally, thanks to Juliette, Déborah, and Hélène, my three precious daughters, for all the love and strength they give me. And thanks to Julia, who shares my life and is also my best reader. Her influence and support at every stage in the writing of this book have been essential. Without them, I would not have had the energy to see this project through to completion.

Note on the Text

In order to avoid burdening the text and footnotes with technical matters, precise details concerning historical sources, bibliographic references, statistical methods, and mathematical models have been included in a technical appendix, which can be accessed on the Internet at http://piketty.pse.ens.fr/capital21c.

In particular, the online technical appendix contains the data from which the graphs in the text were constructed, along with detailed descriptions of the relevant sources and methods. The bibliographic references and footnotes in the text have been pared down as much as possible, with more detailed references relegated to this appendix. It also contains a number of supplementary tables and figures, some of which are referred to in the notes (e.g., "see Supplementary Figure S1.1," in Chapter 1, note 21). The online technical appendix and Internet site were designed as a complement to the book, which can thus be read on several levels.

Interested readers will also find online all relevant data files (mainly in Excel or Stata format), programs, mathematical formulas and equations, references to primary sources, and links to more technical papers on which this book draws.

My goal in writing was to make this book accessible to people without any special technical training, while the book together with the technical appendix should satisfy the demands of specialists in the field. This procedure will also allow me to post revised online versions and updates of the tables, graphs, and technical apparatus. I welcome input from readers of the book or website, who can send comments and criticisms to piketty@ens.fr.

Capital in the Twenty-First Century

Introduction

"Social distinctions can be based only on common utility."
—Declaration of the Rights of Man and the Citizen, article 1, 1789

The distribution of wealth is one of today's most widely discussed and controversial issues. But what do we really know about its evolution over the long term? Do the dynamics of private capital accumulation inevitably lead to the concentration of wealth in ever fewer hands, as Karl Marx believed in the nineteenth century? Or do the balancing forces of growth, competition, and technological progress lead in later stages of development to reduced inequality and greater harmony among the classes, as Simon Kuznets thought in the twentieth century? What do we really know about how wealth and income have evolved since the eighteenth century, and what lessons can we derive from that knowledge for the century now under way?

These are the questions I attempt to answer in this book. Let me say at once that the answers contained herein are imperfect and incomplete. But they are based on much more extensive historical and comparative data than were available to previous researchers, data covering three centuries and more than twenty countries, as well as on a new theoretical framework that affords a deeper understanding of the underlying mechanisms. Modern economic growth and the diffusion of knowledge have made it possible to avoid the Marxist apocalypse but have not modified the deep structures of capital and inequality—or in any case not as much as one might have imagined in the optimistic decades following World War II. When the rate of return on capital exceeds the rate of growth of output and income, as it did in the nineteenth century and seems quite likely to do again in the twenty-first, capitalism automatically generates arbitrary and unsustainable inequalities that radically undermine the meritocratic values on which democratic societies are based. There are nevertheless ways democracy can regain control over capitalism and ensure that the general interest takes precedence over private interests, while preserving economic openness and avoiding protectionist and nationalist reactions. The policy recommendations I propose later in the book tend in this direction. They are based on lessons derived from historical experience, of which what follows is essentially a narrative.

A Debate without Data?

Intellectual and political debate about the distribution of wealth has long been based on an abundance of prejudice and a paucity of fact.

To be sure, it would be a mistake to underestimate the importance of the intuitive knowledge that everyone acquires about contemporary wealth and income levels, even in the absence of any theoretical framework or statistical analysis. Film and literature, nineteenth-century novels especially, are full of detailed information about the relative wealth and living standards of different social groups, and especially about the deep structure of inequality, the way it is justified, and its impact on individual lives. Indeed, the novels of Jane Austen and Honoré de Balzac paint striking portraits of the distribution of wealth in Britain and France between 1790 and 1830. Both novelists were intimately acquainted with the hierarchy of wealth in their respective societies. They grasped the hidden contours of wealth and its inevitable implications for the lives of men and women, including their marital strategies and personal hopes and disappointments. These and other novelists depicted the effects of inequality with a verisimilitude and evocative power that no statistical or theoretical analysis can match.

Indeed, the distribution of wealth is too important an issue to be left to economists, sociologists, historians, and philosophers. It is of interest to everyone, and that is a good thing. The concrete, physical reality of inequality is visible to the naked eye and naturally inspires sharp but contradictory political judgments. Peasant and noble, worker and factory owner, waiter and banker: each has his or her own unique vantage point and sees important aspects of how other people live and what relations of power and domination exist between social groups, and these observations shape each person's judgment of what is and is not just. Hence there will always be a fundamentally subjective and psychological dimension to inequality, which inevitably gives rise to political conflict that no purportedly scientific analysis can alleviate. Democracy will never be supplanted by a republic of experts—and that is a very good thing.

Nevertheless, the distribution question also deserves to be studied in a systematic and methodical fashion. Without precisely defined sources, methods, and concepts, it is possible to see everything and its opposite. Some people believe that inequality is always increasing and that the world is by definition always becoming more unjust. Others believe that inequality is naturally decreasing, or that harmony comes about automatically, and that in any case nothing should be done that might risk disturbing this happy equilibrium. Given this dialogue of the deaf, in which each camp justifies its own intellectual laziness by pointing to the laziness of the other, there is a role for research that is at least systematic and methodical if not fully scientific. Expert analysis will never put an end to the violent political conflict that inequality inevitably instigates. Social scientific research is and always will be tentative and imperfect. It does not claim to transform economics, sociology, and history into exact sciences. But by patiently searching for facts and patterns and calmly analyzing the economic, social, and political mechanisms that might explain them, it can inform democratic debate and focus attention on the right questions. It can help to redefine the terms of debate, unmask certain preconceived or fraudulent notions, and subject all positions to constant critical scrutiny. In my view, this is the role that intellectuals, including social scientists, should play, as citizens like any other but with the good fortune to have more time than others to devote themselves to study (and even to be paid for it—a signal privilege).

There is no escaping the fact, however, that social science research on the distribution of wealth was for a long time based on a relatively limited set of firmly established facts together with a wide variety of purely theoretical speculations. Before turning in greater detail to the sources I tried to assemble in preparation for writing this book, I want to give a quick historical overview of previous thinking about these issues.

Malthus, Young, and the French Revolution

When classical political economy was born in England and France in the late eighteenth and early nineteenth century, the issue of distribution was already one of the key questions. Everyone realized that radical transformations were under way, precipitated by sustained demographic growth—a previously unknown phenomenon—coupled with a rural exodus and the advent of the Industrial Revolution. How would these upheavals affect the distribution of wealth, the social structure, and the political equilibrium of European society?

For Thomas Malthus, who in 1798 published his *Essay on the Principle of Population,* there could be no doubt: the primary threat was overpopulation.[1] Although his sources were thin, he made the best he could of them. One particularly important influence was the travel diary published by Arthur Young, an English agronomist who traveled extensively in France, from Calais to the Pyrenees and from Brittany to Franche-Comté, in 1787–1788, on the eve of the Revolution. Young wrote of the poverty of the French countryside.

His vivid essay was by no means totally inaccurate. France at that time was by far the most populous country in Europe and therefore an ideal place to observe. The kingdom could already boast of a population of 20 million in 1700, compared to only 8 million for Great Britain (and 5 million for England alone). The French population increased steadily throughout the eighteenth century, from the end of

---

1. The English economist Thomas Malthus (1766–1834) is considered to be one of the most influential members of the "classical" school, along with Adam Smith (1723–1790) and David Ricardo (1772–1823).

Louis XIV's reign to the demise of Louis XVI, and by 1780 was close to 30 million. There is every reason to believe that this unprecedentedly rapid population growth contributed to a stagnation of agricultural wages and an increase in land rents in the decades prior to the explosion of 1789. Although this demographic shift was not the sole cause of the French Revolution, it clearly contributed to the growing unpopularity of the aristocracy and the existing political regime.

Nevertheless, Young's account, published in 1792, also bears the traces of nationalist prejudice and misleading comparison. The great agronomist found the inns in which he stayed thoroughly disagreeable and disliked the manners of the women who waited on him. Although many of his observations were banal and anecdotal, he believed he could derive universal consequences from them. He was mainly worried that the mass poverty he witnessed would lead to political upheaval. In particular, he was convinced that only the English political system, with separate houses of Parliament for aristocrats and commoners and veto power for the nobility, could allow for harmonious and peaceful development led by responsible people. He was convinced that France was headed for ruin when it decided in 1789–1790 to allow both aristocrats and commoners to sit in a single legislative body. It is no exaggeration to say that his whole account was overdetermined by his fear of revolution in France. Whenever one speaks about the distribution of wealth, politics is never very far behind, and it is difficult for anyone to escape contemporary class prejudices and interests.

When Reverend Malthus published his famous *Essay* in 1798, he reached conclusions even more radical than Young's. Like his compatriot, he was very afraid of the new political ideas emanating from France, and to reassure himself that there would be no comparable upheaval in Great Britain he argued that all welfare assistance to the poor must be halted at once and that reproduction by the poor should be severely scrutinized lest the world succumb to overpopulation leading to chaos and misery. It is impossible to understand Malthus's exaggeratedly somber predictions without recognizing the way fear gripped much of the European elite in the 1790s.

Ricardo: The Principle of Scarcity

In retrospect, it is obviously easy to make fun of these prophecies of doom. It is important to realize, however, that the economic and social transformations of the late eighteenth and early nineteenth centuries were objectively quite impressive, not to say traumatic, for those who witnessed them. Indeed, most contemporary observers—and not only Malthus and Young—shared relatively dark or even apocalyptic views of the long-run evolution of the distribution of wealth and class structure of society. This was true in particular of David Ricardo and Karl Marx, who were surely the two most influential economists of the nineteenth century and who both believed that a small social group—landowners for Ricardo, industrial capitalists for Marx—would inevitably claim a steadily increasing share of output and income.[2]

For Ricardo, who published his *Principles of Political Economy and Taxation* in 1817, the chief concern was the long-term evolution of land prices and land rents. Like Malthus, he had virtually no genuine statistics at his disposal. He nevertheless had intimate knowledge of the capitalism of his time. Born into a family of Jewish financiers with Portuguese roots, he also seems to have had fewer political prejudices than Malthus, Young, or Smith. He was influenced by the Malthusian model but pushed the argument farther. He was above all interested in the following logical paradox. Once both population and output begin to grow steadily, land tends to become increasingly scarce relative to other goods. The law of supply and demand then implies that the price of land will rise continuously, as will the rents paid to landlords. The landlords will therefore claim a growing share of national income, as the share available to the rest of the population decreases, thus upsetting the social equilibrium. For Ricardo, the only logically

---

2. There is of course a more optimistic school of liberals: Adam Smith seems to belong to it, and in fact he never really considered the possibility that the distribution of wealth might grow more unequal over the long run. The same is true of Jean-Baptiste Say (1767–1832), who also believed in natural harmony.

and politically acceptable answer was to impose a steadily increasing tax on land rents.

This somber prediction proved wrong: land rents did remain high for an extended period, but in the end the value of farm land inexorably declined relative to other forms of wealth as the share of agriculture in national income decreased. Writing in the 1810s, Ricardo had no way of anticipating the importance of technological progress or industrial growth in the years ahead. Like Malthus and Young, he could not imagine that humankind would ever be totally freed from the alimentary imperative.

His insight into the price of land is nevertheless interesting: the "scarcity principle" on which he relied meant that certain prices might rise to very high levels over many decades. This could well be enough to destabilize entire societies. The price system plays a key role in coordinating the activities of millions of individuals—indeed, today, billions of individuals in the new global economy. The problem is that the price system knows neither limits nor morality.

It would be a serious mistake to neglect the importance of the scarcity principle for understanding the global distribution of wealth in the twenty-first century. To convince oneself of this, it is enough to replace the price of farmland in Ricardo's model by the price of urban real estate in major world capitals, or, alternatively, by the price of oil. In both cases, if the trend over the period 1970–2010 is extrapolated to the period 2010–2050 or 2010–2100, the result is economic, social, and political disequilibria of considerable magnitude, not only between but within countries—disequilibria that inevitably call to mind the Ricardian apocalypse.

To be sure, there exists in principle a quite simple economic mechanism that should restore equilibrium to the process: the mechanism of supply and demand. If the supply of any good is insufficient, and its price is too high, then demand for that good should decrease, which should lead to a decline in its price. In other words, if real estate and oil prices rise, then people should move to the country or take to traveling about by bicycle (or both). Never mind that such adjustments might be unpleasant or complicated; they might also take decades, during which landlords and oil well owners might well accumulate claims on the rest of the population so extensive that they could easily come to own everything that can be owned, including rural real estate and bicycles, once and for all.[3] As always, the worst is never certain to arrive. It is much too soon to warn readers that by 2050 they may be paying rent to the emir of Qatar. I will consider the matter in due course, and my answer will be more nuanced, albeit only moderately reassuring. But it is important for now to understand that the interplay of supply and demand in no way rules out the possibility of a large and lasting divergence in the distribution of wealth linked to extreme changes in certain relative prices. This is the principal implication of Ricardo's scarcity principle. But nothing obliges us to roll the dice.

Marx: The Principle of Infinite Accumulation

By the time Marx published the first volume of *Capital* in 1867, exactly one-half century after the publication of Ricardo's *Principles,* economic and social realities had changed profoundly: the question was no longer whether farmers could feed a growing population or land prices would rise sky high but rather how to understand the dynamics of industrial capitalism, now in full blossom.

The most striking fact of the day was the misery of the industrial proletariat. Despite the growth of the economy, or perhaps in part because of it, and because, as well, of the vast rural exodus owing to both population growth and increasing agricultural productivity, workers crowded into urban slums. The working day was long, and wages were very low. A new urban misery emerged, more visible, more shocking, and in some respects even more extreme than the rural misery of the

---

3. The other possibility is to increase supply of the scarce good, for example by finding new oil deposits (or new sources of energy, if possible cleaner than oil), or by moving toward a more dense urban environment (by constructing high-rise housing, for example), which raises other difficulties. In any case, this, too, can take decades to accomplish.

Old Regime. *Germinal, Oliver Twist,* and *Les Misérables* did not spring from the imaginations of their authors, any more than did laws limiting child labor in factories to children older than eight (in France in 1841) or ten in the mines (in Britain in 1842). Dr. Villermé's *Tableau de l'état physique et moral des ouvriers employés dans les manufactures,* published in France in 1840 (leading to the passage of a timid new child labor law in 1841), described the same sordid reality as *The Condition of the Working Class in England,* which Friedrich Engels published in 1845.[4]

In fact, all the historical data at our disposal today indicate that it was not until the second half—or even the final third—of the nineteenth century that a significant rise in the purchasing power of wages occurred. From the first to the sixth decade of the nineteenth century, workers' wages stagnated at very low levels—close or even inferior to the levels of the eighteenth and previous centuries. This long phase of wage stagnation, which we observe in Britain as well as France, stands out all the more because economic growth was accelerating in this period. The capital share of national income—industrial profits, land rents, and building rents—insofar as can be estimated with the imperfect sources available today, increased considerably in both countries in the first half of the nineteenth century.[5] It would decrease slightly in the final decades of the nineteenth century, as wages partly caught up with growth. The data we have assembled nevertheless reveal no structural decrease in inequality prior to World War I. What we see in the period 1870–1914 is at best a stabilization of inequality at an

---

4. Friedrich Engels (1820–1895), who had direct experience of his subject, would become the friend and collaborator of the German philosopher and economist Karl Marx (1818–1883). He settled in Manchester in 1842, where he managed a factory owned by his father.

5. The historian Robert Allen recently proposed to call this long period of wage stagnation "Engels' pause." See Allen, "Engels' Pause: A Pessimist's Guide to the British Industrial Revolution," Oxford University Department of Economics Working Papers 315 (2007). See also "Engels' Pause: Technical Change, Capital Accumulation, and Inequality in the British Industrial Revolution," in *Explorations in Economic History* 46, no. 4 (October 2009): 418–35.

extremely high level, and in certain respects an endless inegalitarian spiral, marked in particular by increasing concentration of wealth. It is quite difficult to say where this trajectory would have led without the major economic and political shocks initiated by the war. With the aid of historical analysis and a little perspective, we can now see those shocks as the only forces since the Industrial Revolution powerful enough to reduce inequality.

In any case, capital prospered in the 1840s and industrial profits grew, while labor incomes stagnated. This was obvious to everyone, even though in those days aggregate national statistics did not yet exist. It was in this context that the first communist and socialist movements developed. The central argument was simple: What was the good of industrial development, what was the good of all the technological innovations, toil, and population movements if, after half a century of industrial growth, the condition of the masses was still just as miserable as before, and all lawmakers could do was prohibit factory labor by children under the age of eight? The bankruptcy of the existing economic and political system seemed obvious. People therefore wondered about its long-term evolution: What could one say about it?

This was the task Marx set himself. In 1848, on the eve of the "spring of nations" (that is, the revolutions that broke out across Europe that spring), he published *The Communist Manifesto,* a short, hard-hitting text whose first chapter began with the famous words "A specter is haunting Europe—the specter of communism."[6] The text ended with the equally famous prediction of revolution: "The development of Modern Industry, therefore, cuts from under its feet the very foundation on which the bourgeoisie produces and appropriates products. What the bourgeoisie therefore produces, above all, are its own gravediggers. Its fall and the victory of the proletariat are equally inevitable."

---

6. The opening passage continues: "All the powers of old Europe have entered into a holy alliance to exorcise this specter: Pope and Tsar, Metternich and Guizot, French Radicals and German police-spies." No doubt Marx's literary talent partially accounts for his immense influence.

Over the next two decades, Marx labored over the voluminous treatise that would justify this conclusion and propose the first scientific analysis of capitalism and its collapse. This work would remain unfinished: the first volume of *Capital* was published in 1867, but Marx died in 1883 without having completed the two subsequent volumes. His friend Engels published them posthumously after piecing together a text from the sometimes obscure fragments of manuscript Marx had left behind.

Like Ricardo, Marx based his work on an analysis of the internal logical contradictions of the capitalist system. He therefore sought to distinguish himself from both bourgeois economists (who saw the market as a self-regulated system, that is, a system capable of achieving equilibrium on its own without major deviations, in accordance with Adam Smith's image of "the invisible hand" and Jean-Baptiste Say's "law" that production creates its own demand), and utopian socialists and Proudhonians, who in Marx's view were content to denounce the misery of the working class without proposing a truly scientific analysis of the economic processes responsible for it.[7] In short, Marx took the Ricardian model of the price of capital and the principle of scarcity as the basis of a more thorough analysis of the dynamics of capitalism in a world where capital was primarily industrial (machinery, plants, etc.) rather than landed property, so that in principle there was no limit to the amount of capital that could be accumulated. In fact, his principal conclusion was what one might call the "principle of infinite accumulation," that is, the inexorable tendency for capital to accumulate and become concentrated in ever fewer hands, with no natural limit to the process. This is the basis of Marx's prediction of an apocalyptic end to capitalism: either the rate of return on capital would steadily diminish (thereby killing the engine of accumulation and leading to violent conflict among capitalists), or capital's share of national income would increase indefinitely (which sooner or later would unite the

---

7. In 1847 Marx published *The Misery of Philosophy*, in which he mocked Proudhon's *Philosophy of Misery*, which was published a few years earlier.

workers in revolt). In either case, no stable socioeconomic or political equilibrium was possible.

Marx's dark prophecy came no closer to being realized than Ricardo's. In the last third of the nineteenth century, wages finally began to increase: the improvement in the purchasing power of workers spread everywhere, and this changed the situation radically, even if extreme inequalities persisted and in some respects continued to increase until World War I. The communist revolution did indeed take place, but in the most backward country in Europe, Russia, where the Industrial Revolution had scarcely begun, whereas the most advanced European countries explored other, social democratic avenues—fortunately for their citizens. Like his predecessors, Marx totally neglected the possibility of durable technological progress and steadily increasing productivity, which is a force that can to some extent serve as a counterweight to the process of accumulation and concentration of private capital. He no doubt lacked the statistical data needed to refine his predictions. He probably suffered as well from having decided on his conclusions in 1848, before embarking on the research needed to justify them. Marx evidently wrote in great political fervor, which at times led him to issue hasty pronouncements from which it was difficult to escape. That is why economic theory needs to be rooted in historical sources that are as complete as possible, and in this respect Marx did not exploit all the possibilities available to him.[8] What is more, he devoted little thought to the question of how a society in which private capital had been totally abolished would be organized politically and economically—a complex issue if ever there was one, as shown by the tragic totalitarian experiments undertaken in states where private capital was abolished.

Despite these limitations, Marx's analysis remains relevant in several respects. First, he began with an important question (concerning

---

8. In Chapter 6 I return to the theme of Marx's use of statistics. To summarize: he occasionally sought to make use of the best available statistics of the day (which were better than the statistics available to Malthus and Ricardo but still quite rudimentary), but he usually did so in a rather impressionistic way and without always establishing a clear connection to his theoretical argument.

the unprecedented concentration of wealth during the Industrial Revolution) and tried to answer it with the means at his disposal: economists today would do well to take inspiration from his example. Even more important, the principle of infinite accumulation that Marx proposed contains a key insight, as valid for the study of the twenty-first century as it was for the nineteenth and in some respects more worrisome than Ricardo's principle of scarcity. If the rates of population and productivity growth are relatively low, then accumulated wealth naturally takes on considerable importance, especially if it grows to extreme proportions and becomes socially destabilizing. In other words, low growth cannot adequately counterbalance the Marxist principle of infinite accumulation: the resulting equilibrium is not as apocalyptic as the one predicted by Marx but is nevertheless quite disturbing. Accumulation ends at a finite level, but that level may be high enough to be destabilizing. In particular, the very high level of private wealth that has been attained since the 1980s and 1990s in the wealthy countries of Europe and in Japan, measured in years of national income, directly reflects the Marxian logic.

From Marx to Kuznets, or Apocalypse to Fairy Tale

Turning from the nineteenth-century analyses of Ricardo and Marx to the twentieth-century analyses of Simon Kuznets, we might say that economists' no doubt overly developed taste for apocalyptic predictions gave way to a similarly excessive fondness for fairy tales, or at any rate happy endings. According to Kuznets's theory, income inequality would automatically decrease in advanced phases of capitalist development, regardless of economic policy choices or other differences between countries, until eventually it stabilized at an acceptable level. Proposed in 1955, this was really a theory of the magical postwar years referred to in France as the "Trente Glorieuses," the thirty glorious years from 1945 to 1975.[9] For

---

9. Simon Kuznets, "Economic Growth and Income Inequality," *American Economic Review* 45, no. 1 (1955): 1–28.

Kuznets, it was enough to be patient, and before long growth would benefit everyone. The philosophy of the moment was summed up in a single sentence: "Growth is a rising tide that lifts all boats." A similar optimism can also be seen in Robert Solow's 1956 analysis of the conditions necessary for an economy to achieve a "balanced growth path," that is, a growth trajectory along which all variables—output, incomes, profits, wages, capital, asset prices, and so on—would progress at the same pace, so that every social group would benefit from growth to the same degree, with no major deviations from the norm.[10] Kuznets's position was thus diametrically opposed to the Ricardian and Marxist idea of an inegalitarian spiral and antithetical to the apocalyptic predictions of the nineteenth century.

In order to properly convey the considerable influence that Kuznets's theory enjoyed in the 1980s and 1990s and to a certain extent still enjoys today, it is important to emphasize that it was the first theory of this sort to rely on a formidable statistical apparatus. It was not until the middle of the twentieth century, in fact, that the first historical series of income distribution statistics became available with the publication in 1953 of Kuznets's monumental *Shares of Upper Income Groups in Income and Savings*. Kuznets's series dealt with only one country (the United States) over a period of thirty-five years (1913–1948). It was nevertheless a major contribution, which drew on two sources of data totally unavailable to nineteenth-century authors: US federal income tax returns (which did not exist before the creation of the income tax in 1913) and Kuznets's own estimates of US national income from a few years earlier. This was the very first attempt to measure social inequality on such an ambitious scale.[11]

---

10. Robert Solow, "A Contribution to the Theory of Economic Growth," *Quarterly Journal of Economics* 70, no. 1 (February 1956): 65–94.

11. See Simon Kuznets, *Shares of Upper Income Groups in Income and Savings* (Cambridge, MA: National Bureau of Economic Research, 1953). Kuznets was an American economist, born in Ukraine in 1901, who settled in the United States in 1922 and became a professor at Harvard after studying at Columbia University. He died in 1985. He was the first person to study the national accounts of the United States and the first to publish historical data on inequality.

It is important to realize that without these two complementary and indispensable datasets, it is simply impossible to measure inequality in the income distribution or to gauge its evolution over time. To be sure, the first attempts to estimate national income in Britain and France date back to the late seventeenth and early eighteenth century, and there would be many more such attempts over the course of the nineteenth century. But these were isolated estimates. It was not until the twentieth century, in the years between the two world wars, that the first yearly series of national income data were developed by economists such as Kuznets and John W. Kendrick in the United States, Arthur Bowley and Colin Clark in Britain, and L. Dugé de Bernonville in France. This type of data allows us to measure a country's total income. In order to gauge the share of high incomes in national income, we also need statements of income. Such information became available when many countries adopted a progressive income tax around the time of World War I (1913 in the United States, 1914 in France, 1909 in Britain, 1922 in India, 1932 in Argentina).[12]

It is crucial to recognize that even where there is no income tax, there are still all sorts of statistics concerning whatever tax basis exists at a given point in time (for example, the distribution of the number of doors and windows by *département* in nineteenth-century France, which is not without interest), but these data tell us nothing about incomes. What is more, before the requirement to declare one's income to the tax authorities was enacted in law, people were often unaware of the amount of their own income. The same is true of the corporate tax and wealth tax. Taxation is not only a way of requiring all citizens to contribute to the financing of public expenditures and projects and to distribute the tax burden as fairly as possible; it is also useful for establishing classifications and promoting knowledge as well as democratic transparency.

---

12. Because it is often the case that only a portion of the population is required to file income tax returns, we also need national accounts in order to measure total income.

In any event, the data that Kuznets collected allowed him to calculate the evolution of the share of each decile, as well as of the upper centiles, of the income hierarchy in total US national income. What did he find? He noted a sharp reduction in income inequality in the United States between 1913 and 1948. More specifically, at the beginning of this period, the upper decile of the income distribution (that is, the top 10 percent of US earners) claimed 45–50 percent of annual national income. By the late 1940s, the share of the top decile had decreased to roughly 30–35 percent of national income. This decrease of nearly 10 percentage points was considerable: for example, it was equal to half the income of the poorest 50 percent of Americans.[13] The reduction of inequality was clear and incontrovertible. This was news of considerable importance, and it had an enormous impact on economic debate in the postwar era in both universities and international organizations.

Malthus, Ricardo, Marx, and many others had been talking about inequalities for decades without citing any sources whatsoever or any methods for comparing one era with another or deciding between competing hypotheses. Now, for the first time, objective data were available. Although the information was not perfect, it had the merit of existing. What is more, the work of compilation was extremely well documented: the weighty volume that Kuznets published in 1953 revealed his sources and methods in the most minute detail, so that every calculation could be reproduced. And besides that, Kuznets was the bearer of good news: inequality was shrinking.

The Kuznets Curve: Good News in the Midst of the Cold War

In fact, Kuznets himself was well aware that the compression of high US incomes between 1913 and 1948 was largely accidental. It stemmed in large part from multiple shocks triggered by the Great Depression

---

13. Put differently, the middle and working classes, defined as the poorest 90 percent of the US population, saw their share of national income increase from 50–55 percent in the 1910s and 1920s to 65–70 percent in the late 1940s.

and World War II and had little to do with any natural or automatic process. In his 1953 work, he analyzed his series in detail and warned readers not to make hasty generalizations. But in December 1954, at the Detroit meeting of the American Economic Association, of which he was president, he offered a far more optimistic interpretation of his results than he had given in 1953. It was this lecture, published in 1955 under the title "Economic Growth and Income Inequality," that gave rise to the theory of the "Kuznets curve."

According to this theory, inequality everywhere can be expected to follow a "bell curve." In other words, it should first increase and then decrease over the course of industrialization and economic development. According to Kuznets, a first phase of naturally increasing inequality associated with the early stages of industrialization, which in the United States meant, broadly speaking, the nineteenth century, would be followed by a phase of sharply decreasing inequality, which in the United States allegedly began in the first half of the twentieth century.

Kuznets's 1955 paper is enlightening. After reminding readers of all the reasons for interpreting the data cautiously and noting the obvious importance of exogenous shocks in the recent reduction of inequality in the United States, Kuznets suggests, almost innocently in passing, that the internal logic of economic development might also yield the same result, quite apart from any policy intervention or external shock. The idea was that inequalities increase in the early phases of industrialization, because only a minority is prepared to benefit from the new wealth that industrialization brings. Later, in more advanced phases of development, inequality automatically decreases as a larger and larger fraction of the population partakes of the fruits of economic growth.[14]

---

14. See Kuznets, *Shares of Upper Income Groups*, 12–18. The Kuznets curve is sometimes referred to as "the inverted-U curve." Specifically, Kuznets suggests that growing numbers of workers move from the poor agricultural sector into the rich industrial sector. At first, only a minority benefits from the wealth of the industrial sector, hence inequality increases. But eventually everyone benefits, so inequality

The "advanced phase" of industrial development is supposed to have begun toward the end of the nineteenth or the beginning of the twentieth century in the industrialized countries, and the reduction of inequality observed in the United States between 1913 and 1948 could therefore be portrayed as one instance of a more general phenomenon, which should theoretically reproduce itself everywhere, including underdeveloped countries then mired in postcolonial poverty. The data Kuznets had presented in his 1953 book suddenly became a powerful political weapon.[15] He was well aware of the highly speculative nature of his theorizing.[16] Nevertheless, by presenting such an optimistic theory in the context of a "presidential address" to the main professional association of US economists, an audience that was inclined to believe and disseminate the good news delivered by their prestigious leader, he knew that he would wield considerable influence: thus the "Kuznets curve" was born. In order to make sure that everyone understood what was at stake, he took care to remind his listeners that the intent of his optimistic predictions was quite simply to maintain the underdeveloped countries "within the orbit of the free world."[17] In large part, then, the theory of the Kuznets curve was a product of the Cold War.

To avoid any misunderstanding, let me say that Kuznets's work in establishing the first US national accounts data and the first historical series of inequality measures was of the utmost importance, and it is clear from reading his books (as opposed to his papers) that he shared

---

decreases. It should be obvious that this highly stylized mechanism can be generalized. For example, labor can be transferred between industrial sectors or between jobs that are more or less well paid.

15. It is interesting to note that Kuznets had no data to demonstrate the increase of inequality in the nineteenth century, but it seemed obvious to him (as to most observers) that such an increase had occurred.

16. As Kuznets himself put it: "This is perhaps 5 percent empirical information and 95 percent speculation, some of it possibly tainted by wishful thinking." See Kuznets, *Economic Growth and Income Inequality*, 24–26.

17. "The future prospect of underdeveloped countries within the orbit of the free world" (28).

the true scientific ethic. In addition, the high growth rates observed in all the developed countries in the post–World War II period were a phenomenon of great significance, as was the still more significant fact that all social groups shared in the fruits of growth. It is quite understandable that the Trente Glorieuses fostered a certain degree of optimism and that the apocalyptic predictions of the nineteenth century concerning the distribution of wealth forfeited some of their popularity.

Nevertheless, the magical Kuznets curve theory was formulated in large part for the wrong reasons, and its empirical underpinnings were extremely fragile. The sharp reduction in income inequality that we observe in almost all the rich countries between 1914 and 1945 was due above all to the world wars and the violent economic and political shocks they entailed (especially for people with large fortunes). It had little to do with the tranquil process of intersectoral mobility described by Kuznets.

Putting the Distributional Question Back at the Heart of Economic Analysis

The question is important, and not just for historical reasons. Since the 1970s, income inequality has increased significantly in the rich countries, especially the United States, where the concentration of income in the first decade of the twenty-first century regained— indeed, slightly exceeded—the level attained in the second decade of the previous century. It is therefore crucial to understand clearly why and how inequality decreased in the interim. To be sure, the very rapid growth of poor and emerging countries, especially China, may well prove to be a potent force for reducing inequalities at the global level, just as the growth of the rich countries did during the period 1945–1975. But this process has generated deep anxiety in the emerging countries and even deeper anxiety in the rich countries. Furthermore, the impressive disequilibria observed in recent decades in the financial, oil, and real estate markets have naturally aroused doubts as to the inevitability of the "balanced growth path" described by Solow and Kuznets, according to whom all key economic variables are supposed to move at the same pace. Will the world in 2050 or 2100 be owned by traders, top managers, and the superrich, or will it belong to the oil-producing countries or the Bank of China? Or perhaps it will be owned by the tax havens in which many of these actors will have sought refuge. It would be absurd not to raise the question of who will own what and simply to assume from the outset that growth is naturally "balanced" in the long run.

In a way, we are in the same position at the beginning of the twenty-first century as our forebears were in the early nineteenth century: we are witnessing impressive changes in economies around the world, and it is very difficult to know how extensive they will turn out to be or what the global distribution of wealth, both within and between countries, will look like several decades from now. The economists of the nineteenth century deserve immense credit for placing the distributional question at the heart of economic analysis and for seeking to study long-term trends. Their answers were not always satisfactory, but at least they were asking the right questions. There is no fundamental reason why we should believe that growth is automatically balanced. It is long since past the time when we should have put the question of inequality back at the center of economic analysis and begun asking questions first raised in the nineteenth century. For far too long, economists have neglected the distribution of wealth, partly because of Kuznets's optimistic conclusions and partly because of the profession's undue enthusiasm for simplistic mathematical models based on so-called representative agents.[18] If the question of

---

18. In these representative-agent models, which have become ubiquitous in economic teaching and research since the 1960s, one assumes from the outset that each agent receives the same wage, is endowed with the same wealth, and enjoys the same sources of income, so that growth proportionately benefits all social groups by definition. Such a simplification of reality may be justified for the study of certain very specific problems but clearly limits the set of economic questions one can ask.

inequality is again to become central, we must begin by gathering as extensive as possible a set of historical data for the purpose of understanding past and present trends. For it is by patiently establishing facts and patterns and then comparing different countries that we can hope to identify the mechanisms at work and gain a clearer idea of the future.

The Sources Used in This Book

This book is based on sources of two main types, which together make it possible to study the historical dynamics of wealth distribution: sources dealing with the inequality and distribution of income, and sources dealing with the distribution of wealth and the relation of wealth to income.

To begin with income: in large part, my work has simply broadened the spatial and temporal limits of Kuznets's innovative and pioneering work on the evolution of income inequality in the United States between 1913 and 1948. In this way I have been able to put Kuznets's findings (which are quite accurate) into a wider perspective and thus radically challenge his optimistic view of the relation between economic development and the distribution of wealth. Oddly, no one has ever systematically pursued Kuznets's work, no doubt in part because the historical and statistical study of tax records falls into a sort of academic no-man's-land, too historical for economists and too economistic for historians. That is a pity, because the dynamics of income inequality can only be studied in a long-run perspective, which is possible only if one makes use of tax records.[19]

---

19. Household income and budget studies by national statistical agencies rarely date back before 1970 and tend to seriously underestimate higher incomes, which is problematic because the upper income decile often owns as much as half the national wealth. Tax records, for all their limitations, tell us more about high incomes and enable us to look back a century in time.

I began by extending Kuznets's methods to France, and I published the results of that study in a book that appeared in 2001.[20] I then joined forces with several colleagues—Anthony Atkinson and Emmanuel Saez foremost among them—and with their help was able to expand the coverage to a much wider range of countries. Anthony Atkinson looked at Great Britain and a number of other countries, and together we edited two volumes that appeared in 2007 and 2010, in which we reported the results for some twenty countries throughout the world.[21] Together with Emmanuel Saez, I extended Kuznets's series for the United States by half a century.[22] Saez himself looked at a number of other key countries, such as Canada and Japan. Many other investigators contributed to this joint effort: in particular, Facundo Alvaredo studied Argentina, Spain, and Portugal; Fabien Dell looked at Germany and Switzerland; and Abhijit Banerjee and I investigated the Indian case. With the help of Nancy Qian I was able to work on China. And so on.[23]

In each case, we tried to use the same types of sources, the same methods, and the same concepts. Deciles and centiles of high incomes were estimated from tax data based on stated incomes (corrected in various ways to ensure temporal and geographic homogeneity of data and concepts). National income and average income were derived from national accounts, which in some cases had to be fleshed out or

---

20. See Thomas Piketty, *Les hauts revenus en France au 20e siècle: Inégalités et redistributions 1901–1998* (Paris: Grasset, 2001). For a summary, see "Income Inequality in France, 1901–1998," *Journal of Political Economy* 111, no. 5 (2003): 1004–42.

21. See Anthony Atkinson and Thomas Piketty, *Top Incomes over the Twentieth Century: A Contrast between Continental-European and English-Speaking Countries* (Oxford: Oxford University Press, 2007), and *Top Incomes: A Global Perspective* (Oxford: Oxford University Press, 2010).

22. See Thomas Piketty and Emmanuel Saez, "Income Inequality in the United States, 1913–1998," *Quarterly Journal of Economics* 118, no. 1 (February 2003): 1–39.

23. A complete bibliography is available in the online technical appendix. For an overview, see also Anthony Atkinson, Thomas Piketty, and Emmanuel Saez, "Top Incomes in the Long-Run of History," *Journal of Economic Literature* 49, no. 1 (March 2011): 3–71.

extended. Broadly speaking, our data series begin in each country when an income tax was established (generally between 1910 and 1920 but in some countries, such as Japan and Germany, as early as the 1880s and in other countries somewhat later). These series are regularly updated and at this writing extend to the early 2010s.

Ultimately, the World Top Incomes Database (WTID), which is based on the joint work of some thirty researchers around the world, is the largest historical database available concerning the evolution of income inequality; it is the primary source of data for this book.[24]

The book's second most important source of data, on which I will actually draw first, concerns wealth, including both the distribution of wealth and its relation to income. Wealth also generates income and is therefore important on the income study side of things as well. Indeed, income consists of two components: income from labor (wages, salaries, bonuses, earnings from nonwage labor, and other remuneration statutorily classified as labor related) and income from capital (rent, dividends, interest, profits, capital gains, royalties, and other income derived from the mere fact of owning capital in the form of land, real estate, financial instruments, industrial equipment, etc., again regardless of its precise legal classification). The WTID contains a great deal of information about the evolution of income from capital over the course of the twentieth century. It is nevertheless essential to complete this information by looking at sources directly concerned with wealth. Here I rely on three distinct types of historical data and methodology, each of which is complementary to the others.[25]

---

24. It is obviously impossible to give a detailed account of each country in this book, which offers a general overview. Interested readers can turn to the complete data series, which are available online at the WTID website (http://topincomes.paris schoolofeconomics.eu) as well as in the more technical books and articles cited above. Many texts and documents are also available in the online technical appendix (http://piketty.pse.ens.fr/capital21c).

25. The WTID is currently being transformed into the World Wealth and Income Database (WWID), which will integrate the three subtypes of complementary data. In this book I will present an overview of the information that is currently available.

In the first place, just as income tax returns allow us to study changes in income inequality, estate tax returns enable us to study changes in the inequality of wealth.[26] This approach was introduced by Robert Lampman in 1962 to study changes in the inequality of wealth in the United States from 1922 to 1956. Later, in 1978, Anthony Atkinson and Alan Harrison studied the British case from 1923 to 1972.[27] These results were recently updated and extended to other countries such as France and Sweden. Unfortunately, data are available for fewer countries than in the case of income inequality. In a few cases, however, estate tax data extend back much further in time, often to the beginning of the nineteenth century, because estate taxes predate income taxes. In particular, I have compiled data collected by the French government at various times and, together with Gilles Postel-Vinay and Jean-Laurent Rosenthal, have put together a huge collection of individual estate tax returns, with which it has been possible to establish homogeneous series of data on the concentration of wealth in France since the Revolution.[28] This will allow us to see the shocks due to World War I in a much broader context than the series dealing with income inequality (which unfortunately date back only as far as 1910 or so). The work of Jesper Roine and Daniel Waldenström on Swedish historical sources is also instructive.[29]

The data on wealth and inheritance also enable us to study changes in the relative importance of inherited wealth and savings in the con-

---

26. One can also use annual wealth tax returns in countries where such a tax is imposed in living individuals, but over the long run estate tax data are easier to come by.

27. See the following pioneering works: R. J. Lampman, *The Share of Top Wealth-Holders in National Wealth, 1922–1956* (Princeton: Princeton University Press, 1962); Anthony Atkinson and A. J. Harrison, *Distribution of Personal Wealth in Britain, 1923–1972* (Cambridge: Cambridge University Press, 1978).

28. See Thomas Piketty, Gilles Postel-Vinay, and Jean-Laurent Rosenthal, "Wealth Concentration in a Developing Economy: Paris and France, 1807–1994," *American Economic Review* 96, no. 1 (March 2006): 236–56.

29. See Jesper Roine and Daniel Waldenström, "Wealth Concentration over the Path of Development: Sweden, 1873–2006," *Scandinavian Journal of Economics* 111, no. 1 (March 2009): 151–87.

stitution of fortunes and the dynamics of wealth inequality. This work is fairly complete in the case of France, where the very rich historical sources offer a unique vantage point from which to observe changing inheritance patterns over the long run.[30] To one degree or another, my colleagues and I have extended this work to other countries, especially Great Britain, Germany, Sweden, and the United States. These materials play a crucial role in this study, because the significance of inequalities of wealth differs depending on whether those inequalities derive from inherited wealth or savings. In this book, I focus not only on the level of inequality as such but to an even greater extent on the structure of inequality, that is, on the origins of disparities in income and wealth between social groups and on the various systems of economic, social, moral, and political justification that have been invoked to defend or condemn those disparities. Inequality is not necessarily bad in itself: the key question is to decide whether it is justified, whether there are reasons for it.

Last but not least, we can also use data that allow us to measure the total stock of national wealth (including land, other real estate, and industrial and financial capital) over a very long period of time. We can measure this wealth for each country in terms of the number of years of national income required to amass it. This type of global study of the capital / income ratio has its limits. It is always preferable to analyze wealth inequality at the individual level as well, and to gauge the relative importance of inheritance and saving in capital formation. Nevertheless, the capital / income approach can give us an overview of the importance of capital to the society as a whole. Moreover, in some cases (especially Britain and France) it is possible to collect and compare estimates for different periods and thus push the analysis back to the early eighteenth century, which allows us to view the Industrial Revolution in relation to the history of capital. For this I will

---

30. See Thomas Piketty, "On the Long-Run Evolution of Inheritance: France 1820–2050," École d'économie de Paris, PSE Working Papers (2010). Summary version published in *Quarterly Journal of Economics* 126, no. 3 (2011): 1071–1131.

rely on historical data Gabriel Zucman and I recently collected.[31] Broadly speaking, this research is merely an extension and generalization of Raymond Goldsmith's work on national balance sheets in the 1970s.[32]

Compared with previous works, one reason why this book stands out is that I have made an effort to collect as complete and consistent a set of historical sources as possible in order to study the dynamics of income and wealth distribution over the long run. To that end, I had two advantages over previous authors. First, this work benefits, naturally enough, from a longer historical perspective than its predecessors had (and some long-term changes did not emerge clearly until data for the 2000s became available, largely owing to the fact that certain shocks due to the world wars persisted for a very long time). Second, advances in computer technology have made it much easier to collect and process large amounts of historical data.

Although I have no wish to exaggerate the role of technology in the history of ideas, the purely technical issues are worth a moment's reflection. Objectively speaking, it was far more difficult to deal with large volumes of historical data in Kuznets's time than it is today. This was true to a large extent as recently as the 1980s. In the 1970s, when Alice Hanson Jones collected US estate inventories from the colonial era and Adeline Daumard worked on French estate records from the nineteenth century,[33] they worked mainly by hand, using index cards. When we reread their remarkable work today, or look at François Siminad's work on the evolution of wages in the nineteenth century

---

31. See Thomas Piketty and Gabriel Zucman, "Capital Is Back: Wealth-Income Ratios in Rich Countries, 1700–2010" (Paris: École d'économie de Paris, 2013).

32. See esp. Raymond Goldsmith, *Comparative National Balance Sheets: A Study of Twenty Countries, 1688–1978* (Chicago: University of Chicago Press, 1985). More complete references may be found in the online technical appendix.

33. See A. H. Jones, *American Colonial Wealth: Documents and Methods* (New York: Arno Press, 1977), and Adeline Daumard, *Les fortunes françaises au 19e siècle: Enquête sur la répartition et la composition des capitaux privés à Paris, Lyon, Lille, Bordeaux et Toulouse d'après l'enregistrement des déclarations de successions* (Paris: Mouton, 1973).

or Ernest Labrousse's work on the history of prices and incomes in the eighteenth century or Jean Bouvier and François Furet's work on the variability of profits in the nineteenth century, it is clear that these scholars had to overcome major material difficulties in order to compile and process their data.[34] In many cases, the technical difficulties absorbed much of their energy, taking precedence over analysis and interpretation, especially since the technical problems imposed strict limits on their ability to make international and temporal comparisons. It is much easier to study the history of the distribution of wealth today than in the past. This book is heavily indebted to recent improvements in the technology of research.[35]

The Major Results of This Study

What are the major conclusions to which these novel historical sources have led me? The first is that one should be wary of any economic determinism in regard to inequalities of wealth and income. The history of the distribution of wealth has always been deeply political, and it cannot be reduced to purely economic mechanisms. In particular, the reduction of inequality that took place in most developed countries between 1910 and 1950 was above all a consequence of war and of policies adopted to cope with the shocks of war. Similarly, the resurgence of inequality after 1980 is due largely to the political shifts of the past several decades, especially in regard to taxation and finance. The history of inequality is shaped by the way economic, social, and

---

34. See in particular François Simiand, *Le salaire, l'évolution sociale et la monnaie* (Paris: Alcan, 1932); Ernest Labrousse, *Esquisse du mouvement des prix et des revenus en France au 18e siècle* (Paris: Librairie Dalloz, 1933); Jean Bouvier, François Furet, and M. Gillet, *Le mouvement du profit en France au 19e siècle: Matériaux et études* (Paris: Mouton, 1965).

35. There are also intrinsically intellectual reasons for the decline of economic and social history based on the evolution of prices, incomes, and fortunes (sometimes referred to as "serial history"). In my view, this decline is unfortunate as well as reversible. I will come back to this point.

political actors view what is just and what is not, as well as by the relative power of those actors and the collective choices that result. It is the joint product of all relevant actors combined.

The second conclusion, which is the heart of the book, is that the dynamics of wealth distribution reveal powerful mechanisms pushing alternately toward convergence and divergence. Furthermore, there is no natural, spontaneous process to prevent destabilizing, inegalitarian forces from prevailing permanently.

Consider first the mechanisms pushing toward convergence, that is, toward reduction and compression of inequalities. The main forces for convergence are the diffusion of knowledge and investment in training and skills. The law of supply and demand, as well as the mobility of capital and labor, which is a variant of that law, may always tend toward convergence as well, but the influence of this economic law is less powerful than the diffusion of knowledge and skill and is frequently ambiguous or contradictory in its implications. Knowledge and skill diffusion is the key to overall productivity growth as well as the reduction of inequality both within and between countries. We see this at present in the advances made by a number of previously poor countries, led by China. These emergent economies are now in the process of catching up with the advanced ones. By adopting the modes of production of the rich countries and acquiring skills comparable to those found elsewhere, the less developed countries have leapt forward in productivity and increased their national incomes. The technological convergence process may be abetted by open borders for trade, but it is fundamentally a process of the diffusion and sharing of knowledge—the public good par excellence—rather than a market mechanism.

From a strictly theoretical standpoint, other forces pushing toward greater equality might exist. One might, for example, assume that production technologies tend over time to require greater skills on the part of workers, so that labor's share of income will rise as capital's share falls: one might call this the "rising human capital hypothesis."

In other words, the progress of technological rationality is supposed to lead automatically to the triumph of human capital over financial capital and real estate, capable managers over fat-cat stockholders, and skill over nepotism. Inequalities would thus become more meritocratic and less static (though not necessarily smaller): economic rationality would then in some sense automatically give rise to democratic rationality.

Another optimistic belief, which is current at the moment, is the idea that "class warfare" will automatically give way, owing to the recent increase in life expectancy, to "generational warfare" (which is less divisive because everyone is first young and then old). Put differently, this inescapable biological fact is supposed to imply that the accumulation and distribution of wealth no longer presage an inevitable clash between dynasties of rentiers and dynasties owning nothing but their labor power. The governing logic is rather one of saving over the life cycle: people accumulate wealth when young in order to provide for their old age. Progress in medicine together with improved living conditions has therefore, it is argued, totally transformed the very essence of capital.

Unfortunately, these two optimistic beliefs (the human capital hypothesis and the substitution of generational conflict for class warfare) are largely illusory. Transformations of this sort are both logically possible and to some extent real, but their influence is far less consequential than one might imagine. There is little evidence that labor's share in national income has increased significantly in a very long time: "nonhuman" capital seems almost as indispensable in the twenty-first century as it was in the eighteenth or nineteenth, and there is no reason why it may not become even more so. Now as in the past, moreover, inequalities of wealth exist primarily within age cohorts, and inherited wealth comes close to being as decisive at the beginning of the twenty-first century as it was in the age of Balzac's *Père Goriot*. Over a long period of time, the main force in favor of greater equality has been the diffusion of knowledge and skills.

Forces of Convergence, Forces of Divergence

The crucial fact is that no matter how potent a force the diffusion of knowledge and skills may be, especially in promoting convergence between countries, it can nevertheless be thwarted and overwhelmed by powerful forces pushing in the opposite direction, toward greater inequality. It is obvious that lack of adequate investment in training can exclude entire social groups from the benefits of economic growth. Growth can harm some groups while benefiting others (witness the recent displacement of workers in the more advanced economies by workers in China). In short, the principal force for convergence—the diffusion of knowledge—is only partly natural and spontaneous. It also depends in large part on educational policies, access to training and to the acquisition of appropriate skills, and associated institutions.

I will pay particular attention in this study to certain worrisome forces of divergence—particularly worrisome in that they can exist even in a world where there is adequate investment in skills and where all the conditions of "market efficiency" (as economists understand that term) appear to be satisfied. What are these forces of divergence? First, top earners can quickly separate themselves from the rest by a wide margin (although the problem to date remains relatively localized). More important, there is a set of forces of divergence associated with the process of accumulation and concentration of wealth when growth is weak and the return on capital is high. This second process is potentially more destabilizing than the first, and it no doubt represents the principal threat to an equal distribution of wealth over the long run.

To cut straight to the heart of the matter: in Figures I.1 and I.2 I show two basic patterns that I will try to explain in what follows. Each graph represents the importance of one of these divergent processes. Both graphs depict "U-shaped curves," that is, a period of decreasing inequality followed by one of increasing inequality. One might assume that the realities the two graphs represent are similar. In fact

FIGURE I.I. Income inequality in the United States, 1910–2010

The top decile share in US national income dropped from 45–50 percent in the 1910s–1920s to less than 35 percent in the 1950s (this is the fall documented by Kuznets); it then rose from less than 35 percent in the 1970s to 45–50 percent in the 2000s–2010s.

Sources and series: see piketty.pse.ens.fr/capital21c.

they are not. The phenomena underlying the various curves are quite different and involve distinct economic, social, and political processes. Furthermore, the curve in Figure I.1 represents income inequality in the United States, while the curves in Figure I.2 depict the capital / income ratio in several European countries (Japan, though not shown, is similar). It is not out of the question that the two forces of divergence will ultimately come together in the twenty-first century. This has already happened to some extent and may yet become a global phenomenon, which could lead to levels of inequality never before seen, as well as to a radically new structure of inequality. Thus far, however, these striking patterns reflect two distinct underlying phenomena.

The US curve, shown in Figure I.1, indicates the share of the upper decile of the income hierarchy in US national income from 1910 to 2010. It is nothing more than an extension of the historical series

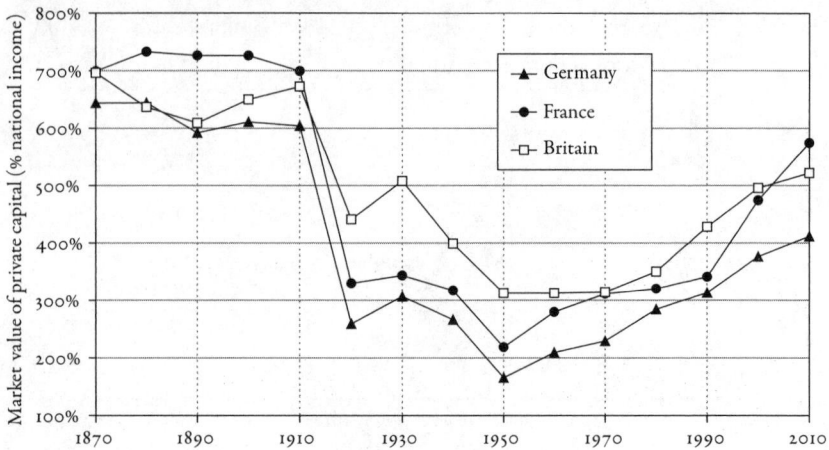

FIGURE I.2. The capital/income ratio in Europe, 1870–2010

Aggregate private wealth was worth about six to seven years of national income in Europe in 1910, between two and three years in 1950, and between four and six years in 2010.

Sources and series: see piketty.pse.ens.fr/capital21c.

Kuznets established for the period 1913–1948. The top decile claimed as much as 45–50 percent of national income in the 1910s–1920s before dropping to 30–35 percent by the end of the 1940s. Inequality then stabilized at that level from 1950 to 1970. We subsequently see a rapid rise in inequality in the 1980s, until by 2000 we have returned to a level on the order of 45–50 percent of national income. The magnitude of the change is impressive. It is natural to ask how far such a trend might continue.

I will show that this spectacular increase in inequality largely reflects an unprecedented explosion of very elevated incomes from labor, a veritable separation of the top managers of large firms from the rest of the population. One possible explanation of this is that the skills and productivity of these top managers rose suddenly in relation to those of other workers. Another explanation, which to me seems more plausible and turns out to be much more consistent with the evidence, is that these top managers by and large have the power to set their own remuneration, in some cases without limit and in many cases without any clear relation to their individual productivity, which in any case is very difficult to estimate in a large organization. This phenomenon is seen mainly in the United States and to a lesser degree in Britain, and it may be possible to explain it in terms of the history of social and fiscal norms in those two countries over the past century. The tendency is less marked in other wealthy countries (such as Japan, Germany, France, and other continental European states), but the trend is in the same direction. To expect that the phenomenon will attain the same proportions elsewhere as it has done in the United States would be risky until we have subjected it to a full analysis—which unfortunately is not that simple, given the limits of the available data.

The Fundamental Force for Divergence: $r > g$

The second pattern, represented in Figure I.2, reflects a divergence mechanism that is in some ways simpler and more transparent and no doubt exerts greater influence on the long-run evolution of the wealth distribution. Figure I.2 shows the total value of private wealth (in real estate, financial assets, and professional capital, net of debt) in Britain, France and Germany, expressed in years of national income, for the period 1870–2010. Note, first of all, the very high level of private wealth in Europe in the late nineteenth century: the total amount of private wealth hovered around six or seven years of national income, which is a lot. It then fell sharply in response to the shocks of the period 1914–1945: the capital / income ratio decreased to just 2 or 3. We then observe a steady rise from 1950 on, a rise so sharp that private fortunes in the early twenty-first century seem to be on the verge of returning to five or six years of national income in both Britain and France. (Private wealth in Germany, which started at a lower level, remains lower, but the upward trend is just as clear.)

This "U-shaped curve" reflects an absolutely crucial transformation, which will figure largely in this study. In particular, I will show that the return of high capital / income ratios over the past few decades can be explained in large part by the return to a regime of relatively slow growth. In slowly growing economies, past wealth naturally takes on disproportionate importance, because it takes only a small flow of new savings to increase the stock of wealth steadily and substantially.

If, moreover, the rate of return on capital remains significantly above the growth rate for an extended period of time (which is more likely when the growth rate is low, though not automatic), then the risk of divergence in the distribution of wealth is very high.

This fundamental inequality, which I will write as $r > g$ (where r stands for the average annual rate of return on capital, including profits, dividends, interest, rents, and other income from capital, expressed as a percentage of its total value, and g stands for the rate of growth of the economy, that is, the annual increase in income or output), will play a crucial role in this book. In a sense, it sums up the overall logic of my conclusions.

When the rate of return on capital significantly exceeds the growth rate of the economy (as it did through much of history until the nineteenth century and as is likely to be the case again in the twenty-first century), then it logically follows that inherited wealth grows faster than output and income. People with inherited wealth need save only a portion of their income from capital to see that capital grow more quickly than the economy as a whole. Under such conditions, it is almost inevitable that inherited wealth will dominate wealth amassed from a lifetime's labor by a wide margin, and the concentration of capital will attain extremely high levels—levels potentially incompatible with the meritocratic values and principles of social justice fundamental to modern democratic societies.

What is more, this basic force for divergence can be reinforced by other mechanisms. For instance, the savings rate may increase sharply with wealth.[36] Or, even more important, the average effective rate of

---

36. This destabilizing mechanism (the richer one is, the wealthier one gets) worried Kuznets a great deal, and this worry accounts for the title of his 1953 book *Shares of Upper Income Groups in Income and Savings*. But he lacked the historical dis-

return on capital may be higher when the individual's initial capital endowment is higher (as appears to be increasingly common). The fact that the return on capital is unpredictable and arbitrary, so that wealth can be enhanced in a variety of ways, also poses a challenge to the meritocratic model. Finally, all of these factors can be aggravated by the Ricardian scarcity principle: the high price of real estate or petroleum may contribute to structural divergence.

To sum up what has been said thus far: the process by which wealth is accumulated and distributed contains powerful forces pushing toward divergence, or at any rate toward an extremely high level of inequality. Forces of convergence also exist, and in certain countries at certain times, these may prevail, but the forces of divergence can at any point regain the upper hand, as seems to be happening now, at the beginning of the twenty-first century. The likely decrease in the rate of growth of both the population and the economy in coming decades makes this trend all the more worrisome.

My conclusions are less apocalyptic than those implied by Marx's principle of infinite accumulation and perpetual divergence (since Marx's theory implicitly relies on a strict assumption of zero productivity growth over the long run). In the model I propose, divergence is not perpetual and is only one of several possible future directions for the distribution of wealth. But the possibilities are not heartening. Specifically, it is important to note that the fundamental $r > g$ inequality, the main force of divergence in my theory, has nothing to do with any market imperfection. Quite the contrary: the more perfect the capital market (in the economist's sense), the more likely r is to be greater than g. It is possible to imagine public institutions and policies that would counter the effects of this implacable logic: for instance, a progressive global tax on capital. But establishing such institutions

---

tance to analyze it fully. This force for divergence was also central to James Meade's classic *Efficiency, Equality, and the Ownership of Property* (London: Allen and Unwin, 1964), and to Atkinson and Harrison, *Distribution of Personal Wealth in Britain,* which in a way was the continuation of Meade's work. Our work follows in the footsteps of these authors.

and policies would require a considerable degree of international coordination. It is unfortunately likely that actual responses to the problem—including various nationalist responses—will in practice be far more modest and less effective.

The Geographical and Historical Boundaries of This Study

What will the geographical and historical boundaries of this study be? To the extent possible, I will explore the dynamics of the distribution of wealth between and within countries around the world since the eighteenth century. However, the limitations of the available data will often make it necessary to narrow the scope of inquiry rather severely. In regard to the between-country distribution of output and income, the subject of the first part of the book, a global approach is possible from 1700 on (thanks in particular to the national accounts data compiled by Angus Maddison). When it comes to studying the capital / income ratio and capital-labor split in Part Two, the absence of adequate historical data will force me to focus primarily on the wealthy countries and proceed by extrapolation to poor and emerging countries. The examination of the evolution of inequalities of income and wealth, the subject of Part Three, will also be narrowly constrained by the limitations of the available sources. I try to include as many poor and emergent countries as possible, using data from the WTID, which aims to cover five continents as thoroughly as possible. Nevertheless, the long-term trends are far better documented in the rich countries. To put it plainly, this book relies primarily on the historical experience of the leading developed countries: the United States, Japan, Germany, France, and Great Britain.

The British and French cases turn out to be particularly significant, because the most complete long-run historical sources pertain to these two countries. We have multiple estimates of both the magnitude and structure of national wealth for Britain and France as far back as the early eighteenth century. These two countries were also the leading colonial and financial powers in the nineteenth and early twentieth centuries. It is therefore clearly important to study them if we wish to understand the dynamics of the global distribution of wealth since the Industrial Revolution. In particular, their history is indispensable for studying what has been called the "first globalization" of finance and trade (1870–1914), a period that is in many ways similar to the "second globalization," which has been under way since the 1970s. The period of the first globalization is as fascinating as it was prodigiously inegalitarian. It saw the invention of the electric light as well as the heyday of the ocean liner (the *Titanic* sailed in 1912), the advent of film and radio, and the rise of the automobile and international investment. Note, for example, that it was not until the coming of the twenty-first century that the wealthy countries regained the same level of stock-market capitalization relative to GDP that Paris and London achieved in the early 1900s. This comparison is quite instructive for understanding today's world.

Some readers will no doubt be surprised that I accord special importance to the study of the French case and may suspect me of nationalism. I should therefore justify my decision. One reason for my choice has to do with sources. The French Revolution did not create a just or ideal society, but it did make it possible to observe the structure of wealth in unprecedented detail. The system established in the 1790s for recording wealth in land, buildings, and financial assets was astonishingly modern and comprehensive for its time. The Revolution is the reason why French estate records are probably the richest in the world over the long run.

My second reason is that because France was the first country to experience the demographic transition, it is in some respects a good place to observe what awaits the rest of the planet. Although the country's population has increased over the past two centuries, the rate of increase has been relatively low. The population of the country was roughly 30 million at the time of the Revolution, and it is slightly more than 60 million today. It is the same country, with a population whose order of magnitude has not changed. By contrast, the population of the United States at the time of the Declaration of Independence was barely 3 million. By 1900 it was 100 million, and today it is above 300 million. When a country goes from a population of 3 million to a population of 300 million (to say nothing of the radical increase in territory owing to westward expansion in the nineteenth century), it is clearly no longer the same country.

The dynamics and structure of inequality look very different in a country whose population increases by a factor of 100 compared with a country whose population merely doubles. In particular, the inheritance factor is much less important in the former than in the latter. It has been the demographic growth of the New World that has ensured that inherited wealth has always played a smaller role in the United States than in Europe. This factor also explains why the structure of inequality in the United States has always been so peculiar, and the same can be said of US representations of inequality and social class. But it also suggests that the US case is in some sense not generalizable (because it is unlikely that the population of the world will increase a hundredfold over the next two centuries) and that the French case is more typical and more pertinent for understanding the future. I am convinced that detailed analysis of the French case, and more generally of the various historical trajectories observed in other developed countries in Europe, Japan, North America, and Oceania, can tell us a great deal about the future dynamics of global wealth, including such emergent economies as China, Brazil, and India, where demographic and economic growth will undoubtedly slow in the future (as they have done already).

Finally, the French case is interesting because the French Revolution— the "bourgeois" revolution par excellence—quickly established an ideal of legal equality in relation to the market. It is interesting to look at how this ideal affected the dynamics of wealth distribution. Although the English Revolution of 1688 established modern parliamentarism, it left standing a royal dynasty, primogeniture on landed estates (ended only in the 1920s), and political privileges for the hereditary nobility (reform of the House of Lords is still under discussion, a bit late in the day). Although the American Revolution established the republican principle, it allowed slavery to continue for nearly a century and legal racial discrimination for nearly two centuries. The race question still has a disproportionate influence on the social question in the United States today. In a way, the French Revolution of 1789 was more ambitious. It abolished all legal privileges and sought to create a political and social order based entirely on equality of rights and opportunities. The Civil Code guaranteed absolute equality before the laws of property as well as freedom of contract (for men, at any rate). In the late nineteenth century, conservative French economists such as Paul Leroy-Beaulieu often used this argument to explain why republican France, a nation of "small property owners" made egalitarian by the Revolution, had no need of a progressive or confiscatory income tax or estate tax, in contrast to aristocratic and monarchical Britain. The data show, however, that the concentration of wealth was as large at that time in France as in Britain, which clearly demonstrates that equality of rights in the marketplace cannot ensure equality of rights tout court. Here again, the French experience is quite relevant to today's world, where many commentators continue to believe, as Leroy-Beaulieu did a little more than a century ago, that ever more fully guaranteed property rights, ever freer markets, and ever "purer and more perfect" competition are enough to ensure a just, prosperous, and harmonious society. Unfortunately, the task is more complex.

The Theoretical and Conceptual Framework

Before proceeding, it may be useful to say a little more about the theoretical and conceptual framework of this research as well as the intellectual itinerary that led me to write this book.

I belong to a generation that turned eighteen in 1989, which was not only the bicentennial of the French Revolution but also the year when the Berlin Wall fell. I belong to a generation that came of age listening to news of the collapse of the Communist dictatorships and never felt the slightest affection or nostalgia for those regimes or for the Soviet Union. I was vaccinated for life against the conventional but lazy rhetoric of anticapitalism, some of which simply ignored the historic failure of Communism and much of which turned its back on the intellectual means necessary to push beyond it. I have no interest in denouncing inequality or capitalism per se—especially since social inequalities are not in themselves a problem as long as they are justified, that is, "founded only upon common utility," as article 1 of the 1789 Declaration of the Rights of Man and the Citizen proclaims. (Although this definition of social justice is imprecise but seductive, it is rooted in history. Let us accept it for now. I will return to this point later on.) By contrast, I am interested in contributing, however modestly, to the debate about the best way to organize society and the most appropriate institutions and policies to achieve a just social order. Furthermore, I would like to see justice achieved effectively and efficiently under the rule of law, which should apply equally to all and derive from universally understood statutes subject to democratic debate.

I should perhaps add that I experienced the American dream at the age of twenty-two, when I was hired by a university near Boston just after finishing my doctorate. This experience proved to be decisive in more ways than one. It was the first time I had set foot in the United States, and it felt good to have my work recognized so quickly. Here was a country that knew how to attract immigrants when it wanted to! Yet I also realized quite soon that I wanted to return to France and Europe, which I did when I was twenty-five. Since then, I have not left Paris, except for a few brief trips. One important reason for my choice has a direct bearing on this book: I did not find the work of US economists entirely convincing. To be sure, they were all very intelligent, and I still have many friends from that period of my life. But something strange happened: I was only too aware of the fact that I knew nothing at all about the world's economic problems. My thesis consisted of several relatively abstract mathematical theorems. Yet the profession liked my work. I quickly realized that there had been no significant effort to collect historical data on the dynamics of inequality since Kuznets, yet the profession continued to churn out purely theoretical results without even knowing what facts needed to be explained. And it expected me to do the same. When I returned to France, I set out to collect the missing data.

To put it bluntly, the discipline of economics has yet to get over its childish passion for mathematics and for purely theoretical and often highly ideological speculation, at the expense of historical research and collaboration with the other social sciences. Economists are all too often preoccupied with petty mathematical problems of interest only to themselves. This obsession with mathematics is an easy way of acquiring the appearance of scientificity without having to answer the far more complex questions posed by the world we live in. There is one great advantage to being an academic economist in France: here, economists are not highly respected in the academic and intellectual world or by political and financial elites. Hence they must set aside their contempt for other disciplines and their absurd claim to greater scientific legitimacy, despite the fact that they know almost nothing about anything. This, in any case, is the charm of the discipline and of the social sciences in general: one starts from square one, so that there is some hope of making major progress. In France, I believe, economists are slightly more interested in persuading historians and sociologists, as well as people outside the academic world, that what they are doing is interesting (although they are not always successful). My dream when I was teaching in Boston was to teach at the École des Hautes Études en Sciences Sociales, whose faculty has included such leading lights as Lucien Febvre, Fernand Braudel, Claude Lévi-Strauss, Pierre Bourdieu, Françoise Héritier, and Maurice Godelier, to name a few. Dare I admit this, at the risk of seeming chauvinistic in my view of the social sciences? I probably admire these scholars more than Robert Solow or even Simon Kuznets, even though I regret the fact that the social sciences have largely lost interest in the distribution of wealth and questions of social class since the 1970s. Before that, statistics about income, wages, prices, and wealth played an important part in historical and sociological research. In any case, I hope that both professional social scientists and amateurs of all fields will find something of interest in this book, starting with those who claim to "know nothing about economics" but who nevertheless have very strong opinions about inequality of income and wealth, as is only natural.

The truth is that economics should never have sought to divorce itself from the other social sciences and can advance only in conjunction with them. The social sciences collectively know too little to waste time on foolish disciplinary squabbles. If we are to progress in our understanding of the historical dynamics of the wealth distribution and the structure of social classes, we must obviously take a pragmatic approach and avail ourselves of the methods of historians, sociologists, and political scientists as well as economists. We must start with fundamental questions and try to answer them. Disciplinary disputes and turf wars are of little or no importance. In my mind, this book is as much a work of history as of economics.

As I explained earlier, I began this work by collecting sources and establishing historical time series pertaining to the distribution of income and wealth. As the book proceeds, I sometimes appeal to theory and to abstract models and concepts, but I try to do so sparingly, and only to the extent that theory enhances our understanding of the changes we observe. For example, income, capital, the economic growth rate, and the rate of return on capital are abstract concepts— theoretical constructs rather than mathematical certainties. Yet I will show that these concepts allow us to analyze historical reality in interesting ways, provided that we remain clear-eyed and critical about the limited precision with which we can measure these things. I will also use a few equations, such as $\alpha = r \times \beta$ (which says that the share of capital in national income is equal to the product of the return on capital and the capital / income ratio), or $\beta = s/g$ (which says that the capital / income ratio is equal in the long run to the savings rate divided by the growth rate). I ask readers not well versed in mathematics to be patient and not immediately close the book: these are elementary equations, which can be explained in a simple, intuitive way and can be understood without any specialized technical knowledge.

Above all, I try to show that this minimal theoretical framework is sufficient to give a clear account of what everyone will recognize as important historical developments.

Outline of the Book

The remainder of the book consists of sixteen chapters divided into four parts. Part One, titled "Income and Capital," contains two chapters and introduces basic ideas that are used repeatedly in the remainder of the book. Specifically, Chapter 1 presents the concepts of national income, capital, and the capital / income ratio and then describes in broad brushstrokes how the global distribution of income and output has evolved. Chapter 2 gives a more detailed analysis of how the growth rates of population and output have evolved since the Industrial Revolution. This first part of the book contains nothing really new, and the reader familiar with these ideas and with the history of global growth since the eighteenth century may wish to skip directly to Part Two.

The purpose of Part Two, titled "The Dynamics of the Capital / Income Ratio," which consists of four chapters, is to examine the prospects for the long-run evolution of the capital / income ratio and the global division of national income between labor and capital in the twenty-first century. Chapter 3 looks at the metamorphoses of capital since the eighteenth century, starting with the British and French cases, about which we possess the most data over the long run. Chapter 4 introduces the German and US cases. Chapters 5 and 6 extend the geographical range of the analysis to the entire planet, insofar as the sources allow, and seek to draw the lessons from all of these historical experiences that can enable us to anticipate the possible evolution of the capital / income ratio and the relative shares of capital and labor in the decades to come.

Part Three, titled "The Structure of Inequality," consists of six chapters. Chapter 7 familiarizes the reader with the orders of magnitude of inequality attained in practice by the distribution of income from labor on the one hand and of capital ownership and income from capital on the other. Chapter 8 then analyzes the historical dynamics of these inequalities, starting with a comparison of France and the United States. Chapters 9 and 10 extend the analysis to all the countries for which we have historical data (in the WTID), looking separately at inequalities related to labor and capital, respectively. Chapter 11 studies the changing importance of inherited wealth over the long run. Finally, Chapter 12 looks at the prospects for the global distribution of wealth over the first few decades of the twenty-first century.

The purpose of Part Four, titled "Regulating Capital in the Twenty-First Century" and consisting of four chapters, is to draw normative and policy lessons from the previous three parts, whose purpose is primarily to establish the facts and understand the reasons for the observed changes. Chapter 13 examines what a "social state" suited to present conditions might look like. Chapter 14 proposes a rethinking of the progressive income tax based on past experience and recent trends. Chapter 15 describes what a progressive tax on capital adapted to twenty-first century conditions might look like and compares this idealized tool to other types of regulation that might emerge from the political process, ranging from a wealth tax in Europe to capital controls in China, immigration reform in the United States, and revival of protectionism in many countries. Chapter 16 deals with the pressing question of public debt and the related issue of the optimal accumulation of public capital at a time when natural capital may be deteriorating.

One final word. It would have been quite presumptuous in 1913 to publish a book called "Capital in the Twentieth Century." I beg the reader's indulgence for giving the title *Capital in the Twenty-First Century* to this book, which appeared in French in 2013 and in English in 2014. I am only too well aware of my total inability to predict what form capital will take in 2063 or 2113. As I already noted, and as I will frequently show in what follows, the history of income and wealth is always deeply political, chaotic, and unpredictable. How this history plays out depends on how societies view inequalities and what kinds of policies and institutions they adopt to measure and transform them. No one can foresee how these things will change in the decades to come. The lessons of history are nevertheless useful, because they help us to see a little more clearly what kinds of choices we will face in the coming century and what sorts of dynamics will be at work. The sole purpose of the book, which logically speaking should have been entitled "Capital at the Dawn of the Twenty-First Century," is to draw from the past a few modest keys to the future. Since history always invents its own pathways, the actual usefulness of these lessons from the past remains to be seen. I offer them to readers without presuming to know their full import.

PART ONE

INCOME AND CAPITAL

ONE

Income and Output

On August 16, 2012, the South African police intervened in a labor conflict between workers at the Marikana platinum mine near Johannesburg and the mine's owners: the stockholders of Lonmin, Inc., based in London. Police fired on the strikers with live ammunition. Thirty-four miners were killed.[1] As often in such strikes, the conflict primarily concerned wages: the miners had asked for a doubling of their wage from 500 to 1,000 euros a month. After the tragic loss of life, the company finally proposed a monthly raise of 75 euros.[2]

This episode reminds us, if we needed reminding, that the question of what share of output should go to wages and what share to profits—in other words, how should the income from production be divided between labor and capital?—has always been at the heart of distributional conflict. In traditional societies, the basis of social inequality and most common cause of rebellion was the conflict of interest between landlord and peasant, between those who owned land and those who cultivated it with their labor, those who received land rents and those who paid them. The Industrial Revolution exacerbated the conflict between capital and labor, perhaps because production became more capital intensive than in the past (making use of machinery

---

1. "South African Police Open Fire on Striking Miners," *New York Times,* August 17, 2012.
2. See the company's official communiqué, "Lonmin Seeks Sustainable Peace at Marikana," August 25, 2012, www.lonmin.com. According to this document, the base wage of miners before the strike was 5,405 rand per month, and the raise granted was 750 rand per month (1 South African rand is roughly equal to 0.1 euro). These figures seem consistent with those reported by the strikers and published in the press.

and exploiting natural resources more than ever before) and perhaps, too, because hopes for a more equitable distribution of income and a more democratic social order were dashed. I will come back to this point.

The Marikana tragedy calls to mind earlier instances of violence. At Haymarket Square in Chicago on May 1, 1886, and then at Fourmies, in northern France, on May 1, 1891, police fired on workers striking for higher wages. Does this kind of violent clash between labor and capital belong to the past, or will it be an integral part of twenty-first-century history?

The first two parts of this book focus on the respective shares of global income going to labor and capital and on how those shares have changed since the eighteenth century. I will temporarily set aside the issue of income inequality between workers (for example, between an ordinary worker, an engineer, and a plant manager) and between capitalists (for example, between small, medium, and large stockholders or landlords) until Part Three. Clearly, each of these two dimensions of the distribution of wealth—the "factorial" distribution in which labor and capital are treated as "factors of production," viewed in the abstract as homogeneous entities, and the "individual" distribution, which takes account of inequalities of income from labor and capital at the individual level—is in practice fundamentally important. It is impossible to achieve a satisfactory understanding of the distributional problem without analyzing both.[3]

In any case, the Marikana miners were striking not only against what they took to be Lonmin's excessive profits but also against the apparently fabulous salary awarded to the mine's manager and the difference

---

3. The "factorial" distribution is sometimes referred to as "functional" or "macro-economic," and the "individual" distribution is sometimes called "personal" or "microeconomic." In reality, both types of distribution depend on both micro-economic mechanisms (which must be analyzed at the level of the firm or individual agents) and macroeconomic mechanisms (which can be understood only at the level of the national or global economy).

between his compensation and theirs.[4] Indeed, if capital ownership were equally distributed and each worker received an equal share of profits in addition to his or her wages, virtually no one would be interested in the division of earnings between profits and wages. If the capital-labor split gives rise to so many conflicts, it is due first and foremost to the extreme concentration of the ownership of capital. Inequality of wealth—and of the consequent income from capital—is in fact always much greater than inequality of income from labor. I will analyze this phenomenon and its causes in Part Three. For now, I will take the inequality of income from labor and capital as given and focus on the global division of national income between capital and labor.

To be clear, my purpose here is not to plead the case of workers against owners but rather to gain as clear as possible a view of reality. Symbolically, the inequality of capital and labor is an issue that arouses strong emotions. It clashes with widely held ideas of what is and is not just, and it is hardly surprising if this sometimes leads to physical violence. For those who own nothing but their labor power and who often live in humble conditions (not to say wretched conditions in the case of eighteenth-century peasants or the Marikana miners), it is difficult to accept that the owners of capital—some of whom have inherited at least part of their wealth—are able to appropriate so much of the wealth produced by their labor. Capital's share can be quite large: often as much as one-quarter of total output and sometimes as high as one-half in capital-intensive sectors such as mining, or even more where local monopolies allow the owners of capital to demand an even larger share.

Of course, everyone can also understand that if all the company's earnings from its output went to paying wages and nothing to profits, it would probably be difficult to attract the capital needed to finance new investments, at least as our economies are currently organized (to

---

4. One million euros per year (equivalent to the wages of 200 miners), according to the strikers. Unfortunately, no information about this is available on the company's website.

be sure, one can imagine other forms of organization). Furthermore, it is not necessarily just to deny any remuneration to those who choose to save more than others—assuming, of course, that differences in saving are an important reason for the inequality of wealth. Bear in mind, too, that a portion of what is called "the income of capital" may be remuneration for "entrepreneurial" labor, and this should no doubt be treated as we treat other forms of labor. This classic argument deserves closer scrutiny. Taking all these elements into account, what is the "right" split between capital and labor? Can we be sure that an economy based on the "free market" and private property always and everywhere leads to an optimal division, as if by magic? In an ideal society, how would one arrange the division between capital and labor? How should one think about the problem?

The Capital-Labor Split in the Long Run: Not So Stable

If this study is to make even modest progress on these questions and at least clarify the terms of a debate that appears to be endless, it will be useful to begin by establishing some facts as accurately and carefully as possible. What exactly do we know about the evolution of the capital-labor split since the eighteenth century? For a long time, the idea accepted by most economists and uncritically repeated in textbooks was that the relative shares of labor and capital in national income were quite stable over the long run, with the generally accepted figure being two-thirds for labor and one-third for capital.[5] Today, with the advantage of greater historical perspective and newly available data, it is clear that the reality was quite a bit more complex.

For one thing, the capital-labor split varied widely over the course of the twentieth century. The changes observed in the nineteenth century, which I touched on in the Introduction (an increase in the capital share in the first half of the century, followed by a slight decrease

---

5. Roughly 65–70 percent for wages and other income from labor and 30–35 percent for profits, rents, and other income from capital.

and then a period of stability), seem mild by comparison. Briefly, the shocks that buffeted the economy in the period 1914–1945—World War I, the Bolshevik Revolution of 1917, the Great Depression, World War II, and the consequent advent of new regulatory and tax policies along with controls on capital—reduced capital's share of income to historically low levels in the 1950s. Very soon, however, capital began to reconstitute itself. The growth of capital's share accelerated with the victories of Margaret Thatcher in England in 1979 and Ronald Reagan in the United States in 1980, marking the beginning of a conservative revolution. Then came the collapse of the Soviet bloc in 1989, followed by financial globalization and deregulation in the 1990s. All of these events marked a political turn in the opposite direction from that observed in the first half of the twentieth century. By 2010, and despite the crisis that began in 2007–2008, capital was prospering as it had not done since 1913. Not all of the consequences of capital's renewed prosperity were negative; to some extent it was a natural and desirable development. But it has changed the way we look at the capital-labor split since the beginning of the twenty-first century, as well as our view of changes likely to occur in the decades to come.

Furthermore, if we look beyond the twentieth century and adopt a very long-term view, the idea of a stable capital-labor split must somehow deal with the fact that the nature of capital itself has changed radically (from land and other real estate in the eighteenth century to industrial and financial capital in the twenty-first century). There is also the idea, widespread among economists, that modern economic growth depends largely on the rise of "human capital." At first glance, this would seem to imply that labor should claim a growing share of national income. And one does indeed find that there may be a tendency for labor's share to increase over the very long run, but the gains are relatively modest: capital's share (excluding human capital) in the early decades of the twenty-first century is only slightly smaller than it was at the beginning of the nineteenth century. The importance of capital in the wealthy countries today is primarily due to a slowing of both demographic growth and productivity growth, coupled with political regimes that objectively favor private capital.

The most fruitful way to understand these changes is to analyze the evolution of the capital / income ratio (that is, the ratio of the total stock of capital to the annual flow of income) rather than focus exclusively on the capital-labor split (that is, the share of income going to capital and labor, respectively). In the past, scholars have mainly studied the latter, largely owing to the lack of adequate data to do anything else.

Before presenting my results in detail, it is best to proceed by stages. The purpose of Part One of this book is to introduce certain basic notions. In the remainder of this chapter, I will begin by presenting the concepts of domestic product and national income, capital and labor, and the capital / income ratio. Then I will look at how the global distribution of income has changed since the Industrial Revolution. In Chapter 2, I will analyze the general evolution of growth rates over time. This will play a central role in the subsequent analysis.

With these preliminaries out of the way, Part Two takes up the dynamics of the capital / income ratio and the capital-labor split, once again proceeding by stages. Chapter 3 will look at changes in the composition of capital and the capital / income ratio since the eighteenth century, beginning with Britain and France, about which we have the best long-run data. Chapter 4 introduces the German case and above all looks at the United States, which serves as a useful complement to the European prism. Finally, Chapters 5 and 6 attempt to extend the analysis to all the rich countries of the world and, insofar as possible, to the entire planet. I also attempt to draw conclusions relevant to the global dynamics of the capital / income ratio and capital-labor split in the twenty-first century.

The Idea of National Income

It will be useful to begin with the concept of "national income," to which I will frequently refer in what follows. National income is defined as the sum of all income available to the residents of a given country in a given year, regardless of the legal classification of that income.

National income is closely related to the idea of GDP, which comes up often in public debate. There are, however, two important differences between GDP and national income. GDP measures the total of goods and services produced in a given year within the borders of a given country. In order to calculate national income, one must first subtract from GDP the depreciation of the capital that made this production possible: in other words, one must deduct wear and tear on buildings, infrastructure, machinery, vehicles, computers, and other items during the year in question. This depreciation is substantial, today on the order of 10 percent of GDP in most countries, and it does not correspond to anyone's income: before wages are distributed to workers or dividends to stockholders, and before genuinely new investments are made, worn-out capital must be replaced or repaired. If this is not done, wealth is lost, resulting in negative income for the owners. When depreciation is subtracted from GDP, one obtains the "net domestic product," which I will refer to more simply as "domestic output" or "domestic production," which is typically 90 percent of GDP.

Then one must add net income received from abroad (or subtract net income paid to foreigners, depending on each country's situation). For example, a country whose firms and other capital assets are owned by foreigners may well have a high domestic product but a much lower national income, once profits and rents flowing abroad are deducted from the total. Conversely, a country that owns a large portion of the capital of other countries may enjoy a national income much higher than its domestic product.

Later I will give examples of both of these situations, drawn from the history of capitalism as well as from today's world. I should say at once that this type of international inequality can give rise to great political tension. It is not an insignificant thing when one country works for another and pays out a substantial share of its output as dividends and rent to foreigners over a long period of time. In many cases, such a system can survive (to a point) only if sustained by relations of political domination, as was the case in the colonial era, when Europe effectively owned much of the rest of the world. A key question of this research is the following: Under what conditions is this type of situation likely to recur in the twenty-first century, possibly in some novel geographic configuration? For example, Europe, rather than being the owner, may find itself owned. Such fears are currently widespread in the Old World—perhaps too widespread. We shall see.

At this stage, suffice it to say that most countries, whether wealthy or emergent, are currently in much more balanced situations than one sometimes imagines. In France as in the United States, Germany as well as Great Britain, China as well as Brazil, and Japan as well as Italy, national income is within 1 or 2 percent of domestic product. In all these countries, in other words, the inflow of profits, interest, dividends, rent, and so on is more or less balanced by a comparable outflow. In wealthy countries, net income from abroad is generally slightly positive. To a first approximation, the residents of these countries own as much in foreign real estate and financial instruments as foreigners own of theirs. Contrary to a tenacious myth, France is not owned by California pension funds or the Bank of China, any more than the United States belongs to Japanese and German investors. The fear of getting into such a predicament is so strong today that fantasy often outstrips reality. The reality is that inequality with respect to capital is a far greater domestic issue than it is an international one. Inequality in the ownership of capital brings the rich and poor within each country into conflict with one another far more than it pits one country against another. This has not always been the case, however, and it is perfectly legitimate to ask whether our future may not look more like our past, particularly since certain countries—Japan, Germany, the oil-exporting countries, and to a lesser degree China—have in recent years accumulated substantial claims on the rest of the world (though by no means as large as the record claims of the colonial era). Furthermore, the very substantial increase in cross-ownership, in which various countries own substantial shares of one another, can give rise to a legitimate sense of dispossession, even when net asset positions are close to zero.

To sum up, a country's national income may be greater or smaller than its domestic product, depending on whether net income from abroad is positive or negative.

National income = domestic output + net income from abroad[6]

At the global level, income received from abroad and paid abroad must balance, so that income is by definition equal to output:

Global income = global output[7]

This equality between two annual flows, income and output, is an accounting identity, yet it reflects an important reality. In any given year, it is impossible for total income to exceed the amount of new wealth that is produced (globally speaking; a single country may of course borrow from abroad). Conversely, all production must be distributed as income in one form or another, to either labor or capital: whether as wages, salaries, honoraria, bonuses, and so on (that is, as payments to workers and others who contributed labor to the process of production) or else as profits, dividends, interest, rents, royalties, and so on (that is, as payments to the owners of capital used in the process of production).

What Is Capital?

To recapitulate: regardless of whether we are looking at the accounts of a company, a nation, or the global economy, the associated output

---

6. National income is also called "net national product" (as opposed to "gross national product" [GNP], which includes the depreciation of capital). I will use the expression "national income," which is simpler and more intuitive. Net income from abroad is defined as the difference between income received from abroad and income paid out to foreigners. These opposite flows consist primarily of income from capital but also include income from labor and unilateral transfers (such as remittances by immigrant workers to their home countries). See the online appendix for details.

7. World income is naturally defined as the sum of national income in different countries, and world output as the sum of domestic output in different countries.

and income can be decomposed as the sum of income to capital and income to labor:

National income = capital income + labor income

But what is capital? What are its limits? What forms does it take? How has its composition changed over time? This question, central to this investigation, will be examined in greater detail in subsequent chapters. For now it will suffice to make the following points:

First, throughout this book, when I speak of "capital" without further qualification, I always exclude what economists often call (unfortunately, to my mind) "human capital," which consists of an individual's labor power, skills, training, and abilities. In this book, capital is defined as the sum total of nonhuman assets that can be owned and exchanged on some market. Capital includes all forms of real property (including residential real estate) as well as financial and professional capital (plants, infrastructure, machinery, patents, and so on) used by firms and government agencies.

There are many reasons for excluding human capital from our definition of capital. The most obvious is that human capital cannot be owned by another person or traded on a market (not permanently, at any rate). This is a key difference from other forms of capital. One can of course put one's labor services up for hire under a labor contract of some sort. In all modern legal systems, however, such an arrangement has to be limited in both time and scope. In slave societies, of course, this is obviously not true: there, a slaveholder can fully and completely own the human capital of another person and even of that person's offspring. In such societies, slaves can be bought and sold on the market and conveyed by inheritance, and it is common to include slaves in calculating a slaveholder's wealth. I will show how this worked when I examine the composition of private capital in the southern United States before 1865. Leaving such special (and for now historical) cases aside, it makes little sense to attempt to add human and nonhuman capital. Throughout history, both forms of wealth have played fundamental and complementary roles in economic growth and development and will continue to do so in the twenty-first century. But in order to understand the growth process and the inequalities it engenders, we must distinguish carefully between human and nonhuman capital and treat each one separately.

Nonhuman capital, which in this book I will call simply "capital," includes all forms of wealth that individuals (or groups of individuals) can own and that can be transferred or traded through the market on a permanent basis. In practice, capital can be owned by private individuals (in which case we speak of "private capital") or by the government or government agencies (in which case we speak of "public capital"). There are also intermediate forms of collective property owned by "moral persons" (that is, entities such as foundations and churches) pursuing specific aims. I will come back to this. The boundary between what private individuals can and cannot own has evolved considerably over time and around the world, as the extreme case of slavery indicates. The same is true of property in the atmosphere, the sea, mountains, historical monuments, and knowledge. Certain private interests would like to own these things, and sometimes they justify this desire on grounds of efficiency rather than mere self-interest. But there is no guarantee that this desire coincides with the general interest. Capital is not an immutable concept: it reflects the state of development and prevailing social relations of each society.

Capital and Wealth

To simplify the text, I use the words "capital" and "wealth" interchangeably, as if they were perfectly synonymous. By some definitions, it would be better to reserve the word "capital" to describe forms of wealth accumulated by human beings (buildings, machinery, infrastructure, etc.) and therefore to exclude land and natural resources, with which humans have been endowed without having to accumulate them. Land would then be a component of wealth but not of capital. The problem is that it is not always easy to distinguish the value of buildings from the value of the land on which they are built. An even greater difficulty is that it is very hard to gauge the value of "virgin" land (as humans found it centuries or millennia ago) apart from improvements due to human intervention, such as drainage, irrigation, fertilization, and so on. The same problem arises in connection with natural resources such as petroleum, gas, rare earth elements, and the like, whose pure value is hard to distinguish from the value added by the investments needed to discover new deposits and prepare them for exploitation. I therefore include all these forms of wealth in capital. Of course, this choice does not eliminate the need to look closely at the origins of wealth, especially the boundary line between accumulation and appropriation.

Some definitions of "capital" hold that the term should apply only to those components of wealth directly employed in the production process. For instance, gold might be counted as part of wealth but not of capital, because gold is said to be useful only as a store of value. Once again, this limitation strikes me as neither desirable nor practical (because gold can be a factor of production, not only in the manufacture of jewelry but also in electronics and nanotechnology). Capital in all its forms has always played a dual role, as both a store of value and a factor of production. I therefore decided that it was simpler not to impose a rigid distinction between wealth and capital.

Similarly, I ruled out the idea of excluding residential real estate from capital on the grounds that it is "unproductive," unlike the "productive capital" used by firms and government: industrial plants, office buildings, machinery, infrastructure, and so on. The truth is that all these forms of wealth are useful and productive and reflect capital's two major economic functions. Residential real estate can be seen as a capital asset that yields "housing services," whose value is measured by their rental equivalent. Other capital assets can serve as factors of production for firms and government agencies that produce goods and services (and need plants, offices, machinery, infrastructure, etc. to do so). Each of these two types of capital currently accounts for roughly half the capital stock in the developed countries.

To summarize, I define "national wealth" or "national capital" as the total market value of everything owned by the residents and government of a given country at a given point in time, provided that it can be traded on some market.[8] It consists of the sum total of nonfinancial assets (land, dwellings, commercial inventory, other buildings, machinery, infrastructure, patents, and other directly owned professional assets) and financial assets (bank accounts, mutual funds, bonds, stocks, financial investments of all kinds, insurance policies, pension funds, etc.), less the total amount of financial liabilities (debt).[9] If we look only at the assets and liabilities of private individuals, the result is private wealth or private capital. If we consider assets and liabilities held by the government and other governmental entities (such as towns, social insurance agencies, etc.), the result is public wealth or public capital. By definition, national wealth is the sum of these two terms:

National wealth = private wealth + public wealth

Public wealth in most developed countries is currently insignificant (or even negative, where the public debt exceeds public assets). As I will show, private wealth accounts for nearly all of national wealth almost everywhere. This has not always been the case, however, so it is important to distinguish clearly between the two notions.

To be clear, although my concept of capital excludes human capital (which cannot be exchanged on any market in nonslave societies), it is not limited to "physical" capital (land, buildings, infrastructure, and other material goods). I include "immaterial" capital such as patents and other intellectual property, which are counted either as nonfinancial assets (if individuals hold patents directly) or as financial assets (when an

---

8. In English one speaks of "national wealth" or "national capital." In the eighteenth and nineteenth centuries, French authors spoke of *fortune nationale* and English authors of "national estate" (with a distinction in English between "real estate" and other property referred to as "personal estate").

9. I use essentially the same definitions and the same categories of assets and liabilities as the current international standards for national accounts, with slight differences that are discussed in the online appendix.

individual owns shares of a corporation that holds patents, as is more commonly the case). More broadly, many forms of immaterial capital are taken into account by way of the stock market capitalization of corporations. For instance, the stock market value of a company often depends on its reputation and trademarks, its information systems and modes of organization, its investments, whether material or immaterial, for the purpose of making its products and services more visible and attractive, and so on. All of this is reflected in the price of common stock and other corporate financial assets and therefore in national wealth.

To be sure, the price that the financial markets set on a company's or even a sector's immaterial capital at any given moment is largely arbitrary and uncertain. We see this in the collapse of the Internet bubble in 2000, in the financial crisis that began in 2007–2008, and more generally in the enormous volatility of the stock market. The important fact to note for now is that this is a characteristic of all forms of capital, not just immaterial capital. Whether we are speaking of a building or a company, a manufacturing firm or a service firm, it is always very difficult to set a price on capital. Yet as I will show, total national wealth, that is, the wealth of a country as a whole and not of any particular type of asset, obeys certain laws and conforms to certain regular patterns.

One further point: total national wealth can always be broken down into domestic capital and foreign capital:

National wealth = national capital = domestic capital
+ net foreign capital

Domestic capital is the value of the capital stock (buildings, firms, etc.) located within the borders of the country in question. Net foreign capital—or net foreign assets—measures the country's position vis-à-vis the rest of the world: more specifically, it is the difference between assets owned by the country's citizens in the rest of the world and assets of the country owned by citizens of other countries. On the eve of World War I, Britain and France both enjoyed significant net positive asset positions vis-à-vis the rest of the world. One characteristic of the financial globalization that has taken place since the 1980s is that many countries have more or less balanced net asset positions, but those positions are quite large in absolute terms. In other words, many countries have large capital stakes in other countries, but those other countries also have stakes in the country in question, and the two positions are more or less equal, so that net foreign capital is close to zero. Globally, of course, all the net positions must add up to zero, so that total global wealth equals the "domestic" capital of the planet as a whole.

The Capital/Income Ratio

Now that income and capital have been defined, I can move on to the first basic law tying these two ideas together. I begin by defining the capital/income ratio.

Income is a flow. It corresponds to the quantity of goods produced and distributed in a given period (which we generally take to be a year).

Capital is a stock. It corresponds to the total wealth owned at a given point in time. This stock comes from the wealth appropriated or accumulated in all prior years combined.

The most natural and useful way to measure the capital stock in a particular country is to divide that stock by the annual flow of income. This gives us the capital/income ratio, which I denote by the Greek letter β.

For example, if a country's total capital stock is the equivalent of six years of national income, we write $\beta = 6$ (or $\beta = 600\%$).

In the developed countries today, the capital/income ratio generally varies between 5 and 6, and the capital stock consists almost entirely of private capital. In France and Britain, Germany and Italy, the United States and Japan, national income was roughly 30,000–35,000 euros per capita in 2010, whereas total private wealth (net of debt) was typically on the order of 150,000–200,000 euros per capita, or five to six times annual national income. There are interesting variations both within Europe and around the world. For instance, β is greater than 6 in Japan and Italy and less than 5 in the United States and Germany. Public wealth is just barely positive in some countries and slightly negative in others. And so on. I examine all this in detail in the next few chapters. At this point, it is enough to keep these orders of magnitude in mind, in order to make the ideas as concrete as possible.[10]

The fact that national income in the wealthy countries of the world in 2010 was on the order of 30,000 euros per capita per annum (or 2,500 euros per month) obviously does not mean that everyone earns that amount. Like all averages, this average income figure hides enormous disparities. In practice, many people earn much less than 2,500 euros a month, while others earn dozens of times that much. Income disparities are partly the result of unequal pay for work and partly of much larger inequalities in income from capital, which are themselves a consequence of the extreme concentration of wealth. The average national income per capita is simply the amount that one could distribute to each individual if it were possible to equalize the income distribution without altering total output or national income.[11]

Similarly, private per capita wealth on the order of 180,000 euros, or six years of national income, does not mean that everyone owns that much capital. Many people have much less, while some own millions or tens of millions of euros' worth of capital assets. Much of the population has very little accumulated wealth—significantly less than one year's income: a few thousand euros in a bank account, the equivalent of a few weeks' or months' worth of wages. Some people even have negative wealth: in other words, the goods they own are worth

---

10. Detailed figures for each country can be consulted in the tables available in the online appendix.

11. In practice, the median income (that is, the income level below which 50 percent of the population sits) is generally on the order of 20–30 percent less than average income. This is because the upper tail of the income distribution is much more drawn out than the lower tail and the middle, which raises the average (but not the median). Note, too, that "per capita national income" refers to average income before taxes and transfers. In practice, citizens of the rich countries have chosen to pay one-third to one-half of their national income in taxes and other charges in order to pay for public services, infrastructure, social protection, a substantial share of expenditures for health and education, etc. The issue of taxes and public expenditures is taken up primarily in Part Four.

less than the debts they owe. By contrast, others have considerable fortunes, ranging from ten to twenty times their annual income or even more. The capital / income ratio for the country as a whole tells us nothing about inequalities within the country. But β does measure the overall importance of capital in a society, so analyzing this ratio is a necessary first step in the study of inequality. The main purpose of Part Two is to understand how and why the capital / income ratio varies from country to country, and how it has evolved over time.

To appreciate the concrete form that wealth takes in today's world, it is useful to note that the capital stock in the developed countries currently consists of two roughly equal shares: residential capital and professional capital used by firms and government. To sum up, each citizen of one of the wealthy countries earned an average of 30,000 euros per year in 2010, owned approximately 180,000 euros of capital, 90,000 in the form of a dwelling and another 90,000 in stocks, bonds, savings, or other investments.[12] There are interesting variations across countries, which I will analyze in Chapter 2. For now, the fact that capital can be divided into two roughly equal shares will be useful to keep in mind.

The First Fundamental Law of Capitalism: $\alpha = r \times \beta$

I can now present the first fundamental law of capitalism, which links the capital stock to the flow of income from capital. The capital / income ratio β is related in a simple way to the share of income from capital in national income, denoted α. The formula is

$$\alpha = r \times \beta$$

where r is *the rate of return on capital.*

---

12. Cash holdings (including in financial assets) accounted for only a minuscule part of total wealth, a few hundred euros per capita, or a few thousand if one includes gold, silver, and other valuable objects, or about 1–2 percent of total wealth. See the online technical appendix. Moreover, public assets are today approximately equal to public debts, so it is not absurd to say that households can include them in their financial assets.

For example, if $\beta = 600\%$ and $r = 5\%$, then $\alpha = r \times \beta = 30\%$.[13]

In other words, if national wealth represents the equivalent of six years of national income, and if the rate of return on capital is 5 percent per year, then capital's share in national income is 30 percent.

The formula $\alpha = r \times \beta$ is a pure accounting identity. It can be applied to all societies in all periods of history, by definition. Though tautological, it should nevertheless be regarded as the first fundamental law of capitalism, because it expresses a simple, transparent relationship among the three most important concepts for analyzing the capitalist system: the capital / income ratio, the share of capital in income, and the rate of return on capital.

The rate of return on capital is a central concept in many economic theories. In particular, Marxist analysis emphasizes the falling rate of profit—a historical prediction that turned out to be quite wrong, although it does contain an interesting intuition. The concept of the rate of return on capital also plays a central role in many other theories. In any case, the rate of return on capital measures the yield on capital over the course of a year regardless of its legal form (profits, rents, dividends, interest, royalties, capital gains, etc.), expressed as a percentage of the value of capital invested. It is therefore a broader notion than the "rate of profit,"[14] and much broader than the "rate of interest,"[15] while incorporating both.

---

13. The formula $\alpha = r \times \beta$ is read as "α equals r times β." Furthermore, "$\beta = 600\%$" is the same as "$\beta = 6$," and "$\alpha = 30\%$" is the same as "$\alpha = 0.30$" and "$r = 5\%$" is the same as "$r = 0.05$."

14. I prefer "rate of return on capital" to "rate of profit" in part because profit is only one of the legal forms that income from capital may take and in part because the expression "rate of profit" has often been used ambiguously, sometimes referring to the rate of return and other times (mistakenly) to the share of profits in income or output (that is, to denote what I am calling α rather than r, which is quite different). Sometimes the expression "marginal rate" is used to denote the share of profits α.

15. Interest is a very special form of the income from capital, much less representative than profits, rents, and dividends (which account for much larger sums than interest, given the typical composition of capital). The "rate of interest" (which, moreover, varies widely depending on the identity of the borrower) is therefore

Obviously, the rate of return can vary widely, depending on the type of investment. Some firms generate rates of return greater than 10 percent per year; others make losses (negative rate of return). The average long-run rate of return on stocks is 7–8 percent in many countries. Investments in real estate and bonds frequently return 3–4 percent, while the real rate of interest on public debt is sometimes much lower. The formula $\alpha = r \times \beta$ tells us nothing about these subtleties, but it does tell us how to relate these three quantities, which can be useful for framing discussion.

For example, in the wealthy countries around 2010, income from capital (profits, interests, dividends, rents, etc.) generally hovered around 30 percent of national income. With a capital / income ratio on the order of 600 percent, this meant that the rate of return on capital was around 5 percent.

Concretely, this means that the current per capita national income of 30,000 euros per year in rich countries breaks down as 21,000 euros per year income from labor (70 percent) and 9,000 euros income from capital (30 percent). Each citizen owns an average of 180,000 euros of capital, and the 9,000 euros of income from capital thus corresponds to an average annual return on capital of 5 percent.

Once again, I am speaking here only of averages: some individuals receive far more than 9,000 euros per year in income from capital, while others receive nothing while paying rent to their landlords and interest to their creditors. Considerable country-to-country variation also exists. In addition, measuring the share of income from capital is often difficult in both a conceptual and a practical sense, because there are some categories of income (such as nonwage self-employment income and entrepreneurial income) that are hard to break down into income from capital and income from labor. In some cases this can make comparison misleading. When such problems arise, the least imperfect method of measuring the capital share of income may be to

---

not representative of the average rate of return on capital and is often much lower. This idea will prove useful when it comes to analyzing the public debt.

apply a plausible average rate of return to the capital / income ratio. At this stage, the orders of magnitude given above ($\beta = 600\%$, $\alpha = 30\%$, $r = 5\%$) may be taken as typical.

For the sake of concreteness, let us note, too, that the average rate of return on land in rural societies is typically on the order of 4–5 percent. In the novels of Jane Austen and Honoré de Balzac, the fact that land (like government bonds) yields roughly 5 percent of the amount of capital invested (or, equivalently, that the value of capital corresponds to roughly twenty years of annual rent) is so taken for granted that it often goes unmentioned. Contemporary readers were well aware that it took capital on the order of 1 million francs to produce an annual rent of 50,000 francs. For nineteenth-century novelists and their readers, the relation between capital and annual rent was self-evident, and the two measuring scales were used interchangeably, as if rent and capital were synonymous, or perfect equivalents in two different languages.

Now, at the beginning of the twenty-first century, we find roughly the same return on real estate, 4–5 percent, sometimes a little less, especially where prices have risen rapidly without dragging rents upward at the same rate. For example, in 2010, a large apartment in Paris, valued at 1 million euros, typically rents for slightly more than 2,500 euros per month, or annual rent of 30,000 euros, which corresponds to a return on capital of only 3 percent per year from the landlord's point of view. Such a rent is nevertheless quite high for a tenant living solely on income from labor (one hopes he or she is paid well) while it represents a significant income for the landlord. The bad news (or good news, depending on your point of view) is that things have always been like this. This type of rent tends to rise until the return on capital is around 4 percent (which in this example would correspond to a rent of 3,000–3,500 euros per month, or 40,000 per year). Hence this tenant's rent is likely to rise in the future. The landlord's annual return on investment may eventually be enhanced by a long-term capital gain on the value of the apartment. Smaller apartments yield a similar or perhaps slightly higher return. An apartment valued at 100,000 euros may yield 400 euros a month in rent, or nearly 5,000 per year (5 percent). A person who owns such an apartment and chooses to live in it can save the rental equivalent and devote that money to other uses, which yields a similar return on investment.

Capital invested in businesses is of course at greater risk, so the average return is often higher. The stock-market capitalization of listed companies in various countries generally represents 12 to 15 years of annual profits, which corresponds to an annual return on investment of 6–8 percent (before taxes).

The formula $\alpha = r \times \beta$ allows us to analyze the importance of capital for an entire country or even for the planet as a whole. It can also be used to study the accounts of a specific company. For example, take a firm that uses capital valued at 5 million euros (including offices, infrastructure, machinery, etc.) to produce 1 million euros worth of goods annually, with 600,000 euros going to pay workers and 400,000 euros in profits.[16] The capital / income ratio of this company is $\beta = 5$ (its capital is equivalent to five years of output), the capital share α is 40 percent, and the rate of return on capital is $r = 8$ percent.

Imagine another company that uses less capital (3 million euros) to produce the same output (1 million euros), but using more labor (700,000 euros in wages, 300,000 in profits). For this company, $\beta = 3$, $\alpha = 30$ percent, and $r = 10$ percent. The second firm is less capital intensive than the first, but it is more profitable (the rate of return on its capital is significantly higher).

---

16. The annual output to which I refer here corresponds to what is sometimes called the firm's "value added," that is, the difference between what the firm earns by selling goods and services ("gross revenue") and what it pays other firms for goods and services ("intermediate consumption"). Value added measures the firm's contribution to the domestic product. By definition, value added also measures the sum available to the firm to pay the labor and capital used in production. I refer here to value added net of capital depreciation (that is, after deducting the cost of wear and tear on capital and infrastructure) and profits net of depreciation.

In all countries, the magnitudes of β, α, and r vary a great deal from company to company. Some sectors are more capital intensive than others: for example, the metal and energy sectors are more capital intensive than the textile and food processing sectors, and the manufacturing sector is more capital intensive than the service sector. There are also significant variations between firms in the same sector, depending on their choice of production technology and market position. The levels of β, α, and r in a given country also depend on the relative shares of residential real estate and natural resources in total capital.

It bears emphasizing that the law $α = r × β$ does not tell us how each of these three variables is determined, or, in particular, how the national capital / income ratio (β) is determined, the latter being in some sense a measure of how intensely capitalistic the society in question is. To answer that question, we must introduce additional ideas and relationships, in particular the savings and investment rates and the rate of growth. This will lead us to the second fundamental law of capitalism: the higher the savings rate and the lower the growth rate, the higher the capital / income ratio (β). This will be shown in the next few chapters; at this stage, the law $α = r × β$ simply means that regardless of what economic, social, and political forces determine the level of the capital / income ratio (β), capital's share in income (α), and the rate of return on capital (r), these three variables are not independent of one another. Conceptually, there are two degrees of freedom, not three.

National Accounts: An Evolving Social Construct

Now that the key concepts of output and income, capital and wealth, capital / income ratio, and rate of return on capital have been explained, I will examine in greater detail how these abstract quantities can be measured and what such measurements can tell us about the historical evolution of the distribution of wealth in various countries. I will briefly review the main stages in the history of national accounts and then present a portrait in broad brushstrokes of how the global distribution of output and income has changed since the eighteenth century, along with a discussion of how demographic and economic growth rates have changed over the same period. These growth rates will play an important part in the analysis.

As noted, the first attempts to measure national income and capital date back to the late seventeenth and early eighteenth century. Around 1700, several isolated estimates appeared in Britain and France (apparently independently of one another). I am speaking primarily of the work of William Petty (1664) and Gregory King (1696) for England and Pierre le Pesant, sieur de Boisguillebert (1695), and Sébastien Le Prestre de Vauban (1707) for France. Their work focused on both the national stock of capital and the annual flow of national income. One of their primary objectives was to calculate the total value of land, by far the most important source of wealth in the agrarian societies of the day, and then to relate the quantity of landed wealth to the level of agricultural output and land rents.

It is worth noting that these authors often had a political objective in mind, generally having to do with modernization of the tax system. By calculating the nation's income and wealth, they hoped to show the sovereign that it would be possible to raise tax receipts considerably while keeping tax rates relatively low, provided that all property and goods produced were subject to taxation and everyone was required to pay, including landlords of both aristocratic and common descent. This objective is obvious in Vauban's *Projet de dîme royale* (Plan for a Royal Tithe), but it is just as clear in the works of Boisguillebert and King (though less so in Petty's writing).

The late eighteenth century saw further attempts to measure income and wealth, especially around the time of the French Revolution. Antoine Lavoisier published his estimates for the year 1789 in his book *La Richesse territoriale du Royaume de France* (The Territorial Wealth of the Kingdom of France), published in 1791. The new tax system established after the Revolution, which ended the privileges of the nobility and imposed a tax on all property in land, was largely inspired by this work, which was widely used to estimate expected receipts from new taxes.

It was above all in the nineteenth century, however, that estimates of national wealth proliferated. From 1870 to 1900, Robert Giffen regularly updated his estimates of Britain's stock of national capital, which he compared to estimates by other authors (especially Patrick Colquhoun) from the early 1800s. Giffen marveled at the size of Britain's stock of industrial capital as well as the stock of foreign assets acquired since the Napoleonic wars, which was many times larger than the entire public debt due to those wars.[17] In France at about the same time, Alfred de Foville and Clément Colson published estimates of "national wealth" and "private wealth," and, like Giffen, both writers also marveled at the considerable accumulation of private capital over the course of the nineteenth century. It was glaringly obvious to everyone that private fortunes were prospering in the period 1870–1914. For the economists of the day, the problem was to measure that wealth and compare different countries (the Franco-British rivalry was never far from their minds). Until World War I, estimates of wealth received much more attention than estimates of income and output, and there were in any case more of them, not only in Britain and France but also in Germany, the United States, and other industrial powers. In those days, being an economist meant first and foremost being able to estimate the national capital of one's country: this was almost a rite of initiation.

It was not until the period between the two world wars that national accounts began to be established on an annual basis. Previous estimates had always focused on isolated years, with successive estimates separated by ten or more years, as in the case of Giffen's calculations of British national capital in the nineteenth century. In the 1930s, improvements in the primary statistical sources made the first annual series of national income data possible. These generally went back as far as the beginning of the twentieth century or the last decades of the nineteenth. They were established for the United States by Kuznets and Kendrick, for Britain by Bowley and Clark, and for France by

---

17. See esp. Robert Giffen, *The Growth of Capital* (London: George Bell and Sons, 1889). For more detailed bibliographic data, see the online appendix.

Dugé de Bernonville. After World War II, government statistical offices supplanted economists and began to compile and publish official annual data on GDP and national income. These official series continue to this day.

Compared with the pre–World War I period, however, the focal point of the data had changed entirely. From the 1940s on, the primary motivation was to respond to the trauma of the Great Depression, during which governments had no reliable annual estimates of economic output. There was therefore a need for statistical and political tools in order to steer the economy properly and avoid a repeat of the catastrophe. Governments thus insisted on annual or even quarterly data on output and income. Estimates of national wealth, which had been so prized before 1914, now took a backseat, especially after the economic and political chaos of 1914–1945 made it difficult to interpret their meaning. Specifically, the prices of real estate and financial assets fell to extremely low levels, so low that private capital seemed to have evaporated. In the 1950s and 1960s, a period of reconstruction, the main goal was to measure the remarkable growth of output in various branches of industry.

In the 1990s–2000s, wealth accounting again came to the fore. Economists and political leaders were well aware that the financial capitalism of the twenty-first century could not be properly analyzed with the tools of the 1950s and 1960s. In collaboration with central banks, government statistical agencies in various developed countries compiled and published annual series of data on the assets and liabilities of different groups, in addition to the usual income and output data. These wealth accounts are still far from perfect: for example, natural capital and damages to the environment are not well accounted for. Nevertheless, they represent real progress in comparison with national accounts from the early postwar years, which were concerned solely with endless growth in output.[18] These are the official series that I use in this book

---

18. The advantage of the ideas of national wealth and income is that they give a more balanced view of a country's enrichment than the idea of GDP, which in some

to analyze aggregate wealth and the current capital / income ratio in the wealthy countries.

One conclusion stands out in this brief history of national accounting: national accounts are a social construct in perpetual evolution. They always reflect the preoccupations of the era when they were conceived.[19] We should be careful not to make a fetish of the published figures. When a country's national income per capita is said to be 30,000 euros, it is obvious that this number, like all economic and social statistics, should be regarded as an estimate, a construct, and not a mathematical certainty. It is simply the best estimate we have. National accounts represent the only consistent, systematic attempt to analyze a country's economic activity. They should be regarded as a limited and imperfect research tool, a compilation and arrangement of data from highly disparate sources. In all developed countries, national accounts are currently compiled by government statistical offices and central banks from the balance sheets and account books of financial and nonfinancial corporations together with many other statistical sources and surveys. We have no reason to think a priori that the officials involved in these efforts do not do their best to spot inconsistencies in the data in order to achieve the best possible estimates. Provided we use these data with caution and in a critical spirit

---

respects is too "productivist." For instance, if a natural disaster destroys a great deal of wealth, the depreciation of capital will reduce national income, but GDP will be increased by reconstruction efforts.

19. For a history of official systems of national accounting since World War II, written by one of the principal architects of the new system adopted by the United Nations in 1993 (the so-called System of National Accounts [SNA] 1993, which was the first to propose consistent definitions for capital accounts), see André Vanoli, *Une histoire de la comptabilité nationale* (Paris: La Découverte, 2002). See also the instructive comments of Richard Stone, "Nobel Memorial Lecture, 1984: The Accounts of Society," *Journal of Applied Econometrics* 1, no. 1 (January 1986): 5–28. Stone was one of the pioneers of British and UN accounts in the postwar period. See also François Fourquet, *Les comptes de la puissance— Histoire de la comptabilité nationale et du plan* (Paris: Recherches, 1980), an anthology of contributions by individuals involved in constructing French national accounts in the period 1945–1975.

and complement them with other data where there are errors or gaps (say, in dealing with tax havens), these national accounts are an indispensable tool for estimating aggregate income and wealth.

In particular, as I will show in Part Two, we can put together a consistent analysis of the historical evolution of the capital / income ratio by meticulously compiling and comparing national wealth estimates by many authors from the eighteenth to the early twentieth century and connecting them up with official capital accounts from the late twentieth and early twenty-first century. The other major limitation of official national accounts, apart from their lack of historical perspective, is that they are deliberately concerned only with aggregates and averages and not with distributions and inequalities. We must therefore draw on other sources to measure the distribution of income and wealth and to study inequalities. National accounts thus constitute a crucial element of our analyses, but only when completed with additional historical and distributional data.

The Global Distribution of Production

I begin by examining the evolution of the global distribution of production, which is relatively well known from the early nineteenth century on. For earlier periods, estimates are more approximate, but we know the broad outlines, thanks most notably to the historical work of Angus Maddison, especially since the overall pattern is relatively simple.[20]

From 1900 to 1980, 70–80 percent of the global production of goods and services was concentrated in Europe and America, which

---

20. Angus Maddison (1926–2010) was a British economist who specialized in reconstituting national accounts at the global level over a very long run. Note that Maddison's historical series are concerned solely with the flow of output (GDP, population, and GDP per capita) and say nothing about national income, the capital-labor split, or the stock of capital. On the evolution of the global distribution of output and income, see also the pioneering work of François Bourguignon and Branko Milanovic. See the online technical appendix.

incontestably dominated the rest of the world. By 2010, the European–American share had declined to roughly 50 percent, or approximately the same level as in 1860. In all probability, it will continue to fall and may go as low as 20–30 percent at some point in the twenty-first century. This was the level maintained up to the turn of the nineteenth century and would be consistent with the European–American share of the world's population (see Figures 1.1 and 1.2).

In other words, the lead that Europe and America achieved during the Industrial Revolution allowed these two regions to claim a share of global output that was two to three times as large as their share of the world's population simply because their output per capita was two to three times as large as the global average.[21] All signs are that this phase of divergence in per capita output is over and that we have embarked on a period of convergence. The resulting "catch-up" phenomenon is far from over, however (see Figure 1.3). It is far too early to predict when it might end, especially since the possibility of economic and / or political reversals in China and elsewhere obviously cannot be ruled out.

From Continental Blocs to Regional Blocs

The general pattern just described is well known, but a number of points need to be clarified and refined. First, putting Europe and the Americas together as a single "Western bloc" simplifies the presentation but is largely artificial. Europe attained its maximal economic weight on the eve of World War I, when it accounted for nearly 50 percent of global output, and it has declined steadily since then, whereas America attained its peak in the 1950s, when it accounted for nearly 40 percent of global output.

---

21. The series presented here go back only as far as 1700, but Maddison's estimates go back all the way to antiquity. His results suggest that Europe began to move ahead of the rest of the world as early as 1500. By contrast, around the year 1000, Asia and Africa (and especially the Arab world) enjoyed a slight advantage. See Supplemental Figures S1.1, S1.2, and S1.3 (available online).

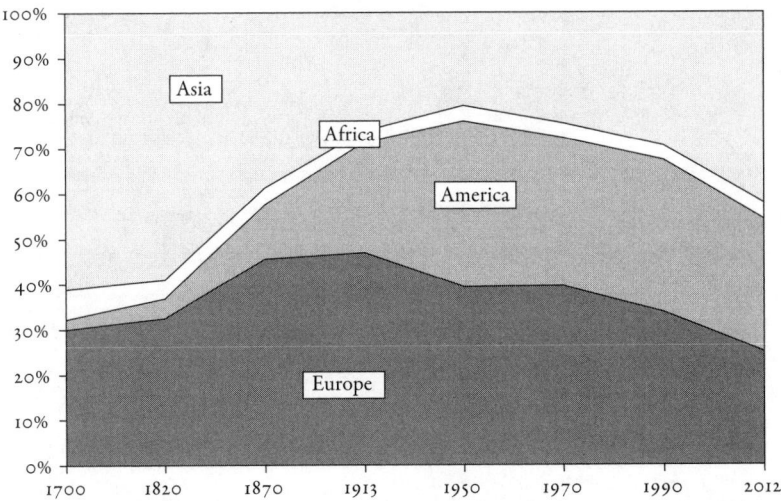

FIGURE I.I. The distribution of world output, 1700–2012

Europe's GDP made 47 percent of world GDP in 1913, down to 25 percent in 2012.
Sources and series: see piketty.pse.ens.fr/capital21c.

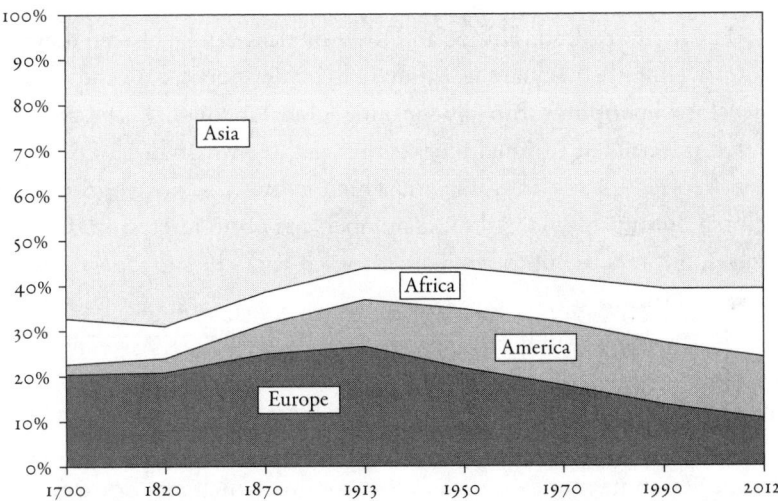

FIGURE I.2. The distribution of world population, 1700–2012

Europe's population made 26 percent of world population in 1913, down to 10 percent in 2012.
Sources and series: see piketty.pse.ens.fr/capital21c.

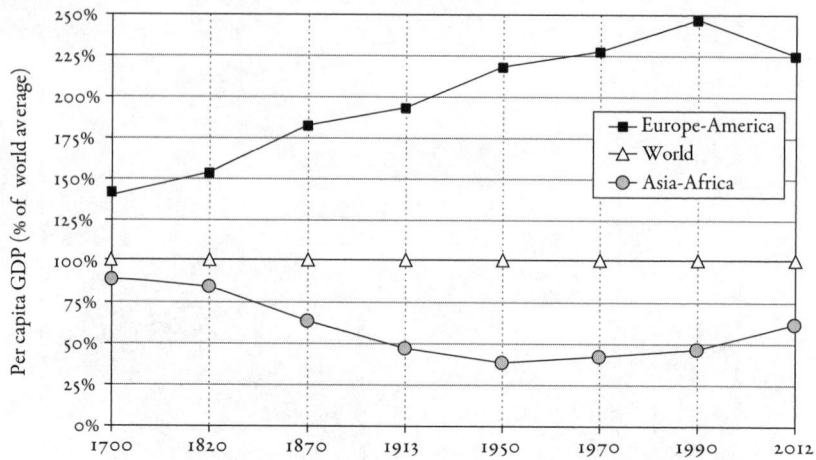

FIGURE 1.3. Global inequality, 1700–2012: divergence then convergence?
Per capita GDP in Asia-Africa went from 37 percent of world average in 1950 to 61 percent in 2012.
Sources and series: see piketty.pse.ens.fr/capital21c.

Furthermore, both Europe and the Americas can be broken down into two highly unequal subregions: a hyperdeveloped core and a less developed periphery. Broadly speaking, global inequality is best analyzed in terms of regional blocs rather than continental blocs. This can be seen clearly in Table 1.1, which shows the distribution of global output in 2012. All these numbers are of no interest in themselves, but it is useful to familiarize oneself with the principal orders of magnitude.

The population of the planet is close to 7 billion in 2012, and global output is slightly greater than 70 trillion euros, so that global output per capita is almost exactly 10,000 euros. If we subtract 10 percent for capital depreciation and divide by 12, we find that this yields an average per capita monthly income of 760 euros, which may be a clearer way of making the point. In other words, if global output and the income to which it gives rise were equally divided, each individual in the world would have an income of about 760 euros per month.

TABLE I.I.

Distribution of world GDP, 2012

Region	Population (million inhabitants)		GDP (billion euros 2012)		Per capita GDP (euros 2012)	Equivalent per capita monthly income (euros 2012)
World	7,050	100%	71,200	100%	10,100	760
Europe	740	10%	17,800	25%	24,000	1,800
incl. European Union	540	8%	14,700	21%	27,300	2,040
incl. Russia / Ukraine	200	3%	3,100	4%	15,400	1,150
America	950	13%	20,600	29%	21,500	1,620
incl. United States / Canada	350	5%	14,300	20%	40,700	3,050
incl. Latin America	600	9%	6,300	9%	10,400	780
Africa	1,070	15%	2,800	4%	2,600	200
incl. North Africa	170	2%	1,000	1%	5,700	430
incl. Sub-Saharan Africa	900	13%	1,800	3%	2,000	150
Asia	4,290	61%	30,000	42%	7,000	520
incl. China	1,350	19%	10,400	15%	7,700	580
incl. India	1,260	18%	4,000	6%	3,200	240
incl. Japan	130	2%	3,800	5%	30,000	2,250
incl. other	1,550	22%	11,800	17%	7,600	570

Note: World GDP, estimated in purchasing power parity, was about 71,200 billion euros in 2012. World population was about 7,050 billion inhabitants, hence a per capita GDP of €10,100 (equivalent to a monthly income of about €760 per month). All numbers were rounded to the closest dozen or hundred.

Sources: See piketty.pse.ens.fr/capital21c.

The population of Europe is about 740 million, about 540 million of whom live in member countries of the European Union, whose per capita output exceeds 27,000 euros per year. The remaining 200 million people live in Russia and Ukraine, where the per capita output is about 15,000 euros per year, barely 50 percent above the global average.[22] The European Union itself is relatively heterogeneous: 410 million of its citizens live in what used to be called Western Europe, three-quarters of them in the five most populous countries of the Union, namely Germany, France, Great Britain, Italy, and Spain, with an average per capita GDP of 31,000 euros per year, while the remaining 130 million live in what used to be Eastern Europe, with an average per capita output on the order of 16,000 euros per year, not very different from the Russia-Ukraine bloc.[23]

The Americas can also be divided into distinct regions that are even more unequal than the European center and periphery: the US-Canada bloc has 350 million people with a per capita output of 40,000 euros, while Latin America has 600 million people with a per capita output of 10,000 euros, exactly equal to the world average.

Sub-Saharan Africa, with a population of 900 million and an annual output of only 1.8 trillion euros (less than the French GDP of 2 trillion), is economically the poorest region of the world, with a per capita output of only 2,000 euros per year. India is slightly higher, while North Africa does markedly better, and China even better than that: with a per capita output of 8,000 euros per year, China in 2012 is not far below the world average. Japan's annual per capita output is equal to that of the wealthiest European countries (approximately 30,000 euros), but its population is such a small minority in the

---

22. To simplify the exposition, I include in the European Union smaller European countries such as Switzerland, Norway, and Serbia, which are surrounded by the European Union but not yet members (the population of the European Union in the narrow sense was 510 million in 2012, not 540 million). Similarly, Belarus and Moldavia are included in the Russia-Ukraine bloc. Turkey, the Caucasus, and Central Asia are included in Asia. Detailed figures for each country are available online.

23. See Supplemental Table S1.1 (available online).

greater Asian population that it has little influence on the continental average, which is close to that of China.[24]

Global Inequality: From 150 Euros per Month to 3,000 Euros per Month

To sum up, global inequality ranges from regions in which the per capita income is on the order of 150–250 euros per month (sub-Saharan Africa, India) to regions where it is as high as 2,500–3,000 euros per month (Western Europe, North America, Japan), that is, ten to twenty times higher. The global average, which is roughly equal to the Chinese average, is around 600–800 euros per month.

These orders of magnitude are significant and worth remembering. Bear in mind, however, that the margin of error in these figures is considerable: it is always much more difficult to measure inequalities between countries (or between different periods) than within them.

For example, global inequality would be markedly higher if we used current exchange rates rather than purchasing power parities, as I have done thus far. To understand what these terms mean, first consider the euro / dollar exchange rate. In 2012, a euro was worth about $1.30 on the foreign exchange market. A European with an income of 1,000 euros per month could go to his or her bank and exchange that amount for $1,300. If that person then took that money to the United States to spend, his or her purchasing power would be $1,300. But according to the official International Comparison Program (ICP), European prices are about 10 percent higher than American prices, so that if this same European spent the same money in Europe, his or her purchasing power would be closer to an American income of $1,200. Thus we say that $1.20 has "purchasing power parity" with 1 euro. I used

---

24. The same can be said of Australia and New Zealand (with a population of barely 30 million, or less than 0.5 percent of the world's population, with a per capita GDP of around 30,000 euros per year). For simplicity's sake, I include these two countries in Asia. See Supplemental Table S1.1 (available online).

this parity rather than the exchange rate to convert American GDP to euros in Table 1.1, and I did the same for the other countries listed. In other words, we compare the GDP of different countries on the basis of the actual purchasing power of their citizens, who generally spend their income at home rather than abroad.[25]

The other advantage of using purchasing power parities is that they are more stable than exchange rates. Indeed, exchange rates reflect not only the supply and demand for the goods and services of different countries but also sudden changes in the investment strategies of international investors and volatile estimates of the political and / or financial stability of this or that country, to say nothing of unpredictable changes in monetary policy. Exchange rates are therefore extremely volatile, as a glance at the large fluctuations of the dollar over the past few decades will show. The dollar / euro rate went from $1.30 per euro in the 1990s to less than $0.90 in 2001 before rising to around $1.50 in 2008 and then falling back to $1.30 in 2012. During that time, the purchasing power parity of the euro rose gently from roughly $1 per euro in the early 1990s to roughly $1.20 in 2010 (see Figure 1.4).[26]

Despite the best efforts of the international organizations involved in the ICP, there is no escaping the fact that these purchasing power parity estimates are rather uncertain, with margins of error on the

---

25. If the current exchange rate of $1.30 per euro to convert American GDP had been used, the United States would have appeared to be 10 percent poorer, and GDP per capital would have declined from 40,000 to about 35,000 euros (which would in fact be a better measure of the purchasing power of an American tourist in Europe). See Supplemental Table S1.1. The official ICP estimates are made by a consortium of international organizations, including the World Bank, Eurostat, and others. Each country is treated separately. There are variations within the Eurozone, and the euro / dollar parity of $1.20 is an average. See the online technical appendix.

26. The secular decline of US dollar purchasing power vis-à-vis the euro since 1990 simply reflects the fact that inflation in the United States was slightly higher (0.8 percent, or nearly 20 percent over 20 years). The current exchange rates shown in Figure 1.4 are annual averages and thus obscure the enormous short-term volatility.

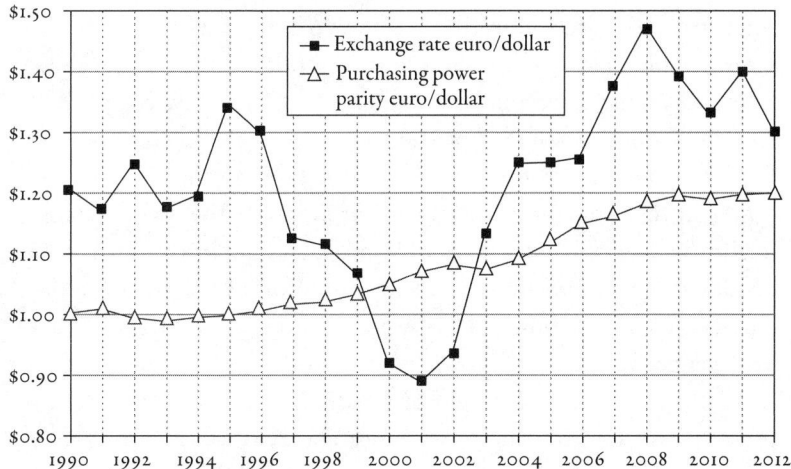

FIGURE 1.4. Exchange rate and purchasing power parity: euro / dollar

In 2012, 1 euro was worth $1.30 according to current exchange rate, but $1.20 in purchasing power parity.

Sources and series: see piketty.pse.ens.fr/capital21c.

order of 10 percent if not higher, even between countries at comparable levels of development. For example, the most recent available survey shows that while some European prices (for energy, housing, hotels, and restaurants) are indeed higher than comparable American prices, others are sharply lower (for health and education, for instance).[27] In theory, the official estimates weight all prices according to the weight of various goods and services in a typical budget for each country, but such calculations clearly leave a good deal of room for error, particularly

---

27. See *Global Purchasing Power Parities and Real Expenditures—2005 International Comparison Programme* (Washington, DC: World Bank, 2008), table 2, pp. 38–47. Note that in these official accounts, free or reduced-price public services are measured in terms of their production cost (for example, teachers' wages in education), which is ultimately paid by taxpayers. This is the result of a statistical protocol that is ultimately paid by the taxpayer. It is an imperfect statistical contract, albeit still more satisfactory than most. A statistical convention that refused to take any of these national statistics into account would be worse, resulting in highly distorted international comparisons.

since it is very hard to measure qualitative differences for many services. In any case, it is important to emphasize that each of these price indices measures a different aspect of social reality. The price of energy measures purchasing power for energy (which is greater in the United States), while the price of health care measures purchasing power in that area (which is greater in Europe). The reality of inequality between countries is multidimensional, and it is misleading to say that it can all be summed up with a single index leading to an unambiguous classification, especially between countries with fairly similar average incomes.

In the poorer countries, the corrections introduced by purchasing power parity are even larger: in Africa and Asia, prices are roughly half what they are in the rich countries, so that GDP roughly doubles when purchasing power parity is used for comparisons rather than the market exchange rate. This is chiefly a result of the fact that the prices of goods and services that cannot be traded internationally are lower, because these are usually relatively labor intensive and involve relatively unskilled labor (a relatively abundant factor of production in less developed countries), as opposed to skilled labor and capital (which are relatively scarce in less developed countries).[28] Broadly speaking, the poorer a country is, the greater the correction: in 2012, the correction coefficient was 1.6 in China and 2.5 in India.[29] At this moment, the euro is worth 8 Chinese yuan on the foreign exchange market but only 5 yuan in purchasing power parity. The gap is shrinking as China de-

---

28. This is the usual expectation (in the so-called Balassa-Samuelson model), which seems to explain fairly well why the purchasing-power parity adjustment is greater than 1 for poor countries vis-à-vis rich countries. Within rich countries, however, things are not so clear: the richest country in the world (the United States) had a purchasing-power parity correction greater than 1 until 1970, but it was less than 1 in the 1980s. Apart from measurement error, one possible explanation would be the high degree of wage inequality observed in the United States in recent years, which might lead to lower prices in the unskilled, labor-intensive, nontradable service sector (just as in the poor countries). See the online technical appendix.

29. See Supplementary Table S1.2 (available online).

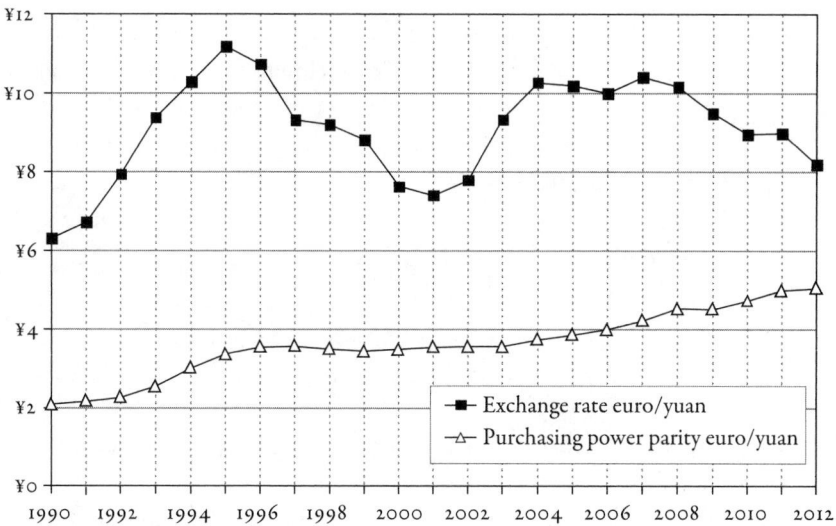

FIGURE 1.5. Exchange rate and purchasing power parity: euro / yuan

In 2012, 1 euro was worth 8 yuan according to current exchange rate, but 5 yuan in purchasing power parity.

Sources and series: see piketty.pse.ens.fr/capital21c.

velops and revalues the yuan (see Figure 1.5). Some writers, including Angus Maddison, argue that the gap is not as small as it might appear and that official international statistics underestimate Chinese GDP.[30]

Because of the uncertainties surrounding exchange rates and purchasing power parities, the average per capita monthly incomes discussed earlier (150–250 euros for the poorest countries, 600–800 euros for middling countries, and 2,500–3,000 euros for the richest countries) should be treated as approximations rather than mathematical certainties. For example, the share of the rich countries (European Union, United States, Canada, and Japan) in global income was 46 percent in 2012 if we use purchasing power parity but 57 percent if

---

30. I have used official estimates for the recent period, but it is entirely possible that the next ICP survey will result in a reevaluation of Chinese GDP. On the Maddison / ICP controversy, see the online technical appendix.

we use current exchange rates.[31] The "truth" probably lies somewhere between these two figures and is probably closer to the first. Still, the orders of magnitude remain the same, as does the fact that the share of income going to the wealthy countries has been declining steadily since the 1970s. Regardless of what measure is used, the world clearly seems to have entered a phase in which rich and poor countries are converging in income.

The Global Distribution of Income Is More Unequal Than the Distribution of Output

To simplify the exposition, the discussion thus far has assumed that the national income of each continental or regional grouping coincided with its domestic product: the monthly incomes indicated in Table 1.1 were obtained simply by deducting 10 percent from GDP (to account for depreciation of capital) and dividing by twelve.

In fact, it is valid to equate income and output only at the global level and not at the national or continental level. Generally speaking, the global income distribution is more unequal than the output distribution, because the countries with the highest per capita output are also more likely to own part of the capital of other countries and therefore to receive a positive flow of income from capital originating in countries with a lower level of per capita output. In other words, the rich countries are doubly wealthy: they both produce more at home and invest more abroad, so that their national income per head is greater than their output per head. The opposite is true for poor countries.

More specifically, all of the major developed countries (the United States, Japan, Germany, France, and Britain) currently enjoy a level of national income that is slightly greater than their domestic product.

---

31. See Supplemental Table S1.2 (available online). The European Union's share would rise from 21 to 25 percent, that of the US–Canada bloc from 20 to 24 percent, and that of Japan from 5 to 8 percent.

As noted, however, net income from abroad is just slightly positive and does not radically alter the standard of living in these countries. It amounts to about 1 or 2 percent of GDP in the United States, France, and Britain and 2–3 percent of GDP in Japan and Germany. This is nevertheless a significant boost to national income, especially for Japan and Germany, whose trade surpluses have enabled them to accumulate over the past several decades substantial reserves of foreign capital, the return on which is today considerable.

I turn now from the wealthiest countries taken individually to continental blocs taken as a whole. What we find in Europe, America, and Asia is something close to equilibrium: the wealthier countries in each bloc (generally in the north) receive a positive flow of income from capital, which is partly canceled by the flow out of other countries (generally in the south and east), so that at the continental level, total income is almost exactly equal to total output, generally within 0.5 percent.[32]

The only continent not in equilibrium is Africa, where a substantial share of capital is owned by foreigners. According to the balance of payments data compiled since 1970 by the United Nations and other international organizations such as the World Bank and International Monetary Fund, the income of Africans is roughly 5 percent less than the continent's output (and as high as 10 percent lower in some individual countries).[33] With capital's share of income at about 30 percent, this means that nearly 20 percent of African capital is owned by foreigners: think of the London stockholders of the Marikana platinum mine discussed at the beginning of this chapter.

---

32. This of course does not mean that each continent is hermetically sealed off from the others: these net flows hide large cross-investments between continents.

33. This 5 percent figure for the African continent appears to have remained fairly stable during the period 1970–2012. It is interesting to note that the outflow of income from capital was on the order of three times greater than the inflow of international aid (the measurement of which is open to debate, moreover). For further details on all these estimates, see the online technical appendix.

It is important to realize what such a figure means in practice. Since some kinds of wealth (such as residential real estate and agricultural capital) are rarely owned by foreign investors, it follows that the foreign-owned share of Africa's manufacturing capital may exceed 40–50 percent and may be higher still in other sectors. Despite the fact that there are many imperfections in the balance of payments data, foreign ownership is clearly an important reality in Africa today.

If we look back farther in time, we find even more marked international imbalances. On the eve of World War I, the national income of Great Britain, the world's leading investor, was roughly 10 percent above its domestic product. The gap was more than 5 percent in France, the number two colonial power and global investor, and Germany was a close third, even though its colonial empire was insignificant, because its highly developed industrial sector accumulated large claims on the rest of the world. British, French, and German investment went partly to other European countries and the United States and partly to Asia and Africa. Overall, the European powers in 1913 owned an estimated one-third to one-half of the domestic capital of Asia and Africa and more than three-quarters of their industrial capital.[34]

What Forces Favor Convergence?

In theory, the fact that the rich countries own part of the capital of poor countries can have virtuous effects by promoting convergence. If the rich countries are so flush with savings and capital that there is little reason to build new housing or add new machinery (in which case economists say that the "marginal productivity of capital," that is, the additional output due to adding one new unit of capital "at the margin," is very low), it can be collectively efficient to invest some part

---

34. In other words, the Asian and African share of world output in 1913 was less than 30 percent, and their share of world income was closer to 25 percent. See the on-line technical appendix.

of domestic savings in poorer countries abroad. Thus the wealthy countries—or at any rate the residents of wealthy countries with capital to spare—will obtain a better return on their investment by investing abroad, and the poor countries will increase their productivity and thus close the gap between them and the rich countries. According to classical economic theory, this mechanism, based on the free flow of capital and equalization of the marginal productivity of capital at the global level, should lead to convergence of rich and poor countries and an eventual reduction of inequalities through market forces and competition.

This optimistic theory has two major defects, however. First, from a strictly logical point of view, the equalization mechanism does not guarantee global convergence of per capita income. At best it can give rise to convergence of per capita output, provided we assume perfect capital mobility and, even more important, total equality of skill levels and human capital across countries—no small assumption. In any case, the possible convergence of output per head does *not* imply convergence of income per head. After the wealthy countries have invested in their poorer neighbors, they may continue to own them indefinitely, and indeed their share of ownership may grow to massive proportions, so that the per capita national income of the wealthy countries remains permanently greater than that of the poorer countries, which must continue to pay to foreigners a substantial share of what their citizens produce (as African countries have done for decades). In order to determine how likely such a situation is to arise, we must compare the rate of return on capital that the poor countries must pay to the rich to the growth rates of rich and poor economies. Before proceeding down this road, we must first gain a better understanding of the dynamics of the capital / income ratio within a given country.

Furthermore, if we look at the historical record, it does not appear that capital mobility has been the primary factor promoting convergence of rich and poor nations. None of the Asian countries that have moved closer to the developed countries of the West in recent years has benefited from large foreign investments, whether it be Japan, South Korea, or Taiwan and more recently China. In essence, all of these countries themselves financed the necessary investments in physical capital and, even more, in human capital, which the latest research holds to be the key to long-term growth.[35] Conversely, countries owned by other countries, whether in the colonial period or in Africa today, have been less successful, most notably because they have tended to specialize in areas without much prospect of future development and because they have been subject to chronic political instability.

Part of the reason for that instability may be the following. When a country is largely owned by foreigners, there is a recurrent and almost irrepressible social demand for expropriation. Other political actors respond that investment and development are possible only if existing property rights are unconditionally protected. The country is thus caught in an endless alternation between revolutionary governments (whose success in improving actual living conditions for their citizens is often limited) and governments dedicated to the protection of existing property owners, thereby laying the groundwork for the next revolution or coup. Inequality of capital ownership is already difficult to accept and peacefully maintain within a single national community. Internationally, it is almost impossible to sustain without a colonial type of political domination.

Make no mistake: participation in the global economy is not negative in itself. Autarky has never promoted prosperity. The Asian coun-

---

35. It has been well known since the 1950s that accumulation of physical capital explains only a small part of long-term productivity growth; the essential thing is the accumulation of human capital and new knowledge. See in particular Robert M. Solow, "A Contribution to the Theory of Economic Growth," *Quarterly Journal of Economics* 70, no. 1 (February 1956): 65–94. The recent articles of Charles I. Jones and Paul M. Romer, "The New Kaldor Facts: Ideas, Institutions, Population and Human Capital," *American Economic Journal: Macroeconomics* 2, no. 1 (January 2010): 224–45, and Robert J. Gordon, "Is U.S. Economic Growth Over? Faltering Innovation Confronts the Six Headwinds," NBER Working Paper 18315 (August 2012), are good points of entry into the voluminous literature on the determinants of long-run growth.

tries that have lately been catching up with the rest of the world have clearly benefited from openness to foreign influences. But they have benefited far more from open markets for goods and services and advantageous terms of trade than from free capital flows. China, for example, still imposes controls on capital: foreigners cannot invest in the country freely, but that has not hindered capital accumulation, for which domestic savings largely suffice. Japan, South Korea, and Taiwan all financed investment out of savings. Many studies also show that gains from free trade come mainly from the diffusion of knowledge and from the productivity gains made necessary by open borders, not from static gains associated with specialization, which appear to be fairly modest.[36]

To sum up, historical experience suggests that the principal mechanism for convergence at the international as well as the domestic level is the diffusion of knowledge. In other words, the poor catch up with the rich to the extent that they achieve the same level of technological know-how, skill, and education, not by becoming the property of the wealthy. The diffusion of knowledge is not like manna from heaven: it is often hastened by international openness and trade (autarky does not encourage technological transfer). Above all, knowledge diffusion depends on a country's ability to mobilize financing as well as institutions that encourage large-scale investment in education and training of the population while guaranteeing a stable legal framework that various economic actors can reliably count on. It is therefore closely associated with the achievement of legitimate and efficient government. Concisely stated, these are the main lessons that history has to teach about global growth and international inequalities.

---

36. According to one recent study, the static gains from the opening of India and China to global commerce amount to just 0.4 percent of global GDP, 3.5 percent of GDP for China, and 1.6 percent for India. In view of the enormous redistributive effects between sectors and countries (with very large numbers of losers in all countries), it seems difficult to justify trade openness (to which these countries nevertheless seem attached) solely on the basis of such gains. See the online technical appendix.

TWO

Growth: Illusions and Realities

A global convergence process in which emerging countries are catching up with developed countries seems well under way today, even though substantial inequalities between rich and poor countries remain. There is, moreover, no evidence that this catch-up process is primarily a result of investment by the rich countries in the poor. Indeed, the contrary is true: past experience shows that the promise of a good outcome is greater when poor countries are able to invest in themselves. Beyond the central issue of convergence, however, the point I now want to stress is that the twenty-first century may see a return to a low-growth regime. More precisely, what we will find is that growth has in fact always been relatively slow except in exceptional periods or when catch-up is occurring. Furthermore, all signs are that growth—or at any rate its demographic component—will be even slower in the future.

To understand what is at issue here and its relation to the convergence process and the dynamics of inequality, it is important to decompose the growth of output into two terms: population growth and per capita output growth. In other words, growth always includes a purely demographic component and a purely economic component, and only the latter allows for an improvement in the standard of living. In public debate this decomposition is too often forgotten, as many people seem to assume that population growth has ceased entirely, which is not yet the case—far from it, actually, although all signs indicate that we are headed slowly in that direction. In 2013–2014, for example, global economic growth will probably exceed 3 percent, thanks to very rapid progress in the emerging countries. But global population is still growing at an annual rate close to 1 percent, so that global output per capita is actually growing at a rate barely above 2 percent (as is global income per capita).

Growth over the Very Long Run

Before turning to present trends, I will go back in time and present the stages and orders of magnitude of global growth since the Industrial Revolution. Consider first Table 2.1, which indicates growth rates over a very long period of time. Several important facts stand out. First, the takeoff in growth that began in the eighteenth century involved relatively modest annual growth rates. Second, the demographic and economic components of growth were roughly similar in magnitude. According to the best available estimates, global output grew at an average annual rate of 1.6 percent between 1700 and 2012, 0.8 percent of which reflects population growth, while another 0.8 percent came from growth in output per head.

Such growth rates may seem low compared to what one often hears in current debates, where annual growth rates below 1 percent are frequently dismissed as insignificant and it is commonly assumed that real growth doesn't begin until one has achieved 3–4 percent a year or even more, as Europe did in the thirty years after World War II and as China is doing today.

In fact, however, growth on the order of 1 percent a year in both population and per capita output, if continued over a very long period of time, as was the case after 1700, is extremely rapid, especially when compared with the virtually zero growth rate that we observe in the centuries prior to the Industrial Revolution.

Indeed, according to Maddison's calculations, both demographic and economic growth rates between year 0 and 1700 were below 0.1 percent (more precisely, 0.06 percent for population growth and 0.02 percent for per capita output).[1]

---

1. See Supplemental Table S2.1, available online, for detailed results by subperiod.

TABLE 2.1.

World growth since the Industrial Revolution (average annual growth rate)

Years	World output (%)	World population (%)	Per capita output (%)
0–1700	0.1	0.1	0.0
1700–2012	1.6	0.8	0.8
1700–1820	0.5	0.4	0.1
1820–1913	1.5	0.6	0.9
1913–2012	3.0	1.4	1.6

Note: Between 1913 and 2012, the growth rate of world GDP was 3.0 percent per year on average. This growth rate can be broken down between 1.4 percent for world population and 1.6 percent for per capita GDP.

Sources: See piketty.pse.ens.fr/capital21c.

To be sure, the precision of such estimates is illusory. We actually possess very little information about the growth of the world's population between 0 and 1700 and even less about output per head. Nevertheless, no matter how much uncertainty there is about the exact figures (which are not very important in any case), there is no doubt whatsoever that the pace of growth was quite slow from antiquity to the Industrial Revolution, certainly no more than 0.1–0.2 percent per year. The reason is quite simple: higher growth rates would imply, implausibly, that the world's population at the beginning of the Common Era was minuscule, or else that the standard of living was very substantially below commonly accepted levels of subsistence. For the same reason, growth in the centuries to come is likely to return to very low levels, at least insofar as the demographic component is concerned.

The Law of Cumulative Growth

In order to understand this argument better, it may be helpful to pause a moment to consider what might be called "the law of cumula-

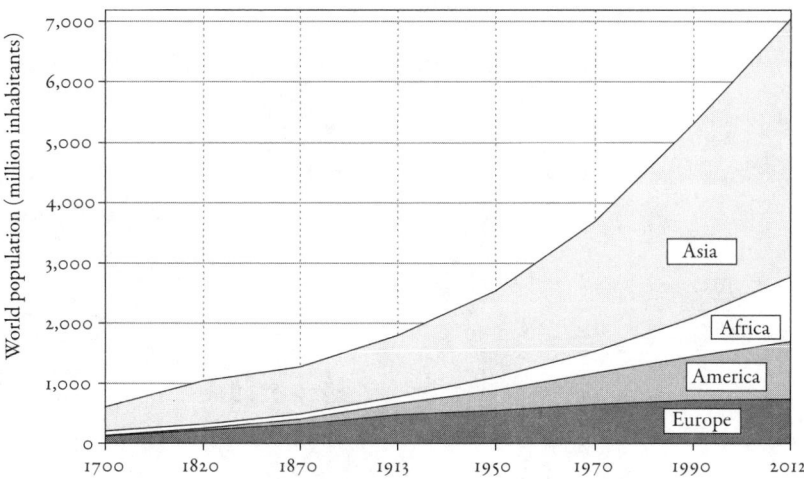

FIGURE 2.1. The growth of world population, 1700–2012

World population rose from 600 million inhabitants in 1700 to 7 billion in 2012. Sources and series: see piketty.pse.ens.fr/capital21c.

tive growth," which holds that a low annual growth rate over a very long period of time gives rise to considerable progress.

Concretely, the population of the world grew at an average annual rate of barely 0.8 percent between 1700 and 2012. Over three centuries, however, this meant that the global population increased more than tenfold. A planet with about 600 million inhabitants in 1700 had more than 7 billion in 2012 (see Figure 2.1). If this pace were to continue for the next three centuries, the world's population would exceed 70 billion in 2300.

To give a clear picture of the explosive effects of the law of cumulative growth, I have indicated in Table 2.2 the correspondence between the annual growth rate (the figure usually reported) and the long-term growth multiplier. For example, a growth rate of 1 percent per year will multiply the population by a factor of 1.35 after thirty years, 3 after one hundred years, 20 after three hundred years, and more than 20,000 after one thousand years. The simple conclusion that jumps out from this table is that growth rates greater than 1–1.5 percent a

TABLE 2.2.
The law of cumulated growth

An annual growth rate equal to . . .	. . . is equivalent to a generational growth rate (30 years) of . . .	. . . i.e., a multiplication by a coefficient equal to . . .	. . . and a multiplication after 100 years by a coefficient equal to . . .	. . . and a multiplication after 1,000 years by a coefficient equal to . . .
0.1%	3%	1.03	1.11	2.72
0.2%	6%	1.06	1.22	7.37
0.5%	16%	1.16	1.65	147
1.0%	35%	1.35	2.70	20,959
1.5%	56%	1.56	4.43	2,924,437
2.0%	81%	1.81	7.24	398,264,652
2.5%	110%	2.10	11.8	52,949,930,179
3.5%	181%	2.81	31.2	. . .
5.0%	332%	4.32	131.5	. . .

Note: An annual growth rate of 1% is equivalent to a cumulative growth rate of 35% per generation (30 years), a multiplication by 2.7 every 100 years, and by over 20,000 every 1,000 years.
Sources: See piketty.pse.ens.fr/capital21c.

year cannot be sustained indefinitely without generating vertiginous population increases.

We see clearly how different choices of time frame lead to contradictory perceptions of the growth process. Over a period of one year, 1 percent growth seems very low, almost imperceptible. People living at the time might not notice any change at all. To them, such growth might seem like complete stagnation, in which each year is virtually identical to the previous one. Growth might therefore seem like a fairly abstract notion, a purely mathematical and statistical construct. But if we expand the time frame to that of a generation, that is, about thirty years, which is the most relevant time scale for evaluating change in the society we live in, the same growth rate results in an increase of about a third, which represents a transformation of quite substantial magnitude. Although this is less impressive than growth of 2–2.5 percent per year, which leads to a doubling in every generation, it is still enough to alter society regularly and profoundly and in the very long run to transform it radically.

The law of cumulative growth is essentially identical to the law of cumulative returns, which says that an annual rate of return of a few percent, compounded over several decades, automatically results in a very large increase of the initial capital, provided that the return is constantly reinvested, or at a minimum that only a small portion of it is consumed by the owner of the capital (small in comparison with the growth rate of the society in question).

The central thesis of this book is precisely that an apparently small gap between the return on capital and the rate of growth can in the long run have powerful and destabilizing effects on the structure and dynamics of social inequality. In a sense, everything follows from the laws of cumulative growth and cumulative returns, and that is why the reader will find it useful at this point to become familiar with these notions.

The Stages of Demographic Growth

I return now to the examination of global population growth.

If the rhythm of demographic growth observed between 1700 and 2012 (0.8 percent per year on average) had started in antiquity and continued ever since, the world's population would have been multiplied by nearly 100,000 between 0 and 1700. Given that the population in 1700 is estimated to have been approximately 600 million, we would have to assume a ridiculously small global population at the time of Christ's birth (fewer than ten thousand people). Even a growth rate of 0.2 percent, extended over 1700 years, would imply a global population of only 20 million in year 0, whereas the best available information suggests that the figure was actually greater than 200 million, with 50 million living in the Roman Empire alone. Regardless of any flaws that may exist in the historical sources and global population estimates for these two dates, there is not a shadow of a doubt that the average demographic growth rate between 0 and 1700 was less than 0.2 percent and almost certainly less than 0.1 percent.

Contrary to a widely held belief, this Malthusian regime of very low growth was not one of complete demographic stagnation. The rate of growth was admittedly quite slow, and the cumulative growth of several generations was often wiped out in a few years by epidemic and famine.[2] Still, world population seems to have increased by a quarter between 0 and 1000, then by a half between 1000 and 1500, and by half again between 1500 and 1700, during which the demographic growth rate was close to 0.2 percent. The acceleration of growth was most likely a very gradual process, which proceeded hand in hand with growth in medical knowledge and sanitary improvements, that is to say, extremely slowly.

Demographic growth accelerated considerably after 1700, with average growth rates on the order of 0.4 percent per year in the eighteenth

---

2. The emblematic example is the Black Plague of 1347, which ostensibly claimed more than a third of the European population, thus negating several centuries of slow growth.

century and 0.6 percent in the nineteenth. Europe (including its American offshoot) experienced its most rapid demographic growth between 1700 and 1913, only to see the process reverse in the twentieth century: the rate of growth of the European population fell by half, to 0.4 percent, in the period 1913–2012, compared with 0.8 percent between 1820 and 1913. Here we see the phenomenon known as the demographic transition: the continual increase in life expectancy is no longer enough to compensate for the falling birth rate, and the pace of population growth slowly reverts to a lower level.

In Asia and Africa, however, the birth rate remained high far longer than in Europe, so that demographic growth in the twentieth century reached vertiginous heights: 1.5–2 percent per year, which translates into a fivefold or more increase in the population over the course of a century. Egypt had a population of slightly more than 10 million at the turn of the twentieth century but now numbers more than 80 million. Nigeria and Pakistan each had scarcely more than 20 million people, but today each has more than 160 million.

It is interesting to note that the growth rates of 1.5–2 percent a year attained by Asia and Africa in the twentieth century are roughly the same as those observed in America in the nineteenth and twentieth centuries (see Table 2.3). The United States thus went from a population of less than 3 million in 1780 to 100 million in 1910 and more than 300 million in 2010, or more than a hundredfold increase in just over two centuries, as mentioned earlier. The crucial difference, obviously, is that the demographic growth of the New World was largely due to immigration from other continents, especially Europe, whereas the 1.5–2 percent growth in Asia and Africa is due entirely to natural increase (the surplus of births over deaths).

As a consequence of this demographic acceleration, global population growth reached the record level of 1.4 percent in the twentieth century, compared with 0.4–0.6 percent in the eighteenth and nineteenth centuries (see Table 2.3).

It is important to understand that we are just emerging from this period of open-ended demographic acceleration. Between 1970 and

TABLE 2.3.

Demographic growth since the Industrial Revolution
(average annual growth rate)

Years	World population (%)	Europe (%)	America (%)	Africa (%)	Asia (%)
0–1700	0.1	0.1	0.0	0.1	0.1
1700–2012	0.8	0.6	1.4	0.9	0.8
1700–1820	0.4	0.5	0.7	0.2	0.5
1820–1913	0.6	0.8	1.9	0.6	0.4
1913–2012	1.4	0.4	1.7	2.2	1.5
Projections 2012–2050	*0.7*	*−0.1*	*0.6*	*1.9*	*0.5*
Projections 2050–2100	*0.2*	*−0.1*	*0.0*	*1.0*	*−0.2*

Note: Between 1913 and 2012, the growth rate of world population was 1.4% per year, including 0.4% for Europe, 1.7% for America, etc.

Sources: See piketty.pse.ens.fr/capital21c. Projections for 2012–2100 correspond to the UN central scenario.

1990, global population was still growing 1.8 percent annually, almost as high as the absolute historical record of 1.9 percent achieved in the period 1950–1970. For the period 1990–2012, the average rate is still 1.3 percent, which is extremely high.[3]

According to official forecasts, progress toward the demographic transition at the global level should now accelerate, leading to eventual stabilization of the planet's population. According to a UN forecast, the demographic growth rate should fall to 0.4 percent by the 2030s and settle around 0.1 percent in the 2070s. If this forecast is correct, the

---

3. If we take aging into account, the growth rate of the global adult population was even higher: 1.9 percent in the period 1990–2012 (during which the proportion of adults in the population rose from 57 percent to 65 percent, reaching close to 80 percent in Europe and Japan and 75 percent in North America in 2012). See the online technical appendix.

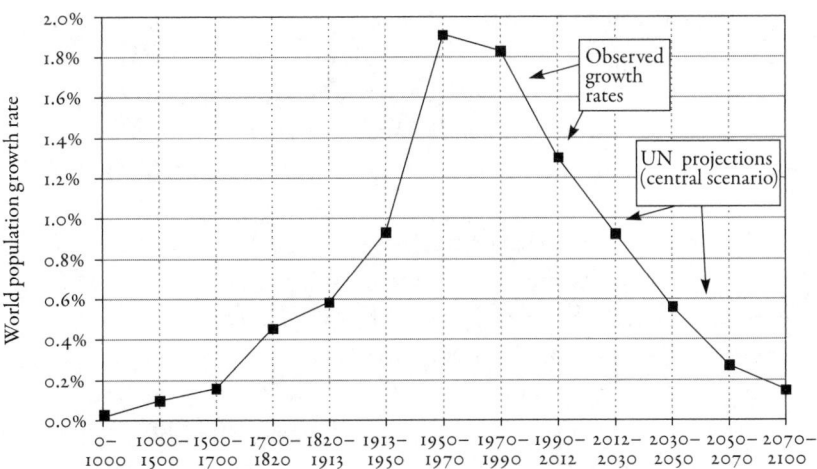

FIGURE 2.2. The growth rate of world population from Antiquity to 2100

The growth rate of world population was above 1 percent per year from 1950 to 2012 and should return toward 0 percent by the end of the twenty-first century.
Sources and series: see piketty.pse.ens.fr/capital21c.

world will return to the very low-growth regime of the years before 1700. The global demographic growth rate would then have followed a gigantic bell curve in the period 1700–2100, with a spectacular peak of close to 2 percent in the period 1950–1990 (see Figure 2.2).

Note, moreover, that the demographic growth anticipated for the second half of the twenty-first century (0.2 percent in the period 2050–2100) is entirely due to the continent of Africa (with annual growth of 1 percent). On the three other continents, the population will probably either stagnate (0.0 percent in America) or decrease (−0.1 percent in Europe and −0.2 percent in Asia). Such a prolonged period of negative demographic growth in peacetime would be unprecedented (see Table 2.3).

Negative Demographic Growth?

These forecasts are obviously rather uncertain. They depend first on the evolution of life expectancy (and thus in part on advances in medical science) and second on the decisions that future generations will make in regard to childbearing. If life expectancy is taken as given, the fertility rate determines the demographic growth rate. The important point to bear in mind is that small variations in the number of children couples decide to have can have significant consequences for society writ large.[4]

What demographic history teaches us is that these childbearing decisions are largely unpredictable. They are influenced by cultural, economic, psychological, and personal factors related to the life goals that individuals choose for themselves. These decisions may also depend on the material conditions that different countries decide to provide, or not provide, for the purpose of making family life compatible with professional life: schools, day care, gender equality, and so on. These issues will undoubtedly play a growing part in twenty-first-century political debate and public policy. Looking beyond the general schema just outlined, we find numerous regional differences and stunning changes in demographic patterns, many of them linked to specific features of each country's history.[5]

---

4. If the fertility rate is 1.8 (surviving) children per woman, or 0.9 per adult, than the population will automatically decrease by 10 percent every generation, or roughly −0.3 percent per year. Conversely, a fertility rate of 2.2 children per woman, or 1.1 per adult, yields a growth rate of 10 percent per generation (or +0.3 percent per year). With 1.5 children per woman, the growth rate is −1.0 percent per year, and with 2.5 children per woman, it is +0.7 percent.

5. It is impossible to do justice here to the large number of works of history, sociology, and anthropology that have tried to analyze, by country and region, the evolution and variations of demographic behavior (which, broadly speaking, encompasses questions of fertility, marriage, family structure, and so on). To take just one example, consider the work of Emmanuel Todd and Hervé Le Bras in mapping family systems in France, Europe, and around the world, from *L'Invention de la France* (Paris: Livre de Poche, 1981; reprint, Paris: Gallimard, 2012) to *L'origine des systèmes familiaux* (Paris: Gallimard, 2011). Or, to take a totally different perspective, see the work of Gosta Esping Andersen on the different types of welfare state and the growing importance of policies designed to make work life and family life compatible: for example, *The Three Worlds of Welfare Capitalism* (Princeton: Princeton University Press, 1990).

The most spectacular reversal no doubt involves Europe and America. In 1780, when the population of Western Europe was already greater than 100 million and that of North America barely 3 million, no one could have guessed the magnitude of the change that lay ahead. By 2010, the population of Western Europe was just above 410 million, while the North American population had increased to 350 million. According to UN projections, the catch-up process will be complete by 2050, at which time the Western European population will have grown to around 430 million, compared with 450 million for North America. What explains this reversal? Not just the flow of immigrants to the New World but also the markedly higher fertility rate there compared with old Europe. The gap persists to this day, even among groups that came originally from Europe, and the reasons for it remain largely a mystery to demographers. One thing is sure: the higher fertility rate in North America is not due to more generous family policies, since such policies are virtually nonexistent there.

Should the difference be interpreted as reflecting a greater North American faith in the future, a New World optimism, and a greater propensity to think of one's own and one's children's futures in terms of a perpetually growing economy? When it comes to decisions as complex as those related to fertility, no psychological or cultural explanation can be ruled out in advance, and anything is possible. Indeed, US demographic growth has been declining steadily, and current trends could be reversed if immigration into the European Union continues to increase, or fertility increases, or the European life expectancy widens the gap with the United States. United Nations forecasts are not certainties.

We also find spectacular demographic turnarounds within each continent. France was the most populous country in Europe in the eighteenth century (and, as noted, both Young and Malthus saw this as the reason for French rural poverty and even as the cause of the French Revolution). But the demographic transition occurred unusually early in France: a fall in the birth rate led to a virtually stagnant population as early as the nineteenth century. This is generally attributed to de-Christianization, which also came early. Yet an equally unusual leap in the birth rate took place in the twentieth century—a leap often attributed to pronatal policies adopted after the two world wars and to the trauma of defeat in 1940. France's wager may well pay off, since UN forecasts predict that the population of France will exceed that of Germany by 2050 or so. It is difficult, however, to distinguish the various causes of this reversal: economic, political, cultural, and psychological factors all play a part.[6]

On a grander scale, everyone knows the consequences of the Chinese policy to allow only one child per family (a decision made in the 1970s, when China feared being condemned to remain an underdeveloped country, and now in the process of being relaxed). The Chinese population, which was roughly 50 percent greater than India's when this radical policy was adopted, is now close to being surpassed by that of its neighbor. According to the United Nations, India will be the most populous country in the world by 2020. Yet here, too, nothing is set in stone: population history invariably combines individual choices, developmental strategies, and national psychologies—private motives and power motives. No one at this point can seriously claim to know what demographic turnarounds may occur in the twenty-first century.

It would therefore be presumptuous to regard the official UN predictions as anything other than a "central scenario." In any case, the United Nations has also published two other sets of predictions, and the gaps between these various scenarios at the 2100 horizon are, unsurprisingly, quite large.[7]

The central scenario is nevertheless the most plausible we have, given the present state of our knowledge. Between 1990 and 2012, the population of Europe was virtually stagnant, and the population of several countries actually decreased. Fertility rates in Germany, Italy,

---

6. See the online technical appendix for detailed series by country.

7. The global population growth rate from 2070 to 2100 will be 0.1 percent according to the central scenario, −1.0 percent according to the low scenario, and +1.2 percent according to the high scenario. See the online technical appendix.

Spain, and Poland fell below 1.5 children per woman in the 2000s, and only an increase in life expectancy coupled with a high level of immigration prevented a rapid decrease of population. In view of these facts, the UN prediction of zero demographic growth in Europe until 2030 and slightly negative rates after that is by no means extravagant. Indeed, it seems to be the most reasonable forecast. The same is true for UN predictions for Asia and other regions: the generations being born now in Japan and China are roughly one-third smaller than the generations born in the 1990s. The demographic transition is largely complete. Changes in individual decisions and government policies may slightly alter these trends: for example, slightly negative rates (such as we see in Japan and Germany) may become slightly positive (as in France and Scandinavia), which would be a significant change, but we are unlikely to see anything more than that, at least for the next several decades.

Of course the very long-run forecasts are much more uncertain. Note, however, that if the rate of population growth observed from 1700 to 2012—0.8 percent per year—were to continue for the next three centuries, the world's population would be on the order of 70 billion in 2300. To be sure, this cannot be ruled out: childbearing behavior could change, or technological advances might allow growth with much less pollution than is possible to imagine now, with output consisting of new, almost entirely nonmaterial goods and services produced with renewable energy sources exhibiting a negligible carbon footprint. At this point, however, it is hardly an exaggeration to say that a world population of 70 billion seems neither especially plausible nor particularly desirable. The most likely hypothesis is that the global population growth rate over the next several centuries will be significantly less than 0.8 percent. The official prediction of 0.1–0.2 percent per year over the very long run seems rather plausible a priori.

Growth as a Factor for Equalization

In any case, it is not the purpose of this book to make demographic predictions but rather to acknowledge these various possibilities and analyze their implications for the evolution of the wealth distribution. Beyond the consequences for the development and relative power of nations, demographic growth also has important implications for the structure of inequality. Other things being equal, strong demographic growth tends to play an equalizing role because it decreases the importance of inherited wealth: every generation must in some sense construct itself.

To take an extreme example, in a world in which each couple has ten children, it is clearly better as a general rule not to count too much on inherited wealth, because the family wealth will be divided by ten with each new generation. In such a society, the overall influence of inherited wealth would be strongly diminished, and most people would be more realistic to rely on their own labor and savings.

The same would be true in a society where the population is constantly replenished by immigration from other countries, as was the case in America. Assuming that most immigrants arrive without much wealth, the amount of wealth passed down from previous generations is inherently fairly limited in comparison with new wealth accumulated through savings. Demographic growth via immigration has other consequences, however, especially in regard to inequality between immigrants and natives as well as within each group. Such a society is thus not globally comparable to a society in which the primary source of population growth is natural increase (that is, from new births).

I will show that the intuition concerning the effects of strong demographic growth can to a certain extent be generalized to societies with very rapid economic (and not just demographic) growth. For example, in a society where output per capita grows tenfold every generation, it is better to count on what one can earn and save from one's own labor: the income of previous generations is so small compared with current income that the wealth accumulated by one's parents and grandparents doesn't amount to much.

Conversely, a stagnant or, worse, decreasing population increases the influence of capital accumulated in previous generations. The same is true of economic stagnation. With low growth, moreover, it is fairly plausible that the rate of return on capital will be substantially higher than the growth rate, a situation that, as I noted in the introduction, is the main factor leading toward very substantial inequality in the distribution of wealth over the long run. Capital-dominated societies in the past, with hierarchies largely determined by inherited wealth (a category that includes both traditional rural societies and the countries of nineteenth-century Europe) can arise and subsist only in low-growth regimes. I will consider the extent to which the probable return to a low-growth regime, if it occurs, will affect the dynamics of capital accumulation and the structure of inequality. In particular, inherited wealth will make a comeback—a long-term phenomenon whose effects are already being felt in Europe and that could extend to other parts of the world as well. That is why it is important for present purposes to become familiar with the history of demographic and economic growth.

There is another mechanism whereby growth can contribute to the reduction of inequality, or at least to a more rapid circulation of elites, which must also be discussed. This mechanism is potentially complementary to the first, although it is less important and more ambiguous. When growth is zero or very low, the various economic and social functions as well as types of professional activity, are reproduced virtually without change from generation to generation. By contrast, constant growth, even if it is only 0.5 or 1 or 1.5 percent per year, means that new functions are constantly being created and new skills are needed in every generation. Insofar as tastes and capabilities are only partially transmitted from generation to generation (or are transmitted much less automatically and mechanically than capital in land, real estate, or financial assets are transmitted by inheritance), growth can thus increase social mobility for individuals whose parents did not belong to the elite of the previous generation. This increased social mobility need not imply decreased income inequality, but in theory it does limit the reproduction and amplification of inequalities of wealth and therefore over the long run also limits income inequality to a certain extent.

One should be wary, however, of the conventional wisdom that modern economic growth is a marvelous instrument for revealing individual talents and aptitudes. There is some truth in this view, but since the early nineteenth century it has all too often been used to justify inequalities of all sorts, no matter how great their magnitude and no matter what their real causes may be, while at the same time gracing the winners in the new industrial economy with every imaginable virtue. For instance, the liberal economist Charles Dunoyer, who served as a prefect under the July Monarchy, had this to say in his 1845 book *De la liberté du travail* (in which he of course expressed his opposition to any form of labor law or social legislation): "one consequence of the industrial regime is to destroy artificial inequalities, but this only highlights natural inequalities all the more clearly." For Dunoyer, natural inequalities included differences in physical, intellectual, and moral capabilities, differences that were crucial to the new economy of growth and innovation that he saw wherever he looked. This was his reason for rejecting state intervention of any kind: "superior abilities . . . are the source of everything that is great and useful. . . . Reduce everything to equality and you will bring everything to a standstill."[8] One sometimes hears the same thought expressed today in the idea that the new information economy will allow the most talented individuals to increase their productivity many times over. The plain fact is that this argument is often used to justify extreme inequalities and to defend the privileges of the winners without much consideration for the losers, much less for the facts, and without any real effort to verify whether this very convenient principle can actually explain the changes we observe. I will come back to this point.

The Stages of Economic Growth

I turn now to the growth of per capita output. As noted, this was of the same order as population growth over the period 1700–2012: 0.8 percent per year on average, which equates to a multiplication of output by a factor of roughly ten over three centuries. Average global per

---

8. See Pierre Rosanvallon, *The Society of Equals,* trans. Arthur Goldhammer (Cambridge, MA: Harvard University Press, 2013), 93.

capita income is currently around 760 euros per month; in 1700, it was less than 70 euros per month, roughly equal to income in the poorest countries of Sub-Saharan Africa in 2012.[9]

This comparison is suggestive, but its significance should not be exaggerated. When comparing very different societies and periods, we must avoid trying to sum everything up with a single figure, for example "the standard of living in society A is ten times higher than in society B." When growth attains levels such as these, the notion of per capita output is far more abstract than that of population, which at least corresponds to a tangible reality (it is much easier to count people than to count goods and services). Economic development begins with the diversification of ways of life and types of goods and services produced and consumed. It is thus a multidimensional process whose very nature makes it impossible to sum up properly with a single monetary index.

Take the wealthy countries as an example. In Western Europe, North America, and Japan, average per capita income increased from barely 100 euros per month in 1700 to more than 2,500 euros per month in 2012, a more than twentyfold increase.[10] The increase in productivity, or output per hour worked, was even greater, because each person's average working time decreased dramatically: as the developed countries grew wealthier, they decided to work less in order to allow for more free time (the work day grew shorter, vacations grew longer, and so on).[11]

---

9. In 2012, the average per capita GDP in Sub-Saharan Africa was about 2,000 euros, implying an average monthly income of 150 euros per person (cf. Chapter 1, Table 1.1). But the poorest countries (such as Congo-Kinshasa, Niger, Chad, and Ethiopia) stand at one-third to one-half that level, while the richest (such as South Africa) are two to three times better off (and close to North African levels). See the online technical appendix.

10. Maddison's estimates (which are fragile for this period) suggest that in 1700, North America and Japan were closer to the global average than to Western Europe, so that overall growth in average income in the period 1700–2012 would be closer to thirty times than to twenty.

11. Over the long run, the average number of hours worked per capita has been cut by approximately one-half (with significant variation between countries), so that productivity growth has been roughly twice that of per capita output growth.

Much of this spectacular growth occurred in the twentieth century. Globally, the average growth of per capita output of 0.8 percent over the period 1700–2012 breaks down as follows: growth of barely 0.1 percent in the eighteenth century, 0.9 percent in the nineteenth century, and 1.6 percent in the twentieth century (see Table 2.1). In Western Europe, average growth of 1.0 percent in the same period breaks down as 0.2 percent in the eighteenth century, 1.1 percent in the nineteenth century, and 1.9 percent in the twentieth century.[12] Average purchasing power in Europe barely increased at all from 1700 to 1820, then more than doubled between 1820 and 1913, and increased more than sixfold between 1913 and 2012. Basically, the eighteenth century suffered from the same economic stagnation as previous centuries. The nineteenth century witnessed the first sustained growth in per capita output, although large segments of the population derived little benefit from this, at least until the last three decades of the century. It was not until the twentieth century that economic growth became a tangible, unmistakable reality for everyone. Around the turn of the twentieth century, average per capita income in Europe stood at just under 400 euros per month, compared with 2,500 euros in 2010.

But what does it mean for purchasing power to be multiplied by a factor of twenty, ten, or even six? It clearly does not mean that Europeans in 2012 produced and consumed six times more goods and services than they produced and consumed in 1913. For example, average food consumption obviously did not increase sixfold. Basic dietary needs would long since have been satisfied if consumption had increased that much. Not only in Europe but everywhere, improvements in purchasing power and standard of living over the long run depend primarily on a transformation of the structure of consumption: a consumer basket initially filled mainly with foodstuffs gradually gave way to a much more diversified basket of goods, rich in manufactured products and services.

---

12. See Supplemental Table S2.2, available online.

Furthermore, even if Europeans in 2012 wished to consume six times the amount of goods and services they consumed in 1913, they could not: some prices have risen more rapidly than the "average" price, while others have risen more slowly, so that purchasing power has not increased sixfold for all types of goods and services. In the short run, the problem of "relative prices" can be neglected, and it is reasonable to assume that the indices of "average" prices published by government agencies allow us to correctly gauge changes in purchasing power. In the long run, however, relative prices shift dramatically, as does the composition of the typical consumer's basket of goods, owing largely to the advent of new goods and services, so that average price indices fail to give an accurate picture of the changes that have taken place, no matter how sophisticated the techniques used by the statisticians to process the many thousands of prices they monitor and to correct for improvements in product quality.

What Does a Tenfold Increase in Purchasing Power Mean?

In fact, the only way to accurately gauge the spectacular increase in standards of living since the Industrial Revolution is to look at income levels in today's currency and compare these to price levels for the various goods and services available in different periods. For now, I will simply summarize the main lessons derived from such an exercise.[13]

It is standard to distinguish the following three types of goods and services. For industrial goods, productivity growth has been more rapid than for the economy as a whole, so that prices in this sector

---

13. Interested readers will find in the online technical appendix historical series of average income for many countries since the turn of the eighteenth century, expressed in today's currency. For detailed examples of the price of foodstuffs, manufactured goods, and services in nineteenth- and twentieth-century France (taken from various historical sources including official indices and compilations of prices published by Jean Fourastié), along with analysis of the corresponding increases in purchasing power, see Thomas Piketty, *Les hauts revenus en France au 20e siècle* (Paris: Grasset, 2001), 80–92.

have fallen relative to the average of all prices. Foodstuffs is a sector in which productivity has increased continuously and crucially over the very long run (thereby allowing a greatly increased population to be fed by ever fewer hands, liberating a growing portion of the workforce for other tasks), even though the increase in productivity has been less rapid in the agricultural sector than in the industrial sector, so that food prices have evolved at roughly the same rate as the average of all prices. Finally, productivity growth in the service sector has generally been low (or even zero in some cases, which explains why this sector has tended to employ a steadily increasing share of the workforce), so that the price of services has increased more rapidly than the average of all prices.

This general pattern is well known. Although it is broadly speaking correct, it needs to be refined and made more precise. In fact, there is a great deal of diversity within each of these three sectors. The prices of many food items did in fact evolve at the same rate as the average of all prices. For example, in France, the price of a kilogram of carrots evolved at the same rate as the overall price index in the period 1900–2010, so that purchasing power expressed in terms of carrots evolved in the same way as average purchasing power (which increased approximately sixfold). An average worker could afford slightly less than ten kilos of carrots per day at the turn of the twentieth century, while he could afford nearly sixty kilos per day at the turn of the twenty-first century.[14] For other foodstuffs, however, such as milk, butter, eggs, and dairy products in general, major technological advances in processing, manufacturing, conservation, and so on led to relative price decreases and thus to increases in purchasing power greater than sixfold. The same is true for products that benefited from the significant reduction in transport costs over the course of the twentieth century: for example, French purchasing power expressed in terms of oranges increased tenfold, and expressed in terms of bananas, twentyfold. Con-

---

14. Of course, everything depended on where carrots were purchased. I am speaking here of the average price.

versely, purchasing power measured in kilos of bread or meat rose less than fourfold, although there was a sharp increase in the quality and variety of products on offer.

Manufactured goods present an even more mixed picture, primarily because of the introduction of radically new goods and spectacular improvements in performance. The example often cited in recent years is that of electronics and computer technology. Advances in computers and cell phones in the 1990s and of tablets and smartphones in the 2000s and beyond have led to tenfold increases in purchasing power in a very short period of time: prices have fallen by half, while performance has increased by a factor of 5.

It is important to note that equally impressive examples can be found throughout the long history of industrial development. Take the bicycle. In France in the 1880s, the cheapest model listed in catalogs and sales brochures cost the equivalent of six months of the average worker's wage. And this was a relatively rudimentary bicycle, "which had wheels covered with just a strip of solid rubber and only one brake that pressed directly against the front rim." Technological progress made it possible to reduce the price to one month's wages by 1910. Progress continued, and by the 1960s one could buy a quality bicycle (with "detachable wheel, two brakes, chain and mud guards, saddle bags, lights, and reflector") for less than a week's average wage. All in all, and leaving aside the prodigious improvement in the quality and safety of the product, purchasing power in terms of bicycles rose by a factor of 40 between 1890 and 1970.[15]

One could easily multiply examples by comparing the price history of electric light bulbs, household appliances, table settings, clothing, and automobiles to prevailing wages in both developed and emerging economies.

All of these examples show how futile and reductive it is to try to sum up all these changes with a single index, as in "the standard of living increased tenfold between date A and date B." When family

---

15. See Piketty, *Les hauts revenus en France,* 83–85.

budgets and lifestyles change so radically and purchasing power varies so much from one good to another, it makes little sense to take averages, because the result depends heavily on the weights and measures of quality one chooses, and these are fairly uncertain, especially when one is attempting comparisons across several centuries.

None of this in any way challenges the reality of growth. Quite the contrary: the material conditions of life have clearly improved dramatically since the Industrial Revolution, allowing people around the world to eat better, dress better, travel, learn, obtain medical care, and so on. It remains interesting to measure growth rates over shorter periods such as a generation or two. Over a period of thirty to sixty years, there are significant differences between a growth rate of 0.1 percent per year (3 percent per generation), 1 percent per year (35 percent per generation), or 3 percent per year (143 percent per generation). It is only when growth statistics are compiled over very long periods leading to multiplications by huge factors that the numbers lose a part of their significance and become relatively abstract and arbitrary quantities.

Growth: A Diversification of Lifestyles

To conclude this discussion, consider the case of services, where diversity is probably the most extreme. In theory, things are fairly clear: productivity growth in the service sector has been less rapid, so that purchasing power expressed in terms of services has increased much less. As a typical case—a "pure" service benefiting from no major technological innovation over the centuries—one often takes the example of barbers: a haircut takes just as long now as it did a century ago, so that the price of a haircut has increased by the same factor as the barber's pay, which has itself progressed at the same rate as the average wage and average income (to a first approximation). In other words, an hour's work of the typical wage-earner in the twenty-first century can buy just as many haircuts as an hour's work a hundred years ago, so

TABLE 2.4.

Employment by sector in France and the United States, 1800–2012
(% of total employment)

Year	France			United States		
	Agriculture	Manufacturing	Services	Agriculture	Manufacturing	Services
1800	64	22	14	68	18	13
1900	43	29	28	41	28	31
1950	32	33	35	14	33	53
2012	3	21	76	2	18	80

Note: In 2012, agriculture made up 3% of total employment in France v. 21% in manufacturing and 76% in services. Construction—7% of employment in France and the United States in 2012—was included in manufacturing.
Sources: See piketty.pse.ens.fr/capital21c.

that purchasing power expressed in terms of haircuts has not increased (and may in fact have decreased slightly).[16]

In fact, the diversity of services is so extreme that the very notion of a service sector makes little sense. The decomposition of the economy into three sectors—primary, secondary, and tertiary—was an idea of the mid-twentieth century in societies where each sector included similar, or at any rate comparable, fractions of economic activity and the workforce (see Table 2.4). But once 70–80 percent of the workforce in the developed countries found itself working in the service sector, the category ceased to have the same meaning: it provided little information about the nature of the trades and services produced in a given society.

In order to find our way through this vast aggregate of activities, whose growth accounts for much of the improvement in living conditions since the nineteenth century, it will be useful to distinguish several subsectors.

16. Ibid., 86–87.

Consider first services in health and education, which by themselves account for more than 20 percent of total employment in the most advanced countries (or as much as all industrial sectors combined). There is every reason to think that this fraction will continue to increase, given the pace of medical progress and the steady growth of higher education. The number of jobs in retail; hotels, cafés, and restaurants; and culture and leisure activities also increased rapidly, typically accounting for 20 percent of total employment. Services to firms (consulting, accounting, design, data processing, etc.) combined with real estate and financial services (real estate agencies, banks, insurance, etc.) and transportation add another 20 percent of the job total. If you then add government and security services (general administration, courts, police, armed forces, etc.), which account for nearly 10 percent of total employment in most countries, you reach the 70–80 percent figure given in official statistics.[17]

Note that an important part of these services, especially in health and education, is generally financed by taxes and provided free of charge. The details of financing vary from country to country, as does the exact share financed by taxes, which is higher in Europe, for example, than in the United States or Japan. Still, it is quite high in all developed countries: broadly speaking, at least half of the total cost of health and education services is paid for by taxes, and in a number of European countries it is more than three-quarters. This raises poten-

---

17. For a historical analysis of the constitution of these various strata of services from the late nineteenth century to the late twentieth, starting with the examples of France and the United States, see Thomas Piketty, "Les Créations d'emploi en France et aux Etats-Unis: Services de proximité contre petits boulots?" *Les Notes de la Fondation Saint-Simon* 93, 1997. See also "L'Emploi dans les services en France et aux Etats-Unis: Une analyse structurelle sur longue période," *Economie et statistique* 318, no. 1 (1998): 73–99. Note that in government statistics the pharmaceutical industry is counted in industry and not in health services, just as the automobile and aircraft industries are counted in industry and not transport services, etc. It would probably be more perspicuous to group activities in terms of their ultimate purpose (health, transport, housing, etc.) and give up on the distinction agriculture / industry / services.

tial new difficulties and uncertainties when it comes to measuring and comparing increases in the standard of living in different countries over the long run. This is not a minor point: not only do these two sectors account for more than 20 percent of GDP and employment in the most advanced countries—a percentage that will no doubt increase in the future—but health and education probably account for the most tangible and impressive improvement in standards of living over the past two centuries. Instead of living in societies where the life expectancy was barely forty years and nearly everyone was illiterate, we now live in societies where it is common to reach the age of eighty and everyone has at least minimal access to culture.

In national accounts, the value of public services available to the public for free is always estimated on the basis of the production costs assumed by the government, that is, ultimately, by taxpayers. These costs include the wages paid to health workers and teachers employed by hospitals, schools, and public universities. This method of valuing services has its flaws, but it is logically consistent and clearly more satisfactory than simply excluding free public services from GDP calculations and concentrating solely on commodity production. It would be economically absurd to leave public services out entirely, because doing so would lead in a totally artificial way to an underestimate of the GDP and national income of a country that chose a public system of health and education rather than a private system, even if the available services were strictly identical.

The method used to compute national accounts has the virtue of correcting this bias. Still, it is not perfect. In particular, there is no objective measure of the quality of services rendered (although various correctives for this are under consideration). For example, if a private health insurance system costs more than a public system but does not yield truly superior quality (as a comparison of the United States with Europe suggests), then GDP will be artificially overvalued in countries that rely mainly on private insurance. Note, too, that the convention in national accounting is not to count any remuneration for public capital such as hospital buildings and equipment or schools and universities.[18] The consequence of this is that a country that privatized its health and education services would see its GDP rise artificially, even if the services produced and the wages paid to employees remained exactly the same.[19] It may be that this method of accounting by costs underestimates the fundamental "value" of education and health and therefore the growth achieved during periods of rapid expansion of services in these areas.[20]

Hence there is no doubt that economic growth led to a significant improvement in standard of living over the long run. The best available estimates suggest that global per capita income increased by a factor of more than 10 between 1700 and 2012 (from 70 euros to 760 euros per month) and by a factor of more than 20 in the wealthiest countries (from 100 to 2,500 euros per month). Given the difficulties of measuring such radical transformations, especially if we try to sum them up with a single index, we must be careful not to make a fetish of the numbers, which should rather be taken as indications of orders of magnitude and nothing more.

The End of Growth?

Now to consider the future. Will the spectacular increase in per capita output I have just described inexorably slow in the twenty-first century? Are we headed toward the end of growth for technological or ecological reasons, or perhaps both at once?

Before trying to answer this question, it is important to recall that past growth, as spectacular as it was, almost always occurred at rela-

---

18. Only the depreciation of capital (replacement of used buildings and equipment) is taken into account in calculating costs of production. But the remuneration of public capital, net of depreciation, is conventionally set at zero.

19. In Chapter 6 I take another look at the magnitude of the bias thus introduced into international comparisons.

20. Hervé Le Bras and Emmanuel Todd say much the same thing when they speak of the "Trente glorieuses culturelles" in describing the period 1980–2010 in France. This was a time of rapid educational expansion, in contrast to the "Trente glorieuses économiques" of 1950–1980. See *Le mystère français* (Paris: Editions du Seuil, 2013).

tively slow annual rates, generally no more than 1–1.5 percent per year. The only historical examples of noticeably more rapid growth— 3–4 percent or more—occurred in countries that were experiencing accelerated catch-up with other countries. This is a process that by definition ends when catch-up is achieved and therefore can only be transitional and time limited. Clearly, moreover, such a catch-up process cannot take place globally.

At the global level, the average rate of growth of per capita output was 0.8 percent per year from 1700 to 2012, or 0.1 percent in the period 1700–1820, 0.9 percent in 1820–1913, and 1.6 percent in 1913–2012. As indicated in Table 2.1, we find the same average growth rate—0.8 percent—when we look at world population 1700–2012.

Table 2.5 shows the economic growth rates for each century and each continent separately. In Europe, per capita output grew at a rate of 1.0 percent 1820–1913 and 1.9 percent 1913–2012. In America, growth reached 1.5 percent 1820–1913 and 1.5 percent again 1913–2012.

The details are unimportant. The key point is that there is no historical example of a country at the world technological frontier whose growth in per capita output exceeded 1.5 percent over a lengthy period of time. If we look at the last few decades, we find even lower growth rates in the wealthiest countries: between 1990 and 2012, per capita output grew at a rate of 1.6 percent in Western Europe, 1.4 percent in North America, and 0.7 percent in Japan.[21] It is important to bear this reality in mind as I proceed, because many people think that growth ought to be at least 3 or 4 percent per year. As noted, both history and logic show this to be illusory.

With these preliminaries out of the way, what can we say about future growth rates? Some economists, such as Robert Gordon, believe

---

21. To be sure, growth was close to zero in the period 2007–2012 because of the 2008–2009 recession. See Supplemental Table S2.2, available online, for detailed figures for Western Europe and North America (not very different from the figures indicated here for Europe and North America as a whole) and for each country separately.

TABLE 2.5.

*Per capita output growth since the Industrial Revolution
(average annual growth rate)*

Years	Per capita world output (%)	Europe (%)	America (%)	Africa (%)	Asia (%)
0–1700	0.0	0.0	0.0	0.0	0.0
1700–2012	0.8	1.0	1.1	0.5	0.7
1700–1820	0.1	0.1	0.4	0.0	0.0
1820–1913	0.9	1.0	1.5	0.4	0.2
1913–2012	1.6	1.9	1.5	1.1	2.0
1913–1950	0.9	0.9	1.4	0.9	0.2
1950–1970	2.8	3.8	1.9	2.1	3.5
1970–1990	1.3	1.9	1.6	0.3	2.1
1990–2012	2.1	1.9	1.5	1.4	3.8
1950–1980	2.5	3.4	2.0	1.8	3.2
1980–2012	1.7	1.8	1.3	0.8	3.1

Note: Between 1910 and 2012, the growth rate of per capita output was 1.7% per year on average at the world level, including 1.9% in Europe, 1.6% in America, etc.

Sources: See piketty.pse.ens.fr/capital21c.

that the rate of growth of per capita output is destined to slow in the most advanced countries, starting with the United States, and may sink below 0.5 percent per year between 2050 and 2100.[22] Gordon's analysis is based on a comparison of the various waves of innovation that have succeeded one another since the invention of the steam engine and introduction of electricity, and on the finding that the most recent waves—including the revolution in information technology— have a much lower growth potential than earlier waves, because they

---

22. See Robert J. Gordon, *Is U.S. Economic Growth Over? Faltering Innovation Confronts the Six Headwinds,* NBER Working Paper 18315 (August 2012).

are less disruptive to modes of production and do less to improve productivity across the economy.

Just as I refrained earlier from predicting demographic growth, I will not attempt now to predict economic growth in the twenty-first century. Rather, I will attempt to draw the consequences of various possible scenarios for the dynamics of the wealth distribution. To my mind, it is as difficult to predict the pace of future innovations as to predict future fertility. The history of the past two centuries makes it highly unlikely that per capita output in the advanced countries will grow at a rate above 1.5 percent per year, but I am unable to predict whether the actual rate will be 0.5 percent, 1 percent, or 1.5 percent. The median scenario I will present here is based on a long-term per capita output growth rate of 1.2 percent in the wealthy countries, which is relatively optimistic compared with Robert Gordon's predictions (which I think are a little too dark). This level of growth cannot be achieved, however, unless new sources of energy are developed to replace hydrocarbons, which are rapidly being depleted.[23] This is only one scenario among many.

An Annual Growth of 1 Percent Implies Major Social Change

In my view, the most important point—more important than the specific growth rate prediction (since, as I have shown, any attempt to reduce long-term growth to a single figure is largely illusory)—is that a per capita output growth rate on the order of 1 percent is in fact extremely rapid, much more rapid than many people think.

The right way to look at the problem is once again in generational terms. Over a period of thirty years, a growth rate of 1 percent per year corresponds to cumulative growth of more than 35 percent. A growth rate of 1.5 percent per year corresponds to cumulative growth of more than 50 percent. In practice, this implies major changes in lifestyle and employment. Concretely, per capita output growth in Europe, North

---

23. I return to this question later. See esp. Part Four, Chapter 11.

America, and Japan over the past thirty years has ranged between 1 and 1.5 percent, and people's lives have been subjected to major changes. In 1980 there was no Internet or cell phone network, most people did not travel by air, most of the advanced medical technologies in common use today did not yet exist, and only a minority attended college. In the areas of communication, transportation, health, and education, the changes have been profound. These changes have also had a powerful impact on the structure of employment: when output per head increases by 35 to 50 percent in thirty years, that means that a very large fraction—between a quarter and a third—of what is produced today, and therefore between a quarter and a third of occupations and jobs, did not exist thirty years ago.

What this means is that today's societies are very different from the societies of the past, when growth was close to zero, or barely 0.1 percent per year, as in the eighteenth century. A society in which growth is 0.1–0.2 percent per year reproduces itself with little or no change from one generation to the next: the occupational structure is the same, as is the property structure. A society that grows at 1 percent per year, as the most advanced societies have done since the turn of the nineteenth century, is a society that undergoes deep and permanent change. This has important consequences for the structure of social inequalities and the dynamics of the wealth distribution. Growth can create new forms of inequality: for example, fortunes can be amassed very quickly in new sectors of economic activity. At the same time, however, growth makes inequalities of wealth inherited from the past less apparent, so that inherited wealth becomes less decisive. To be sure, the transformations entailed by a growth rate of 1 percent are far less sweeping than those required by a rate of 3–4 percent, so that the risk of disillusionment is considerable—a reflection of the hope invested in a more just social order, especially since the Enlightenment. Economic growth is quite simply incapable of satisfying this democratic and meritocratic hope, which must create specific institutions for the purpose and not rely solely on market forces or technological progress.

The Posterity of the Postwar Period: Entangled Transatlantic Destinies

Continental Europe and especially France have entertained considerable nostalgia for what the French call the Trente Glorieuses, the thirty years from the late 1940s to the late 1970s during which economic growth was unusually rapid. People still do not understand what evil spirit condemned them to such a low rate of growth beginning in the late 1970s. Even today, many people believe that the last thirty (soon to be thirty-five or forty) "pitiful years" will soon come to an end, like a bad dream, and things will once again be as they were before.

In fact, when viewed in historical perspective, the thirty postwar years were the exceptional period, quite simply because Europe had fallen far behind the United States over the period 1914–1945 but rapidly caught up during the Trente Glorieuses. Once this catch-up was complete, Europe and the United States both stood at the global technological frontier and began to grow at the same relatively slow pace, characteristic of economics at the frontier.

A glance at Figure 2.3, which shows the comparative evolution of European and North American growth rates, will make this point clear. In North America, there is no nostalgia for the postwar period, quite simply because the Trente Glorieuses never existed there: per capita output grew at roughly the same rate of 1.5–2 percent per year throughout the period 1820–2012. To be sure, growth slowed a bit between 1930 and 1950 to just over 1.5 percent, then increased again to just over 2 percent between 1950 and 1970, and then slowed to less than 1.5 percent between 1990 and 2012. In Western Europe, which suffered much more from the two world wars, the variations are considerably greater: per capita output stagnated between 1913 and 1950 (with a growth rate of just over 0.5 percent) and then leapt ahead to more than 4 percent from 1950 to 1970, before falling sharply to just slightly above US levels (a little more than 2 percent) in the period 1970–1990 and to barely 1.5 percent between 1990 and 2012.

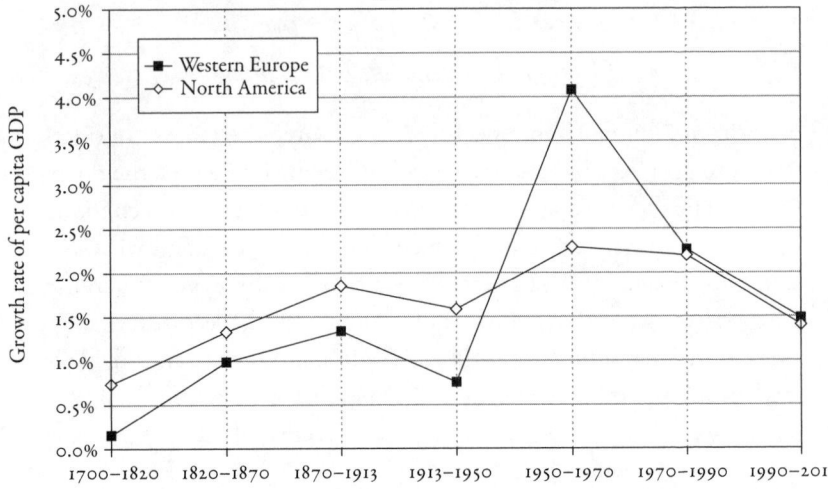

FIGURE 2.3. The growth rate of per capita output since the Industrial Revolution

The growth rate of per capita output surpassed 4 percent per year in Europe between 1950 and 1970, before returning to American levels.

Sources and series: see piketty.pse.ens.fr/capital21c.

Western Europe experienced a golden age of growth between 1950 and 1970, only to see its growth rate diminish to one-half or even one-third of its peak level during the decades that followed. Note that Figure 2.3 underestimates the depth of the fall, because I included Britain in Western Europe (as it should be), even though British growth in the twentieth century adhered fairly closely to the North American pattern of quasi stability. If we looked only at continental Europe, we would find an average per capita output growth rate of 5 percent between 1950 and 1970—a level well beyond that achieved in other advanced countries over the past two centuries.

These very different collective experiences of growth in the twentieth century largely explain why public opinion in different countries varies so widely in regard to commercial and financial globalization and indeed to capitalism in general. In continental Europe and especially France, people quite naturally continue to look on the first three postwar decades—a period of strong state intervention in the economy—as a period blessed with rapid growth, and many regard the liberalization of the economy that began around 1980 as the cause of a slowdown.

In Great Britain and the United States, postwar history is interpreted quite differently. Between 1950 and 1980, the gap between the English-speaking countries and the countries that had lost the war closed rapidly. By the late 1970s, US magazine covers often denounced the decline of the United States and the success of German and Japanese industry. In Britain, GDP per capita fell below the level of Germany, France, Japan, and even Italy. It may even be the case that this sense of being rivaled (or even overtaken in the case of Britain) played an important part in the "conservative revolution." Margaret Thatcher in Britain and Ronald Reagan in the United States promised to "roll back the welfare state" that had allegedly sapped the animal spirits of Anglo-Saxon entrepreneurs and thus to return to pure nineteenth-century capitalism, which would allow the United States and Britain to regain the upper hand. Even today, many people in both countries believe that the conservative revolution was remarkably successful, because their growth rates once again matched continental European and Japanese levels.

In fact, neither the economic liberalization that began around 1980 nor the state interventionism that began in 1945 deserves such praise or blame. France, Germany, and Japan would very likely have caught up with Britain and the United States following their collapse of 1914–1945 regardless of what policies they had adopted (I say this with only slight exaggeration). The most one can say is that state intervention did no harm. Similarly, once these countries had attained the global technological frontier, it is hardly surprising that they ceased to grow more rapidly than Britain and the United States or that growth rates in all of these wealthy countries more or less equalized, as Figure 2.3 shows (I will come back to this). Broadly speaking, the US and British policies of economic liberalization appear to have had little effect on this simple reality, since they neither increased growth nor decreased it.

The Double Bell Curve of Global Growth

To recapitulate, global growth over the past three centuries can be pictured as a bell curve with a very high peak. In regard to both population growth and per capita output growth, the pace gradually accelerated over the course of the eighteenth and nineteenth centuries, and especially the twentieth, and is now most likely returning to much lower levels for the remainder of the twenty-first century.

There are, however, fairly clear differences between the two bell curves. If we look at the curve for population growth, we see that the rise began much earlier, in the eighteenth century, and the decrease also began much earlier. Here we see the effects of the demographic transition, which has already largely been completed. The rate of global population growth peaked in the period 1950–1970 at nearly 2 percent per year and since then has decreased steadily. Although one can never be sure of anything in this realm, it is likely that this process will continue and that global demographic growth rates will decline to near zero in the second half of the twenty-first century. The shape of the bell curve is quite well defined (see Figure 2.2).

When it comes to the growth rate of per capita output, things are more complicated. It took longer for "economic" growth to take off: it remained close to zero throughout the eighteenth century, began to climb only in the nineteenth, and did not really become a shared reality until the twentieth. Global growth in per capita output exceeded 2 percent between 1950 and 1990, notably thanks to European catch-up, and again between 1990 and 2012, thanks to Asian and especially Chinese catch-up, with growth in China exceeding 9 percent per year in that period, according to official statistics (a level never before observed).[24]

---

24. Note that global per capita output, estimated to have grown at a rate of 2.1 percent between 1990 and 2012, drops to 1.5 percent if we look at output growth per adult rather than per capita. This is a logical consequence of the fact that demographic growth rose from 1.3 to 1.9 percent per year during this period, which allows us to calculate both the total population and the adult population. This

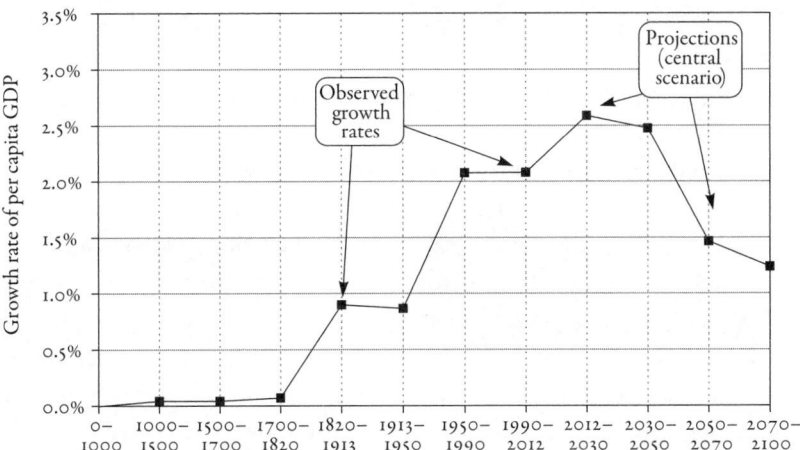

FIGURE 2.4. The growth rate of world per capita output from Antiquity to 2100

The growth rate of per capita output surpassed 2 percent from 1950 to 2012. If the convergence process goes on, it will surpass 2.5 percent from 2012 to 2050, and then will drop below 1.5 percent.

Sources and series: see piketty.pse.ens.fr/capital21c.

What will happen after 2012? In Figure 2.4 I have indicated a "median" growth prediction. In fact, this is a rather optimistic forecast, since I have assumed that the richest countries (Western Europe, North America, and Japan) will grow at a rate of 1.2 percent from 2012 to 2100 (markedly higher than many other economists predict), while poor and emerging countries will continue the convergence process without stumbling, attaining growth of 5 percent per year from 2012 to 2030 and 4 percent from 2030 to 2050. If this were to occur as predicted, per capita output in China, Eastern Europe, South America, North Africa, and the Middle East would match that of the wealthiest countries by 2050.[25] After that, the distribution of global output

---

shows the importance of the demographic issue when it comes to breaking down global output growth (3.4 percent per year). See the online technical appendix.

25. Only Sub-Saharan Africa and India continue to lag. See the online technical appendix.

described in Chapter 1 would approximate the distribution of the population.[26]

In this optimistic median scenario, global growth of per capita output would slightly exceed 2.5 percent per year between 2012 and 2030 and again between 2030 and 2050, before falling below 1.5 percent initially and then declining to around 1.2 percent in the final third of the century. By comparison with the bell curve followed by the rate of demographic growth (Figure 2.2), this second bell curve has two special features. First, it peaks much later than the first one (almost a century later, in the middle of the twenty-first century rather than the twentieth), and second, it does not decrease to zero or near-zero growth but rather to a level just above 1 percent per year, which is much higher than the growth rate of traditional societies (see Figure 2.4).

By adding these two curves, we can obtain a third curve showing the rate of growth of total global output (Figure 2.5). Until 1950, this had always been less than 2 percent per year, before leaping to 4 percent in the period 1950–1990, an exceptionally high level that reflected both the highest demographic growth rate in history and the highest growth rate in output per head. The rate of growth of global output then began to fall, dropping below 3.5 percent in the period 1990–2012, despite extremely high growth rates in emerging countries, most notably China. According to my median scenario, this rate will continue through 2030 before dropping to 3 percent in 2030–2050 and then to roughly 1.5 percent during the second half of the twenty-first century.

I have already conceded that these "median" forecasts are highly hypothetical. The key point is that regardless of the exact dates and growth rates (details that are obviously important), the two bell curves of global growth are in large part already determined. The median forecast shown on Figures 2.2–5 is optimistic in two respects: first, because it assumes that productivity growth in the wealthy countries

---

26. See Chapter 1, Figures 1.1–2.

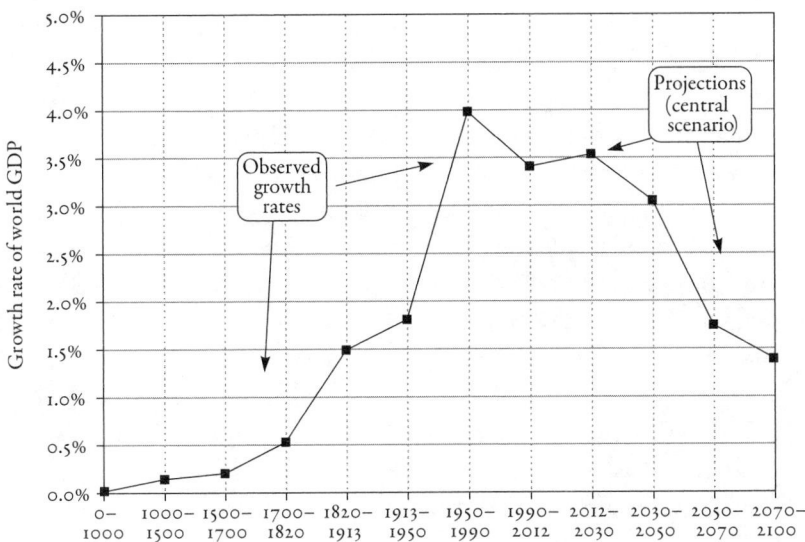

FIGURE 2.5. The growth rate of world output from Antiquity to 2100

The growth rate of world output surpassed 4 percent from 1950 to 1990. If the convergence process goes on, it will drop below 2 percent by 2050.

Sources and series: see piketty.pse.ens.fr/capital21c.

will continue at a rate of more than 1 percent per year (which assumes significant technological progress, especially in the area of clean energy), and second, perhaps more important, because it assumes that emerging economies will continue to converge with the rich economies, without major political or military impediments, until the process is complete, around 2050, which is very rapid. It is easy to imagine less optimistic scenarios, in which case the bell curve of global growth could fall faster to levels lower than those indicated on these graphs.

The Question of Inflation

The foregoing overview of growth since the Industrial Revolution would be woefully incomplete if I did not discuss the question of inflation. Some would say that inflation is a purely monetary phenomenon with which we do not need to concern ourselves. In fact, all the growth rates I have discussed thus far are so-called real growth rates, which are obtained by subtracting the rate of inflation (derived from the consumer price index) from the so-called nominal growth rate (measured in terms of consumer prices).

In reality, inflation plays a key role in this investigation. As noted, the use of a price index based on "averages" poses a problem, because growth always brings forth new goods and services and leads to enormous shifts in relative prices, which are difficult to summarize in a single index. As a result, the concepts of inflation and growth are not always very well defined. The decomposition of nominal growth (the only kind that can be observed with the naked eye, as it were) into a real component and an inflation component is in part arbitrary and has been the source of numerous controversies.

For example, if the nominal growth rate is 3 percent per year and prices increase by 2 percent, then we say that the real growth rate is 1 percent. But if we revise the inflation estimate downward because, for example, we believe that the real price of smartphones and tablets has decreased much more than we thought previously (given the considerable increase in their quality and performance, which statisticians try to measure carefully—no mean feat), so that we now think that prices rose by only 1.5 percent, then we conclude that the real growth rate is 1.5 percent. In fact, when differences are this small, it is difficult to be certain about the correct figure, and each estimate captures part of the truth: growth was no doubt closer to 1.5 percent for aficionados of smartphones and tablets and closer to 1 percent for others.

Relative price movements can play an even more decisive role in Ricardo's theory based on the principle of scarcity: if certain prices, such as those for land, buildings, or gasoline, rise to very high levels for a prolonged period of time, this can permanently alter the distribution of wealth in favor of those who happen to be the initial owners of those scarce resources.

In addition to the question of relative prices, I will show that inflation per se—that is, a generalized increase of all prices—can also play a fundamental role in the dynamics of the wealth distribution. Indeed, it was essentially inflation that allowed the wealthy countries to get rid of the public debt they owed at the end of World War II. Inflation also led to various redistributions among social groups over the course of the twentieth century, often in a chaotic, uncontrolled manner. Conversely, the wealth-based society that flourished in the eighteenth and nineteenth centuries was inextricably linked to the very stable monetary conditions that persisted over this very long period.

The Great Monetary Stability of the Eighteenth and Nineteenth Centuries

To back up a bit: the first crucial fact to bear in mind is that inflation is largely a twentieth-century phenomenon. Before that, up to World War I, inflation was zero or close to it. Prices sometimes rose or fell sharply for a period of several years or even decades, but these price movements generally balanced out in the end. This was the case in all countries for which we possess long-run price series.

More precisely, if we look at average price increases over the periods 1700–1820 and 1820–1913, we find that inflation was insignificant in France, Britain, the United States, and Germany: at most 0.2–0.3 percent per year. We even find periods of slightly negative price movements: for example, Britain and the United States in the nineteenth century (−0.2 percent per year if we average the two cases between 1820 and 1913).

To be sure, there were a few exceptions to the general rule of monetary stability, but each of them was short-lived, and the return to normal came quickly, as though it were inevitable. One particularly emblematic case was that of the French Revolution. Late in 1789, the revolutionary government issued its famous assignats, which became a true circulating currency and medium of exchange by 1790 or 1791. It was one of the first historical examples of paper money. This gave rise to high inflation (measured in assignats) until 1794 or 1795. The important point, however, is that the return to metal coinage, after creation of the franc germinal, took place at the same parity as the currency of the Ancien Régime. The law of 18 germinal, Year III (April 7, 1795), did away with the old livre tournois (which reminded people too much of the monarchy) and replaced it with the franc, which became the country's new official monetary unit. It had the same metal content as its predecessor. A 1-franc coin was supposed to contain exactly 4.5 grams of fine silver (as the livre tournois had done since 1726). This was confirmed by the law of 1796 and again by the law of 1803, which permanently established bimetallism in France (based on gold and silver).[27]

Ultimately, prices measured in francs in the period 1800–1810 were roughly the same as prices expressed in livres tournois in the period 1770–1780, so that the change of monetary unit during the Revolution did not alter the purchasing power of money in any way. The novelists of the early nineteenth century, starting with Balzac, moved constantly from one unit to another when characterizing income and wealth: for contemporary readers, the franc germinal (or "franc-or") and livre tournois were one and the same. For Père Goriot, "a thousand two hundred livres" of rent was perfectly equivalent to "twelve hundred francs," and no further specification was needed.

The gold value of the franc set in 1803 was not officially changed until June 25, 1928, when a new monetary law was adopted. In fact, the Banque de France had been relieved of the obligation to exchange its notes for gold or silver since August 1914, so that the "franc-or" had already become a "paper franc" and remained such until the monetary stabilization of 1926–1928. Nevertheless, the same parity with metal remained in effect from 1726 to 1914—a not insignificant period of time.

---

27. The law of 25 germinal, Year IV (April 14, 1796), confirmed the silver parity of the franc, and the law of 17 germinal, Year XI (April 7, 1803), set a double parity: the franc was equal to 4.5 grams of fine silver and 0.29 grams of gold (for a gold:silver ratio of 1/15.5). It was the law of 1803, promulgated a few years after the creation of the Banque de France in 1800, that give rise to the appellation "franc germinal." See the online technical appendix.

We find the same degree of monetary stability in the British pound sterling. Despite slight adjustments, the conversion rate between French and British currencies remained quite stable for two centuries: the pound sterling continued to be worth 20–25 livres tournois or francs germinal from the eighteenth century until 1914.[28] For British novelists of the time, the pound sterling and its strange offspring, such as shillings and guineas, seemed as solid as marble, just as the livre tournois and franc-or did to French novelists.[29] Each of these units seemed to measure quantities that did not vary with time, thus laying down markers that bestowed an aura of eternity on monetary magnitudes and a kind of permanence to social distinctions.

The same was true in other countries: the only major changes concerned the definition of new units of currency or the creation of new currencies, such as the US dollar in 1775 and the gold mark in 1873. But once the parities with metal were set, nothing changed: in the nineteenth and early twentieth centuries, everyone knew that a pound sterling was worth about 5 dollars, 20 marks, and 25 francs. The value of money had not changed for decades, and no one saw any reason to think it would be different in the future.

---

28. Under the gold standard observed from 1816 to 1914, a pound sterling was worth 7.3 grams of fine gold, or exactly 25.2 times the gold parity of the franc. Gold-silver bimetallism introduced several complications, about which I will say nothing here.

29. Until 1971, the pound sterling was divided into 20 shillings, each of which was further divided into 12 pence (so that there were 240 pence in a pound). A guinea was worth 21 shillings, or 1.05 pounds. It was often used to quote prices for professional services and in fashionable stores. In France, the livre tournois was also divided into 20 deniers and 240 sous until the decimal reform of 1795. After that, the franc was divided into 100 centimes, sometimes called "sous" in the nineteenth century. In the eighteenth century, a louis d'or was a coin worth 20 livres tournois, or approximately 1 pound sterling. An écu was worth 3 livres tournois until 1795, after which it referred to a silver coin worth 5 francs from 1795 to 1878. To judge by the way novelists shifted from one unit to another, it would seem that contemporaries were perfectly aware of these subtleties.

The Meaning of Money in Literary Classics

In eighteenth- and nineteenth-century novels, money was everywhere, not only as an abstract force but above all as a palpable, concrete magnitude. Writers frequently described the income and wealth of their characters in francs or pounds, not to overwhelm us with numbers but because these quantities established a character's social status in the mind of the reader. Everyone knew what standard of living these numbers represented.

These monetary markers were stable, moreover, because growth was relatively slow, so that the amounts in question changed only very gradually, over many decades. In the eighteenth century, per capita income grew very slowly. In Great Britain, the average income was on the order of 30 pounds a year in the early 1800s, when Jane Austen wrote her novels.[30] The same average income could have been observed in 1720 or 1770. Hence these were very stable reference points, with which Austen had grown up. She knew that to live comfortably and elegantly, secure proper transportation and clothing, eat well, and find amusement and a necessary minimum of domestic servants, one needed—by her lights—at least twenty to thirty times that much. The characters in her novels consider themselves free from need only if they dispose of incomes of 500 to 1,000 pounds a year.

I will have a lot more to say about the structure of inequality and standards of living that underlies these realities and perceptions, and in particular about the distribution of wealth and income that flowed from them. At this stage, the important point is that absent inflation and in view of very low growth, these sums reflect very concrete and stable realities. Indeed, a half century later, in the 1850s, the average income was barely 40–50 pounds a year. Readers probably found the amounts mentioned by Jane Austen somewhat too small to live comfortably but were not totally confused by them. By the turn of

---

30. The estimates referred to here concern national income per adult, which I believe is more significant than national income per capita. See the online technical appendix.

the twentieth century, the average income in Great Britain had risen to 80–90 pounds a year. The increase was noticeable, but annual incomes of 1,000 pounds or more—the kind that Austen talked about—still marked a significant divide.

We find the same stability of monetary references in the French novel. In France, the average income was roughly 400–500 francs per year in the period 1810–1820, in which Balzac set *Père Goriot*. Expressed in livres tournois, the average income was just slightly lower in the Ancien Régime. Balzac, like Austen, described a world in which it took twenty to thirty times that much to live decently: with an income of less than 10–20,000 francs, a Balzacian hero would feel that he lived in misery. Again, these orders of magnitude would change only very gradually over the course of the nineteenth century and into the Belle Époque: they would long seem familiar to readers.[31] These amounts allowed the writer to economically set the scene, hint at a way of life, evoke rivalries, and, in a word, describe a civilization.

One could easily multiply examples by drawing on American, German, and Italian novels, as well as on the literature of all the other countries that experienced this long period of monetary stability. Until World War I, money had meaning, and novelists did not fail to exploit it, explore it, and turn it into a literary subject.

The Loss of Monetary Bearings in the Twentieth Century

This world collapsed for good with World War I. To pay for this war of extraordinary violence and intensity, to pay for soldiers and for the ever more costly and sophisticated weapons they used, governments went deeply into debt. As early as August 1914, the principal belligerents ended the convertibility of their currency into gold. After the war, all countries resorted to one degree or another to the printing press to deal with their enormous public debts. Attempts to reintroduce the

---

31. Average annual income in France ranged from 700 to 800 francs in the 1850s and from 1300 to 1400 francs in 1900–1910. See the online technical appendix.

gold standard in the 1920s did not survive the crisis of the 1930s: Britain abandoned the gold standard in 1931, the United States in 1933, France in 1936. The post–World War II gold standard would prove to be barely more robust: established in 1946, it ended in 1971 when the dollar ceased to be convertible into gold.

Between 1913 and 1950, inflation in France exceeded 13 percent per year (so that prices rose by a factor of 100), and inflation in Germany was 17 percent per year (so that prices rose by a factor of more than 300). In Britain and the United States, which suffered less damage and less political destabilization from the two wars, the rate of inflation was significantly lower: barely 3 percent per year in the period 1913–1950. Yet this still means that prices were multiplied by three, following two centuries in which prices had barely moved at all.

In all countries the shocks of the period 1914–1945 disrupted the monetary certitudes of the prewar world, not least because the inflationary process unleashed by war has never really ended.

We see this very clearly in Figure 2.6, which shows the evolution of inflation by subperiod for four countries in the period 1700–2012. Note that inflation ranged between 2 and 6 percent per year on average from 1950 to 1970, before rising sharply in the 1970s to the point where average inflation reached 10 percent in Britain and 8 percent in France in the period 1970–1990, despite the beginnings of significant disinflation nearly everywhere after 1980. If we compare this behavior of inflation with that of the previous decades, it is tempting to think that the period 1990–2012, with average inflation of around 2 percent in the four countries (a little less in Germany and France, a little more in Britain and the United States), signified a return to the zero inflation of the pre–World War I years.

To make this inference, however, one would have to forget that inflation of 2 percent per year is quite different from zero inflation. If we add annual inflation of 2 percent to real growth of 1–2 percent, then all of our key amounts—output, income, wages—must be increasing 3–4 percent a year, so that after ten or twenty years, the sums we are dealing with will bear no relation to present quantities. Who remem-

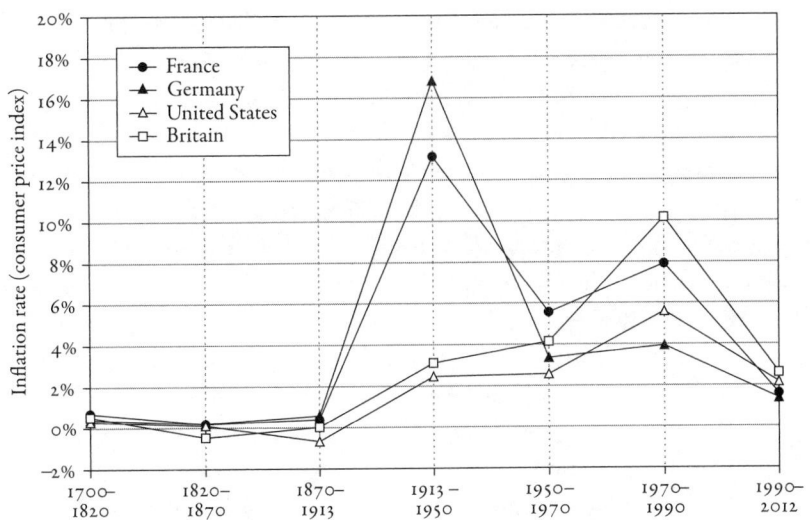

FIGURE 2.6. Inflation since the Industrial Revolution

Inflation in the rich countries was zero in the eighteenth and nineteenth centuries, high in the twentieth century, and roughly 2 percent a year since 1990.

Sources and series: see piketty.pse.ens.fr/capital21c.

bers the prevailing wages of the late 1980s or early 1990s? Furthermore, it is perfectly possible that this inflation of 2 percent per year will rise somewhat in the coming years, in view of the changes in monetary policy that have taken place since 2007–2008, especially in Britain and the United States. The monetary regime today differs significantly from the monetary regime in force a century ago. It is also interesting to note that Germany and France, the two countries that resorted most to inflation in the twentieth century, and more specifically between 1913 and 1950, today seem to be the most hesitant when it comes to using inflationary policy. What is more, they built a monetary zone, the Eurozone, that is based almost entirely on the principle of combating inflation.

I will have more to say later about the role played by inflation in the dynamics of wealth distribution, and in particular about the accumulation and distribution of fortunes, in various periods of time.

At this stage, I merely want to stress the fact that the loss of stable monetary reference points in the twentieth century marks a significant rupture with previous centuries, not only in the realms of economics and politics but also in regard to social, cultural, and literary matters. It is surely no accident that money—at least in the form of specific amounts—virtually disappeared from literature after the shocks of 1914–1945. Specific references to wealth and income were omnipresent in the literature of all countries before 1914; these references gradually dropped out of sight between 1914 and 1945 and never truly reemerged. This is true not only of European and American novels but also of the literature of other continents. The novels of Naguib Mahfouz, or at any rate those that unfold in Cairo between the two world wars, before prices were distorted by inflation, lavish attention on income and wealth as a way of situating characters and explaining their anxieties. We are not far from the world of Balzac and Austen. Obviously, the social structures are very different, but it is still possible to orient perceptions, expectations, and hierarchies in relation to monetary references. The novels of Orhan Pamuk, set in Istanbul in the 1970s, that is, in a period during which inflation had long since rendered the meaning of money ambiguous, omit mention of any specific sums. In *Snow,* Pamuk even has his hero, a novelist like himself, say that there is nothing more tiresome for a novelist than to speak about money or discuss last year's prices and incomes. The world has clearly changed a great deal since the nineteenth century.

PART TWO

THE DYNAMICS OF THE CAPITAL / INCOME RATIO

THREE

The Metamorphoses of Capital

In Part One, I introduced the basic concepts of income and capital and reviewed the main stages of income and output growth since the Industrial Revolution.

In this part, I am going to concentrate on the evolution of the capital stock, looking at both its overall size, as measured by the capital / income ratio, and its breakdown into different types of assets, whose nature has changed radically since the eighteenth century. I will consider various forms of wealth (land, buildings, machinery, firms, stocks, bonds, patents, livestock, gold, natural resources, etc.) and examine their development over time, starting with Great Britain and France, the countries about which we possess the most information over the long run. But first I want to take a brief detour through literature, which in the cases of Britain and France offers a very good introduction to the subject of wealth.

The Nature of Wealth: From Literature to Reality

When Honoré de Balzac and Jane Austen wrote their novels at the beginning of the nineteenth century, the nature of wealth was relatively clear to all readers. Wealth seemed to exist in order to produce rents, that is, dependable, regular payments to the owners of certain assets, which usually took the form of land or government bonds. Père Goriot owned the latter, while the small estate of the Rastignacs consisted of the former. The vast Norland estate that John Dashwood inherits in *Sense and Sensibility* is also agricultural land, from which he is quick to expel his half-sisters Elinor and Marianne, who must make do with the interest on the small capital in government bonds left to them by their father. In the classic novels of the nineteenth century, wealth is everywhere, and no matter how large or small the capital, or who owns it, it generally takes one of two forms: land or government bonds.

From the perspective of the twenty-first century, these types of assets may seem old-fashioned, and it is tempting to consign them to the remote and supposedly vanished past, unconnected with the economic and social realities of the modern era, in which capital is supposedly more "dynamic." Indeed, the characters in nineteenth-century novels often seem like archetypes of the rentier, a suspect figure in the modern era of democracy and meritocracy. Yet what could be more natural to ask of a capital asset than that it produce a reliable and steady income: that is in fact the goal of a "perfect" capital market as economists define it. It would be quite wrong, in fact, to assume that the study of nineteenth-century capital has nothing to teach us today.

When we take a closer look, the differences between the nineteenth and twenty-first centuries are less apparent than they might seem at first glance. In the first place, the two types of capital asset—land and government bonds—raise very different issues and probably should not be added together as cavalierly as nineteenth-century novelists did for narrative convenience. Ultimately, a government bond is nothing more than a claim of one portion of the population (those who receive interest) on another (those who pay taxes): it should therefore be excluded from national wealth and included solely in private wealth. The complex question of government debt and the nature of the wealth associated with it is no less important today than it was in 1800, and by studying the past we can learn a lot about an issue of great contemporary concern. Although today's public debt is nowhere near the astronomical levels attained at the beginning of the nineteenth century, at least in Britain, it is at or near a historical record in France and many other countries and is probably the source of as much confusion today as in the Napoleonic era. The process of financial intermediation (whereby individuals deposit money in a bank, which then invests it elsewhere) has become so complex that people are often unaware of who owns what. To be sure, we are in debt. How can we possibly forget it, when the media remind us every day? But to whom exactly do we owe money? In the nineteenth century, the rentiers who lived off the public debt were clearly identified. Is that still the case today? This mystery needs to be dispelled, and studying the past can help us do so.

There is also another, even more important complication: many other forms of capital, some of them quite "dynamic," played an essential role not only in classic novels but in the society of the time. After starting out as a noodle maker, Père Goriot made his fortune as a pasta manufacturer and grain merchant. During the wars of the revolutionary and Napoleonic eras, he had an unrivaled eye for the best flour and a knack for perfecting pasta production technologies and setting up distribution networks and warehouses so that he could deliver the right product to the right place at the right time. Only after making a fortune as an entrepreneur did he sell his share of the business, much in the manner of a twenty-first-century startup founder exercising his stock options and pocketing his capital gains. Goriot then invested the proceeds in safer assets: perpetual government bonds that paid interest indefinitely. With this capital he was able to arrange good marriages for his daughters and secure an eminent place for them in Parisian high society. On his deathbed in 1821, abandoned by his daughters Delphine and Anastasie, old Goriot still dreamt of juicy investments in the pasta business in Odessa.

César Birotteau, another Balzac character, made his money in perfumes. He was the ingenious inventor of any number of beauty products—Sultan's Cream, Carminative Water, and so on—that Balzac tells us were all the rage in late imperial and Restoration France. But this was not enough for him: when the time came to retire, he sought to triple his capital by speculating boldly on real estate in the neighborhood of La Madeleine, which was developing rapidly in the 1820s. After rejecting the sage advice of his wife, who urged him to invest in good farmland near Chinon and government bonds, he ended in ruin.

Jane Austen's heroes were more rural than Balzac's. Prosperous landowners all, they were nevertheless wiser than Balzac's characters in appearance only. In *Mansfield Park,* Fanny's uncle, Sir Thomas, has to travel out to the West Indies for a year with his eldest son for the purpose of managing his affairs and investments. After returning to Mansfield, he is obliged to set out once again for the islands for a period of many months. In the early 1800s it was by no means simple to manage plantations several thousand miles away. Tending to one's wealth was not a tranquil matter of collecting rent on land or interest on government debt.

So which was it: quiet capital or risky investments? Is it safe to conclude that nothing has really changed since 1800? What actual changes have occurred in the structure of capital since the eighteenth century? Père Goriot's pasta may have become Steve Jobs's tablet, and investments in the West Indies in 1800 may have become investments in China or South Africa in 2010, but has the deep structure of capital really changed? Capital is never quiet: it is always risk-oriented and entrepreneurial, at least at its inception, yet it always tends to transform itself into rents as it accumulates in large enough amounts—that is its vocation, its logical destination. What, then, gives us the vague sense that social inequality today is very different from social inequality in the age of Balzac and Austen? Is this just empty talk with no purchase on reality, or can we identify objective factors to explain why some people think that modern capital has become more "dynamic" and less "rent-seeking?"

The Metamorphoses of Capital in Britain and France

I will begin by looking at changes in the capital structure of Britain and France since the eighteenth century. These are the countries for which we possess the richest historical sources and have therefore been able to construct the most complete and homogeneous estimates over the long run. The principal results of this work are shown in Figures 3.1 and 3.2, which attempt to summarize several key aspects of three centuries in the history of capitalism. Two clear conclusions emerge.

We find, to begin with, that the capital / income ratio followed quite similar trajectories in both countries, remaining relatively stable

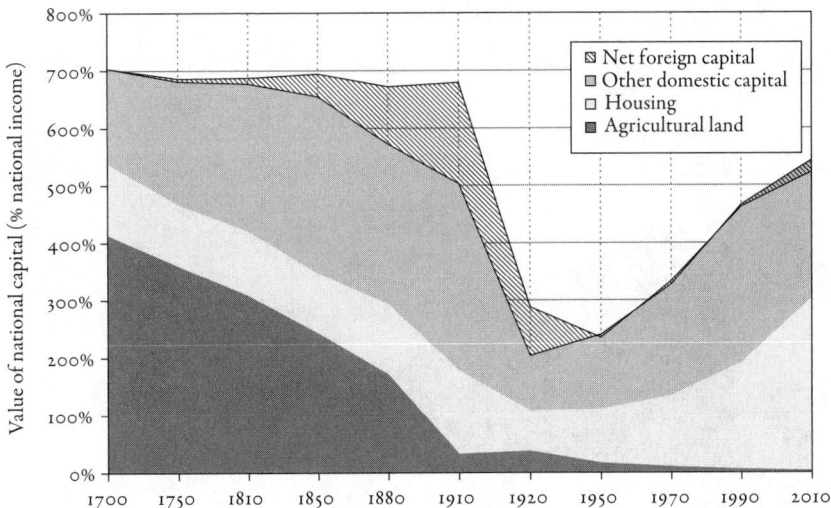

FIGURE 3.1. Capital in Britain, 1700–2010

National capital is worth about seven years of national income in Britain in 1700 (including four in agricultural land).

Sources and series: see piketty.pse.ens.fr/capital21c.

in the eighteenth and nineteenth centuries, followed by an enormous shock in the twentieth century, before returning to levels similar to those observed on the eve of World War I. In both Britain and France, the total value of national capital fluctuated between six and seven years of national income throughout the eighteenth and nineteenth centuries, up to 1914. Then, after World War I, the capital / income ratio suddenly plummeted, and it continued to fall during the Depression and World War II, to the point where national capital amounted to only two or three years of national income in the 1950s. The capital / income ratio then began to climb and has continued to do so ever since. In both countries, the total value of national capital in 2010 is roughly five to six years' worth of national income, indeed a bit more than six in France, compared with less than four in the 1980s and barely more than two in the 1950s. The measurements are of course not perfectly precise, but the general shape of the curve is clear.

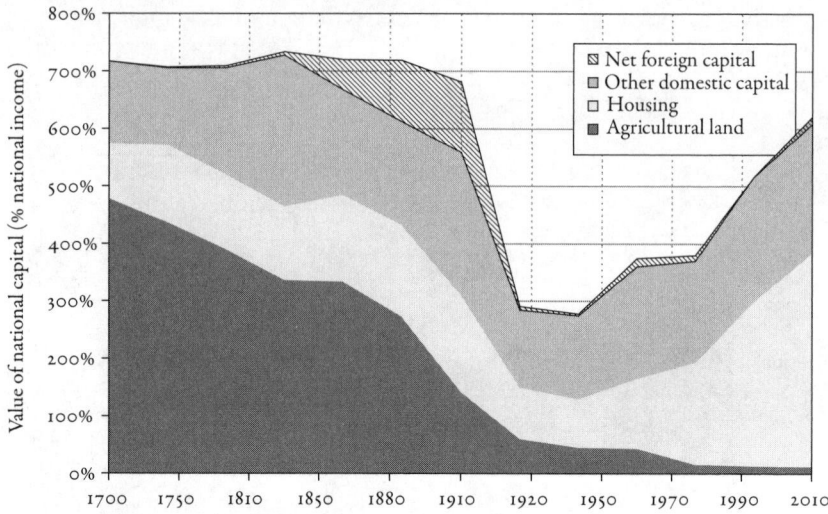

FIGURE 3.2. Capital in France, 1700–2010

National capital is worth almost seven years of national income in France in 1910 (including one invested abroad).

Sources and series: see piketty.pse.ens.fr/capital21c.

In short, what we see over the course of the century just past is an impressive "U-shaped curve." The capital / income ratio fell by nearly two-thirds between 1914 and 1945 and then more than doubled in the period 1945–2012.

These are very large swings, commensurate with the violent military, political, and economic conflicts that marked the twentieth century. Capital, private property, and the global distribution of wealth were key issues in these conflicts. The eighteenth and nineteenth centuries look tranquil by comparison.

In the end, by 2010, the capital / income ratio had returned to its pre–World War I level—or even surpassed it if we divide the capital stock by disposable household income rather than national income (a dubious methodological choice, as will be shown later). In any case, regardless of the imperfections and uncertainties of the available measures, there can be no doubt that Britain and France in the 1990s and 2000s regained a level of wealth not seen since the early twentieth century, at the conclusion of a process that originated in the 1950s. By the middle of the twentieth century, capital had largely disappeared. A little more than half a century later, it seems about to return to levels equal to those observed in the eighteenth and nineteenth centuries. Wealth is once again flourishing. Broadly speaking, it was the wars of the twentieth century that wiped away the past to create the illusion that capitalism had been structurally transformed.

As important as it is, this evolution of the overall capital/income ratio should not be allowed to obscure sweeping changes in the composition of capital since 1700. This is the second conclusion that emerges clearly from Figures 3.1 and 3.2. In terms of asset structure, twenty-first-century capital has little in common with eighteenth-century capital. The evolutions we see are again quite close to what we find happening in Britain and France. To put it simply, we can see that over the very long run, agricultural land has gradually been replaced by buildings, business capital, and financial capital invested in firms and government organizations. Yet the overall value of capital, measured in years of national income, has not really changed.

More precisely, remember that national capital, which is shown in Figures 3.1 and 3.2, is defined as the sum of private capital and public capital. Government debt, which is an asset for the private sector and a liability for the public sector, therefore nets out to zero (if each country owns its own government debt). As noted in Chapter 1, national capital, so defined, can be decomposed into domestic capital and net foreign capital. Domestic capital measures the value of the capital stock (buildings, firms, etc.) located within the territory of the country in question. Net foreign capital (or net foreign assets) measures the wealth of the country in question with respect to the rest of the world, that is, the difference between assets owned by residents of the country in the rest of the world and assets owned by the rest of the world in the country in question (including assets in the form of government bonds).

Domestic capital can in turn be broken down into three categories: farmland, housing (including the value of the land on which buildings stand), and other domestic capital, which covers the capital of firms and government organizations (including buildings used for business and the associated land, infrastructure, machinery, computers, patents, etc.). These assets, like any asset, are evaluated in terms of market value: for example, in the case of a corporation that issues stock, the value depends on the share price. This leads to the following decomposition of national capital, which I have used to create Figures 3.1 and 3.2:

National capital = farmland + housing + other domestic capital
+ net foreign capital

A glance at these graphs shows that at the beginning of the eighteenth century, the total value of farmland represented four to five years of national income, or nearly two-thirds of total national capital. Three centuries later, farmland was worth less than 10 percent of national income in both France and Britain and accounted for less than 2 percent of total wealth. This impressive change is hardly surprising: agriculture in the eighteenth century accounted for nearly three-quarters of all economic activity and employment, compared with just a few percent today. It is therefore natural that the share of capital involved in agriculture has evolved in a similar direction.

This collapse in the value of farmland (proportionate to national income and national capital) was counterbalanced on the one hand by a rise in the value of housing, which rose from barely one year of national income in the eighteenth century to more than three years today, and on the other hand by an increase in the value of other domestic capital, which rose by roughly the same amount (actually slightly less, from 1.5 years of national income in the eighteenth century to a little less than 3 years today).[1] This very long-term structural

---

1. According to available estimates (especially King's and Petty's for Britain and Vauban's and Boisguillebert's for France), farm buildings and livestock accounted for nearly half of what I am classifying as "other domestic capital" in the eigh-

transformation reflects on the one hand the growing importance of housing, not only in size but also in quality and value, in the process of economic and industrial development;[2] and on the other the very substantial accumulation since the Industrial Revolution of buildings used for business purposes, infrastructure, machinery, warehouses, offices, tools, and other material and immaterial capital, all of which is used by firms and government organizations to produce all sorts of nonagricultural goods and services.[3] The nature of capital has changed: it once was mainly land but has become primarily housing plus industrial and financial assets. Yet it has lost none of its importance.

The Rise and Fall of Foreign Capital

What about foreign capital? In Britain and France, it evolved in a very distinctive way, shaped by the turbulent history of these two leading colonial powers over the past three centuries. The net assets these two countries owned in the rest of the world increased steadily during the eighteenth and nineteenth centuries and attained an extremely high level on the eve of World War I, before literally collapsing in the period 1914–1945 and stabilizing at a relatively low level since then, as Figures 3.1 and 3.2 show.

Foreign possessions first became important in the period 1750–1800, as we know, for instance, from Sir Thomas's investments in the West Indies in Jane Austen's *Mansfield Park*. But the share of foreign assets remained modest: when Austen wrote her novel in 1812, they represented, as far as we can tell from the available sources, barely 10 percent of Britain's national income, or one-thirtieth of the value of

---

teenth century. If we subtracted these items in order to concentrate on industry and services, then the increase in other domestic capital not associated with agriculture would be as large as the increase in housing capital, indeed slightly higher.

2. César Birotteau's real estate speculation in the Madeleine quarter is a good example.

3. Think of Père Goriot's pasta factories or César Birotteau's perfume operation.

agricultural land (which amounted to more than three years of national income). Hence it comes as no surprise to discover that most of Austen's characters lived on the rents from their rural properties.

It was during the nineteenth century that British subjects began to accumulate considerable assets in the rest of the world, in amounts previously unknown and never surpassed to this day. By the eve of World War I, Britain had assembled the world's preeminent colonial empire and owned foreign assets equivalent to nearly two years of national income, or 6 times the total value of British farmland (which at that point was worth only 30 percent of national income).[4] Clearly, the structure of wealth had been utterly transformed since the time of *Mansfield Park,* and one has to hope that Austen's heroes and their descendants were able to adjust in time and follow Sir Thomas's lead by investing a portion of their land rents abroad. By the turn of the twentieth century, capital invested abroad was yielding around 5 percent a year in dividends, interest, and rent, so that British national income was about 10 percent higher than its domestic product. A fairly significant social group were able to live off this boon.

France, which commanded the second most important colonial empire, was in a scarcely less enviable situation: it had accumulated foreign assets worth more than a year's national income, so that in the first decade of the twentieth century its national income was 5–6 percent higher than its domestic product. This was equal to the total industrial output of the northern and eastern *départements,* and it came to France in the form of dividends, interest, royalties, rents, and other revenue on assets that French citizens owned in the country's foreign possessions.[5]

It is important to understand that these very large net positions in foreign assets allowed Britain and France to run structural trade deficits in the late nineteenth and early twentieth century. Between 1880 and 1914, both countries received significantly more in goods and ser-

---

4. For further details, see the online technical appendix.
5. See the online technical appendix.

vices from the rest of the world than they exported themselves (their trade deficits averaged 1–2 percent of national income throughout this period). This posed no problem, because their income from foreign assets totaled more than 5 percent of national income. Their balance of payments was thus strongly positive, which enabled them to increase their holdings of foreign assets year after year.[6] In other words, the rest of the world worked to increase consumption by the colonial powers and at the same time became more and more indebted to those same powers. This may seem shocking. But it is essential to realize that the goal of accumulating assets abroad by way of commercial surpluses and colonial appropriations was precisely to be in a position later to run trade deficits. There would be no interest in running trade surpluses forever. The advantage of owning things is that one can continue to consume and accumulate without having to work, or at any rate continue to consume and accumulate more than one could produce on one's own. The same was true on an international scale in the age of colonialism.

In the wake of the cumulative shocks of two world wars, the Great Depression, and decolonization, these vast stocks of foreign assets would eventually evaporate. In the 1950s, both France and Great Britain found themselves with net foreign asset holdings close to zero, which means that their foreign assets were just enough to balance the assets of the two former colonial powers owned by the rest of the world. Broadly speaking, this situation did not change much over the next half century. Between 1950 and 2010, the net foreign asset holdings of France and Britain varied from slightly positive to slightly negative while remaining quite close to zero, at least when compared with the levels observed previously.[7]

---

6. Detailed annual series of trade and payment balances for Britain and France are available in the online technical appendix.

7. Since 1950, the net foreign holdings of both countries have nearly always ranged between −10 and +10 percent of national income, which is one-tenth to one-twentieth of the level attained around the turn of the twentieth century. The difficulty of measuring net foreign holdings today does not undermine this finding.

Finally, when we compare the structure of national capital in the eighteenth century to its structure now, we find that net foreign assets play a negligible role in both periods, and that the real long-run structural change is to be found in the gradual replacement of farmland by real estate and working capital, while the total capital stock has remained more or less unchanged relative to national income.

Income and Wealth: Some Orders of Magnitude

To sum up these changes, it is useful to take today's world as a reference point. The current per capita national income in Britain and France is on the order of 30,000 euros per year, and national capital is about 6 times national income, or roughly 180,000 euros per head. In both countries, farmland is virtually worthless today (a few thousand euros per person at most), and national capital is broadly speaking divided into two nearly equal parts: on average, each citizen has about 90,000 euros in housing (for his or her own use or for rental to others) and about 90,000 euros worth of other domestic capital (primarily in the form of capital invested in firms by way of financial instruments).

As a thought experiment, let us go back three centuries and apply the national capital structure as it existed around 1700 but with the average amounts we find today: 30,000 euros annual income per capita and 180,000 euros of capital. Our representative French or British citizen would then own around 120,000 euros worth of land, 30,000 euros worth of housing, and 30,000 euros in other domestic assets.[8] Clearly, some of these people (for example, Jane Austen's characters: John Dashwood with his Norland estate and Fitzwilliam Darcy with Pemberley) owned hundreds of hectares—capital worth tens or hundreds of millions of euros—while many others owned nothing at all.

---

8. More precisely, for an average income of 30,000 euros in 1700, average wealth would have been on the order of 210,000 euros (seven years of income rather than six), 150,000 of which would have been in land (roughly five years of income if one includes farm buildings and livestock), 30,000 in housing, and 30,000 in other domestic assets.

But these averages give us a somewhat more concrete idea of the way the structure of national capital has been utterly transformed since the eighteenth century while preserving roughly the same value in terms of annual income.

Now imagine this British or French person at the turn of the twentieth century, still with an average income of 30,000 euros and an average capital of 180,000. In Britain, farmland already accounted for only a small fraction of this wealth: 10,000 for each British subject, compared with 50,000 euros worth of housing and 60,000 in other domestic assets, together with nearly 60,000 in foreign investments. France was somewhat similar, except that each citizen still owned on average between 30,000 and 40,000 euros worth of land and roughly the same amount of foreign assets.[9] In both countries, foreign assets had taken on considerable importance. Once again, it goes without saying that not everyone owned shares in the Suez Canal or Russian bonds. But by averaging over the entire population, which contained many people with no foreign assets at all and a small minority with substantial portfolios, we are able to measure the vast quantity of accumulated wealth in the rest of the world that French and British foreign asset holdings represented.

Public Wealth, Private Wealth

Before studying more precisely the nature of the shocks sustained by capital in the twentieth century and the reasons for the revival of capital since World War II, it will be useful at this point to broach the issue of the public debt, and more generally the division of national capital between public and private assets. Although it is difficult today, in an age where rich countries tend to accumulate substantial public debts, to

---

9. Again, for an average income of 30,000 euros, average wealth in 1910 would have been closer to 210,000 euros (seven years of national income), with other domestic assets closer to 90,000 (three years income) than 60,000 (two years). All the figures given here are deliberately simplified and rounded off. See the online technical appendix for further details.

remember that the public sector balance sheet includes assets as well as liabilities, we should be careful to bear this fact in mind.

To be sure, the distinction between public and private capital changes neither the total amount nor the composition of national capital, whose evolution I have just traced. Nevertheless, the division of property rights between the government and private individuals is of considerable political, economic, and social importance.

I will begin, then, by recalling the definitions introduced in Chapter 1. National capital (or wealth) is the sum of public capital and private capital. Public capital is the difference between the assets and liabilities of the state (including all public agencies), and private capital is of course the difference between the assets and liabilities of private individuals. Whether public or private, capital is always defined as net wealth, that is, the difference between the market value of what one owns (assets) and what one owes (liabilities, or debts).

Concretely, public assets take two forms. They can be nonfinancial (meaning essentially public buildings, used for government offices or for the provision of public services, primarily in health and education: schools, universities, hospitals, etc.) or financial. Governments can own shares in firms, in which they can have a majority or minority stake. These firms may be located within the nation's borders or abroad. In recent years, for instance, so-called sovereign wealth funds have arisen to manage the substantial portfolios of foreign financial assets that some states have acquired.

In practice, the boundary between financial and nonfinancial assets need not be fixed. For example, when the French government transformed France Telecom and the French Post Office into shareholder-owned corporations, state-owned buildings used by both firms began to be counted as financial assets of the state, whereas previously they were counted as nonfinancial assets.

At present, the total value of public assets (both financial and nonfinancial) is estimated to be almost one year's national income in Britain and a little less than 1 1/2 times that amount in France. Since the public debt of both countries amounts to about one year's national

TABLE 3.1.

Public wealth and private wealth in France in 2012

	Value of capital (% national income)[a]		Value of capital (% national capital)	
ational capital (public pital + private capital)	605		100	
blic capital (net public wealth: fference between assets and bt held by government and her public agencies)	31 Assets 145%	Debt 114%	5 Assets 24%	Debt 19%
vate capital (net private wealth: ference between assets and debt ld by private individuals ouseholds])	574 Assets 646%	Debt 72%	95 Assets 107%	Debt 12%

te: In 2012, the total value of national capital in France was equal to 605% of national income (6.05 times
:ional income), including 31% for public capital (5% of total) and 574% for private capital (95% of total).
ı. National income is equal to GDP minus capital depreciation plus net foreign income; in practice, it is
ically equal to about 90% of GDP in France in 2012; see Chapter 1 and the online technical appendix.
Sources: See piketty.pse.ens.fr/capital21c.

income, net public wealth (or capital) is close to zero. According to
the most recent official estimates by the statistical services and central
banks of both countries, Britain's net public capital is almost exactly
zero and France's is slightly less than 30 percent of national income (or
one-twentieth of total national capital: see Table 3.1).[10]

In other words, if the governments of both countries decided to sell
off all their assets in order to immediately pay off their debts, nothing
would be left in Britain and very little in France.

---

10. More precisely, Britain's public assets amount to 93 percent of national income,
and its public debts amount to 92 percent, for a net public wealth of +1 percent
of national income. In France, public assets amount to 145 percent of national
income and debts to 114 percent, for a net public wealth of +31 percent. See the
online technical appendix for detailed annual series for both countries.

Once again, we should not allow ourselves to be misled by the precision of these estimates. Countries do their best to apply the standardized concepts and methods established by the United Nations and other international organizations, but national accounting is not, and never will be, an exact science. Estimating public debts and financial assets poses no major problems. By contrast, it is not easy to set a precise market value on public buildings (such as schools and hospitals) or transportation infrastructure (such as railway lines and highways) since these are not regularly sold. In theory, such items are priced by observing the sales of similar items in the recent past, but such comparisons are not always reliable, especially since market prices frequently fluctuate, sometimes wildly. Hence these figures should be taken as rough estimates, not mathematical certainties.

In any event, there is absolutely no doubt that net public wealth in both countries is quite small and certainly insignificant compared with total private wealth. Whether net public wealth represents less than 1 percent of national wealth, as in Britain, or about 5 percent, as in France, or even 10 percent if we assume that the value of public assets is seriously underestimated, is ultimately of little or no importance for present purposes. Regardless of the imperfections of measurement, the crucial fact here is that private wealth in 2010 accounts for virtually all of national wealth in both countries: more than 99 percent in Britain and roughly 95 percent in France, according to the latest available estimates. In any case, the true figure is certainly greater than 90 percent.

Public Wealth in Historical Perspective

If we examine the history of public wealth in Britain and France since the eighteenth century, as well as the evolution of the public-private division of national capital, we find that the foregoing description has almost always been accurate (see Figures 3.3–6). To a first approximation, public assets and liabilities, and a fortiori the difference between the two, have generally represented very limited amounts compared

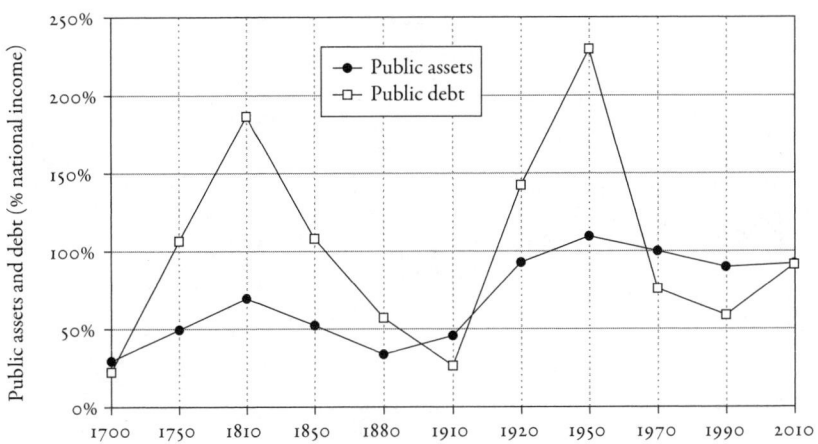

FIGURE 3.3. Public wealth in Britain, 1700–2010

Public debt surpassed two years of national income in 1950 (versus one year for public assets).

Sources and series: see piketty.pse.ens.fr/capital21c.

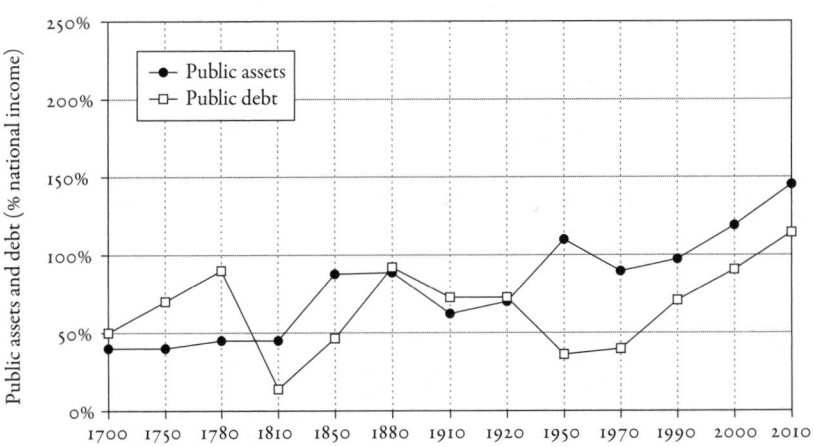

FIGURE 3.4. Public wealth in France, 1700–2010

Public debt is about one year of national income in France in 1780 as well as in 1880 and in 2000–2010.

Sources and series: see piketty.pse.ens.fr/capital21c.

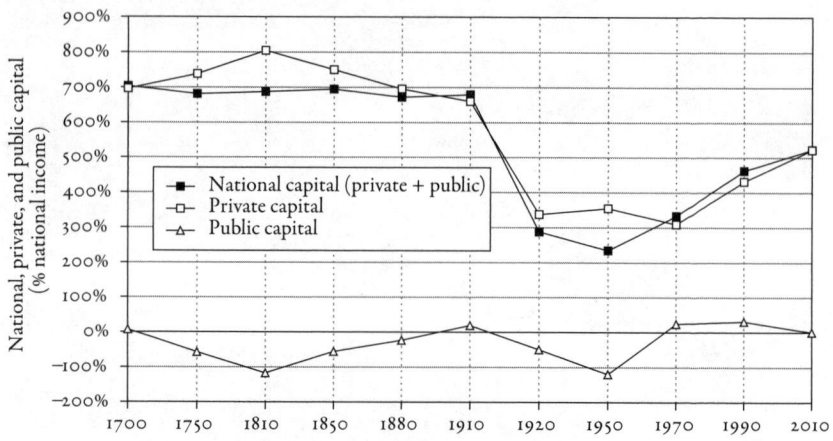

FIGURE 3.5. Private and public capital in Britain, 1700–2010

In 1810, private capital is worth eight years of national income in Britain (versus seven years for national capital).

Sources and series: see piketty.pse.ens.fr/capital21c.

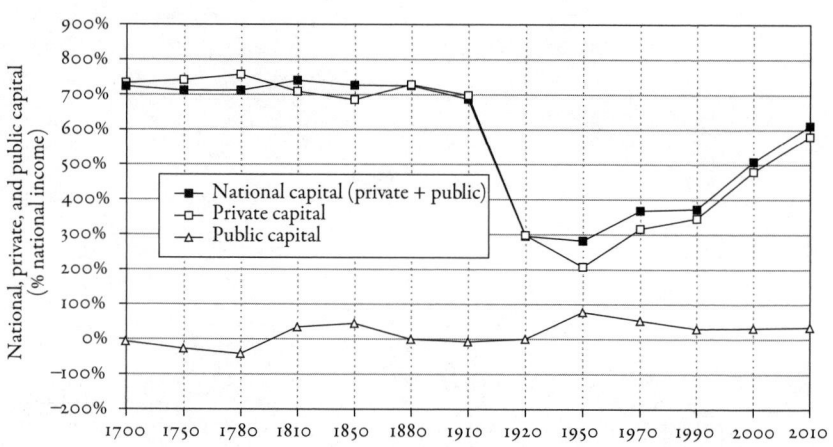

FIGURE 3.6. Private and public capital in France, 1700–2010

In 1950, public capital is worth almost one year of national income versus two years for private capital.

Sources and series: see piketty.pse.ens.fr/capital21c.

with the enormous mass of private wealth. In both countries, net public wealth over the past three centuries has sometimes been positive, sometimes negative. But the oscillations, which have ranged, broadly speaking, between +100 and −100 percent of national income (and more often than not between +50 and −50) have all in all been limited in amplitude compared to the high levels of private wealth (as much as 700–800 percent of national income).

In other words, the history of the ratio of national capital to national income in France and Britain since the eighteenth century, summarized earlier, has largely been the history of the relation between private capital and national income (see Figures 3.5 and 3.6).

The crucial fact here is of course well known: France and Britain have always been countries based on private property and never experimented with Soviet-style communism, where the state takes control of most capital. Hence it is not surprising that private wealth has always dominated public wealth. Conversely, neither country has ever amassed public debts sufficiently large to radically alter the magnitude of private wealth.

With this central fact in mind, it behooves us to push the analysis a bit farther. Even though public policy never went to extremes in either country, it did have a nonnegligible impact on the accumulation of private wealth at several points, and in different directions.

In eighteenth- and nineteenth-century Britain, the government tended at times to increase private wealth by running up large public debts. The French government did the same under the Ancien Régime and in the Belle Époque. At other times, however, the government tried to reduce the magnitude of private wealth. In France after World War II, public debts were canceled, and a large public sector was created; the same was true to a lesser extent in Britain during the same period. At present, both countries (along with most other wealthy countries) are running large public debts. Historical experience shows, however, that this can change fairly rapidly. It will therefore be useful to lay some groundwork by studying historical reversals of policy in Britain and France. Both countries offer a rich and varied historical experience in this regard.

Great Britain: Public Debt and the Reinforcement of Private Capital

I begin with the British case. On two occasions—first at the end of the Napoleonic wars and again after World War II—Britain's public debt attained extremely high levels, around 200 percent of GDP or even slightly above that. Although no country has sustained debt levels as high as Britain's for a longer period of time, Britain never defaulted on its debt. Indeed, the latter fact explains the former: if a country does not default in one way or another, either directly by simply repudiating its debt or indirectly through high inflation, it can take a very long time to pay off such a large public debt.

In this respect, Britain's public debt in the nineteenth century is a textbook case. To look back a little farther in time: even before the Revolutionary War in America, Britain had accumulated large public debts in the eighteenth century, as had France. Both monarchies were frequently at war, both with each other and with other European countries, and they did not manage to collect enough in taxes to pay for their expenditures, so that public debt rose steeply. Both countries thus managed to amass debts on the order of 50 percent of national income in the period 1700–1720 and 100 percent of national income in the period 1760–1770.

The French monarchy's inability to modernize its tax system and eliminate the fiscal privileges of the nobility is well known, as is the ultimate revolutionary resolution, initiated by the convocation of the Estates General in 1789, that led eventually to the introduction of a new tax system in 1790–1791. A land tax was imposed on all landowners and an estate tax on all inherited wealth. In 1797 came what was called the "banqueroute des deux tiers," or "two-thirds bankruptcy," which was in fact a massive default on two-thirds of the outstanding public debt, compounded by high inflation triggered by the issuance of assignats (paper money backed by nationalized land). This was how the debts of the Ancien Régime were ultimately dealt with.[11] The French public debt was thus quickly reduced to a very low level in the first decades of the nineteenth century (less than 20 percent of national income in 1815).

Britain followed a totally different trajectory. In order to finance its war with the American revolutionaries as well as its many wars with France in the revolutionary and Napoleonic eras, the British monarchy chose to borrow without limit. The public debt consequently rose to 100 percent of national income in the early 1770s and to nearly 200 percent in the 1810s—10 times France's debt in the same period. It would take a century of budget surpluses to gradually reduce Britain's debt to under 30 percent of national income in the 1910s (see Figure 3.3).

What lessons can we draw from this historical experience? First, there is no doubt that Britain's high level of public debt enhanced the influence of private wealth in British society. Britons who had the necessary means lent what the state demanded without appreciably reducing private investment: the very substantial increase in public debt in the period 1770–1810 was financed largely by a corresponding increase in private saving (proving that the propertied class in Britain was indeed prosperous and that yields on government bonds were attractive), so that national capital remained stable overall at around seven years of national income throughout the period, whereas private wealth rose to more than eight years of national income in the 1810s, as net public capital fell into increasingly negative territory (see Figure 3.5).

Hence it is no surprise that wealth is ubiquitous in Jane Austen's novels: traditional landlords were joined by unprecedented numbers of government bondholders. (These were largely the same people, if literary sources count as reliable historical sources.) The result was an exceptionally high level of overall private wealth. Interest on British

11. See François Crouzet, *La Grande inflation: La monnaie en France de Louis XVI à Napoléon* (Paris: Fayard, 1993).

government bonds supplemented land rents as private capital grew to dimensions never before seen.

Second, it is also quite clear that, all things considered, this very high level of public debt served the interests of the lenders and their descendants quite well, at least when compared with what would have happened if the British monarchy had financed its expenditures by making them pay taxes. From the standpoint of people with the means to lend to the government, it is obviously far more advantageous to lend to the state and receive interest on the loan for decades than to pay taxes without compensation. Furthermore, the fact that the government's deficits increased the overall demand for private wealth inevitably increased the return on that wealth, thereby serving the interests of those whose prosperity depended on the return on their investment in government bonds.

The central fact—and the essential difference from the twentieth century—is that the compensation to those who lent to the government was quite high in the nineteenth century: inflation was virtually zero from 1815 to 1914, and the interest rate on government bonds was generally around 4–5 percent; in particular, it was significantly higher than the growth rate. Under such conditions, investing in public debt can be very good business for wealthy people and their heirs.

Concretely, imagine a government that runs deficits on the order of 5 percent of GDP every year for twenty years (to pay, say, the wages of a large number of soldiers from 1795 to 1815) without having to increase taxes by an equivalent amount. After twenty years, an additional public debt of 100 percent of GDP will have been accumulated. Suppose that the government does not seek to repay the principal and simply pays the annual interest due on the debt. If the interest rate is 5 percent, it will have to pay 5 percent of GDP every year to the owners of this additional public debt, and must continue to do so until the end of time.

In broad outline, this is what Britain did in the nineteenth century. For an entire century, from 1815 to 1914, the British budget was always in substantial primary surplus: in other words, tax revenues always exceeded expenditures by several percent of GDP—an amount greater, for example, than the total expenditure on education throughout this period. It was only the growth of Britain's domestic product and national income (nearly 2.5 percent a year from 1815 to 1914) that ultimately, after a century of penance, allowed the British to significantly reduce their public debt as a percentage of national income.[12]

Who Profits from Public Debt?

This historical record is fundamental for a number of reasons. First, it enables us to understand why nineteenth-century socialists, beginning with Marx, were so wary of public debt, which they saw—not without a certain perspicacity—as a tool of private capital.

This concern was all the greater because in those days investors in public debt were paid handsomely, not only in Britain but also in many other countries, including France. There was no repeat of the revolutionary bankruptcy of 1797, and the rentiers in Balzac's novels do not seem to have worried any more about their government bonds than those in Jane Austen's works. Indeed, inflation was as low in France as in Britain in the period 1815–1914, and interest on government bonds was always paid in a timely manner. French sovereign debt was a good investment throughout the nineteenth century, and private investors prospered on the proceeds, just as in Britain. Although the total outstanding public debt in France was quite limited in 1815, the amount grew over the next several decades, particularly during the Restoration and July Monarchy (1815–1848), during which the right to vote was based on a property qualification.

The French government incurred large debts in 1815–1816 to pay for an indemnity to the occupying forces and then again in 1825 to fi-

---

12. In the period 1815–1914, Britain's primary budget surplus varied between 2 and 3 percent of GDP, and this went to pay interest on government debt of roughly the same amount. The total budget for education in this period was less than 2 percent of GDP. For detailed annual series of primary and secondary public deficits, see the online technical appendix.

nance the notorious "émigrés' billion," a sum paid to aristocrats who fled France during the Revolution (to compensate them for the rather limited redistribution of land that took place in their absence). Under the Second Empire, financial interests were well served. In the fierce articles that Marx penned in 1849–1850, published in *The Class Struggle in France,* he took offense at the way Louis-Napoleon Bonaparte's new minister of finance, Achille Fould, representing bankers and financiers, peremptorily decided to increase the tax on drinks in order to pay rentiers their due. Later, after the Franco-Prussian War of 1870–1871, the French government once again had to borrow from its population to pay for a transfer of funds to Germany equivalent to approximately 30 percent of national income.[13] In the end, during the period 1880–1914, the French public debt was even higher than the British: 70 to 80 percent of national income compared with less than 50 percent. In French novels of the Belle Époque, interest on government bonds figured significantly. The government paid roughly 2–3 percent of national income in interest every year (more than the budget for national education), and a very substantial group of people lived on that interest.[14]

In the twentieth century, a totally different view of public debt emerged, based on the conviction that debt could serve as an instrument of policy aimed at raising public spending and redistributing wealth for the benefit of the least well-off members of society. The difference between these two views is fairly simple: in the nineteenth century, lenders were handsomely reimbursed, thereby increasing private wealth; in the twentieth century, debt was drowned by inflation and repaid with money of decreasing value. In practice, this allowed deficits to be financed by those who had lent money to the state, and

---

13. These two series of transfers explain most of the increase in French public debt in the nineteenth century. On the amounts and sources, see the online technical appendix.

14. Between 1880 and 1914, France paid more interest on its debt than Britain did. For detailed annual series of government deficits in both countries and on the evolution of the rate of return on public debt, see the online technical appendix.

taxes did not have to be raised by an equivalent amount. This "progressive" view of public debt retains its hold on many minds today, even though inflation has long since declined to a rate not much above the nineteenth century's, and the distributional effects are relatively obscure.

It is interesting to recall that redistribution via inflation was much more significant in France than in Britain. As noted in Chapter 2, French inflation in the period 1913–1950 averaged more than 13 percent a year, which multiplied prices by a factor of 100. When Proust published *Swann's Way* in 1913, government bonds seemed as indestructible as the Grand Hotel in Cabourg, where the novelist spent his summers. By 1950, the purchasing power of those bonds was a hundredth of what it had been, so that the rentiers of 1913 and their progeny had virtually nothing left.

What did this mean to the government? Despite a large initial public debt (nearly 80 percent of national income in 1913), and very high deficits in the period 1913–1950, especially during the war years, by 1950 French public debt once again stood at a relatively low level (about 30 percent of national income), just as in 1815. In particular, the enormous deficits of the Liberation were almost immediately canceled out by inflation above 50 percent per year in the four years 1945–1948, in a highly charged political climate. In a sense, this was the equivalent of the "two-thirds bankruptcy" of 1797: past loans were wiped off the books in order to rebuild the country with a low level of public debt (see Figure 3.4).

In Britain, things were done differently: more slowly and with less passion. Between 1913 and 1950, the average rate of inflation was a little more than 3 percent a year, which meant that prices increased by a factor of 3 (less than one-thirtieth as much as in France). For British rentiers, this was nevertheless a spoliation of a sort that would have been unimaginable in the nineteenth century, indeed right up to World War I. Still, it was hardly sufficient to prevent an enormous accumulation of public deficits during two world wars: Britain was fully mobilized to pay for the war effort without undue dependence on the printing press, with the result that by 1950 the country found itself saddled with a colossal debt, more than 200 percent of GDP, even higher than in 1815. Only with the inflation of the 1950s (more than 4 percent a year) and above all of the 1970s (nearly 15 percent a year) did Britain's debt fall to around 50 percent of GDP (see Figure 3.3).

The mechanism of redistribution via inflation is extremely powerful, and it played a crucial historical role in both Britain and France in the twentieth century. It nevertheless raises two major problems. First, it is relatively crude in its choice of targets: among people with some measure of wealth, those who own government bonds (whether directly or indirectly via bank deposits) are not always the wealthiest: far from it. Second, the inflation mechanism cannot work indefinitely. Once inflation becomes permanent, lenders will demand a higher nominal interest rate, and the higher price will not have the desired effects. Furthermore, high inflation tends to accelerate constantly, and once the process is under way, its consequences can be difficult to master: some social groups saw their incomes rise considerably, while others did not. It was in the late 1970s—a decade marked by a mix of inflation, rising unemployment, and relative economic stagnation ("stagflation")—that a new consensus formed around the idea of low inflation. I will return to this issue later.

The Ups and Downs of Ricardian Equivalence

This long and tumultuous history of public debt, from the tranquil rentiers of the eighteenth and nineteenth centuries to the expropriation by inflation of the twentieth century, has indelibly marked collective memories and representations. The same historical experiences have also left their mark on economists. For example, when David Ricardo formulated in 1817 the hypothesis known today as "Ricardian equivalence," according to which, under certain conditions, public debt has no effect on the accumulation of national capital, he was obviously strongly influenced by what he witnessed around him. At the moment he wrote, British public debt was close to 200 percent of

GDP, yet it seemed not to have dried up the flow of private investment or the accumulation of capital. The much feared "crowding out" phenomenon had not occurred, and the increase in public debt seemed to have been financed by an increase in private saving. To be sure, it does not follow from this that Ricardian equivalence is a universal law, valid in all times and places. Everything of course depended on the prosperity of the social group involved (in Ricardo's day, a minority of Britons with enough wealth to generate the additional savings required), on the rate of interest that was offered, and of course on confidence in the government. But it is a fact worth noting that Ricardo, who had no access to historical time series or measurements of the type indicated in Figure 3.3 but who had intimate knowledge of the British capitalism of his time, clearly recognized that Britain's gigantic public debt had no apparent impact on national wealth and simply constituted a claim of one portion of the population on another.[15]

Similarly, when John Maynard Keynes wrote in 1936 about "the euthanasia of the rentier," he was also deeply impressed by what he observed around him: the pre–World War I world of the rentier was collapsing, and there was in fact no other politically acceptable way out of the economic and budgetary crisis of the day. In particular, Keynes clearly felt that inflation, which the British were still reluctant to accept because of strong conservative attachment to the pre-1914 gold standard, would be the simplest though not necessarily the most just way to reduce the burden of public debt and the influence of accumulated wealth.

Since the 1970s, analyses of the public debt have suffered from the fact that economists have probably relied too much on so-called representative agent models, that is, models in which each agent is

---

15. Ricardo's discussion of this issue in *Principles of Political Economy and Taxation* (London: George Bell and Sons, 1817) is not without ambiguity, however. On this point, see Gregory Clark's interesting historical analysis, "Debt, Deficits, and Crowding Out: England, 1716–1840," *European Review of Economic History* 5, no. 3 (December 2001): 403–36.

assumed to earn the same income and to be endowed with the same amount of wealth (and thus to own the same quantity of government bonds). Such a simplification of reality can be useful at times in order to isolate logical relations that are difficult to analyze in more complex models. Yet by totally avoiding the issue of inequality in the distribution of wealth and income, these models often lead to extreme and unrealistic conclusions and are therefore a source of confusion rather than clarity. In the case of public debt, representative agent models can lead to the conclusion that government debt is completely neutral, in regard not only to the total amount of national capital but also to the distribution of the fiscal burden. This radical reinterpretation of Ricardian equivalence, which was first proposed by the American economist Robert Barro,[16] fails to take account of the fact that the bulk of the public debt is in practice owned by a minority of the population (as in nineteenth-century Britain but not only there), so that the debt is the vehicle of important internal redistributions when it is repaid as well as when it is not. In view of the high degree of concentration that has always been characteristic of the wealth distribution, to study these questions without asking about inequalities between social groups is in fact to say nothing about significant aspects of the subject and what is really at stake.

France: A Capitalism without Capitalists in the Postwar Period

I return now to the history of public wealth and to the question of assets held by the government. Compared with the history of government debt, the history of public assets is seemingly less tumultuous.

---

16. See Robert Barro, "Are Government Bonds Net Wealth?" *Journal of Political Economy* 82, no. 6 (1974): 1095–1117, and "Government Spending, Interest Rates, Prices, and Budget Deficits in the United Kingdom, 1701–1918," *Journal of Monetary Economics* 20, no. 2 (1987): 221–48.

To simplify, one can say that the total value of public assets increased over the long run in both France and Britain, rising from barely 50 percent of national income in the eighteenth and nineteenth centuries to roughly 100 percent at the end of the twentieth century (see Figures 3.3 and 3.4).

To a first approximation, this increase reflects the steady expansion of the economic role of the state over the course of history, including in particular the development of ever more extensive public services in the areas of health and education (necessitating major investments in buildings and equipment) together with public or semipublic infrastructural investments in transportation and communication. These public services and infrastructures are more extensive in France than in Britain: the total value of public assets in France in 2010 is close to 150 percent of national income, compared with barely 100 percent across the Channel.

Nevertheless, this simplified, tranquil view of the accumulation of public assets over the long run omits an important aspect of the history of the last century: the accumulation of significant public assets in the industrial and financial sectors in the period 1950–1980, followed by major waves of privatization of the same assets after 1980. Both phenomena can be observed to varying degrees in most developed countries, especially in Europe, as well as in many emerging economies.

The case of France is emblematic. To understand it, we can look back in time. Not only in France but in countries around the world, faith in private capitalism was greatly shaken by the economic crisis of the 1930s and the cataclysms that followed. The Great Depression, triggered by the Wall Street crash of October 1929, struck the wealthy countries with a violence that has never been repeated to this day: a quarter of the working population in the United States, Germany, Britain, and France found themselves out of work. The traditional doctrine of "laissez faire," or nonintervention by the state in the economy, to which all countries adhered in the nineteenth century and to a large extent until the early 1930s, was durably discredited. Many countries opted for a greater degree of interventionism. Naturally enough, governments and the general public questioned the wisdom of financial and economic elites who had enriched themselves while leading the world to disaster. People began to think about different types of "mixed" economy, involving varying degrees of public ownership of firms alongside traditional forms of private property, or else, at the very least, a strong dose of public regulation and supervision of the financial system and of private capitalism more generally.

Furthermore, the fact that the Soviet Union joined the victorious Allies in World War II enhanced the prestige of the statist economic system the Bolsheviks had put in place. Had not that system allowed the Soviets to lead a notoriously backward country, which in 1917 had only just emerged from serfdom, on a forced march to industrialization? In 1942, Joseph Schumpeter believed that socialism would inevitably triumph over capitalism. In 1970, when Paul Samuelson published the eighth edition of his famous textbook, he was still predicting that the GDP of the Soviet Union might outstrip that of the United States sometime between 1990 and 2000.[17]

In France, this general climate of distrust toward private capitalism was deepened after 1945 by the fact that many members of the economic elite were suspected of having collaborated with the German occupiers and indecently enriched themselves during the war. It was in this highly charged post-Liberation climate that major sectors of the economy were nationalized, including in particular the banking sector, the coal mines, and the automobile industry. The Renault factories were punitively seized after their owner, Louis Renault, was arrested as a collaborator in September 1944. The provisional government nationalized the firm in January 1945.[18]

---

17. Paul Samuelson, *Economics,* 8th ed. (New York: McGraw-Hill, 1970), 831.
18. See Claire Andrieu, L. Le Van, and Antoine Prost, *Les Nationalisations de la Libération: De l'utopie au compromis* (Paris: FNSP, 1987), and Thomas Piketty, *Les hauts revenus en France au 20e siècle* (Paris: Grasset, 2001), 137–138.

In 1950, according to available estimates, the total value of French public assets exceeded one year's national income. Since the value of public debt had been sharply reduced by inflation, net public wealth was close to one year's national income, at a time when total private wealth was worth barely two years of national income (see Figure 3.6). As usual, one should not be misled by the apparent precision of these estimates: it is difficult to measure the value of capital in this period, when asset prices had attained historic lows, and it is possible that public assets are slightly undervalued compared with private assets. But the orders of magnitude may be taken as significant: in 1950, the government of France owned 25–30 percent of the nation's wealth, and perhaps even a little more.

This is a significant proportion, especially in view of the fact that public ownership left small and medium firms untouched, along with agriculture, and never claimed more than a minority share (less than 20 percent) of residential real estate. In the industrial and financial sectors most directly affected by the postwar nationalizations, the state's share of national wealth exceeded 50 percent from 1950 to 1980.

Although this historical episode was relatively brief, it is important for understanding the complex attitude of the French people toward private capitalism even today. Throughout the Trente Glorieuses, during which the country was rebuilt and economic growth was strong (stronger that at any other time in the nation's history), France had a mixed economy, in a sense a capitalism without capitalists, or at any rate a state capitalism in which private owners no longer controlled the largest firms.

To be sure, waves of nationalization also occurred in this same period in many other countries, including Britain, where the value of public assets also exceeded a year's national income in 1950—a level equal to that of France. The difference is that British public debt at the time exceeded two years of national income, so that net public wealth was significantly negative in the 1950s, and private wealth was that much greater. Net public wealth did not turn positive in Britain until the 1960s–1970s, and even then it remained less than 20 percent of national income (which is already quite large).[19]

What is distinctive about the French trajectory is that public ownership, having thrived from 1950 to 1980, dropped to very low levels after 1980, even as private wealth—both financial and real estate—rose to levels even higher than Britain's: nearly six years of national income in 2010, or 20 times the value of public wealth. Following a period of state capitalism after 1950, France became the promised land of the new private-ownership capitalism of the twenty-first century.

What makes the change all the more striking is that it was never clearly acknowledged for what it was. The privatization of the economy, including both liberalization of the market for goods and services and deregulation of financial markets and capital flows, which affected countries around the world in the 1980s, had multiple and complex origins. The memory of the Great Depression and subsequent disasters had faded. The "stagflation" of the 1970s demonstrated the limits of the postwar Keynesian consensus. With the end of postwar reconstruction and the high growth rates of the Trente Glorieuses, it was only natural to question the wisdom of indefinitely expanding the role of the state and its increasing claims on national output. The deregulation movement began with the "conservative revolutions" of 1979–1980 in the United States and Britain, as both countries increasingly chafed at being overtaken by others (even though the catch-up

---

19. It is instructive to reread British estimates of national capital at various points during the twentieth century, as the form and magnitude of public assets and liabilities changed utterly. See in particular H. Campion, *Public and Private Property in Great Britain* (Oxford: Oxford University Press, 1939), and J. Revell, *The Wealth of the Nation: The National Balance Sheet of the United Kingdom, 1957–1961* (Cambridge: Cambridge University Press, 1967). The question barely arose in Giffen's time, since private capital so clearly outweighed public capital. We find the same evolution in France, for example in the 1956 work published by François Divisia, Jean Dupin, and René Roy and quite aptly entitled *A la recherche du franc perdu* (Paris: Société d'édition de revues et de publications, 1954), whose third volume is titled *La fortune de la France* and attempts, not without difficulty, to update Clément Colson's estimates for the Belle Époque.

was a largely inevitable process, as noted in Chapter 2). Meanwhile, the increasingly obvious failure of statist Soviet and Chinese models in the 1970s led both communist giants to begin a gradual liberalization of their economic systems in the 1980s by introducing new forms of private property in firms.

Despite these converging international currents, French voters in 1981 displayed a certain desire to sail against the wind. Every country has its own history, of course, and its own political timetable. In France, a coalition of Socialists and Communists won a majority on a platform that promised to continue the nationalization of the industrial and banking sectors begun in 1945. This proved to be a brief intermezzo, however, since in 1986 a liberal majority initiated a very important wave of privatization in all sectors. This initiative was then continued and amplified by a new socialist majority in the period 1988–1993. The Renault Company became a joint-stock corporation in 1990, as did the public telecommunications administration, which was transformed into France Telecom and opened to private investment in 1997–1998. In a context of slower growth, high unemployment, and large government deficits, the progressive sale of publicly held shares after 1990 brought additional funds into public coffers, although it did not prevent a steady increase in the public debt. Net public wealth fell to very low levels. Meanwhile, private wealth slowly returned to levels not seen since the shocks of the twentieth century. In this way, France totally transformed its national capital structure at two different points in time without really understanding why.

FOUR

From Old Europe to the New World

In the previous chapter, I examined the metamorphoses of capital in Britain and France since the eighteenth century. The lessons to be learned from each country proved consistent and complementary. The nature of capital was totally transformed, but in the end its total amount relative to income scarcely changed at all. To gain a better understanding of the different historical processes and mechanisms involved, the analysis must now extend to other countries. I will begin by looking at Germany, which will round out the European panorama. Then I will turn my attention to capital in North America (the United States and Canada). Capital in the New World took some quite unusual and specific forms, in the first place because land was so abundant that it did not cost very much; second, because of the existence of slavery; and finally, because this region of perpetual demographic growth tended to accumulate structurally smaller amounts of capital (relative to annual income and output) than Europe did. This will lead to the question of what fundamentally determines the capital / income ratio in the long run, which will be the subject of Chapter 5. I will approach that question by extending the analysis first to all the wealthy countries and then to the entire globe, insofar as the sources allow.

Germany: Rhenish Capitalism and Social Ownership

I begin with the case of Germany. It is interesting to compare the British and French trajectories with the German, especially in regard to the issue of mixed economy, which became important, as noted, after World War II. Unfortunately, the historical data for Germany are

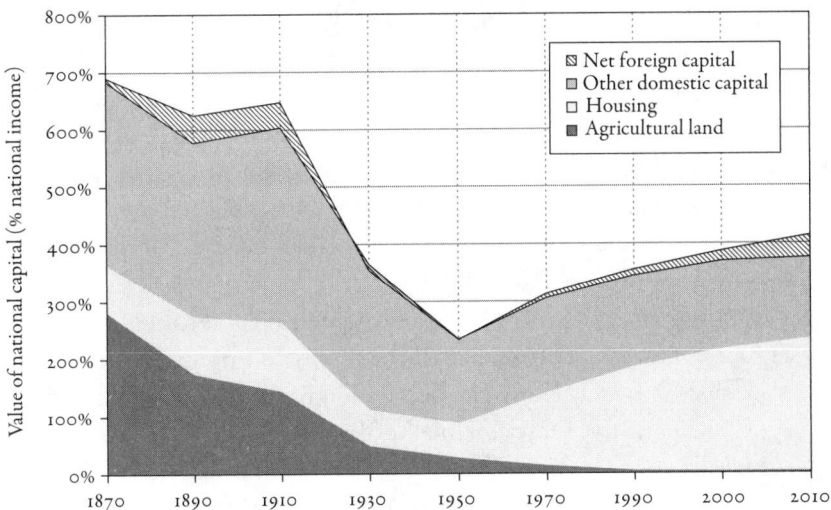

FIGURE 4.1. Capital in Germany, 1870–2010

National capital is worth 6.5 years of national income in Germany in 1910 (including about 0.5 year invested abroad).

Sources and series: see piketty.pse.ens.fr/capital21c.

more diverse, owing to the lateness of German unification and numerous territorial changes, so there is no satisfactory way to trace the history back beyond 1870. Still, the estimates we have for the period after 1870 reveal clear similarities with Britain and France, as well as a number of differences.

The first thing to notice is that the overall evolution is similar: first, agricultural land gave way in the long run to residential and commercial real estate and industrial and financial capital, and second, the capital / income ratio has grown steadily since World War II and appears to be on its way to regaining the level it had attained prior to the shocks of 1914–1945 (see Figure 4.1).

Note that the importance of farmland in late nineteenth-century Germany made the German case resemble the French more than the British one (agriculture had not yet disappeared east of the Rhine), and the value of industrial capital was higher than in either France or

Britain. By contrast, Germany on the eve of World War I had only half as much in foreign assets as France (roughly 50 percent of national income versus a year's worth of income for France) and only a quarter as much as Britain (whose foreign assets were worth two years of national income). The main reason for this is of course that Germany had no colonial empire, a fact that was the source of some very powerful political and military tensions: think, for example, of the Moroccan crises of 1905 and 1911, when the Kaiser sought to challenge French supremacy in Morocco. The heightened competition among European powers for colonial assets obviously contributed to the climate that ultimately led to the declaration of war in the summer of 1914: one need not subscribe to all of Lenin's theses in *Imperialism, the Highest Stage of Capitalism* (1916) to share this conclusion.

Note, too, that Germany over the past several decades has amassed substantial foreign assets thanks to trade surpluses. By 2010, Germany's net foreign asset position was close to 50 percent of national income (more than half of which has been accumulated since 2000). This is almost the same level as in 1913. It is a small amount compared to the foreign asset positions of Britain and France at the end of the nineteenth century, but it is substantial compared to the current positions of the two former colonial powers, which are close to zero. A comparison of Figure 4.1 with Figures 3.1–2 shows how different the trajectories of Germany, France, and Britain have been since the nineteenth century: to a certain extent they have inverted their respective positions. In view of Germany's very large current trade surpluses, it is not impossible that this divergence will increase. I will come back to this point.

In regard to public debt and the split between public and private capital, the German trajectory is fairly similar to the French. With average inflation of nearly 17 percent between 1913 and 1950, which means that prices were multiplied by a factor of 300 between those dates (compared with barely 100 in France), Germany was the country that, more than any other, drowned its public debt in inflation in the twentieth century. Despite running large deficits during both world

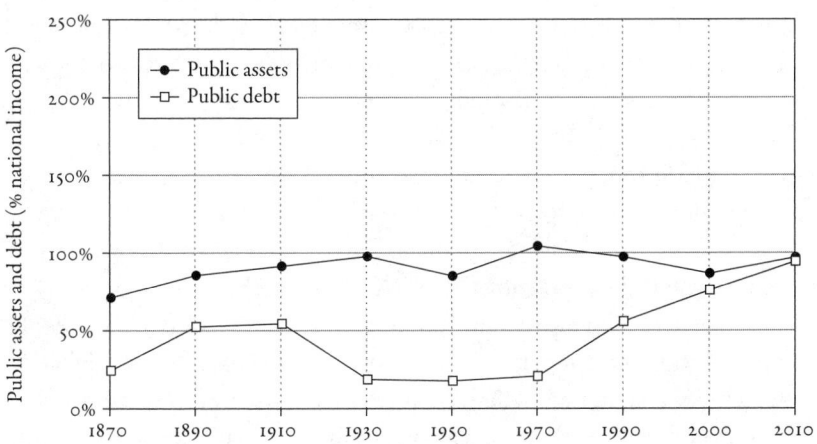

FIGURE 4.2. Public wealth in Germany, 1870–2010
Public debt is worth almost one year of national income in Germany in 2010 (as much as assets).
Sources and series: see piketty.pse.ens.fr/capital21c.

wars (the public debt briefly exceeded 100 percent of GDP in 1918–1920 and 150 percent of GDP in 1943–1944), inflation made it possible in both instances to shrink the debt very rapidly to very low levels: barely 20 percent of GDP in 1930 and again in 1950 (see Figure 4.2).[1] Yet the recourse to inflation was so extreme and so violently destabilized German society and economy, especially during the hyperinflation of the 1920s, that the German public came away from these experiences with a strongly antiinflationist attitude.[2] That is why the following paradoxical situation exists today: Germany, the country that made the most dramatic use of inflation to rid itself of debt in the twentieth century, refuses to countenance any rise in prices greater than 2 percent a year, whereas Britain, whose government has always

---

1. In order to concentrate on long-run evolutions, the figures accompanying this chapter indicate values by decade only and thus ignore extremes that lasted for only a few years. For complete annual series, see the online technical appendix.

2. The average inflation figure of 17 percent for the period 1913–1950 omits the year 1923, when prices increased by a factor of 100 million over the course of the year.

paid its debts, even more than was reasonable, has a more flexible attitude and sees nothing wrong with allowing its central bank to buy a substantial portion of its public debt even if it means slightly higher inflation.

In regard to the accumulation of public assets, the German case is again similar to the French: the government took large positions in the banking and industrial sectors in the period 1950–1980, then partially sold off those positions between 1980 and 2000, but substantial holdings remain. For example, the state of Lower Saxony today owns more than 15 percent of the shares (and 20 percent of the voting rights, which are guaranteed by law, despite objections from the European Union) of Volkswagen, the leading automobile manufacturer in Europe and the world.[3] In the period 1950–1980, when public debt was close to zero, net public capital was close to one year's national income in Germany, compared with barely two years for private capital, which then stood at a very low level (see Figure 4.3). Just as in France, the government owned 25–30 percent of Germany's national capital during the decades of postwar reconstruction and the German economic miracle. Just as in France, the slowdown in economic growth after 1970 and the accumulation of public debt (which began well before reunification and has continued since) led to a complete turnaround over the course of the past few decades. Net public wealth was almost exactly zero in 2010, and private wealth, which has grown steadily since 1950, accounts for nearly all of national wealth.

There is, however, a significant difference between the value of private capital in Germany compared to that in France and Britain. German private wealth has increased enormously since World War II: it was exceptionally low in 1950 (barely a year and a half of national income), but today it stands at more than four years of national in-

---

3. Virtually equal to General Motors, Toyota, and Renault-Nissan, with sales of around 8 million vehicles each in 2011. The French government still holds about 15 percent of the capital of Renault (the third leading European manufacturer after Volkswagen and Peugeot).

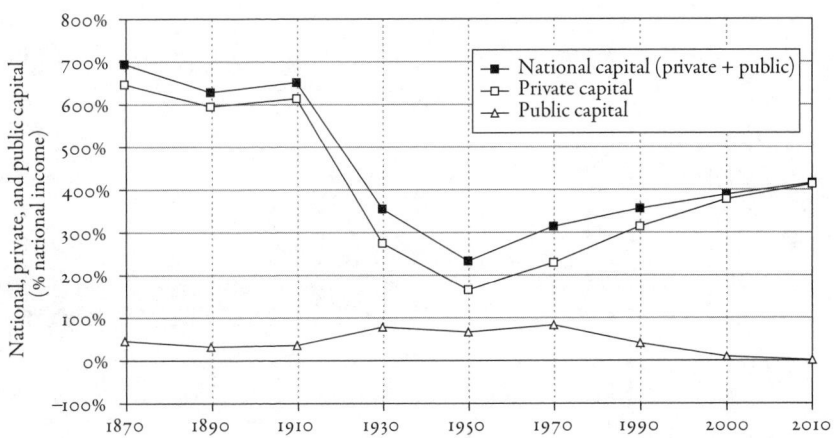

FIGURE 4.3. Private and public capital in Germany, 1870–2010
In 1970, public capital is worth almost one year of national income, versus slightly more than two for private capital.
Sources and series: see piketty.pse.ens.fr/capital21c.

come. The reconstitution of private wealth in all three countries emerges clearly from Figure 4.4. Nevertheless, German private wealth in 2010 was noticeably lower than private wealth in Britain and France: barely four years of national income in Germany compared with five or six in France and Britain and more than six in Italy and Spain (as we will see in Chapter 5). Given the high level of German saving, this low level of German wealth compared to other European countries is to some extent a paradox, which may be transitory and can be explained as follows.[4]

The first factor to consider is the low price of real estate in Germany compared to other European countries, which can be explained in part by the fact that the sharp price increases seen everywhere else after 1990 were checked in Germany by the effects of German reunification,

---

4. Given the limitations of the available sources, it is also possible that this gap can be explained in part by various statistical biases. See the online technical appendix.

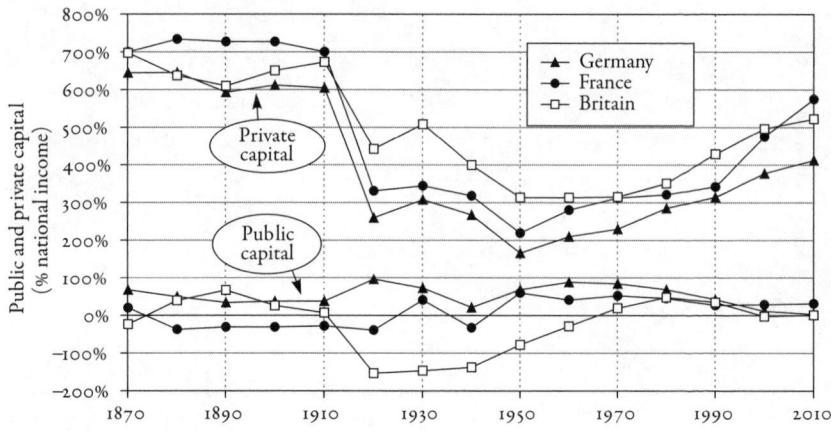

FIGURE 4.4. Private and public capital in Europe, 1870–2010

The fluctuations of national capital in Europe in the long run are mostly due to the fluctuations of private capital.

Sources and series: see piketty.pse.ens.fr/capital21c.

which brought a large number of low-cost houses onto the market. To explain the discrepancy over the long term, however, we would need more durable factors, such as stricter rent control.

In any case, most of the gap between Germany on the one hand and France and Britain on the other stems not from the difference in the value of the housing stock but rather from the difference in the value of other domestic capital, and primarily the capital of firms (see Figure 4.1). In other words, the gap arises not from the low valuation of German real estate but rather from the low stock market valuation of German firms. If, in measuring total private wealth, we used not stock market value but book value (obtained by subtracting a firm's debt from the cumulative value of its investments), the German paradox would disappear: German private wealth would immediately rise to French and British levels (between five and six years of national income rather than four). These complications may appear to be purely matters of accounting but are in fact highly political.

At this stage, suffice it to say that the lower market values of German firms appear to reflect the character of what is sometimes called

"Rhenish capitalism" or "the stakeholder model," that is, an economic model in which firms are owned not only by shareholders but also by certain other interested parties known as "stakeholders," starting with representatives of the firms' workers (who sit on the boards of directors of German firms not merely in a consultative capacity but as active participants in deliberations, even though they may not be shareholders), as well as representatives of regional governments, consumers' associations, environmental groups, and so on. The point here is not to idealize this model of shared social ownership, which has its limits, but simply to note that it can be at least as efficient economically as Anglo-Saxon market capitalism or "the shareholder model" (in which all power lies in theory with shareholders, although in practice things are always more complex), and especially to observe that the stakeholder model inevitably implies a lower market valuation but not necessarily a lower social valuation. The debate about different varieties of capitalism erupted in the early 1990s after the collapse of the Soviet Union.[5] Its intensity later waned, in part no doubt because the German economic model seemed to be losing steam in the years after reunification (between 1998 and 2002, Germany was often presented as the sick man of Europe). In view of Germany's relatively good health in the midst of the global financial crisis (2007–2012), it is not out of the question that this debate will be revived in the years to come.[6]

Shocks to Capital in the Twentieth Century

Now that I have presented a first look at the general evolution of the capital / income ratio and the public-private split over the long run, I must return to the question of chronology and in particular attempt to understand the reasons first for the collapse of the capital / income

---

5. See, for example, Michel Albert, *Capitalisme contre capitalisme* (Paris: Le Seuil, 1991).
6. See, for example, Guillaume Duval, *Made in Germany* (Paris: Le Seuil, 2013).

ratio over the course of the twentieth century and then for its spectacular recovery.

Note first of all that this was a phenomenon that affected all European countries. All available sources indicate that the changes observed in Britain, France, and Germany (which together in 1910 and again in 2010 account for more than two-thirds of the GDP of Western Europe and more than half of the GDP of all of Europe) are representative of the entire continent: although interesting variations between countries do exist, the overall pattern is the same. In particular, the capital / income ratio in Italy and Spain has risen quite sharply since 1970, even more sharply than in Britain and France, and the available historical data suggest that it was on the order of six or seven years of national income around the turn of the twentieth century. Available estimates for Belgium, the Netherlands, and Austria indicate a similar pattern.[7]

Next, we must insist on the fact that the fall in the capital / income ratio between 1914 and 1945 is explained to only a limited extent by the physical destruction of capital (buildings, factories, infrastructure, etc.) due to the two world wars. In Britain, France, and Germany, the value of national capital was between six and a half and seven years of national income in 1913 and fell to around two and a half years in 1950: a spectacular drop of more than four years of national income (see Figures 4.4 and 4.5). To be sure, there was substantial physical destruction of capital, especially in France during World War I (during which the northeastern part of the country, on the front lines, was severely battered) and in both France and Germany during World War II owing to massive bombing in 1944–1945 (although the periods of combat were shorter than in World War I, the technology was considerably more destructive). All in all, capital worth nearly a year of national income was destroyed in France (accounting for one-fifth to one-quarter of the total decline in the capital / income ratio), and a year and a half in Germany (or roughly a third of the total decline).

---

7. See the online technical appendix.

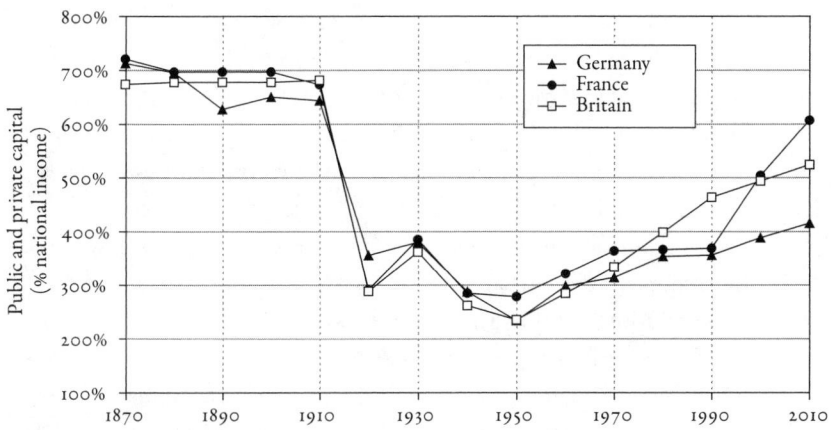

FIGURE 4.5. National capital in Europe, 1870–2010

National capital (sum of public and private capital) is worth between two and three years of national income in Europe in 1950.

Sources and series: see piketty.pse.ens.fr/capital21c.

Although these losses were quite significant, they clearly explain only a fraction of the total drop, even in the two countries most directly affected by the conflicts. In Britain, physical destruction was less extensive—insignificant in World War I and less than 10 percent of national income owing to German bombing in World War II—yet national capital fell by four years of national income (or more than 40 times the loss due to physical destruction), as much as in France and Germany.

In fact, the budgetary and political shocks of two wars proved far more destructive to capital than combat itself. In addition to physical destruction, the main factors that explain the dizzying fall in the capital / income ratio between 1913 and 1950 were on the one hand the collapse of foreign portfolios and the very low savings rate characteristic of the time (together, these two factors, plus physical destruction, explain two-thirds to three-quarters of the drop) and on the other the low asset prices that obtained in the new postwar political context of mixed ownership and regulation (which accounted for one-quarter to one-third of the drop).

I have already mentioned the importance of losses on foreign assets, especially in Britain, where net foreign capital dropped from two years of national income on the eve of World War I to a slightly negative level in the 1950s. Britain's losses on its international portfolio were thus considerably greater than French or German losses through physical destruction of domestic capital, and these more than made up for the relatively low level of physical destruction on British soil.

The decline of foreign capital stemmed in part from expropriations due to revolution and the process of decolonization (think of the Russian loans to which many French savers subscribed in the Belle Époque and that the Bolsheviks repudiated in 1917, or the nationalization of the Suez Canal by Nasser in 1956, to the dismay of the British and French shareholders who owned the canal and had been collecting dividends and royalties on it since 1869) and in even greater part to the very low savings rate observed in various European countries between 1914 and 1945, which led British and French (and to a lesser degree German) savers to gradually sell off their foreign assets. Owing to low growth and repeated recessions, the period 1914–1945 was a dark one for all Europeans but especially for the wealthy, whose income dwindled considerably in comparison with the Belle Époque. Private savings rates were therefore relatively low (especially if we deduct the amount of reparations and replacement of war-damaged property), and some people consequently chose to maintain their standard of living by gradually selling off part of their capital. When the Depression came in the 1930s, moreover, many stock- and bondholders were ruined as firm after firm went bankrupt.

Furthermore, the limited amount of private saving was largely absorbed by enormous public deficits, especially during the wars: national saving, the sum of private and public saving, was extremely low in Britain, France, and Germany between 1914 and 1945. Savers lent massively to their governments, in some cases selling their foreign assets, only to be ultimately expropriated by inflation, very quickly in France and Germany and more slowly in Britain, which created the illusion that private wealth in Britain was faring better in 1950 than private wealth on the continent. In fact, national wealth was equally affected in both places (see Figures 4.4 and 4.5). At times governments borrowed directly from abroad: that is how the United States went from a negative position on the eve of World War I to a positive position in the 1950s. But the effect on the national wealth of Britain or France was the same.[8]

Ultimately, the decline in the capital / income ratio between 1913 and 1950 is the history of Europe's suicide, and in particular of the euthanasia of European capitalists.

This political, military, and budgetary history would be woefully incomplete, however, if we did not insist on the fact that the low level of the capital / income ratio after World War II was in some ways a positive thing, in that it reflected in part a deliberate policy choice aimed at reducing—more or less consciously and more or less efficaciously—the market value of assets and the economic power of their owners. Concretely, real estate values and stocks fell to historically low levels in the 1950s and 1960s relative to the price of goods and services, and this goes some way toward explaining the low capital / income ratio. Remember that all forms of wealth are evaluated in terms of market prices at a given point in time. This introduces an element of arbitrariness (markets are often capricious), but it is the only method we have for calculating the national capital stock: how else could one possibly add up hectares of farmland, square meters of real estate, and blast furnaces?

In the postwar period, housing prices stood at historic lows, owing primarily to rent control policies that were adopted nearly everywhere in periods of high inflation such as the early 1920s and especially the 1940s. Rents rose less sharply than other prices. Housing became less

---

8. The difference from Ricardo's day was that wealthy Britons in the 1800s and 1810s were prosperous enough to generate the additional private saving needed to absorb public deficits without affecting national capital. By contrast, the European deficits of 1914–1945 occurred in a context where private wealth and saving had already been subjected to repeated negative shocks, so that public indebtedness aggravated the decline of national capital.

expensive for tenants, while landlords earned less on their properties, so real estate prices fell. Similarly, the value of firms, that is, the value of the stock of listed firms and shares of partnerships, fell to relatively low levels in the 1950s and 1960s. Not only had confidence in the stock markets been strongly shaken by the Depression and the nationalizations of the postwar period, but new policies of financial regulation and taxation of dividends and profits had been established, helping to reduce the power of stockholders and the value of their shares.

Detailed estimates for Britain, France, and Germany show that low real estate and stock prices after World War II account for a nonnegligible but still minority share of the fall in the capital / income ratio between 1913 and 1950: between one-quarter and one-third of the drop depending on the country, whereas volume effects (low national savings rate, loss of foreign assets, destructions) account for two-thirds to three-quarters of the decline.[9] Similarly, as I will show in the next chapter, the very strong rebound of real estate and stock market prices in the 1970s and 1980s and especially the 1990s and 2000s explains a significant part of the rebound in the capital / income ratio, though still less important than volume effects, linked this time to a structural decrease in the rate of growth.

Capital in America: More Stable Than in Europe

Before studying in greater detail the rebound in the capital / income ratio in the second half of the twentieth century and analyzing the prospects for the twenty-first century, I now want to move beyond the European framework to examine the historical forms and levels of capital in America.

Several facts stand out clearly. First, America was the New World, where capital mattered less than in the Old World, meaning old Europe. More precisely, the value of the stock of national capital, based

---

9. See the online technical appendix.

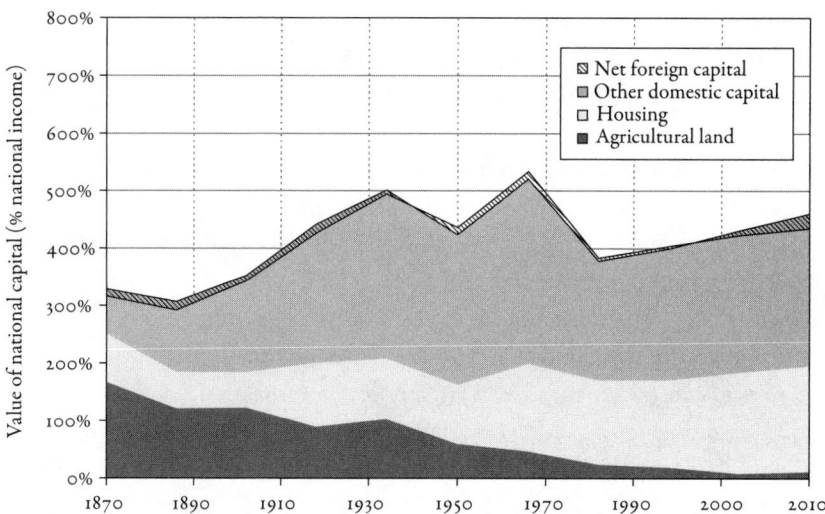

FIGURE 4.6. Capital in the United States, 1770–2010

National capital is worth three years of national income in the United States in 1770 (including 1.5 years in agricultural land).

Sources and series: see piketty.pse.ens.fr/capital21c.

on numerous contemporary estimates I have collected and compared, as for other countries, was scarcely more than three years of national income around the time that the United States gained its independence, in the period 1770–1810. Farmland was valued at between one and one and a half years of national income (see Figure 4.6). Uncertainties notwithstanding, there is no doubt that the capital / income ratio was much lower in the New World colonies than in Britain or France, where national capital was worth roughly seven years of national income, of which farmland accounted for nearly four (see Figures 3.1 and 3.2).

The crucial point is that the number of hectares per person was obviously far greater in North America than in old Europe. In volume, capital per capita was therefore higher in the United States. Indeed, there was so much land that its market value was very low: anyone could own vast quantities, and therefore it was not worth very much. In other words, the price effect more than counterbalanced the volume effect: when the volume of a given type of capital exceeds certain thresholds, its price will inevitably fall to a level so low that the product of the price and volume, which is the value of the capital, is lower than it would be if the volume were smaller.

The considerable difference between the price of land in the New World and in Europe at the end of the eighteenth century and the beginning of the nineteenth is confirmed by all available sources concerning land purchases and inheritances (such as probate records and wills).

Furthermore, the other types of capital—housing and other domestic capital—were also relatively less important in the colonial era and during the early years of the American republic (in comparison to Europe). The reason for this is different, but the fact is not surprising. New arrivals, who accounted for a very large proportion of the US population, did not cross the Atlantic with their capital of homes or tools or machinery, and it took time to accumulate the equivalent of several years of national income in real estate and business capital.

Make no mistake: the low capital / income ratio in America reflected a fundamental difference in the structure of social inequalities compared with Europe. The fact that total wealth amounted to barely three years of national income in the United States compared with more than seven in Europe signified in a very concrete way that the influence of landlords and accumulated wealth was less important in the New World. With a few years of work, the new arrivals were able to close the initial gap between themselves and their wealthier predecessors—or at any rate it was possible to close the wealth gap more rapidly than in Europe.

In 1840, Tocqueville noted quite accurately that "the number of large fortunes [in the United States] is quite small, and capital is still scarce," and he saw this as one obvious reason for the democratic spirit that in his view dominated there. He added that, as his observations showed, all of this was a consequence of the low price of agricultural land: "In America, land costs little, and anyone can easily become a landowner."[10] Here we can see at work the Jeffersonian ideal of a society of small landowners, free and equal.

Things would change over the course of the nineteenth century. The share of agriculture in output decreased steadily, and the value of farmland also declined, as in Europe. But the United States accumulated a considerable stock of real estate and industrial capital, so that national capital was close to five years of national income in 1910, versus three in 1810. The gap with old Europe remained, but it had shrunk by half in one century (see Figure 4.6). The United States had become capitalist, but wealth continued to have less influence than in Belle Époque Europe, at least if we consider the vast US territory as a whole. If we limit our gaze to the East Coast, the gap is smaller still. In the film *Titanic,* the director, James Cameron, depicted the social structure of 1912. He chose to make wealthy Americans appear just as prosperous—and arrogant—as their European counterparts: for instance, the detestable Hockley, who wants to bring young Rose to Philadelphia in order to marry her. (Heroically, she refuses to be treated as property and becomes Rose Dawson.) The novels of Henry James that are set in Boston and New York between 1880 and 1910 also show social groups in which real estate and industrial and financial capital matter almost as much as in European novels: times had indeed changed since the Revolutionary War, when the United States was still a land without capital.

The shocks of the twentieth century struck America with far less violence than Europe, so that the capital / income ratio remained far more stable: it oscillated between four and five years of national income from 1910 to 2010 (see Figure 4.6), whereas in Europe it dropped from more than seven years to less than three before rebounding to five or six (see Figures 3.1–2).

To be sure, US fortunes were also buffeted by the crises of 1914–1945. Public debt rose sharply in the United States due to the cost of

---

10. See Alexis de Tocqueville, *Democracy in America,* trans. Arthur Goldhammer (New York: Library of America, 2004), II.2.19, p. 646, and II.3.6, p. 679.

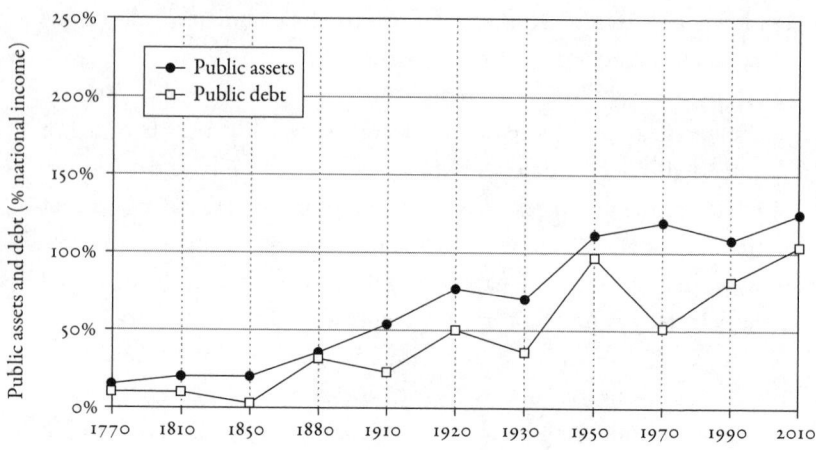

FIGURE 4.7. Public wealth in the United States, 1770–2010

Public debt is worth one year of national income in the United States in 1950 (almost as much as assets).

Sources and series: see piketty.pse.ens.fr/capital21c.

waging war, especially during World War II, and this affected national saving in a period of economic instability: the euphoria of the 1920s gave way to the Depression of the 1930s. (Cameron tells us that the odious Hockley commits suicide in October 1929.). Under Franklin D. Roosevelt, moreover, the United States adopted policies designed to reduce the influence of private capital, such as rent control, just as in Europe. After World War II, real estate and stock prices stood at historic lows. When it came to progressive taxation, the United States went much farther than Europe, possibly demonstrating that the goal there was more to reduce inequality than to eradicate private property. No sweeping policy of nationalization was attempted, although major public investments were initiated in the 1930s and 1940s, especially in infrastructures. Inflation and growth eventually returned public debt to a modest level in the 1950s and 1960s, so that public wealth was distinctly positive in 1970 (see Figure 4.7). In the end, American private wealth decreased from nearly five years of national

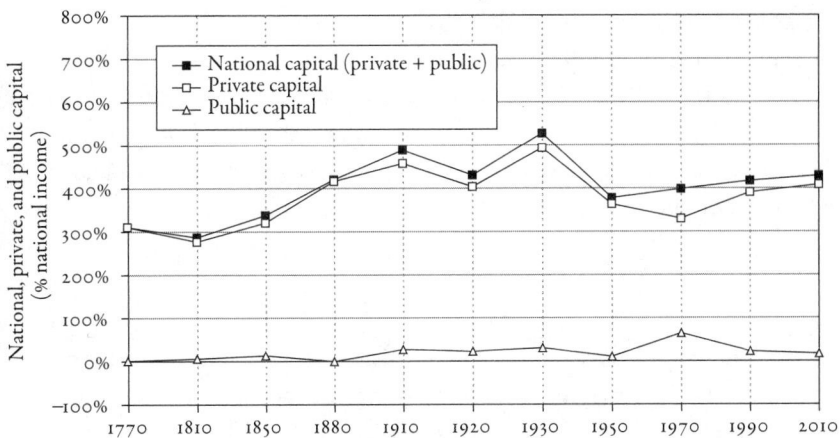

FIGURE 4.8. Private and public capital in the United States, 1770–2010

In 2010, public capital is worth 20 percent of national income, versus over 400 percent for private capital.

Sources and series: see piketty.pse.ens.fr/capital21c.

income in 1930 to less than three and a half in 1970, a not insignificant decline (see Figure 4.8).

Nevertheless, the "U-shaped curve" of the capital / income ratio in the twentieth century is smaller in amplitude in the United States than in Europe. Expressed in years of income or output, capital in the United States seems to have achieved virtual stability from the turn of the twentieth century on—so much so that a stable capital / income or capital / output ratio is sometimes treated as a universal law in US textbooks (like Paul Samuelson's). In comparison, Europe's relation to capital, and especially private capital, was notably chaotic in the century just past. In the Belle Époque capital was king. In the years after World War II many people thought capitalism had been almost eradicated. Yet at the beginning of the twenty-first century Europe seems to be in the avant-garde of the new patrimonial capitalism, with private fortunes once again surpassing US levels. This is fairly well explained by the lower rate of economic and especially demographic growth in Europe compared with the United States, leading automatically to increased influence of wealth accumulated in the past, as we will see in Chapter 5. In any case, the key fact is that the United States enjoyed a much more stable capital / income ratio than Europe in the twentieth century, perhaps explaining why Americans seem to take a more benign view of capitalism than Europeans.

The New World and Foreign Capital

Another key difference between the history of capital in America and Europe is that foreign capital never had more than a relatively limited importance in the United States. This is because the United States, the first colonized territory to have achieved independence, never became a colonial power itself.

Throughout the nineteenth century, the United States' net foreign capital position was slightly negative: what US citizens owned in the rest of the world was less than what foreigners, mainly British, owned in the United States. The difference was quite small, however, at most 10–20 percent of the US national income, and generally less than 10 percent between 1770 and 1920.

For example, on the eve of World War I, US domestic capital—farmland, housing, other domestic capital—stood at 500 percent of national income. Of this total, the assets owned by foreign investors (minus foreign assets held by US investors) represented the equivalent of 10 percent of national income. The national capital, or net national wealth, of the United States was thus about 490 percent of national income. In other words, the United States was 98 percent US-owned and 2 percent foreign-owned. The net foreign asset position was close to balanced, especially when compared to the enormous foreign assets held by Europeans: between one and two years of national income in France and Britain and half a year in Germany. Since the GDP of the United States was barely more than half of the GDP of Western Europe in 1913, this also means that the Europeans of 1913 held only a small proportion of their foreign asset portfolios (less than 5 percent) in the United States. To sum up, the world of 1913 was one in which Europe owned a large part of Africa, Asia, and Latin America, while the United States owned itself.

With the two world wars, the net foreign asset position of the United States reversed itself: it was negative in 1913 but turned slightly positive in the 1920s and remained so into the 1970s and 1980s. The United States financed the belligerents and thus ceased to be a debtor of Europe and became a creditor. It bears emphasizing, however, that the United States' net foreign assets holdings remained relatively modest: barely 10 percent of national income (see Figure 4.6).

In the 1950s and 1960s in particular, the net foreign capital held by the United States was still fairly limited (barely 5 percent of national income, whereas domestic capital was close to 400 percent, or 80 times greater). The investments of US multinational corporations in Europe and the rest of the world attained levels that seemed considerable at the time, especially to Europeans, who were accustomed to owning the world and who chafed at the idea of owing their reconstruction in part to Uncle Sam and the Marshall Plan. In fact, despite these national traumas, US investments in Europe would always be fairly limited compared to the investments the former colonial powers had held around the globe a few decades earlier. Furthermore, US investments in Europe and elsewhere were balanced by continued strong foreign investment in the United States, particularly by Britain. In the series *Mad Men,* which is set in the early 1960s, the New York advertising agency Sterling Cooper is bought out by distinguished British stockholders, which does not fail to cause a culture shock in the small world of Madison Avenue advertising: it is never easy to be owned by foreigners.

The net foreign capital position of the United States turned slightly negative in the 1980s and then increasingly negative in the 1990s and 2000s as a result of accumulating trade deficits. Nevertheless, US investments abroad continued to yield a far better return than the nation paid on its foreign-held debt—such is the privilege due to confidence in the dollar. This made it possible to limit the degradation of the negative US position, which amounted to roughly 10 percent of national income in the 1990s and slightly more than 20 percent in the early 2010s. All in all, the current situation is therefore fairly close to that obtained on the eve of World War I. The domestic capital of the United States is worth about 450 percent of national income. Of this total, assets held by foreign investors (minus foreign assets held by US investors) represent the equivalent of 20 percent of national income. The net national wealth of the United States is therefore about 430 percent of national income. In other words, the United States is more than 95 percent American owned and less than 5 percent foreign owned.

To sum up, the net foreign asset position of the United States has at times been slightly negative, at other times slightly positive, but these positions were always of relatively limited importance compared with the total stock of capital owned by US citizens (always less than 5 percent and generally less than 2 percent).

Canada: Long Owned by the Crown

It is interesting to observe that things took a very different course in Canada, where a very significant share of domestic capital—as much as a quarter in the late nineteenth and early twentieth century—was owned by foreign investors, mainly British, especially in the natural resources sector (copper, zinc, and aluminum mines as well as hydrocarbons). In 1910, Canada's domestic capital was valued at 530 percent of national income. Of this total, assets owned by foreign investors (less foreign assets owned by Canadian investors) represented the equivalent of 120 percent of national income, somewhere between one-fifth and one-quarter of the total. Canada's net national wealth was thus equal to about 410 percent of national income (see Figure 4.9).[11]

---

11. On Figures 3.1–2, 4.1, 4.6, and 4.9, positive positions relative to the rest of the world are unshaded (indicating periods of net positive foreign capital) and negative positions are shaded (periods of net positive foreign debt). The complete

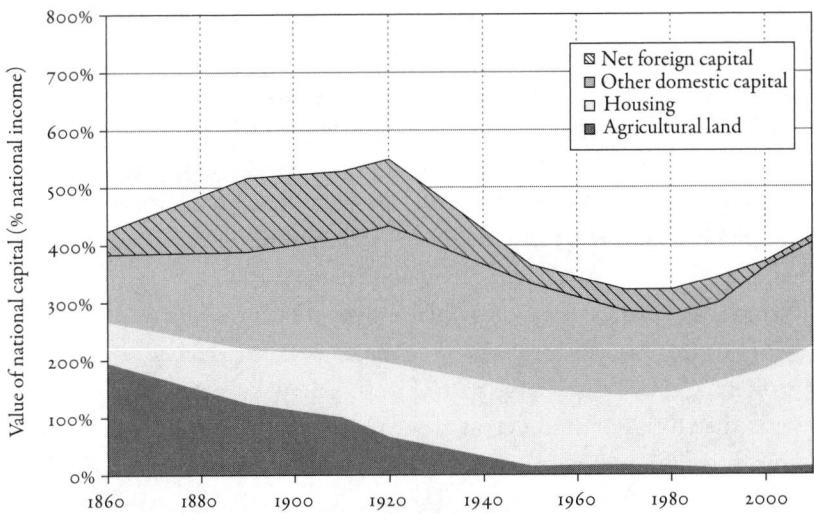

FIGURE 4.9. Capital in Canada, 1860–2010
In Canada, a substantial part of domestic capital has always been held by the rest of the world, so that national capital has always been less than domestic capital.
Sources and series: see piketty.pse.ens.fr/capital21c.

Two world wars changed this situation considerably, as Europeans were forced to sell many foreign assets. This took time, however: from 1950 to 1990, Canada's net foreign debt represented roughly 10 percent of its domestic capital. Public debt rose toward the end of the period before being consolidated after 1990.[12] Today, Canada's situation is fairly close to that of the United States. Its domestic capital is worth roughly 410 percent of its national income. Of this total, assets owned by foreign investors (less foreign assets own by Canadian investors) represent less than 10 percent of national income. Canada is thus more than 98 percent Canadian owned and less than 2 percent foreign owned. (Note, however, that this view of net foreign capital

series used to establish all these figures are available in the online technical appendix.

12. See Supplemental Figures S4.1–2, available online.

masks the magnitude of cross-ownership between countries, about which I will say more in the next chapter.)

This comparison of the United States with Canada is interesting, because it is difficult to find purely economic reasons why these two North American trajectories should differ so profoundly. Clearly, political factors played a central role. Although the United States has always been quite open to foreign investment, it is fairly difficult to imagine that nineteenth-century US citizens would have tolerated a situation in which one-quarter of the country was owned by its former colonizer.[13] This posed less of a problem in Canada, which remained a British colony: the fact that a large part of the country was owned by Britain was therefore not so different from the fact that Londoners owned much of the land and many of the factories in Scotland or Sussex. Similarly, the fact that Canada's net foreign assets remained negative for so long is linked to the absence of any violent political rupture (Canada gradually gained independence from Britain, but its head of state remained the British monarch) and hence to the absence of expropriations of the kind that elsewhere in the world generally accompanied access to independence, especially in regard to natural resources.

New World and Old World: The Importance of Slavery

I cannot conclude this examination of the metamorphoses of capital in Europe and the United States without examining the issue of slavery and the place of slaves in US fortunes.

Thomas Jefferson owned more than just land. He also owned more than six hundred slaves, mostly inherited from his father and father-in-law, and his political attitude toward the slavery question was always extremely ambiguous. His ideal republic of small landowners enjoying equal rights did not include people of color, on whose forced

---

13. On reactions to European investments in the United States during the nineteenth century, see, for example, Mira Wilkins, *The History of Foreign Investment in the United States to 1914* (Cambridge, MA: Harvard University Press, 1989), chap. 16.

labor the economy of his native Virginia largely depended. After becoming president of the United States in 1801 thanks to the votes of the southern states, he nevertheless signed a law ending the import of new slaves to US soil after 1808. This did not prevent a sharp increase in the number of slaves (natural increase was less costly than buying new slaves), which rose from around 400,000 in the 1770s to 1 million in the 1800 census. The number more than quadrupled again between 1800 and the census of 1860, which counted more than 4 million slaves: in other words, the number of slaves had increased tenfold in less than a century. The slave economy was growing rapidly when the Civil War broke out in 1861, leading ultimately to the abolition of slavery in 1865.

In 1800, slaves represented nearly 20 percent of the population of the United States: roughly 1 million slaves out of a total population of 5 million. In the South, where nearly all of the slaves were held,[14] the proportion reached 40 percent: 1 million slaves and 1.5 million whites for a total population of 2.5 million. Not all whites owned slaves, and only a tiny minority owned as many as Jefferson: fortunes based on slavery were among the most concentrated of all.

By 1860, the proportion of slaves in the overall population of the United States had fallen to around 15 percent (about 4 million slaves in a total population of 30 million), owing to rapid population growth in the North and West. In the South, however, the proportion remained at 40 percent: 4 million slaves and 6 million whites for a total population of 10 million.

We can draw on any number of historical sources to learn about the price of slaves in the United States between 1770 and 1865. These include probate records assembled by Alice Hanson Jones, tax and census data used by Raymond Goldsmith, and data on slave market transactions collected primarily by Robert Fogel. By comparing these various sources, which are quite consistent with one another, I compiled the estimates shown in Figures 4.10 and 4.11.

---

14. Only a few tens of thousands of slaves were held in the North. See the online technical appendix.

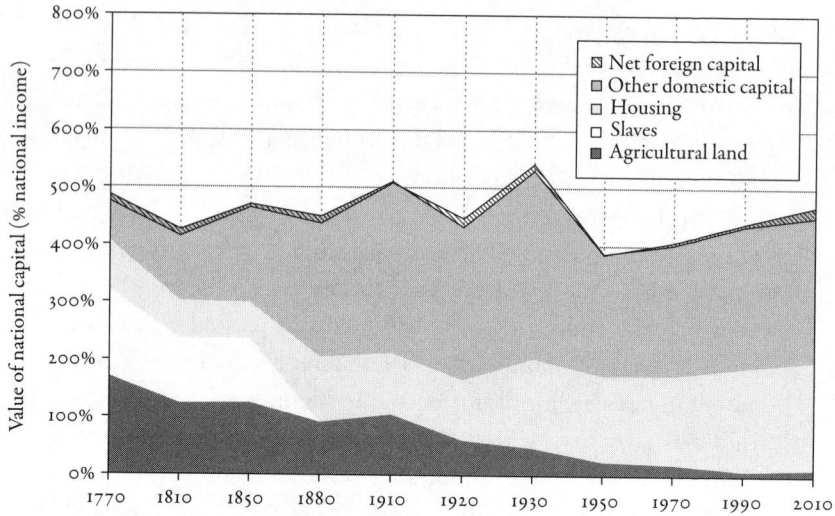

FIGURE 4.10. Capital and slavery in the United States

The market value of slaves was about 1.5 years of US national income around 1770 (as much as land).

Sources and series: see piketty.pse.ens.fr/capital21c.

What one finds is that the total market value of slaves represented nearly a year and a half of US national income in the late eighteenth century and the first half of the nineteenth century, which is roughly equal to the total value of farmland. If we include slaves along with other components of wealth, we find that total American wealth has remained relatively stable from the colonial era to the present, at around four and a half years of national income (see Figure 4.10). To add the value of slaves to capital in this way is obviously a dubious thing to do in more ways than one: it is the mark of a civilization in which some people were treated as chattel rather than as individuals endowed with rights, including in particular the right to own property.[15] But it does allow us to measure the importance of slave capital for slave owners.

15. If each person is treated as an individual subject, then slavery (which can be seen as an extreme form of debt between individuals) does not increase national

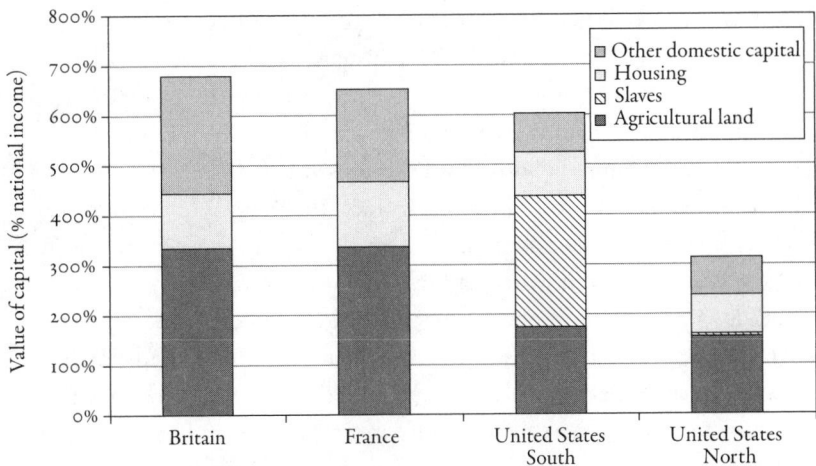

FIGURE 4.11. Capital around 1770–1810: Old and New World

The combined value of agricultural land and slaves in the Southern United States surpassed four years of national income around 1770–1810.

Sources and series: see piketty.pse.ens.fr/capital21c.

This emerges even more clearly when we distinguish southern from northern states and compare the capital structure in the two regions (slaves included) in the period 1770–1810 with the capital structure in Britain and France in the same period (Figure 4.11). In the American South, the total value of slaves ranged between two and a half and three years of national income, so that the combined value of farmland and slaves exceeded four years of national income. All told, southern slave owners in the New World controlled more wealth than the landlords of old Europe. Their farmland was not worth very much, but since they had the bright idea of owning not just the land but also the labor force needed to work that land, their total capital was even greater.

If one adds the market value of slaves to other components of wealth, the value of southern capital exceeds six years of the southern

wealth, like any other private or public debt (debts are liabilities for some individuals and assets for others, hence they cancel out at the global level).

states' income, or nearly as much as the total value of capital in Britain and France. Conversely, in the North, where there were virtually no slaves, total wealth was indeed quite small: barely three years of the northern states' income, half as much as in the South or Europe.

Clearly, the antebellum United States was far from the country without capital discussed earlier. In fact, the New World combined two diametrically opposed realities. In the North we find a relatively egalitarian society in which capital was indeed not worth very much, because land was so abundant that anyone could became a landowner relatively cheaply, and also because recent immigrants had not had time to accumulate much capital. In the South we find a world where inequalities of ownership took the most extreme and violent form possible, since one half of the population owned the other half: here, slave capital largely supplanted and surpassed landed capital.

This complex and contradictory relation to inequality largely persists in the United States to this day: on the one hand this is a country of egalitarian promise, a land of opportunity for millions of immigrants of modest background; on the other it is a land of extremely brutal inequality, especially in relation to race, whose effects are still quite visible. (Southern blacks were deprived of civil rights until the 1960s and subjected to a regime of legal segregation that shared some features in common with the system of apartheid that was maintained in South Africa until the 1980s.) This no doubt accounts for many aspects of the development—or rather nondevelopment—of the US welfare state.

Slave Capital and Human Capital

I have not tried to estimate the value of slave capital in other slave societies. In the British Empire, slavery was abolished in 1833–1838. In the French Empire it was abolished in two stages (first abolished in 1792, restored by Napoleon in 1803, abolished definitively in 1848). In both empires, in the eighteenth and early nineteenth centuries a portion of foreign capital was invested in plantations in the West Indies (think of Sir Thomas in *Mansfield Park*) or in slave estates on islands in the Indian Ocean (the Ile Bourbon and Ile de France, which became Réunion and Mauritius after the French Revolution). Among the assets of these plantations were slaves, whose value I have not attempted to calculate separately. Since total foreign assets did not exceed 10 percent of national income in these two countries at the beginning of the nineteenth century, the share of slaves in total wealth was obviously smaller than in the United States.[16]

Conversely, in societies where slaves represent a large share of the population, their market value can easily reach very high levels, potentially even higher than it did in the United States in 1770–1810 and greater than the value of all other forms of wealth. Take an extreme case in which virtually an entire population is owned by a tiny minority. Assume for the sake of argument that the income from labor (that is, the yield to slave owners on the labor of their slaves) represents 60 percent of national income, the income on capital (meaning the return on land and other capital in the form of rents, profits, etc.) represents 40 percent of national income, and the return on all forms of nonhuman capital is 5 percent a year.

By definition, the value of national capital (excluding slaves) is equal to eight years of national income: this is the first fundamental law of capitalism ($\beta = \alpha / r$), introduced in Chapter 1.

In a slave society, we can apply the same law to slave capital: if slaves yield the equivalent of 60 percent of national income, and the return on all forms of capital is 5 percent a year, then the market value of the

---

16. The number of slaves in French colonies emancipated in 1848 has been estimated at 250,000 (or less than 10 percent of the number of slaves in the United States). As in the United States, however, forms of legal inequality continued well after formal emancipation: in Réunion, for example, after 1848 former slaves could be arrested and imprisoned as indigents unless they could produce a labor contract as a servant or worker on a plantation. Compared with the previous legal regime, under which fugitive slaves were hunted down and returned to their masters if caught, the difference was real, but it represented a shift in policy rather than a complete break with the previous regime.

total stock of slaves is equal to twelve years of national income—or half again more than national nonhuman capital, simply because slaves yield half again as much as nonhuman capital. If we add the value of slaves to the value of capital, we of course obtain twenty years of national income, since the total annual flow of income and output is capitalized at a rate of 5 percent.

In the case of the United States in the period 1770–1810, the value of slave capital was on the order of one and a half years of national income (and not twelve years), in part because the proportion of slaves in the population was 20 percent (and not 100 percent) and in part because the average productivity of slaves was slightly below the average productivity of free labor and the rate of return on slave capital was generally closer to 7 or 8 percent, or even higher, than it was to 5 percent, leading to a lower capitalization. In practice, in the antebellum United States, the market price of a slave was typically on the order of ten to twelve years of an equivalent free worker's wages (and not twenty years, as equal productivity and a return of 5 percent would require). In 1860, the average price of a male slave of prime working age was roughly $2,000, whereas the average wage of a free farm laborer was on the order of $200.[17] Note, however, that the price of a slave varied widely depending on various characteristics and on the owner's evaluation; for example, the wealthy planter Quentin Tarantino portrays in *Django Unchained* is prepared to sell beautiful Broomhilda for only $700 but wants $12,000 for his best fighting slaves.

In any case, it is clear that this type of calculation makes sense only in a slave society, where human capital can be sold on the market, permanently and irrevocably. Some economists, including the authors of a recent series of World Bank reports on "the wealth of nations," choose to calculate the total value of "human capital" by capitalizing the value of the income flow from labor on the basis of a more or less arbitrary annual rate of return (typically 4–5 percent). These reports conclude with amazement that human capital is the leading form of

---

17. See the online technical appendix.

capital in the enchanted world of the twenty-first century. In reality, this conclusion is perfectly obvious and would also have been true in the eighteenth century: whenever more than half of national income goes to labor and one chooses to capitalize the flow of labor income at the same or nearly the same rate as the flow of income to capital, then by definition the value of human capital is greater than the value of all other forms of capital. There is no need for amazement and no need to resort to a hypothetical capitalization to reach this conclusion. (It is enough to compare the flows.)[18] Attributing a monetary value to the stock of human capital makes sense only in societies where it is actually possible to own other individuals fully and entirely—societies that at first sight have definitively ceased to exist.

---

18. For example, if national income consists of 70 percent income from labor and 30 percent income from capital and one capitalizes these incomes at 5 percent, then the total value of the stock of human capital will equal fourteen years of national income, that of the stock of nonhuman capital will equal six years of national income, and the whole will by construction equal twenty years. With a 60–40 percent split of national income, which is closer to what we observe in the eighteenth century (at least in Europe), we obtain twelve years and eight years, respectively, again for a total of twenty years.

{ FIVE }

The Capital / Income Ratio over the Long Run

In the previous chapter I examined the metamorphoses of capital in Europe and North America since the eighteenth century. Over the long run, the nature of wealth was totally transformed: capital in the form of agricultural land was gradually replaced by industrial and financial capital and urban real estate. Yet the most striking fact was surely that in spite of these transformations, the total value of the capital stock, measured in years of national income—the ratio that measures the overall importance of capital in the economy and society—appears not to have changed very much over a very long period of time. In Britain and France, the countries for which we possess the most complete historical data, national capital today represents about five or six years of national income, which is just slightly less than the level of wealth observed in the eighteenth and nineteenth centuries and right up to the eve of World War I (about six or seven years of national income). Given the strong, steady increase of the capital / income ratio since the 1950s, moreover, it is natural to ask whether this increase will continue in the decades to come and whether the capital / income ratio will regain or even surpass past levels before the end of the twenty-first century.

The second salient fact concerns the comparison between Europe and the United States. Unsurprisingly, the shocks of the 1914–1945 period affected Europe much more strongly, so that the capital / income ratio was lower there from the 1920s into the 1980s. If we except this lengthy period of war and its aftermath, however, we find that the capital / income ratio has always tended to be higher in Europe. This was true in the nineteenth and early twentieth centuries (when the capital / income ratio was 6 to 7 in Europe compared with 4 to 5 in the United States) and again in the late twentieth and early twenty-first centuries: private wealth in Europe again surpassed US levels in the early 1990s, and the capital / income ratio there is close to 6 today, compared with slightly more than 4 in the United States (see Figures 5.1 and 5.2).[1]

These facts remain to be explained. Why did the capital / income ratio return to historical highs in Europe, and why should it be structurally higher in Europe than in the United States? What magical forces imply that capital in one society should be worth six or seven years of national income rather than three or four? Is there an equilibrium level for the capital / income ratio, and if so how is it determined, what are the consequences for the rate of return on capital, and what is the relation between it and the capital-labor split of national income? To answer these questions, I will begin by presenting the dynamic law that allows us to relate the capital / income ratio in an economy to its savings and growth rates.

The Second Fundamental Law of Capitalism: $\beta = s/g$

In the long run, the capital / income ratio β is related in a simple and transparent way to the savings rate s and the growth rate g according to the following formula:

$$\beta = s/g$$

---

1. The European capital / income ratio indicated in Figures 5.1 and 5.2 was estimated by calculating the average of the available series for the four largest European economies (Germany, France, Britain, and Italy), weighted by the national income of each country. Together, these four countries represent more than three-quarters of Western European GDP and nearly two-thirds of European GDP. Including other countries (especially Spain) would yield an even steeper rise in the capital / income ratio over the last few decades. See the online technical appendix.

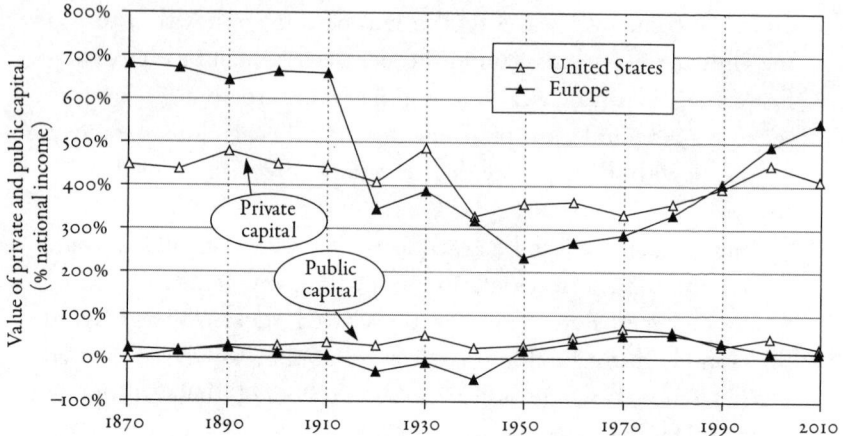

FIGURE 5.1. Private and public capital: Europe and America, 1870–2010

The fluctuations of national capital in the long run correspond mostly to the fluctuations of private capital (both in Europe and in the United States).

Sources and series: see piketty.pse.ens.fr/capital21c.

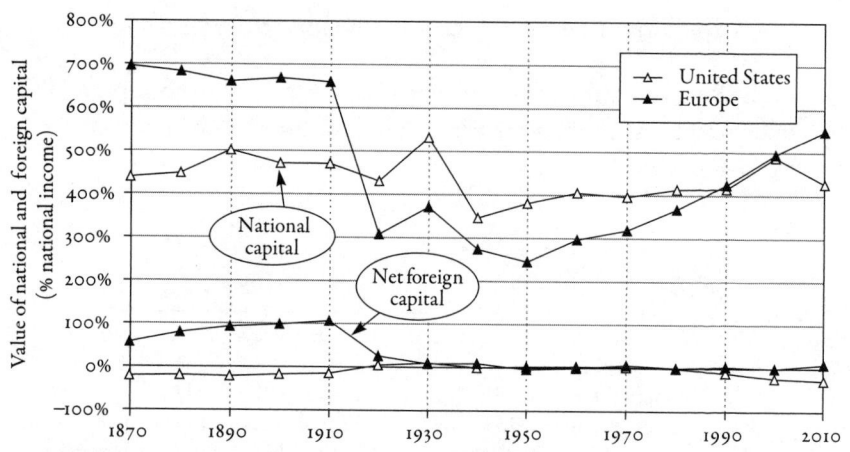

FIGURE 5.2. National capital in Europe and America, 1870–2010

National capital (public and private) is worth 6.5 years of national income in Europe in 1910, versus 4.5 years in America.

Sources and series: see piketty.pse.ens.fr/capital21c.

For example, if $s = 12\%$ and $g = 2\%$, then $\beta = s/g = 600\%$.[2]

In other words, if a country saves 12 percent of its national income every year, and the rate of growth of its national income is 2 percent per year, then in the long run the capital / income ratio will be equal to 600 percent: the country will have accumulated capital worth six years of national income.

This formula, which can be regarded as the second fundamental law of capitalism, reflects an obvious but important point: a country that saves a lot and grows slowly will over the long run accumulate an enormous stock of capital (relative to its income), which can in turn have a significant effect on the social structure and distribution of wealth.

Let me put it another way: in a quasi-stagnant society, wealth accumulated in the past will inevitably acquire disproportionate importance.

The return to a structurally high capital / income ratio in the twenty-first century, close to the levels observed in the eighteenth and nineteenth centuries, can therefore be explained by the return to a slow-growth regime. Decreased growth—especially demographic growth—is thus responsible for capital's comeback.

The basic point is that small variations in the rate of growth can have very large effects on the capital / income ratio over the long run.

For example, given a savings rate of 12 percent, if the rate of growth falls to 1.5 percent a year (instead of 2 percent), then the long-term capital / income ratio $\beta = s/g$ will rise to eight years of national income (instead of six). If the growth rate falls to 1 percent, then $\beta = s/g$ will rise to twelve years, indicative of a society twice as capital intensive as when the growth rate was 2 percent. In one respect, this is good news: capital is potentially useful to everyone, and provided that things are properly organized, everyone can benefit from it. In another respect, however, what this means is that the owners of capital—for a

---

2. The formula $\beta = s/g$ is read as "β equals s divided by g." Recall, too, that "$\beta = 600\%$" is equivalent to "$\beta = 6$," just as "$s = 12\%$" is equivalent to "$s = 0.12$" and "$g = 2\%$" is equivalent to "$g = 0.02$." The savings rate represents truly new savings—hence net of depreciation of capital—divided by national income. I will come back to this point.

given distribution of wealth—potentially control a larger share of total economic resources. In any event, the economic, social, and political repercussions of such a change are considerable.

On the other hand if the growth rate increases to 3 percent, then $\beta = s/g$ will fall to just four years of national income. If the savings rate simultaneously decreases slightly to $s = 9$ percent, then the long-run capital / income ratio will decline to 3.

These effects are all the more significant because the growth rate that figures in the law $\beta = s/g$ is the overall rate of growth of national income, that is, the sum of the per capita growth rate and the population growth rate.[3] In other words, for a savings rate on the order of 10–12 percent and a growth rate of national income per capita on the order of 1.5–2 percent a year, it follows immediately that a country that has near-zero demographic growth and therefore a total growth rate close to 1.5–2 percent, as in Europe, can expect to accumulate a capital stock worth six to eight years of national income, whereas a country with demographic growth on the order of 1 percent a year and therefore a total growth rate of 2.5–3 percent, as in the United States, will accumulate a capital stock worth only three to four years of national income. And if the latter country tends to save a little less than the former, perhaps because its population is not aging as rapidly, this mechanism will be further reinforced as a result. In other words, countries with similar growth rates of income per capita can end up with very different capital / income ratios simply because their demographic growth rates are not the same.

This law allows us to give a good account of the historical evolution of the capital / income ratio. In particular, it enables us to explain why the capital / income ratio seems now—after the shocks of 1914–1945 and the exceptionally rapid growth phase of the second half of the twentieth century—to be returning to very high levels. It also enables

---

3. Sometimes g is used to denote the growth rate of national income per capita and n the population growth rate, in which case the formula would be written $\beta = s / (g+n)$. To keep the notation simple, I have chosen to use g for the overall growth rate of the economy, so that my formula is $\beta = s/g$.

us to understand why Europe tends for structural reasons to accumulate more capital than the United States (or at any rate will tend to do so as long as the US demographic growth rate remains higher than the European, which probably will not be forever). But before I can explain this phenomenon, I must make several conceptual and theoretical points more precise.

A Long-Term Law

First, it is important to be clear that the second fundamental law of capitalism, $\beta = s/g$, is applicable only if certain crucial assumptions are satisfied. First, this is an asymptotic law, meaning that it is valid only in the long run: if a country saves a proportion s of its income indefinitely, and if the rate of growth of its national income is g permanently, then its capital / income ratio will tend closer and closer to $\beta = s/g$ and stabilize at that level. This won't happen in a day, however: if a country saves a proportion s of its income for only a few years, it will not be enough to achieve a capital / income ratio of $\beta = s/g$.

For example, if a country starts with zero capital and saves 12 percent of its national income for a year, it obviously will not accumulate a capital stock worth six years of its income. With a savings rate of 12 percent a year, starting from zero capital, it will take fifty years to save the equivalent of six years of income, and even then the capital / income ratio will not be equal to 6, because national income will itself have increased considerably after half a century (unless we assume that the growth rate is actually zero).

The first principle to bear in mind is, therefore, that the accumulation of wealth takes time: it will take several decades for the law $\beta = s/g$ to become true. Now we can understand why it took so much time for the shocks of 1914–1945 to fade away, and why it is so important to take a very long historical view when studying these questions. At the individual level, fortunes are sometimes amassed very quickly, but at the country level, the movement of the capital / income ratio described by the law $\beta = s/g$ is a long-run phenomenon.

Hence there is a crucial difference between this law and the law $\alpha = r \times \beta$, which I called the first fundamental law of capitalism in Chapter 1. According to that law, the share of capital income in national income, α, is equal to the average rate of return on capital, r, times the capital / income ratio, β. It is important to realize that the law $\alpha = r \times \beta$ is actually a pure accounting identity, valid at all times in all places, by construction. Indeed, one can view it as a definition of the share of capital in national income (or of the rate of return on capital, depending on which parameter is easiest to measure) rather than as a law. By contrast, the law $\beta = s/g$ is the result of a dynamic process: it represents a state of equilibrium toward which an economy will tend if the savings rate is s and the growth rate g, but that equilibrium state is never perfectly realized in practice.

Second, the law $\beta = s/g$ is valid only if one focuses on those forms of capital that human beings can accumulate. If a significant fraction of national capital consists of pure natural resources (i.e., natural resources whose value is independent of any human improvement and any past investment), then β can be quite high without any contribution from savings. I will say more later about the practical importance of nonaccumulable capital.

Finally, the law $\beta = s/g$ is valid only if asset prices evolve on average in the same way as consumer prices. If the price of real estate or stocks rises faster than other prices, then the ratio β between the market value of national capital and the annual flow of national income can again be quite high without the addition of any new savings. In the short run, variations (capital gains or losses) of relative asset prices (i.e., of asset prices relative to consumer prices) are often quite a bit larger than volume effects (i.e., effects linked to new savings). If we assume, however, that price variations balance out over the long run, then the law $\beta = s/g$ is necessarily valid, regardless of the reasons why the country in question chooses to save a proportion s of its national income.

This point bears emphasizing: the law $\beta = s/g$ is totally independent of the reasons why the residents of a particular country—or their government—accumulate wealth. In practice, people accumulate capital for all sorts of reasons: for instance, to increase future consumption (or to avoid a decrease in consumption after retirement), or to amass or preserve wealth for the next generation, or again to acquire the power, security, or prestige that often come with wealth. In general, all these motivations are present at once in proportions that vary with the individual, the country, and the age. Quite often, all these motivations are combined in single individuals, and individuals themselves may not always be able to articulate them clearly. In Part Three I discuss in depth the significant implications of these various motivations and mechanisms of accumulation for inequality and the distribution of wealth, the role of inheritance in the structure of inequality, and, more generally, the social, moral, and political justification of disparities in wealth. At this stage I am simply explaining the dynamics of the capital / income ratio (a question that can be studied, at least initially, independently of the question of how wealth is distributed). The point I want to stress is that the law $\beta = s/g$ applies in all cases, regardless of the exact reasons for a country's savings rate.

This is due to the simple fact that $\beta = s/g$ is the only stable capital / income ratio in a country that saves a fraction s of its income, which grows at a rate g.

The argument is elementary. Let me illustrate it with an example. In concrete terms: if a country is saving 12 percent of its income every year, and if its initial capital stock is equal to six years of income, then the capital stock will grow at 2 percent a year,[4] thus at exactly the same rate as national income, so that the capital / income ratio will remain stable.

By contrast, if the capital stock is less than six years of income, then a savings rate of 12 percent will cause the capital stock to grow at a rate greater than 2 percent a year and therefore faster than income, so that the capital / income ratio will increase until it attains its equilibrium level.

---

4. Twelve percent of income gives 12 divided by 6 or 2 percent of capital. More generally, if the savings rate is s and the capital / income ratio is β, then the capital stock grows at a rate equal to s / β.

Conversely, if the capital stock is greater than six years of annual income, then a savings rate of 12 percent implies that capital is growing at less than 2 percent a year, so that the capital / income ratio cannot be maintained at that level and will therefore decrease until it reaches equilibrium.

In each case, the capital / income ratio tends over the long run toward its equilibrium level $\beta = s/g$ (possibly augmented by pure natural resources), provided that the average price of assets evolves at the same rate as consumption prices over the long run.[5]

To sum up: the law $\beta = s/g$ does not explain the short-term shocks to which the capital / income ratio is subject, any more than it explains the existence of world wars or the crisis of 1929—events that can be taken as examples of extreme shocks—but it does allow us to understand the potential equilibrium level toward which the capital / income ratio tends in the long run, when the effects of shocks and crises have dissipated.

Capital's Comeback in Rich Countries since the 1970s

In order to illustrate the difference between short-term and long-term movements of the capital / income ratio, it is useful to examine the annual changes observed in the wealthiest countries between 1970 and 2010, a period for which we have reliable and homogeneous data for a large number of countries. To begin, here is a look at the ratio of private capital to national income, whose evolution is shown in Figure 5.3 for the eight richest countries in the world, in order of decreasing GDP: the United States, Japan, Germany, France, Britain, Italy, Canada, and Australia.

Compared with Figures 5.1 and 5.2, as well as with the figures that accompanied previous chapters, which presented decennial averages

---

5. The simple mathematical equation describing the dynamics of the capital / income ratio β and its convergence toward $\beta = s/g$ is given in the online technical appendix.

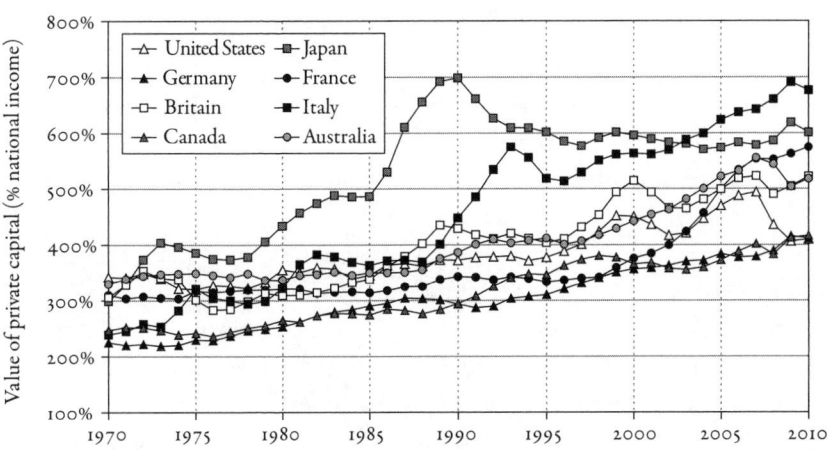

FIGURE 5.3. Private capital in rich countries, 1970–2010

Private capital is worth between two and 3.5 years of national income in rich countries in 1970, and between four and seven years of national income in 2010.

Sources and series: see piketty.pse.ens.fr/capital21c.

in order to focus attention on long-term trends, Figure 5.3 displays annual series and shows that the capital / income ratio in all countries varied constantly in the very short run. These erratic changes are due to the fact that the prices of real estate (including housing and business real estate) and financial assets (especially shares of stock) are notoriously volatile. It is always very difficult to set a price on capital, in part because it is objectively complex to foresee the future demand for the goods and services generated by a firm or by real estate and therefore to predict the future flows of profit, dividends, royalties, rents, and so on that the assets in question will yield, and in part because the present value of a building or corporation depends not only on these fundamental factors but also on the price at which one can hope to sell these assets if the need arises (that is, on the anticipated capital gain or loss).

Indeed, these anticipated future prices themselves depend on the general enthusiasm for a given type of asset, which can give rise to so-called self-fulfilling beliefs: as long as one can hope to sell an asset for more than one paid for it, it may be individually rational to pay a good deal more than the fundamental value of that asset (especially since the fundamental value is itself uncertain), thus giving in to the general enthusiasm for that type of asset, even though it may be excessive. That is why speculative bubbles in real estate and stocks have existed as long as capital itself; they are consubstantial with its history.

As it happens, the most spectacular bubble in the period 1970–2010 was surely the Japanese bubble of 1990 (see Figure 5.3). During the 1980s, the value of private wealth shot up in Japan from slightly more than four years of national income at the beginning of the decade to nearly seven at the end. Clearly, this enormous and extremely rapid increase was partly artificial: the value of private capital fell sharply in the early 1990s before stabilizing at around six years of national income from the mid-1990s on.

I will not rehearse the history of the numerous real estate and stock market bubbles that inflated and burst in the rich countries after 1970, nor will I attempt to predict future bubbles, which I am quite incapable of doing in any case. Note, however, the sharp correction in the Italian real estate market in 1994–1995 and the bursting of the Internet bubble in 2000–2001, which caused a particularly sharp drop in the capital / income ratio in the United States and Britain (though not as sharp as the drop in Japan ten years earlier). Note, too, that the subsequent US real estate and stock market boom continued until 2007, followed by a deep drop in the recession of 2008–2009. In two years, US private fortunes shrank from five to four years of national income, a drop of roughly the same size as the Japanese correction of 1991–1992. In other countries, and particularly in Europe, the correction was less severe or even nonexistent: in Britain, France, and Italy, the price of assets, especially in real estate, briefly stabilized in 2008 before starting upward again in 2009–2010, so that by the early 2010s private wealth had returned to the level attained in 2007, if not slightly higher.

The important point I want to emphasize is that beyond these erratic and unpredictable variations in short-term asset prices, variations whose amplitude seems to have increased in recent decades (and we will see later that this can be related to the increase in the potential capital / income ratio), there is indeed a long-term trend at work in all of the rich countries in the period 1970–2010 (see Figure 5.3). At the beginning of the 1970s, the total value of private wealth (net of debt) stood between two and three and a half years of national income in all the rich countries, on all continents.[6] Forty years later, in 2010, private wealth represented between four and seven years of national income in all the countries under study.[7] The general evolution is clear: bubbles aside, what we are witnessing is a strong comeback of private capital in the rich countries since 1970, or, to put it another way, the emergence of a new patrimonial capitalism.

This structural evolution is explained by three sets of factors, which complement and reinforce one another to give the phenomenon a very significant amplitude. The most important factor in the long run is slower growth, especially demographic growth, which, together with a high rate of saving, automatically gives rise to a structural increase in the long-run capital / income ratio, owing to the law $\beta = s/g$. This mechanism is the dominant force in the very long run but should not be allowed to obscure the two other factors that have substantially reinforced its effects over the last few decades: first, the gradual privatization and transfer of public wealth into private hands in the 1970s and 1980s, and second, a long-term catch-up phenomenon affecting real estate and stock market prices, which also accelerated in the 1980s and 1990s in a political context that was on the whole more favorable to private wealth than that of the immediate postwar decades.

---

6. From 2.2 years in Germany to 3.4 years in the United States in 1970. See Supplemental Table S5.1, available online, for the complete series.

7. From 4.1 years in Germany and the United States to 6.1 years in Japan and 6.8 years in Italy in 2010. The values indicated for each year are annual averages. (For example, the value indicated for 2010 is the average of the wealth estimates on January 1, 2010, and January 1, 2011.) The first available estimates for 2012–2013 are not very different. See the online technical appendix.

Beyond Bubbles: Low Growth, High Saving

I begin with the first mechanism, based on slower growth coupled with continued high saving and the dynamic law $\beta = s/g$. In Table 5.1 I have indicated the average values of the growth rates and private savings rates in the eight richest countries during the period 1970–2010. As noted in Chapter 2, the rate of growth of per capita national income (or the virtually identical growth rate of per capita domestic product) has been quite similar in all the developed countries over the last few decades. If comparisons are made over periods of a few years, the differences can be significant, and these often spur national pride or jealousy. But if one takes averages over longer periods, the fact is that all the rich countries are growing at approximately the same rate. Between 1970 and 2010, the average annual rate of growth of per capita national income ranged from 1.6 to 2.0 percent in the eight most developed countries and more often than not remained between 1.7 and 1.9 percent. Given the imperfections of the available statistical measures (especially price indices), it is by no means certain that such small differences are statistically significant.[8]

In any case, these differences are very small compared with differences in the demographic growth rate. In the period 1970–2010, population grew at less than 0.5 percent per year in Europe and Japan (and closer to 0 percent in the period 1990–2010, or in Japan even at a negative rate), compared with 1.0–1.5 percent in the United States, Canada, and Australia (see Table 5.1). Hence the overall growth rate for the period 1970–2010 was significantly higher in the United States and the other new countries than in Europe or Japan: around 3 percent a year in the former (or perhaps even a bit more), compared with barely 2 percent in the latter (or even just barely 1.5 percent in the most recent subperiod). Such differences may seem small, but over

---

8. In particular, it would suffice to change from one price index to another (there are several of them, and none is perfect) to alter the relative rank of these various countries. See the online technical appendix.

TABLE 5.1.

Growth rates and saving rates in rich countries, 1970–2010

Country	Growth rate of national income (%)	Growth rate of population (%)	Growth rate of per capita national income (%)	Private saving (net of depreciation) (% national income)
United States	2.8	1.0	1.8	7.7
Japan	2.5	0.5	2.0	14.6
Germany	2.0	0.2	1.8	12.2
France	2.2	0.5	1.7	11.1
Britain	2.2	0.3	1.9	7.3
Italy	1.9	0.3	1.6	15.0
Canada	2.8	1.1	1.7	12.1
Australia	3.2	1.4	1.7	9.9

Note: Saving rates and demographic growth vary a lot within rich countries; growth rates of per capita national income vary much less.

Sources: See piketty.pse.ens.fr/capital21c.

the long run they mount up, so that in fact they are quite significant. The new point I want to stress here is that such differences in growth rates have enormous effects on the long-run accumulation of capital and largely explain why the capital / income ratio is structurally higher in Europe and Japan than in the United States.

Turning now to average savings rates in the period 1970–2010, again one finds large variations between countries: the private savings rate generally ranges between 10 and 12 percent of national income, but it is as low as 7 to 8 percent in the United States and Britain and as high as 14–15 percent in Japan and Italy (see Table 5.1). Over forty years, these differences mount up to create significant variation. Note, too, that the countries that save the most are often those whose population is stagnant and aging (which may justify saving for the purpose of retirement and bequest), but the relation is far from systematic. As noted, there are many reasons why one might choose to save more or less, and it comes as no surprise that many factors (linked to, among other things, culture, perceptions of the future, and distinctive national histories) come into play, just as they do in regard to decisions concerning childbearing and immigration, which ultimately help to determine the demographic growth rate.

If one now combines variations in growth rates with variations in savings rate, it is easy to explain why different countries accumulate very different quantities of capital, and why the capital / income ratio has risen sharply since 1970. One particularly clear case is that of Japan: with a savings rate close to 15 percent a year and a growth rate barely above 2 percent, it is hardly surprising that Japan has over the long run accumulated a capital stock worth six to seven years of national income. This is an automatic consequence of the dynamic law of accumulation, $\beta = s/g$. Similarly, it is not surprising that the United States, which saves much less than Japan and is growing faster, has a significantly lower capital / income ratio.

More generally, if one compares the level of private wealth in 2010 predicted by the savings flows observed between 1970 and 2010 (together with the initial wealth observed in 1970) with the actual observed levels of wealth in 2010, one finds that the two numbers are quite similar for most countries.[9] The correspondence is not perfect, which shows that other factors also play a significant role. For instance, in the British case, the flow of savings seems quite inadequate to explain the very steep rise in private wealth in this period.

Looking beyond the particular circumstances of this or that country, however, the results are overall quite consistent: it is possible to explain the main features of private capital accumulation in the rich countries between 1970 and 2010 in terms of the quantity of savings between those two dates (along with the initial capital endowment) without assuming a significant structural increase in the relative price of assets. In other words, movements in real estate and stock market prices always domi-

9. See Supplemental Figure S5.1, available online.

nate in the short and even medium run but tend to balance out over the long run, where volume effects appear generally to be decisive.

Once again, the Japanese case is emblematic. If one tries to understand the enormous increase in the capital / income ratio in the 1980s and the sharp drop in the early 1990s, it is clear that the dominant phenomenon was the formation of a bubble in real estate and stocks, which then collapsed. But if one seeks to understand the evolution observed over the entire period 1970–2010, it is clear that volume effects outweighed price effects: the fact that private wealth in Japan rose from three years of national income in 1970 to six in 2010 is predicted almost perfectly by the flow of savings.[10]

The Two Components of Private Saving

For the sake of completeness, I should make clear that private saving consists of two components: savings made directly by private individuals (this is the part of disposable household income that is not consumed immediately) and savings by firms on behalf of the private individuals who own them, directly in the case of individual firms or indirectly via their financial investments. This second component consists of profits reinvested by firms (also referred to as "retained earnings") and in some countries accounts for as much as half the total amount of private savings (see Table 5.2).

If one were to ignore this second component of savings and consider only household savings strictly defined, one would conclude that savings flows in all countries are clearly insufficient to account

---

10. More precisely: the series show that the private capital / national income ratio rose from 299 percent in 1970 to 601 percent in 2010, whereas the accumulated flows of savings would have predicted an increase from 299 to 616 percent. The error is therefore 15 percent of national income out of an increase on the order of 300 percent, or barely 5 percent: the flow of savings explains 95 percent of the increase in the private capital / national income ratio in Japan between 1970 and 2010. Detailed calculations for all countries are available in the online technical appendix.

TABLE 5.2.

Private saving in rich countries, 1970–2010

Country	Private saving (net of depreciation) (% national income)	Incl. household net saving (%)	Incl. corporate net saving (net retained earnings) (%)
United States	7.7	4.6	3.1
Japan	14.6	6.8	7.8
Germany	12.2	9.4	2.8
France	11.1	9.0	2.1
Britain	7.4	2.8	4.6
Italy	15.0	14.6	0.4
Canada	12.1	7.2	4.9
Australia	9.9	5.9	3.9

Note: A large part (variable across countries) of private saving comes from corporate retained earnings (undistributed profits).

Sources: See piketty.pse.ens.fr/capital21c.

for the growth of private wealth, which one would then explain largely in terms of a structural increase in the relative price of assets, especially shares of stock. Such a conclusion would be correct in accounting terms but artificial in economic terms: it is true that stock prices tend to rise more quickly than consumption prices over the long run, but the reason for this is essentially that retained earnings allow firms to increase their size and capital (so that we are looking at a volume effect rather than a price effect). If retained earnings are included in private savings, however, the price effect largely disappears.

In practice, from the standpoint of shareholders, profits paid out directly as dividends are often more heavily taxed than retained earnings: hence it may be advantageous for the owners of capital to pay only a limited share of profits as dividends (to meet their immediate consumption needs) and leave the rest to accumulate and be reinvested in the firm and its subsidiaries. Later, some shares can be sold in order to realize the capital gains (which are generally taxed less heavily than dividends).[11] The variation between countries with respect to the proportion of retained earnings in total private savings can be explained, moreover, largely by differences in legal and tax systems; these are accounting differences rather than actual economic differences. Under these conditions, it is better to treat retained earnings as savings realized on behalf of the firm's owners and therefore as a component of private saving.

I should also be clear that the notion of savings relevant to the dynamic law $\beta = s/g$ is savings net of capital depreciation, that is, truly new savings, or the part of total savings left over after we deduct the amount needed to compensate for wear and tear on buildings and equipment (to repair a hole in the roof or a pipe or to replace a worn-out automobile, computer, machine, or what have you). The difference is important, because annual capital depreciation in the developed economies is on the order of 10–15 percent of national income and absorbs nearly half of total savings, which generally run around 25–30 percent of national income, leaving net savings of 10–15 percent of national income (see Table 5.3). In particular, the bulk of retained earnings often goes to maintaining buildings and equipment, and frequently the amount left over to finance net investment is quite small—at most a few percent of national income—or even negative, if retained earnings are insufficient to cover the depreciation of capital. By definition, only net savings can increase the capital stock: savings used to cover depreciation simply ensure that the existing capital stock will not decrease.[12]

---

11. When a firm buys its own shares, it enables its shareholders to realize capital gains, which will generally be taxed less heavily than if the firm had used the same sum of money to distribute dividends. It is important to realize that the same is true when a firm buys the stock of other firms, so that overall the business sector allows the individual sector to realize capital gains by purchasing financial instruments.

12. One can also write the law $\beta = s/g$ with s standing for the total rather than the net rate of saving. In that case the law becomes $\beta = s / (g + \delta)$ (where δ now stands for

TABLE 5.3.

Gross and net saving in rich countries, 1970–2010

Country	Gross private savings (% national income)	Minus: Capital depreciation (%)	Equals: Net private saving (%)
United States	18.8	11.1	7.7
Japan	33.4	18.9	14.6
Germany	28.5	16.2	12.2
France	22.0	10.9	11.1
Britain	19.7	12.3	7.3
Italy	30.1	15.1	15.0
Canada	24.5	12.4	12.1
Australia	25.1	15.2	9.9

Note: A large part of gross saving (generally about half) corresponds to capital depreciation; i.e., it is used solely to repair or replace used capital.

Sources: See piketty.pse.ens.fr/capital21c.

Durable Goods and Valuables

Finally, I want to make it clear that private saving as defined here, and therefore private wealth, does not include household purchases of durable goods: furniture, appliances, automobiles, and so on. In this respect I am following international standards for national accounting, under which durable household goods are treated as items of immediate consumption (although the same goods, when purchased by firms, are counted as investments with a high rate of annual depreciation). This is of limited importance for my purposes, however, because durable goods have always represented a relatively small proportion of total wealth, which has not varied much over time: in all rich countries, available estimates indicate that the total value of durable

---

the rate of depreciation of capital expressed as a percentage of the capital stock). For example, if the raw savings rate is $s = 24\%$, and if the depreciation rate of the capital stock is $\delta = 2\%$, for a growth rate of $g = 2\%$, then we obtain a capital/income ratio $\beta = s / (g + \delta) = 600\%$. See the online technical appendix.

household goods is generally between 30 and 50 percent of national income throughout the period 1970–2010, with no apparent trend.

In other words, everyone owns on average between a third and half a year's income worth of furniture, refrigerators, cars, and so on, or 10,000–15,000 euros per capita for a national income on the order of 30,000 euros per capita in the early 2010s. This is not a negligible amount and accounts for most of the wealth owned by a large segment of the population. Compared, however, with overall private wealth of five to six years of national income, or 150,000–200,000 euros per person (excluding durable goods), about half of which is in the form of real estate and half in net financial assets (bank deposits, stocks, bonds, and other investments, net of debt) and business capital, this is only a small supplementary amount. Concretely, if we were to include durable goods in private wealth, the only effect would be to add 30–50 percent of national income to the curves shown in Figure 5.3 without significantly modifying the overall evolution.[13]

Note in passing that apart from real estate and business capital, the only nonfinancial assets included in national accounts under international standards (which I have followed scrupulously in order to ensure consistency in my comparisons of private and national wealth between countries) are "valuables," including items such as works of art, jewelry, and precious metals such as gold and silver, which households acquire as a pure reservoir of value (or for their aesthetic value) and which in principle do not deteriorate (or deteriorate very little) over time. These valuables are worth much less than du-

---

13. With a growth of $g = 2\%$, it would take a net expenditure on durable goods equal to $s = 1\%$ of national income per year to accumulate a stock of durable goods equal to $\beta = s/g = 50\%$ of national income. Durable goods need to be replaced frequently, however, so the gross expenditure would be considerably higher. For example, if average replacement time is five years, one would need a gross expenditure on durable goods of 10 percent of national income per year simply to replace used goods, and 11 percent a year to generate a net expenditure of 1% and an equilibrium stock of 50% of national income (still assuming growth $g = 2\%$). See the online technical appendix.

rable goods by most estimates, however (between 5 and 10 percent of national income, depending on the country, or between 1,500 and 3,000 per person for a per capita national income of 30,000 euros), hence their share of total private wealth is relatively small, even after the recent rise in the price of gold.[14]

It is interesting to note that according to available historical estimates, these orders of magnitude do not seem to have changed much over the long run. Estimates of the value of durable goods are generally around 30–50 percent of national income for both the nineteenth and twentieth centuries. Gregory King's estimates of British national wealth around 1700 show the same thing: the total value of furniture, china, and so on was about 30 percent of national income. The amount of wealth represented by valuables and precious objects seems to have decreased over the long run, however, from 10–15 percent of national income in the late nineteenth and early twentieth century to 5–10 percent today. According to King, the total value of such goods (including metal coin) was as high as 25–30 percent of national income around 1700. In all cases, these are relatively limited amounts compared to total accumulated wealth in Britain of around seven years of national income, primarily in the form of farmland, dwellings, and other capital goods (shops, factories, warehouses, livestock, ships, etc.), at which King does not fail to rejoice and marvel.[15]

---

14. The total value of the world's gold stock has decreased over the long run (it was 2 to 3 percent of total private wealth in the nineteenth century but less than 0.5 percent at the end of the twentieth century). It tends to rise during periods of crisis, however, because gold serves as a refuge, so that it currently accounts for 1.5 percent of total private wealth, of which roughly one-fifth is held by central banks. These are impressive variations, yet they are minor compared with the overall value of the capital stock. See the online technical appendix.

15. Even though it does not make much difference, for the sake of consistency I have used the same conventions for the historical series discussed in Chapters 3 and 4 and for the series discussed here for the period 1970–2010: durable goods have been excluded from wealth, and valuables have been included in the category labeled "other domestic capital."

Private Capital Expressed in Years of Disposable Income

Note, moreover, that the capital / income ratio would have attained even higher levels—no doubt the highest ever recorded—in the rich countries in the 2000s and 2010s if I had expressed total private wealth in terms of years of disposable income rather than national income, as I have done thus far. This seemingly technical issue warrants further discussion.

As the name implies, disposable household income (or simply "disposable income") measures the monetary income that households in a given country dispose of directly. To go from national income to disposable income, one must deduct all taxes, fees, and other obligatory payments and add all monetary transfers (pensions, unemployment insurance, aid to families, welfare payments, etc.). Until the turn of the twentieth century, governments played a limited role in social and economic life (total tax payments were on the order of 10 percent of national income, which went essentially to pay for traditional state functions such as police, army, courts, highways, and so on, so that disposable income was generally around 90 percent of national income). The state's role increased considerably over the course of the twentieth century, so that disposable income today amounts to around 70–80 percent of national income in the rich countries. As a result, total private wealth expressed in years of disposable income (rather than national income) is significantly higher. For example, private capital in the 2000s represented four to seven years of national income in the rich countries, which would correspond to five to nine years of disposable income (see Figure 5.4).

Both ways of measuring the capital / income ratio can be justified, depending on how one wants to approach the question. When expressed in terms of disposable income, the ratio emphasizes strictly monetary realities and shows us the magnitude of wealth in relation to the income actually available to households (to save, for instance). In a way, this reflects the concrete reality of the family bank account, and it is important to keep these orders of magnitude in mind. It is also important to note, however, that the gap between disposable

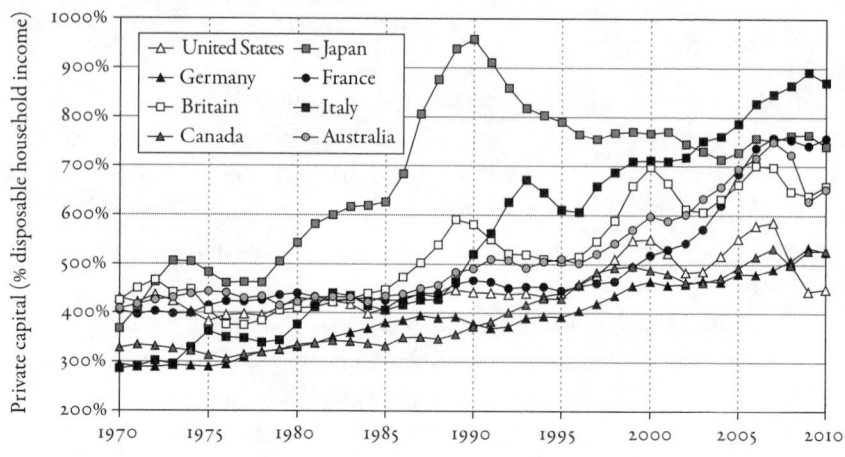

FIGURE 5.4. Private capital measured in years of disposable income

Expressed in years of household disposable income (about 70–80 percent of national income), the capital / income ratio appears to be larger than when it is expressed in years of national income.

Sources and series: see piketty.pse.ens.fr/capital21c.

income and national income measures by definition the value of public services from which households benefit, especially health and education services financed directly by the public treasury. Such "transfers in kind" are just as valuable as the monetary transfers included in disposable income: they allow the individuals concerned to avoid spending comparable (or even greater) sums on private producers of health and education services. Ignoring such transfers in kind might well distort certain evolutions or international comparisons. That is why it seemed to me preferable to express wealth in years of national income: to do so is to adopt an economic (rather than strictly monetary) view of income. In this book, whenever I refer to the capital / income ratio without further qualification, I am always referring to the ratio of the capital stock to the flow of national income.[16]

---

16. In Part Four I return to the question of taxes, transfers, and redistributions effected by the government, and in particular to the question of their impact on inequality and on the accumulation and distribution of capital.

The Question of Foundations and Other Holders of Capital

Note also that for the sake of completeness I have included in private wealth not only the assets and liabilities of private individuals ("households" in national accounting terminology) but also assets and liabilities held by foundations and other nonprofit organizations. To be clear, this category includes only foundations and other organizations financed primarily by gifts from private individuals or income from their properties. Organizations that depend primarily on public subsidies are classified as governmental organizations, and those that depend primarily on the sale of goods are classified as corporations.

In practice, all of these distinctions are malleable and porous. It is rather arbitrary to count the wealth of foundations as part of private wealth rather than public wealth or to place it in a category of its own, since it is in fact a novel form of ownership, intermediate between purely private and strictly public ownership. In practice, when we think of the property owned by churches over the centuries, or the property owned today by organizations such as Doctors without Borders or the Bill and Melinda Gates Foundation, it is clear that we are dealing with a wide variety of moral persons pursuing a range of specific objectives.

Note, however, that the stakes are relatively limited, since the amount of wealth owned by moral persons is generally rather small compared with what physical persons retain for themselves. Available estimates for the various rich countries in the period 1970–2010 show that foundations and other nonprofit organizations always own less than 10 percent and generally less than 5 percent of total private wealth, though with interesting variations between countries: barely 1 percent in France, around 3–4 percent in Japan, and as much as 6–7 percent in the United States (with no apparent trend). Available historical sources indicate that the total value of church-owned property in eighteenth-century France amounted to about 7–8 percent of total private wealth, or approximately 50–60 percent of national income (some of this property was confiscated and sold during the French

Revolution to pay off debts incurred by the government of the Ancien Régime).[17] In other words, the Catholic Church owned more property in Ancien Régime France (relative to the total private wealth of the era) than prosperous US foundations own today. It is interesting to observe that the two levels are nevertheless fairly close.

These are quite substantial holdings of wealth, especially if we compare them with the meager (and sometimes negative) net wealth owned by the government at various points in time. Compared with total private wealth, however, the wealth of foundations remains fairly modest. In particular, it matters little whether or not we include foundations when considering the general evolution of the ratio of private capital to national income over the long run. Inclusion is justified, moreover, by the fact that it is never easy to define the boundary line between on the one hand various legal structures such as foundations, trust funds, and the like used by wealthy individuals to manage their assets and further their private interests (which are in principle counted in national accounts as individual holdings, assuming they are identified as such) and on the other hand foundations and nonprofits said to be in the public interest. I will come back to this delicate issue in Part Three, where I will discuss the dynamics of global inequality of wealth, and especially great wealth, in the twenty-first century.

The Privatization of Wealth in the Rich Countries

The very sharp increase in private wealth observed in the rich countries, and especially in Europe and Japan, between 1970 and 2010 thus can be explained largely by slower growth coupled with continued high savings, using the law $\beta = s/g$. I will now return to the two other complementary phenomena that amplified this mechanism, which I mentioned earlier: the privatization or gradual transfer of public wealth into private hands and the "catch-up" of asset prices over the long run.

---

17. See the online technical appendix.

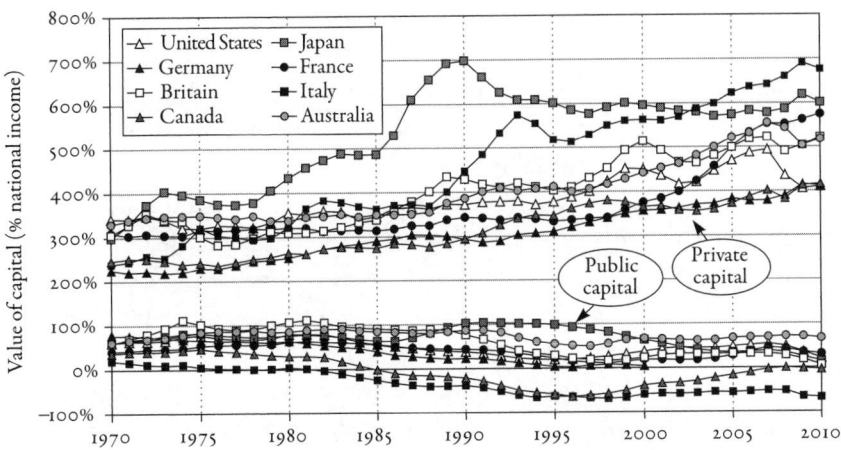

FIGURE 5.5. Private and public capital in rich countries, 1970–2010

In Italy, private capital rose from 240 percent to 680 percent of national income between 1970 and 2010, while public capital dropped from 20 percent to −70 percent. Sources and series: see piketty.pse.ens.fr/capital21c.

I begin with privatization. As noted, the proportion of public capital in national capital has dropped sharply in recent decades, especially in France and Germany, where net public wealth represented as much as a quarter or even a third of total national wealth in the period 1950–1970, whereas today it represents just a few percent (public assets are just enough to balance public debt). This evolution reflects a quite general phenomenon that has affected all eight leading developed economies: a gradual decrease in the ratio of public capital to national income in the period 1970–2010, accompanied by an increase in the ratio of private capital to national income (see Figure 5.5). In other words, the revival of private wealth is partly due to the privatization of national wealth. To be sure, the increase in private capital in all countries was greater than the decrease in public capital, so national capital (measured in years of national income) did indeed increase. But it increased less rapidly than private capital owing to privatization.

The case of Italy is particularly clear. Net public wealth was slightly positive in the 1970s, then turned slightly negative in the 1980s as large government deficits mounted. All told, public wealth decreased by an amount equal to nearly a year of national income over the period 1970–2010. At the same time, private wealth rose from barely two and a half years of national income in 1970 to nearly seven in 2010, an increase of roughly four and a half years. In other words, the decrease in public wealth represented between one-fifth and one-quarter of the increase in private wealth—a nonnegligible share. Italian national wealth did indeed rise significantly, from around two and a half years of national income in 1970 to about six in 2010, but this was a smaller increase than in private wealth, whose exceptional growth was to some extent misleading, since nearly a quarter of it reflected a growing debt that one portion of the Italian population owed to another. Instead of paying taxes to balance the government's budget, the Italians—or at any rate those who had the means—lent money to the government by buying government bonds or public assets, which increased their private wealth without increasing the national wealth.

Indeed, despite a very high rate of private saving (roughly 15 percent of national income), national saving in Italy was less than 10 percent of national income in the period 1970–2010. In other words, more than a third of private saving was absorbed by government deficits. A similar pattern exists in all the rich countries, but one generally less extreme than in Italy: in most countries, public saving was negative (which means that public investment was less than the public deficit: the government invested less than it borrowed or used borrowed money to pay current expenses). In France, Britain, Germany, and the United States, government deficits exceeded public investment by 2–3 percent of national income on average over the period 1970–2010, compared with more than 6 percent in Italy (see Table 5.4).[18]

---

18. Net public investment is typically rather low (generally around 0.5–1 percent of national income, of which 1.5–2 percent goes to gross public investment and 0.5–1 percent to depreciation of public capital), so negative public saving is often fairly close to the government deficit. (There are exceptions, however: public investment is higher in Japan, which is the reason why public saving is slightly positive despite significant government deficits.) See the online technical appendix.

TABLE 5.4.

Private and public saving in rich countries, 1970–2010

Country	National saving (private + public) (net of depreciation) (% national income)	Private saving (%)	Public saving (%)
United States	5.2	7.6	−2.4
Japan	14.6	14.5	0.1
Germany	10.2	12.2	−2.0
France	9.2	11.1	−1.9
Britain	5.3	7.3	−2.0
Italy	8.5	15.0	−6.5
Canada	10.1	12.1	−2.0
Australia	8.9	9.8	−0.9

Note: A large part (variable across countries) of private saving is absorbed by public deficits, so that national saving (private + public) is less than private saving.
   Sources: See piketty.pse.ens.fr/capital21c.

In all the rich countries, public dissaving and the consequent decrease in public wealth accounted for a significant portion of the increase in private wealth (between one-tenth and one-quarter, depending on the country). This was not the primary reason for the increase in private wealth, but it should not be neglected.

It is possible, moreover, that the available estimates somewhat undervalue public assets in the 1970s, especially in Britain (and perhaps Italy and France as well), which would lead us to underestimate the magnitude of the transfers of public wealth to private hands.[19] If true, this would allow us to explain why British private wealth increased so much between 1970 and 2010, despite a clearly insufficient private savings rate, and in particular during the waves of privatizations of public firms in the 1980s and 1990s, privatizations that often involved

---

19. This possible undervaluation is linked to the small number of public asset transactions in this period. See the online technical appendix.

notoriously low prices, which of course guaranteed that the policy would be popular with buyers.

It is important to note that these transfers of public sector wealth to the private sector were not limited to rich countries after 1970—far from it. The same general pattern exists on all continents. At the global level, the most extensive privatization in recent decades, and indeed in the entire history of capital, obviously took place in the countries of the former Soviet bloc.

The highly imperfect estimates available to us indicate that private wealth in Russia and the former Eastern bloc countries stood at about four years of national income in the late 2000s and early 2010s, and net public wealth was extremely low, just as in the rich countries. Available estimates for the 1970s and 1980s, prior to the fall of the Berlin Wall and the collapse of the Communist regimes, are even more imperfect, but all signs are that the distribution was strictly the opposite: private wealth was insignificant (limited to individual plots of land and perhaps some housing in the Communist countries least averse to private property but in all cases less than a year's national income), and public capital represented the totality of industrial capital and the lion's share of national capital, amounting, as a first approximation, to between three and four years of national income. In other words, at first sight, the stock of national capital did not change, but the public-private split was totally reversed.

To sum up: the very considerable growth of private wealth in Russia and Eastern Europe between the late 1980s and the present, which led in some cases to the spectacularly rapid enrichment of certain individuals (I am thinking mainly of the Russian "oligarchs"), obviously had nothing to do with saving or the dynamic law $\beta = s/g$. It was purely and simply the result of a transfer of ownership of capital from the government to private individuals. The privatization of national wealth in the developed countries since 1970 can be regarded as a very attenuated form of this extreme case.

The Historic Rebound of Asset Prices

The last factor explaining the increase in the capital / income ratio over the past few decades is the historic rebound of asset prices. In other words, no correct analysis of the period 1970–2010 is possible unless we situate this period in the longer historical context of 1910–2010. Complete historical records are not available for all developed countries, but the series I have established for Britain, France, Germany, and the United States yield consistent results, which I summarize below.

If we look at the whole period 1910–2010, or 1870–2010, we find that the global evolution of the capital / income ratio is very well explained by the dynamic law $\beta = s/g$. In particular, the fact that the capital / income ratio is structurally higher over the long run in Europe than in the United States is perfectly consistent with the differences in the saving rate and especially the growth rate over the past century.[20] The decline we see in the period 1910–1950 is consistent with low national savings and wartime destruction, and the fact that the capital / income ratio rose more rapidly between 1980 and 2010 than between 1950 and 1980 is well explained by the decrease in the growth rate between these two periods.

Nevertheless, the low point of the 1950s was lower than the simple logic of accumulation summed up by the law $\beta = s/g$ would have predicted. In order to understand the depth of the mid-twentieth-century low, we need to add the fact that the price of real estate and stocks fell to historically low levels in the aftermath of World War II for any number of reasons (rent control laws, financial regulation, a political climate unfavorable to private capitalism). After 1950, these asset prices gradually recovered, with an acceleration after 1980.

---

20. Between 1870 and 2010, the average rate of growth of national income was roughly 2–2.2 percent in Europe (of which 0.4–0.5 percent came from population growth) compared with 3.4 percent in the United States (of which 1.5 percent came from population growth). See the online technical appendix.

According to my estimates, this historical catch-up process is now complete: leaving aside erratic short-term price movements, the increase in asset prices between 1950 and 2010 seems broadly speaking to have compensated for the decline between 1910 and 1950. It would be risky to conclude from this that the phase of structural asset price increases is definitively over, however, and that asset prices will henceforth progress at exactly the same pace as consumer prices. For one thing, the historical sources are incomplete and imperfect, and price comparisons over such long periods of time are approximate at best. For another, there are many theoretical reasons why asset prices may evolve differently from other prices over the long run: for example, some types of assets, such as buildings and infrastructure, are affected by technological progress at a rate different from those of other parts of the economy. Furthermore, the fact that certain natural resources are nonrenewable can also be important.

Last but not least, it is important to stress that the price of capital, leaving aside the perennial short- and medium-term bubbles and possible long-term structural divergences, is always in part a social and political construct: it reflects each society's notion of property and depends on the many policies and institutions that regulate relations among different social groups, and especially between those who own capital and those who do not. This is obvious, for example, in the case of real estate prices, which depend on laws regulating the relations between landlords and tenants and controlling rents. The law also affects stock market prices, as I noted when I discussed why stock prices in Germany are relatively low.

In this connection, it is interesting to analyze the ratio between the stock market value and the accounting value of firms in the period 1970–2010 in those countries for which such data are available (see Figure 5.6). (Readers who find these issues too technical can easily skip over the remainder of this section and go directly to the next.)

The market value of a company listed on the stock exchange is its stock market capitalization. For companies not so listed, either because they are too small or because they choose not to finance them-

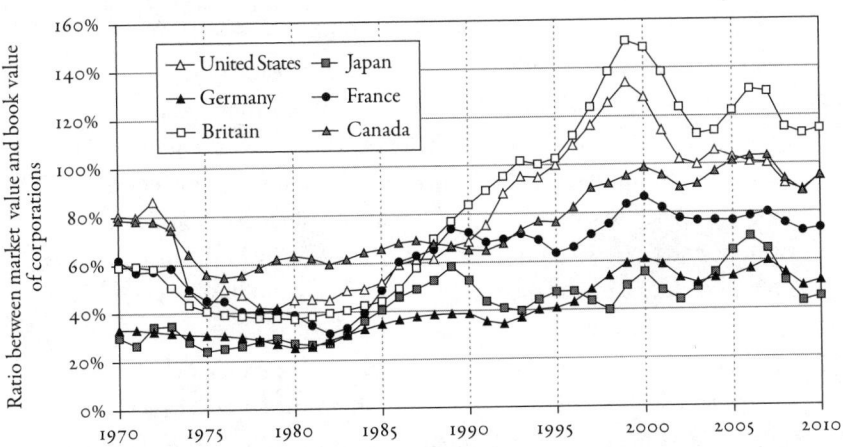

FIGURE 5.6. Market value and book value of corporations

Tobin's Q (i.e. the ratio between market value and book value of corporations) has risen in rich countries since the 1970s–1980s.

Sources and series: see piketty.pse.ens.fr/capital21c.

selves via the stock market (perhaps in order to preserve family ownership, which can happen even in very large firms), the market value is calculated for national accounting purposes with reference to observed stock prices for listed firms as similar as possible (in terms of size, sector of activity, and so on) to the unlisted firm, while taking into account the "liquidity" of the relevant market.[21] Thus far I have used market values to measure stocks of private wealth and national wealth. The accounting value of a firm, also called book value or net assets or own capital, is equal to the accumulated value of all assets— buildings, infrastructure, machinery, patents, majority or minority stakes in subsidiaries and other firms, vault cash, and so on—included in the firm's balance sheet, less the total of all outstanding debt.

---

21. An unlisted firm whose shares are difficult to sell because of the small number of transactions, so that it takes a long time to find an interested buyer, may be valued 10 to 20 percent lower than a similar company listed on the stock exchange, for which it is always possible to find an interested buyer or seller on the same day.

In theory, in the absence of all uncertainty, the market value and book value of a firm should be the same, and the ratio of the two should therefore be equal to 1 (or 100 percent). This is normally the case when a company is created. If the shareholders subscribe to 100 million euros worth of shares, which the firm uses to buy offices and equipment worth 100 million euros, then the market value and book value will both be equal to 100 million euros. The same is true if the firm borrows 50 million euros to buy new machinery worth 50 million euros: the net asset value will still be 100 million euros (150 million in assets minus 50 million in debt), as will the stock market capitalization. The same will be true if the firm earns 50 million in profits and decides to create a reserve to finance new investments worth 50 million: the stock price will rise by the same amount (because everyone knows that the firm has new assets), so that both the market value and the book value will increase to 150 million.

The difficulty arises from the fact that anticipating the future of the firm quickly becomes more complex and uncertain. After a certain time, for example, no one is really sure whether the investment of 50 million euros several years earlier is really economically useful to the firm. The book value may then diverge from the market value. The firm will continue to list investments—in new offices, machinery, infrastructure, patents, and so on—on its balance sheet at their market value, so the book value of the firm remains unchanged.[22] The market value of the firm, that is, its stock market capitalization, may be significantly lower or higher, depending on whether financial markets have

---

22. The harmonized international norms used for national accounts—which I use here—prescribe that assets and liabilities must always be recorded at their market value as of the date of the balance sheet (that is, the value that could be obtained if the firm decided to liquidate its assets, estimated if need be by using recent transactions for similar goods). The private accounting norms that firms use when publishing their balance sheets are not exactly the same as the norms for national accounts and vary from country to country, raising multiple problems for financial and prudential regulation as well as for taxation. In Part Four I come back to the crucial issue of harmonization of accounting standards.

suddenly become more optimistic or pessimistic about the firm's ability to use its investments to generate new business and profits. That is why, in practice, one always observes enormous variations in the ratio of the market value to the book value of individual firms. This ratio, which is also known as "Tobin's Q" (for the economist James Tobin, who was the first to define it), varied from barely 20 percent to more than 340 percent for French firms listed in the CAC 40 in 2012.[23]

It is more difficult to understand why Tobin's Q, when measured for all firms in a given country taken together, should be systematically greater or smaller than 1. Classically, two explanations have been given.

If certain immaterial investments (such as expenditures to increase the value of a brand or for research and development) are not counted on the balance sheet, then it is logical for the market value to be structurally greater than the book value. This may explain the ratios slightly greater than 1 observed in the United States (100–120 percent) and especially Britain (120–140 percent) in the late 1990s and 2000s. But these ratios greater than 1 also reflect stock market bubbles in both countries: Tobin's Q fell rapidly toward 1 when the Internet bubble burst in 2001–2002 and in the financial crisis of 2008–2009 (see Figure 5.6).

Conversely, if the stockholders of a company do not have full control, say, because they have to compromise in a long-term relationship with other "stakeholders" (such as worker representatives, local or national governments, consumer groups, and so on), as we saw earlier is the case in "Rhenish capitalism," then it is logical that the market value should be structurally less than the book value. This may explain the ratios slightly below one observed in France (around 80 percent) and especially Germany and Japan (around 50–70 percent) in the 1990s and 2000s, when English and US firms were at or above 100 percent (see Figure 5.6). Note, too, that stock market capitalization is calculated on the basis of prices observed in current stock transactions,

---

23. See, for example, "Profil financier du CAC 40," a report by the accounting firm Ricol Lasteyrie, June 26, 2012. The same extreme variation in Tobin's Q is found in all countries and all stock markets.

which generally correspond to buyers seeking small minority positions and not buyers seeking to take control of the firm. In the latter case, it is common to pay a price significantly higher than the current market price, typically on the order of 20 percent higher. This difference may be enough to explain a Tobin's Q of around 80 percent, even when there are no stakeholders other than minority shareholders.

Leaving aside these interesting international variations, which reflect the fact that the price of capital always depends on national rules and institutions, one can note a general tendency for Tobin's Q to increase in the rich countries since 1970. This is a consequence of the historic rebound of asset prices. All told, if we take account of both higher stock prices and higher real estate prices, we can say that the rebound in asset prices accounts for one-quarter to one-third of the increase in the ratio of national capital to national income in the rich countries between 1970 and 2010 (with large variations between countries).[24]

National Capital and Net Foreign Assets in the Rich Countries

As noted, the enormous amounts of foreign assets held by the rich countries, especially Britain and France, on the eve of World War I totally disappeared following the shocks of 1914–1945, and net foreign asset positions have never returned to their previous high levels. In fact, if we look at the levels of national capital and net foreign capital in the rich countries between 1970 and 2010, it is tempting to conclude that foreign assets were of limited importance. The net foreign asset position is sometimes slightly positive and sometimes slightly negative, depending on the country and the year, but the balance is generally fairly small compared with total national capital. In other words, the sharp increase in the level of national capital in the rich countries reflects mainly the increase of domestic capital,

---

24. See the online technical appendix.

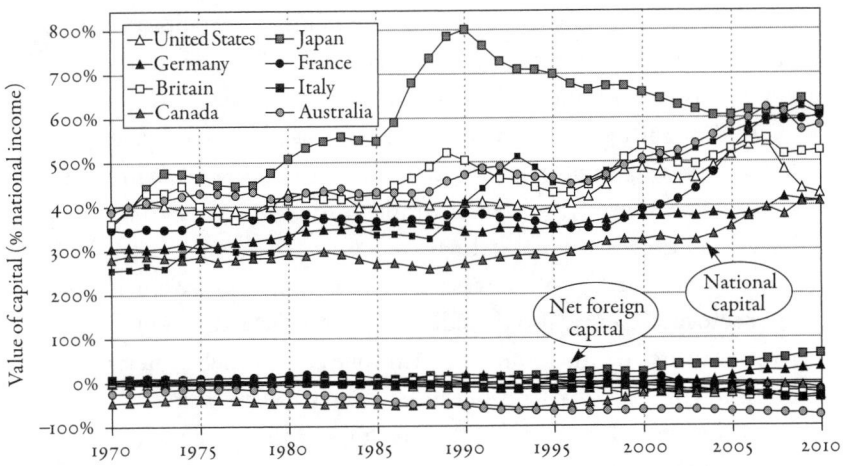

FIGURE 5.7. National capital in rich countries, 1970–2010

Net foreign assets held by Japan and Germany are worth between 0.5 and one year of national income in 2010.

Sources and series: see piketty.pse.ens.fr/capital21c.

and to a first approximation net foreign assets would seem to have played only a relatively minor role (see Figure 5.7).

This conclusion is not quite accurate, however. For example, Japan and Germany have accumulated quite significant quantities of net foreign assets over the past few decades, especially in the 2000s (largely as an automatic consequence of their trade surpluses). In the early 2010s, Japan's net foreign assets totaled about 70 percent of national income, and Germany's amounted to nearly 50 percent. To be sure, these amounts are still substantially lower than the net foreign assets of Britain and France on the eve of World War I (nearly two years of national income for Britain and more than one for France). Given the rapid pace of accumulation, however, it is natural to ask whether this will continue.[25] To what extent will some countries find themselves

---

25. Germany's trade surplus attained 6 percent of GDP in the early 2010s, and this enabled the Germans to rapidly amass claims on the rest of the world. By comparison,

owned by other countries over the course of the twenty-first century? Are the substantial net foreign asset positions observed in the colonial era likely to return or even to be surpassed?

To deal correctly with this question, we need to bring the petroleum exporting countries and emerging economies (starting with China) back into the analysis. Although historical data concerning these countries is limited (which is why I have not discussed them much to this point), our sources for the current period are much more satisfactory. We must also consider inequality within and not just between countries. I therefore defer this question, which concerns the dynamics of the global distribution of capital, to Part Three.

At this stage, I note simply that the logic of the law $\beta = s/g$ can automatically give rise to very large international capital imbalances, as the Japanese case clearly illustrates. For a given level of development, slight differences in growth rates (particularly demographic growth rates) or savings rates can leave some countries with a much higher capital / income ratio than others, in which case it is natural to expect that the former will invest massively in the latter. This can create serious political tensions. The Japanese case also indicates a second type of risk, which can arise when the equilibrium capital / income ratio $\beta = s/g$ rises to a very high level. If the residents of the country in question strongly prefer domestic assets—say, Japanese real estate—this can

---

the Chinese trade surplus is only 2 percent of GDP (both Germany and China have trade surpluses of 170–180 billion euros a year, but China's GDP is three times that of Germany: 10 trillion euros versus 3 trillion). Note, too, that five years of German trade surpluses would be enough to buy all the real estate in Paris, and five more years would be enough to buy the CAC 40 (around 800–900 billion euros for each purchase). Germany's very large trade surplus seems to be more a consequence of the vagaries of German competitiveness than of an explicit policy of accumulation. It is therefore possible that domestic demand will increase and the trade surplus will decrease in coming years. In the oil exporting countries, which are explicitly seeking to accumulate foreign assets, the trade surplus is more than 10 percent of GDP (in Saudi Arabia and Russia, for example) and even multiples of that in some of the smaller petroleum exporters. See Chapter 12 and the online technical appendix.

drive the price of those preferred assets to unprecedentedly high levels. In this respect, it is interesting to note that the Japanese record of 1990 was recently beaten by Spain, where the total amount of net private capital reached eight years of national income on the eve of the crisis of 2007–2008, which is a year more than in Japan in 1990. The Spanish bubble began to shrink quite rapidly in 2010–2011, just as the Japanese bubble did in the early 1990s.[26] It is quite possible that even more spectacular bubbles will form in the future, as the potential capital / income ratio $\beta = s/g$ rises to new heights. In passing, note how useful it is to represent the historical evolution of the capital / income ratio in this way and thus to exploit stocks and flows in the national accounts. Doing so might make it possible to detect obvious overvaluations in time to apply prudential policies and financial regulations designed to temper the speculative enthusiasm of financial institutions in the relevant countries.[27]

One should also note that small net positions may hide enormous gross positions. Indeed, one characteristic of today's financial globalization is that every country is to a large extent owned by other countries, which not only distorts perceptions of the global distribution of wealth but also represents an important vulnerability for smaller countries as well as a source of instability in the global distribution of net positions. Broadly speaking, the 1970s and 1980s witnessed an extensive "financialization" of the global economy, which altered the structure of wealth in the sense that the total amount of financial assets and liabilities held by various sectors (households, corporations, government agencies) increased more rapidly than net wealth. In most countries, the total amount of financial assets and liabilities in the early 1970s did not exceed four to five years of national income. By

---

26. See Supplemental Figure S5.2, available online.

27. In the case of Spain, many people noticed the very rapid rise of real estate and stock market indices in the 2000s. Without a precise point of reference, however, it is very difficult to determine when valuations have truly climbed to excessive heights. The advantage of the capital / income ratio is that it provides a precise point of reference useful for making comparisons in time and space.

2010, this amount had increased to ten to fifteen years of national income (in the United States, Japan, Germany, and France in particular) and to twenty years of national income in Britain, which set an absolute historical record.[28] This reflects the unprecedented development of cross-investments involving financial and nonfinancial corporations in the same country (and, in particular, a significant inflation of bank balance sheets, completely out of proportion with the growth of the banks' own capital), as well as cross-investments between countries.

In this respect, note that the phenomenon of international cross-investments is much more prevalent in European countries, led by Britain, Germany, and France (where financial assets held by other countries represent between one-quarter and one-half of total domestic financial assets, which is considerable), than in larger economies such as the United States and Japan (where the proportion of foreign-held assets is not much more than one-tenth).[29] This increases the feeling of dispossession, especially in Europe, in part for good reasons,

---

28. See Supplemental Figures S5.3–4, available online. It bears emphasizing, moreover, that the balances established by central banks and government statistical agencies concern only primary financial assets (notes, shares, bonds, and other securities) and not derivatives (which are like insurance contracts indexed to these primary assets or, perhaps better, like wagers, depending on how one sees the problem), which would bring the total to even higher levels (twenty to thirty years of national income, depending on the definitions one adopts). It is nevertheless important to realize that these quantities of financial assets and liabilities, which are higher today than ever in the past (in the nineteenth century and until World War I, the total amount of financial assets and liabilities did not exceed four to five years of national income) by definition have no impact on net wealth (any more than the amount of bets placed on a sporting event influences the level of national wealth). See the online technical appendix.

29. For example, the financial assets held in France by the rest of the world amounted to 310 percent of national income in 2010, and financial assets held by French residents in the rest of the world amounted to 300 percent of national income, for a negative net position of −10 percent. In the United States, a negative net position of −20 percent corresponds to financial assets on the order of 120 percent of national income held by the rest of the world in the United States and 100 percent of national income owned by US residents in other countries. See Supplemental Figures S5.5–11, available online, for detailed series by country.

though often to an exaggerated degree. (People quickly forget that while domestic companies and government debt are largely owned by the rest of the world, residents hold equivalent assets abroad through annuities and other financial products.) Indeed, balance sheets structured in this way subject small countries, especially in Europe, to an important vulnerability, in that small "errors" in the valuation of financial assets and liabilities can lead to enormous variations in the net foreign asset position.[30] Furthermore, the evolution of a country's net foreign asset position is determined not only by the accumulation of trade surpluses or deficits but also by very large variations in the return on the country's financial assets and liabilities.[31] I should also point out that these international positions are in substantial part the result of fictitious financial flows associated not with the needs of the real economy but rather with tax optimization strategies and regulatory arbitrage (using screen corporations set up in countries where the tax structure and / or regulatory environment is particularly attractive).[32]

---

30. In this regard, note that one key difference between the Japanese and Spanish bubbles is that Spain now has a net negative foreign asset position of roughly one year's worth of national income (which seriously complicates Spain's situation), whereas Japan has a net positive position of about the same size. See the online technical appendix.

31. In particular, in view of the very large trade deficits the United States has been running, its net foreign asset position ought to be far more negative than it actually is. The gap is explained in part by the very high return on foreign assets (primarily stocks) owned by US citizens and the low return paid on US liabilities (especially US government bonds). On this subject, see the work of Pierre-Olivier Gourinchas and Hélène Rey cited in the online technical appendix. Conversely, Germany's net position should be higher than it is, and this discrepancy is explained by the low rates of return on Germany's investments abroad, which may partially account for Germany's current wariness. For a global decomposition of the accumulation of foreign assets by rich countries between 1970 and 2010, which distinguishes between the effects of trade balances and the effects of returns on the foreign asset portfolio, see the online technical appendix (esp. Supplemental Table S5.13, available online).

32. For example, it is likely that a significant part of the US trade deficit simply corresponds to fictitious transfers to US firms located in tax havens, transfers that are subsequently repatriated in the form of profits realized abroad (which

I come back to these questions in Part Three, where I will examine the importance of tax havens in the global dynamics of wealth distribution.

What Will the Capital / Income Ratio Be in the Twenty-First Century?

The dynamic law $\beta = s/g$ also enables us to think about what level the global capital / income ratio might attain in the twenty-first century.

First consider what we can say about the past. Concerning Europe (or at any rate the leading economies of Western Europe) and North America, we have reliable estimates for the entire period 1870–2010. For Japan, we have no comprehensive estimate of total private or national wealth prior to 1960, but the incomplete data we do have, in particular Japanese probate records going back to 1905, clearly show that Japanese wealth can be described by the same type of "U-curve" as in Europe, and that the capital / income ratio in the period 1910–1930 rose quite high, to 600–700 percent, before falling to just 200–300 percent in the 1950s and 1960s and then rebounding spectacularly to levels again close to 600–700 percent in the 1990s and 2000s.

For other countries and continents, including Asia (apart from Japan), Africa, and South America, relatively complete estimates exist from 1990 on, and these show a capital / income ratio of about four years on average. For the period 1870–1990 there are no truly reliable estimates, and I have simply assumed that the overall level was about the same. Since these countries account for just over a fifth of global output throughout this period, their impact on the global capital / income ratio is in any case fairly limited.

The results I have obtained are shown in Figure 5.8. Given the weight of the rich countries in this total, it comes as no surprise to discover that the global capital / income ratio followed the same type

---

restores the balance of payments). Clearly, such accounting games can interfere with the analysis of the most basic economic phenomena.

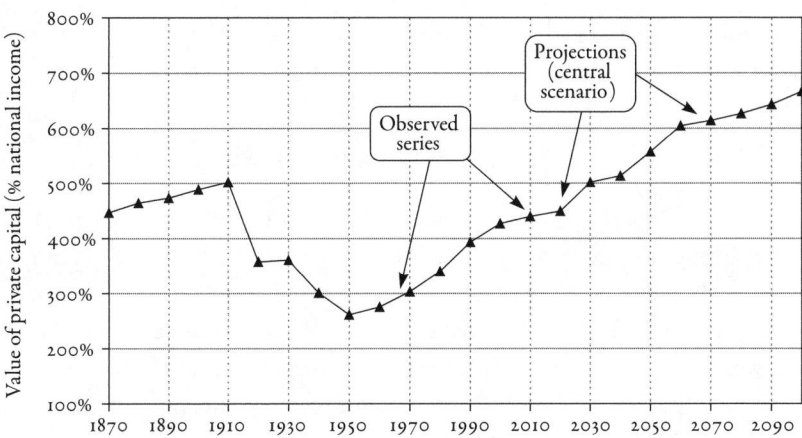

FIGURE 5.8. The world capital / income ratio, 1870–2100

According to simulations (central scenario), the world capital / income ratio could be close to 700 percent by the end of the twenty-first century.

Sources and series: see piketty.pse.ens.fr/capital21c.

of "U-curve": it seems today to be close to 500 percent, which is roughly the same level as that attained on the eve of World War I.

The most interesting question concerns the extrapolation of this curve into the future. Here I have used the demographic and economic growth predictions presented in Chapter 2, according to which global output will gradually decline from the current 3 percent a year to just 1.5 percent in the second half of the twenty-first century. I also assume that the savings rate will stabilize at about 10 percent in the long run. With these assumptions, the dynamic law $\beta = s/g$ implies that the global capital / income ratio will quite logically continue to rise and could approach 700 percent before the end of the twenty-first century, or approximately the level observed in Europe from the eighteenth century to the Belle Époque. In other words, by 2100, the entire planet could look like Europe at the turn of the twentieth century, at least in terms of capital intensity. Obviously, this is just one possibility among others. As noted, these growth predictions are extremely uncertain, as is the prediction of the rate of saving. These simulations are nevertheless plausible and valuable as a way of illustrating the crucial role of slower growth in the accumulation of capital.

The Mystery of Land Values

By definition, the law $\beta = s/g$ applies only to those forms of capital that can be accumulated. It does not take account of the value of pure natural resources, including "pure land," that is, land prior to any human improvements. The fact that the law $\beta = s/g$ allows us to explain nearly the entirety of the observed capital stock in 2010 (between 80 and 100 percent, depending on the country) suggests that pure land constitutes only a small part of national capital. But exactly how much? The available data are insufficient to give a precise answer to this question.

Consider first the case of farmland in a traditional rural society. It is very difficult to say precisely what portion of its value represents "pure land value" prior to any human exploitation and what corresponds to the many investments in and improvements to this land over the centuries (including clearing, drainage, fencing, and so on). In the eighteenth century, the value of farmland in France and Britain attained the equivalent of four years of national income.[33] According to contemporary estimates, investments and improvements represented at least three-quarters of this value and probably more. The value of pure land represented at most one year of national income, and probably less than half a year. This conclusion follows primarily from the

---

33. It is difficult to make comparisons with ancient societies, but the rare available estimates suggest that the value of land sometimes reached even higher levels: six years of national income in ancient Rome, according to R. Goldsmith, *Premodern Financial Systems: A Historical Comparative Study* (Cambridge: Cambridge University Press, 1987), 58. Estimates of the intergenerational mobility of wealth in small primitive societies suggest that the importance of transmissible wealth varied widely depending on the nature of economic activity (hunting, herding, farming, etc.). See Monique Borgerhoff Mulder et al., "Intergenerational Wealth Transmission and the Dynamics of Inequality in Small-Scale Societies," *Science* 326, no. 5953 (October 2009): 682–88.

fact that the annual value of the labor required to clear, drain, and otherwise improve the land was considerable, on the order of 3–4 percent of national income. With relatively slow growth, less than 1 percent a year, the cumulative value of such investments was undoubtedly close to the total value of the land (if not greater).[34]

It is interesting that Thomas Paine, in his famous "Agrarian Justice" proposal to French legislators in 1795, also concluded that "unimproved land" accounted for roughly one-tenth of national wealth, or a little more than half a year of national income.

Nevertheless, estimates of this sort are inevitably highly approximate. When the growth rate is low, small variations in the rate of investment produce enormous differences in the long-run value of the capital / income ratio $\beta = s/g$. The key point to remember is that even in a traditional society, the bulk of national capital already stemmed from accumulation and investment: nothing has really changed, except perhaps the fact that the depreciation of land was quite small compared with that of modern real estate or business capital, which has to be repaired or replaced much more frequently. This may contribute to the impression that modern capital is more "dynamic." But since the data we have concerning investment in traditional rural societies are limited and imprecise, it is difficult to say more.

In particular, it seems impossible to compare in any precise way the value of pure land long ago with its value today. The principal issue today is urban land: farmland is worth less than 10 percent of national income in both France and Britain. But it is no easier to measure the value of pure urban land today, independent not only of buildings and construction but also of infrastructure and other improvements needed to make the land attractive, than to measure the value of pure farmland in the eighteenth century. According to my estimates, the annual flow of investment over the past few decades can account for almost all the value of wealth, including wealth in real estate, in 2010. In other words, the rise in the capital / income ratio cannot be explained in

---

34. See the online technical appendix.

terms of an increase in the value of pure urban land, which to a first approximation seems fairly comparable to the value of pure farmland in the eighteenth century: half to one year of national income. The margin of uncertainty is nevertheless substantial.

Two further points are worth mentioning. First, the fact that total capital, especially in real estate, in the rich countries can be explained fairly well in terms of the accumulation of flows of saving and investment obviously does not preclude the existence of large local capital gains linked to the concentration of population in particular areas, such as major capitals. It would not make much sense to explain the increase in the value of buildings on the Champs-Elysées or, for that matter, anywhere in Paris exclusively in terms of investment flows. Our estimates suggest, however, that these large capital gains on real estate in certain areas were largely compensated by capital losses in other areas, which became less attractive, such as smaller cities or decaying neighborhoods.

Second, the fact that the increase in the value of pure land does not seem to explain much of the historic rebound of the capital / income ratio in the rich countries in no way implies that this will continue to be true in the future. From a theoretical point of view, there is nothing that guarantees long-term stability of the value of land, much less of all natural resources. I will come back to this point when I analyze the dynamics of wealth and foreign asset holdings in the petroleum exporting countries.[35]

---

35. See Chapter 12.

SIX

The Capital-Labor Split in the Twenty-First Century

We now have a fairly good understanding of the dynamics of the capital / income ratio, as described by the law $\beta = s/g$. In particular, the long-run capital / income ratio depends on the savings rate s and the growth rate g. These two macrosocial parameters themselves depend on millions of individual decisions influenced by any number of social, economic, cultural, psychological, and demographic factors and may vary considerably from period to period and country to country. Furthermore, they are largely independent of each other. These facts enable us to understand the wide historical and geographic variations in the capital / income ratio, independent of the fact that the relative price of capital can also vary widely over the long term as well as the short term, as can the relative price of natural resources.

From the Capital / Income Ratio to the Capital-Labor Split

I turn now from the analysis of the capital / income ratio to the division of national income between labor and capital. The formula $\alpha = r \times \beta$, which in Chapter 1 I called the first fundamental law of capitalism, allows us to move transparently between the two. For example, if the capital stock is equal to six years of national income ($\beta = 6$), and if the average return on capital is 5 percent a year ($r = 5\%$), then the share of income from capital, α, in national income is 30 percent (and the share of income from labor is therefore 70 percent). Hence the central question is the following: How is the rate of return on capital determined? I shall begin by briefly examining the evolutions observed

FIGURE 6.1. The capital-labor split in Britain, 1770–2010

During the nineteenth century, capital income (rent, profits, dividends, interest ...) absorbed about 40 percent of national income versus 60 percent for labor income (including both wage and nonwage income).

Sources and series: see piketty.pse.ens.fr/capital21c.

FIGURE 6.2. The capital-labor split in France, 1820–2010

In the twenty-first century, capital income (rent, profits, dividends, interest ...) absorbs about 30 percent of national income versus 70 percent for labor income (including both wage and nonwage income).

Sources and series: see piketty.pse.ens.fr/capital21c.

over the very long run before analyzing the theoretical mechanisms and economic and social forces that come into play.

The two countries for which we have the most complete historical data from the eighteenth century on are once again Britain and France. We find that the general evolution of capital's share of income, α, is described by the same U-shaped curve as the capital / income ratio, β, although the depth of the U is less pronounced. In other words, the rate of return on capital, r, seems to have attenuated the evolution of the quantity of capital, β: r is higher in periods when β is lower, and vice versa, which seems natural.

More precisely: we find that capital's share of income was on the order of 35–40 percent in both Britain and France in the late eighteenth century and throughout the nineteenth, before falling to 20–25 percent in the middle of the twentieth century and then rising again to 25–30 percent in the late twentieth and early twenty-first centuries (see Figures 6.1 and 6.2). This corresponds to an average rate of return on capital of around 5–6 percent in the eighteenth and nineteenth centuries, rising to 7–8 percent in the mid-twentieth century, and then falling to 4–5 percent in the late twentieth and early twenty-first centuries (see Figures 6.3 and 6.4).

The overall curve and the orders of magnitude described here may be taken as reliable and significant, at least to a first approximation. Nevertheless, the limitations and weaknesses of the data should be noted immediately. First, as noted, the very notion of an "average" rate of return on capital is a fairly abstract construct. In practice, the rate of return varies widely with the type of asset, as well as with the size of individual fortunes (it is generally easier to obtain a good return if one begins with a large stock of capital), and this tends to amplify inequalities. Concretely, the yield on the riskiest assets, including industrial capital (whether in the form of partnerships in family firms in the nineteenth century or shares of stock in listed corporations in the twentieth century), is often greater than 7–8 percent, whereas the yield on less risky assets is significantly lower, on the order of 4–5 percent for farmland in the eighteenth and nineteenth centuries and as

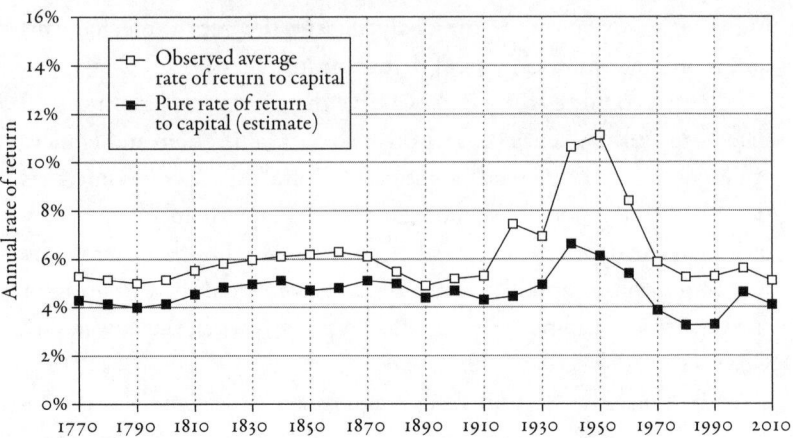

FIGURE 6.3. The pure rate of return on capital in Britain, 1770–2010

The pure rate of return to capital is roughly stable around 4–5 percent in the long run.
Sources and series: see piketty.pse.ens.fr/capital21c.

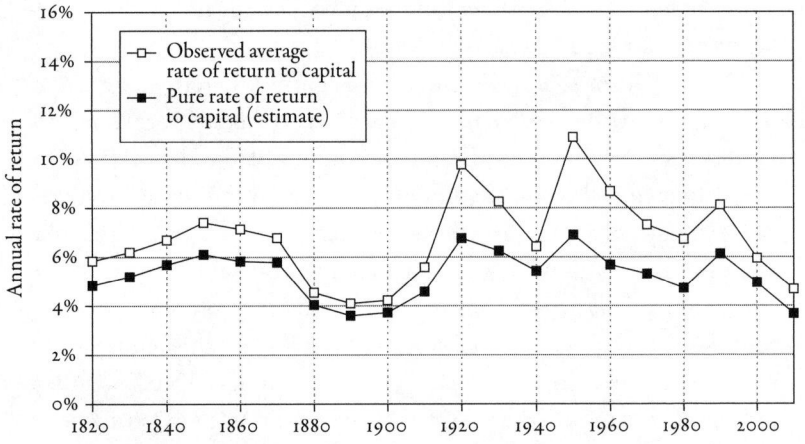

FIGURE 6.4. The pure rate of return on capital in France, 1820–2010

The observed average rate of return displays larger fluctuations than the pure rate of return during the twentieth century.
Sources and series: see piketty.pse.ens.fr/capital21c.

low as 3–4 percent for real estate in the early twenty-first century. Small nest eggs held in checking or savings accounts often yield a real rate of return closer to 1–2 percent or even less, perhaps even negative, when the inflation rate exceeds the meager nominal interest rate on such accounts. This is a crucial issue about which I will have more to say later on.

At this stage it is important to point out that the capital shares and average rates of return indicated in Figures 6.1–4 were calculated by adding the various amounts of income from capital included in national accounts, regardless of legal classification (rents, profits, dividends, interest, royalties, etc., excluding interest on public debt and before taxes) and then dividing this total by national income (which gives the share of capital income in national income, denoted α) or by the national capital stock (which gives the average rate of return on capital, denoted r).[1] By construction, this average rate of return aggregates the returns on very different types of assets and investments: the goal is in fact to measure the average return on capital in a given society taken as a whole, ignoring differences in individual situations. Obviously some people earn more than the average return and others less. Before looking at the distribution of individual returns around the mean, it is natural to begin by analyzing the location of the mean.

Flows: More Difficult to Estimate Than Stocks

Another important caveat concerns the income of nonwage workers, which may include remuneration of capital that is difficult to distinguish from other income.

---

1. Interest on the public debt, which is not part of national income (because it is a pure transfer) and which remunerates capital that is not included in national capital (because public debt is an asset for private bondholders and a liability for the government), is not included in Figures 6.1–4. If it were included, capital's share of income would be a little higher, generally on the order of one to two percentage points (and up to four to five percentage points in periods of unusually high public debt). For the complete series, see the online technical appendix.

To be sure, this problem is less important now than in the past because most private economic activity today is organized around corporations or, more generally, joint-stock companies, so a firm's accounts are clearly separate from the accounts of the individuals who supply the capital (who risk only the capital they have invested and not their personal fortunes, thanks to the revolutionary concept of the "limited liability corporation," which was adopted almost everywhere in the latter half of the nineteenth century). On the books of such a corporation, there is a clear distinction between remuneration of labor (wages, salaries, bonuses, and other payments to employees, including managers, who contribute labor to the company's activities) and remuneration of capital (dividends, interest, profits reinvested to increase the value of the firm's capital, etc.).

Partnerships and sole proprietorships are different: the accounts of the business are sometimes mingled with the personal accounts of the firm head, who is often both the owner and operator. Today, around 10 percent of domestic production in the rich countries is due to nonwage workers in individually owned businesses, which is roughly equal to the proportion of nonwage workers in the active population. Nonwage workers are mostly found in small businesses (merchants, craftsmen, restaurant workers, etc.) and in the professions (doctors, lawyers, etc.). For a long time this category also included a large number of independent farmers, but today these have largely disappeared. On the books of these individually owned firms, it is generally impossible to distinguish the remuneration of capital: for example, the profits of a radiologist remunerate both her labor and the equipment she uses, which can be costly. The same is true of the hotel owner or small farmer. We therefore say that the income of nonwage workers is "mixed," because it combines income from labor with income from capital. This is also referred to as "entrepreneurial income."

To apportion mixed incomes between capital and labor, I have used the same average capital-labor split as for the rest of the economy. This is the least arbitrary choice, and it appears to yield results close to those obtained with the other two commonly used methods.[2] It remains an approximation, however, since the very notion of a clear boundary between income from capital and income from labor is not clearly defined for mixed incomes. For the current period, this makes virtually no difference: because the share of mixed income in national income is small, the uncertainty about capital's share of mixed income affects no more than 1–2 percent of national income. In earlier periods, and especially for the eighteenth and nineteenth centuries when mixed incomes may have accounted for more than half of national income, the uncertainties are potentially much greater.[3] That is why available estimates of the capital share for the eighteenth and nineteenth centuries can only be counted as approximations.[4]

Despite these caveats, my estimates for capital's share of national income in this period (at least 40 percent) appear to be valid: in both Britain and France, the rents paid to landlords alone accounted for 20 percent of national income in the eighteenth and early nineteenth centuries, and all signs are that the return on farmland (which accounted for about half of national capital) was slightly less than the average return on capital and significantly less than the return on industrial capital, to judge by the very high level of industrial profits, especially during the first half of the nineteenth century. Because of imperfec-

---

2. One can either attribute to nonwage workers the same average labor income as wage workers, or one can attribute to the business capital used by nonwage workers the same average return as for other forms of capital. See the online technical appendix.

3. In the rich countries, the share of individually owned businesses in domestic output fell from 30–40 percent in the 1950s (and from perhaps 50 percent in the nineteenth and early twentieth centuries) to around 10 percent in the 1980s (reflecting mainly the decline in the share of agriculture) and then stabilized at around that level, at times rising to about 12–15 percent in response to changing fiscal advantages and disadvantages. See the online technical appendix.

4. The series depicted in Figures 6.1 and 6.2 are based on the historical work of Robert Allen for Britain and on my own work for France. All details on sources and methods are available in the online technical appendix.

tions in the available data, however, it is better to give an interval—between 35 and 40 percent—than a single estimate.

For the eighteenth and nineteenth centuries, estimates of the value of the capital stock are probably more accurate than estimates of the flows of income from labor and capital. This remains largely true today. That is why I chose to emphasize the evolution of the capital / income ratio rather than the capital-labor split, as most economic researchers have done in the past.

The Notion of the Pure Return on Capital

The other important source of uncertainties, which leads me to think that the average rates of return indicated in Figures 6.3 and 6.4 are somewhat overestimated, so that I also indicate what might be called the "pure" rate of return on capital, is the fact that national accounts do not allow for the labor, or at any rate attention, that is required of anyone who wishes to invest. To be sure, the cost of managing capital and of "formal" financial intermediation (that is, the investment advice and portfolio management services provided by a bank or official financial institution or real estate agency or managing partner) is obviously taken into account and deducted from the income on capital in calculating the average rate of return (as presented here). But this is not the case with "informal" financial intermediation: every investor spends time—in some cases a lot of time—managing his own portfolio and affairs and determining which investments are likely to be the most profitable. This effort can in certain cases be compared to genuine entrepreneurial labor or to a form of business activity.

It is of course quite difficult—and to some extent arbitrary—to calculate the value of this informal labor in any precise way, which explains why it is omitted from national accounts. In theory, one would have to measure the time spent on investment-related activities and ascribe an hourly value to that time, based perhaps on the remuneration of equivalent labor in the formal financial or real estate sector. One might also imagine that these informal costs are greater in periods of very rapid economic growth (or high inflation), for such times are likely to require more frequent reallocation of investments and more time researching the best investment opportunities than in a quasi-stagnant economy. For example, it is difficult to believe that the average returns on capital of close to 10 percent that we observe in France (and to a lesser degree in Britain) during periods of postwar reconstruction are simply pure returns on capital. It is likely that such high returns also include a nonnegligible portion of remuneration for informal entrepreneurial labor. (Similar returns are also observed in emerging economies such as China today, where growth rates are also very rapid.)

For illustrative purposes, I have indicated in Figures 6.3 and 6.4 my estimates of the pure return on capital in Britain and France at various times. I obtained these estimates by deducting from the observed average return a plausible (although perhaps too high) estimate of the informal costs of portfolio management (that is, the value of the time spent managing one's wealth). The pure rates of return obtained in this way are generally on the order of one or two percentage points lower than the observed returns and should probably be regarded as minimum values.[5] In particular, the available data on the rates of return earned by fortunes of different sizes suggest that there are important economies of scale in the management of wealth, and that the pure returns earned by the largest fortunes are significantly higher than the levels indicated here.[6]

The Return on Capital in Historical Perspective

The principal conclusion that emerges from my estimates is the following. In both France and Britain, from the eighteenth century to the twenty-first, the pure return on capital has oscillated around a central value of 4–5 percent a year, or more generally in an interval from 3–6

---

5. See also Supplemental Figures S6.1 and S6.2, available online, on which I have indicated upper and lower bounds for capital's share of income in Britain and France.
6. See in particular Chapter 12.

percent a year. There has been no pronounced long-term trend either upward or downward. The pure return rose significantly above 6 percent following the massive destruction of property and numerous shocks to capital in the two world wars but subsequently returned fairly rapidly to the lower levels observed in the past. It is possible, however, that the pure return on capital has decreased slightly over the very long run: it often exceeded 4–5 percent in the eighteenth and nineteenth centuries, whereas in the early twenty-first century it seems to be approaching 3–4 percent as the capital / income ratio returns to the high levels observed in the past.

We nevertheless lack the distance needed to be certain about this last point. We cannot rule out the possibility that the pure return on capital will rise to higher levels over the next few decades, especially in view of the growing international competition for capital and the equally increasing sophistication of financial markets and institutions in generating high yields from complex, diversified portfolios.

In any case, this virtual stability of the pure return on capital over the very long run (or more likely this slight decrease of about one-quarter to one-fifth, from 4–5 percent in the eighteenth and nineteenth centuries to 3–4 percent today) is a fact of major importance for this study.

In order to put these figures in perspective, recall first of all that the traditional rate of conversion from capital to rent in the eighteenth and nineteenth centuries, for the most common and least risky forms of capital (typically land and public debt) was generally on the order of 5 percent a year: the value of a capital asset was estimated to be equal to twenty years of the annual income yielded by that asset. Sometimes this was increased to twenty-five years (corresponding to a return of 4 percent a year).[7]

---

7. The interest rate on the public debt of Britain and France in the eighteenth and nineteenth centuries was typically on the order of 4–5 percent. It sometimes went as low as 3 percent (for example, during the economic slowdown of the late nineteenth century). Conversely, it rose to 5–6 percent or even higher during periods of high political tension, when there was doubt about the credibility of the

In classic novels of the early nineteenth century, such as those of Balzac and Jane Austen, the equivalence between capital and rent at a rate of 5 percent (or more rarely 4 percent) is taken for granted. Novelists frequently failed to mention the nature of the capital and generally treated land and public debt as almost perfect substitutes, mentioning only the yield in rent. We are told, for example, that a major character has 50,000 francs or 2,000 pounds sterling of rent but not whether it comes from land or from government bonds. It made no difference, since in both cases the income was certain and steady and sufficient to finance a very definite lifestyle and to reproduce across generations a familiar and well-understood social status.

Similarly, neither Austen nor Balzac felt it necessary to specify the rate of return needed to transform a specific amount of capital into an annual rent: every reader knew full well that it took a capital on the order of 1 million francs to produce an annual rent of 50,000 francs (or a capital of 40,000 pounds to produce an income of 2,000 pounds a year), no matter whether the investment was in government bonds or land or something else entirely. For nineteenth-century novelists and their readers, the equivalence between wealth and annual rent was obvious, and there was no difficulty in moving from one measuring scale to the other, as if the two were perfectly synonymous.

It was also obvious to novelists and their readers that some kinds of investment required greater personal involvement, whether it was Père Goriot's pasta factories or Sir Thomas's plantations in the West Indies in *Mansfield Park*. What is more, the return on such investments was naturally higher, typically on the order of 7–8 percent or even more if one struck an especially good bargain, as César Birotteau hoped to do by investing in real estate in the Madeleine district of

government budget, for example, during the decades prior to and during the French Revolution. See F. Velde and D. Weir, "The Financial Market and Government Debt Policy in France 1746–1793," *Journal of Economic History* 52, no. 1 (March 1992): 1–39. See also K. Béguin, *Financer la guerre au 17e siècle: La dette publique et les rentiers de l'absolutisme* (Seyssel: Champ Vallon, 2012). See online appendix.

Paris after earlier successes in the perfume business. But it was also perfectly clear to everyone that when the time and energy devoted to organizing such affairs was deducted from the profits (think of the long months that Sir Thomas is forced to spend in the West Indies), the pure return obtained in the end was not always much more than the 4–5 percent earned by investments in land and government bonds. In other words, the additional yield was largely remuneration for the labor devoted to the business, and the pure return on capital, including the risk premium, was generally not much above 4–5 percent (which was not in any case a bad rate of return).

The Return on Capital in the Early Twenty-First Century

How is the pure return on capital determined (that is, what is the annual return on capital after deducting all management costs, including the value of the time spent in portfolio management)? Why did it decrease over the long run from roughly 4–5 percent in the age of Balzac and Austen to roughly 3–4 percent today?

Before attempting to answer these questions, another important issue needs to be clarified. Some readers may find the assertion that the average return on capital today is 3–4 percent quite optimistic in view of the paltry return that they obtain on their meager savings. A number of points need to be made.

First, the returns indicated in Figures 6.3 and 6.4 are pretax returns. In other words, they are the returns that capital would earn if there were no taxes on capital or income. In Part Four I will consider the role such taxes have played in the past and may play in the future as fiscal competition between states increases. At this stage, let me say simply that fiscal pressure was virtually nonexistent in the eighteenth and nineteenth centuries. It was sharply higher in the twentieth century and remains higher today, so that the average after-tax return on capital has decreased much more over the long run than the average pretax return. Today, the level of taxation of capital and its income may be fairly low if one adopts the correct strategy of fiscal optimization (and some particularly persuasive investors even manage to obtain subsidies), but in most cases the tax is substantial. In particular, it is important to remember that there are many taxes other than income tax to consider: for instance, real estate taxes cut into the return on investments in real estate, and corporate taxes do the same for the income on financial capital invested in firms. Only if all these taxes were eliminated (as may happen someday, but we are still a long way from that) that the returns on capital actually accruing to its owners would reach the levels indicated in Figures 6.3 and 6.4. When all taxes are taken into account, the average tax rate on income from capital is currently around 30 percent in most of the rich countries. This is the primary reason for the large gap between the pure economic return on capital and the return actually accruing to individual owners.

The second important point to keep in mind is that a pure return of around 3–4 percent is an average that hides enormous disparities. For individuals whose only capital is a small balance in a checking account, the return is negative, because such balances yield no interest and are eaten away by inflation. Savings accounts often yield little more than the inflation rate.[8] But the important point is that even if there are many such individuals, their total wealth is relatively small. Recall that wealth in the rich countries is currently divided into two approximately equal (or comparable) parts: real estate and financial assets. Nearly all financial assets are accounted for by stocks, bonds, mutual funds, and long-term financial contracts such as annuities or pension funds. Non-interest-bearing checking accounts currently represent only about 10–20 percent of national income, or at most 3–4 percent of total wealth (which, as readers will recall, is 500–600 percent of national income). If we add savings accounts, we increase the total to just above 30 percent of national income, or barely more than

---

8. The French "livret A" savings account paid a nominal interest of barely 2 percent in 2013, for a real return of close to zero.

5 percent of total wealth.[9] The fact that checking and savings accounts yield only very meager interest is obviously of some concern to depositors, but in terms of the average return on capital, this fact is not very important.

In regard to average return, it is far more important to observe that the annual rental value of housing, which accounts for half of total national wealth, is generally 3–4 percent of the value of the property. For example, an apartment worth 500,000 euros will yield rent of 15,000–20,000 euros per year (or about 1,500 euros per month). Those who prefer to own their property can save that amount in rent. This is also true for more modest housing: an apartment worth 100,000 euros yields 3,000–4,000 euros of rent a year (or allows the owner to avoid paying that amount). And, as noted, the rental yield on small apartments is as high as 5 percent. The returns on financial investments, which are the predominant asset in larger fortunes, are higher still. Taken together, it is these kinds of investments, in real estate and financial instruments, that account for the bulk of private wealth, and this raises the average rate of return.

Real and Nominal Assets

The third point that needs to be clarified is that the rates of return indicated in Figures 6.3 and 6.4 are *real* rates of return. In other words, it would be a serious mistake to try to deduce the rate of inflation (typically 1–2 percent in the rich countries today) from these yields.

The reason is simple and was touched on earlier: the lion's share of household wealth consists of "real assets" (that is, assets directly related to a real economic activity, such as a house or shares in a corporation, the price of which therefore evolves as the related activity evolves) rather than "nominal assets" (that is, assets whose value is fixed at a nominal initial value, such as a sum of money deposited in a

---

9. See the online technical appendix. In most countries, checking account deposits earn interest (but this is forbidden in France).

checking or savings account or invested in a government bond that is not indexed to inflation).

Nominal assets are subject to a substantial inflation risk: if you invest 10,000 euros in a checking or savings account or a nonindexed government or corporate bond, that investment is still worth 10,000 euros ten years later, even if consumer prices have doubled in the meantime. In that case, we say that the real value of the investment has fallen by half: you can buy only half as much in goods and services as you could have bought with the initial investment, so that your return after ten years is −50 percent, which may or may not have been compensated by the interest you earned in the interim. In periods during which prices are rising sharply, the "nominal" rate of interest, that is, the rate of interest prior to deduction of the inflation rate, will rise to a high level, usually greater than the inflation rate. But the investor's results depend on when the investment was made, how the parties to the transaction anticipated future inflation at that point in time, and so on: the "real" interest rate, that is, the return actually obtained after inflation has been deducted, may be significantly negative or significantly positive, depending on the case.[10] In any case, the inflation rate must be deducted from the interest rate if one wants to know the real return on a nominal asset.

With real assets, everything is different. The price of real estate, like the price of shares of stock or parts of a company or investments in a mutual fund, generally rises at least as rapidly as the consumer price index. In other words, not only must we not subtract inflation from the annual rents or dividends received on such assets, but we often need to add to the annual return the capital gains earned when the asset is sold (or subtract the capital loss, as the case may be). The crucial point is that real assets are far more representative than nominal

---

10. For example, a nominal interest rate of 5 percent with an inflation rate of 10 percent corresponds to a real interest rate of −5 percent, whereas a nominal interest rate of 15 percent and an inflation rate of 5 percent corresponds to a real interest rate of +10 percent.

assets: they generally account for more than three-quarters of total household assets and in some cases as much as nine-tenths.[11]

When I examined the accumulation of capital in Chapter 5, I concluded that these various effects tend to balance out over the long run. Concretely, if we look at all assets over the period 1910–2010, we find that their average price seems to have increased at about the same rate as the consumer price index, at least to a first approximation. To be sure, there may have been large capital gains or losses for a given category of assets (and nominal assets, in particular, generate capital losses, which are compensated by capital gains on real assets), which vary greatly from period to period: the relative price of capital decreased sharply in the period 1910–1950 before trending upward between 1950 and 2010. Under these conditions, the most reasonable approach is to take the view that the average returns on capital indicated in Figures 6.3 and 6.4, which I obtained by dividing the annual flow of income on capital (from rents, dividends, interest, profits, etc.) by the stock of capital, thus neglecting both capital gains and capital losses, is a good estimate of the average return on capital over the long run.[12] Of course, this does not mean that when we study the yield of a particular asset we need not add any capital gain or subtract any capital loss (and, in particular, deduct inflation in the case of a nominal asset). But it would not make much sense to deduct inflation from the return on all forms of capital without adding capital gains, which on average amply make up for the effects of inflation.

Make no mistake: I am obviously not denying that inflation can in some cases have real effects on wealth, the return on wealth, and the distribution of wealth. The effect, however, is largely one of re-

---

11. Real estate assets alone account for roughly half of total assets, and among financial assets, real assets generally account for more than half of the total and often more than three-quarters. See the online technical appendix.

12. As I explained in Chapter 5, however, this approach includes in the return of capital the structural capital gain due to capitalization of retained earnings as reflected in the stock price, which is an important component of the return on stocks over the long run.

distributing wealth among asset categories rather than a long-term structural effect. For example, I showed earlier that inflation played a central role in virtually wiping out the value of public debt in the rich countries in the wake of the two world wars. But when inflation remains high for a considerable period of time, investors will try to protect themselves by investing in real assets. There is every reason to believe that the largest fortunes are often those that are best indexed and most diversified over the long run, while smaller fortunes—typically checking or savings accounts—are the most seriously affected by inflation.

To be sure, one could argue that the transition from virtually zero inflation in the nineteenth century to 2 percent inflation in the late twentieth and early twenty-first centuries led to a slight decrease in the pure return on capital, in the sense that it is easier to be a rentier in a regime of zero inflation (where wealth accumulated in the past runs no risk of being whittled away by rising prices), whereas today's investor must spend more time reallocating her wealth among different asset categories in order to achieve the best investment strategy. Again, however, there is no certainty that the largest fortunes are the ones most affected by inflation or that relying on inflation to reduce the influence of wealth accumulated in the past is the best way of attaining that goal. I will come back to this key question in the next Part Three, when I turn to the way the effective returns obtained by different investors vary with size of fortune, and in Part Four, when I compare the various institutions and policies that may influence the distribution of wealth, including primarily taxes and inflation. At this stage, let me note simply that inflation primarily plays a role—sometimes desirable, sometimes not—in redistributing wealth among those who have it. In any case, the potential impact of inflation on the average return on capital is fairly limited and much smaller than the apparent nominal effect.[13]

---

13. In other words, an increase of inflation from 0 to 2 percent in a society where the return on capital is initially 4 percent is certainly not equivalent to a 50 percent

What Is Capital Used For?

Using the best available historical data, I have shown how the return on capital evolved over time. I will now try to explain the changes observed. How is the rate of return on capital determined in a particular society at a particular point in time? What are the main social and economic forces at work, why do these forces change over time, and what can we predict about how the rate of return on capital will evolve in the twenty-first century?

According to the simplest economic models, assuming "pure and perfect" competition in both capital and labor markets, the rate of return on capital should be exactly equal to the "marginal productivity" of capital (that is, the additional output due to one additional unit of capital). In more complex models, which are also more realistic, the rate of return on capital also depends on the relative bargaining power of the various parties involved. Depending on the situation, it may be higher or lower than the marginal productivity of capital (especially since this quantity is not always precisely measurable).

In any case, the rate of return on capital is determined by the following two forces: first, technology (what is capital used for?), and second, the abundance of the capital stock (too much capital kills the return on capital).

Technology naturally plays a key role. If capital is of no use as a factor of production, then by definition its marginal productivity is zero. In the abstract, one can easily imagine a society in which capital is of no use in the production process: no investment can increase the productivity of farmland, no tool or machine can increase output, and having a roof over one's head adds nothing to well-being compared with sleeping outdoors. Yet capital might still play an important role

---

tax on income from capital, for the simple reason that the price of real estate and stocks will begin to increase at 2 percent a year, so that only a small proportion of the assets owned by households—broadly speaking, cash deposits and some nominal assets—will pay the inflation tax. I will return to this question in Chapter 12.

in such a society as a pure store of value: for example, people might choose to accumulate piles of food (assuming that conditions allow for such storage) in anticipation of a possible future famine or perhaps for purely aesthetic reasons (adding piles of jewels and other ornaments to the food piles, perhaps). In the abstract, nothing prevents us from imagining a society in which the capital / income ratio β is quite high but the return on capital r is strictly zero. In that case, the share of capital in national income, $\alpha = r \times \beta$, would also be zero. In such a society, all of national income and output would go to labor.

Nothing prevents us from imagining such a society, but in all known human societies, including the most primitive, things have been arranged differently. In all civilizations, capital fulfills two economic functions: first, it provides housing (more precisely, capital produces "housing services," whose value is measured by the equivalent rental value of dwellings, defined as the increment of well-being due to sleeping and living under a roof rather than outside), and second, it serves as a factor of production in producing other goods and services (in processes of production that may require land, tools, buildings, offices, machinery, infrastructure, patents, etc.). Historically, the earliest forms of capital accumulation involved both tools and improvements to land (fencing, irrigation, drainage, etc.) and rudimentary dwellings (caves, tents, huts, etc.). Increasingly sophisticated forms of industrial and business capital came later, as did constantly improved forms of housing.

The Notion of Marginal Productivity of Capital

Concretely, the marginal productivity of capital is defined by the value of the additional production due to one additional unit of capital. Suppose, for example, that in a certain agricultural society, a person with the equivalent of 100 euros' worth of additional land or tools (given the prevailing price of land and tools) can increase food production by the equivalent of 5 euros per year (all other things being equal, in particular the quantity of labor utilized). We then say that the marginal productivity of capital is 5 euros for an investment of 100 euros, or 5 percent a year. Under conditions of pure and perfect competition, this is the annual rate of return that the owner of the capital (land or tools) should obtain from the agricultural laborer. If the owner seeks to obtain more than 5 percent, the laborer will rent land and tools from another capitalist. And if the laborer wants to pay less than 5 percent, then the land and tools will go to another laborer. Obviously, there can be situations in which the landlord is in a monopoly position when it comes to renting land and tools or purchasing labor (in the latter case one speaks of "monopsony" rather than monopoly), in which case the owner of capital can impose a rate of return greater than the marginal productivity of his capital.

In a more complex economy, where there are many more diverse uses of capital—one can invest 100 euros not only in farming but also in housing or in an industrial or service firm—the marginal productivity of capital may be difficult to determine. In theory, this is the function of the system of financial intermediation (banks and financial markets): to find the best possible uses for capital, such that each available unit of capital is invested where it is most productive (at the opposite ends of the earth, if need be) and pays the highest possible return to the investor. A capital market is said to be "perfect" if it enables each unit of capital to be invested in the most productive way possible and to earn the maximal marginal product the economy allows, if possible as part of a perfectly diversified investment portfolio in order to earn the average return risk-free while at the same time minimizing intermediation costs.

In practice, financial institutions and stock markets are generally a long way from achieving this ideal of perfection. They are often sources of chronic instability, waves of speculation, and bubbles. To be sure, it is not a simple task to find the best possible use for each unit of capital around the world, or even within the borders of a single country. What is more, "short-termism" and "creative accounting" are sometimes the shortest path to maximizing the immediate private return on capital. Whatever institutional imperfections may exist, however, it is clear that systems of financial intermediation have played a central and irreplaceable role in the history of economic development. The process has always involved a very large number of actors, not just banks and formal financial markets: for example, in the eighteenth and nineteenth centuries, notaries played a central role in bringing investors together with entrepreneurs in need of financing, such as Père Goriot with his pasta factories and César Birotteau with his desire to invest in real estate.[14]

It is important to state clearly that the notion of marginal productivity of capital is defined independently of the institutions and rules—or absence of rules—that define the capital-labor split in a given society. For example, if an owner of land and tools exploits his own capital, he probably does not account separately for the return on the capital that he invests in himself. Yet this capital is nevertheless useful, and his marginal productivity is the same as if the return were paid to an outside investor. The same is true if the economic system chooses to collectivize all or part of the capital stock, and in extreme cases (the Soviet Union, for example) to eliminate all private return on capital. In that case, the private return is less than the "social" return on capital, but the latter is still defined as the marginal productivity of an additional unit of capital. Is it useful and just for the owners of capital to receive this marginal product as payment for their ownership of property (whether their own past savings or that of their ancestors) even if they contribute no new work? This is clearly a crucial question, but not the one I am asking here.

Too Much Capital Kills the Return on Capital

Too much capital kills the return on capital: whatever the rules and institutions that structure the capital-labor split may be, it is natural

---

14. See P. Hoffman, Gilles Postel-Vinay, and Jean-Laurent Rosenthal, *Priceless Markets: The Political Economy of Credit in Paris 1660–1870* (Chicago: University of Chicago Press, 2000).

to expect that the marginal productivity of capital decreases as the stock of capital increases. For example, if each agricultural worker already has thousands of hectares to farm, it is likely that the extra yield of an additional hectare of land will be limited. Similarly, if a country has already built a huge number of new dwellings, so that every resident enjoys hundreds of square feet of living space, then the increase to well-being of one additional building—as measured by the additional rent an individual would be prepared to pay in order to live in that building—would no doubt be very small. The same is true for machinery and equipment of any kind: marginal productivity decreases with quantity beyond a certain threshold. (Although it is possible that some minimum number of tools are needed to begin production, saturation is eventually reached.) Conversely, in a country where an enormous population must share a limited supply of land, scarce housing, and a small supply of tools, then the marginal product of an additional unit of capital will naturally be quite high, and the fortunate owners of that capital will not fail to take advantage of this.

The interesting question is therefore not whether the marginal productivity of capital decreases when the stock of capital increases (this is obvious) but rather how fast it decreases. In particular, the central question is how much the return on capital r decreases (assuming that it is equal to the marginal productivity of capital) when the capital / income ratio β increases. Two cases are possible. If the return on capital r falls more than proportionately when the capital / income ratio β increases (for example, if r decreases by more than half when β is doubled), then the share of capital income in national income $\alpha = r \times \beta$ decreases when β increases. In other words, the decrease in the return on capital more than compensates for the increase in the capital / income ratio. Conversely, if the return r falls less than proportionately when β increases (for example, if r decreases by less than half when β is doubled), then capital's share $\alpha = r \times \beta$ increases when β increases. In that case, the effect of the decreased return on capital is simply to cushion and moderate the increase in the capital share compared to the increase in the capital / income ratio.

Based on historical evolutions observed in Britain and France, the second case seems more relevant over the long run: the capital share of income, α, follows the same U-shaped curve as the capital/income ratio, β (with a high level in the eighteenth and nineteenth centuries, a drop in the middle of the twentieth century, and a rebound in the late twentieth and early twenty-first centuries). The evolution of the rate of return on capital, r, significantly reduces the amplitude of this U-curve, however: the return on capital was particularly high after World War II, when capital was scarce, in keeping with the principle of decreasing marginal productivity. But this effect was not strong enough to invert the U-curve of the capital / income ratio, β, and transform it into an inverted U-curve for the capital share α.

It is nevertheless important to emphasize that both cases are theoretically possible. Everything depends on the vagaries of technology, or more precisely, everything depends on the range of technologies available to combine capital and labor to produce the various types of goods and services that society wants to consume. In thinking about these questions, economists often use the concept of a "production function," which is a mathematical formula reflecting the technological possibilities that exist in a given society. One characteristic of a production function is that it defines an elasticity of substitution between capital and labor: that is, it measures how easy it is to substitute capital for labor, or labor for capital, to produce required goods and services.

For example, if the coefficients of the production function are completely fixed, then the elasticity of substitution is zero: it takes exactly one hectare and one tool per agricultural worker (or one machine per industrial worker), neither more nor less. If each worker has as little as 1/100 hectare too much or one tool too many, the marginal productivity of the additional capital will be zero. Similarly, if the number of workers is one too many for the available capital stock, the extra worker cannot be put to work in any productive way.

Conversely, if the elasticity of substitution is infinite, the marginal productivity of capital (and labor) is totally independent of the available quantity of capital and labor. In particular, the return on capital is fixed and does not depend on the quantity of capital: it is always possible to accumulate more capital and increase production by a fixed percentage, for example, 5 or 10 percent a year per unit of additional capital. Think of an entirely robotized economy in which one can increase production at will simply by adding more capital.

Neither of these two extreme cases is really relevant: the first sins by want of imagination and the second by excess of technological optimism (or pessimism about the human race, depending on one's point of view). The relevant question is whether the elasticity of substitution between labor and capital is greater or less than one. If the elasticity lies between zero and one, then an increase in the capital / income ratio β leads to a decrease in the marginal productivity of capital large enough that the capital share $\alpha = r \times \beta$ decreases (assuming that the return on capital is determined by its marginal productivity).[15] If the elasticity is greater than one, an increase in the capital / income ratio β leads instead to a drop in the marginal productivity of capital, so that the capital share $\alpha = r \times \beta$ increases (again assuming that the return on capital is equal to marginal productivity).[16] If the elasticity is exactly equal to one, then the two effects cancel each other out: the return on capital decreases in exactly the same proportion as the capital / income ratio β increases, so that the product $\alpha = r \times \beta$ does not change.

Beyond Cobb-Douglas: The Question of the Stability of the Capital-Labor Split

The case of an elasticity of substitution exactly equal to one corresponds to the so-called Cobb-Douglas production function, named for the economists Charles Cobb and Paul Douglas, who first proposed it in 1928. With a Cobb-Douglas production function, no matter what hap-

---

15. In the extreme case of zero elasticity, the return on capital and therefore the capital share of income fall to zero if there is even a slight excess of capital.

16. In the extreme case of infinite elasticity, the return on capital does not change, so that the capital share of income increases in the same proportion as the capital / income ratio.

pens, and in particular no matter what quantities of capital and labor are available, the capital share of income is always equal to the fixed coefficient α, which can be taken as a purely technological parameter.[17]

For example, if α = 30 percent, then no matter what the capital / income ratio is, income from capital will account for 30 percent of national income (and income from labor for 70 percent). If the savings rate and growth rate are such that the long-term capital / income ratio $\beta = s/g$ corresponds to six years of national income, then the rate of return on capital will be 5 percent, so that the capital share of income will be 30 percent. If the long-term capital stock is only three years of national income, then the return on capital will rise to 10 percent. And if the savings and growth rates are such that the capital stock represents ten years of national income, then the return on capital will fall to 3 percent. In all cases, the capital share of income will be 30 percent.

The Cobb-Douglas production function became very popular in economics textbooks after World War II (after being popularized by Paul Samuelson), in part for good reasons but also in part for bad ones, including simplicity (economists like simple stories, even when they are only approximately correct), but above all because the stability of the capital-labor split gives a fairly peaceful and harmonious view of the social order. In fact, the stability of capital's share of income—assuming it turns out to be true—in no way guarantees harmony: it is compatible with extreme and untenable inequality of the ownership of capital and distribution of income. Contrary to a widespread idea, moreover, stability of capital's share of national income in no way implies stability of the capital / income ratio, which can easily

---

17. It can be shown that the Cobb-Douglas production function takes the mathematical form $Y = F(K, L) = K^{\alpha} L^{1-\alpha}$, where Y is output, K is capital, and L is labor. There are other mathematical forms to represent the cases where the elasticity of substitution is greater than one or less than one. The case of infinite elasticity corresponds to a linear production function: output is given $Y = F(K, L) = rK + vL$ (so that the return on capital r does not depend on the quantities of capital and labor involved, nor does the return on labor v, which is just the wage rate, also fixed in this example). See the online technical appendix.

take on very different values at different times and in different countries, so that, in particular, there can be substantial international imbalances in the ownership of capital.

The point I want to emphasize, however, is that historical reality is more complex than the idea of a completely stable capital-labor split suggests. The Cobb-Douglas hypothesis is sometimes a good approximation for certain subperiods or sectors and, in any case, is a useful point of departure for further reflection. But this hypothesis does not satisfactorily explain the diversity of the historical patterns we observe over the long, short, or medium run, as the data I have collected show.

Furthermore, there is nothing really surprising about this, given that economists had very little historical data to go on when Cobb and Douglas first proposed their hypothesis. In their original article, published in 1928, these two American economists used data about US manufacturing in the period 1899–1922, which did indeed show a certain stability in the share of income going to profits.[18] This idea appears to have been first introduced by the British economist Arthur Bowley, who in 1920 published an important book on the distribution of British national income in the period 1880–1913 whose primary conclusion was that the capital-labor split remained relatively stable during this period.[19] Clearly, however, the periods analyzed by these authors were relatively short: in particular, they did not try to compare their results with estimates from the early nineteenth century (much less the eighteenth).

As noted, moreover, these questions aroused very strong political tensions in the late nineteenth and early twentieth centuries, as well as throughout the Cold War, that were not conducive to a calm consideration of the facts. Both conservative and liberal economists were

18. See Charles Cobb and Paul Douglas, "A Theory of Production," *American Economic Review* 18, no. 1 (March 1928): 139–65.

19. According to Bowley's calculations, capital's share of national income throughout the period was about 37 percent and labor's share about 63 percent. See Arthur Bowley, *The Change in the Distribution of National Income, 1880–1913* (Oxford: Clarendon Press, 1920). These estimates are consistent with my findings for this period. See the online technical appendix.

keen to show that growth benefited everyone and thus were very attached to the idea that the capital-labor split was perfectly stable, even if believing this sometimes meant neglecting data or periods that suggested an increase in the share of income going to capital. By the same token, Marxist economists liked to show that capital's share was always increasing while wages stagnated, even if believing this sometimes required twisting the data. In 1899, Eduard Bernstein, who had the temerity to argue that wages were increasing and the working class had much to gain from collaborating with the existing regime (he was even prepared to become vice president of the Reichstag), was roundly outvoted at the congress of the German Social Democratic Party in Hanover. In 1937, the young German historian and economist Jürgen Kuczynski, who later became a well-known professor of economic history at Humboldt University in East Berlin and who in 1960–1972 published a monumental thirty-eight-volume universal history of wages, attacked Bowley and other bourgeois economists. Kuczynski argued that labor's share of national income had decreased steadily from the advent of industrial capitalism until the 1930s. This was true for the first half—indeed, the first two-thirds—of the nineteenth century but wrong for the entire period.[20] In the years that followed, controversy raged in the pages of academic journals. In 1939, in *Economic History Review,* where calmer debates where the norm, Frederick Brown unequivocally backed Bowley, whom he characterized as a "great scholar" and "serious statistician," whereas Kuczynski in his view was nothing more than a "manipulator," a charge

---

20. See Jürgen Kuczynski, *Labour Conditions in Western Europe 1820 to 1935* (London: Lawrence and Wishart, 1937). That same year, Bowley extended his work from 1920: see Arthur Bowley, *Wages and Income in the United Kingdom since 1860* (Cambridge: Cambridge University Press, 193). See also Jürgen Kuczynski, *Geschichte der Lage der Arbeiter unter dem Kapitalismus,* 38 vols. (Berlin, 1960–72). Volumes 32, 33, and 34 are devoted to France. For a critical analysis of Kuczynski's series, which remain a valuable historical source despite their lacunae, see Thomas Piketty, *Les hauts revenus en France au 20e siècle: Inégalités et redistribution 1901–1998* (Paris: Grasset, 2001), 677–681. See the online technical appendix for additional references.

that was wide of the mark.[21] Also in 1939, Keynes took the side of the bourgeois economists, calling the stability of the capital-labor split "one of the best-established regularities in all of economic science." This assertion was hasty to say the least, since Keynes was essentially relying on data from British manufacturing industry in the 1920s, which were insufficient to establish a universal regularity.[22]

In textbooks published in the period 1950–1970 (and indeed as late as 1990), a stable capital-labor split is generally presented as an uncontroversial fact, but unfortunately the period to which this supposed law applies is not always clearly specified. Most authors are content to use data going back no further than 1950, avoiding comparison with the interwar period or the early twentieth century, much less with the eighteenth and nineteenth centuries. From the 1990s on, however, numerous studies mention a significant increase in the share of national income in the rich countries going to profits and capital after 1970, along with the concomitant decrease in the share going to wages and labor. The universal stability thesis thus began to be questioned, and in the 2000s several official reports published by the Organisation for Economic Cooperation and Development (OECD) and International Monetary Fund (IMF) took note of the phenomenon (a sign that the question was being taken seriously).[23]

The novelty of this study is that it is to my knowledge the first attempt to place the question of the capital-labor split and the recent increase of capital's share of national income in a broader historical context by focusing on the evolution of the capital / income ratio from

---

21. See Frederick Brown, "Labour and Wages," *Economic History Review* 9, no. 2 (May 1939): 215–17.

22. See J. M. Keynes, "Relative Movement of Wages and Output," *Economic Journal* 49 (1939): 48. It is interesting to note that in those days the proponents of a stable capital-labor split were still unsure about the supposedly stable level of this split. In this instance Keynes insisted on the fact that the share of income going to "manual labor" (a category difficult to define over the long run) seemed stable at 40 percent of national income between 1920 and 1930.

23. See the online technical appendix for a complete bibliography.

the eighteenth century until now. The exercise admittedly has its limits, in view of the imperfections of the available historical sources, but I believe that it gives us a better view of the major issues and puts the question in a whole new light.

Capital-Labor Substitution in the Twenty-First Century: An Elasticity Greater Than One

I begin by examining the inadequacy of the Cobb-Douglas model for studying evolutions over the very long run. Over a very long period of time, the elasticity of substitution between capital and labor seems to have been greater than one: an increase in the capital / income ratio β seems to have led to a slight increase in α, capital's share of national income, and vice versa. Intuitively, this corresponds to a situation in which there are many different uses for capital in the long run. Indeed, the observed historical evolutions suggest that it is always possible—up to a certain point, at least—to find new and useful things to do with capital: for example, new ways of building and equipping houses (think of solar panels on rooftops or digital lighting controls), ever more sophisticated robots and other electronic devices, and medical technologies requiring larger and larger capital investments. One need not imagine a fully robotized economy in which capital would reproduce itself (corresponding to an infinite elasticity of substitution) to appreciate the many uses of capital in a diversified advanced economy in which the elasticity of substitution is greater than one.

It is obviously quite difficult to predict how much greater than one the elasticity of substitution of capital for labor will be in the twenty-first century. On the basis of historical data, one can estimate an elasticity between 1.3 and 1.6.[24] But not only is this estimate uncertain and imprecise. More than that, there is no reason why the technologies of the future should exhibit the same elasticity as those of the past. The only thing that appears to be relatively well established is that the

---

24. See the online technical appendix.

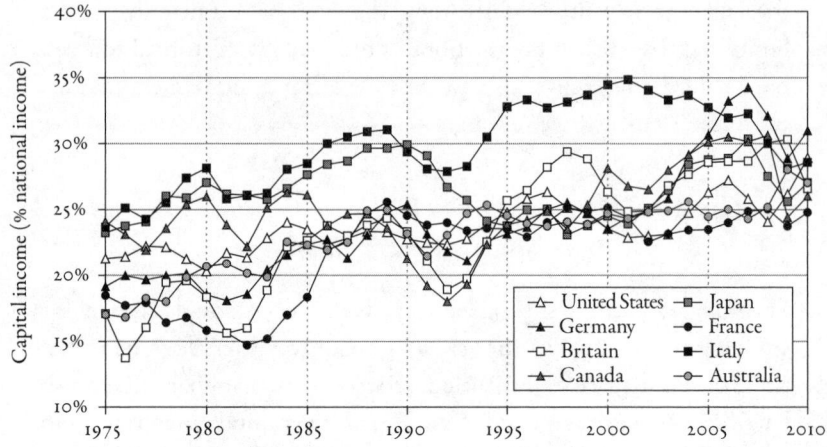

FIGURE 6.5. The capital share in rich countries, 1975–2010

Capital income absorbs between 15 percent and 25 percent of national income in rich countries in 1970, and between 25 percent and 30 percent in 2000–2010.

Sources and series: see piketty.pse.ens.fr/capital21c.

tendency for the capital / income ratio β to rise, as has been observed in the rich countries in recent decades and might spread to other countries around the world if growth (and especially demographic growth) slows in the twenty-first century, may well be accompanied by a durable increase in capital's share of national income, α. To be sure, it is likely that the return on capital, r, will decrease as β increases. But on the basis of historical experience, the most likely outcome is that the volume effect will outweigh the price effect, which means that the accumulation effect will outweigh the decrease in the return on capital.

Indeed, the available data indicate that capital's share of income increased in most rich countries between 1970 and 2010 to the extent that the capital / income ratio increased (see Figure 6.5). Note, however, that this upward trend is consistent not only with an elasticity of substitution greater than one but also with an increase in capital's bargaining power vis-à-vis labor over the past few decades, which have seen increased mobility of capital and heightened competition between states eager to attract investments. It is likely that the two effects have reinforced each other in recent years, and it is also possible that this will continue to be the case in the future. In any event, it is important to point out that no self-corrective mechanism exists to prevent a steady increase of the capital / income ratio, β, together with a steady rise in capital's share of national income, α.

Traditional Agricultural Societies: An Elasticity Less Than One

I have just shown that an important characteristic of contemporary economies is the existence of many opportunities to substitute capital for labor. It is interesting that this was not at all the case in traditional economies based on agriculture, where capital existed mainly in the form of land. The available historical data suggest very clearly that the elasticity of substitution was significantly less than one in traditional agricultural societies. In particular, this is the only way to explain why, in the eighteenth and nineteenth centuries, the value of land in the United States, as measured by the capital / income ratio and land rents, was much lower than in Europe, even though land was much more plentiful in the New World.

This is perfectly logical, moreover: if capital is to serve as a ready substitute for labor, then it must exist in different forms. For any given form of capital (such as farmland in the case in point), it is inevitable that beyond a certain point, the price effect will outweigh the volume effect. If a few hundred individuals have an entire continent at their disposal, then it stands to reason that the price of land and land rents will fall to near-zero levels. There is no better illustration of the maxim "Too much capital kills the return on capital" than the relative value of land and land rents in the New World and the Old.

Is Human Capital Illusory?

The time has come to turn to a very important question: Has the apparently growing importance of human capital over the course of history been an illusion? Let me rephrase the question in more precise terms. Many people believe that what characterizes the process of development and economic growth is the increased importance of human labor, skill, and know-how in the production process. Although this hypothesis is not always formulated in explicit terms, one reasonable interpretation would be that technology has changed in such a way that the labor factor now plays a greater role.[25] Indeed, it seems plausible to interpret in this way the decrease in capital's share of income over the very long run, from 35–40 percent in 1800–1810 to 25–30 percent in 2000–2010, with a corresponding increase in labor's share from 60–65 percent to 70–75 percent. Labor's share increased simply because labor became more important in the production process. Thus it was the growing power of human capital that made it possible to decrease the share of income going to land, buildings, and financial capital.

If this interpretation is correct, then the transformation to which it points was indeed quite significant. Caution is in order, however. For one thing, as noted earlier, we do not have sufficient perspective at this point in history to reach an adequate judgment about the very long-run evolution of capital's share of income. It is quite possible that capital's share will increase in coming decades to the level it reached at the beginning of the nineteenth century. This may happen even if the structural form of technology—and the relative importance of capital and labor—does not change (although the relative bargaining power of labor and capital may change) or if technology changes only slightly (which seems to me the more plausible alternative) yet the increase in the capital / income ratio drives capital's share of income toward or perhaps beyond historic peaks because the long-run elasticity of substitution of capital for labor is apparently greater than one. This is

---

25. This might take the form of an increase in the exponent $1 - \alpha$ in the Cobb-Douglas production function (and a corresponding decrease in α) or similar modifications to the more general production functions in which elasticities of substitution are greater or smaller than one. See the online technical appendix.

perhaps the most important lesson of this study thus far: modern technology still uses a great deal of capital, and even more important, because capital has many uses, one can accumulate enormous amounts of it without reducing its return to zero. Under these conditions, there is no reason why capital's share must decrease over the very long run, even if technology changes in a way that is relatively favorable to labor.

A second reason for caution is the following. The probable long-run decrease in capital's share of national income from 35–40 percent to 25–30 percent is, I think, quite plausible and surely significant but does not amount to a change of civilization. Clearly, skill levels have increased markedly over the past two centuries. But the stock of industrial, financial, and real estate capital has also increased enormously. Some people think that capital has lost its importance and that we have magically gone from a civilization based on capital, inheritance, and kinship to one based on human capital and talent. Fat-cat stockholders have supposedly been replaced by talented managers thanks solely to changes in technology. I will come back to this question in Part Three when I turn to the study of individual inequalities in the distribution of income and wealth: a correct answer at this stage is impossible. But I have already shown enough to warn against such mindless optimism: capital has not disappeared for the simple reason that it is still useful—hardly less useful than in the era of Balzac and Austen, perhaps—and may well remain so in the future.

Medium-Term Changes in the Capital-Labor Split

I have just shown that the Cobb-Douglas hypothesis of a completely stable capital-labor split cannot give a totally satisfactory explanation of the long-term evolution of the capital-labor split. The same can be said, perhaps even more strongly, about short- and medium-term evolutions, which can in some cases extend over fairly long periods, particularly as seen by contemporary witnesses to these changes.

The most important case, which I discussed briefly in the Introduction, is no doubt the increase in capital's share of income during the early phases of the Industrial Revolution, from 1800 to 1860. In Britain, for which we have the most complete data, the available historical studies, in particular those of Robert Allen (who gave the name "Engels' pause" to the long stagnation of wages), suggest that capital's share increased by something like 10 percent of national income, from 35–40 percent in the late eighteenth and early nineteenth centuries to around 45–50 percent in the middle of the nineteenth century, when Marx wrote *The Communist Manifesto* and set to work on *Capital*. The sources also suggest that this increase was roughly compensated by a comparable decrease in capital's share in the period 1870–1900, followed by a slight increase between 1900 and 1910, so that in the end the capital share was probably not very different around the turn of the twentieth century from what it was during the French Revolution and Napoleonic era (see Figure 6.1). We can therefore speak of a "medium-term" movement rather than a durable long-term trend. Nevertheless, this transfer of 10 percent of national income to capital during the first half of the nineteenth century was by no means negligible: to put it in concrete terms, the lion's share of economic growth in this period went to profits, while wages—objectively miserable—stagnated. According to Allen, the main explanation for this was the exodus of labor from the countryside and into the cities, together with technological changes that increased the productivity of capital (reflected by a structural change in the production function)—the caprices of technology, in short.[26]

Available historical data for France suggest a similar chronology. In particular, all the sources indicate a serious stagnation of wages in the period 1810–1850 despite robust industrial growth. The data collected by Jean Bouvier and François Furet from the books of leading French industrial firms confirm this chronology: the share of profits increased until 1860, then decreased from 1870 to 1900, and rose again between 1900 and 1910.[27]

---

26. See the online technical appendix.

27. See Jean Bouvier, François Furet, and M. Gillet, *Le mouvement du profit en France au 19e siècle: Matériaux et études* (Paris: Mouton, 1965).

The data we have for the eighteenth century and the period of the French Revolution also suggest an increase in the share of income going to land rent in the decades preceding the revolution (which seems consistent with Arthur Young's observations about the misery of French peasants),[28] and substantial wage increases between 1789 and 1815 (which can conceivably be explained by the redistribution of land and the mobilization of labor to meet the needs of military conflict).[29] When the lower classes of the Restoration and July Monarchy looked back on the revolutionary period and the Napoleonic era, they accordingly remembered good times.

To remind ourselves that these short- and medium-term changes in the capital-labor split occur at many different times, I have shown the annual evolution in France from 1900 to 2010 in Figures 6.6–8, in which I distinguish the evolution of the wage-profit split in value added by firms from the evolution of the share of rent in national income.[30] Note, in particular, that the wage-profit split has gone through three distinct phases since World War II, with a sharp rise in profits from 1945 to 1968 followed by a very pronounced drop in the share of profits from 1968 to 1983 and then a very rapid rise after 1983 leading

---

28. See François Simiand, *Le salaire, l'évolution sociale et la monnaie* (Paris: Alcan, 1932); Ernest Labrousse, *Esquisse du mouvement des prix et des revenus en France au 18e siècle* (Paris: Librairie Dalloz, 1933). The historical series assembled by Jeffrey Williamson and his colleagues on the long-term evolution of land rents and wages also suggest an increase in the share of national income going to land rent in the eighteenth and early nineteenth centuries. See the online technical appendix.

29. See A. Chabert, *Essai sur les mouvements des prix et des revenus en France de 1798 à 1820*, 2 vols. (Paris: Librairie de Médicis, 1945–49). See also Gilles Postel-Vinay, "A la recherche de la révolution économique dans les campagnes (1789–1815)," *Revue économique*, 1989.

30. A firm's "value added" is defined as the difference between what it earns by selling goods and services (called "sales revenue" in English) and what it pays other firms for its purchases (called "intermediate consumption"). As the name indicates, this sum measures the value the firm adds in the process of production. Wages are paid out of value added, and what is left over is by definition the firm's profit. The study of the capital-labor split is too often limited to the wage-profit split, which neglects rent.

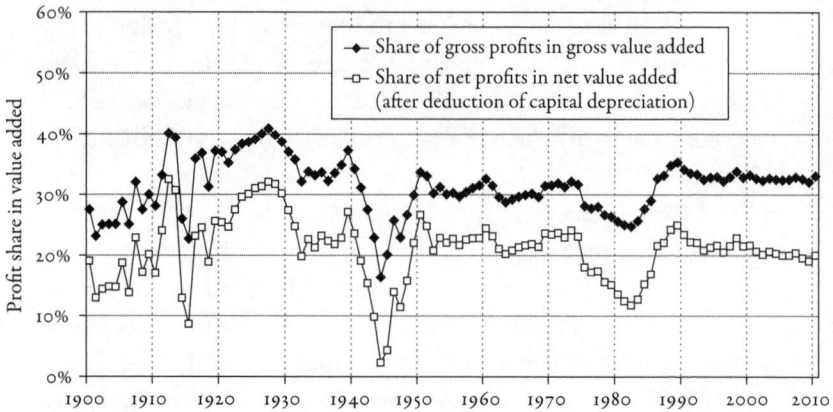

FIGURE 6.6. The profit share in the value added of corporations in France, 1900–2010

The share of gross profits in gross value added of corporations rose from 25 percent in 1982 to 33 percent in 2010; the share of net profits in net value added rose from 12 percent to 20 percent.

Sources and series: see piketty.pse.ens.fr/capital21c.

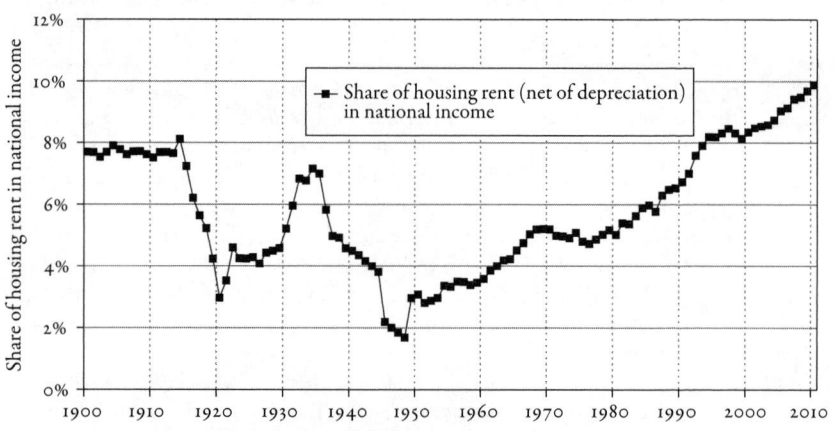

FIGURE 6.7. The share of housing rent in national income in France, 1900–2010

The share of housing rent (rental value of dwellings) rose from 2 percent of national income in 1948 to 10 percent in 2010.

Sources and series: see piketty.pse.ens.fr/capital21c.

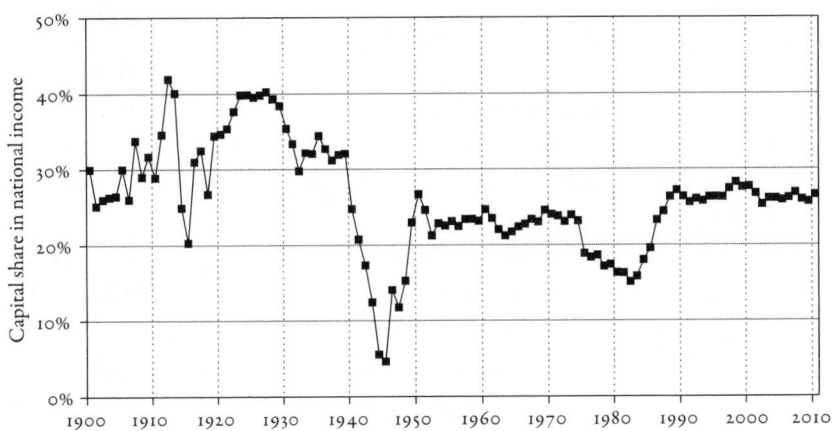

FIGURE 6.8. The capital share in national income in France, 1900–2010
The share of capital income (net profits and rents) rose from 15 percent of national income in 1982 to 27 percent in 2010.
Sources and series: see piketty.pse.ens.fr/capital21c.

to stabilization in the early 1990s. I will have more to say about this highly political chronology in subsequent chapters, where I will discuss the dynamics of income inequality. Note the steady rise of the share of national income going to rent since 1945, which implies that the share going to capital overall continued to increase between 1990 and 2010, despite the stabilization of the profit share.

Back to Marx and the Falling Rate of Profit

As I come to the end of this examination of the historical dynamics of the capital / income ratio and the capital-labor split, it is worth pointing out the relation between my conclusions and the theses of Karl Marx.

For Marx, the central mechanism by which "the bourgeoisie digs its own grave" corresponded to what I referred to in the Introduction as "the principle of infinite accumulation": capitalists accumulate ever increasing quantities of capital, which ultimately leads inexorably to a falling rate of profit (i.e., return on capital) and eventually to their own downfall. Marx did not use mathematical models, and his prose was not always limpid, so it is difficult to be sure what he had in mind. But one logically consistent way of interpreting his thought is to consider the dynamic law $\beta = s/g$ in the special case where the growth rate g is zero or very close to zero.

Recall that g measures the long-term structural growth rate, which is the sum of productivity growth and population growth. In Marx's mind, as in the minds of all nineteenth- and early twentieth-century economists before Robert Solow did his work on growth in the 1950s, the very idea of structural growth, driven by permanent and durable growth of productivity, was not clearly identified or formulated.[31] In those days, the implicit hypothesis was that growth of production, and especially of manufacturing output, was explained mainly by the accumulation of industrial capital. In other words, output increased solely because every worker was backed by more machinery and equipment and not because productivity as such (for a given quantity of labor and capital) increased. Today we know that long-term structural growth is possible only because of productivity growth. But this was not obvious in Marx's time, owing to lack of historical perspective and good data.

Where there is no structural growth, and the productivity and population growth rate g is zero, we run up against a logical contradiction very close to what Marx described. If the savings rate s is positive, meaning the capitalists insist on accumulating more and more capital every year in order to increase their power and perpetuate their advantages or simply because their standard of living is already so high, then the capital / income ratio will increase indefinitely. More generally, if g is close to zero, the long-term capital / income ratio $\beta = s/g$ tends toward

---

31. The notion of permanent and durable population growth was no clearer, and the truth is that it remains as confused and frightening today as it ever was, which is why the hypothesis of stabilization of the global population is generally accepted. See Chapter 2.

infinity. And if β is extremely large, then the return on capital r must get smaller and smaller and closer and closer to zero, or else capital's share of income, $\alpha = r \times \beta$, will ultimately devour all of national income.[32] The dynamic inconsistency that Marx pointed out thus corresponds to a real difficulty, from which the only logical exit is structural growth, which is the only way of balancing the process of capital accumulation (to a certain extent). Only permanent growth of productivity and population can compensate for the permanent addition of new units of capital, as the law $\beta = s/g$ makes clear. Otherwise, capitalists do indeed dig their own grave: either they tear each other apart in a desperate attempt to combat the falling rate of profit (for instance, by waging war over the best colonial investments, as Germany and France did in the Moroccan crises of 1905 and 1911), or they force labor to accept a smaller and smaller share of national income, which ultimately leads to a proletarian revolution and general expropriation. In any event, capital is undermined by its internal contradictions.

That Marx actually had a model of this kind in mind (i.e., a model based on infinite accumulation of capital) is confirmed by his use on several occasions of the account books of industrial firms with very high capital intensities. In volume 1 of *Capital,* for instance, he uses the books of a textile factory, which were conveyed to him, he says, "by the owner," and seem to show an extremely high ratio of the total amount of fixed and variable capital used in the production process to the value of a year's output—apparently greater than ten. A capital / income ratio of this level is indeed rather frightening. If the rate of return on capital is 5 percent, then more than half the value of the firm's output goes to profits. It was natural for Marx and many other anxious contemporary observers to ask where all this might lead (especially because wages had been stagnant since the beginning of the nineteenth

---

32. The only case in which the return on capital does not tend toward zero is in a "robotized" economy with an infinite elasticity of substitution between capital and labor, so that production ultimately uses capital alone. See the online technical appendix.

century) and what type of long-run socioeconomic equilibrium such hyper-capital-intensive industrial development would produce.

Marx was also an assiduous reader of British parliamentary reports from the period 1820–1860. He used these reports to document the misery of wage workers, workplace accidents, deplorable health conditions, and more generally the rapacity of the owners of industrial capital. He also used statistics derived from taxes imposed on profits from different sources, which showed a very rapid increase of industrial profits in Britain during the 1840s. Marx even tried—in a very impressionistic fashion, to be sure—to make use of probate statistics in order to show that the largest British fortunes had increased dramatically since the Napoleonic wars.[33]

The problem is that despite these important intuitions, Marx usually adopted a fairly anecdotal and unsystematic approach to the available statistics. In particular, he did not try to find out whether the very high capital intensity that he observed in the account books of certain factories was representative of the British economy as a whole or even of some particular sector of the economy, as he might have done by collecting just a few dozen similar accounts. The most surprising thing, given that his book was devoted largely to the question of capital accumulation, is that he makes no reference to the numerous attempts to estimate the British capital stock that had been carried out since the beginning of the eighteenth century and extended in the nineteenth century by work beginning with Patrick Colqhoun between 1800 and 1810 and continuing through Giffen in the 1870s.[34] Marx seems to have missed entirely the work on national accounting that

---

33. The most interesting tax data are presented in appendix 10 of book 1 of *Capital*. See the online technical appendix for an analysis of some of the calculations of profit shares and rates of exploitation based on the account books presented by Marx. In *Wages, Price, and Profit* (1865) Marx also used the accounts of a highly capitalistic factory in which profits attained 50 percent of value added (as large a proportion as wages). Although he does not say so explicitly, this seems to be the type of overall split he had in mind for an industrial economy.

34. See Chapter 1.

was developing around him, and this is all the more unfortunate in that it would have enabled him to some extent to confirm his intuitions concerning the vast accumulation of private capital in this period and above all to clarify his explanatory model.

Beyond the "Two Cambridges"

It is important to recognize, however, that the national accounts and other statistical data available in the late nineteenth and early twentieth centuries were wholly inadequate for a correct understanding of the dynamics of the capital / income ratio. In particular, there were many more estimates of the stock of national capital than of national income or domestic product. By the mid-twentieth century, following the shocks of 1914–1945, the reverse was true. This no doubt explains why the question of capital accumulation and a possible dynamic equilibrium continued to stir controversy and arouse a good deal of confusion for so long. A good example of this is the famous "Cambridge capital controversy" of the 1950s and 1960s (also called the "Two Cambridges Debate" because it pitted Cambridge, England, against Cambridge, Massachusetts).

To briefly recall the main points of this debate: when the formula $\beta = s/g$ was explicitly introduced for the first time by the economists Roy Harrod and Evsey Domar in the late 1930s, it was common to invert it as $g = s / \beta$. Harrod, in particular, argued in 1939 that β was fixed by the available technology (as in the case of a production function with fixed coefficients and no possible substitution between labor and capital), so that the growth rate was entirely determined by the savings rate. If the savings rate is 10 percent and technology imposes a capital / income ratio of 5 (so that it takes exactly five units of capital, neither more nor less, to produce one unit of output), then the growth rate of the economy's productive capacity is 2 percent per year. But since the growth rate must also be equal to the growth rate of the population (and of productivity, which at the time was still ill defined), it follows that growth is an intrinsically unstable process, balanced "on a razor's edge." There is always either too much or too little capital, which therefore gives rise either to excess capacity and speculative bubbles or else to unemployment, or perhaps both at once, depending on the sector and the year.

Harrod's intuition was not entirely wrong, and he was writing in the midst of the Great Depression, an obvious sign of great macroeconomic instability. Indeed, the mechanism he described surely helps to explain why the growth process is always highly volatile: to bring savings into line with investment at the national level, when savings and investment decisions are generally made by different individuals for different reasons, is a structurally complex and chaotic phenomenon, especially since it is often difficult in the short run to alter the capital intensity and organization of production.[35] Nevertheless, the capital / income ratio is relatively flexible in the long run, as is unambiguously demonstrated by the very large historical variations that are observed in the data, together with the fact that the elasticity of substitution of capital for labor has apparently been greater than one over a long period of time.

In 1948, Domar developed a more optimistic and flexible version of the law $g = s / \beta$ than Harrod's. Domar stressed the fact that the savings rate and capital / income ratio can to a certain extent adjust to each other. Even more important was Solow's introduction in 1956 of a production function with substitutable factors, which made it possible to invert the formula and write $\beta = s/g$. In the long run, the capital / income ratio adjusts to the savings rate and structural growth rate of the economy rather than the other way around. Controversy continued, however, in the 1950s and 1960s between economists based primarily in Cambridge, Massachusetts (including Solow and Samuelson, who defended the production function with substitutable factors) and economists working in Cambridge, England (including Joan Robinson, Nicholas Kaldor, and Luigi Pasinetti), who (not without a certain confusion at times) saw in Solow's model a claim

---

35. Some recent theoretical models attempt to make this intuition explicit. See the online technical appendix.

that growth is always perfectly balanced, thus negating the importance Keynes had attributed to short-term fluctuations. It was not until the 1970s that Solow's so-called neoclassical growth model definitively carried the day.

If one rereads the exchanges in this controversy with the benefit of hindsight, it is clear that the debate, which at times had a marked postcolonial dimension (as American economists sought to emancipate themselves from the historic tutelage of their British counterparts, who had reigned over the profession since the time of Adam Smith, while the British sought to defend the memory of Lord Keynes, which they thought the American economists had betrayed), did more to cloud economic thinking than to enlighten it. There was no real justification for the suspicions of the British. Solow and Samuelson were fully convinced that the growth process is unstable in the short term and that macroeconomic stabilization requires Keynesian policies, and they viewed $\beta = s/g$ solely as a long-term law. Nevertheless, the American economists, some of whom (for example Franco Modigliani) were born in Europe, tended at times to exaggerate the implications of the "balanced growth path" they had discovered.[36] To be sure, the law $\beta = s/g$ describes a growth path in which all macroeconomic quantities—capital stock, income and output flows—progress at the same pace over the long run. Still, apart from the question of short-term volatility, such balanced growth does not guarantee a harmonious distribution of wealth and in no way implies the disappearance or even reduction of inequality in the ownership of capital. Furthermore, contrary to an idea that until recently was widespread, the law $\beta = s/g$ in no way precludes very large variations in the capital/income ratio over time and between countries. Quite the contrary. In my view, the virulence—and at times sterility—of the

---

36. To say nothing of the fact that some of the US economists (starting with Modigliani) argued that capital had totally changed its nature (so that it now stemmed from accumulation over the life cycle), while the British (starting with Kaldor) continued to see wealth in terms of inheritance, which was significantly less reassuring. I return to this crucial question in Part Three.

Cambridge capital controversy was due in part to the fact that participants on both sides lacked the historical data needed to clarify the terms of the debate. It is striking to see how little use either side made of national capital estimates done prior to World War I; they probably believed them to be incompatible with the realities of the 1950s and 1960s. The two world wars created such a deep discontinuity in both conceptual and statistical analysis that for a while it seemed impossible to study the issue in a long-run perspective, especially from a European point of view.

Capital's Comeback in a Low-Growth Regime

The truth is that only since the end of the twentieth century have we had the statistical data and above all the indispensable historical distance to correctly analyze the long-run dynamics of the capital / income ratio and the capital-labor split. Specifically, the data I have assembled and the historical distance we are fortunate enough to enjoy (still insufficient, to be sure, but by definition greater than that which previous authors had) lead to the following conclusions.

First, the return to a historic regime of low growth, and in particular zero or even negative demographic growth, leads logically to the return of capital. This tendency for low-growth societies to reconstitute very large stocks of capital is expressed by the law $\beta = s/g$ and can be summarized as follows: in stagnant societies, wealth accumulated in the past naturally takes on considerable importance.

In Europe today, the capital / income ratio has already risen to around five to six years of national income, scarcely less than the level observed in the eighteenth and nineteenth centuries and up to the eve of World War I.

At the global level, it is entirely possible that the capital / income ratio will attain or even surpass this level during the twenty-first century. If the savings rate is now around 10 percent and the growth rate stabilizes at around 1.5 percent in the very long run, then the global stock of capital will logically rise to six or seven years of income. And if growth falls to 1 percent, the capital stock could rise as high as ten years of income.

As for capital's share in national and global income, which is given by the law $\alpha = r \times \beta$, experience suggests that the predictable rise in the capital / income ratio will not necessarily lead to a significant drop in the return on capital. There are many uses for capital over the very long run, and this fact can be captured by noting that the long-run elasticity of substitution of capital for labor is probably greater than one. The most likely outcome is thus that the decrease in the rate of return will be smaller than the increase in the capital / income ratio, so that capital's share will increase. With a capital / income ratio of seven to eight years and a rate of return on capital of 4–5 percent, capital's share of global income could amount to 30 or 40 percent, a level close to that observed in the eighteenth and nineteenth centuries, and it might rise even higher.

As noted, it is also possible that technological changes over the very long run will slightly favor human labor over capital, thus lowering the return on capital and the capital share. But the size of this long-term effect seems limited, and it is possible that it will be more than compensated by other forces tending in the opposite direction, such as the creation of increasingly sophisticated systems of financial intermediation and international competition for capital.

The Caprices of Technology

The principal lesson of this second part of the book is surely that there is no natural force that inevitably reduces the importance of capital and of income flowing from ownership of capital over the course of history. In the decades after World War II, people began to think that the triumph of human capital over capital in the traditional sense (land, buildings, and financial capital) was a natural and irreversible process, due perhaps to technology and to purely economic forces. In fact, however, some people were already saying that political forces were central. My results fully confirm this view. Progress toward economic and technological rationality need not imply progress toward democratic and meritocratic rationality. The primary reason for this is simple: technology, like the market, has neither limits nor morality. The evolution of technology has certainly increased the need for human skills and competence. But it has also increased the need for buildings, homes, offices, equipment of all kinds, patents, and so on, so that in the end the total value of all these forms of nonhuman capital (real estate, business capital, industrial capital, financial capital) has increased almost as rapidly as total income from labor. If one truly wishes to found a more just and rational social order based on common utility, it is not enough to count on the caprices of technology.

To sum up: modern growth, which is based on the growth of productivity and the diffusion of knowledge, has made it possible to avoid the apocalypse predicted by Marx and to balance the process of capital accumulation. But it has not altered the deep structures of capital—or at any rate has not truly reduced the macroeconomic importance of capital relative to labor. I must now examine whether the same is true for inequality in the distribution of income and wealth. How much has the structure of inequality with respect to both labor and capital actually changed since the nineteenth century?

PART THREE

THE STRUCTURE OF INEQUALITY

SEVEN

Inequality and Concentration: Preliminary Bearings

In Part Two I examined the dynamics of both the capital / income ratio at the country level and the overall split of national income between capital and labor, but I did not look directly at income or wealth inequality at the individual level. In particular, I analyzed the importance of the shocks of 1914–1945 in order to understand changes in the capital / income ratio and the capital-labor split over the course of the twentieth century. The fact that Europe—and to some extent the entire world—have only just gotten over these shocks has given rise to the impression that patrimonial capitalism—which is flourishing in these early years of the twenty-first century—is something new, whereas it is in large part a repetition of the past and characteristic of a low-growth environment like the nineteenth century.

Here begins my examination of inequality and distribution at the individual level. In the next few chapters, I will show that the two world wars, and the public policies that followed from them, played a central role in reducing inequalities in the twentieth century. There was nothing natural or spontaneous about this process, in contrast to the optimistic predictions of Kuznets's theory. I will also show that inequality began to rise sharply again since the 1970s and 1980s, albeit with significant variation between countries, again suggesting that institutional and political differences played a key role. I will also analyze, from both a historical and a theoretical point of view, the evolution of the relative importance of inherited wealth versus income from labor over the very long run. Many people believe that modern growth naturally favors labor over inheritance and competence over birth. What is the source of this widespread belief, and how sure can we be that it is correct? Finally, in Chapter 12, I will consider how the global distribution of wealth might evolve in the decades to come. Will the twenty-first century be even more inegalitarian than the nineteenth, if it is not already so? In what respects is the structure of inequality in the world today really different from that which existed during the Industrial Revolution or in traditional rural societies? Part Two has already suggested some interesting leads to follow in this regard, but the only way to answer this crucial question is by analyzing the structure of inequality at the individual level.

Before proceeding farther, in this chapter I must first introduce certain ideas and orders of magnitude. I begin by noting that in all societies, income inequality can be decomposed into three terms: inequality in income from labor; inequality in the ownership of capital and the income to which it gives rise; and the interaction between these two terms. Vautrin's famous lesson to Rastignac in Balzac's *Père Goriot* is perhaps the clearest introduction to these issues.

Vautrin's Lesson

Balzac's *Père Goriot,* published in 1835, could not be clearer. Père Goriot, a former spaghetti maker, has made a fortune in pasta and grain during the Revolution and Napoleonic era. A widower, he sacrifices everything he has to find husbands for his daughters Delphine and Anastasie in the best Parisian society of the 1810s. He keeps just enough to pay his room and board in a shabby boardinghouse, where he meets Eugène de Rastignac, a penniless young noble who has come up from the provinces to study law in Paris. Full of ambition and humiliated by his poverty, Eugène avails himself of the help of a distant cousin to worm his way into the luxurious salons where the aristocracy, *grande bourgeoisie,* and high finance of the Restoration mingle. He quickly falls in love with Delphine, who has been abandoned by her husband, Baron de Nucingen, a banker who has already used his wife's dowry in any number of speculative ventures. Rastignac soon sheds his illusions as he discovers the cynicism of a society entirely corrupted by money. He is appalled to learn how Père Goriot has been abandoned by his daughters, who, preoccupied as they are with social success, are ashamed of their father and have seen little of him since availing themselves of his fortune. The old man dies in sordid poverty and solitude. Only Rastignac attends his burial. But no sooner has he left Père Lachaise cemetery than he is overwhelmed by the sight of Parisian wealth on display along the Seine and decides to set out in conquest of the capital: "It's just you and me now!" he apostrophizes the city. His sentimental and social education is over. From this point on he, too, will be ruthless.

The darkest moment in the novel, when the social and moral dilemmas Rastignac faces are rawest and clearest, comes at the midpoint, when the shady character Vautrin offers him a lesson about his future prospects.[1] Vautrin, who resides in the same shabby boardinghouse as Rastignac and Goriot, is a glib talker and seducer who is concealing a dark past as a convict, much like Edmond Dantès in *Le Comte de Monte-Cristo* or Jean Valjean in *Les Misérables*. In contrast to those two characters, who are on the whole worthy fellows, Vautrin is deeply wicked and cynical. He attempts to lure Rastignac into committing a murder in order to lay hands on a large legacy. Before that, Vautrin offers Rastignac an extremely lurid, detailed lesson about the different fates that might befall a young man in the French society of the day.

In substance, Vautrin explains to Rastignac that it is illusory to think that social success can be achieved through study, talent, and effort. He paints a detailed portrait of the various possible careers that await his young friend if he pursues studies in law or medicine, fields in which professional competence counts more than inherited wealth. In particular, Vautrin explains very clearly to Rastignac what yearly income he can aspire to in each of these professions. The verdict is clear: even if he ranks at the top of his class and quickly achieves a brilliant career in law, which will require many compromises, he will still

---

1. Honoré de Balzac, *Le père Goriot* (Paris: Livre de Poche, 1983), 123–35.

have to get by on a mediocre income and give up all hope of becoming truly wealthy:

> By the age of thirty, you will be a judge making 1,200 francs a year, if you haven't yet tossed away your robes. When you reach forty, you will marry a miller's daughter with an income of around 6,000 livres. Thank you very much. If you're lucky enough to find a patron, you will become a royal prosecutor at thirty, with compensation of a thousand écus [5,000 francs], and you will marry the mayor's daughter. If you're willing to do a little political dirty work, you will be a prosecutor-general by the time you're forty.... It is my privilege to point out to you, however, that there are only twenty prosecutors-general in France, while 20,000 of you aspire to the position, and among them are a few clowns who would sell their families to move up a rung. If this profession disgusts you, consider another. Would Baron de Rastignac like to be a lawyer? Very well then! You will need to suffer ten years of misery, spend a thousand francs a month, acquire a library and an office, frequent society, kiss the hem of a clerk to get cases, and lick the courthouse floor with your tongue. If the profession led anywhere, I wouldn't advise you against it. But can you name five lawyers in Paris who earn more than 50,000 francs a year at the age of fifty?[2]

By contrast, the strategy for social success that Vautrin proposes to Rastignac is quite a bit more efficient. By marrying Mademoiselle Victorine, a shy young woman who lives in the boardinghouse and has eyes only for the handsome Eugène, he will immediately lay hands on a fortune of a million francs. This will enable him to draw at age

---

2. See Balzac, *Le père Goriot*, 131. To measure income and wealth, Balzac usually used francs or livres tournois (which became equivalent once the franc "germinal" was in place) as well as écus (an écu was a silver coin worth 5 francs in the nineteenth century), and more rarely louis d'or (a louis was a gold coin worth 20 francs, which was already worth 20 livres under the Ancien Régime). Because inflation was nonexistent at the time, all these units were so stable that readers could move easily from one to another. See Chapter 2. I discuss the amounts mentioned by Balzac in greater detail in Chapter 11.

twenty an annual income of 50,000 francs (5 percent of the capital) and thus immediately achieve ten times the level of comfort to which he could hope to aspire only years later on a royal prosecutor's salary (and as much as the most prosperous Parisian lawyers of the day earned at age fifty after years of effort and intrigue).

The conclusion is clear: he must lose no time in marrying young Victorine, ignoring the fact that she is neither very pretty nor very appealing. Eugène eagerly heeds Vautrin's lesson right up to the ultimate coup de grâce: if the illegitimate child Victorine is to be recognized by her wealthy father and become the heiress of the million francs Vautrin has mentioned, her brother must first be killed. The ex-convict is ready to take on this task in exchange for a commission. This is too much for Rastignac: although he is quite amenable to Vautrin's arguments concerning the merits of inheritance over study, he is not prepared to commit murder.

The Key Question: Work or Inheritance?

What is most frightening about Vautrin's lecture is that his brisk portrait of Restoration society contains such precise figures. As I will soon show, the structure of the income and wealth hierarchies in nineteenth-century France was such that the standard of living the wealthiest French people could attain greatly exceeded that to which one could aspire on the basis of income from labor alone. Under such conditions, why work? And why behave morally at all? Since social inequality was in itself immoral and unjustified, why not be thoroughly immoral and appropriate capital by whatever means are available?

The detailed income figures Vautrin gives are unimportant (although quite realistic): the key fact is that in nineteenth-century France and, for that matter, into the early twentieth century, work and study alone were not enough to achieve the same level of comfort afforded by inherited wealth and the income derived from it. This was so obvious to everyone that Balzac needed no statistics to prove it, no detailed figures concerning the deciles and centiles of the income hierarchy.

Conditions were similar, moreover, in eighteenth- and nineteenth-century Britain. For Jane Austen's heroes, the question of work did not arise: all that mattered was the size of one's fortune, whether acquired through inheritance or marriage. Indeed, the same was true almost everywhere before World War I, which marked the suicide of the patrimonial societies of the past. One of the few exceptions to this rule was the United States, or at any rate the various "pioneer" microsocieties in the northern and western states, where inherited capital had little influence in the eighteenth and nineteenth centuries—a situation that did not last long, however. In the southern states, where capital in the form of slaves and land predominated, inherited wealth mattered as much as it did in old Europe. In *Gone with the Wind*, Scarlett O'Hara's suitors cannot count on their studies or talents to assure their future comfort any more than Rastignac can: the size of one's father's (or father-in-law's) plantation matters far more. Vautrin, to show how little he thinks of morality, merit, or social justice, points out to young Eugène that he would be glad to end his days as a slave owner in the US South, living in opulence on what his Negroes produced.[3] Clearly, the America that appeals to the French ex-convict is not the America that appealed to Tocqueville.

To be sure, income from labor is not always equitably distributed, and it would be unfair to reduce the question of social justice to the importance of income from labor versus income from inherited wealth. Nevertheless, democratic modernity is founded on the belief that inequalities based on individual talent and effort are more justified than other inequalities—or at any rate we hope to be moving in that direction. Indeed, Vautrin's lesson to some extent ceased to be valid in twentieth-century Europe, at least for a time. During the decades that followed World War II, inherited wealth lost much of its importance, and for the first time in history, perhaps, work and study became the surest routes to the top. Today, even though all sorts of inequalities have reemerged, and many beliefs in social and democratic

---

3. See Balzac, *Le père Goriot*, 131.

progress have been shaken, most people still believe that the world has changed radically since Vautrin lectured Rastignac. Who today would advise a young law student to abandon his or her studies and adopt the ex-convict's strategy for social advancement? To be sure, there may exist rare cases where a person would be well advised to set his or her sights on inheriting a large fortune.[4] In the vast majority of cases, however, it is not only more moral but also more profitable to rely on study, work, and professional success.

Vautrin's lecture focuses our attention on two questions, which I will try to answer in the next few chapters with the imperfect data at my disposal. First, can we be sure that the relative importance of income from labor versus income from inherited wealth has been transformed since the time of Vautrin, and if so, to what extent? Second, and even more important, if we assume that such a transformation has to some degree occurred, why exactly did it happen, and can it be reversed?

Inequalities with Respect to Labor and Capital

To answer these questions, I must first introduce certain basic ideas and the fundamental patterns of income and wealth inequality in different societies at different times. I showed in Part One that income can always be expressed as the sum of income from labor and income from capital. Wages are one form of income from labor, and to simplify the exposition I will sometimes speak of wage inequality when I mean inequality of income from labor more generally. To be sure, income from labor also includes income from nonwage labor, which for a long time played a crucial role and still plays a nonnegligible role today. Income from capital can also take different forms: it includes all income derived from the ownership of capital independent of any

---

4. According to the press, the son of a former president of France, while studying law in Paris, recently married the heiress of the Darty chain of appliance stores, but he surely did not meet her at the Vauquer boardinghouse.

labor and regardless of its legal classification (rents, dividends, interest, royalties, profits, capital gains, etc.).

By definition, in all societies, income inequality is the result of adding up these two components: inequality of income from labor and inequality of income from capital. The more unequally distributed each of these two components is, the greater the total inequality. In the abstract, it is perfectly possible to imagine a society in which inequality with respect to labor is high and inequality with respect to capital is low, or vice versa, as well as a society in which both components are highly unequal or highly egalitarian.

The third decisive factor is the relation between these two dimensions of inequality: to what extent do individuals with high income from labor also enjoy high income from capital? Technically speaking, this relation is a statistical correlation, and the greater the correlation, the greater the total inequality, all other things being equal. In practice, the correlation in question is often low or negative in societies in which inequality with respect to capital is so great that the owners of capital do not need to work (for example, Jane Austen's heroes usually eschew any profession). How do things stand today, and how will they stand in the future?

Note, too, that inequality of income from capital may be greater than inequality of capital itself, if individuals with large fortunes somehow manage to obtain a higher return than those with modest to middling fortunes. This mechanism can be a powerful multiplier of inequality, and this is especially true in the century that has just begun. In the simple case where the average rate of return is the same at all levels of the wealth hierarchy, then by definition the two inequalities coincide.

When analyzing the unequal distribution of income, it is essential to carefully distinguish these various aspects and components of inequality, first for normative and moral reasons (the justification of inequality is quite different for income from labor, from inherited wealth, and from differential returns on capital), and second, because the economic, social, and political mechanisms capable of explaining the observed evolutions are totally distinct. In the case of unequal incomes from labor, these mechanisms include the supply of and demand for different skills, the state of the educational system, and the various rules and institutions that affect the operation of the labor market and the determination of wages. In the case of unequal incomes from capital, the most important processes involve savings and investment behavior, laws governing gift-giving and inheritance, and the operation of real estate and financial markets. The statistical measures of income inequality that one finds in the writings of economists as well as in public debate are all too often synthetic indices, such as the Gini coefficient, which mix very different things, such as inequality with respect to labor and capital, so that it is impossible to distinguish clearly among the multiple dimensions of inequality and the various mechanisms at work. By contrast, I will try to distinguish these things as precisely as possible.

Capital: Always More Unequally Distributed Than Labor

The first regularity we observe when we try to measure income inequality in practice is that inequality with respect to capital is always greater than inequality with respect to labor. The distribution of capital ownership (and of income from capital) is always more concentrated than the distribution of income from labor.

Two points need to be clarified at once. First, we find this regularity in all countries in all periods for which data are available, without exception, and the magnitude of the phenomenon is always quite striking. To give a preliminary idea of the order of magnitude in question, the upper 10 percent of the labor income distribution generally receives 25–30 percent of total labor income, whereas the top 10 percent of the capital income distribution always owns more than 50 percent of all wealth (and in some societies as much as 90 percent). Even more strikingly, perhaps, the bottom 50 percent of the wage distribution always receives a significant share of total labor income (generally between one-quarter and one-third, or approximately as much as the top 10 percent), whereas the bottom 50 percent of the wealth distribution owns nothing at all, or almost nothing (always less than 10 percent and generally less than 5 percent of total wealth, or one-tenth as much as the wealthiest 10 percent). Inequalities with respect to labor usually seem mild, moderate, and almost reasonable (to the extent that inequality can be reasonable—this point should not be overstated). In comparison, inequalities with respect to capital are always extreme.

Second, this regularity is by no means foreordained, and its existence tells us something important about the nature of the economic and social processes that shape the dynamics of capital accumulation and the distribution of wealth.

Indeed, it is not difficult to think of mechanisms that would lead to a distribution of wealth more egalitarian than the distribution of income from labor. For example, suppose that at a given point in time, labor incomes reflect not only permanent wage inequalities among different groups of workers (based on the skill level and hierarchical position of each group) but also short-term shocks (for instance: wages and working hours in different sectors might fluctuate considerably from year to year or over the course of an individual's career). Labor incomes would then be highly unequal in the short run, although this inequality would diminish if measured over a long period (say ten years rather than one, or even over the lifetime of an individual, although this is rarely done because of the lack of long-term data). A longer-term perspective would be ideal for studying the true inequalities of opportunity and status that are the subject of Vautrin's lecture but are unfortunately often quite difficult to measure.

In a world with large short-term wage fluctuations, the main reason for accumulating wealth might be precautionary (as a reserve against a possible negative shock to income), in which case inequality of wealth would be smaller than wage inequality. For example, inequality of wealth might be of the same order of magnitude as the permanent inequality of wage income (measured over the length of an individual career) and therefore significantly lower than the instantaneous wage inequality (measured at a given point in time). All of this is logically possible but clearly not very relevant to the real world, since inequality of wealth is always and everywhere much greater than inequality of income from labor. Although precautionary saving in anticipation of short-term shocks does indeed exist in the real world, it is clearly not the primary explanation for the observed accumulation and distribution of wealth.

We can also imagine mechanisms that would imply an inequality of wealth comparable in magnitude to the inequality of income from labor. Specifically, if wealth is accumulated primarily for life-cycle reasons (saving for retirement, say), as Modigliani reasoned, then everyone would be expected to accumulate a stock of capital more or less proportional to his or her wage level in order to maintain approximately the same standard of living (or the same proportion thereof) after retirement. In that case, inequality of wealth would be a simple translation in time of inequality of income from labor and would as such have only limited importance, since the only real source of social inequality would be inequality with respect to labor.

Once again, such a mechanism is theoretically plausible, and its real-world role is of some significance, especially in aging societies. In quantitative terms, however, it is not the primary mechanism at work. Life-cycle saving cannot explain the very highly concentrated ownership of capital we observe in practice, any more than precautionary saving can. To be sure, older individuals are certainly richer on average than younger ones. But the concentration of wealth is actually nearly as great within each age cohort as it is for the population as a whole. In other words, and contrary to a widespread belief, intergenerational warfare has not replaced class warfare. The very high concentration of capital is explained mainly by the importance of inherited wealth and its cumulative effects: for example, it is easier to save if you inherit an apartment and do not have to pay rent. The fact that the return on capital often takes on extreme values also plays a significant role in this dynamic process. In the remainder of Part Three, I examine these various mechanisms in greater detail and consider how their relative importance has evolved in time and space. At this stage, I note simply that the magnitude of inequality of wealth, both in absolute terms and relative to inequality of income from labor—points toward certain mechanisms rather than others.

Inequalities and Concentration: Some Orders of Magnitude

Before analyzing the historical evolutions that can be observed in different countries, it will be useful to give a more precise account of the characteristic orders of magnitude of inequality with respect to labor and capital. The goal is to familiarize the reader with numbers and notions such as deciles, centiles, and the like, which may seem somewhat technical and even distasteful to some but are actually quite useful for analyzing and understanding changes in the structure of inequality in different societies—provided we use them correctly.

To that end, I have charted in Tables 7.1–3 the distributions actually observed in various countries at various times. The figures indicated are approximate and deliberately rounded off but at least give us a preliminary idea of what the terms "low," "medium," and "high" inequality mean today and have meant in the past, with respect to both income from labor and ownership of capital, and finally with respect to total income (the sum of income from labor and income from capital).

For example, with respect to inequality of income from labor, we find that in the most egalitarian societies, such as the Scandinavian countries in the 1970s and 1980s (inequalities have increased in northern Europe since then, but these countries nevertheless remain the least inegalitarian), the distribution is roughly as follows. Looking at the entire adult population, we see that the 10 percent receiving the highest incomes from labor claim a little more than 20 percent of the total income from labor (and in practice this means essentially wages); the least well paid 50 percent get about 35 percent of the total; and the 40 percent in the middle therefore receive roughly 45 percent of the total (see Table 7.1).[5] This is not perfect equality, for in that case each group

---

5. I define deciles in terms of the adult population (minors generally earn no income) and, insofar as possible, at the individual level. The estimates in Tables

TABLE 7.1.

Inequality of labor income across time and space

Share of different groups in total labor income	Low inequality (≈ Scandinavia, 1970s–1980s)	Medium inequality (≈ Europe 2010)	High inequality (≈ US 2010)	Very high inequality (≈ US 2030?)
The top 10% ("upper class")	20%	25%	35%	45%
Including the top 1% ("dominant class")	5%	7%	12%	17%
Including the next 9% ("well-to-do class")	15%	18%	23%	28%
The middle 40% ("middle class")	45%	45%	40%	35%
The bottom 50% ("lower class")	35%	30%	25%	20%
Corresponding Gini coefficient (synthetic inequality index)	0.19	0.26	0.36	0.46

Note: In societies where labor income inequality is relatively low (such as in Scandinavian countries in the 1970s–1980s), the top 10% most well paid receive about 20% of total labor income; the bottom 50% least well paid about 35%; the middle 40% about 45%. The corresponding Gini index (a synthetic inequality index with values from 0 to 1) is equal to 0.19. See the online technical appendix.

TABLE 7.2.

Inequality of capital ownership across time and space

Share of different groups in total capital	Low inequality (never observed; ideal society?)	Medium inequality (≈ Scandinavia, 1970s–1980s)	Medium–high inequality (≈ Europe 2010)	High inequality (≈ US 2010)	Very high inequality (≈ Europe 1910)
The top 10% "upper class"	30%	50%	60%	70%	90%
Including the top 1% ("dominant class")	10%	20%	25%	35%	50%
Including the next 9% ("well-to-do class")	20%	30%	35%	35%	40%
The middle 40% ("middle class")	45%	40%	35%	25%	5%
The bottom 50% ("lower class")	25%	10%	5%	5%	5%
Corresponding Gini coefficient (synthetic inequality index)	0.33	0.58	0.67	0.73	0.85

Note: In societies with "medium" inequality of capital ownership (such as Scandinavian countries in the 1970s–1980s), the top 10% richest in wealth own about 50% of aggregate wealth; the bottom 50% poorest about 10%; and the middle 40% about 40%. The corresponding Gini coefficient is equal to 0.58. See the online technical appendix.

TABLE 7.3.

Inequality of total income (labor and capital) across time and space

Share of different groups in total income (labor + capital)	Low inequality (≈ Scandinavia, 1970s–1980s)	Medium inequality (≈ Europe 2010)	High inequality (≈ US 2010, Europe 1910)	Very high inequality (≈ US 2030?)
The top 10% ("upper class")	25%	35%	50%	60%
Including the top 1% ("dominant class")	7%	10%	20%	25%
Including the next 9% ("well-to-do class")	18%	25%	30%	35%
The middle 40% ("middle class")	45%	40%	30%	25%
The bottom 50% ("lower class")	30%	25%	20%	15%
Corresponding Gini coefficient (synthetic inequality index)	0.26	0.36	0.49	0.58

Note: In societies where the inequality of total income is relatively low (such as Scandinavian countries during the 1970s–1980s), the 10% highest incomes receive about 20% of total income; the 50% lowest incomes receive about 30%. The corresponding Gini coefficient is equal to 0.26. See the online technical appendix.

should receive the equivalent of its share of the population (the best paid 10 percent should get exactly 10 percent of the income, and the worst paid 50 percent should get 50 percent). But the inequality we see here is not too extreme, at least in comparison to what we observe in other countries or at other times, and it is not too extreme especially when compared with what we find almost everywhere for the ownership of capital, even in the Scandinavian countries.

In order to have a clear idea of what these figures really mean, we need to relate distributions expressed as percentages of total income to the paychecks that flesh-and-blood workers actually receive as well as to the fortunes in real estate and financial assets owned by the people who actually make up these wealth hierarchies.

Concretely, if the best paid 10 percent receive 20 percent of total wages, then it follows mathematically that each person in this group earns on average twice the average pay in the country in question. Similarly, if the least well paid 50 percent receive 35 percent of total wages, it follows that each person in this group earns on average 70 percent of the average wage. And if the middle 40 percent receive 45 percent of the total wage, this means that the average wage of this group is slightly higher than the average pay for society as a whole (45/40 of the average, to be precise).

For example, if the average pay in a country is 2,000 euros per month, then this distribution implies that the top 10 percent earn 4,000 euros a month on average, the bottom 50 percent 1,400 euros a month, and the middle 40 percent 2,250 a month.[6] This intermediate group may be regarded as a vast "middle class" whose standard of living is determined by the average wage of the society in question.

7.1–3 are based on this definition. For some countries, such as France and the United States, the historical data on income are available only at the household level (so that the incomes of both partners in a couple are added). This slightly modifies the shares of the various deciles but has little effect on the long-term evolutions that are of interest here. For wages, the historical data are generally available at the individual level. See the online technical appendix.

6. See the online technical appendix and Supplemental Table S7.1, available online.

Lower, Middle, and Upper Classes

To be clear, the designations "lower class" (defined as the bottom 50 percent), "middle class" (the middle 40 percent), and "upper class" (top 10 percent) that I use in Tables 7.1–3 are quite obviously arbitrary and open to challenge. I introduce these terms purely for illustrative purposes, to pin down my ideas, but in fact they play virtually no role in the analysis, and I might just as well have called them "Class A," "Class B," and "Class C." In political debate, however, such terminological issues are generally far from innocent. The way the population is divided up usually reflects an implicit or explicit position concerning the justice and legitimacy of the amount of income or wealth claimed by a particular group.

For example, some people use the term "middle class" very broadly to encompass individuals who clearly fall within the upper decile (that is, the top 10 percent) of the social hierarchy and who may even be quite close to the upper centile (the top 1 percent). Generally, the purpose of such a broad definition of the middle class is to insist that even though such individuals dispose of resources considerably above the average for the society in question, they nevertheless retain a certain proximity to the average: in other words, the point is to say that such individuals are not privileged and fully deserve the indulgence of the government, particularly in regard to taxes.

Other commentators reject any notion of "middle class" and prefer to describe the social structure as consisting of just two groups: "the people," who constitute the vast majority, and a tiny "elite" or "upper class." Such a description may be accurate for some societies, or it may be applicable to certain political or historical contexts. For example, in France in 1789, it is generally estimated that the aristocracy represented 1–2 percent of the population, the clergy less than 1 percent, and the "Third Estate," meaning (under the political system of the Ancien Régime) all the rest, from peasantry to bourgeoisie, more than 97 percent.

It is not my purpose to police dictionaries or linguistic usage. When it comes to designating social groups, everyone is right and wrong at the same time. Everyone has good reasons for using certain terms but is wrong to denigrate the terms used by others. My definition of "middle class" (as the "middle" 40 percent) is highly contestable, since the income (or wealth) of everyone in the group is, by construction, above the median for the society in question.[7] One might equally well choose to divide society into three thirds and call the middle third the "middle class." Still, the definition I have given seems to me to correspond more closely to common usage: the expression "middle class" is generally used to refer to people who are doing distinctly better than the bulk of the population yet still a long way from the true "elite." Yet all such designations are open to challenge, and there is no need for me to take a position on this delicate issue, which is not just linguistic but also political.

The truth is that any representation of inequality that relies on a small number of categories is doomed to be crudely schematic, since the underlying social reality is always a continuous distribution. At any given level of wealth or income there is always a certain number of flesh-and-blood individuals, and the number of such individuals varies slowly and gradually in accordance with the shape of the distribution in the society in question. There is never a discontinuous break between social classes or between "people" and "elite." For that reason, my analysis is based entirely on statistical concepts such as deciles (top 10 percent, middle 40 percent, lower 50 percent, etc.), which are defined in exactly the same way in different societies. This allows me to make rigorous and objective comparisons across time and space

---

7. The median is the level below which half the population lies. In practice, the median is always lower than the mean, or average, because real-world distributions always have long upper tails, which raises the mean but not the median. For incomes from labor, the median is typically around 80 percent of the mean (e.g., if the average wage is 2,000 euros a month, the median is around 1,600 euros). For wealth, the median can be extremely low, often less than 50 percent of mean wealth, or even zero if the poorer half of the population owns almost nothing.

without denying the intrinsic complexity of each particular society or the fundamentally continuous structure of social inequality.

Class Struggle or Centile Struggle?

My fundamental goal is to compare the structure of inequality in societies remote from one another in time and space, societies that are very different a priori, and in particular societies that use totally different words and concepts to refer to the social groups that compose them. The concepts of deciles and centiles are rather abstract and undoubtedly lack a certain poetry. It is easier for most people to identify with groups with which they are familiar: peasants or nobles, proletarians or bourgeois, office workers or top managers, waiters or traders. But the beauty of deciles and centiles is precisely that they enable us to compare inequalities that would otherwise be incomparable, using a common language that should in principle be acceptable to everyone.

When necessary, we will break down our groups even more finely, using centiles or even thousandths to register more precisely the continuous character of social inequality. Specifically, in every society, even the most egalitarian, the upper decile is truly a world unto itself. It includes some people whose income is just two or three times greater than the mean and others whose resources are ten or twenty times greater, if not more. To start with, it is always enlightening to break the top decile down into two subgroups: the upper centile (which we might call the "dominant class" for the sake of concreteness, without claiming that this term is better than any other) and the remaining nine centiles (which we might call the "wealthy class" or "well-to-do").

For example, if we look at the case where inequality of income from labor is relatively low (think Scandinavia), represented in Table 7.1, with 20 percent of wages going to the best paid 10 percent of workers, we find that the share going to the top 1 percent is typically on the order of 5 percent of total wages. This means that the top 1 percent of earners make on average five times the mean wage, or

10,000 euros per month, in a society in which the average wage is 2,000 euros per month. In other words, the best paid 10 percent earn 4,000 euros a month on average, but within that group the top 1 percent earn an average of 10,000 euros a month (and the next 9 percent earn on average 3,330 euros a month). If we break this down even further and looked at the top thousandth (the best paid 0.1 percent) in the top centile, we find individuals earning tens of thousands of euros a month and a few earning hundreds of thousands, even in the Scandinavian countries in the 1970s and 1980s. Of course there would not be many such people, so their weight in the sum total of all wages would be relatively small.

Thus to judge the inequality of a society, it is not enough to observe that some individuals earn very high incomes. For example, to say that the "income scale goes from 1 to 10" or even "1 to 100" does not actually tell us very much. We also need to know how many people earn the incomes at each level. The share of income (or wealth) going to the top decile or centile is a useful index for judging how unequal a society is, because it reflects not just the existence of extremely high incomes or extremely large fortunes but also the number of individuals who enjoy such rewards.

The top centile is a particularly interesting group to study in the context of my historical investigation. Although it constitutes (by definition) a very small minority of the population, it is nevertheless far larger than the superelites of a few dozen or hundred individuals on whom attention is sometimes focused (such as the "200 families" of France, to use the designation widely applied in the interwar years to the 200 largest stockholders of the Banque de France, or the "400 richest Americans" or similar rankings established by magazines like *Forbes*). In a country of almost 65 million people such as France in 2013, of whom some 50 million are adults, the top centile comprises some 500,000 people. In a country of 320 million like the United States, of whom 245 million are adults, the top centile consists of 2.6 million individuals. These are numerically quite large groups who inevitably stand out in society, especially when the individuals included in them tend to live in the same cities and even to congregate in the same neighborhoods. In every country the upper centile occupies a prominent place in the social landscape and not just in the income distribution.

Thus in every society, whether France in 1789 (when 1–2 percent of the population belonged to the aristocracy) or the United States in 2011 (when the Occupy Wall Street movement aimed its criticism at the richest 1 percent of the population), the top centile is a large enough group to exert a significant influence on both the social landscape and the political and economic order.

This shows why deciles and centiles are so interesting to study. How could one hope to compare inequalities in societies as different as France in 1789 and the United States in 2011 other than by carefully examining deciles and centiles and estimating the shares of national wealth and income going to each? To be sure, this procedure will not allow us to eliminate every problem or settle every question, but at least it will allow us to say something—and that is far better than not being able to say anything at all. We can therefore try to determine whether "the 1 percent" had more power under Louis XVI or under George Bush and Barack Obama.

To return for a moment to the Occupy Wall Street movement, what it shows is that the use of a common terminology, and in particular the concept of the "top centile," though it may at first glance seem somewhat abstract, can be helpful in revealing the spectacular growth of inequality and may therefore serve as a useful tool for social interpretation and criticism. Even mass social movements can avail themselves of such a tool to develop unusual mobilizing themes, such as "We are the 99 percent!" This might seem surprising at first sight, until we remember that the title of the famous pamphlet that Abbé Sieyès published in January 1789 was "What Is the Third Estate?"[8]

---

8. "What is the Third Estate? Everything. What has it been in the political order until now? Nothing. What does it want? To become something."

I should also make it clear that the hierarchies (and therefore centiles and deciles) of income are not the same as those of wealth. The top 10 percent or bottom 50 percent of the labor income distribution are not the same people who constitute the top 10 percent or bottom 50 percent of the wealth distribution. The "1 percent" who earn the most are not the same as the "1 percent" who own the most. Deciles and centiles are defined separately for income from labor, ownership of capital, and total income (from both labor and capital), with the third being a synthesis of the first two dimensions and thus defining a composite social hierarchy. It is always essential to be clear about which hierarchy one is referring to. In traditional societies, the correlation between the two dimensions was often negative (because people with large fortunes did not work and were therefore at the bottom of the labor income hierarchy). In modern societies, the correlation is generally positive but never perfect (the coefficient of correlation is always less than one). For example, many people belong to the upper class in terms of labor income but to the lower class in terms of wealth, and vice versa. Social inequality is multidimensional, just like political conflict.

Note, finally, that the income and wealth distributions described in Tables 7.1–3 and analyzed in this and subsequent chapters are in all cases "primary" distributions, meaning before taxes. Depending on whether the tax system (and the public services and transfer payments it finances) is "progressive" or "regressive" (meaning that it weighs more or less heavily on different groups depending on whether they stand high or low in the income or wealth hierarchy), the after-tax distribution may be more or less egalitarian than the before-tax distribution. I will come back to this in Part Four, along with many other questions related to redistribution. At this stage only the before-tax distribution requires consideration.[9]

---

9. As is customary, I have included replacement incomes (i.e., pensions and unemployment insurance intended to replace lost income from labor and financed by wage deductions) in primary income from labor. Had I not done

Inequalities with Respect to Labor: Moderate Inequality?

To return to the question of orders of magnitude of inequality: To what extent are inequalities of income from labor moderate, reasonable, or even no longer an issue today? It is true that inequalities with respect to labor are always much smaller than inequalities with respect to capital. It would be quite wrong, however, to neglect them, first because income from labor generally accounts for two-thirds to three-quarters of national income, and second because there are quite substantial differences between countries in the distribution of income from labor, which suggests that public policies and national differences can have major consequences for these inequalities and for the living conditions of large numbers of people.

In countries where income from labor is most equally distributed, such as the Scandinavian countries between 1970 and 1990, the top 10 percent of earners receive about 20 percent of total wages and the bottom 50 percent about 35 percent. In countries where wage inequality is average, including most European countries (such as France and Germany) today, the first group claims 25–30 percent of total wages, and the second around 30 percent. And in the most inegalitarian countries, such as the United States in the early 2010s (where, as will emerge later, income from labor is about as unequally distributed as has ever been observed anywhere), the top decile gets 35 percent of the total, whereas the bottom half gets only 25 percent. In other words, the equilibrium between the two groups is almost completely reversed. In the most egalitarian countries, the bottom 50 percent receive nearly twice as much total income as the top 10 percent (which some will say is still too little, since the former group is five

---

this, inequality of adult income from labor would be noticeably—and to some extent artificially—greater than indicated in Tables 7.1 and 7.3 (given the large number of retirees and unemployed workers whose income from labor is zero). In Part Four I will come back to the question of redistribution by way of pensions and unemployment insurance, which for the time being I treat simply as "deferred wages."

times as large as the latter), whereas in the most inegalitarian countries the bottom 50 percent receive one-third less than the top group. If the growing concentration of income from labor that has been observed in the United States over the last few decades were to continue, the bottom 50 percent could earn just half as much in total compensation as the top 10 percent by 2030 (see Table 7.1). Obviously there is no certainty that this evolution will in fact continue, but the point illustrates the fact that recent changes in the income distribution have by no means been painless.

In concrete terms, if the average wage is 2,000 euros a month, the egalitarian (Scandinavian) distribution corresponds to 4,000 euros a month for the top 10 percent of earners (and 10,000 for the top 1 percent), 2,250 a month for the 40 percent in the middle, and 1,400 a month for the bottom 50 percent, where the more inegalitarian (US) distribution corresponds to a markedly steeper hierarchy: 7,000 euros a month for the top 10 percent (and 24,000 for the top 1 percent), 2,000 for the middle 40 percent, and just 1,000 for the bottom 50 percent.

For the least-favored half of the population, the difference between the two income distributions is therefore far from negligible: if a person earns 1,400 euros a month instead of 1,000—40 percent additional income—even leaving taxes and transfers aside, the consequences for lifestyle choices, housing, vacation opportunities, and money to spend on projects, children, and so on are considerable. In most countries, moreover, women are in fact significantly overrepresented in the bottom 50 percent of earners, so that these large differences between countries reflect in part differences in the male-female wage gap, which is smaller in northern Europe than elsewhere.

The gap between the two distributions is also significant for the top-earning group: a person who all his or her life earns 7,000 euros a month rather than 4,000 (or, even better, 24,000 instead of 10,000), will not spend money on the same things and will have greater power not only over what he or she buys but also over other people: for instance, this person can hire less well paid individuals to serve his or her needs. If the trend observed in the United States were to continue, then by 2030 the top 10 percent of earners will be making 9,000 euros a month (and the top 1 percent, 34,000 euros), the middle 40 percent will earn 1,750, and the bottom 50 percent just 800 a month. The top 10 percent could therefore use a small portion of their incomes to hire many of the bottom 50 percent as domestic servants.[10]

Clearly, then, the same mean wage is compatible with very different distributions of income from labor, which can result in very disparate social and economic realities for different social groups. In some cases, these inequalities may give rise to conflict. It is therefore important to understand the economic, social, and political forces that determine the degree of labor income inequality in different societies.

Inequalities with Respect to Capital: Extreme Inequality

Although inequality with respect to income from labor is sometimes seen—incorrectly—as moderate inequality that no longer gives rise to conflict, this is largely a consequence of comparing it with the distribution of capital ownership, which is extremely inegalitarian everywhere (see Table 7.2).

In the societies where wealth is most equally distributed (once again, the Scandinavian countries in the 1970s and 1980s), the richest 10 percent own around 50 percent of national wealth or even a bit more, somewhere between 50 and 60 percent, if one properly accounts for the largest fortunes. Currently, in the early 2010s, the richest 10 percent own around 60 percent of national wealth in most European countries, and in particular in France, Germany, Britain, and Italy.

The most striking fact is no doubt that in all these societies, half of the population own virtually nothing: the poorest 50 percent

---

10. These basic calculations are detailed in Supplemental Table S7.1, available online.

invariably own less than 10 percent of national wealth, and generally less than 5 percent. In France, according to the latest available data (for 2010–2011), the richest 10 percent command 62 percent of total wealth, while the poorest 50 percent own only 4 percent. In the United States, the most recent survey by the Federal Reserve, which covers the same years, indicates that the top decile own 72 percent of America's wealth, while the bottom half claim just 2 percent. Note, however, that this source, like most surveys in which wealth is self-reported, underestimates the largest fortunes.[11] As noted, moreover, it is also important to add that we find the same concentration of wealth within each age cohort.[12]

Ultimately, inequalities of wealth in the countries that are most egalitarian in that regard (such as the Scandinavian countries in the 1970s and 1980s) appear to be considerably greater than wage inequalities in the countries that are most inegalitarian with respect to wages (such as the United States in the early 2010s: see Tables 7.1 and 7.2). To my knowledge, no society has ever existed in which ownership of capital can reasonably be described as "mildly" inegalitarian, by which I mean a distribution in which the poorest half of society would own a significant share (say, one-fifth to one-quarter) of total wealth.[13] Optimism is not forbidden, however, so I have indicated in Table 7.2 a virtual example of a possible distribution of wealth in which inequality would be "low," or at any rate lower than it is in Scandinavia (where it is "medium"), Europe ("medium-to-high"), or the United States ("high"). Of course, how one might go about establishing such an "ideal society"—assuming that such low inequality of wealth is in-

---

11. The top decile in the United States most likely owns something closer to 75 percent of all wealth.

12. See the online technical appendix.

13. It is difficult to say whether this criterion was met in the Soviet Union and other countries of the former Communist bloc, because the data are not available. In any case, the government owned most of the capital, a fact that considerably diminishes the interest of the question.

deed a desirable goal—remains to be seen (I will return to this central question in Part Four).[14]

As in the case of wage inequality, it is important to have a good grasp of exactly what these wealth figures mean. Imagine a society in which average net wealth is 200,000 euros per adult,[15] which is roughly the case today in the richest European countries.[16] As noted in Part Two, this private wealth can be divided into two roughly equal parts: real estate on the one hand and financial and business assets on the other (these include bank deposits, savings plans, portfolios of stocks and bonds, life insurance, pension funds, etc., net of debts). Of course these are average figures, and there are large variations between countries and enormous variations between individuals.

If the poorest 50 percent own 5 percent of total wealth, then by definition each member of that group owns on average the equivalent of 10 percent of the average individual wealth of society as a whole. In the example in the previous paragraph, it follows that each person among the poorest 50 percent possesses on average a net wealth of 20,000 euros. This is not nothing, but it is very little compared with the wealth of the rest of society.

Concretely, in such a society, the poorest half of the population will generally comprise a large number of people—typically a quarter of the population—with no wealth at all or perhaps a few thousand euros at most. Indeed, a nonnegligible number of people—perhaps one-twentieth to one-tenth of the population—will have slightly negative net wealth (their debts exceed their assets). Others will own small amounts of wealth up to about 60,000 or 70,000 euros or

---

14. Note that inequality remains high even in the "ideal society" described in Table 7.2. (The richest 10 percent own more capital than the poorest 50 percent, even though the latter group is 5 times larger; the average wealth of the richest 1 percent is 20 times greater than that of the poorest 50 percent.) There is nothing preventing us from aiming at more ambitious goals.

15. Or 400,000 euros on average per couple.

16. See Chapters 3–5. The exact figures are available in the online technical appendix.

perhaps a bit more. This range of situations, including the existence of a large number of people with very close to zero absolute wealth, results in an average wealth of about 20,000 euros for the poorest half of the population. Some of these people may own real estate that remains heavily indebted, while others may possess very small nest eggs. Most, however, are renters whose only wealth consists of a few thousand euros of savings in a checking or savings account. If we included durable goods such as cars, furniture, appliances, and the like in wealth, then the average wealth of the poorest 50 percent would increase to no more than 30,000 or 40,000 euros.[17]

For this half of the population, the very notions of wealth and capital are relatively abstract. For millions of people, "wealth" amounts to little more than a few weeks' wages in a checking account or low-interest savings account, a car, and a few pieces of furniture. The inescapable reality is this: wealth is so concentrated that a large segment of society is virtually unaware of its existence, so that some people imagine that it belongs to surreal or mysterious entities. That is why it is so essential to study capital and its distribution in a methodical, systematic way.

At the other end of the scale, the richest 10 percent own 60 percent of total wealth. It therefore follows that each member of this group owns on average 6 times the average wealth of the society in question. In the example, with an average wealth of 200,000 euros per adult, each of the richest 10 percent therefore owns on average the equivalent of 1.2 million euros.

The upper decile of the wealth distribution is itself extremely unequal, even more so than the upper decile of the wage distribution. When the upper decile claims about 60 percent of total wealth, as is the case in most European countries today, the share of the upper centile is generally around 25 percent and that of the next 9 percent of the population is about 35 percent. The members of the first group are therefore on average 25 times as rich as the average member of society,

---

17. On durable goods, see Chapter 5 and the online technical appendix.

while the members of the second group are barely 4 times richer. Concretely, in the example, the average wealth of the top 10 percent is 1.2 million euros each, with 5 million euros each for the top 1 percent and a little less than 800,000 each for the next 9 percent.[18]

In addition, the composition of wealth varies widely within this group. Nearly everyone in the top decile owns his or her own home, but the importance of real estate decreases sharply as one moves higher in the wealth hierarchy. In the "9 percent" group, at around 1 million euros, real estate accounts for half of total wealth and for some individuals more than three-quarters. In the top centile, by contrast, financial and business assets clearly predominate over real estate. In particular, shares of stock or partnerships constitute nearly the totality of the largest fortunes. Between 2 and 5 million euros, the share of real estate is less than one-third; above 5 million euros, it falls below 20 percent; above 10 million euros, it is less than 10 percent and wealth consists primarily of stock. Housing is the favorite investment of the middle class and moderately well-to-do, but true wealth always consists primarily of financial and business assets.

Between the poorest 50 percent (who own 5 percent of total wealth, or an average of 20,000 euros each in the example) and the richest 10 percent (who own 60 percent of total wealth, or an average of 1.2 million euros each) lies the middle 40 percent: this "middle class of wealth" owns 35 percent of total national wealth, which means that their average net wealth is fairly close to the average for society as a whole—in the example, it comes to exactly 175,000 euros per adult. Within this vast group, where individual wealth ranges from barely 100,000 euros to more than 400,000, a key role is often played by ownership of a primary residence and the way it is acquired and paid for. Sometimes, in addition to a home, there is also a substantial amount of savings. For example, a net capital of 200,000 euros may consist of a house valued at 250,000 euros, from which an outstanding mortgage balance

---

18. Exactly 35/9 × 200,000 euros, or 777,778 euros. See Supplemental Table S7.2, available online.

of 100,000 euros must be deducted, together with savings of 50,000 euros invested in a life insurance policy or retirement savings account. When the mortgage is fully paid off, net wealth in this case will rise to 300,000 euros, or even more if the savings account has grown in the meantime. This is a typical trajectory in the middle class of the wealth hierarchy, who are richer than the poorest 50 percent (who own practically nothing) but poorer than the richest 10 percent (who own much more).

A Major Innovation: The Patrimonial Middle Class

Make no mistake: the growth of a true "patrimonial (or propertied) middle class" was the principal structural transformation of the distribution of wealth in the developed countries in the twentieth century.

To go back a century in time, to the decade 1900–1910: in all the countries of Europe, the concentration of capital was then much more extreme than it is today. It is important to bear in mind the orders of magnitude indicated in Table 7.2. In this period in France, Britain, and Sweden, as well as in all other countries for which we have data, the richest 10 percent owned virtually all of the nation's wealth: the share owned by the upper decile reached 90 percent. The wealthiest 1 percent alone owned more than 50 percent of all wealth. The upper centile exceeded 60 percent in some especially inegalitarian countries, such as Britain. On the other hand, the middle 40 percent owned just over 5 percent of national wealth (between 5 and 10 percent depending on the country), which was scarcely more than the poorest 50 percent, who then as now owned less than 5 percent.

In other words, there was no middle class in the specific sense that the middle 40 percent of the wealth distribution were almost as poor as the bottom 50 percent. The vast majority of people owned virtually nothing, while the lion's share of society's assets belonged to a minority. To be sure, this was not a tiny minority: the upper decile comprised an elite far larger than the upper centile, which even so included a substantial number of people. Nevertheless, it was a minority. Of course, the distribution curve was continuous, as it is in all societies, but its slope was extremely steep in the neighborhood of the top decile and centile, so that there was an abrupt transition from the world of the poorest 90 percent (whose members had at most a few tens of thousands of euros' worth of wealth in today's currency) to that of the richest 10 percent, whose members owned the equivalent of several million euros or even tens of millions of euros.[19]

The emergence of a patrimonial middle class was an important, if fragile, historical innovation, and it would be a serious mistake to underestimate it. To be sure, it is tempting to insist on the fact that wealth is still extremely concentrated today: the upper decile own 60 percent of Europe's wealth and more than 70 percent in the United States.[20] And the poorer half of the population are as poor today as they were in the past, with barely 5 percent of total wealth in 2010, just as in 1910. Basically, all the middle class managed to get its hands on was a few crumbs: scarcely more than a third of Europe's wealth and barely a quarter in the United States. This middle group has four times as many members as the top decile yet only one-half to one-third as much wealth. It is tempting to conclude that nothing has really changed: inequalities in the ownership of capital are still extreme (see Table 7.2).

None of this is false, and it is essential to be aware of these things: the historical reduction of inequalities of wealth is less substantial than many people believe. Furthermore, there is no guarantee that the

---

19. To get a clearer idea of what this means, we can continue the arithmetic exercise described above. With an average wealth of 200,000 euros, "very high" inequality of wealth as described in Table 7.2 meant an average wealth of 20,000 euros for the poorest 50 percent, 25,000 euros for the middle 40 percent, and 1.8 million euros for the richest 10 percent (with 890,000 for the 9 percent and 10 million for the top 1 percent). See the online technical appendix and Supplemental Tables S7.1–3, available online.

20. If we look only at financial and business capital, that is, at control of firms and work-related tools, then the upper decile's share is 70–80 percent or more. Firm ownership remains a relatively abstract concept for the vast majority of the population.

limited compression of inequality that we have seen is irreversible. Nevertheless, the crumbs that the middle class has collected are important, and it would be wrong to underestimate the historical significance of the change. A person who has a fortune of 200,000 to 300,000 euros may not be rich but is a long way from being destitute, and most of these people do not like to be treated as poor. Tens of millions of individuals—40 percent of the population represents a large group, intermediate between rich and poor—individually own property worth hundreds of thousands of euros and collectively lay claim to one-quarter to one-third of national wealth: this is a change of some moment. In historical terms, it was a major transformation, which deeply altered the social landscape and the political structure of society and helped to redefine the terms of distributive conflict. It is therefore essential to understand why it occurred.

The rise of a propertied middle class was accompanied by a very sharp decrease in the wealth share of the upper centile, which fell by more than half, going from more than 50 percent in Europe at the turn of the twentieth century to around 20–25 percent at the end of that century and beginning of the next. As we will see, this partly invalidated Vautrin's lesson, in that the number of fortunes large enough to allow a person to live comfortably on annual rents decreased dramatically: an ambitious young Rastignac could no longer live better by marrying Mademoiselle Victorine than by studying law. This was historically important, because the extreme concentration of wealth in Europe around 1900 was in fact characteristic of the entire nineteenth century. All available sources agree that these orders of magnitude—90 percent of wealth for the top decile and at least 50 percent for the top centile—were also characteristic of traditional rural societies, whether in Ancien Régime France or eighteenth-century England. Such concentration of capital is in fact a necessary condition for societies based on accumulated and inherited wealth, such as those described in the novels of Austen and Balzac, to exist and prosper. Hence one of the main goals of this book is to understand the conditions under which such concentrated wealth can emerge, persist, vanish, and perhaps reappear.

Inequality of Total Income: Two Worlds

Finally, let us turn now to inequality of total income, that is, of income from both labor and capital (see Table 7.3). Unsurprisingly, the level of inequality of total income falls between inequality of income from labor and inequality of ownership of capital. Note, too, that inequality of total income is closer to inequality of income from labor than to inequality of capital, which comes as no surprise, since income from labor generally accounts for two-thirds to three-quarters of total national income. Concretely, the top decile of the income hierarchy received about 25 percent of national income in the egalitarian societies of Scandinavia in the 1970s and 1980s (it was 30 percent in Germany and France at that time and is more than 35 percent now). In more inegalitarian societies, the top decile claimed as much as 50 percent of national income (with about 20 percent going to the top centile). This was true in France and Britain during the Ancien Régime as well as the Belle Époque and is true in the United States today.

Is it possible to imagine societies in which the concentration of income is much greater? Probably not. If, for example, the top decile appropriates 90 percent of each year's output (and the top centile took 50 percent just for itself, as in the case of wealth), a revolution will likely occur, unless some peculiarly effective repressive apparatus exists to keep it from happening. When it comes to the ownership of capital, such a high degree of concentration is already a source of powerful political tensions, which are often difficult to reconcile with universal suffrage. Yet such capital concentration might be tenable if the income from capital accounts for only a small part of national income: perhaps one-fourth to one-third, or sometimes a bit more, as in the Ancien Régime (which made the extreme concentration of wealth at that time particularly oppressive). But if the same level of inequality applies to the totality of national income, it is hard to imagine that those at the bottom will accept the situation permanently.

That said, there are no grounds for asserting that the upper decile can never claim more than 50 percent of national income or that a country's economy would collapse if this symbolic threshold were crossed. In fact, the available historical data are far from perfect, and it is not out of the question that this symbolic limit has already been exceeded. In particular, it is possible that under the Ancien Régime, right up to the eve of the French Revolution, the top decile did take more than 50 percent and even as much as 60 percent or perhaps slightly more of national income. More generally, this may have been the case in other traditional rural societies. Indeed, whether such extreme inequality is or is not sustainable depends not only on the effectiveness of the repressive apparatus but also, and perhaps primarily, on the effectiveness of the apparatus of justification. If inequalities are seen as justified, say because they seem to be a consequence of a choice by the rich to work harder or more efficiently than the poor, or because preventing the rich from earning more would inevitably harm the worst-off members of society, then it is perfectly possible for the concentration of income to set new historical records. That is why I indicate in Table 7.3 that the United States may set a new record around 2030 if inequality of income from labor—and to a lesser extent inequality of ownership of capital—continue to increase as they have done in recent decades. The top decile would then claim about 60 percent of national income, while the bottom half would get barely 15 percent.

I want to insist on this point: the key issue is the justification of inequalities rather than their magnitude as such. That is why it is essential to analyze the structure of inequality. In this respect, the principal message of Tables 7.1–3 is surely that there are two different ways for a society to achieve a very unequal distribution of total income (around 50 percent for the top decile and 20 percent for the top centile).

The first of these two ways of achieving such high inequality is through a "hyperpatrimonial society" (or "society of rentiers"): a society in which inherited wealth is very important and where the concentration of wealth attains extreme levels (with the upper decile owning typically 90 percent of all wealth, with 50 percent belonging to the upper centile alone). The total income hierarchy is then dominated by very high incomes from capital, especially inherited capital. This is the pattern we see in Ancien Régime France and in Europe during the Belle Époque, with on the whole minor variations. We need to understand how such structures of ownership and inequality emerged and persisted and to what extent they belong to the past—unless of course they are also pertinent to the future.

The second way of achieving such high inequality is relatively new. It was largely created by the United States over the past few decades. Here we see that a very high level of total income inequality can be the result of a "hypermeritocratic society" (or at any rate a society that the people at the top like to describe as hypermeritocratic). One might also call this a "society of superstars" (or perhaps "supermanagers," a somewhat different characterization). In other words, this is a very inegalitarian society, but one in which the peak of the income hierarchy is dominated by very high incomes from labor rather than by inherited wealth. I want to be clear that at this stage I am not making a judgment about whether a society of this kind really deserves to be characterized as "hypermeritocratic." It is hardly surprising that the winners in such a society would wish to describe the social hierarchy in this way, and sometimes they succeed in convincing some of the losers. For present purposes, however, hypermeritocracy is not a hypothesis but one possible conclusion of the analysis—bearing in mind that the opposite conclusion is equally possible. I will analyze in what follows how far the rise of labor income inequality in the United States has obeyed a "meritocratic" logic (insofar as it is possible to answer such a complex normative question).

At this point it will suffice to note that the stark contrast I have drawn here between two types of hyperinegalitarian society—a society of rentiers and a society of supermanagers—is naïve and overdrawn. The two types of inequality can coexist: there is no reason why a person can't be both a supermanager and a rentier—and the fact that the concentration of wealth is currently much higher in the United States than in Europe suggests that this may well be the case in the United States today. And of course there is nothing to prevent the children of supermanagers from becoming rentiers. In practice, we find both logics at work in every society. Nevertheless, there is more than one way of achieving the same level of inequality, and what primarily characterizes the United States at the moment is a record level of inequality of income from labor (probably higher than in any other society at any time in the past, anywhere in the world, including societies in which skill disparities were extremely large) together with a level of inequality of wealth less extreme than the levels observed in traditional societies or in Europe in the period 1900–1910. It is therefore essential to understand the conditions under which each of these two logics could develop, while keeping in mind that they may complement each other in the century ahead and combine their effects. If this happens, the future could hold in store a new world of inequality more extreme than any that preceded it.[21]

Problems of Synthetic Indices

Before turning to a country-by-country examination of the historical evolution of inequality in order to answer the questions posed above, several methodological issues remain to be discussed. In particular, Tables 7.1–3 include indications of the Gini coefficients of the various distributions considered. The Gini coefficient—named for the Italian statistician Corrado Gini (1884–1965)—is one of the more commonly used synthetic indices of inequality, frequently found in official re-

---

21. The increasing association of the two dimensions of inequality might, for example, be a consequence of the increase in university attendance. I will come back to this point later.

ports and public debate. By construction, it ranges from 0 to 1: it is equal to 0 in case of complete equality and to 1 when inequality is absolute, that is, when a very tiny group owns all available resources.

In practice, the Gini coefficient varies from roughly 0.2 to 0.4 in the distributions of labor income observed in actual societies, from 0.6 to 0.9 for observed distributions of capital ownership, and from 0.3 to 0.5 for total income inequality. In Scandinavia in the 1970s and 1980s, the Gini coefficient of the labor income distribution was 0.19, not far from absolute equality. Conversely, the wealth distribution in Belle Époque Europe exhibited a Gini coefficient of 0.85, not far from absolute inequality.[22]

These coefficients—and there are others, such as the Theil index—are sometimes useful, but they raise many problems. They claim to summarize in a single numerical index all that a distribution can tell us about inequality—the inequality between the bottom and the middle of the hierarchy as well as between the middle and the top or between the top and the very top. This is very simple and appealing at first glance but inevitably somewhat misleading. Indeed, it is impossible to summarize a multidimensional reality with a unidimensional index without unduly simplifying matters and mixing up things that should not be treated together. The social reality and economic and political significance of inequality are very different at different levels of the distribution, and it is important to analyze these separately. In addition, Gini coefficients and other synthetic indices tend to confuse inequality in regard to labor with inequality in regard to capital, even though the economic mechanisms at work, as well as the normative justifications of inequality, are very different in the two cases. For all these reasons, it seemed to me far better to analyze inequalities in terms of distribution tables indicating the shares of various deciles

---

22. These calculations slightly underestimate the true Gini coefficients, because they are based on the hypothesis of a finite number of social groups (those indicated in Tables 7.1–3), whereas the underlying reality is a continuous wealth distribution. See the online technical appendix and Supplemental Tables S7.4–6 for the detailed results obtained with different numbers of social groups.

and centiles in total income and total wealth rather than using synthetic indices such as the Gini coefficient.

Distribution tables are also valuable because they force everyone to take note of the income and wealth levels of the various social groups that make up the existing hierarchy. These levels are expressed in cash terms (or as a percentage of average income and wealth levels in the country concerned) rather than by way of artificial statistical measures that can be difficult to interpret. Distribution tables allow us to have a more concrete and visceral understanding of social inequality, as well as an appreciation of the data available to study these issues and the limits of those data. By contrast, statistical indices such as the Gini coefficient give an abstract and sterile view of inequality, which makes it difficult for people to grasp their position in the contemporary hierarchy (always a useful exercise, particularly when one belongs to the upper centiles of the distribution and tends to forget it, as is often the case with economists). Indices often obscure the fact that there are anomalies or inconsistencies in the underlying data, or that data from other countries or other periods are not directly comparable (because, for example, the tops of the distribution have been truncated or because income from capital is omitted for some countries but not others). Working with distribution tables forces us to be more consistent and transparent.

The Chaste Veil of Official Publications

For similar reasons, caution is in order when using indices such as the interdecile ratios often cited in official reports on inequality from the OECD or national statistical agencies. The most frequently used interdecile ratio is the P90/P10, that is, the ratio between the ninetieth percentile of the income distribution and the tenth percentile.[23] For

---

23. Other ratios such as P90/P50, P50/P10, P75/P25, etc. are also used. (P50 indicates the fiftieth percentile, that is, the median, while P25 and P75 refer to the twenty-fifth and seventy-fifth percentiles, respectively.

example, if one needs to earn more than 5,000 euros a month to belong to the top 10 percent of the income distribution and less than 1,000 euros a month to belong to the bottom 10 percent, then the P90/P10 ratio is 5.

Such indices can be useful. It is always valuable to have more information about the complete shape of the distribution in question. One should bear in mind, however, that by construction these ratios totally ignore the evolution of the distribution beyond the ninetieth percentile. Concretely, no matter what the P90/P10 ratio may be, the top decile of the income or wealth distribution may have 20 percent of the total (as in the case of Scandinavian incomes in the 1970s and 1980s) or 50 percent (as in the case of US incomes in the 2010s) or 90 percent (as in the case of European wealth in the Belle Époque). We will not learn any of this by consulting the publications of the international organizations or national statistical agencies who compile these statistics, however, because they usually focus on indices that deliberately ignore the top end of the distribution and give no indication of income or wealth beyond the ninetieth percentile.

This practice is generally justified on the grounds that the available data are "imperfect." This is true, but the difficulties can be overcome by using adequate sources, as the historical data collected (with limited means) in the World Top Incomes Database (WTID) show. This work has begun, slowly, to change the way things are done. Indeed, the methodological decision to ignore the top end is hardly neutral: the official reports of national and international agencies are supposed to inform public debate about the distribution of income and wealth, but in practice they often give an artificially rosy picture of inequality. It is as if an official government report on inequalities in France in 1789 deliberately ignored everything above the ninetieth percentile—a group 5 to 10 times larger than the entire aristocracy of the day—on the grounds that it was too complex to say anything about. Such a chaste approach is all the more regrettable in that it inevitably feeds the wildest fantasies and tends to discredit official statistics and statisticians rather than calm social tensions.

Conversely, interdecile ratios are sometimes quite high for largely artificial reasons. Take the distribution of capital ownership, for example: the bottom 50 percent of the distribution generally own next to nothing. Depending on how small fortunes are measured—for example, whether or not durable goods and debts are counted—one can come up with apparently quite different evaluations of exactly where the tenth percentile of the wealth hierarchy lies: for the same underlying social reality, one might put it at 100 euros, 1,000 euros, or even 10,000 euros, which in the end isn't all that different but can lead to very different interdecile ratios, depending on the country and the period, even though the bottom half of the wealth distribution owns less than 5 percent of total wealth. The same is only slightly less true of the labor income distribution: depending on how one chooses to treat replacement incomes and pay for short periods of work (for example, depending on whether one uses the average weekly, monthly, annual, or decadal income) one can come up with highly variable P10 thresholds (and therefore interdecile ratios), even though the bottom 50 percent of the labor income distribution actually draws a fairly stable share of the total income from labor.[24]

This is perhaps one of the main reasons why it is preferable to study distributions as I have presented them in Tables 7.1–3, that is, by emphasizing the shares of income and wealth claimed by different groups, particularly the bottom half and the top decile in each society, rather than the threshold levels defining given percentiles. The shares give a much more stable picture of reality than the interdecile ratios.

---

24. Similarly, the decision whether to measure inequalities at the individual or household level can have a much larger—and especially more volatile—effect on interdecile ratios of the P90/P10 type (owing in particular to the fact that in many cases women do not work outside the home) than on the bottom half's share of total income.

Back to "Social Tables" and Political Arithmetic

These, then, are my reasons for believing that the distribution tables I have been examining in this chapter are the best tool for studying the distribution of wealth, far better than synthetic indices and interdecile ratios.

In addition, I believe that my approach is more consistent with national accounting methods. Now that national accounts for most countries enable us to measure national income and wealth every year (and therefore average income and wealth, since demographic sources provide easy access to population figures), the next step is naturally to break down these total income and wealth figures by decile and centile. Many reports have recommended that national accounts be improved and "humanized" in this way, but little progress has been made to date.[25] A useful step in this direction would be a breakdown indicating the poorest 50 percent, the middle 40 percent, and the richest 10 percent. In particular, such an approach would allow any observer to see just how much the growth of domestic output and national income is or is not reflected in the income actually received by these different social groups. For instance, only by knowing the share going to the top decile can we determine the extent to which a disproportionate share of growth has been captured by the top end of the distribution. Neither a Gini coefficient nor an interdecile ratio permits such a clear and precise response to this question.

I will add, finally, that the distribution tables whose use I am recommending are in some ways fairly similar to the "social tables" that were in vogue in the eighteenth and early nineteenth centuries. First developed in Britain and France in the late seventeenth century, these social tables were widely used, improved, and commented on in France during the Enlightenment: for example, in the celebrated article on

---

25. See in particular Joseph E. Stiglitz, Amartya Sen, and Jean-Paul Fitoussi, Report by the Commission on the Measurement of Economic Performance and Social Progress, 2009 (www.stiglitz-sen-fitoussi.fr).

"political arithmetic" in Diderot's *Encyclopedia*. From the earliest versions established by Gregory King in 1688 to the more elaborate examples compiled by Expilly and Isnard on the eve of the French Revolution or by Peuchet, Colqhoun, and Blodget during the Napoleonic era, social tables always aimed to provide a comprehensive vision of the social structure: they indicated the number of nobles, bourgeois, gentlemen, artisans, farmers, and so on along with their estimated income (and sometimes wealth); the same authors also compiled the earliest estimates of national income and wealth. There is, however, one essential difference between these tables and mine: the old social tables used the social categories of their time and did not seek to ascertain the distribution of wealth or income by deciles and centiles.[26]

Nevertheless, social tables sought to portray the flesh-and-blood aspects of inequality by emphasizing the shares of national wealth held by different social groups (and, in particular, the various strata of the elite), and in this respect there are clear affinities with the approach I have taken here. At the same time, social tables are remote in spirit from the sterile, atemporal statistical measures of inequality such as those employed by Gini and Pareto, which were all too commonly used in the twentieth century and tend to naturalize the distribution of wealth. The way one tries to measure inequality is never neutral.

---

26. Social tables were similar, in spirit at least, to the famous *Tableau économique* that François Quesnay published in 1758, which provided the first synthetic picture of the economy and of exchanges between social groups. One can also find much older social tables from any number of countries from antiquity on. See the interesting tables described by B. Milanovic, P. Lindert, and J. Williamson in "Measuring Ancient Inequality," NBER Working Paper 13550 (October 2007). See also B. Milanovic, *The Haves and the Have-Nots: A Brief and Idiosyncratic History of Global Inequality* (New York: Basic Books, 2010). Unfortunately, the data in these early tables are not always satisfactory from the standpoint of homogeneity and comparability. See the online technical appendix.

EIGHT

Two Worlds

I have now precisely defined the notions needed for what follows, and I have introduced the orders of magnitude attained in practice by inequality with respect to labor and capital in various societies. The time has now come to look at the historical evolution of inequality around the world. How and why has the structure of inequality changed since the nineteenth century? The shocks of the period 1914–1945 played an essential role in the compression of inequality, and this compression was in no way a harmonious or spontaneous occurrence. The increase in inequality since 1970 has not been the same everywhere, which again suggests that institutional and political factors played a key role.

A Simple Case: The Reduction of Inequality in France in the Twentieth Century

I will begin by examining at some length the case of France, which is particularly well documented (thanks to a rich lode of readily available historical sources). It is also relatively simple and straightforward (as far as it is possible for a history of inequality to be straightforward) and, above all, broadly representative of changes observed in several other European countries. By "European" I mean "continental European," because in some respects the British case is intermediate between the European and the US cases. To a large extent the continental European pattern is also representative of what happened in Japan. After France I will turn to the United States, and finally I will extend the analysis to the entire set of developed and emerging economies for which adequate historical data exist.

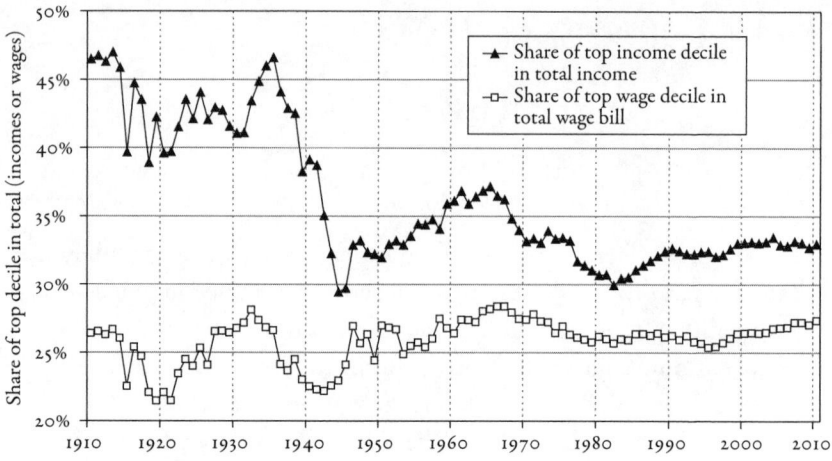

FIGURE 8.1. Income inequality in France, 1910–2010

Inequality of total income (labor and capital) has dropped in France during the twentieth century, while wage inequality has remained the same.

Sources and series: see piketty.pse.ens.fr/capital21c.

Figure 8.1 depicts the upper decile's share of both national income and wages over time. Three facts stand out.

First, income inequality has greatly diminished in France since the Belle Époque: the upper decile's share of national income decreased from 45–50 percent on the eve of World War I to 30–35 percent today.

This drop of 15 percentage points of national income is considerable. It represents a decrease of about one-third in the share of each year's output going to the wealthiest 10 percent of the population and an increase of about a third in the share going to the other 90 percent. Note, too, that this is roughly equivalent to three-quarters of what the bottom half of the population received in the Belle Époque and more than half of what it receives today.[1] Recall, moreover, that in this part of the book, I am examining inequality of primary incomes (that

---

1. See Table 7.3.

is, before taxes and transfers). In Part Four, I will show how taxes and transfers reduced inequality even more. To be clear, the fact that inequality decreased does not mean that we are living today in an egalitarian society. It mainly reflects the fact that the society of the Belle Époque was extremely inegalitarian—indeed, one of the most inegalitarian societies of all time. The form that this inequality took and the way it came about would not, I think, be readily accepted today.

Second, the significant compression of income inequality over the course of the twentieth century was due entirely to diminished top incomes from capital. If we ignore income from capital and concentrate on wage inequality, we find that the distribution remained quite stable over the long run. In the first decade of the twentieth century as in the second decade of the twenty-first, the upper decile of the wage hierarchy received about 25 percent of total wages. The sources also indicate long-term stability of wage inequality at the bottom end of the distribution. For example, the least well paid 50 percent always received 25–30 percent of total wages (so that the average pay of a member of this group was 50–60 percent of the average wage overall), with no clear long-term trend.[2] The wage level has obviously changed a great deal over the past century, and the composition and skills of the workforce have been totally transformed, but the wage hierarchy has remained more or less the same. If top incomes from capital had not decreased, income inequality would not have diminished in the twentieth century.

This fact stands out even more boldly when we climb the rungs of the social ladder. Look, in particular, at the evolution of the top centile (Figure 8.2).[3] Compared with the peak inequality of the Belle Époque, the top centile's share of income literally collapsed in France

---

2. See Table 7.1 and the online technical appendix.

3. For complete series for the various centiles and up to the top ten-thousandth, as well as a detailed analysis of the overall evolution, see Thomas Piketty, *Les hauts revenus en France au 20e siècle: Inégalités et redistribution 1901–1998* (Paris: Grasset, 2001). Here I will confine myself to the broad outlines of the story,

FIGURE 8.2. The fall of rentiers in France, 1910–2010

The fall in the top percentile share (the top 1 percent highest incomes) in France between 1914 and 1945 is due to the fall of top capital incomes.

Sources and series: see piketty.pse.ens.fr/capital21c.

over the course of the twentieth century, dropping from more than 20 percent of national income in 1900–1910 to 8 or 9 percent in 2000–2010. This represents a decrease of more than half in one century, indeed nearly two-thirds if we look at the bottom of the curve in the early 1980s, when the top centile's share of national income was barely 7 percent.

Again, this collapse was due solely to the decrease of very high incomes from capital (or, crudely put, the fall of the rentier). If we look only at wages, we find that the upper centile's share remains almost totally stable over the long run at around 6 or 7 percent of total wages. On the eve of World War I, income inequality (as measured by the share of the upper centile) was nearly three times greater than wage inequality. Today it is a nearly a third higher and largely identical with wage inequality, to the point where one might imagine—

taking account of more recent research. The updated series are also available online in the WTID.

incorrectly—that top incomes from capital have virtually disappeared (see Figure 8.2).

To sum up: the reduction of inequality in France during the twentieth century is largely explained by the fall of the rentier and the collapse of very high incomes from capital. No generalized structural process of inequality compression (and particularly wage inequality compression) seems to have operated over the long run, contrary to the optimistic predictions of Kuznets's theory.

Herein lies a fundamental lesson about the historical dynamics of the distribution of wealth, no doubt the most important lesson the twentieth century has to teach. This is all the more true when we recognize that the factual picture is more or less the same in all developed countries, with minor variations.

The History of Inequality: A Chaotic Political History

The third important fact to emerge from Figures 8.1 and 8.2 is that the history of inequality has not been a long, tranquil river. There have been many twists and turns and certainly no irrepressible, regular tendency toward a "natural" equilibrium. In France and elsewhere, the history of inequality has always been chaotic and political, influenced by convulsive social changes and driven not only by economic factors but by countless social, political, military, and cultural phenomena as well. Socioeconomic inequalities—disparities of income and wealth between social groups—are always both causes and effects of other developments in other spheres. All these dimensions of analysis are inextricably intertwined. Hence the history of the distribution of wealth is one way of interpreting a country's history more generally.

In the case of France, it is striking to see the extent to which the compression of income inequality is concentrated in one highly distinctive period: 1914–1945. The shares of both the upper decile and upper centile in total income reached their nadir in the aftermath of World War II and seem never to have recovered from the extremely violent shocks of the war years (see Figures 8.1 and 8.2). To a large extent, it was the chaos of war, with its attendant economic and political shocks, that reduced inequality in the twentieth century. There was no gradual, consensual, conflict-free evolution toward greater equality. In the twentieth century it was war, and not harmonious democratic or economic rationality, that erased the past and enabled society to begin anew with a clean slate.

What were these shocks? I discussed them in Part Two: destruction caused by two world wars, bankruptcies caused by the Great Depression, and above all new public policies enacted in this period (from rent control to nationalizations and the inflation-induced euthanasia of the rentier class that lived on government debt). All of these things led to a sharp drop in the capital / income ratio between 1914 and 1945 and a significant decrease in the share of income from capital in national income. But capital is far more concentrated than labor, so income from capital is substantially overrepresented in the upper decile of the income hierarchy (even more so in the upper centile). Hence there is nothing surprising about the fact that the shocks endured by capital, especially private capital, in the period 1914–1945 diminished the share of the upper decile (and upper centile), ultimately leading to a significant compression of income inequality.

France first imposed a tax on income in 1914 (the Senate had blocked this reform since the 1890s, and it was not finally adopted until July 15, 1914, a few weeks before war was declared, in an extremely tense climate). For that reason, we unfortunately have no detailed annual data on the structure of income before that date. In the first decade of the twentieth century, numerous estimates were made of the distribution of income in anticipation of the imposition of a general income tax, in order to predict how much revenue such a tax might bring in. We therefore have a rough idea of how concentrated income was in the Belle Époque. But these estimates are not sufficient to give us historical perspective on the shock of World War I (for that, the income tax would have to have been adopted several decades earlier).[4] Fortunately, data on estate taxes, which have been levied since 1791, allow us to study the evolution of the wealth distribution throughout the nineteenth and twentieth centuries, and we are therefore able to confirm the central role played by the shocks of 1914–1945. For these data indicate that on the eve of World War I, nothing presaged a spontaneous reduction of the concentration of capital ownership—on the contrary. From the same source we also know that income from capital accounted for the lion's share of the upper centile's income in the period 1900–1910.

From a "Society of Rentiers" to a "Society of Managers"

In 1932, despite the economic crisis, income from capital still represented the main source of income for the top 0.5 percent of the distribution (see Figure 8.3).[5] But when we look at the composition of the top income group today, we find that a profound change has occurred. To be sure, today as in the past, income from labor gradually disappears as one moves higher in the income hierarchy, and income from

---

4. The estimates shown in Figures 8.1 and 8.2 are based on declarations of income and wages (the general income tax was instituted in France in 1914, and the so-called cédulaire tax on wages was adopted in 1917, so we have separate annual measures of high incomes and high wages starting from those two dates) and on national accounts (which tell us about total national income and total wages paid), using a method initially introduced by Kuznets and described briefly in the introduction. The fiscal data begin only with income for 1915 (the first year in which the new tax was levied), and I have completed the series for 1910–1914 using estimates carried out before the war by the tax authorities and contemporary economists. See the online technical appendix.

5. In Figure 8.3 (and subsequent figures of similar type) I have used the same notations as in Les hauts revenus en France and the WTID to designate the various "fractiles" of the income hierarchy: P90–95 includes everyone between the ninetieth and ninety-fifth percentile (the poorer half of the richest 10 percent), P95–99 includes those between the ninety-fifth and ninety-ninth percentile (the next higher 4 percent), P99–99.5 the next 0.5 percent (the poorer half of the top 1 percent), P99.5–99.9 the next 0.4 percent, P99.9–99.99 the next 0.09 percent, and P99.99–100 the richest 0.01 percent (the top ten-thousandth).

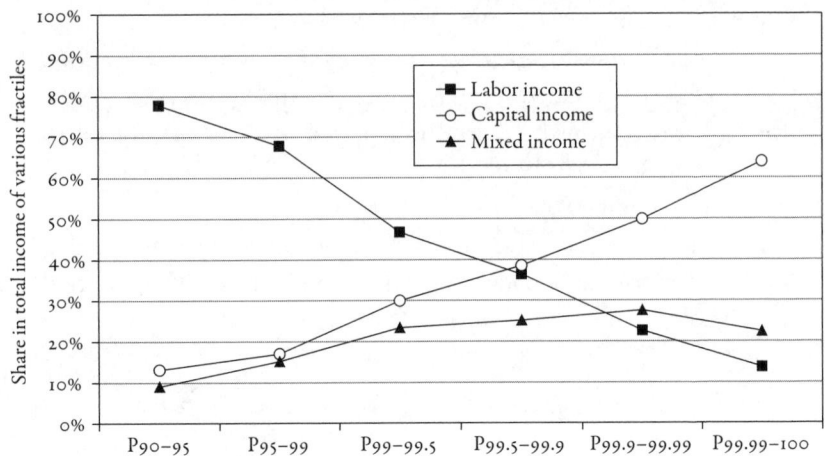

FIGURE 8.3. The composition of top incomes in France in 1932
Labor income becomes less and less important as one goes up within the top decile of total income. Notes: (i) "P90–95" includes individuals between percentiles 90 to 95, "P95–99" includes the next 4 percent, "P99–99.5" the next 0.5 percent, etc.; (ii) Labor income: wages, bonuses, pensions. Capital income: dividends, interest, rent. Mixed income: self-employment income.
Sources and series: see piketty.pse.ens.fr/capital21c.

capital becomes more and more predominant in the top centiles and thousandths of the distribution: this structural feature has not changed. There is one crucial difference, however: today one has to climb much higher in the social hierarchy before income from capital outweighs income from labor. Currently, income from capital exceeds income from labor only in the top 0.1 percent of the income distribution (see Figure 8.4). In 1932, this social group was 5 times larger; in the Belle Époque it was 10 times larger.

Make no mistake: this is a significant change. The top centile occupies a very prominent place in any society. It structures the economic and political landscape. This is much less true of the top thousandth.[6] Although this is a matter of degree, it is nevertheless im-

---

6. As a reminder, the top centile in France in 2010 consists of 500,000 adults out of an adult population of 50 million.

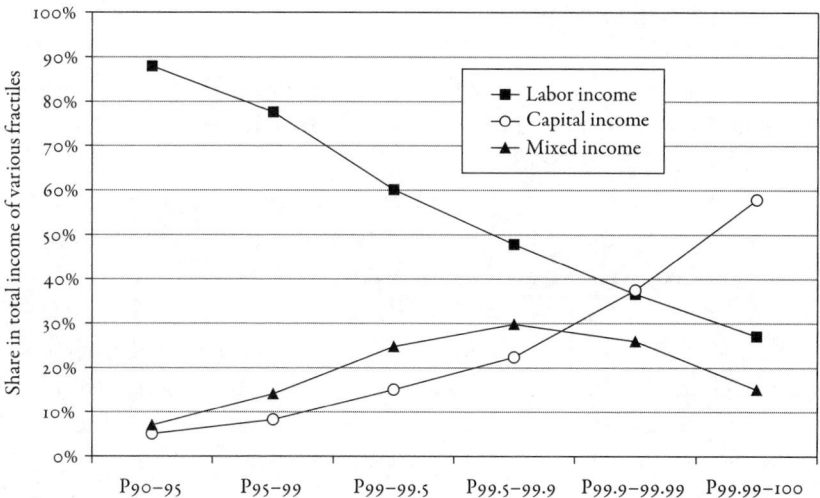

FIGURE 8.4. The composition of top incomes in France in 2005

Capital income becomes dominant at the level of the top 0.1 percent in France in 2005, as opposed to the top 0.5 percent in 1932.

Sources and series: see piketty.pse.ens.fr/capital21c.

portant: there are moments when the quantitative becomes qualitative. This change also explains why the share of income going to the upper centile today is barely higher than the upper centile's share of total wages: income from capital assumes decisive importance only in the top thousandth or top ten-thousandth. Its influence in the top centile as a whole is relatively insignificant.

To a large extent, we have gone from a society of rentiers to a society of managers, that is, from a society in which the top centile is dominated by rentiers (people who own enough capital to live on the annual income from their wealth) to a society in which the top of the income hierarchy, including to the upper centile, consists mainly of highly paid individuals who live on income from labor. One might also say, more correctly (if less positively), that we have gone from a society of superrentiers to a less extreme form of rentier society, with a better balance between success through work and success through capital. It is important, however, to be clear that this major upheaval came about, in France at any rate, without any expansion of the wage hierarchy (which has been globally stable for a long time: the universe of individuals who are paid for their labor has never been as homogeneous as many people think); it was due entirely to the decrease in high incomes from capital.

To sum up: what happened in France is that rentiers (or at any rate nine-tenths of them) fell behind managers; managers did not race ahead of rentiers. We need to understand the reasons for this long-term change, which are not obvious at first glance, since I showed in Part Two that the capital / income ratio has lately returned to Belle Époque levels. The collapse of the rentier between 1914 and 1945 is the obvious part of the story. Exactly why rentiers have not come back is the more complex and in some ways more important and interesting part. Among the structural factors that may have limited the concentration of wealth since World War II and to this day have helped prevent the resurrection of a society of rentiers as extreme as that which existed on the eve of World War I, we can obviously cite the creation of highly progressive taxes on income and inheritances (which for the most part did not exist prior to 1920). But other factors may also have played a significant and potentially equally important role.

The Different Worlds of the Top Decile

But first, let me dwell a moment on the very diverse social groups that make up the top decile of the income hierarchy. The boundaries between the various subgroups have changed over time: income from capital used to predominate in the top centile but today predominates only in the top thousandth. More than that, the coexistence of several worlds within the top decile can help us to understand the often chaotic short- and medium-term evolutions we see in the data. Income statements required by the new tax laws have proved to be a rich historical source, despite their many imperfections. With their help, it is possible to precisely describe and analyze the diversity at the top of the income distribution and its evolution over time. It is particularly striking to note that in all the countries for which we have this type of data, in all periods, the composition of the top income group can be characterized by intersecting curves like those shown in Figures 8.3 and 8.4 for France in 1932 and 2005, respectively: the share of income from labor always decreases rapidly as one moves progressively higher in the top decile, and the share of income from capital always rises sharply.

In the poorer half of the top decile, we are truly in the world of managers: 80–90 percent of income comes from compensation for labor.[7] Moving up to the next 4 percent, the share of income from labor decreases slightly but remains clearly dominant at 70–80 percent of total income in the interwar period as well as today (see Figures 8.3 and 8.4). In this large "9 percent" group (that is, the upper decile exclusive of the top centile), we find mainly individuals living primarily on income from labor, including both private sector managers and engineers and senior officials and teachers from the public sector. Here, pay is usually 2 to 3 times the average wage for society as a whole: if average wages are 2,000 euros a month, in other words, this group earns 4,000–6,000 a month.

Obviously, the types of jobs and levels of skill required at this level have changed considerably over time: in the interwar years, high school teachers and even late-career grade school teachers belonged to "the 9 percent," whereas today one has to be a college professor or researcher or, better yet, a senior government official to make the grade.[8] In the past, a foreman or skilled technician came close to

---

7. As is also the case for the nine-tenths of the population below the ninetieth percentile, but here compensation in the form of wages (or replacement pay in the form of retirement income or unemployment insurance) is lower.

8. The pay scales for civil servants are among the pay hierarchies about which we have the most long-term data. In France in particular, we have detailed information from state budgets and legislative reports going back to the beginning of the nineteenth century. Private sector pay has to be divined from tax records, hence little is known about the period prior to the creation of the income tax in 1914–1917. The data we have about civil service pay suggest that the wage hierarchy in the nineteenth century was roughly similar to what we see in the period

making it into this group. Today one has to be at least a middle manager and increasingly a top manager with a degree from a prestigious university or business school. The same is true lower down the pay scale: once upon a time, the least well paid workers (typically paid about half the average wage, or 1,000 euros a month if the average is 2,000) were farm laborers and domestic servants. At a later point, these were replaced by less skilled industrial workers, many of whom were women in the textile and food processing industries. This group still exists today, but the lowest paid workers are now in the service sector, employed as waiters and waitresses in restaurants or as shop clerks (again, many of these are women). Thus the labor market was totally transformed over the past century, but the structure of wage inequality across the market barely changed over the long run, with "the 9 percent" just below the top and the 50 percent at the bottom still drawing about the same shares of income from labor over a very considerable period of time.

Within "the 9 percent" we also find doctors, lawyers, merchants, restaurateurs, and other self-employed entrepreneurs. Their number grows as we move closer to "the 1 percent," as is shown by the curve indicating the share of "mixed incomes" (that is, incomes of nonwage workers, which includes both compensation for labor and income from business capital, which I have shown separately in Figures 8.3 and 8.4). Mixed incomes account for 20–30 percent of total income in the neighborhood of the top centile threshold, but this percentage decreases as we move higher into the top centile, where pure capital income (rent, interest, and dividends) clearly predominates. To make it into "the 9 percent" or even rise into the lower strata of "the 1 percent," which means attaining an income 4–5 times higher than the average (that is, 8,000–10,000 euros a month in a society where the average income is 2,000), choosing to become a doctor, lawyer, or suc-

---

1910–2010 for both the top decile and the bottom half, although the top centile may have been slightly higher (without reliable private sector data we cannot be more precise). See the online technical appendix.

cessful restaurateur may therefore be a good strategy, and it is almost as common (actually about half as common) as the choice to become a top manager in a large firm.[9] But to reach the stratosphere of "the 1 percent" and enjoy an income several tens of times greater than average (hundreds of thousands if not millions of euros per year), such a strategy is unlikely to be enough. A person who owns substantial amounts of assets is more likely to reach the top of the income hierarchy.[10]

It is interesting that it was only in the immediate postwar years (1919–1920 in France and then again 1945–1946) that this hierarchy was reversed: mixed incomes very briefly surpassed income from capital in the upper levels of the top centile. This apparently reflects rapid accumulation of new fortunes in connection with postwar reconstruction.[11]

To sum up: the top decile always encompasses two very different worlds: "the 9 percent," in which income from labor clearly predominates, and "the 1 percent," in which income from capital becomes progressively more important (more or less rapidly and massively, depending on the period). The transition between the two groups is always gradual, and the frontiers are of course porous, but the differences are nevertheless clear and systematic.

---

9. In 2000–2010, the share of wages in the P99–99.5 and P99.5–99.9 fractiles (which constitute nine-tenths of the top centile) was 50–60 percent, compared with 20–30 percent for mixed incomes (see Figure 8.4). High salaried incomes dominated high mixed incomes to almost the same degree as in the interwar years (see Figure 8.3).

10. As in Chapter 7, the euro figures cited here are deliberately rounded off and approximate, so they are no more than indications of orders of magnitude. The exact thresholds of each centile and thousandth are available in the online technical appendix, year by year.

11. Note, however, that the data on which these boundaries are based are imperfect. As noted in Chapter 6, some entrepreneurial income may be disguised as dividends and therefore classed as income from capital. For a detailed, year-by-year analysis of the composition of the top centiles and thousandths of income in France since 1914, see Piketty, *Les hauts revenus en France*, 93–168.

For example, while income from capital is obviously not altogether absent from the income of "the 9 percent," it is usually not the main source of income but simply a supplement. A manager earning 4,000 euros a month may also own an apartment that she rents for 1,000 euros a month (or lives in, thus avoiding paying a rent of 1,000 euros a month, which comes to the same thing financially). Her total income is then 5,000 euros a month, 80 percent of which is income from labor and 20 percent from capital. Indeed, an 80–20 split between labor and capital is reasonably representative of the structure of income among "the 9 percent"; this was true between the two world wars and remains true today. A part of this group's income from capital may also come from savings accounts, life insurance contracts, and financial investments, but real estate generally predominates.[12]

Conversely, within "the 1 percent," it is labor income that gradually becomes supplementary, while capital increasingly becomes the main source of income. Another interesting pattern is the following: if we break income from capital down into rent on land and structures on the one hand and dividends and interest from mobile capital on the other, we find that the very large share of income from capital in the upper decile is due largely to the latter (especially dividends). For example, in France, the share of income from capital in 1932 as well as 2005 is 20 percent at the level of "the 9 percent" but increases to 60 percent in the top 0.01 percent. In both cases, this sharp increase is explained entirely by income from financial assets (almost all of it in the form of dividends). The share of rent stagnates at around 10 per-

---

12. Income from capital seems to represent less than 10 percent of the income of "the 9 percent" in Figure 8.4, but that is solely a result of the fact that these figures, like the series on the shares of the top decile and centile, are based exclusively on self-declared income statements, which since 1960 have excluded so-called fictive rents (that is, the rental value of owner-occupied housing, which was previously part of taxable income). If we included nontaxable capital income (such as fictive rents), the share of income from capital among "the 9 percent" would reach and even slightly exceed 20 percent in 2000–2010. See the online technical appendix.

cent of total income and even tends to diminish in the top centile. This pattern reflects the fact that large fortunes consist primarily of financial assets (mainly stocks and shares in partnerships).

The Limits of Income Tax Returns

Despite all these interesting patterns, I must stress the limits of the fiscal sources used in this chapter. Figures 8.3 and 8.4 are based solely on income from capital reported in tax returns. Actual capital income is therefore underestimated, owing both to tax evasion (it is easier to hide investment income than wages, for example, by using foreign bank accounts in countries that do not cooperate with the country in which the taxpayer resides) and to the existence of various tax exemptions that allow whole categories of capital income to legally avoid the income tax (which in France and elsewhere was originally intended to include all types of income). Since income from capital is overrepresented in the top decile, this underdeclaration of capital income also implies that the shares of the upper decile and centile indicated on Figures 8.1 and 8.2, which are based solely on income tax returns, are underestimated (for France and other countries). These shares are in any case approximate. They are interesting (like all economic and social statistics) mainly as indicators of orders of magnitude and should be taken as low estimates of the actual level of inequality.

In the French case, we can compare self-declared income on tax returns with other sources (such as national accounts and sources that give a more direct measure of the distribution of wealth) to estimate how much we need to adjust our results to compensate for the underdeclaration of capital income. It turns out that we need to add several percentage points to capital income's share of national income (perhaps as many as 5 percentage points if we choose a high estimate of tax evasion, but more realistically 2 to 3 percentage points). This is not a negligible amount. Put differently, the share of the top decile in national income, which according to Figure 8.1 fell from 45–50 percent in 1900–1910 to 30–35 percent in 2000–2010, was no doubt closer to

50 percent (or even slightly higher) in the Belle Époque and is currently slightly more than 35 percent.[13] Nevertheless, this correction does not significantly affect the overall evolution of income inequality. Even if opportunities for legal tax avoidance and illegal tax evasion have increased in recent years (thanks in particular to the emergence of tax havens about which I will say more later on), we must remember that income from mobile capital was already significantly underreported in the early twentieth century and during the interwar years. All signs are that the copies of dividend and interest coupons requested by the governments of that time were no more effective than today's bilateral agreements as a means of ensuring compliance with applicable tax laws.

To a first approximation, therefore, we may assume that accounting for tax avoidance and evasion would increase the levels of inequality derived from tax returns by similar proportions in different periods and would therefore not substantially modify the time trends and evolutions I have identified.

Note, however, that we have not yet attempted to apply such corrections in a systematic and consistent way in different countries. This is an important limitation of the World Top Incomes Database. One consequence is that our series underestimate—probably slightly—the increase of inequality that can be observed in most countries after 1970, and in particular the role of income from capital. In fact, income tax returns are becoming increasingly less accurate sources for studying capital income, and it is indispensable to make use of other, complementary sources as well. These may be either macroeconomic sources (of the kind used in Part Two to study the dynamics of the capital / income ratio and capital-labor split) or microeconomic sources (with which it is possible to study the distribution of wealth directly, and of which I will make use in subsequent chapters).

Furthermore, different capital taxation laws may bias international comparisons. Broadly speaking, rents, interest, and dividends are treated

---

13. See the online technical appendix.

fairly similarly in different countries.[14] By contrast, there are significant variations in the treatment of capital gains. For instance, capital gains are not fully or consistently reported in French tax data (and I have simply excluded them altogether), while they have always been fairly well accounted for in US tax data. This can make a major difference, because capital gains, especially those realized from the sale of stocks, constitute a form of capital income that is highly concentrated in the very top income groups (in some cases even more than dividends). For example, if Figures 8.3 and 8.4 included capital gains, the share of income from capital in the top ten-thousandth would not be 60 percent but something closer to 70 or 80 percent (depending on the year).[15] So as not to bias comparisons, I will present the results for the United States both with and without capital gains.

The other important limitation of income tax returns is that they contain no information about the origin of the capital whose income is being reported. We can see the income produced by capital owned by the taxpayer at a particular moment in time, but we have no idea whether that capital was inherited or accumulated by the taxpayer during his or her lifetime with income derived from labor (or from other capital). In other words, an identical level of inequality with respect to income from capital can in fact reflect very different situations, and we would never learn anything about these differences if we restricted ourselves to tax return data. Generally speaking, very high incomes from capital usually correspond to fortunes so large that it is hard to imagine that they could have been amassed with savings from labor income alone (even in the case of a very high-level manager or executive). There is every reason to believe that inheritance plays a major role. As we will see in later chapters, however, the relative importance of inheritance and saving has evolved considerably over

---

14. In particular, I always include all rents, interest, and dividends in income declarations, even when some of these types of income are not subject to the same tax schedule and may be covered by specific exemptions or reduced rates.

15. See the online technical appendix.

time, and this is a subject that deserves further study. Once again, I will need to make use of sources bearing directly on the question of inheritance.

The Chaos of the Interwar Years

Consider the evolution of income inequality in France over the last century. Between 1914 and 1945, the share of the top centile of the income hierarchy fell almost constantly, dropping gradually from 20 percent in 1914 to just 7 percent in 1945 (Figure 8.2). This steady decline reflects the long and virtually uninterrupted series of shocks sustained by capital (and income from capital) during this time. By contrast, the share of the top decile of the income hierarchy decreased much less steadily. It apparently fell during World War I, but this was followed by an unsteady recovery in the 1920s and then a very sharp, and at first sight surprising, rise between 1929 and 1935, followed by a steep decline in 1936–1938 and a collapse during World War II.[16] In the end, the top decile's share of national income, which was more than 45 percent in 1914, fell to less than 30 percent in 1944–1945.

If we consider the entire period 1914–1945, the two declines are perfectly consistent: the share of the upper decile decreased by nearly 18 points, according to my estimates, and the upper centile by nearly 14 points.[17] In other words, "the 1 percent" by itself accounts for roughly three-quarters of the decrease in inequality between 1914 and 1945, while "the 9 percent" explains roughly one-quarter. This is hardly sur-

---

16. Note that throughout World War II, the French tax authorities carried on with their work of collecting income statements, recording them, and compiling statistics based on them as if nothing had changed. Indeed, it was a golden age of mechanical data processing: new technologies allowed for automated sorting of punched cards, which made it possible to do rapid cross-tabulations, a great advance over previous manual methods. Hence the statistical publications of the Ministry of Finance during the war years were richer than ever before.

17. The share of the upper decile decreased from 47 to 29 percent of national income, and that of the upper centile from 21 to 7 percent. Details are available in the online technical appendix.

prising in view of the extreme concentration of capital in the hands of "the 1 percent," who in addition often held riskier assets.

By contrast, the differences observed during this period are at first sight more surprising: Why did the share of the upper decile rise sharply after the crash of 1929 and continue at least until 1935, while the share of the top centile fell, especially between 1929 and 1932?

In fact, when we look at the data more closely, year by year, each of these variations has a perfectly good explanation. It is enlightening to revisit the chaotic interwar period, when social tensions ran very high. To understand what happened, we must recognize that "the 9 percent" and "the 1 percent" lived on very different income streams. Most of the income of "the 1 percent" came in the form of income from capital, especially interest and dividends paid by the firms whose stocks and bonds made up the assets of this group. That is why the top centile's share plummeted during the Depression, as the economy collapsed, profits fell, and firm after firm went bankrupt.

By contrast, "the 9 percent" included many managers, who were the great beneficiaries of the Depression, at least when compared with other social groups. They suffered much less from unemployment than the employees who worked under them. In particular, they never experienced the extremely high rates of partial or total unemployment endured by industrial workers. They were also much less affected by the decline in company profits than those who stood above them in the income hierarchy. Within "the 9 percent," midlevel civil servants and teachers fared particularly well. They had only recently been the beneficiaries of civil service raises granted in the period 1927–1931. (Recall that government workers, particularly those at the top of the pay scale, had suffered greatly during World War I and had been hit hard by the inflation of the early 1920s.) These midlevel employees were immune, too, from the risk of unemployment, so that the public sector's wage bill remained constant in nominal terms until 1933 (and decreased only slightly in 1934–1935, when Prime Minister Pierre Laval sought to cut civil service pay). Meanwhile, private sector wages decreased by more than 50 percent between 1929 and 1935. The severe deflation France suffered in this period (prices fell by 25 percent between 1929 and 1935, as both trade and production collapsed) played a key role in the process: individuals lucky enough to hold on to their jobs and their nominal compensation—typically civil servants—enjoyed increased purchasing power in the midst of the Depression as falling prices raised their real wages. Furthermore, such capital income as "the 9 percent" enjoyed—typically in the form of rents, which were extremely rigid in nominal terms—also increased on account of the deflation, so that the real value of this income stream rose significantly, while the dividends paid to "the 1 percent" evaporated.

For all these reasons, the share of national income going to "the 9 percent" increased quite significantly in France between 1929 and 1935, much more than the share of "the 1 percent" decreased, so that the share of the upper decile as a whole increased by more than 5 percent of national income (see Figures 8.1 and 8.2). The process was completely turned around, however, when the Popular Front came to power: workers' wages increased sharply as a result of the Matignon Accords, and the franc was devalued in September 1936, resulting in inflation and a decrease of the shares of both "the 9 percent" and the top decile in 1936–1938.[18]

The foregoing discussion demonstrates the usefulness of breaking income down by centiles and income source. If we had tried to analyze the interwar dynamic by using a synthetic index such as the Gini coefficient, it would have been impossible to understand what was going on. We would not have been able to distinguish between income from labor and income from capital or between short-term and long-term changes. In the French case, what makes the period 1914–1945 so complex is the fact that although the general trend is fairly clear (a sharp drop in the share of national income going to the top decile, induced by a collapse of the top centile's share), many smaller counter-movements were superimposed on this overall pattern in the

---

18. For a detailed analysis of all these evolutions, year by year, see *Les hauts revenus en France,* esp. chaps. 2 and 3, pp. 93–229.

1920s and 1930s. We find similar complexity in other countries in the interwar period, with characteristic features associated with the history of each particular country. For example, deflation ended in the United States in 1933, when President Roosevelt came to power, so that the reversal that occurred in France in 1936 came earlier in America, in 1933. In every country the history of inequality is political—and chaotic.

The Clash of Temporalities

Broadly speaking, it is important when studying the dynamics of the income and wealth distributions to distinguish among several different time scales. In this book I am primarily interested in long-term evolutions, fundamental trends that in many cases cannot be appreciated on time scales of less than thirty to forty years or even longer, as shown, for example, by the structural increase in the capital / income ratio in Europe since World War II, a process that has been going on for nearly seventy years now yet would have been difficult to detect just ten or twenty years ago owing to the superimposition of various other developments (as well as the absence of usable data). But this focus on the long period must not be allowed to obscure the fact that shorter-term trends also exist. To be sure, these are often counterbalanced in the end, but for the people who live through them they often appear, quite legitimately, to be the most significant realities of the age. Indeed, how could it be otherwise, when these "short-term" movements can continue for ten to fifteen years or even longer, which is quite long when measured on the scale of a human lifetime.

The history of inequality in France and elsewhere is replete with these short- and medium-term movements—and not just in the particularly chaotic interwar years. Let me briefly recount the major episodes in the case of France. During both world wars, the wage hierarchy was compressed, but in the aftermath of each war, wage inequalities reasserted themselves (in the 1920s and then again in the late 1940s and on into the 1950s and 1960s). These were movements of considerable magnitude: the share of total wages going to the top 10 percent decreased by about 5 points during each conflict but recovered afterward by the same amount (see Figure 8.1).[19] Wage spreads were reduced in the public as well as the private sector. In each war the scenario was the same: in wartime, economic activity decreases, inflation increases, and real wages and purchasing power begin to fall. Wages at the bottom of the wage scale generally rise, however, and are somewhat more generously protected from inflation than those at the top. This can induce significant changes in the wage distribution if inflation is high. Why are low and medium wages better indexed to inflation than higher wages? Because workers share certain perceptions of social justice and norms of fairness, an effort is made to prevent the purchasing power of the least well-off from dropping too sharply, while their better-off comrades are asked to postpone their demands until the war is over. This phenomenon clearly played a role in setting wage scales in the public sector, and it was probably the same, at least to a certain extent, in the private sector. The fact that large numbers of young and relatively unskilled workers were mobilized for service (or held in prisoner-of-war camps) may also have improved the relative position of low- and medium-wage workers on the labor market.

In any case, the compression of wage inequality was reversed in both postwar periods, and it is therefore tempting to forget that it ever occurred. Nevertheless, for workers who lived through these periods, the changes in the wage distribution made a deep impression. In particular, the issue of restoring the wage hierarchy in both the public and private sectors was one of the most important political, social, and economic issues of the postwar years.

Turning now to the history of inequality in France between 1945 and 2010, we find three distinct phases: income inequality rose sharply between 1945 and 1967 (with the share going to the top decile in-

---

19. In World War II, the compression of the wage hierarchy actually began before the war, in 1936, with the Matignon Accords.

creasing from less than 30 to 36 or 37 percent). It then decreased considerably between 1968 and 1983 (with the share of the top decile dropping back to 30 percent). Finally, inequality increased steadily after 1983, so that the top decile's share climbed to about 33 percent in the period 2000–2010 (see Figure 8.1). We find roughly similar changes of wage inequality at the level of the top centile (see Figures 8.3 and 8.4). Once again, these various increases and decreases more or less balance out, so it is tempting to ignore them and concentrate on the relative stability over the long run, 1945–2010. Indeed, if one were interested solely in very long-term evolutions, the outstanding change in France during the twentieth century would be the significant compression of wage inequality between 1914 and 1945, followed by relative stability afterward. Each way of looking at the matter is legitimate and important in its own right, and to my mind it is essential to keep all of these different time scales in mind: the long term is important, but so are the short and the medium term. I touched on this point previously in my examination of the evolution of the capital / income ratio and the capital-labor split in Part Two (see in particular Chapter 6).

It is interesting to note that the capital-labor split tends to move in the same direction as inequality in income from labor, so that the two reinforce each other in the short to medium term but not necessarily in the long run. For example, each of the two world wars saw a decrease in capital's share of national income (and of the capital / income ratio) as well as a compression of wage inequality. Generally speaking, inequality tends to evolve "procyclically" (that is, it moves in the same direction as the economic cycle, in contrast to "countercyclical" changes). In economic booms, the share of profits in national income tends to increase, and pay at the top end of the scale (including incentives and bonuses) often increases more than wages toward the bottom and middle. Conversely, during economic slowdowns or recessions (of which war can be seen as an extreme form), various noneconomic factors, especially political ones, ensure that these movements do not depend solely on the economic cycle.

The substantial increase in French inequality between 1945 and 1967 was the result of sharp increases in both capital's share of national income and wage inequality in a context of rapid economic growth. The political climate undoubtedly played a role: the country was entirely focused on reconstruction, and decreasing inequality was not a priority, especially since it was common knowledge that inequality had decreased enormously during the war. In the 1950s and 1960s, managers, engineers, and other skilled personnel saw their pay increase more rapidly than the pay of workers at the bottom and middle of the wage hierarchy, and at first no one seemed to care. A national minimum wage was created in 1950 but was seldom increased thereafter and fell farther and farther behind the average wage.

Things changed suddenly in 1968. The events of May 1968 had roots in student grievances and cultural and social issues that had little to do with the question of wages (although many people had tired of the inegalitarian productivist growth model of the 1950s and 1960s, and this no doubt played a role in the crisis). But the most immediate political result of the movement was its effect on wages: to end the crisis, Charles de Gaulle's government signed the Grenelle Accords, which provided, among other things, for a 20 percent increase in the minimum wage. In 1970, the minimum wage was officially (if partially) indexed to the mean wage, and governments from 1968 to 1983 felt obliged to "boost" the minimum significantly almost every year in a seething social and political climate. The purchasing power of the minimum wage accordingly increased by more than 130 percent between 1968 and 1983, while the mean wage increased by only about 50 percent, resulting in a very significant compression of wage inequalities. The break with the previous period was sharp and substantial: the purchasing power of the minimum wage had increased barely 25 percent between 1950 and 1968, while the average wage had more than doubled.[20] Driven by the sharp rise of low wages, the total wage bill

---

20. See *Les hauts revenus en France*, 201–2. The very sharp break in wage inequality that occurred in 1968 was recognized at the time. See in particular the meticulous

rose markedly more rapidly than output between 1968 and 1983, and this explains the sharp decrease in capital's share of national income that I pointed out in Part Two, as well as the very substantial compression of income inequality.

These movements reversed in 1982–1983. The new Socialist government elected in May 1981 surely would have preferred to continue the earlier trend, but it was not a simple matter to arrange for the minimum wage to increase twice as fast as the average wage (especially when the average wage itself was increasing faster than output). In 1982–1983, therefore, the government decided to "turn toward austerity": wages were frozen, and the policy of annual boosts to the minimum wage was definitively abandoned. The results were soon apparent: the share of profits in national income skyrocketed during the remainder of the 1980s, while wage inequalities once again increased, and income inequalities even more so (see Figures 8.1 and 8.2). The break was as sharp as that of 1968, but in the other direction.

The Increase of Inequality in France since the 1980s

How should we characterize the phase of increasing inequality that began in France in 1982–1983? It is tempting to see it in a long-run perspective as a microphenomenon, a simple reversal of the previous trend, especially since by 1990 or so the share of profits in national income had returned to the level achieved on the eve of May 1968.[21] This would be a mistake, however, for several reasons. First, as I showed in Part Two, the profit share in 1966–1967 was historically high, a consequence of the restoration of capital's share that began at the end of World War II. If we include, as we should, rent as well as profit in income from capital, we find that capital's share of national income actually continued to grow in the 1990s and 2000s. A correct under-

work of Christian Baudelot and A. Lebeaupin, *Les salaires de 1950 à 1975* (Paris: INSEE, 1979).

21. See Figure 6.6.

standing of this long-run phenomenon requires that it be placed in the context of the long-term evolution of the capital / income ratio, which by 2010 had returned to virtually the same level it had achieved in France on the eve of World War I. It is impossible to fully appreciate the implications of this restoration of the prosperity of capital simply by looking at the evolution of the upper decile's share of income, in part because income from capital is understated, so that we tend to slightly underestimate the increase in top incomes, and in part because the real issue is the renewed importance of inherited wealth, a long-term process that has only begun to reveal its true effects and can be correctly analyzed only by directly studying the changing role and importance of inherited wealth as such.

But that is not all. A stunning new phenomenon emerged in France in the 1990s: the very top salaries, and especially the pay packages awarded to the top executives of the largest companies and financial firms, reached astonishing heights—somewhat less astonishing in France, for the time being, than in the United States, but still, it would be wrong to neglect this new development. The share of wages going to the top centile, which was less than 6 percent in the 1980s and 1990s, began to increase in the late 1990s and reached 7.5–8 percent of the total by the early 2010s. Thus there was an increase of nearly 30 percent in a little over a decade, which is far from negligible. If we move even higher up the salary and bonus scale to look at the top 0.1 or 0.01 percent, we find even greater increases, with hikes in purchasing power greater than 50 percent in ten years.[22] In a context of very low growth and virtual stagnation of purchasing power for the vast majority of workers, raises of this magnitude for top earners have not failed to attract attention. Furthermore, the phenomenon was radically new, and in order to interpret it correctly, we must view it in international perspective.

---

22. See esp. the work of Camille Landais, "Les hauts revenus en France (1998–2006): Une explosion des inégalités?" (Paris: Paris School of Economics, 2007), and Olivier Godechot, "Is Finance Responsible for the Rise in Wage Inequality in France?" *Socio-Economic Review* 10, no. 3 (2012): 447–70.

A More Complex Case: The Transformation of Inequality in the United States

Indeed, let me turn now to the US case, which stands out precisely because it was there that a subclass of "supermanagers" first emerged over the past several decades. I have done everything possible to ensure that the data series for the United States are as comparable as possible with the French series. In particular, Figures 8.5 and 8.6 represent the same data for the United States as Figures 8.1 and 8.2 for France: the goal is to compare, in the first figure of each pair, the evolution of the shares of income going to the top decile and top centile of the wage hierarchy and to compare, in the second figure, the wage hierarchies themselves. I should add that the United States first instituted a federal income tax in 1913, concluding a long battle with the Supreme Court.[23] The data derived from US income tax returns are on the whole quite comparable to the French data, though somewhat less detailed. In particular, total income can be gleaned from US statements from 1913 on, but we do not have separate information on income from labor until 1927, so the series dealing with the wage distribution in the United States before 1927 are somewhat less reliable.[24]

When we compare the French and US trajectories, a number of similarities stand out, but so do certain important differences. I shall begin by examining the overall evolution of the share of income going to the top decile (Figure 8.6). The most striking fact is that the United States has become noticeably more inegalitarian than France (and Europe as a whole) from the turn of the twentieth century until now, even though the United States was more egalitarian at the beginning of this period. What makes the US case complex is that the end of the

---

23. For the years 1910–1912, I completed the series by using various available data sources, and in particular various estimates carried out by the US government in anticipation of the creation of a federal income tax (just as I did in the case of France). See the online technical appendix.

24. For the years 1913–1926, I used data on income level and categories of income to estimate the evolution of wage inequality. See the online technical appendix.

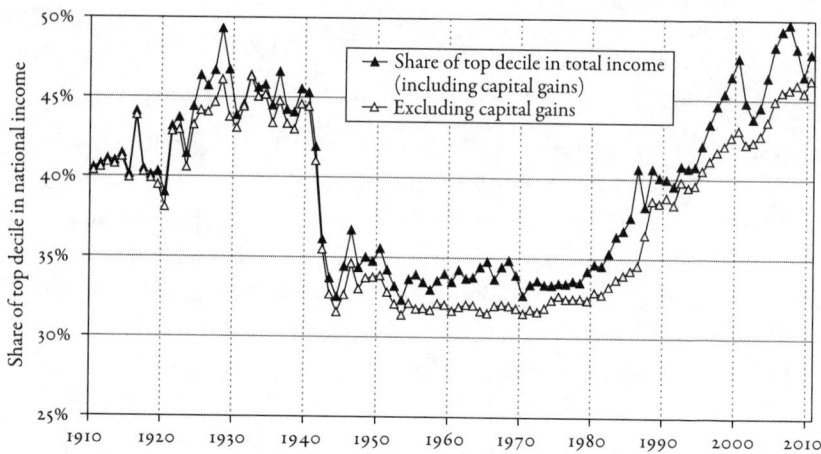

FIGURE 8.5. Income inequality in the United States, 1910–2010

The top decile income share rose from less than 35 percent of total income in the 1970s to almost 50 percent in the 2000s–2010s.

Sources and series: see piketty.pse.ens.fr/capital21c.

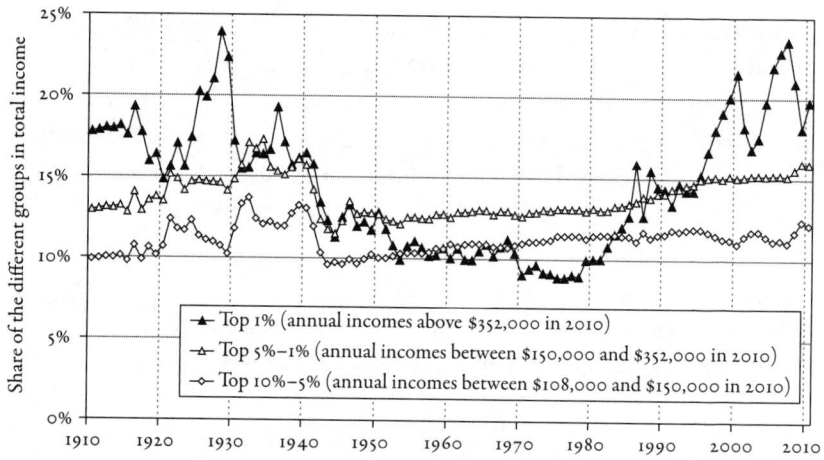

FIGURE 8.6. Decomposition of the top decile, United States, 1910–2010

The rise of the top decile income share since the 1970s is mostly due to the top percentile.

Sources and series: see piketty.pse.ens.fr/capital21c.

process did not simply mark a return to the situation that had existed at the beginning: US inequality in 2010 is quantitatively as extreme as in old Europe in the first decade of the twentieth century, but the structure of that inequality is rather clearly different.

I will proceed systematically. First, European income inequality was significantly greater than US income inequality at the turn of the twentieth century. In 1900–1910, according to the data at our disposal, the top decile of the income hierarchy received a little more than 40 percent of total national income in the United States, compared with 45–50 percent in France (and very likely somewhat more in Britain). This reflects two differences. First, the capital / income ratio was higher in Europe, and so was capital's share of national income. Second, inequality of ownership of capital was somewhat less extreme in the New World. Clearly, this does not mean that American society in 1900–1910 embodied the mythical ideal of an egalitarian society of pioneers. In fact, American society was already highly inegalitarian, much more than Europe today, for example. One has only to reread Henry James or note that the dreadful Hockley who sailed in luxury on *Titanic* in 1912 could have existed in real life and not just in the imagination of James Cameron to convince oneself that a society of rentiers existed not only in Paris and London but also in turn-of-the-century Boston, New York, and Philadelphia. Nevertheless, capital (and therefore the income derived from it) was distributed somewhat less unequally in the United States than in France or Britain. Concretely, US rentiers were fewer in number and not as rich (compared to the average US standard of living) as their European counterparts. I will need to explain why this was so.

Income inequality increased quite sharply in the United States during the 1920s, however, peaking on the eve of the 1929 crash with more than 50 percent of national income going to the top decile—a level slightly higher than in Europe at the same time, as a result of the substantial shocks to which European capital had already been subjected since 1914. Nevertheless, US inequality was not the same as European inequality: note the already crucial importance of capital gains in top US incomes during the heady stock market ascent of the 1920s (see Figure 8.5).

During the Great Depression, which hit the United States particularly hard, and again during World War II, when the nation was fully mobilized behind the war effort (and the effort to end the economic crisis), income inequality was substantially compressed, a compression comparable in some respects to what we observe in Europe in the same period. Indeed, as we saw in Part Two, the shocks to US capital were far from negligible: although there was no physical destruction due to war, the Great Depression was a major shock and was followed by substantial tax shocks imposed by the federal government in the 1930s and 1940s. If we look at the period 1910–1950 as a whole, however, we find that the compression of inequality was noticeably smaller in the United States than in France (and, more generally, Europe). To sum up: inequality in the United States started from a lower peak on the eve of World War I but at its low point after World War II stood above inequality in Europe. Europe in 1914–1945 witnessed the suicide of rentier society, but nothing of the sort occurred in the United States.

The Explosion of US Inequality after 1980

Inequality reached its lowest ebb in the United States between 1950 and 1980: the top decile of the income hierarchy claimed 30 to 35 percent of US national income, or roughly the same level as in France today. This is what Paul Krugman nostalgically refers to as "the America we love"—the America of his childhood.[25] In the 1960s, the period of the TV series *Mad Men* and General de Gaulle, the United States was in fact a more egalitarian society than France

---

25. Two recent books about the rise of inequality in the United States by well-known economists demonstrate the strength of the attachment to this relatively egalitarian period of US history: Paul Krugman, *The Conscience of a Liberal* (New York: Norton, 2007), and Joseph Stiglitz, *The Price of Inequality* (New York: Norton, 2012).

(where the upper decile's share had increased dramatically to well above 35 percent), at least for those US citizens whose skin was white.

Since 1980, however, income inequality has exploded in the United States. The upper decile's share increased from 30–35 percent of national income in the 1970s to 45–50 percent in the 2000s—an increase of 15 points of national income (see Figure 8.5). The shape of the curve is rather impressively steep, and it is natural to wonder how long such a rapid increase can continue: if change continues at the same pace, for example, the upper decile will be raking in 60 percent of national income by 2030.

It is worth taking a moment to clarify several points about this evolution. First, recall that the series represented in Figure 8.5, like all the series in the WTID, take account only of income declared in tax returns and in particular do not correct for any possible understatement of capital income for legal or extralegal reasons. Given the widening gap between the total capital income (especially dividends and interest) included in US national accounts and the amount declared in income tax returns, and given, too, the rapid development of tax havens (flows to which are, in all likelihood, mostly not even included in national accounts), it is likely that Figure 8.5 underestimates the amount by which the upper decile's share actually increased. By comparing various available sources, it is possible to estimate that the upper decile's share slightly exceeded 50 percent of US national income on the eve of the financial crisis of 2008 and then again in the early 2010s.[26]

Note, moreover, that stock market euphoria and capital gains can account for only part of the structural increase in the top decile's share over the past thirty or forty years. To be sure, capital gains in the United States reached unprecedented heights during the Internet bubble in

---

26. The available data, though imperfect, suggest that the correction for understatement of capital income might add two to three points of national income. The uncorrected share of the upper decile was 49.7 percent in 2007 and 47.9 percent in 2010 (with a clear upward trend). See the online technical appendix.

2000 and again in 2007: in both cases, capital gains alone accounted for about five additional points of national income for the upper decile, which is an enormous amount. The previous record, set in 1928 on the eve of the 1929 stock market crash, was roughly 3 points of national income. But such levels cannot be sustained for very long, as the large annual variations evident in Figure 8.5 show. The incessant short-term fluctuations of the stock market add considerable volatility to the evolution of the upper decile's share (and certainly contribute to the volatility of the US economy as a whole) but do not contribute much to the structural increase of inequality. If we simply ignore capital gains (which is not a satisfactory method either, given the importance of this type of remuneration in the United States), we still find almost as great an increase in the top decile's share, which rose from around 32 percent in the 1970s to more than 46 percent in 2010, or fourteen points of national income (see Figure 8.5). Capital gains oscillated around one or two points of additional national income for the top decile in the 1970s and around two to three points between 2000 and 2010 (excluding exceptionally good and bad years). The structural increase is therefore on the order of one point: this is not nothing, but then again it is not much compared with the fourteen-point increase of the top decile's share exclusive of capital gains.[27]

Looking at evolutions without capital gains also allows us to identify the structural character of the increase of inequality in the United States more clearly. In fact, from the late 1970s to 2010, the increase in the upper decile's share (exclusive of capital gains) appears to have been relatively steady and constant: it passed 35 percent in the 1980s, then 40 percent in the 1990s, and finally 45 percent in the 2000s (see Figure 8.5).[28] Much more striking is the fact that the level attained in

---

27. The series "with capital gains" naturally include capital gains in both the numerator (for the top income deciles and centiles) and the denominator (for total national income); the series "without capital gains" exclude them in both cases. See the online technical appendix.

28. The only suspicious jump takes place around the time of the major Reagan tax reform of 1986, when a number of important firms changed their legal form in order

2010 (with more than 46 percent of national income, exclusive of capital gains, going to the top decile) is already significantly higher than the level attained in 2007, on the eve of the financial crisis. Early data for 2011–2012 suggest that the increase is still continuing.

This is a crucial point: the facts show quite clearly that the financial crisis as such cannot be counted on to put an end to the structural increase of inequality in the United States. To be sure, in the immediate aftermath of a stock market crash, inequality always grows more slowly, just as it always grows more rapidly in a boom. The years 2008–2009, following the collapse of Lehman Brothers, like the years 2001–2002, after the bursting of the first Internet bubble, were not great times for taking profits on the stock market. Indeed, capital gains plummeted in those years. But these short-term movements did not alter the long-run trend, which is governed by other forces whose logic I must now try to clarify.

To proceed further, it will be useful to break the top decile of the income hierarchy down into three groups: the richest 1 percent, the next 4 percent, and the bottom 5 percent (see Figure 8.6). The bulk of the growth of inequality came from "the 1 percent," whose share of national income rose from 9 percent in the 1970s to about 20 percent in 2000–2010 (with substantial year-to-year variation due to capital gains)—an increase of 11 points. To be sure, "the 5 percent" (whose annual income ranged from $108,000 to $150,000 per household in 2010) as well as "the 4 percent" (whose income ranged from $150,000 to $352,000) also experienced substantial increases: the share of the former in US national income rose from 11 to 12 percent (or one point), and that of the latter rose from 13 to 16 percent (three points).[29] By definition, that means that since 1980, these social groups have experienced

---

to have their profits taxed as personal rather than corporate income. This transfer between fiscal bases had purely short-term effects (income that should have been realized a little later as capital gains was realized somewhat earlier) and played a secondary role in shaping the long-term trend. See the online technical appendix.

29. The annual pretax incomes mentioned here correspond to household incomes (married income or single individual). Income inequality at the individual level

income growth substantially higher than the average growth of the US economy, which is not negligible.

Among the members of these upper income groups are US academic economists, many of whom believe that the economy of the United States is working fairly well and, in particular, that it rewards talent and merit accurately and precisely. This is a very comprehensible human reaction.[30] But the truth is that the social groups above them did even better: of the 15 additional points of national income going to the top decile, around 11 points, or nearly three-quarters of the total, went to "the 1 percent" (those making more than $352,000 a year in 2010), of which roughly half went to "the 0.1 percent" (those making more than $1.5 million a year).[31]

Did the Increase of Inequality Cause the Financial Crisis?

As I have just shown, the financial crisis as such seems not to have had an impact on the structural increase of inequality. What about the reverse causality? Is it possible that the increase of inequality in the United States helped to trigger the financial crisis of 2008? Given the fact that the share of the upper decile in US national income peaked twice in the past century, once in 1928 (on the eve of the crash of 1929) and again in 2007 (on the eve of the crash of 2008), the question is difficult to avoid.

In my view, there is absolutely no doubt that the increase of inequality in the United States contributed to the nation's financial instability. The reason is simple: one consequence of increasing inequality was virtual stagnation of the purchasing power of the lower and middle classes in the United States, which inevitably made it more likely that modest

---

increased by approximately the same proportion as inequality in terms of household income. See the online technical appendix.

30. This visceral appreciation of the economy is sometimes particularly noticeable among economists teaching in US universities but born in foreign countries (generally poorer than the United States), an appreciation that is again quite comprehensible.

31. All detailed series are available in the online technical appendix.

households would take on debt, especially since unscrupulous banks and financial intermediaries, freed from regulation and eager to earn good yields on the enormous savings injected into the system by the well-to-do, offered credit on increasingly generous terms.[32]

In support of this thesis, it is important to note the considerable transfer of US national income—on the order of 15 points—from the poorest 90 percent to the richest 10 percent since 1980. Specifically, if we consider the total growth of the US economy in the thirty years prior to the crisis, that is, from 1977 to 2007, we find that the richest 10 percent appropriated three-quarters of the growth. The richest 1 percent alone absorbed nearly 60 percent of the total increase of US national income in this period. Hence for the bottom 90 percent, the rate of income growth was less than 0.5 percent per year.[33] These figures are incontestable, and they are striking: whatever one thinks about the fundamental legitimacy of income inequality, the numbers deserve close scrutiny.[34] It is hard to imagine an economy and society that can continue functioning indefinitely with such extreme divergence between social groups.

Quite obviously, if the increase in inequality had been accompanied by exceptionally strong growth of the US economy, things would look quite different. Unfortunately, this was not the case: the economy

---

32. This argument is more and more widely accepted. It is defended, for example, by Michael Kumhof and Romain Rancière, "Inequality, Leverage, and Crises," International Monetary Fund Working Paper (November 2010). See also Raghuram G. Rajan, *Fault Lines* (Princeton, NJ: Princeton University Press, 2010), which nevertheless underestimates the importance of the growing share of US national income claimed by the top of the income hierarchy.

33. See Anthony B. Atkinson, Thomas Piketty, and Emmanuel Saez, "Top Incomes in the Long Run of History," *Journal of Economic Literature* 49, no. 1 (2011): Table 1, p. 9.

34. Remember that these figures all concern the distribution of primary income (before taxes and transfers). I examine the effects of taxes and transfers in Part Four. To put it in a nutshell, the progressivity of the tax system was significantly reduced in this period, which makes the numbers worse, while increases in some transfers to the poorest individuals slightly alleviate them.

grew rather more slowly than in previous decades, so that the increase in inequality led to virtual stagnation of low and medium incomes.

Note, too, that this internal transfer between social groups (on the order of fifteen points of US national income) is nearly four times larger than the impressive trade deficit the United States ran in the 2000s (on the order of four points of national income). The comparison is interesting because the enormous trade deficit, which has its counterpart in Chinese, Japanese, and German trade surpluses, has often been described as one of the key contributors to the "global imbalances" that destabilized the US and global financial system in the years leading up to the crisis of 2008. That is quite possible, but it is important to be aware of the fact that the United States' internal imbalances are four times larger than its global imbalances. This suggests that the place to look for the solutions of certain problems may be more within the United States than in China or other countries.

That said, it would be altogether too much to claim that the increase of inequality in the United States was the sole or even primary cause of the financial crisis of 2008 or, more generally, of the chronic instability of the global financial system. To my mind, a potentially more important cause of instability is the structural increase of the capital / income ratio (especially in Europe), coupled with an enormous increase in aggregate international asset positions.[35]

The Rise of Supersalaries

Let me return now to the causes of rising inequality in the United States. The increase was largely the result of an unprecedented increase in wage inequality and in particular the emergence of extremely high remunerations at the summit of the wage hierarchy, particularly among top managers of large firms (see Figures 8.7 and 8.8).

Broadly speaking, wage inequality in the United States changed in major ways over the past century: the wage hierarchy expanded in the

---

35. See Chapter 5, where the Japanese and Spanish bubbles are discussed.

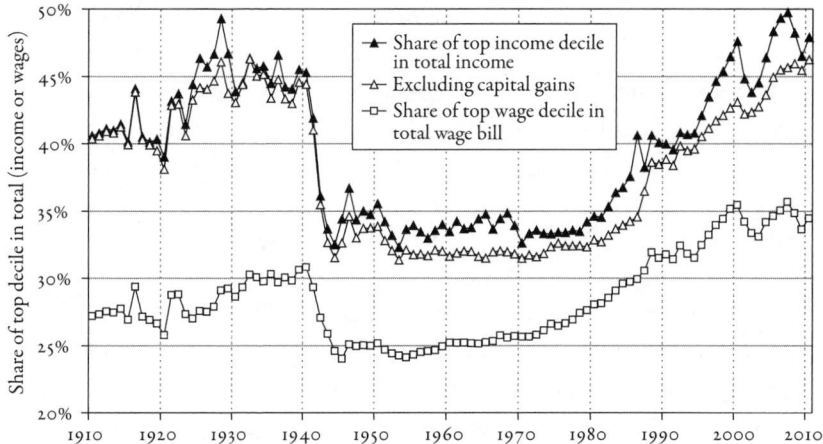

FIGURE 8.7. High incomes and high wages in the United States, 1910–2010

The rise of income inequality since the 1970s is largely due to the rise of wage inequality.

Sources and series: see piketty.pse.ens.fr/capital21c.

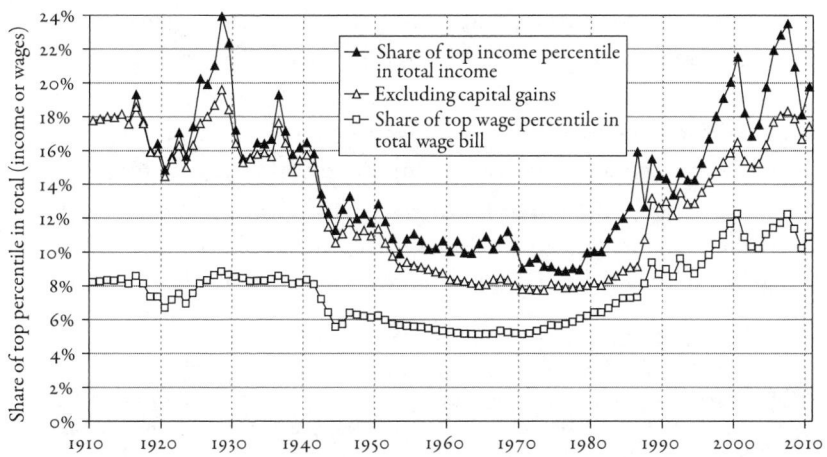

FIGURE 8.8. The transformation of the top 1 percent in the United States

The rise in the top 1 percent highest incomes since the 1970s is largely due to the rise in the top 1 percent highest wages.

Sources and series: see piketty.pse.ens.fr/capital21c.

1920s, was relatively stable in the 1930s, and then experienced severe compression during World War II. The phase of "severe compression" has been abundantly studied. An important role was played by the National War Labor Board, the government agency that had to approve all wage increases in the United States from 1941 to 1945 and generally approved raises only for the lowest paid workers. In particular, managers' salaries were systematically frozen in nominal terms and even at the end of the war were raised only moderately.[36] During the 1950s, wage inequality in the United States stabilized at a relatively low level, lower than in France, for example: the share of income going to the upper decile was about 25 percent, and the share of the upper centile was 5 or 6 percent. Then, from the mid-1970s on, the top 10 percent and, even more, the top 1 percent began to claim a share of labor income that grew more rapidly than the average wage. All told, the upper decile's share rose from 25 to 35 percent, and this increase of ten points explains approximately two-thirds of the increase in the upper decile's share of total national income (see Figures 8.7 and 8.8).

Several points call for additional comment. First, this unprecedented increase in wage inequality does not appear to have been compensated by increased wage mobility over the course of a person's career.[37] This is a significant point, in that greater mobility is often mentioned as a reason to believe that increasing inequality is not that important. In fact, if each individual were to enjoy a very high income for part of his or her life (for example, if each individual spent a year in the upper centile of the income hierarchy), then an increase in the level characterized as "very high pay" would not necessarily imply that inequality

---

36. See Thomas Piketty and Emmanuel Saez, "Income Inequality in the United States, 1913–1998," *Quarterly Journal of Economics* 118, no. 1 (February 2003): 29–30. See also Claudia Goldin and R. Margo, "The Great Compression: The Wage Structure in the United States at Mid-Century," *Quarterly Journal of Economics* 107, no. 1 (February 1992): 1–34.

37. Nor was it compensated by greater intergenerational mobility; quite the contrary. I come back to this point in Chapter 13.

with respect to labor—measured over a lifetime—had truly increased. The familiar mobility argument is powerful, so powerful that it is often impossible to verify. But in the US case, government data allow us to measure the evolution of wage inequality with mobility taken into account: we can compute average wages at the individual level over long periods of time (ten, twenty, or thirty years). And what we find is that the increase in wage inequality is identical in all cases, no matter what reference period we choose.[38] In other words, workers at McDonald's or in Detroit's auto plants do not spend a year of their lives as top managers of large US firms, any more than professors at the University of Chicago or middle managers from California do. One may have felt this intuitively, but it is always better to measure systematically wherever possible.

Cohabitation in the Upper Centile

Furthermore, the fact that the unprecedented increase of wage inequality explains most of the increase in US income inequality does not mean that income from capital played no role. It is important to dispel the notion that capital income has vanished from the summit of the US social hierarchy.

In fact, a very substantial and growing inequality of capital income since 1980 accounts for about one-third of the increase in income inequality in the United States—a far from negligible amount. Indeed, in the United States, as in France and Europe, today as in the past, income from capital always becomes more important as one climbs the rungs of the income hierarchy. Temporal and spatial differences are differences of degree: though large, the general principle remains. As Edward Wolff and Ajit Zacharias have pointed out, the upper

---

38. See Wojciech Kopczuk, Emmanuel Saez, and Jae Song, "Earnings Inequality and Mobility in the United States: Evidence from Social Security Data since 1937," *Quarterly Journal of Economics* 125, no. 1 (2010): 91–128.

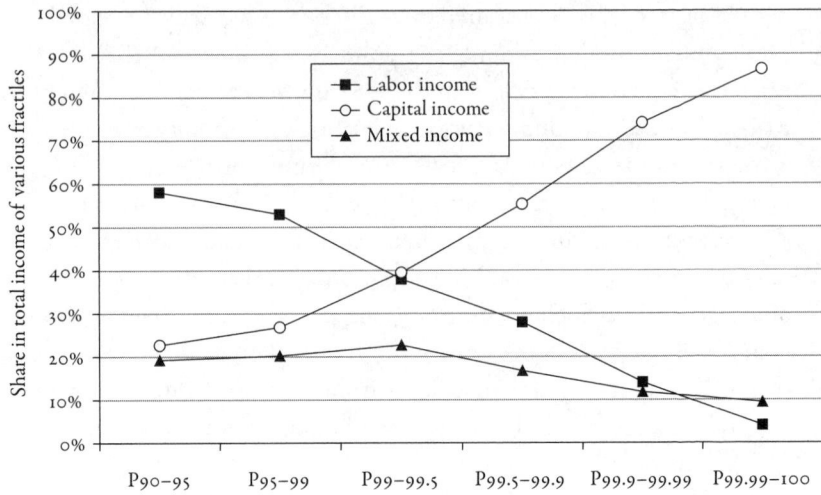

FIGURE 8.9. The composition of top incomes in the United States in 1929
Labor income becomes less and less important as one moves up within the top income decile.
Sources and series: see piketty.pse.ens.fr/capital21c.

centile always consists of several different social groups, some with very high incomes from capital and others with very high incomes from labor; the latter do not supplant the former.[39]

In the US case, as in France but to an even greater degree, the difference today is that one has to climb much further up the income hierarchy before income from capital takes the upper hand. In 1929, income from capital (essentially dividends and capital gains) was the primary resource for the top 1 percent of the income hierarchy (see Figure 8.9). In 2007, one has to climb to the 0.1 percent level be-

---

39. See Edward N. Wolff and Ajit Zacharias, "Household Wealth and the Measurement of Economic Well-Being in the U.S.," *Journal of Economic Inequality* 7, no. 2 (June 2009): 83–115. Wolff and Zacharias correctly remark that my initial article with Emmanuel Saez in 2003 overstated the degree to which the evolutions we observed could be explained by the substitution of "working rich" for "coupon-clipping rentiers," when in fact what one finds is rather a "cohabitation" of the two.

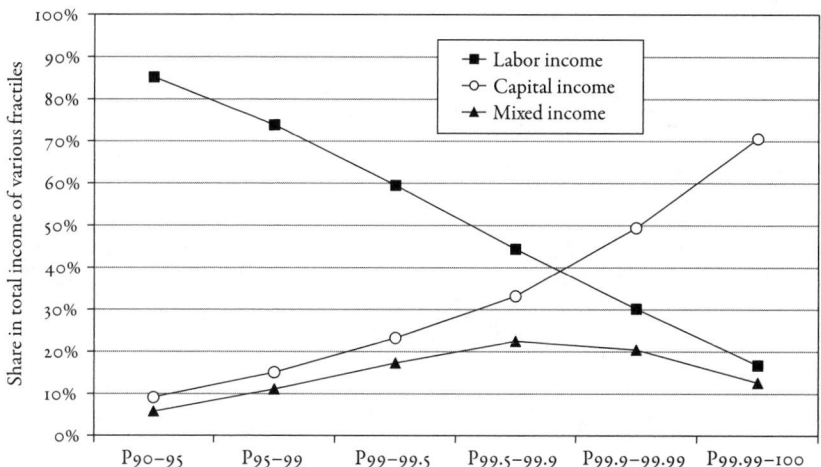

FIGURE 8.10. The composition of top incomes in the United States, 2007
Capital income becomes dominant at the level of top 0.1 percent in 2007, as opposed to the top 1 percent in 1929.
Sources and series: see piketty.pse.ens.fr/capital21c.

fore this is true (see Figure 8.10). Again, I should make it clear that this has to do with the inclusion of capital gains in income from capital: without capital gains, salaries would be the main source of income up to the 0.01 percent level of the income hierarchy.[40]

The final and perhaps most important point in need of clarification is that the increase in very high incomes and very high salaries primarily reflects the advent of "supermanagers," that is, top executives of large firms who have managed to obtain extremely high, historically unprecedented compensation packages for their labor. If we look only at the five highest paid executives in each company listed on the stock exchange (which are generally the only compensation packages that must be made public in annual corporate reports), we come to the paradoxical conclusion that there are not enough top corporate managers to explain the increase in very high US incomes, and it therefore becomes difficult to explain the evolutions we observe in incomes

---

40. See Supplemental Figures S8.1 and S8.2, available online.

stated on federal income tax returns.[41] But the fact is that in many large US firms, there are far more than five executives whose pay places them in the top 1 percent (above \$352,000 in 2010) or even the top 0.1 percent (above \$1.5 million).

Recent research, based on matching declared income on tax returns with corporate compensation records, allows me to state that the vast majority (60 to 70 percent, depending on what definitions one chooses) of the top 0.1 percent of the income hierarchy in 2000–2010 consists of top managers. By comparison, athletes, actors, and artists of all kinds make up less than 5 percent of this group.[42] In this sense, the new US inequality has much more to do with the advent of "supermanagers" than with that of "superstars."[43]

It is also interesting to note that the financial professions (including both managers of banks and other financial institutions and traders operating on the financial markets) are about twice as common in the very high income groups as in the economy overall (roughly 20 percent of top 0.1 percent, whereas finance accounts for less than 10 percent of GDP). Nevertheless, 80 percent of the top income groups are not in finance, and the increase in the proportion of high-earning

---

41. See Steven N. Kaplan and Joshua Rauh, "Wall Street and Main Street: What Contributes to the Rise of the Highest Incomes?" *Review of Financial Studies* 23, no. 3 (March 2009): 1004–1050.

42. See Jon Bakija, Adam Cole, and Bradley T. Heim, "Jobs and Income Growth of Top Earners and the Causes of Changing Income Inequality: Evidence from U.S. Tax Return Data," Department of Economics Working Papers 2010–24, Department of Economics, Williams College, Table 1. Other important professional groups include doctors and lawyers (about 10 percent of the total) and real estate promoters (around 5 percent). These data should be used with caution, however: we do not know the origin of the fortunes involved (whether inherited or not), but income from capital accounts for more than half of all income at the level of the top thousandth if capital gains are included (see Figure 8.10) and about a quarter if they are excluded (see Supplemental Figure S8.2, available online).

43. "Superentrepreneurs" of the Bill Gates type are so few in number that they are not relevant for the analysis of income and are best studied in the context of an analysis of fortunes and in particular the evolution of different classes of fortune. See Chapter 12.

Americans is explained primarily by the skyrocketing pay packages of top managers of large firms in the nonfinancial as well as financial sectors.

Finally, note that in accordance with US tax laws as well as economic logic, I have included in wages all bonuses and other incentives paid to top managers, as well as the value of any stock options (a form of remuneration that has played an important role in the increase of wage inequality depicted in Figures 8.9 and 8.10).[44] The very high volatility of incentives, bonuses, and option prices explains why top incomes fluctuated so much in the period 2000–2010.

---

44. Concretely, if a manager is granted options that allow him to buy for $100 stock in the company valued at $200 when he exercises the option, then the difference between the two prices—in this case $100—is treated as a component of the manager's wage in the year in which the option is exercised. If he later sells the shares of stock for an even higher price, say $250, then the difference, $50, is recorded as a capital gain.

NINE

Inequality of Labor Income

Now that I have introduced the evolution of income and wages in France and the United States since the beginning of the twentieth century, I will examine the changes I have observed and consider how representative they are of long-term changes in other developed and emerging economies.

I will begin by examining in this chapter the dynamics of labor income inequality. What caused the explosion of wage inequalities and the rise of the supermanager in the United States after 1980? More generally, what accounts for the diverse historical evolutions we see in various countries?

In subsequent chapters I will look into the evolution of the capital ownership distribution: How and why has the concentration of wealth decreased everywhere, but especially in Europe, since the turn of the twentieth century? The emergence of a "patrimonial middle class" is a crucial issue for this study, because it largely explains why income inequality decreased during the first half of the twentieth century and why we in the developed countries have gone from a society of rentiers to a society of managers (or, in the less optimistic version, from a society of superrentiers to a somewhat less extreme form of rentier society).

Wage Inequality: A Race between Education and Technology?

Why is inequality of income from labor, and especially wage inequality, greater in some societies and periods than others? The most widely accepted theory is that of a race between education and technology.

To be blunt, this theory does not explain everything. In particular, it does not offer a satisfactory explanation of the rise of the supermanager or of wage inequality in the United States after 1980. The theory does, however, suggest interesting and important clues for explaining certain historical evolutions. I will therefore begin by discussing it.

The theory rests on two hypotheses. First, a worker's wage is equal to his marginal productivity, that is, his individual contribution to the output of the firm or office for which he works. Second, the worker's productivity depends above all on his skill and on supply and demand for that skill in a given society. For example, in a society in which very few people are qualified engineers (so that the "supply" of engineers is low) and the prevailing technology requires many engineers (so that "demand" is high), then it is highly likely that this combination of low supply and high demand will result in very high pay for engineers (relative to other workers) and therefore significant wage inequality between highly paid engineers and other workers.

This theory is in some respects limited and naïve. (In practice, a worker's productivity is not an immutable, objective quantity inscribed on his forehead, and the relative power of different social groups often plays a central role in determining what each worker is paid.) Nevertheless, as simple or even simplistic as the theory may be, it has the virtue of emphasizing two social and economic forces that do indeed play a fundamental role in determining wage inequality, even in more sophisticated theories: the supply and demand of skills. In practice, the supply of skills depends on, among other things, the state of the educational system: how many people have access to this or that track, how good is the training, how much classroom teaching is supplemented by appropriate professional experience, and so on. The demand for skills depends on, among other things, the state of the technologies available to produce the goods and services that society consumes. No matter what other forces may be involved, it seems clear that these two factors—the state of the training system on the one hand, the state of technology on the other—play a crucial role.

At a minimum, they influence the relative power of different social groups.

These two factors themselves depend on many other forces. The educational system is shaped by public policy, criteria of selection for different tracks, the way it is financed, the cost of study for students and their families, and the availability of continuing education. Technological progress depends on the pace of innovation and the rapidity of implementation. It generally increases the demand for new skills and creates new occupations. This leads to the idea of a race between education and technology: if the supply of skills does not increase at the same pace as the needs of technology, then groups whose training is not sufficiently advanced will earn less and be relegated to devalued lines of work, and inequality with respect to labor will increase. In order to avoid this, the educational system must increase its supply of new types of training and its output of new skills at a sufficiently rapid pace. If inequality is to decrease, moreover, the supply of new skills must increase even more rapidly, especially for the least well educated.

Consider, for example, wage inequalities in France. As I have shown, the wage hierarchy was fairly stable over a long period of time. The average wage increased enormously over the course of the twentieth century, but the gap between the best and worst paid deciles remained the same. Why was this the case, despite the massive democratization of the educational system during the same period? The most natural explanation is that all skill levels progressed at roughly the same pace, so that the inequalities in the wage scale were simply translated upward. The bottom group, which had once only finished grade school, moved up a notch on the educational ladder, first completing junior high school, then going on to a high school diploma. But the group that had previously made do with a high school diploma now went on to college or even graduate school. In other words, the democratization of the educational system did not eliminate educational inequality and therefore did not reduce wage inequality. If educational democratization had not taken place, however, and if the children of those who had only finished grade school a century ago (three-quarters of each generation at that time) had remained at that level, inequalities with respect to labor, and especially wage inequalities, would surely have increased substantially.

Now consider the US case. Two economists, Claudia Goldin and Lawrence Katz, systematically compared the following two evolutions in the period 1890–2005: on the one hand the wage gap between workers who graduated from college and those who had only a high school diploma, and on the other the rate of growth of the number of college degrees. For Goldin and Katz, the conclusion is stark: the two curves move in opposite directions. In particular, the wage gap, which decreased fairly regularly until the 1970s, suddenly begins to widen in the 1980s, at precisely the moment when for the first time the number of college graduates stops growing, or at any rate grows much more slowly than before.[1] Goldin and Katz have no doubt that increased wage inequality in the United States is due to a failure to invest sufficiently in higher education. More precisely, too many people failed to receive the necessary training, in part because families could not afford the high cost of tuition. In order to reverse this trend, they conclude, the United States should invest heavily in education so that as many people as possible can attend college.

The lessons of French and US experience thus point in the same direction. In the long run, the best way to reduce inequalities with respect to labor as well as to increase the average productivity of the labor force and the overall growth of the economy is surely to invest in education. If the purchasing power of wages increased fivefold in a century, it was because the improved skills of the workforce, coupled with technological progress, increased output per head fivefold. Over the long run, education and technology are the decisive determinants of wage levels.

---

1. Claudia Dale Goldin and Lawrence F. Katz, *The Race between Education and Technology: The Evolution of U.S. Educational Wage Differentials, 1890–2005* (Cambridge, MA: Belknap Press, 2010).

By the same token, if the United States (or France) invested more heavily in high-quality professional training and advanced educational opportunities and allowed broader segments of the population to have access to them, this would surely be the most effective way of increasing wages at the low to medium end of the scale and decreasing the upper decile's share of both wages and total income. All signs are that the Scandinavian countries, where wage inequality is more moderate than elsewhere, owe this result in large part to the fact that their educational system is relatively egalitarian and inclusive.[2] The question of how to pay for education, and in particular how to pay for higher education, is everywhere one of the key issues of the twenty-first century. Unfortunately, the data available for addressing issues of educational cost and access in the United States and France are extremely limited. Both countries attach a great deal of importance to the central role of schools and vocational training in fostering social mobility, yet theoretical discussion of educational issues and of meritocracy is often out of touch with reality, and in particular with the fact that the most prestigious schools tend to favor students from privileged social backgrounds. I will come back to this point in Chapter 13.

The Limits of the Theoretical Model: The Role of Institutions

Education and technology definitely play a crucial role in the long run. This theoretical model, based on the idea that a worker's wage is always perfectly determined by her marginal productivity and thus primarily by skill, is nevertheless limited in a number of ways. Leave aside the fact that it is not always enough to invest in training: existing technology is sometimes unable to make use of the available supply of skills. Leave aside, too, the fact that this theoretical model, at least in its most simplistic form, embodies a far too instrumental and utilitarian view of training. The main purpose of the health sector is not to

---

2. See Table 7.2.

provide other sectors with workers in good health. By the same token, the main purpose of the educational sector is not to prepare students to take up an occupation in some other sector of the economy. In all human societies, health and education have an intrinsic value: the ability to enjoy years of good health, like the ability to acquire knowledge and culture, is one of the fundamental purposes of civilization.[3] We are free to imagine an ideal society in which all other tasks are almost totally automated and each individual has as much freedom as possible to pursue the goods of education, culture, and health for the benefit of herself and others. Everyone would be by turns teacher or student, writer or reader, actor or spectator, doctor or patient. As noted in Chapter 2, we are to some extent already on this path: a characteristic feature of modern growth is the considerable share of both output and employment devoted to education, culture, and medicine.

While awaiting the ideal society of the future, let us try to gain a better understanding of wage inequality today. In this narrower context, the main problem with the theory of marginal productivity is quite simply that it fails to explain the diversity of the wage distributions we observe in different countries at different times. In order to understand the dynamics of wage inequality, we must introduce other factors, such as the institutions and rules that govern the operation of the labor market in each society. To an even greater extent than other markets, the labor market is not a mathematical abstraction whose workings are entirely determined by natural and immutable mechanisms and implacable technological forces: it is a social construct based on specific rules and compromises.

In the previous chapter I noted several important episodes of compression and expansion of wage hierarchies that are very difficult to explain solely in terms of the supply of and demand for various skills. For example, the compression of wage inequalities that occurred in

---

3. In the language of national accounting, expenditures on health and education are counted as consumption (a source of intrinsic well-being) and not investment. This is yet another reason why the expression "human capital" is problematic.

both France and the United States during World Wars I and II was the result of negotiations over wage scales in both the public and private sectors, in which specific institutions such as the National War Labor Board (created expressly for the purpose) played a central role. I also called attention to the importance of changes in the minimum wage for explaining the evolution of wage inequalities in France since 1950, with three clearly identified subperiods: 1950–1968, during which the minimum wage was rarely adjusted and the wage hierarchy expanded; 1968–1983, during which the minimum wage rose very rapidly and wage inequalities decreased sharply; and finally 1983–2012, during which the minimum wage increased relatively slowly and the wage hierarchy tended to expand.[4] At the beginning of 2013, the minimum wage in France stood at 9.43 euros per hour.

In the United States, a federal minimum wage was introduced in 1933, nearly twenty years earlier than in France.[5] As in France, changes in the minimum wage played an important role in the evolution of wage inequalities in the United States. It is striking to learn that in terms of purchasing power, the minimum wage reached its maximum level nearly half a century ago, in 1969, at $1.60 an hour (or $10.10 in 2013 dollars, taking account of inflation between 1968 and 2013), at a time when the unemployment rate was below 4 percent. From 1980 to 1990, under the presidents Ronald Reagan and George H. W. Bush, the federal minimum wage remained stuck at $3.35, which led to a significant decrease in purchasing power when inflation is factored in. It then rose to $5.25 under Bill Clinton in the 1990s and was

---

4. There were of course multiple subepisodes within each phase: for instance, the minimum wage increased by about 10 percent between 1998 and 2002 in order to compensate for the reduction of the legal work week from 39 hours to 35 hours while preserving the same monthly wage.

5. As in the case of the federal income tax, the minimum wage legislation resulted in a fierce battle between the executive branch and the Supreme Court, which overturned the first minimum wage law in 1935, but Roosevelt reintroduced it in 1938 and ultimately prevailed.

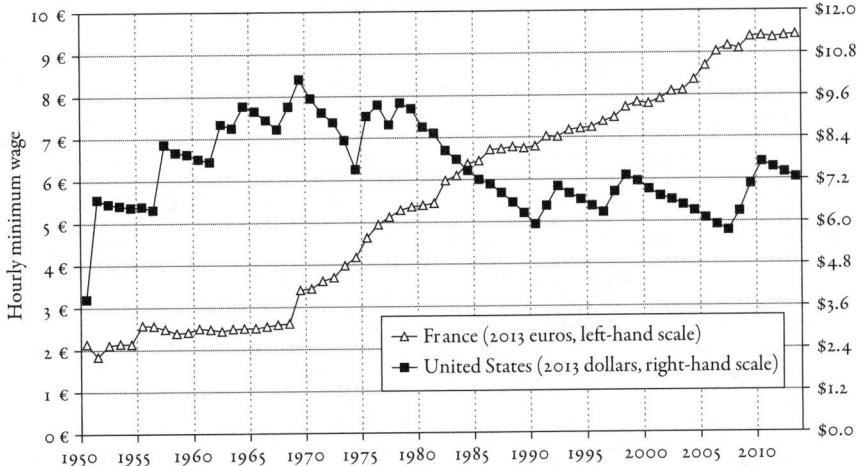

FIGURE 9.1. Minimum wage in France and the United States, 1950–2013

Expressed in 2013 purchasing power, the hourly minimum wage rose from $3.80 to $7.30 between 1950 and 2013 in the United States, and from €2.10 to €9.40 in France.

Sources and series: see piketty.pse.ens.fr/capital21c.

frozen at that level until legislation passed under George W. Bush led to an increase under Barack Obama. At the beginning of 2013 it stood at $7.25 an hour, or barely 6 euros, which is a third below the French minimum wage, the opposite of the situation that obtained in the early 1980s (see Figure 9.1).[6] President Obama, in his State of the Union address in February 2013, announced his intention to raise the minimum wage to about $9 an hour for the period 2013–2016.[7]

Inequalities at the bottom of the US wage distribution have closely followed the evolution of the minimum wage: the gap between the

---

6. In Figure 9.1, I have converted nominal minimum wages into 2013 euros and dollars. See Supplemental Figures S9.1–2, available online, for the nominal minimum wages.

7. Some states have a higher minimum wage than the federal minimum in 2013: in California and Massachusetts, the minimum is $8 an hour; in Washington state it is $9.19.

bottom 10 percent of the wage distribution and the overall average wage widened significantly in the 1980s, then narrowed in the 1990s, and finally increased again in the 2000s. Nevertheless, inequalities at the top of the distribution—for example, the share of total wages going to the top 10 percent—increased steadily throughout this period. Clearly, the minimum wage has an impact at the bottom of the distribution but much less influence at the top, where other forces are at work.

Wage Scales and the Minimum Wage

There is no doubt that the minimum wage plays an essential role in the formation and evolution of wage inequalities, as the French and US experiences show. Each country has its own history in this regard and its own peculiar chronology. There is nothing surprising about that: labor market regulations depend on each society's perceptions and norms of social justice and are intimately related to each country's social, political, and cultural history. The United States used the minimum wage to increase lower-end wages in the 1950s and 1960s but abandoned this tool in the 1970s. In France, it was exactly the opposite: the minimum wage was frozen in the 1950s and 1960s but was used much more often in the 1970s. Figure 9.1 illustrates this striking contrast.

It would be easy to multiply examples from other countries. Britain introduced a minimum wage in 1999, at a level between the United States and France: in 2013 it was £6.19 (or about 8.05 euros).[8] Germany and Sweden have chosen to do without minimum wages at the national level, leaving it to trade unions to negotiate not only minimums but also complete wage schedules with employers in each branch of industry. In practice, the minimum wage in both countries was about 10 euros an hour in 2013 in many branches (and therefore higher than

---

8. At an exchange rate of 1.30 euros per pound. In practice, the gap between the British and French minimum wages is larger because of the difference in employer social security payments (which are added to the gross wage). I come back to this point in Part Four.

in countries with a national minimum wage). But minimum pay can be markedly lower in sectors that are relatively unregulated or under-unionized. In order to set a common floor, Germany is contemplating the introduction of a minimum wage in 2013–2014. This is not the place to write a detailed history of minimum wages and wage schedules around the world or to discuss their impact on wage inequality. My goal here is more modest: simply to indicate briefly what general principles can be used to analyze the institutions that regulate wage setting everywhere.

What is in fact the justification for minimum wages and rigid wage schedules? First, it is not always easy to measure the marginal productivity of a particular worker. In the public sector, this is obvious, but it is also clear in the private sector: in an organization employing dozens or even thousands of workers, it is no simple task to judge each individual worker's contribution to overall output. To be sure, one can estimate marginal productivity, at least for jobs that can be replicated, that is, performed in the same way by any number of employees. For an assembly-line worker or McDonald's server, management can calculate how much additional revenue an additional worker or server would generate. Such an estimate would be approximate, however, yielding a range of productivities rather than an absolute number. In view of this uncertainty, how should the wage be set? There are many reasons to think that granting management absolute power to set the wage of each employee on a monthly or (why not?) daily basis would not only introduce an element of arbitrariness and injustice but would also be inefficient for the firm.

In particular, it may be efficient for the firm to ensure that wages remain relatively stable and do not vary constantly with fluctuations in sales. The owners and managers of the firm usually earn much more and are significantly wealthier than their workers and can therefore more easily absorb short-term shocks to their income. Under such circumstances, it can be in everyone's interest to provide a kind of "wage insurance" as part of the employment contract, in the sense that the worker's monthly wage is guaranteed (which does not preclude the use of bonuses and other incentives). The payment of a monthly rather than a daily wage was a revolutionary innovation that gradually took hold in all the developed countries during the twentieth century. This innovation was inscribed in law and became a feature of wage negotiations between workers and employers. The daily wage, which had been the norm in the nineteenth century, gradually disappeared. This was a crucial step in the constitution of the working class: workers now enjoyed a legal status and received a stable, predictable remuneration for their work. This clearly distinguished them from day laborers and piece workers—the typical employees of the eighteenth and nineteenth centuries.[9]

This justification of setting wages in advance obviously has its limits. The other classic argument in favor of minimum wages and fixed wage schedules is the problem of "specific investments." Concretely, the particular functions and tasks that a firm needs to be performed often require workers to make specific investments in the firm, in the sense that these investments are of no (or limited) value to other firms: for instance, workers might need to learn specific work methods, organizational methods, or skills linked to the firm's production process. If wages can be set unilaterally and changed at any moment by the firm, so that workers do not know in advance how much they will be paid, then it is highly likely that they will not invest as much in the firm as they should. It may therefore be in everyone's interest to set pay scales in advance. The same "specific investments" argument can also apply to other decisions by the firm, and it is the main reason for limiting the power of stockholders (who are seen as having too short-term an outlook in some cases) in favor of a power-sharing arrangement with a broader group of "stakeholders" (including the firm's workers), as in the "Rhenish model" of capitalism discussed earlier, in

---

9. Important differences persist between countries: in Britain, for example, many prices and incomes (including rents, allowances, and some wages) are set by the week and not the month. On these questions, see Robert Castel, *Les Métamorphoses de la question sociale: Une chronique du salariat* (Paris: Fayard, 1995).

Part Two. This is probably the most important argument in favor of fixed wage scales.

More generally, insofar as employers have more bargaining power than workers and the conditions of "pure and perfect" competition that one finds in the simplest economic models fail to be satisfied, it may be reasonable to limit the power of employers by imposing strict rules on wages. For example, if a small group of employers occupies a monopsony position in a local labor market (meaning that they are virtually the only source of employment, perhaps because of the limited mobility of the local labor force), they will probably try to exploit their advantage by lowering wages as much as possible, possibly even below the marginal productivity of the workers. Under such conditions, imposing a minimum wage may be not only just but also efficient, in the sense that the increase in wages may move the economy closer to the competitive equilibrium and increase the level of employment. This theoretical model, based on imperfect competition, is the clearest justification for the existence of a minimum wage: the goal is to make sure that no employer can exploit his competitive advantage beyond a certain limit.

Again, everything obviously depends on the level of the minimum wage. The limit cannot be set in the abstract, independent of the country's general skill level and average productivity. Various studies carried out in the United States between 1980 and 2000, most notably by the economists David Card and Alan Krueger, showed that the US minimum wage had fallen to a level so low in that period that it could be raised without loss of employment, indeed at times with an increase in employment, as in the monopsony model.[10] On the basis

---

10. See in particular David Card and Alan Krueger, *Myth and Measurement: The New Economics of the Minimum Wage* (Princeton: Princeton University Press, 1995). Card and Krueger exploited numerous cases in which neighboring states had different minimum wages. The pure "monopsony" case is one in which a single employer can purchase labor in a given geographical area. (In pure monopoly, there is a single seller rather than a single buyer.) The employer then sets the wage as low as possible, and an increase in the minimum wage does not

of these studies, it seems likely that the increase in the minimum wage of nearly 25 percent (from \$7.25 to \$9 an hour) currently envisaged by the Obama administration will have little or no effect on the number of jobs. Obviously, raising the minimum wage cannot continue indefinitely: as the minimum wage increases, the negative effects on the level of employment eventually win out. If the minimum wage were doubled or tripled, it would be surprising if the negative impact were not dominant. It is more difficult to justify a significant increase in the minimum wage in a country like France, where it is relatively high (compared with the average wage and marginal productivity), than in the United States. To increase the purchasing power of low-paid workers in France, it is better to use other tools, such as training to improve skills or tax reform (these two remedies are complementary, moreover). Nevertheless, the minimum wage should not be frozen. Wage increases cannot exceed productivity increases indefinitely, but it is just as unhealthy to restrain (most) wage increases to below the rate of productivity increase. Different labor market institutions and policies play different roles, and each must be used in an appropriate manner.

To sum up: the best way to increase wages and reduce wage inequalities in the long run is to invest in education and skills. Over the long run, minimum wages and wage schedules cannot multiply wages by factors of five or ten: to achieve that level of progress, education and technology are the decisive forces. Nevertheless, the rules of the labor market play a crucial role in wage setting during periods of time determined by the relative progress of education and technology. In practice, those periods can be fairly long, in part because it is hard to gauge individual marginal productivities with any certainty, and in

---

reduce the level of employment, because the employer's profit margin is so large as to make it possible to continue to hire all who seek employment. Employment may even increase, because more people will seek work, perhaps because at the higher wage they prefer work to illegal activities, which is a good thing, or because they prefer work to school, which may not be such a good thing. This is precisely what Card and Krueger observed.

part because of the problem of specific investments and imperfect competition.

How to Explain the Explosion of Inequality in the United States?

The most striking failure of the theory of marginal productivity and the race between education and technology is no doubt its inability to adequately explain the explosion of very high incomes from labor observed in the United States since 1980. According to this theory, one should be able to explain this change as the result of skill-biased technological change. Some US economists buy this argument, which holds that top labor incomes have risen much more rapidly than average wages simply because unique skills and new technology have made these workers much more productive than the average. There is a certain tautological quality to this explanation (after all, one can "explain" any distortion of the wage hierarchy as the result of some supposed technological change). It also has other major weaknesses, which to my mind make it a rather unconvincing argument.

First, as shown in the previous chapter, the increase in wage inequality in the United States is due mainly to increased pay at the very top end of the distribution: the top 1 percent and even more the top 0.1 percent. If we look at the entire top decile, we find that "the 9 percent" have progressed more rapidly than the average worker but not nearly at the same rate as "the 1 percent." Concretely, those making between $100,000 and $200,000 a year have seen their pay increase only slightly more rapidly than the average, whereas those making more than $500,000 a year have seen their remuneration literally explode (and those above $1 million a year have risen even more rapidly).[11] This very sharp discontinuity at the top income levels is a problem for the theory of marginal productivity: when we look at the changes in the skill levels of different groups in the income distribution, it is hard to

---

11. See in particular Figures 8.6–8.

see any discontinuity between "the 9 percent" and "the 1 percent," regardless of what criteria we use: years of education, selectivity of educational institution, or professional experience. One would expect a theory based on "objective" measures of skill and productivity to show relatively uniform pay increases within the top decile, or at any rate increases within different subgroups much closer to one another than the widely divergent increases we observe in practice.

Make no mistake: I am not denying the decisive importance of the investments in higher education and training that Katz and Goldin have identified. Policies to encourage broader access to universities are indispensable and crucial in the long run, in the United States and elsewhere. As desirable as such policies are, however, they seem to have had limited impact on the explosion of the topmost incomes observed in the United States since 1980.

In short, two distinct phenomena have been at work in recent decades. First, the wage gap between college graduates and those who go no further than high school has increased, as Goldin and Katz showed. In addition, the top 1 percent (and even more the top 0.1 percent) have seen their remuneration take off. This is a very specific phenomenon, which occurs within the group of college graduates and in many cases separates individuals who have pursued their studies at elite universities for many years. Quantitatively, the second phenomenon is more important than the first. In particular, as shown in the previous chapter, the overperformance of the top centile explains most (nearly three-quarters) of the increase in the top decile's share of US national income since 1970.[12] It is therefore

---

12. This fact is crucial but often neglected in US academic debate. In addition to the work of Goldin and Katz, *Race between Education and Technology*, see also the recent work of Rebecca Blank, *Changing Inequality* (Berkeley: University of California Press, 2011), which is almost entirely focused on the evolution of the wage difference associated with a college diploma (and on the evolution of family structures). Raghuram Rajan, *Fault Lines* (Princeton: Princeton University Press, 2010), also seems convinced that the evolution of inequality related to col-

important to find an adequate explanation of this phenomenon, and at first sight the educational factor does not seem to be the right one to focus on.

The Rise of the Supermanager: An Anglo-Saxon Phenomenon

The second difficulty—and no doubt the major problem confronting the marginal productivity theory—is that the explosion of very high salaries occurred in some developed countries but not others. This suggests that institutional differences between countries rather than general and a priori universal causes such as technological change played a central role.

I begin with the English-speaking countries. Broadly speaking, the rise of the supermanager is largely an Anglo-Saxon phenomenon. Since 1980 the share of the upper centile in national income has risen significantly in the United States, Great Britain, Canada, and Australia (see Figure 9.2). Unfortunately, we do not have separate series for wage inequality and total income inequality for all countries as we do for France and the United States. But in most cases we do have data concerning the composition of income in relation to total income, from which we can infer that in all of these countries the explosion of top incomes explains most (generally at least two-thirds) of the increase in the top centile's share of national income; the rest is

---

lege is more significant than the explosion of the 1 percent (which is incorrect). The reason for this is probably that the data normally used by labor and education economists do not give the full measure of the overperformance of the top centile (one needs tax data to see what is happening). The survey data have the advantage of including more sociodemographic data (including data on education) than tax records do. But they are based on relatively small samples and also raise many problems having to do with respondents' self-characterization. Ideally, both types of sources should be used together. On these methodological issues, see the online technical appendix.

explained by robust income from capital. In all the English-speaking countries, the primary reason for increased income inequality in recent decades is the rise of the supermanager in both the financial and nonfinancial sectors.

This family resemblance should not be allowed to obscure the fact that the magnitude of the phenomenon varies widely from country to country, however. Figure 9.2 is quite clear on this point. In the 1970s, the upper centile's share of national income was quite similar across countries. It ranged from 6 to 8 percent in the four English-speaking countries considered, and the United States did not stand out as exceptional: indeed, Canada was slightly higher, at 9 percent, whereas Australia came in last, with just 5 percent of national income going to the top centile in the late 1970s and early 1980s. Thirty years later, in the early 2010s, the situation is totally different. The upper centile's share is nearly 20 percent in the United States, compared with 14–15 percent in Britain and Canada and barely 9–10 percent in Australia (see Figure 9.2).[13] To a first approximation, we can say that the upper centile's share in the United States increased roughly twice as much as in Britain and Canada and about three times as much as in Australia and New Zealand.[14] If the rise of the supermanager were a purely technological phenomenon, it would be difficult to understand why such large differences exist between otherwise quite similar countries.

Let me turn now to the rest of the wealthy world, namely, continental Europe and Japan. The key fact is that the upper centile's share of national income in these countries has increased much less than in

---

13. Note that the curves in Figure 9.2 and subsequent figures do not take account of capital gains (which are not consistently measured across countries). Since capital gains are particularly large in the United States (making the top centile's share of national income more than 20 percent in the 2000s if we count capital gains), the gap is in fact wider than indicated in Figure 9.2. See, for example, Supplemental Figure S9.3, available online.

14. New Zealand followed almost the same trajectory as Australia. See Supplemental Figure S9.4, available online. In order to keep the figures simple, I have presented only some of the countries and series available. Interested readers should consult the online technical appendix or the WTID for the complete series.

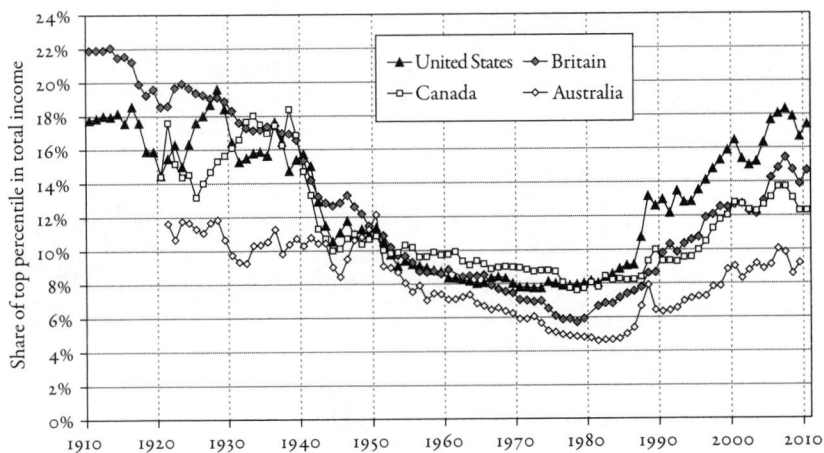

FIGURE 9.2. Income inequality in Anglo-Saxon countries, 1910–2010

The share of top percentile in total income rose since the 1970s in all Anglo-Saxon countries, but with different magnitudes.

Sources and series: see piketty.pse.ens.fr/capital21c.

the English-speaking countries since 1980. The comparison between Figures 9.2 and 9.3 is particularly striking. To be sure, the upper centile's share increased significantly everywhere. In Japan the evolution was virtually the same as in France: the top centile's share of national income was barely 7 percent in the 1980s but is 9 percent or perhaps even slightly higher today. In Sweden, the top centile's share was a little more than 4 percent in the early 1980s (the lowest level recorded in the World Top Incomes Database for any country in any period) but reached 7 percent in the early 2010s.[15] In Germany, the top centile's share rose from about 9 percent to nearly 11 percent of national income between the early 1980s and the early 2010s (see Figure 9.3).

If we look at other European countries, we observe similar evolutions, with the top centile's share increasing by two or three points of

15. Indeed, if we include capital gains, which were strong in Sweden in the period 1990–2010, the top centile's share reached 9 percent. See the online technical appendix.

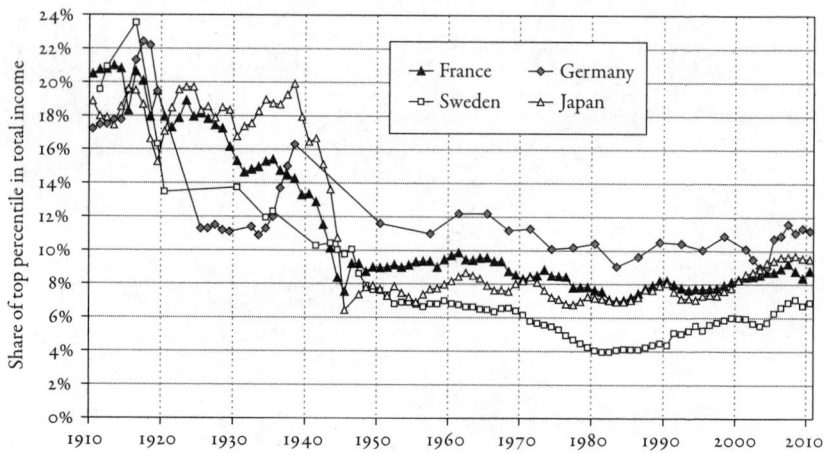

FIGURE 9.3. Income inequality in Continental Europe and Japan, 1910–2010
As compared to Anglo-Saxon countries, the share of top percentile barely increased since the 1970s in Continental Europe and Japan.
Sources and series: see piketty.pse.ens.fr/capital21c.

national income over the past thirty years in both northern and southern Europe. In Denmark and other Nordic countries, top incomes claim a smaller share of the total, but the increase is similar: the top centile received a little more than 5 percent of Danish national income in the 1980s but got close to 7 percent in 2000–2010. In Italy and Spain, the orders of magnitude are very close to those observed in France, with the top centile's share rising from 7 to 9 percent of national income in the same period, again an increase of two points of national income (see Figure 9.4). In this respect, continental Europe is indeed an almost perfect "union." Britain, of course, stands apart, being much closer to the pattern of the United States than that of Europe.[16]

---

16. All the other European countries in the WTID, namely, the Netherlands, Switzerland, Norway, Finland, and Portugal, evolved in ways similar to those observed in other continental European countries. Note that we have fairly complete data for southern Europe. The series for Spain goes back to 1933, when an

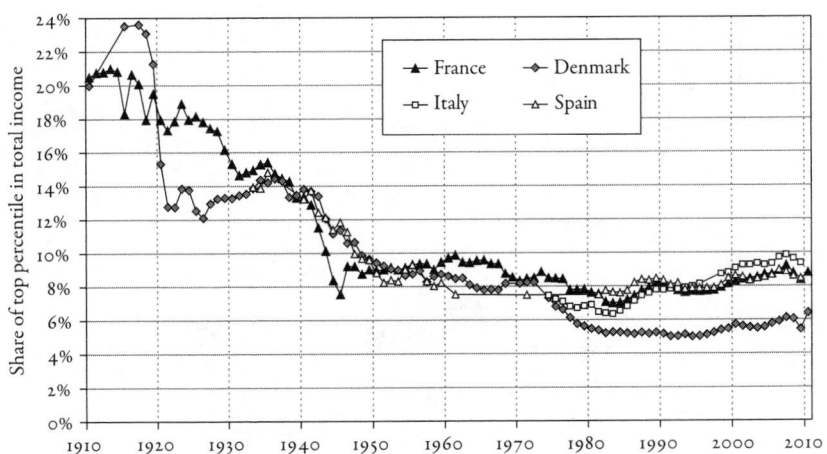

FIGURE 9.4. Income inequality in Northern and Southern Europe, 1910–2010
As compared to Anglo-Saxon countries, the top percentile income share barely increased in Northern and Southern Europe since the 1970s.
Sources and series: see piketty.pse.ens.fr/capital21c.

Make no mistake: these increases on the order of two to three points of national income in Japan and the countries of continental Europe mean that income inequality rose quite significantly. The top 1 percent of earners saw pay increases noticeably more rapid than the average: the upper centile's share increased by about 30 percent, and even more in countries where it started out lower. This was quite striking to contemporary observers, who read in the daily paper or heard on the radio about stupendous raises for "supermanagers." It was particularly striking in the period 1990–2010, when average income stagnated, or at least rose much more slowly than in the past.

Furthermore, the higher one climbs in the income hierarchy, the more spectacular the raises. Even if the number of individuals benefiting

---

income tax was created, but there are several breaks. In Italy, the income tax was created in 1923, but complete data are not available until 1974. See the online technical appendix.

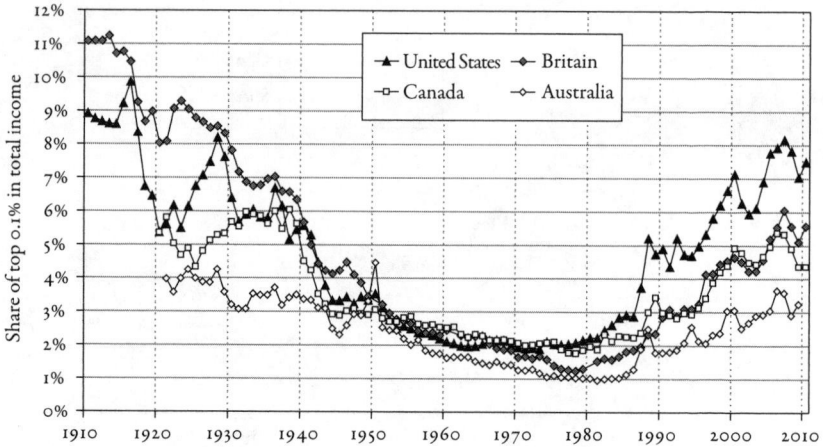

FIGURE 9.5. The top thousandth income share in Anglo-Saxon countries, 1910–2010
The share of the top 0.1 percent highest incomes in total income rose sharply since the 1970s in all Anglo-Saxon countries, but with varying magnitudes.
Sources and series: see piketty.pse.ens.fr/capital21c.

from such salary increases is fairly limited, they are nevertheless quite visible, and this visibility naturally raises the question of what justifies such high levels of compensation. Consider the share of the top thousandth—the best remunerated 0.1 percent—in the national income of the English-speaking countries on the one hand (Figure 9.5) and continental Europe and Japan on the other (Figure 9.6). The differences are obvious: the top thousandth in the United States increased their share from 2 to nearly 10 percent over the past several decades—an unprecedented rise.[17] But there has been a remarkable increase of top incomes everywhere. In France and Japan, the top thousandth's share rose from barely 1.5 percent of national income in the early 1980s to nearly 2.5 percent in the early 2010s—close to double. In Sweden, the

---

17. The share of the top thousandth exceeded 8 percent in the United States in 2000–2010 if we omit capital gains and 12 percent if we include them. See the online technical appendix.

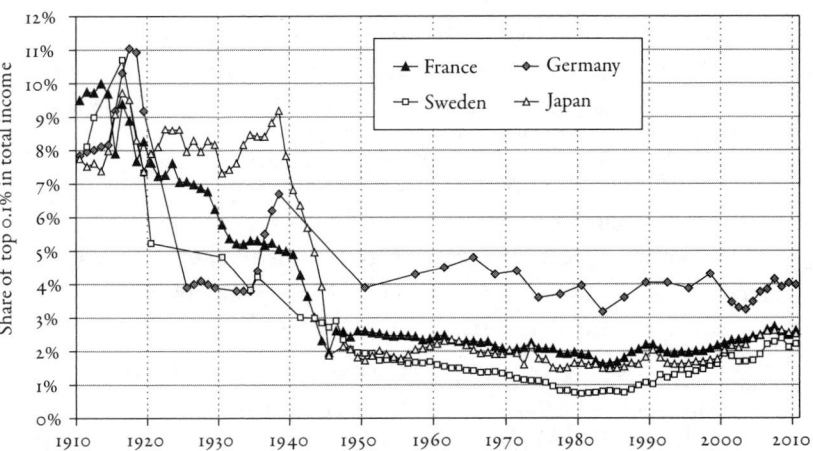

FIGURE 9.6. The top thousandth income share in Continental Europe and Japan, 1910–2010

As compared to Anglo-Saxon countries, the top 0.1 percent income share barely increased in Continental Europe and Japan.

Sources and series: see piketty.pse.ens.fr/capital21c.

same share rose from less than 1 percent to more than 2 percent in the same period.

To make clear what this represents in concrete terms, remember that a 2 percent share of national income for 0.1 percent of the population means that the average individual in this group enjoys an income 20 times higher than the national average (or 600,000 euros a year if the average income is 30,000 per adult). A share of 10 percent means that each individual enjoys an income 100 times the national average (or 3 million euros a year if the average is 30,000).[18] Recall, too, that the top 0.1 percent is by definition a group of 50,000 people in a country with a population of 50 million adults (like France in the

---

18. The "0.1 percent" in France and Japan therefore increased from 15 to 25 times the national average income (that is, from 450,000 to 750,000 euros a year if the average is 30,000), while the top "0.1 percent" in the United States rose from 20 to 100 times the national average (that is, from $600,000 a year to $3 million). These orders of magnitude are approximate, but they give us a better sense of the phenomenon and relate shares to the salaries often quoted in the media.

early 2010s). This is a very small minority ("the 1 percent" is of course 10 times larger), yet it occupies a significant place in the social and political landscape.[19] The central fact is that in all the wealthy countries, including continental Europe and Japan, the top thousandth enjoyed spectacular increases in purchasing power in 1990–2010, while the average person's purchasing power stagnated.

From a macroeconomic point of view, however, the explosion of very high incomes has thus far been of limited importance in continental Europe and Japan: the rise has been impressive, to be sure, but too few people have been affected to have had an impact as powerful as in the United States. The transfer of income to "the 1 percent" involves only two to three points of national income in continental Europe and Japan compared with 10 to 15 points in the United States— 5 to 7 times greater.[20]

The simplest way to express these regional differences is no doubt the following: in the United States, income inequality in 2000–2010 regained the record levels observed in 1910–1920 (although the composition of income was now different, with a larger role played by high incomes from labor and a smaller role by high incomes from capital). In Britain and Canada, things moved in the same direction. In continental Europe and Japan, income inequality today remains far lower than it was at the beginning of the twentieth century and in fact

---

19. The income of "the 1 percent" is distinctly lower: a share of 10 percent of national income for the 1 percent means by definition that their average income is 10 times higher than the national average (a share of 20 percent would indicate an average 20 times higher than the national average, and so on). The Pareto coefficient, about which I will say more in Chapter 10, enables us to relate the shares of the top decile, top centile, and top thousandth: in relatively egalitarian countries (such as Sweden in the 1970s), the top 0.1 percent earned barely twice as much as the top 1 percent, so that the top thousandth's share of national income was barely one-fifth of the top centile's. In highly inegalitarian countries (such as the United States in the 2000s), the top thousandth earns 4 to 5 times what the top centile earns, and the top thousandth's share is 40 to 50 percent of the top centile's share.

20. Depending on whether capital gains are included or not. See the online technical appendix for the complete series.

has not changed much since 1945, if we take a long-run view. The comparison of Figures 9.2 and 9.3 is particularly clear on this point.

Obviously, this does not mean that the European and Japanese evolutions of the past few decades should be neglected. On the contrary: their trajectory resembles that of the United States in some respects, with a delay of one or two decades, and one need not wait until the phenomenon assumes the macroeconomic significance observed in the United States to worry about it.

Nevertheless, the fact remains that the evolution in continental Europe and Japan is thus far much less serious than in the United States (and, to a lesser extent, in the other Anglo-Saxon countries). This may tell us something about the forces at work. The divergence between the various regions of the wealthy world is all the more striking because technological change has been the same more or less everywhere: in particular, the revolution in information technology has affected Japan, Germany, France, Sweden, and Denmark as much as the United States, Britain, and Canada. Similarly, economic growth—or, more precisely, growth in output per capita, which is to say, productivity growth—has been quite similar throughout the wealthy countries, with differences of a few tenths of a percentage point.[21] In view of these facts, this quite large divergence in the way the income distribution has evolved in the various wealthy countries demands an explanation, which the theory of marginal productivity and of the race between technology and education does not seem capable of providing.

Europe: More Inegalitarian Than the New World in 1900–1910

Note, moreover, that the United States, contrary to what many people think today, was not always more inegalitarian than Europe—far from it. Income inequality was actually quite high in Europe at the beginning of the twentieth century. This is confirmed by all the indices

21. See, in particular, Table 5.1.

and historical sources. In particular, the top centile's share of national income exceeded 20 percent in all the countries of Europe in 1900–1910 (see Figures 9.2–4). This was true not only of Britain, France, and Germany but also of Sweden and Denmark (proof that the Nordic countries have not always been models of equality—far from it), and more generally of all European countries for which we have estimates from this period.[22]

The similar levels of income concentration in all European countries during the Belle Époque obviously demand an explanation. Since top incomes in this period consisted almost entirely of income from capital,[23] the explanation must be sought primarily in the realm of concentration of capital. Why was capital so concentrated in Europe in the period 1900–1910?

It is interesting to note that, compared with Europe, inequality was lower not only in the United States and Canada (where the top centile's share of national income was roughly 16–18 percent at the beginning of the twentieth century) but especially in Australia and New Zealand (11–12 percent). Thus it was the New World, and especially the newest and most recently settled parts of the New World, that appear to have been less inegalitarian than Old Europe in the Belle Époque.

It is also interesting to note that Japan, despite its social and cultural differences from Europe, seems to have had the same high level of inequality at the beginning of the twentieth century, with about 20 percent of national income going to the top centile. The available data do not allow me to make all the comparisons I would like to make, but all signs are that in terms of both income structure and income

---

22. For Sweden and Denmark, in some years in the period 1900–1910, we find top centile shares of 25 percent of national income, higher than the levels seen in Britain, France, and Germany at that time (where the maximum was closer to 22 or 23 percent). Given the limitations of the available sources, it is not certain that these differences are truly significant, however. See the online technical appendix.

23. For all the countries for which we have data on the composition of income at different levels, comparable to the data presented for France and the United States in the previous chapter (see Figures 8.3–4 and 8.9–10), we find the same reality.

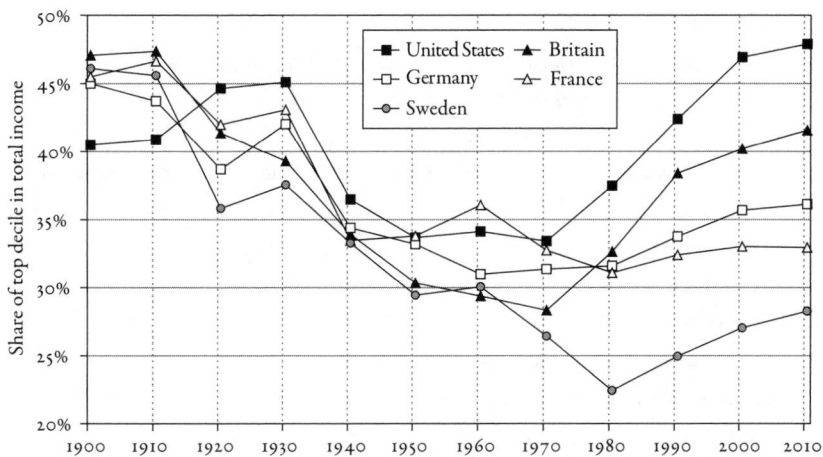

FIGURE 9.7. The top decile income share in Europe and the United States, 1900–2010

In the 1950s–1970s, the top decile income share was about 30–35 percent of total income in Europe as in the United States.

Sources and series: see piketty.pse.ens.fr/capital21c.

inequality, Japan was indeed part of the same "old world" as Europe. It is also striking to note the similar evolution of Japan and Europe over the course of the twentieth century (Figure 9.3).

I will return later to the reasons for the very high concentration of capital in the Belle Époque and to the transformations that took place in various countries over the course of the twentieth century (namely, a reduction of concentration). I will show in particular that the greater inequality of wealth that we see in Europe and Japan is fairly naturally explained by the low demographic growth rate we find in the Old World, which resulted almost automatically in a greater accumulation and concentration of capital.

At this stage, I want simply to stress the magnitude of the changes that have altered the relative standing of countries and continents. The clearest way to make this point is probably to look at the evolution of the top decile's share of national income. Figure 9.7 shows this for the United States and four European countries (Britain, France, Germany, and Sweden) since the turn of the twentieth century. I have indicated decennial averages in order to focus attention on long-term trends.[24]

What we find is that on the eve of World War I, the top decile's share was 45–50 percent of national income in all the European countries, compared with a little more than 40 percent in the United States. By the end of World War II, the United States had become slightly more inegalitarian than Europe: the top decile's share decreased on both continents owing to the shocks of 1914–1945, but the fall was more precipitous in Europe (and Japan). The explanation for this is that the shocks to capital were much larger. Between 1950 and 1970, the upper decile's share was fairly stable and fairly similar in the United States and Europe, around 30–35 percent of national income. The strong divergence that began in 1970–1980 led to the following situation in 2000–2010: the top decile's share of US national income reached 45–50 percent, or roughly the same level as Europe in 1900–1910. In Europe, we see wide variation, from the most inegalitarian case (Britain, with a top decile share of 40 percent) to the most egalitarian (Sweden, less than 30 percent), with France and Germany in between (around 35 percent).

If we calculate (somewhat abusively) an average for Europe based on these four countries, we can make a very clear international comparison: the United States was less inegalitarian than Europe in 1900–1910, slightly more inegalitarian in 1950–1960, and much more inegalitarian in 2000–2010 (see Figure 9.8).[25]

Apart from this long-term picture, there are of course multiple national histories as well as constant short- and medium-term fluctua-

---

24. See Supplemental Figure S9.6, available online, for the same graph using annual series. Series for other countries are similar and available online.

25. Figure 9.8 simply shows the arithmetic mean of the four European countries included in Figure 9.7. These four countries are quite representative of European diversity, and the curve would not look very different if we included other northern and southern European countries for which data are available, or if we weighted the average by the national income of each country. See the online technical appendix.

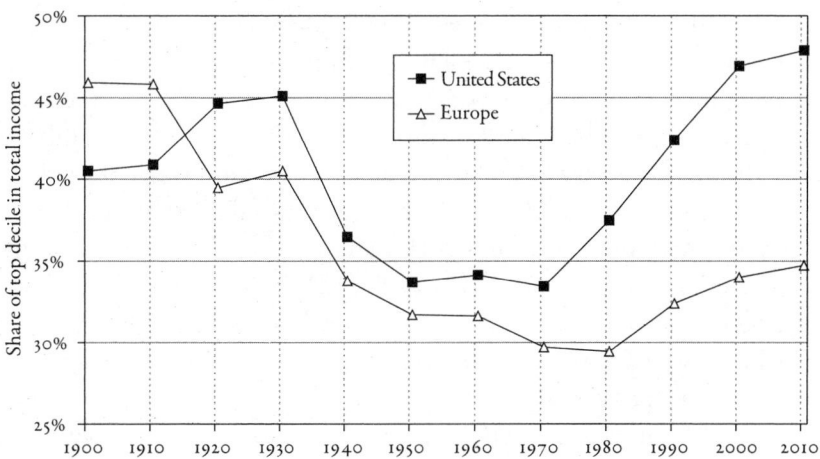

FIGURE 9.8. Income inequality in Europe versus the United States, 1900–2010
The top decile income share was higher in Europe than in the United States in 1900–
1910; it is a lot higher in the United States in 2000–2010.
Sources and series: see piketty.pse.ens.fr/capital21c.

tions linked to social and political developments in each country, as I showed in Chapter 8 and analyzed in some detail in the French and US cases. Space will not permit me to do the same for every country here.[26]

In passing, however, it is worth mentioning that the period between the two world wars seems to have been particularly tumultuous and chaotic almost everywhere, though the chronology of events varied from country to country. In Germany, the hyperinflation of the 1920s followed hard on the heels of military defeat. The Nazis came to power a short while later, after the worldwide depression had plunged the country back into crisis. Interestingly, the top centile's share of

---

26. Interested readers may wish to consult the case studies of twenty-three countries that Anthony Atkinson and I published in two volumes in 2007 and 2010: *Top Incomes over the Twentieth Century: A Contrast Between Continental European and English-Speaking Countries* (Oxford: Oxford University Press, 2007), and *Top Incomes: A Global Perspective* (Oxford: Oxford University Press, 2010).

German national income increased rapidly between 1933 and 1938, totally out of phase with other countries: this reflects the revival of industrial profits (boosted by demand for armaments), as well as a general reestablishment of income hierarchies in the Nazi era. Note, too, that the share of the top centile—and, even more, the top thousandth—in Germany has been noticeably higher since 1950 than in most other continental European countries (including, in particular, France) as well as Japan, even though the overall level of inequality in Germany is not very different. This can be explained in various ways, among which it is difficult to say that one is better than another. (I will come back to this point.)

In addition, there are serious lacunae in German tax records, owing in large part to the country's turbulent history in the twentieth century, so that it is difficult to be sure about certain developments or to make sharp comparisons with other countries. Prussia, Saxony, and most other German states imposed an income tax relatively early, between 1880 and 1890, but there were no national laws or tax records until after World War I. There were frequent breaks in the statistical record during the 1920s, and then the records for 1938 to 1950 are missing altogether, so it is impossible to study how the income distribution evolved during World War II and its immediate aftermath.

This distinguishes Germany from other countries deeply involved in the conflict, especially Japan and France, whose tax administrations continued to compile statistics during the war years without interruption, as if nothing were amiss. If Germany was anything like these two countries, it is likely that the top centile's share of national income reached a nadir in 1945 (the year in which German capital and income from capital were reduced to virtually nothing) before beginning to rise sharply again in 1946–1947. Yet when German tax records return in 1950, they show the income hierarchy already beginning to resemble its appearance in 1938. In the absence of complete sources, it is difficult to say more. The German case is further complicated by the fact that the country's boundaries changed several times during the twentieth century, most recently with the reunification of 1990–1991, in addition to which full tax data are published only every three years (rather than annually as in most other countries).

Inequalities in Emerging Economies: Lower Than in the United States?

Let me turn now to the poor and emerging economies. The historical sources we need in order to study the long-run dynamics of the wealth distribution there are unfortunately harder to come by than in the rich countries. There are, however, a number of poor and emerging economies for which it is possible to find long series of tax data useful for making (rough) comparisons with our results for the more developed economies. Shortly after Britain introduced a progressive income tax at home, it decided to do the same in a number of its colonies. Thus an income tax fairly similar to that introduced in Britain in 1909 was adopted in South Africa in 1913 and in India (including present-day Pakistan) in 1922. Similarly, the Netherlands imposed an income tax on its Indonesian colony in 1920. Several South American countries introduced an income tax between the two world wars: Argentina, for example, did so in 1932. For these four countries—South Africa, India, Indonesia, and Argentina—we have tax data going back, respectively, to 1913, 1922, 1920, and 1932 and continuing (with gaps) to the present. The data are similar to what we have for the rich countries and can be employed using similar methods, in particular national income estimates for each country going back to the turn of the twentieth century.

My estimates are indicated in Figure 9.9. Several points deserve to be emphasized. First, the most striking result is probably that the upper centile's share of national income in poor and emerging economies is roughly the same as in the rich economies. During the most inegalitarian phases, especially 1910–1950, the top centile took around 20 percent of national income in all four countries: 15–18 percent in India and 22–25 percent in South Africa, Indonesia, and Argentina. During more egalitarian phases (essentially 1950–1980), the top centile's share fell to between 6 and 12 percent (barely 5–6 percent in

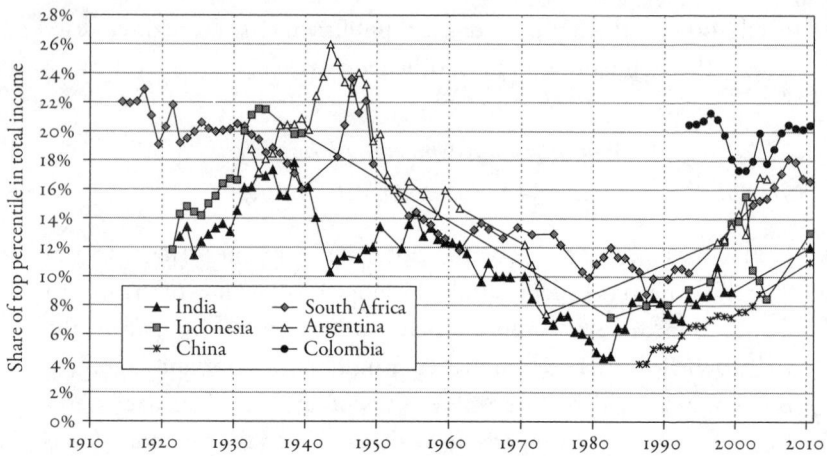

FIGURE 9.9. Income inequality in emerging countries, 1910–2010

Measured by the top percentile income share, income inequality rose in emerging countries since the 1980s, but ranks below the US level in 2000–2010.

Sources and series: see piketty.pse.ens.fr/capital21c.

India, 8–9 percent in Indonesia and Argentina, and 11–12 percent in South Africa). Thereafter, in the 1980s, the top centile's share rebounded, and today it stands at about 15 percent of national income (12–13 percent in India and Indonesia and 16–18 percent in South Africa and Argentina).

Figure 9.9 also shows two countries for which the available tax records allow us only to study how things have changed since the mid-1980s: China and Colombia.[27] In China, the top centile's share of national income rose rapidly over the past several decades but starting from a fairly low (almost Scandinavian) level in the mid-1980s: less

---

27. In China, strictly speaking, there was no income tax before 1980, so there is no way to study the evolution of income inequality for the entire twentieth century (the series presented here began in 1986). For Colombia, the tax records I have collected thus far go back only to 1993, but the income tax existed well before that, and it is entirely possible that we will ultimately find the earlier data (the archives of historical tax records are fairly poorly organized in a number of South American countries).

than 5 percent of national income went to the top centile at that time, according to the available sources. This is not very surprising for a Communist country with a very compressed wage schedule and virtual absence of private capital. Chinese inequality increased very rapidly following the liberalization of the economy in the 1980s and accelerated growth in the period 1990–2000, but according to my estimates, the upper centile's share in 2000–2010 was 10–11 percent, less than in India or Indonesia (12–14 percent, roughly the same as Britain and Canada) and much lower than in South Africa or Argentina (16–18 percent, approximately the same as the United States).

Colombia on the other hand is one of the most inegalitarian societies in the WTID: the top centile's share stood at about 20 percent of national income throughout the period 1990–2010, with no clear trend (see Figure 9.9). This level of inequality is even higher than that attained by the United States in 2000–2010, at least if capital gains are excluded; if they are included, the United States was slightly ahead of Colombia over the past decade.

It is important, however, to be aware of the significant limitations of the data available for measuring the dynamics of the income distribution in poor and emerging countries and for comparing them with the rich countries. The orders of magnitude indicated here are the best I was able to come up with given the available sources, but the truth is that our knowledge remains meager. We have tax data for the entire twentieth century for only a few emerging economies, and there are many gaps and breaks in the data, often in the period 1950–1970, the era of independence (in Indonesia, for example). Work is going forward to update the WTID with historical data from many other countries, especially from among the former British and French colonies, in Indochina and Africa, but data from the colonial era are often difficult to relate to contemporary tax records.[28]

Where tax records do exist, their interest is often reduced by the fact that the income tax in less developed countries generally applies

---

28. The list of ongoing projects is available on the WTID site.

to only a small minority of the population, so that one can estimate the upper centile's share of total income but not the upper decile's. Where the data allow, as in South Africa for certain subperiods, one finds that the highest observed levels for the top decile are on the order of 50–55 percent of national income—a level comparable to or slightly higher than the highest levels of inequality observed in the wealthy countries, in Europe in 1900–1910 and in the United States in 2000–2010.

I have also noticed a certain deterioration of the tax data after 1990. This is due in part to the arrival of computerized records, which in many cases led the tax authorities to interrupt the publication of detailed statistics, which in earlier periods they needed for their own purposes. This sometimes means, paradoxically, that sources have deteriorated since the advent of the information age (we find the same thing happening in the rich countries).[29] Above all, the deterioration of the sources seems to be related to a certain disaffection with the progressive income tax in general on the part of certain governments and international organizations.[30] A case in point is India, which ceased publishing detailed income tax data in the early 2000s, even though such data had been published without interruption since 1922. As a result, it is harder to study the evolution of top incomes in India since 2000 than over the course of the twentieth century.[31]

This lack of information and democratic transparency is all the more regrettable in that the question of the distribution of wealth and

---

29. When digital tax files are accessible, computerization naturally leads to improvement in our sources of information. But when the files are closed or poorly indexed (which often happens), then the absence of statistical data in paper form can impair our "historical memory" of income tax data.

30. The closer the income tax is to being purely proportional, the less the need for detailed information about different income brackets. In Part Four I will discuss changes in taxation itself. The point for now is that such changes have an influence on our observational instruments.

31. The information for the year 2010 in Figure 9.9 is based on very imperfect data concerning the remuneration of firm managers and should be taken as a first approximation. See the online technical appendix.

of the fruits of growth is at least as urgent in the poor and emerging economies as in the rich ones. Note, too, that the very high official growth figures for developing countries (especially India and China) over the past few decades are based almost exclusively on production statistics. If one tries to measure income growth by using household survey data, it is often quite difficult to identify the reported rates of macroeconomic growth: Indian and Chinese incomes are certainly increasing rapidly, but not as rapidly as one would infer from official growth statistics. This paradox—sometimes referred to as the "black hole" of growth—is obviously problematic. It may be due to the overestimation of growth of output (there are many bureaucratic incentives for doing so), or perhaps the underestimation of income growth (household surveys have their own flaws), or most likely both. In particular, the missing income may be explained by the possibility that a disproportionate share of the growth in output has gone to the most highly remunerated individuals, whose incomes are not always captured in the tax data.

In the case of India, it is possible to estimate (using tax return data) that the increase in the upper centile's share of national income explains between one-quarter and one-third of the "black hole" of growth between 1990 and 2000.[32] Given the deterioration of the tax data since 2000, it is impossible to do a proper social decomposition of recent growth. In the case of China, official tax records are even more rudimentary than in India. In the current state of research, the estimates in Figure 9.9 are the most reliable we have.[33] It is nevertheless

---

32. See Abhijit Banerjee and Thomas Piketty, "Top Indian Incomes, 1922–2000," *World Bank Economic Review* 19, no. 1 (May 2005): 1–20. See also A. Banerjee and T. Piketty, "Are the Rich Growing Richer? Evidence from Indian Tax Data," in Angus Deaton and Valerie Kozel, eds., *Data and Dogma: The Great Indian Poverty Debate* (New Delhi: Macmillan India Ltd., 2005): 598–611. The "black hole" itself represents nearly half of total growth in India between 1990 and 2000: per capita income increased by nearly 4 percent a year according to national accounts data but by only 2 percent according to household survey data. The issue is therefore important.

33. See the online technical appendix.

urgent that both countries publish more complete data—and other countries should do so as well. If and when better data become available, we may discover that inequality in India and China has increased more rapidly than we imagined.

In any case, the important point is that whatever flaws the tax authorities in poor and emerging countries may exhibit, the tax data reveal much higher—and more realistic—top income levels than do household surveys. For example, tax returns show that the top centile's share of national income in Colombia in 2000–2010 was more than 20 percent (and almost 20 percent in Argentina). Actual inequality may be even greater. But the fact that the highest incomes declared in household surveys in these same countries are generally only 4 to 5 times as high as the average income (suggesting that no one is really rich)—so that, if we were to trust the household survey, the top centile's share would be less than 5 percent—suggests that the survey data are not very credible. Clearly, household surveys, which are often the only source used by international organizations (in particular the World Bank) and governments for gauging inequality, give a biased and misleadingly complacent view of the distribution of wealth. As long as these official estimates of inequality fail to combine survey data with other data systematically gleaned from tax records and other government sources, it will be impossible to apportion macroeconomic growth properly among various social groups or among the centiles and deciles of the income hierarchy. This is true, moreover, of wealthy countries as well as poor and emerging ones.

The Illusion of Marginal Productivity

Let me now return to the explosion of wage inequality in the United States (and to a lesser extent Britain and Canada) after 1970. As noted, the theory of marginal productivity and of the race between technology and education is not very convincing: the explosion of compensation has been highly concentrated in the top centile (or even the top thousandth) of the wage distribution and has affected some countries while sparing others (Japan and continental Europe are thus far much less affected than the United States), even though one would expect technological change to have altered the whole top end of the skill distribution in a more continuous way and to have worked its effects in all countries at a similar level of development. The fact that income inequality in the United States in 2000–2010 attained a level higher than that observed in the poor and emerging countries at various times in the past—for example, higher than in India or South Africa in 1920–1930, 1960–1970, and 2000–2010—also casts doubt on any explanation based solely on objective inequalities of productivity. Is it really the case that inequality of individual skills and productivities is greater in the United States today than in the half-illiterate India of the recent past (or even today) or in apartheid (or postapartheid) South Africa? If that were the case, it would be bad news for US educational institutions, which surely need to be improved and made more accessible but probably do not deserve such extravagant blame.

To my mind, the most convincing explanation for the explosion of the very top US incomes is the following. As noted, the vast majority of top earners are senior managers of large firms. It is rather naïve to seek an objective basis for their high salaries in individual "productivity." When a job is replicable, as in the case of an assembly-line worker or fast-food server, we can give an approximate estimate of the "marginal product" that would be realized by adding one additional worker or waiter (albeit with a considerable margin of error in our estimate). But when an individual's job functions are unique, or nearly so, then the margin of error is much greater. Indeed, once we introduce the hypothesis of imperfect information into standard economic models (eminently justifiable in this context), the very notion of "individual marginal productivity" becomes hard to define. In fact, it becomes something close to a pure ideological construct on the basis of which a justification for higher status can be elaborated.

To put this discussion in more concrete terms, imagine a large multinational corporation employing 100,000 people and with gross annual revenue of 10 billion euros, or 100,000 euros per worker. Suppose that half of this revenue figure represents purchases of goods and services by the firm (this is a typical figure for the economy as a whole), so that the value added by the firm—the value available to pay the labor and capital that it directly employs—is 5 billion euros, or 50,000 euros per worker. To set the pay of the firm's CFO (or his deputies, or of the director of marketing and her staff, etc.), one would in principle want to estimate his marginal productivity, that is, his contribution to the firm's value-added of 5 billion euros: is it 100,000, 500,000, or 5 million euros per year? A precise, objective answer to this question is clearly impossible. To be sure, one could in theory experiment by trying out several CFOs, each for several years, in order to determine what impact the choice has on the firm's total revenue of 10 billion euros. Obviously, such an estimate would be highly approximate, with a margin of error much greater than the maximum salary one would think of paying, even in a totally stable economic environment.[34] And the whole idea of experimentation looks even more hopeless when one remembers that the environment is in fact changing constantly, as is the nature of the firm and the exact definition of each job.

In view of these informational and cognitive difficulties, how are such remunerations determined in practice? They are generally set by hierarchical superiors, and at the very highest levels salaries are set by the executives themselves or by corporate compensation committees whose members usually earn comparable salaries (such as senior executives of other large corporations). In some companies, stockholders are asked to vote on compensation for senior executives at annual meetings, but the number of posts subject to such approval is small, and not all senior managers are covered. Since it is impossible to give a precise estimate of

---

34. In fact, the principal—and on the whole rather obvious—result of economic models of optimal experimentation in the presence of imperfect information is that it is never in the interest of the agents (in this case the firm) to seek complete information as long as experimentation is costly (and it is costly to try out a number of CFOs before making a final choice), especially when information has a public value greater than its private value to the agent. See the online technical appendix for bibliographic references.

each manager's contribution to the firm's output, it is inevitable that this process yields decisions that are largely arbitrary and dependent on hierarchical relationships and on the relative bargaining power of the individuals involved. It is only reasonable to assume that people in a position to set their own salaries have a natural incentive to treat themselves generously, or at the very least to be rather optimistic in gauging their marginal productivity. To behave in this way is only human, especially since the necessary information is, in objective terms, highly imperfect. It may be excessive to accuse senior executives of having their "hands in the till," but the metaphor is probably more apt than Adam Smith's metaphor of the market's "invisible hand." In practice, the invisible hand does not exist, any more than "pure and perfect" competition does, and the market is always embodied in specific institutions such as corporate hierarchies and compensation committees.

This does not mean that senior executives and compensation committees can set whatever salaries they please and always choose the highest possible figure. "Corporate governance" is subject to certain institutions and rules specific to each country. The rules are generally ambiguous and flawed, but there are certain checks and balances. Each society also imposes certain social norms, which affect the views of senior managers and stockholders (or their proxies, who are often institutional investors such as financial corporations and pension funds) as well as of the larger society. These social norms reflect beliefs about the contributions that different individuals make to the firm's output and to economic growth in general. Since uncertainty about these issues is great, it is hardly surprising that perceptions vary from country to country and period to period and are influenced by each country's specific history. The important point is that it is very difficult for any individual firm to go against the prevailing social norms of the country in which it operates.

Without a theory of this kind, it seems to me quite difficult to explain the very large differences of executive pay that we observe between on the one hand the United States (and to a lesser extent in other English-speaking countries) and on the other continental Europe and

Japan. Simply put, wage inequalities increased rapidly in the United States and Britain because US and British corporations became much more tolerant of extremely generous pay packages after 1970. Social norms evolved in a similar direction in European and Japanese firms, but the change came later (in the 1980s or 1990s) and has thus far not gone as far as in the United States. Executive compensation of several million euros a year is still more shocking today in Sweden, Germany, France, Japan, and Italy than in the United States or Britain. It has not always been this way—far from it: recall that in the 1950s and 1960s the United States was more egalitarian than France, especially in regard to the wage hierarchy. But it has been this way since 1980, and all signs are that this change in senior management compensation has played a key role in the evolution of wage inequalities around the world.

The Takeoff of the Supermanagers: A Powerful Force for Divergence

This approach to executive compensation in terms of social norms and acceptability seems rather plausible a priori, but in fact it only shifts the difficulty to another level. The problem is now to explain where these social norms come from and how they evolve, which is obviously a question for sociology, psychology, cultural and political history, and the study of beliefs and perceptions at least as much as for economics per se. The problem of inequality is a problem for the social sciences in general, not for just one of its disciplines. In the case in point, I noted earlier that the "conservative revolution" that gripped the United States and Great Britain in the 1970s and 1980s, and that led to, among other things, greater tolerance of very high executive pay, was probably due in part to a feeling that these countries were being overtaken by others (even though the postwar period of high growth in Europe and Japan was in reality an almost mechanical consequence of the shocks of the period 1914–1945). Obviously, however, other factors also played an important role.

To be clear, I am not claiming that all wage inequality is determined by social norms of fair remuneration. As noted, the theory of marginal productivity and of the race between technology and education offers a plausible explanation of the long-run evolution of the wage distribution, at least up to a certain level of pay and within a certain degree of precision. Technology and skills set limits within which most wages must be fixed. But to the extent that certain job functions, especially in the upper management of large firms, become more difficult to replicate, the margin of error in estimating the productivity of any given job becomes larger. The explanatory power of the skills-technology logic then diminishes, and that of social norms increases. Only a small minority of employees are affected, a few percent at most and probably less than 1 percent, depending on the country and period.

But the key fact, which was by no means evident a priori, is that the top centile's share of total wages can vary considerably by country and period, as the disparate evolutions in the wealthy countries after 1980 demonstrate. The explosion of supermanager salaries should of course be seen in relation to firm size and to the growing diversity of functions within the firm. But the objectively complex problem of governance of large organizations is not the only issue. It is also possible that the explosion of top incomes can be explained as a form of "meritocratic extremism," by which I mean the apparent need of modern societies, and especially US society, to designate certain individuals as "winners" and to reward them all the more generously if they seem to have been selected on the basis of their intrinsic merits rather than birth or background. (I will come back to this point.)

In any case, the extremely generous rewards meted out to top managers can be a powerful force for divergence of the wealth distribution: if the best paid individuals set their own salaries, (at least to some extent), the result may be greater and greater inequality. It is very difficult to say in advance where such a process might end. Consider again the case of the CFO of a large firm with gross revenue of 10 billion euros a year. It is hard to imagine that the corporate compensation committee would suddenly decide that the CFO's marginal productivity is 1 billion or even 100 million euros (if only because it would then be difficult to find enough money to pay the rest of the management team). By contrast, some people might think that a pay package of 1 million, 10 million, or even 50 million euros a year would be justified (uncertainty about individual marginal productivity being so large that no obvious limit is apparent). It is perfectly possible to imagine that the top centile's share of total wages could reach 15–20 percent in the United States, or 25–30 percent, or even higher.

The most convincing proof of the failure of corporate governance and of the absence of a rational productivity justification for extremely high executive pay is that when we collect data about individual firms (which we can do for publicly owned corporations in all the rich countries), it is very difficult to explain the observed variations in terms of firm performance. If we look at various performance indicators, such as sales growth, profits, and so on, we can break down the observed variance as a sum of other variances: variance due to causes external to the firm (such as the general state of the economy, raw material price shocks, variations in the exchange rate, average performance of other firms in the same sector, etc.) plus other "nonexternal" variances. Only the latter can be significantly affected by the decisions of the firm's managers. If executive pay were determined by marginal productivity, one would expect its variance to have little to do with external variances and to depend solely or primarily on nonexternal variances. In fact, we observe just the opposite: it is when sales and profits increase for external reasons that executive pay rises most rapidly. This is particularly clear in the case of US corporations: Bertrand and Mullainhatan refer to this phenomenon as "pay for luck."[35]

---

35. See Marianne Bertrand and Sendhil Mullainathan, "Are CEOs Rewarded for Luck? The Ones without Principals Are," *Quarterly Journal of Economics* 116, no. 3 (2001): 901–932. See also Lucian Bebchuk and Jesse Fried, *Pay without Performance* (Cambridge, MA: Harvard University Press, 2004).

I return to this question and generalize this approach in Part Four (see Chapter 14). The propensity to "pay for luck" varies widely with country and period, and notably as a function of changes in tax laws, especially the top marginal income tax rate, which seems to serve either as a protective barrier (when it is high) or an incentive to mischief (when it is low)—at least up to a certain point. Of course changes in tax laws are themselves linked to changes in social norms pertaining to inequality, but once set in motion they proceed according to a logic of their own. Specifically, the very large decrease in the top marginal income tax rate in the English-speaking countries after 1980 (despite the fact that Britain and the United States had pioneered nearly confiscatory taxes on incomes deemed to be indecent in earlier decades) seems to have totally transformed the way top executive pay is set, since top executives now had much stronger incentives than in the past to seek large raises. I also analyze the way this amplifying mechanism can give rise to another force for divergence that is more political in nature: the decrease in the top marginal income tax rate led to an explosion of very high incomes, which then increased the political influence of the beneficiaries of the change in the tax laws, who had an interest in keeping top tax rates low or even decreasing them further and who could use their windfall to finance political parties, pressure groups, and think tanks.

{ TEN }

Inequality of Capital Ownership

Let me turn now to the question of inequality of wealth and its historical evolution. The question is important, all the more so because the reduction of this type of inequality, and of the income derived from it, was the only reason why total income inequality diminished during the first half of the twentieth century. As noted, inequality of income from labor did not decrease in a structural sense between 1900–1910 and 1950–1960 in either France or the United States (contrary to the optimistic predictions of Kuznets's theory, which was based on the idea of a gradual and mechanical shift of labor from worse paid to better paid types of work), and the sharp drop in total income inequality was due essentially to the collapse of high incomes from capital. All the information at our disposal indicates that the same is true for all the other developed countries.[1] It is therefore essential to understand how and why this historic compression of inequality of wealth came about.

The question is all the more important because capital ownership is apparently becoming increasingly concentrated once again today, as the capital / income ratio rises and growth slows. The possibility of a widening wealth gap raises many questions as to its long-term consequences. In some respects it is even more worrisome than the widening income gap between supermanagers and others, which to date remains a geographically limited phenomenon.

---

1. In particular, all the data on the composition of income by level of overall income corroborate this finding. The same is true of series beginning in the late nineteenth century (for Germany, Japan, and several Nordic countries). The available data for the poor and emergent countries are more fragmentary but suggest a similar pattern. See the online technical appendix.

Hyperconcentrated Wealth: Europe and America

As noted in Chapter 7, the distribution of wealth—and therefore of income from capital—is always much more concentrated than the distribution of income from labor. In all known societies, at all times, the least wealthy half of the population own virtually nothing (generally little more than 5 percent of total wealth); the top decile of the wealth hierarchy own a clear majority of what there is to own (generally more than 60 percent of total wealth and sometimes as much as 90 percent); and the remainder of the population (by construction, the 40 percent in the middle) own from 5 to 35 percent of all wealth.[2] I also noted the emergence of a "patrimonial middle class," that is, an intermediate group who are distinctly wealthier than the poorer half of the population and own between a quarter and a third of national wealth. The emergence of this middle class is no doubt the most important structural transformation to affect the wealth distribution over the long run.

Why did this transformation occur? To answer this question, one must first take a closer look at the chronology. When and how did inequality of wealth begin to decline? To be candid, because the necessary sources (mainly probate records) are unfortunately not always available, I have thus far not been able to study the historical evolution of wealth inequality in as many countries as I examined in the case of income inequality. We have fairly complete historical estimates for four countries: France, Britain, the United States, and Sweden. The lessons of these four histories are fairly clear and consistent, however, so that we can say something about the similarities and differences between the European and US trajectories.[3] Furthermore, the wealth

---

2. See esp. Table 7.2.

3. The parallel series available for other countries give consistent results. For example, the evolutions we observe in Denmark and Norway since the nineteenth century are very close to the trajectory of Sweden. The data for Japan and Germany suggest a dynamic similar to that of France. A recent study of Australia yields results consistent with those obtained for the United States. See the online technical appendix.

data have one enormous advantage over the income data: they allow us in some cases to go much farther back in time. Let me now examine one by one the four countries I have studied in detail.

France: An Observatory of Private Wealth

France is a particularly interesting case, because it is the only country for which we have a truly homogeneous historical source that allows us to study the distribution of wealth continuously from the late eighteenth century to the present. In 1791, shortly after the fiscal privileges of the nobility were abolished, a tax on estates and gifts was established, together with a wealth registry. These were astonishing innovations at the time, notable for their universal scope. The new estate tax was universal in three ways: first, it applied to all types of property: farmland, other urban and rural real estate, cash, public and private bonds, other kinds of financial assets such as shares of stock or partnerships, furniture, valuables, and so on; second, it applied to all owners of wealth, whether noble or common; and third, it applied to fortunes of all sizes, large or small. Moreover, the purpose of this fundamental reform was not only to fill the coffers of the new regime but also to enable the government to record all transfers of wealth, whether by bequest (at the owner's death) or gift (during the owner's lifetime), in order to guarantee to all the full exercise of their property rights. In official language, the estate and gift tax has always— from 1791 until now—been classified as one of a number of *droits d'enregistrement* (recording fees), and more specifically *droits de mutation* (transfer fees), which included both charges assessed on "free-will transfers," or transfers of title to property made without financial consideration, by bequest or gift, and "transfers for consideration" (that is, transfers made in exchange for cash or other valuable tokens). The purpose of the law was thus to allow every property owner, large or small, to record his title and thus to enjoy his property rights in full security, including the right to appeal to the public authorities in case of difficulty. Thus a fairly complete system of property records was established in the late 1790s and early 1800s, including a cadastre for real estate that still exists today.

In Part Four I say more about the history of estate taxes in different countries. At this stage, taxes are of interest primarily as a historical source. In most other countries, it was not until the end of the nineteenth century or beginning of the twentieth that estate and gift taxes comparable to France's were established. In Britain, the reform of 1894 unified previous taxes on the conveyance of real estate, financial assets, and personal estate, but homogeneous probate statistics covering all types of property go back only to 1919–1920. In the United States, the federal tax on estates and gifts was not created until 1916 and covered only a tiny minority of the population. (Although taxes covering broader segments of the population do exist in some states, these are highly heterogeneous.) Hence it is very difficult to study the evolution of wealth inequalities in these two countries before World War I. To be sure, there are many probate documents and estate inventories, mostly of private origin, dealing with particular subsets of the population and types of property, but there is no obvious way to use these records to draw general conclusions.

This is unfortunate, because World War I was a major shock to wealth and its distribution. One of the primary reasons for studying the French case is precisely that it will allow us to place this crucial turning point in a longer historical perspective. From 1791 to 1901, the estate and gift tax was strictly proportional: it varied with degree of kinship but was the same regardless of the amount transferred and was usually quite low (generally 1–2 percent). The tax was made slightly progressive in 1901 after a lengthy parliamentary battle. The government, which had begun publishing detailed statistics on the annual flow of bequests and donations as far back as the 1820s, began compiling a variety of statistics by size of estate in 1901, and from then until the 1950s, these became increasingly sophisticated (with cross-tabulations by age, size of estate, type of property, etc.). After 1970, digital files containing representative samples from estate and gift tax filings in a specific year became available, so that the data set can be extended to 2000–2010. In addition to the rich sources produced directly by the tax authorities over the past two centuries, I have also collected, together with Postel-Vinay and Rosenthal, tens of thousands of individual declarations (which have been very carefully preserved in national and departmental archives since the early nineteenth century) for the purpose of constructing large samples covering each decade from 1800–1810 to 2000–2010. All in all, French probate records offer an exceptionally rich and detailed view of two centuries of wealth accumulation and distribution.[4]

The Metamorphoses of a Patrimonial Society

Figure 10.1 presents the main results I obtained for the evolution of the wealth distribution from 1810 to 2010.[5] The first conclusion is that prior to the shocks of 1914–1945, there was no visible trend toward reduced inequality of capital ownership. Indeed, there was a slight tendency for capital concentration to rise throughout the nineteenth century (starting from an already very high level) and even an acceleration of the inegalitarian spiral in the period 1880–1913. The top decile of the wealth hierarchy already owned between 80 and 85 percent of all wealth at the beginning of the nineteenth century; by

---

4. For a precise description of the various sources used, see Thomas Piketty, "On the Long-Run Evolution of Inheritance: France 1820–2050," Paris School of Economics, 2010 (a summary version appeared in the *Quarterly Journal of Economics*, 126, no. 3 [August 2011]: 1071–131). The individual statements were collected with Gilles Postel-Vinay and Jean-Laurent Rosenthal from Parisian archives. We also used statements previously collected for all of France under the auspices of the Enquête TRA project, thanks to the efforts of numerous other researchers, in particular Jérôme Bourdieu, Lionel Kesztenbaum, and Akiko Suwa-Eisenmann. See the online technical appendix.

5. For a detailed analysis of these results, see Thomas Piketty, Gilles Postel-Vinay, and Jean-Laurent Rosenthal, "Wealth Concentration in a Developing Economy: Paris and France, 1807–1994," *American Economic Review* 96, no. 1 (February 2006): 236–56. The version presented here is an updated version of these series. Figure 10.1 and subsequent figures focus on means by decade in order to focus attention on long-term evolutions. All the annual series are available online.

the turn of the twentieth, it owned nearly 90 percent. The top centile alone owned 45–50 percent of the nation's wealth in 1800–1810; its share surpassed 50 percent in 1850–1860 and reached 60 percent in 1900–1910.[6]

Looking at these data with the historical distance we enjoy today, we cannot help being struck by the impressive concentration of wealth in France during the Belle Époque, notwithstanding the reassuring rhetoric of the Third Republic's economic and political elites. In Paris, which was home to little more than one-twentieth of the population in 1900–1910 but claimed one-quarter of the wealth, the concentration of wealth was greater still and seems to have increased without limit during the decades leading up to World War I. In the capital, where in the nineteenth century two-thirds of the population died without any wealth to leave to the next generation (compared with half of the population in the rest of the country) but where the largest fortunes were also concentrated, the top centile's share was about 55 percent at the beginning of the century, rose to 60 percent in 1880–1890, and then to 70 percent on the eve of World War I (see Figure 10.2). Looking at this curve, it is natural to ask how high the concentration of wealth might have gone had there been no war.

The probate records also allow us to see that throughout the nineteenth century, wealth was almost as unequally distributed within each age cohort as in the nation as a whole. Note that the estimates indicated in Figures 10.1–2 (and subsequent figures) reflect inequality of wealth in the (living) adult population at each charted date: we start with wealth at the time of death but reweight each observation as a function of the number of living individuals in each age cohort as of the date in question. In practice, this does not make much difference: the concentration of wealth among the living is barely a few points

---

6. The shares of each decile and centile indicated in Figures 10.1 and following were calculated as percentages of total private wealth. But since private fortunes made up nearly all of national wealth, this makes little difference.

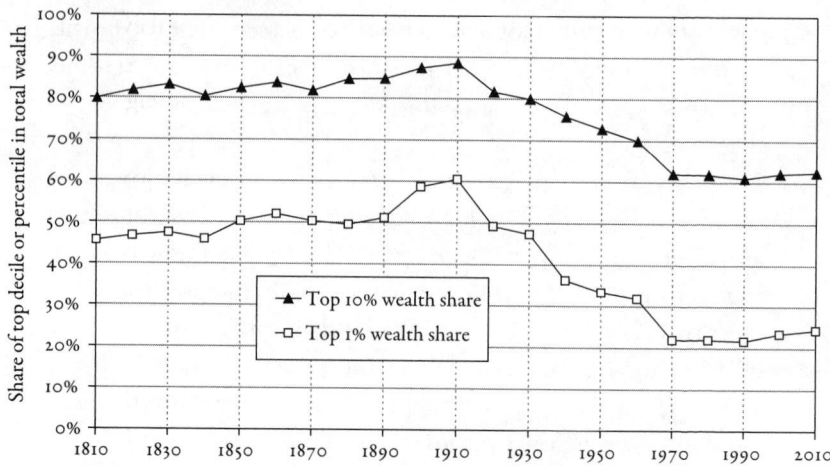

FIGURE 10.1. Wealth inequality in France, 1810–2010

The top decile (the top 10 percent highest wealth holders) owns 80–90 percent of total wealth in 1810–1910, and 60–65 percent today.

Sources and series: see piketty.pse.ens.fr/capital21c.

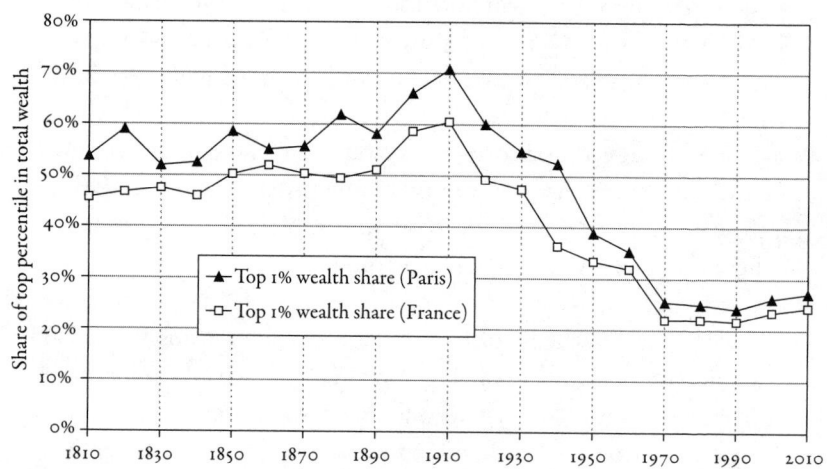

FIGURE 10.2. Wealth inequality in Paris versus France, 1810–2010

The top percentile (the top 1 percent wealth holders) owns 70 percent of aggregate wealth in Paris on the eve of World War I.

Sources and series: see piketty.pse.ens.fr/capital21c.

higher than inequality of wealth at death, and the temporal evolution is nearly identical in each case.[7]

How concentrated was wealth in France during the eighteenth century up to the eve of the Revolution? Without a source comparable to the probate records created by the revolutionary assemblies (for the Ancien Régime we have only heterogeneous and incomplete sets of private data, as for Britain and the United States until the late nineteenth century), it is unfortunately impossible to make precise comparisons. Yet all signs are that inequality of private wealth decreased slightly between 1780 and 1810 owing to redistribution of agricultural land and cancellation of public debt during the Revolution, together with other shocks to aristocratic fortunes. It is possible that the top decile's share attained or even slightly exceeded 90 percent of total wealth on the eve of 1789 and that the upper centile's share attained or exceeded 60 percent. Conversely, the "émigré billion" (the billion francs paid to the nobility in compensation for land confiscated during the Revolution) and the return of the nobility to the forefront of the political scene contributed to the reconstitution of some old fortunes during the period of limited-suffrage monarchy (1815–1848). In fact, our probate data reveal that the percentage of aristocratic names in the top centile of the Parisian wealth hierarchy increased gradually from barely 15 percent in 1800–1810 to nearly 30 percent in 1840–1850 before

---

7. This method, called the "mortality multiplier," involves a reweighting of each observation by the inverse of the mortality rate in each age cohort: a person who dies at age forty represents more living individuals than a person who dies at eighty (one must also take into account mortality differentials by level of wealth). The method was developed by French and British economists and statisticians (especially B. Mallet, M. J. Séaillès, H. C. Strutt, and J. C. Stamp) in 1900–1910 and used in all subsequent historical research. When we have data from wealth surveys or annual wealth taxes on the living (as in the Nordic countries, where such taxes have existed since the beginning of the twentieth century, or in France, with data from the wealth tax of 1990–2010), we can check the validity of this method and refine our hypotheses concerning mortality differentials. On these methodological issues, see the online technical appendix.

embarking on an inexorable decline from 1850–1860 on, falling to less than 10 percent by 1890–1900.[8]

The magnitude of the changes initiated by the French Revolution should not be overstated, however. Beyond the probable decrease of inequality of wealth between 1780 and 1810, followed by a gradual increase between 1810 and 1910, and especially after 1870, the most significant fact is that inequality of capital ownership remained relatively stable at an extremely high level throughout the eighteenth and nineteenth centuries. During this period, the top decile consistently owned 80 to 90 percent of total wealth and the top centile 50 to 60 percent. As I showed in Part Two, the structure of capital was totally transformed between the eighteenth century and the beginning of the twentieth century (landed capital was almost entirely replaced by industrial and financial capital and real estate), but total wealth, measured in years of national income, remained relatively stable. In particular, the French Revolution had relatively little effect on the capital / income ratio. As just shown, the Revolution also had relatively little effect on the distribution of wealth. In 1810–1820, the epoch of Père Goriot, Rastignac, and Mademoiselle Victorine, wealth was probably slightly less unequally distributed than during the Ancien Régime, but the difference was really rather minimal: both before and after the Revolution, France was a patrimonial society characterized by a hyperconcentration of capital, in which inheritance and marriage played a key role and inheriting or marrying a large fortune could procure a level of comfort not obtainable through work or study. In the Belle Époque, wealth was even more concentrated than when Vautrin lectured Rastignac. At bottom, however, France remained the same society, with the same basic structure of inequality, from the Ancien Régime to the Third Republic, despite the vast economic and political changes that took place in the interim.

---

8. See the online technical appendix. This percentage probably exceeded 50 prior to 1789.

Probate records also enable us to observe that the decrease in the upper decile's share of national wealth in the twentieth century benefited the middle 40 percent of the population exclusively, while the share of the poorest 50 percent hardly increased at all (it remained less than 5 percent of total wealth). Throughout the nineteenth and twentieth centuries, the bottom half of the population had virtually zero net wealth. In particular, we find that at the time of death, individuals in the poorest half of the wealth distribution owned no real estate or financial assets that could be passed on to heirs, and what little wealth they had went entirely to expenses linked to death and to paying off debts (in which case the heirs generally chose to renounce their inheritance). The proportion of individuals in this situation at the time of death exceeded two-thirds in Paris throughout the nineteenth century and until the eve of World War I, and there was no downward trend. Père Goriot belonged to this vast group, dying as he did abandoned by his daughters and in abject poverty: his landlady, Madame Vauquer, dunned Rastignac for what the old man owed her, and he also had to pay the cost of burial, which exceeded the value of the deceased's meager personal effects. Roughly half of all French people in the nineteenth century died in similar circumstances, without any wealth to convey to heirs, or with only negative net wealth, and this proportion barely budged in the twentieth century.[9]

Inequality of Capital in Belle Époque Europe

The available data for other European countries, though imperfect, unambiguously demonstrate that extreme concentration of wealth in the eighteenth and nineteenth centuries and until the eve of World War I was a European and not just a French phenomenon.

---

9. On this question, see also Jérôme Bourdieu, Gilles Postel-Vinay, and Akiko Suwa-Eisenmann, "Pourquoi la richesse ne s'est-elle pas diffusée avec la croissance? Le degré zéro de l'inégalité et son évolution en France: 1800–1940," *Histoire et mesure* 18, 1/2 (2003): 147–98.

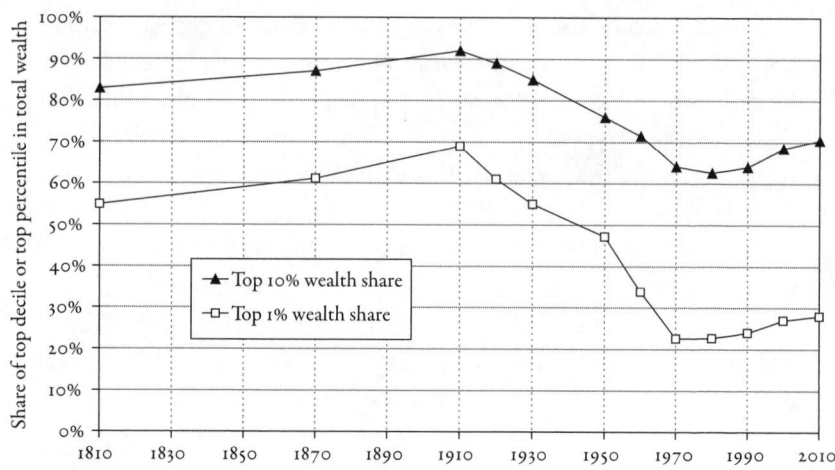

FIGURE 10.3. Wealth inequality in Britain, 1810–2010

The top decile owns 80–90 percent of total wealth in 1810–1910, and 70 percent today. Sources and series: see piketty.pse.ens.fr/capital21c.

In Britain, we have detailed probate data from 1910–1920 on, and these records have been exhaustively studied by many investigators (most notably Atkinson and Harrison). If we complete these statistics with estimates from recent years as well as the more robust but less homogeneous estimates that Peter Linder has made for the period 1810–1870 (based on samples of estate inventories), we find that the overall evolution was very similar to the French case, although the level of inequality was always somewhat greater in Britain. The top decile's share of total wealth was on the order of 85 percent from 1810 to 1870 and surpassed 90 percent in 1900–1910; the uppermost centile's share rose from 55–60 percent in 1810–1870 to nearly 70 percent in 1910–1920 (see Figure 10.3). The British sources are imperfect, especially for the nineteenth century, but the orders of magnitude are quite clear: wealth in Britain was extremely concentrated in the nineteenth century and showed no tendency to decrease before 1914. From a French perspective, the most striking fact is that inequality of capital ownership was only slightly greater in Britain than in France during the Belle Époque,

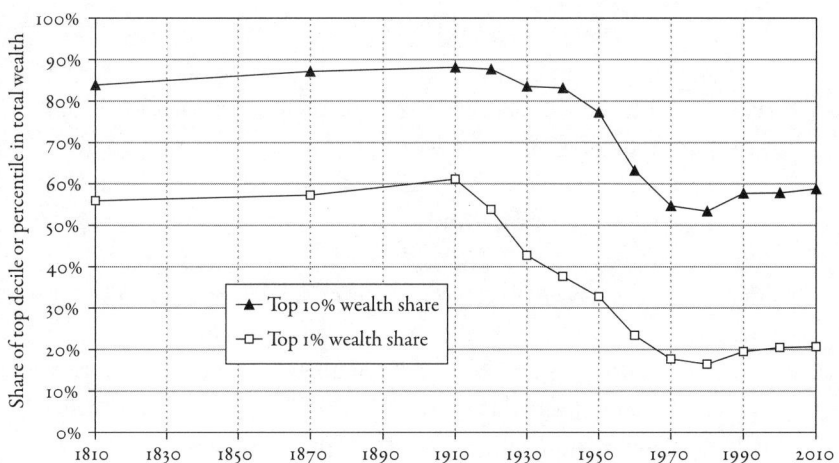

FIGURE 10.4. Wealth inequality in Sweden, 1810–2010

The top 10 percent holds 80–90 percent of total wealth in 1810–1910 and 55–60 percent today.

Sources and series: see piketty.pse.ens.fr/capital21c.

even though Third Republic elites at the time liked to portray France as an egalitarian country compared with its monarchical neighbor across the Channel. In fact, the formal nature of the political regime clearly had very little influence on the distribution of wealth in the two countries.

In Sweden, where the very rich data available from 1910, of which Ohlsson, Roine, and Waldenström have recently made use, and for which we also have estimates for the period 1810–1870 (by Lee Soltow in particular), we find a trajectory very similar to what we observed in France and Britain (see Figure 10.4). Indeed, the Swedish wealth data confirm what we already know from income statements: Sweden was not the structurally egalitarian country that we sometimes imagine. To be sure, the concentration of wealth in Sweden in 1970–1980 attained the lowest level of inequality observed in any of our historical series (with barely 50 percent of total wealth owned by the top decile and slightly more than 15 percent by the top centile). This is still a fairly high level of inequality, however, and, what is more, inequality in

Sweden has increased significantly since 1980–1990 (and in 2010 was just slightly lower than in France). It is worth stressing, moreover, that Swedish wealth was as concentrated as French and British wealth in 1900–1910. In the Belle Époque, wealth was highly concentrated in all European countries. It is essential to understand why this was so, and why things changed so much over the course of the twentieth century.

Note, moreover, that we also find the same extremely high concentration of wealth—with 80 to 90 percent of capital owned by the top decile and 50–60 percent by the top centile—in most societies prior to the nineteenth century, and in particular in traditional agrarian societies in the modern era, as well as in the Middle Ages and antiquity. The available sources are not sufficiently robust to permit precise comparisons or study temporal evolutions, but the orders of magnitude obtained for the shares of the top decile and centile in total wealth (and especially in total farmland) are generally close to what we find in France, Britain, and Sweden in the nineteenth century and Belle Époque.[10]

The Emergence of the Patrimonial Middle Class

Three questions will concern us in the remainder of this chapter. Why were inequalities of wealth so extreme, and increasing, before World War I? And why, despite the fact that wealth is once again prospering at the beginning of the twenty-first century as it did at the beginning of the twentieth century (as the evolution of the capital / income ratio shows), is the concentration of wealth today significantly below its historical record high? Finally, is this state of affairs irreversible?

In fact, the second conclusion that emerges very clearly from the French data presented in Figure 10.1 is that the concentration of

---

10. See for example the interesting data on the distribution of land in Roger S. Bagnall, "Landholding in Late Roman Egypt: The Distribution of Wealth," *Journal of Roman Studies* 82 (November 1992): 128–49. Other work of this type yields similar results. See the online technical appendix.

wealth, as well as the concentration of income from wealth, has never fully recovered from the shocks of 1914–1945. The upper decile's share of total wealth, which attained 90 percent in 1910–1920, fell to 60–70 percent in 1950–1970; the upper centile's share dropped even more precipitously, from 60 percent in 1910–1920 to 20–30 percent in 1950–1970. Compared with the trend prior to World War I, the break is clear and overwhelming. To be sure, inequality of wealth began to increase again in 1980–1990, and financial globalization has made it more and more difficult to measure wealth and its distribution in a national framework: inequality of wealth in the twenty-first century will have to be gauged more and more at the global level. Despite these uncertainties, however, there is no doubt that inequality of wealth today stands significantly below its level of a century ago: the top decile's share is now around 60–65 percent, which, though still quite high, is markedly below the level attained in the Belle Époque. The essential difference is that there is now a patrimonial middle class, which owns about a third of national wealth—a not insignificant amount.

The available data for the other European countries confirm that this has been a general phenomenon. In Britain, the upper decile's share fell from more than 90 percent on the eve of World War I to 60–65 percent in the 1970s; it is currently around 70 percent. The top centile's share collapsed in the wake of the twentieth century's shocks, falling from nearly 70 percent in 1910–1920 to barely more than 20 percent in 1970–1980, then rising to 25–30 percent today (see Figure 10.3). In Sweden, capital ownership was always less concentrated than in Britain, but the overall trajectory is fairly similar (see Figure 10.4). In every case, we find that what the wealthiest 10 percent lost mainly benefited the "patrimonial middle class" (defined as the middle 40 percent of the wealth hierarchy) and did not go to the poorest half of the population, whose share of total wealth has always been minuscule (generally around 5 percent), even in Sweden (where it was never more than 10 percent). In some cases, such as Britain, we find that what the richest 1 percent lost also brought significant gains to the next lower 9 percent. Apart from such national specificities, however, the general similarity of the various European trajectories is quite striking. The major structural transformation was the emergence of a middle group, representing nearly half the population, consisting of individuals who managed to acquire some capital of their own—enough so that collectively they came to own one-quarter to one-third of the nation's total wealth.

Inequality of Wealth in America

I turn now to the US case. Here, too, we have probate statistics from 1910–1920 on, and these have been heavily exploited by researchers (especially Lampman, Kopczuk, and Saez). To be sure, there are important caveats associated with the use of these data, owing to the small percentage of the population covered by the federal estate tax. Nevertheless, estimates based on the probate data can be supplemented by information from the detailed wealth surveys that the Federal Reserve Bank has conducted since the 1960s (used notably by Arthur Kennickell and Edward Wolff), and by less robust estimates for the period 1810–1870 based on estate inventories and wealth census data exploited respectively by Alice Hanson Jones and Lee Soltow.[11]

Several important differences between the European and US trajectories stand out. First, it appears that inequality of wealth in the United States around 1800 was not much higher than in Sweden in 1970–1980. Since the United States was a new country whose population consisted largely of immigrants who came to the New World with little or no wealth, this is not very surprising: not enough time had passed for wealth to be accumulated or concentrated. The data nevertheless leave much to be desired, and there is some variation between the northern states (where estimates suggest a level of inequality lower than that of Sweden in 1970–1980) and southern states (where inequality was closer to contemporary European levels).[12]

---

11. Bibliographic and technical details can be found in the online technical appendix.
12. Some estimates find that the top centile in the United States as a whole owned less than 15 percent of total national wealth around 1800, but that finding de-

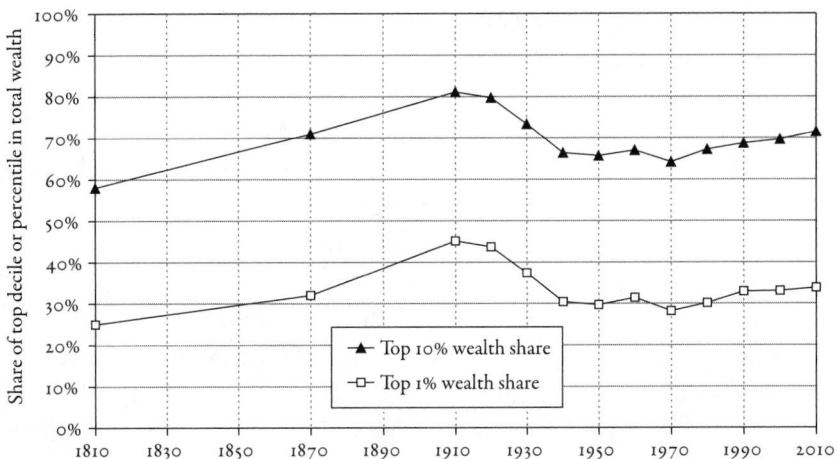

FIGURE 10.5. Wealth inequality in the United States, 1810–2010

The top 10 percent wealth holders own about 80 percent of total wealth in 1910 and 75 percent today.

Sources and series: see piketty.pse.ens.fr/capital21c.

It is a well-established fact that wealth in the United States became increasingly concentrated over the course of the nineteenth century. In 1910, capital inequality there was very high, though still markedly lower than in Europe: the top decile owned about 80 percent of total wealth and the top centile around 45 percent (see Figure 10.5). Interestingly, the fact that inequality in the New World seemed to be catching up with inequality in old Europe greatly worried US economists at the time. Willford King's book on the distribution of wealth in the United States in 1915—the first broad study of the question—is particularly illuminating in this regard.[13] From today's perspective,

---

pends entirely on the decision to focus on free individuals only, which is obviously a controversial choice. The estimates that are reported here refer to the entire population (free and unfree). See the online technical appendix.

13. See Willford I. King, *The Wealth and Income of the People of the United States* (New York: MacMillan, 1915). King, a professor of statistics and economics at the University of Wisconsin, relied on imperfect but suggestive data from several US states and compared them with European estimates, mainly based on Prussian

this may seem surprising: we have been accustomed for several decades now to the fact that the United States is more inegalitarian than Europe and even that many Americans are proud of the fact (often arguing that inequality is a prerequisite of entrepreneurial dynamism and decrying Europe as a sanctuary of Soviet-style egalitarianism). A century ago, however, both the perception and the reality were strictly the opposite: it was obvious to everyone that the New World was by nature less inegalitarian than old Europe, and this difference was also a subject of pride. In the late nineteenth century, in the period known as the Gilded Age, when some US industrialists and financiers (for example John D. Rockefeller, Andrew Carnegie, and J. P. Morgan) accumulated unprecedented wealth, many US observers were alarmed by the thought that the country was losing its pioneering egalitarian spirit. To be sure, that spirit was partly a myth, but it was also partly justified by comparison with the concentration of wealth in Europe. In Part Four we will see that this fear of growing to resemble Europe was part of the reason why the United States in 1910–1920 pioneered a very progressive estate tax on large fortunes, which were deemed to be incompatible with US values, as well as a progressive income tax on incomes thought to be excessive. Perceptions of inequality, redistribution, and national identity changed a great deal over the course of the twentieth century, to put it mildly.

Inequality of wealth in the United States decreased between 1910 and 1950, just as inequality of income did, but much less so than in Europe: of course it started from a lower level, and the shocks of war were less violent. By 2010, the top decile's share of total wealth exceeded 70 percent, and the top centile's share was close to 35 percent.[14]

In the end, the deconcentration of wealth in the United States over the course of the twentieth century was fairly limited: the top decile's

---

tax statistics. He found the differences to be much smaller than he initially imagined.

14. These levels, based on official Federal Reserve Bank surveys, may be somewhat low (given the difficulty of estimating large fortunes), and the top centile's share may have reached 40 percent. See the online technical appendix.

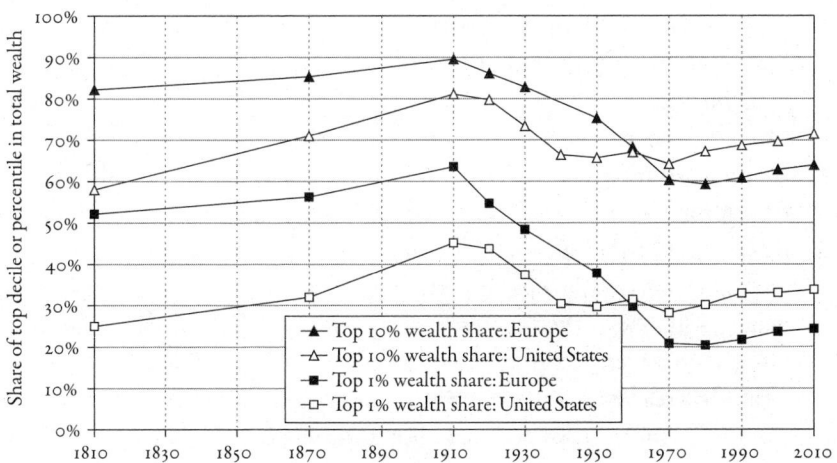

FIGURE 10.6. Wealth inequality in Europe versus the United States, 1810–2010
Until the mid-twentieth century, wealth inequality was higher in Europe than in the
United States.
Sources and series: see piketty.pse.ens.fr/capital21c.

share of total wealth dropped from 80 to 70 percent, whereas in Europe it fell from 90 to 60 percent (see Figure 10.6).[15]

The differences between the European and US experiences are
clear. In Europe, the twentieth century witnessed a total transformation of society: inequality of wealth, which on the eve of World War I
was as great as it had been under the Ancien Régime, fell to an unprecedentedly low level, so low that nearly half the population were able
to acquire some measure of wealth and for the first time to own a significant share of national capital. This is part of the explanation for
the great wave of enthusiasm that swept over Europe in the period
1945–1975. People felt that capitalism had been overcome and that
inequality and class society had been relegated to the past. It also explains why Europeans had a hard time accepting that this seemingly

15. The European average in Figure 10.6 was calculated from the figures for France,
Britain, and Sweden (which appear to have been representative). See the online
technical appendix.

ineluctable social progress ground to a halt after 1980, and why they are still wondering when the evil genie of capitalism will be put back in its bottle.

In the United States, perceptions are very different. In a sense, a (white) patrimonial middle class already existed in the nineteenth century. It suffered a setback during the Gilded Age, regained its health in the middle of the twentieth century, and then suffered another setback after 1980. This "yo-yo" pattern is reflected in the history of US taxation. In the United States, the twentieth century is not synonymous with a great leap forward in social justice. Indeed, inequality of wealth is greater today than it was at the beginning of the nineteenth century. Hence the lost US paradise is associated with the country's beginnings: there is nostalgia for the era of the Boston Tea Party, not for Trente Glorieuses and a heyday of state intervention to curb the excesses of capitalism.

The Mechanism of Wealth Divergence: r *versus* g *in History*

Let me try now to explain the observed facts: the hyperconcentration of wealth in Europe during the nineteenth century and up to World War I; the substantial compression of wealth inequality following the shocks of 1914–1945; and the fact that the concentration of wealth has not—thus far—regained the record heights set in Europe in the past.

Several mechanisms may be at work here, and to my knowledge there is no evidence that would allow us to determine the precise share of each in the overall movement. We can, however, try to hierarchize the different mechanisms with the help of the available data and analyses. Here is the main conclusion that I believe we can draw from what we know.

The primary reason for the hyperconcentration of wealth in traditional agrarian societies and to a large extent in all societies prior to World War I (with the exception of the pioneer societies of the New World, which are for obvious reasons very special and not representative of the rest of the world or the long run) is that these were low-growth societies in which the rate of return on capital was markedly and durably higher than the rate of growth.

This fundamental force for divergence, which I discussed briefly in the Introduction, functions as follows. Consider a world of low growth, on the order of, say, 0.5–1 percent a year, which was the case everywhere before the eighteenth and nineteenth centuries. The rate of return on capital, which is generally on the order of 4 or 5 percent a year, is therefore much higher than the growth rate. Concretely, this means that wealth accumulated in the past is recapitalized much more quickly than the economy grows, even when there is no income from labor.

For example, if $g = 1\%$ and $r = 5\%$, saving one-fifth of the income from capital (while consuming the other four-fifths) is enough to ensure that capital inherited from the previous generation grows at the same rate as the economy. If one saves more, because one's fortune is large enough to live well while consuming somewhat less of one's annual rent, then one's fortune will increase more rapidly than the economy, and inequality of wealth will tend to increase even if one contributes no income from labor. For strictly mathematical reasons, then, the conditions are ideal for an "inheritance society" to prosper— where by "inheritance society" I mean a society characterized by both a very high concentration of wealth and a significant persistence of large fortunes from generation to generation.

Now, it so happens that these conditions existed in any number of societies throughout history, and in particular in the European societies of the nineteenth century. As Figure 10.7 shows, the rate of return on capital was significantly higher than the growth rate in France from 1820 to 1913, around 5 percent on average compared with a growth rate of around 1 percent. Income from capital accounted for nearly 40 percent of national income, and it was enough to save one-quarter of this to generate a savings rate on the order of 10 percent (see Figure 10.8). This was sufficient to allow wealth to grow slightly more rapidly than income, so that the concentration of wealth trended upward. In the next chapter I will show that most wealth in this period did come

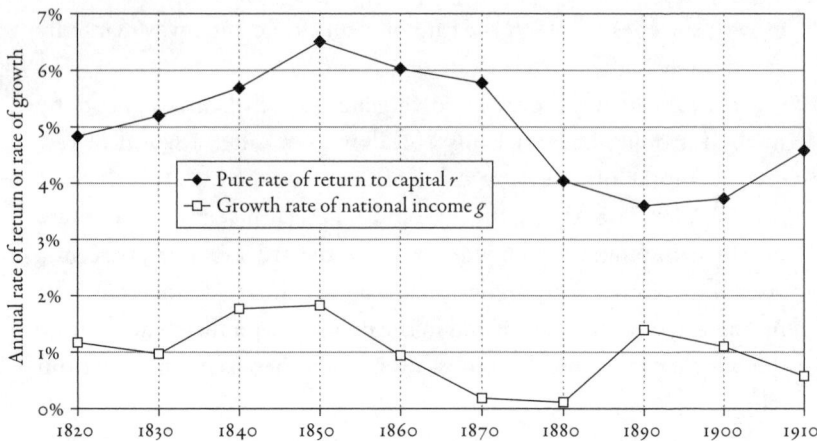

FIGURE 10.7. Return to capital and growth: France, 1820–1913

The rate of return on capital is a lot higher than the growth rate in France between 1820 and 1913.

Sources and series: see piketty.pse.ens.fr/capital21c.

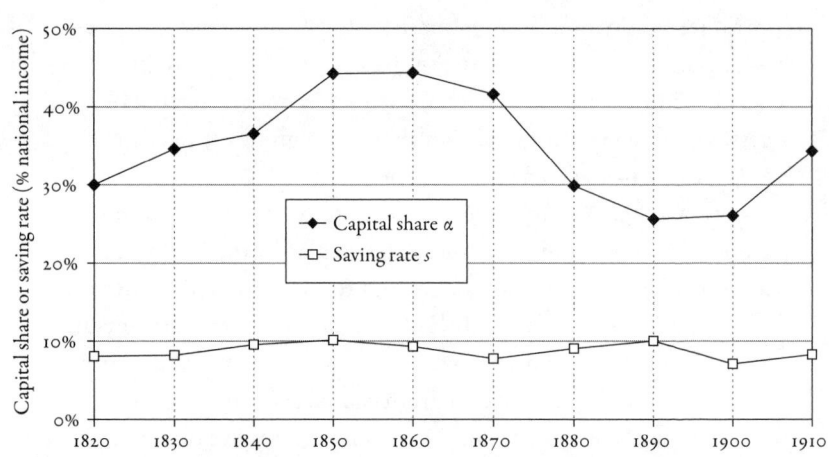

FIGURE 10.8. Capital share and saving rate: France, 1820–1913

The share of capital income in national income is much larger than the saving rate in France between 1820 and 1913.

Sources and series: see piketty.pse.ens.fr/capital21c.

from inheritance, and this supremacy of inherited capital, despite the period's great economic dynamism and impressive financial sophistication, is explained by the dynamic effects of the fundamental inequality $r > g$: the very rich French probate data allow us to be quite precise about this point.

Why Is the Return on Capital Greater Than the Growth Rate?

Let me pursue the logic of the argument. Are there deep reasons why the return on capital should be systematically higher than the rate of growth? To be clear, I take this to be a historical fact, not a logical necessity.

It is an incontrovertible historical reality that r was indeed greater than g over a long period of time. Many people, when first confronted with this claim, express astonishment and wonder why it should be true. The most obvious way to convince oneself that $r > g$ is indeed a historical fact is no doubt the following.

As I showed in Part One, economic growth was virtually nil throughout much of human history: combining demographic with economic growth, we can say that the annual growth rate from antiquity to the seventeenth century never exceeded 0.1–0.2 percent for long. Despite the many historical uncertainties, there is no doubt that the rate of return on capital was always considerably greater than this: the central value observed over the long run is 4–5 percent a year. In particular, this was the return on land in most traditional agrarian societies. Even if we accept a much lower estimate of the pure yield on capital—for example, by accepting the argument that many landowners have made over the years that it is no simple matter to manage a large estate, so that this return actually reflects a just compensation for the highly skilled labor contributed by the owner—we would still be left with a minimum (and to my mind unrealistic and much too low) return on capital of at least 2–3 percent a year, which is still much greater than 0.1–0.2 percent. Thus throughout most of human history,

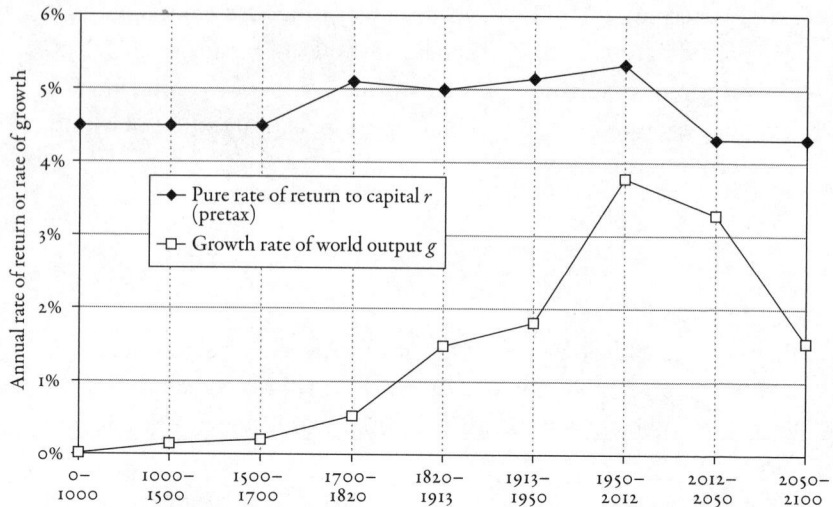

FIGURE 10.9. Rate of return versus growth rate at the world level, from Antiquity until 2100

The rate of return to capital (pretax) has always been higher than the world growth rate, but the gap was reduced during the twentieth century, and might widen again in the twenty-first century.

Sources and series: see piketty.pse.ens.fr/capital21c.

the inescapable fact is that the rate of return on capital was always at least 10 to 20 times greater than the rate of growth of output (and income). Indeed, this fact is to a large extent the very foundation of society itself: it is what allowed a class of owners to devote themselves to something other than their own subsistence.

In order to illustrate this point as clearly as possible, I have shown in Figure 10.9 the evolution of the global rate of return on capital and the growth rate from antiquity to the twenty-first century.

These are obviously approximate and uncertain estimates, but the orders of magnitude and overall evolutions may be taken as valid. For the global growth rate, I have used the historical estimates and projections discussed in Part One. For the global rate of return on capital, I have used the estimates for Britain and France in the period 1700–2010, which were analyzed in Part Two. For early periods, I have used a pure return of 4.5 percent, which should be taken as a minimum value (available historical data suggest average returns on the order of 5–6 percent).[16] For the twenty-first century, I have assumed that the value observed in the period 1990–2010 (about 4 percent) will continue, but this is of course uncertain: there are forces pushing toward a lower return and other forces pushing toward a higher. Note, too, that the returns on capital in Figure 10.8 are pretax returns (and also do not take account of capital losses due to war, or of capital gains and losses, which were especially large in the twentieth century).

As Figure 10.9 shows, the pure rate of return on capital—generally 4–5 percent—has throughout history always been distinctly greater than the global growth rate, but the gap between the two shrank significantly during the twentieth century, especially in the second half of the century, when the global economy grew at a rate of 3.5–4 percent a year. In all likelihood, the gap will widen again in the twenty-first century as growth (especially demographic growth) slows. According to the central scenario discussed in Part One, global growth is likely to be around 1.5 percent a year between 2050 and 2100, roughly the same rate as in the nineteenth century. The gap between r and g would then return to a level comparable to that which existed during the Industrial Revolution.

In such a context, it is easy to see that taxes on capital—and shocks of various kinds—can play a central role. Before World War I, taxes on capital were very low (most countries did not tax either personal income or corporate profits, and estate taxes were generally no more than a few percent). To simplify matters, we may therefore assume that the rate of return on capital was virtually the same after taxes as before. After World War I, the tax rates on top incomes, profits, and

---

16. For land rent, the earliest data available for antiquity and the Middle Ages suggest annual returns of around 5 percent. For interest on loans, we often find rates above 5 percent in earlier periods, typically on the order of 6–8 percent, even for loans with real estate collateral. See, for example, the data collected by S. Homer and R. Sylla, *A History of Interest Rates* (New Brunswick, NJ: Rutgers University Press, 1996).

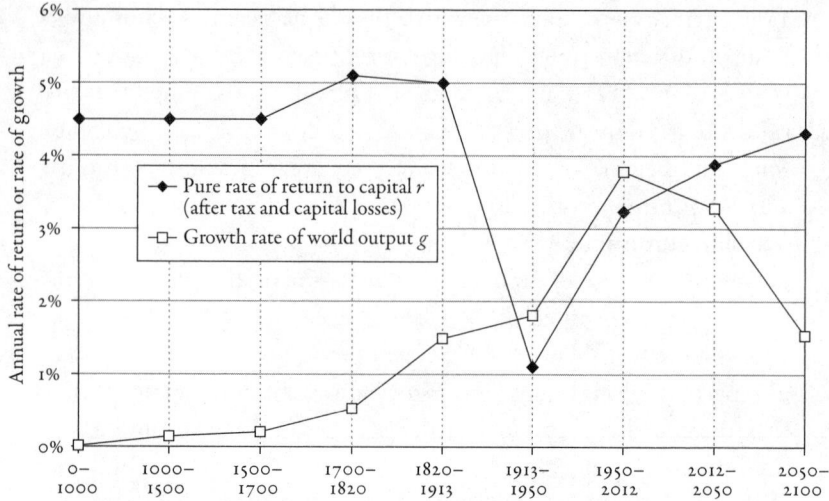

FIGURE 10.10. After tax rate of return versus growth rate at the world level, from Antiquity until 2100

The rate of return to capital (after tax and capital losses) fell below the growth rate during the twentieth century, and may again surpass it in the twenty-first century. Sources and series: see piketty.pse.ens.fr/capital21c.

wealth quickly rose to high levels. Since the 1980s, however, as the ideological climate changed dramatically under the influence of financial globalization and heightened competition between states for capital, these same tax rates have been falling and in some cases have almost entirely disappeared.

Figure 10.10 shows my estimates of the average return on capital after taxes and after accounting for estimated capital losses due to destruction of property in the period 1913–1950. For the sake of argument, I have also assumed that fiscal competition will gradually lead to total disappearance of taxes on capital in the twenty-first century: the average tax rate on capital is set at 30 percent for 1913–2012, 10 percent for 2012–2050, and 0 percent in 2050–2100. Of course, things are more complicated in practice: taxes vary enormously, depending on the country and type of property. At times, they are progressive (meaning that the tax rate increases with the level of income or wealth, at least in theory), and obviously it is not foreordained that fiscal competition must proceed to its ultimate conclusion.

Under these assumptions, we find that the return on capital, net of taxes (and losses), fell to 1–1.5 percent in the period 1913–1950, which was less than the rate of growth. This novel situation continued in the period 1950–2012 owing to the exceptionally high growth rate. Ultimately, we find that in the twentieth century, both fiscal and nonfiscal shocks created a situation in which, for the first time in history, the net return on capital was less than the growth rate. A concatenation of circumstances (wartime destruction, progressive tax policies made possible by the shocks of 1914–1945, and exceptional growth during the three decades following the end of World War II) thus created a historically unprecedented situation, which lasted for nearly a century. All signs are, however, that it is about to end. If fiscal competition proceeds to its logical conclusion—which it may—the gap between r and g will return at some point in the twenty-first century to a level close to what it was in the nineteenth century (see Figure 10.10). If the average tax rate on capital stays at around 30 percent, which is by no means certain, the net rate of return on capital will most likely rise to a level significantly above the growth rate, at least if the central scenario turns out to be correct.

To bring this possible evolution out even more clearly, I have combined in Figure 10.11 the two subperiods 1913–1950 and 1950–2012 into a single average for the century 1913–2012, the unprecedented era during which the net rate of return on capital was less than the growth rate. I have also combined the two subperiods 2012–2050 and 2050–2100 into a single average for 2012–2100 and assumed that the rates for the second half of the twenty-first century would continue into the twenty-second century (which is of course by no means guaranteed). In any case, Figure 10.11 at least brings out the unprecedented—and possibly unique—character of the twentieth century in regard to the relation between r and g. Note, too, that the hypothesis that global growth will continue at a rate of 1.5 percent a year over the very long run is regarded as excessively optimistic by many observers. Recall

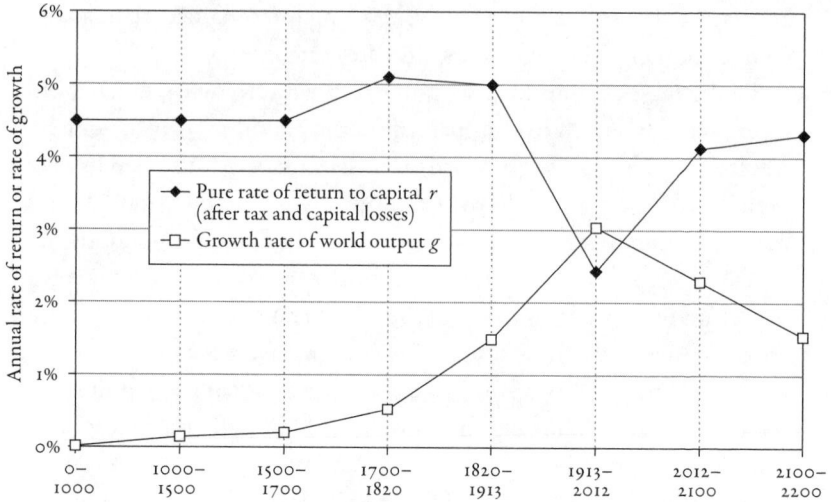

FIGURE 10.11. After tax rate of return versus growth rate at the world level, from Antiquity until 2200

The rate of return to capital (after tax and capital losses) fell below the growth rate during the twentieth century, and might again surpass it in the twenty-first century. Sources and series: see piketty.pse.ens.fr/capital21c.

that the average growth of global per capita output was 0.8 percent a year between 1700 and 2012, and demographic growth (which also averaged 0.8 percent a year over the past three centuries) is expected to drop sharply between now and the end of the twenty-first century (according to most forecasts). Note, however, that the principal short-coming of Figure 10.11 is that it relies on the assumption that no significant political reaction will alter the course of capitalism and financial globalization over the course of the next two centuries. Given the tumultuous history of the past century, this is a dubious and to my mind not very plausible hypothesis, precisely because its inegalitarian consequences would be considerable and would probably not be tolerated indefinitely.

To sum up: the inequality $r > g$ has clearly been true throughout most of human history, right up to the eve of World War I, and it will probably be true again in the twenty-first century. Its truth depends, however, on the shocks to which capital is subject, as well as on what public policies and institutions are put in place to regulate the relationship between capital and labor.

The Question of Time Preference

To recap: the inequality $r > g$ is a contingent historical proposition, which is true in some periods and political contexts and not in others. From a strictly logical point of view, it is perfectly possible to imagine a society in which the growth rate is greater than the return on capital— even in the absence of state intervention. Everything depends on the one hand on technology (what is capital used for?) and on the other on attitudes toward saving and property (why do people choose to hold capital?). As noted, it is perfectly possible to imagine a society in which capital has no uses (other than to serve as a pure store of value, with a return strictly equal to zero), but in which people would choose to hold a lot of it, in anticipation, say, of some future catastrophe or grand potlatch or simply because they are particularly patient and take a generous attitude toward future generations. If, moreover, productivity growth in this society is rapid, either because of constant innovation or because the country is rapidly catching up with more technologically advanced countries, then the growth rate may very well be distinctly higher than the rate of return on capital.

In practice, however, there appears never to have been a society in which the rate of return on capital fell naturally and persistently to less than 2–3 percent, and the mean return we generally see (averaging over all types of investments) is generally closer to 4–5 percent (before taxes). In particular, the return on agricultural land in traditional societies, like the return on real estate in today's societies—these being the most common and least risky forms of investment in each case—is generally around 4–5 percent, with perhaps a slight downward trend over the very long run (to 3–4 percent rather than 4–5).

The economic model generally used to explain this relative stability of the return on capital at around 4–5 percent (as well as the fact that it never falls below 2–3 percent) is based on the notion of "time pref-erence" in favor of the present. In other words, economic actors are characterized by a rate of time preference (usually denoted θ) that mea-sures how impatient they are and how they take the future into ac-count. For example, if $\theta = 5$ percent, the actor in question is prepared to sacrifice 105 euros of consumption tomorrow in order to consume an additional 100 euros today. This "theory," like many theoretical models in economics, is somewhat tautological (one can always explain any observed behavior by assuming that the actors involved have prefer-ences—or "utility functions" in the jargon of the profession—that lead them to act that way), and its predictive power is radical and im-placable. In the case in point, assuming a zero-growth economy, it is not surprising to discover that the rate of return on capital must equal the time preference θ.[17] According to this theory, the reason why the return on capital has been historically stable at 4–5 percent is ulti-mately psychological: since this rate of return reflects the average per-son's impatience and attitude toward the future, it cannot vary much from this level.

In addition to being tautological, the theory raises a number of other difficulties. To be sure, the intuition that lies behind the model (like that which lies behind marginal productivity theory) cannot be entirely wrong. All other things equal, a more patient society, or one that anticipates future shocks, will of course amass greater reserves and accumulate more capital. Similarly, if a society accumulates so much capital that the return on capital is persistently low, say, 1 per-cent a year (or in which all forms of wealth, including the property of the middle and lower classes, are taxed so that the net return is very low), then a significant proportion of property-owning individuals

---

17. If the return on capital were greater than the time preference, everyone would prefer to reduce present consumption and save more (so that the capital stock would grow indefinitely, until the return on capital fell to the rate of time prefer-ence). In the opposite case, everyone would sell a portion of her capital stock in order to increase present consumption (and the capital stock would decrease until the return on capital rose to equal θ). In either case we are left with $r = \theta$.

will seek to sell their homes and financial assets, thus decreasing the capital stock until the yield rises.

The problem with the theory is that it is too simplistic and systematic: it is impossible to encapsulate all savings behavior and all attitudes toward the future in a single inexorable psychological parameter. If we take the most extreme version of the model (called the "infinite horizon" model, because agents calculate the consequences of their savings strategy for all their descendants until the end of time as though they were thinking of themselves, in accordance with their own rate of time preference), it follows that the net rate of return on capital cannot vary by even as little as a tenth of a percent: any attempt to alter the net return (for example, by changing tax policy) will trigger an infinitely powerful reaction in one sense or another (saving or dissaving) in order to force the net return back to its unique equilibrium. Such a prediction is scarcely realistic: history shows that the elasticity of saving is positive but not infinite, especially when the rate of return varies within moderate and reasonable limits.[18]

Another difficulty with this theoretical model (in its strictest interpretation) is that it implies that the rate of return on capital, r, must, in order to maintain the economy in equilibrium, rise very rapidly with the growth rate g, so that the gap between r and g should be greater in a rapidly growing economy than in one that is not growing at all. Once again, this prediction is not very realistic, nor is it compatible with historical experience (the return on capital may rise in a rapidly growing economy but probably not enough to increase the gap $r - g$ significantly, to judge by observed historical experience), and it, too, is a consequence of the infinite horizon hypothesis. Note, however, that the intuition here is again partially valid and in any case interesting from a strictly logical point of view. In the standard economic model, based on the existence of a "perfect" market for capital

---

18. The infinite horizon model implies an infinite elasticity of saving—and thus of the supply of capital—in the long run. It therefore assumes that tax policy cannot affect the supply of capital.

(in which each owner of capital receives a return equal to the highest marginal productivity available in the economy, and everyone can borrow as much as he or she wants at that rate), the reason why the return on capital, r, is systematically and necessarily higher than the growth rate, g, is the following. If r were less than g, economic agents, realizing that their future income (and that of their descendants) will rise faster than the rate at which they can borrow, will feel infinitely wealthy and will therefore wish to borrow without limit in order to consume immediately (until r rises above g). In this extreme form, the mechanism is not entirely plausible, but it shows that $r > g$ is true in the most standard of economic models and is even more likely to be true as capital markets become more efficient.[19]

To recap: savings behavior and attitudes toward the future cannot be encapsulated in a single parameter. These choices need to be analyzed in more complex models, involving not only time preference but also precautionary savings, life-cycle effects, the importance attached to wealth in itself, and many other factors. These choices depend on the social and institutional environment (such as the existence of a public pension system), family strategies and pressures, and limitations that social groups impose on themselves (for example, in some aristocratic societies, heirs are not free to sell family property), in addition to individual psychological and cultural factors.

To my way of thinking, the inequality $r > g$ should be analyzed as a historical reality dependent on a variety of mechanisms and not as an absolute logical necessity. It is the result of a confluence of forces, each largely independent of the others. For one thing, the rate of growth, g, tends to be structurally low (generally not much more than 1 percent a year once the demographic transition is complete and the country

---

19. Formally, in the standard infinite horizon model, the equilibrium rate of return is given by the formula $r = \theta + \gamma \times g$ (where θ is the rate of time preference and γ measures the concavity of the utility function. It is generally estimated that γ lies between 1.5 and 2.5. For example, if $\theta = 5\%$ and $\gamma = 2$, then $r = 5\%$ for $g = 0\%$ and $r = 9\%$ for $g = 2\%$, so that the gap $r - g$ rises from 5% to 7% when growth increases from 0% to 2%. See the online technical appendix.

reaches the world technological frontier, where the pace of innovation is fairly slow). For another, the rate of return on capital, r, depends on many technological, psychological, social, and cultural factors, which together seem to result in a return of roughly 4–5 percent (in any event distinctly greater than 1 percent).

Is There an Equilibrium Distribution?

Let me now turn to the consequences of $r > g$ for the dynamics of the wealth distribution. The fact that the return on capital is distinctly and persistently greater than the growth rate is a powerful force for a more unequal distribution of wealth. For example, if $g = 1$ percent and $r = 5$ percent, wealthy individuals have to reinvest only one-fifth of their annual capital income to ensure that their capital will grow faster than average income. Under these conditions, the only forces that can avoid an indefinite inegalitarian spiral and stabilize inequality of wealth at a finite level are the following. First, if the fortunes of wealthy individuals grow more rapidly than average income, the capital / income ratio will rise indefinitely, which in the long run should lead to a decrease in the rate of return on capital. Nevertheless, this mechanism can take decades to operate, especially in an open economy in which wealthy individuals can accumulate foreign assets, as was the case in Britain and France in the nineteenth century and up to the eve of World War I. In principle, this process always comes to an end (when those who own foreign assets take possession of the entire planet), but this can obviously take time. This process was largely responsible for the vertiginous increase in the top centile's share of wealth in Britain and France during the Belle Époque.

Furthermore, in regard to the trajectories of individual fortunes, this divergent process can be countered by shocks of various kinds, whether demographic (such as the absence of an heir or the presence of too many heirs, leading to dispersal of the family capital, or early death, or prolonged life) or economic (such as a bad investment or a peasant uprising or a financial crisis or a mediocre season, etc.). Shocks of this sort always affect family fortunes, so that changes in the wealth distribution occur even in the most static societies. Note, moreover, the importance of demographic choices (the fewer children the rich choose to have, the more concentrated wealth becomes) and inheritance laws.

Many traditional aristocratic societies were based on the principle of primogeniture: the eldest son inherited all (or at any rate a disproportionately large share) of the family property so as to avoid fragmentation and to preserve or increase the family's wealth. The eldest son's privilege concerned the family's primary estate in particular and often placed heavy constraints on the property: the heir was not allowed to diminish its value and was obliged to live on the income from the capital, which was then conveyed in turn to the next heir in the line of succession, usually the eldest grandson. In British law this was the system of "entails" (the equivalent in French law being the system of *substitution héréditaire* under the Ancien Régime). It was the reason for the misfortune of Elinor and Marianne in *Sense and Sensibility*: the Norland estate passed directly to their father and half-brother, John Dashwood, who decided, after considering the matter with his wife, Fanny, to leave them nothing. The fate of the two sisters is a direct consequence of this sinister conversation. In *Persuasion*, Sir Walter's estate goes directly to his nephew, bypassing his three daughters. Jane Austen, herself disfavored by inheritance and left a spinster along with her sister, knew what she was talking about.

The inheritance law that derived from the French Revolution and the Civil Code that followed rested on two main pillars: the abolition of *substitutions héréditaires* and primogeniture and the adoption of the principle of equal division of property among brothers and sisters (equipartition). This principle has been applied strictly and consistently since 1804: in France, the *quotité disponible* (that is, the share of the estate that parents are free to dispose of as they wish) is only a quarter of total wealth for parents with three or more children,[20] and exemption is granted only in extreme circumstances (for example, if the chil-

---

20. A third for parents with two children and a half for those with only one child.

dren murder their stepmother). It is important to understand that the new law was based not only on a principle of equality (younger children were valued as much as the eldest and protected from the whims of the parents) but also on a principle of liberty and economic efficiency. In particular, the abolition of entails, which Adam Smith disliked and Voltaire, Rousseau, and Montesquieu abhorred, rested on a simple idea: this abolition allowed the free circulation of goods and the possibility of reallocating property to the best possible use in the judgment of the living generation, despite what dead ancestors may have thought. Interestingly, after considerable debate, Americans came to the same conclusion in the years after the Revolution: entails were forbidden, even in the South. As Thomas Jefferson famously put it, "the Earth belongs to the living." And equipartition of estates among siblings became the legal default, that is, the rule that applied in the absence of an explicit will (although the freedom to make one's will as one pleases still prevails in both the United States and Britain, in practice most estates are equally divided among siblings). This was an important difference between France and the United States on the one hand, where the law of equipartition applied from the nineteenth century on, and Britain on the other, where primogeniture remained the default in 1925 for a portion of the parental property, namely, landed and agricultural capital.[21] In Germany, it was not until the Weimar Republic that the German equivalent of entails was abolished in 1919.[22]

During the French Revolution, this egalitarian, antiauthoritarian, liberal legislation (which challenged parental authority while affirming that of the new family head, in some cases to the detriment of his spouse) was greeted with considerable optimism, at least by men—

---

21. Note that in 1807 Napoleon introduced the *majorat* for his imperial nobility. This allowed an increased share of certain landed estates linked to titles of nobility to go the eldest males. Only a few thousand individuals were concerned. Moreover, Charles X tried to restore *substitutions héréditaires* for his own nobility in 1826. These throwbacks to the Ancien Régime affected only a small part of the population and were in any case definitively abolished in 1848.

22. See Jens Beckert, *Inherited Wealth* (Princeton: Princeton University Press, 2008).

despite being quite radical for the time.[23] Proponents of this revolutionary legislation were convinced that they had found the key to future equality. Since, moreover, the Civil Code granted everyone equal rights with respect to the market and property, and guilds had been abolished, the ultimate outcome seemed clear: such a system would inevitably eliminate the inequalities of the past. The marquis de Condorcet gave forceful expression to this optimistic view in his *Esquisse d'un tableau historique des progrès de l'esprit humain* (1794): "It is easy to prove that fortunes tend naturally toward equality, and that excessive differences of wealth either cannot exist or must promptly cease, if the civil laws do not establish artificial ways of perpetuating and amassing such fortunes, and if freedom of commerce and industry eliminate the advantage that any prohibitive law or fiscal privilege gives to acquired wealth."[24]

The Civil Code and the Illusion of the French Revolution

How, then, are we to explain the fact that the concentration of wealth increased steadily in France throughout the nineteenth century and ultimately peaked in the Belle Époque at a level even more extreme than when the Civil Code was introduced and scarcely less than in monarchical and aristocratic Britain? Clearly, equality of rights and opportunities is not enough to ensure an egalitarian distribution of wealth.

Indeed, once the rate of return on capital significantly and durably exceeds the growth rate, the dynamics of the accumulation and trans-

---

23. In theory, women enjoyed the same rights as men when it came to dividing estates, according to the Civil Code. But a wife was not free to dispose of her property as she saw fit: this type of asymmetry, in regard to opening and managing bank accounts, selling property, etc., did not totally disappear until the 1970s. In practice, therefore, the new law favored (male) heads of families: younger sons acquired the same rights as elder sons, but daughters were left behind. See the online technical appendix.

24. See Pierre Rosanvallon, *La société des égaux* (Paris: Le Seuil, 2011), 50.

mission of wealth automatically lead to a very highly concentrated distribution, and egalitarian sharing among siblings does not make much of a difference. As I mentioned a moment ago, there are always economic and demographic shocks that affect the trajectories of individual family fortunes. With the aid of a fairly simple mathematical model, one can show that for a given structure of shocks of this kind, the distribution of wealth tends toward a long-run equilibrium and that the equilibrium level of inequality is an increasing function of the gap $r - g$ between the rate of return on capital and the growth rate. Intuitively, the difference $r - g$ measures the rate at which capital income diverges from average income if none of it is consumed and everything is reinvested in the capital stock. The greater the difference $r - g$, the more powerful the divergent force. If the demographic and economic shocks take a multiplicative form (i.e., the greater the initial capital, the greater the effect of a good or bad investment), the long-run equilibrium distribution is a Pareto distribution (a mathematical form based on a power law, which corresponds fairly well to distributions observed in practice). One can also show fairly easily that the coefficient of the Pareto distribution (which measures the degree of inequality) is a steeply increasing function of the difference $r - g$.[25]

Concretely, what this means is that if the gap between the return on capital and the growth rate is as high as that observed in France in the nineteenth century, when the average rate of return was 5 percent a year and growth was roughly 1 percent, the model predicts that the cumulative dynamics of wealth accumulation will automatically give rise to an extremely high concentration of wealth, with typically around 90 percent of capital owned by the top decile and more than 50 percent by the top centile.[26]

---

25. The equation relating the Pareto coefficient to $r - g$ is given in the online technical appendix.

26. Clearly, this does not imply that the $r > g$ logic is necessarily the only force at work. The model and related calculations are obviously a simplification of reality and do not claim to identify the precise role played by each mechanism (various contradictory forces may balance each other). It does show, however, that the

In other words, the fundamental inequality $r > g$ can explain the very high level of capital inequality observed in the nineteenth century, and thus in a sense the failure of the French Revolution. Although the revolutionary assemblies established a universal tax (and in so doing provided us with a peerless instrument for measuring the distribution of wealth), the tax rate was so low (barely 1–2 percent on directly transmitted estates, no matter how large, throughout the nineteenth century) that it had no measurable impact on the difference between the rate of return on capital and the growth rate. Under these conditions, it is no surprise that inequality of wealth was as great in nineteenth-century France and even during the republican Belle Époque as in monarchical Britain. The formal nature of the regime was of little moment compared with the inequality $r > g$.

Equipartition of estates between siblings did have some effect, but less than the gap $r − g$. Concretely, primogeniture (or, more precisely, primogeniture on agricultural land, which accounted for a decreasing share of British national capital over the course of the nineteenth century), magnified the effects of demographic and economic shocks (creating additional inequality depending on one's rank in the sibling order) and thus increased the Pareto coefficient and gave rise to a more concentrated distribution of wealth. This may help to explain why the top decile's share of total wealth was greater in Britain than in France in 1900–1910 (slightly more than 90 percent, compared with slightly less in France), and especially why the top centile's share was significantly greater on the British side of the Channel (70 percent v. 60 percent), since this appears to have been based on the preservation of a small number of very large landed estates. But this effect was partly compensated by France's low demographic growth rate (cumulative inequality of wealth is structurally greater when the population is stagnant, again because of the difference between r and g), and in

---

$r > g$ logic is by itself sufficient to explain the observed level of concentration. See the online technical appendix.

the end it had only a moderate effect on the overall distribution, which was fairly close in the two countries.[27]

In Paris, where the Napoleonic Civil Code came into effect in 1804 and where inequality cannot be laid at the door of British aristocrats and the queen of England, the top centile owned more than 70 percent of total wealth in 1913, even more than in Britain. The reality was so striking that it even found expression in an animated cartoon, *The Aristocats,* set in Paris in 1910. The size of the old lady's fortune is not mentioned, but to judge by the splendor of her residence and by the zeal of her butler Edgar to get rid of Duchesse and her three kittens, it must have been considerable.

In terms of the $r > g$ logic, the fact that the growth rate increased from barely 0.2 percent prior to 1800 to 0.5 percent in the eighteenth century and then to 1 percent in the nineteenth century does not seem to have made much of a difference: it was still small compared to a return on capital of around 5 percent, especially since the Industrial Revolution appears to have slightly increased that return.[28] According to the theoretical model, if the return on capital is around 5 percent a year, the equilibrium concentration of capital will not decrease significantly unless the growth rate exceeds 1.5–2 percent or taxes on capital reduce the net return to below 3–3.5 percent, or both.

Note, finally, that if the difference $r - g$ surpasses a certain threshold, there is no equilibrium distribution: inequality of wealth will increase

---

27. The Swedish case is interesting, because it combines several contradictory forces that seem to balance one another out: first, the capital / income ratio was lower than in France or Britain in the nineteenth and early twentieth centuries (the value of land was lower, and domestic capital was partly owned by foreigners—in this respect, Sweden was similar to Canada), and second, primogeniture was in force until the end of the nineteenth century, and some entails on large dynastic fortunes in Sweden persist to this day. In the end, wealth was less concentrated in Sweden in 1900–1910 than in Britain and close to the French level. See Figures 10.1–4 and the work of Henry Ohlsson, Jesper Roine, and Daniel Waldenström.

28. Recall that the estimates of the "pure" return on capital indicated in Figure 10.10 should be regarded as minimums and that the average observed return rose as high as 6–7 percent in Britain and France in the nineteenth century (see Chapter 6).

without limit, and the gap between the peak of the distribution and the average will grow indefinitely. The exact level of this threshold of course depends on savings behavior: divergence is more likely to occur if the very wealthy have nothing to spend their money on and no choice but to save and add to their capital stock. *The Aristocats* calls attention to the problem: Adélaïde de Bonnefamille obviously enjoys a handsome income, which she lavishes on piano lessons and painting classes for Duchesse, Marie, Toulouse, and Berlioz, who are somewhat bored by it all.[29] This kind of behavior explains quite well the rising concentration of wealth in France, and particularly in Paris, in the Belle Époque: the largest fortunes increasingly belonged to the elderly, who saved a large fraction of their capital income, so that their capital grew significantly faster than the economy. As noted, such an inegalitarian spiral cannot continue indefinitely: ultimately, there will be no place to invest the savings, and the global return on capital will fall, until an equilibrium distribution emerges. But that can take a very long time, and since the top centile's share of Parisian wealth in 1913 already exceeded 70 percent, it is legitimate to ask how high the equilibrium level would have been had the shocks due to World War I not occurred.

Pareto and the Illusion of Stable Inequality

It is worth pausing a moment to discuss some methodological and historical issues concerning the statistical measurement of inequality. In Chapter 7, I discussed the Italian statistician Corrado Gini and his famous coefficient. Although the Gini coefficient was intended to sum up inequality in a single number, it actually gives a simplistic, overly optimistic, and difficult-to-interpret picture of what is really going on. A more interesting case is that of Gini's compatriot Vilfredo Pa-

---

29. Fortunately, Duchesse and her kittens ultimately meet Thomas O'Malley, an alley cat whose earthy ways they find more amusing than art classes (a little like Jack Dawson, who meets young Rose on the deck of *Titanic* two years later, in 1912).

reto, whose major works, including a discussion of the famous "Pareto law," were published between 1890 and 1910. In the interwar years, the Italian Fascists adopted Pareto as one of their own and promoted his theory of elites. Although they were no doubt seeking to capitalize on his prestige, it is nevertheless true that Pareto, shortly before his death in 1923, hailed Mussolini's accession to power. Of course the Fascists would naturally have been attracted to Pareto's theory of stable inequality and the pointlessness of trying to change it.

What is more striking when one reads Pareto's work with the benefit of hindsight is that he clearly had no evidence to support his theory of stability. Pareto was writing in 1900 or thereabouts. He used available tax tables from 1880–1890, based on data from Prussia and Saxony as well as several Swiss and Italian cities. The information was scanty and covered a decade at most. What is more, it showed a slight trend toward higher inequality, which Pareto intentionally sought to hide.[30] In any case, it is clear that such data provide no basis whatsoever for any conclusion about the long-term behavior of inequality around the world.

Pareto's judgment was clearly influenced by his political prejudices: he was above all wary of socialists and what he took to be their redistributive illusions. In this respect he was hardly different from any number of contemporary colleagues, such as the French economist Pierre Leroy-Beaulieu, whom he admired. Pareto's case is interesting because it illustrates the powerful illusion of eternal stability, to which the uncritical use of mathematics in the social sciences sometimes leads. Seeking to find out how rapidly the number of taxpayers decreases as one climbs higher in the income hierarchy, Pareto discovered that the rate of decrease could be approximated by a mathematical law that subsequently became known as "Pareto's law" or, alternatively, as an instance of a general class of functions known as "power laws."[31] Indeed, this family of functions is still used today to study distributions of

---

30. For an analysis of Pareto's data, see my *Les hauts revenus en France au 20e siècle: Inégalités et redistribution 1901–1998* (Paris: Grasset, 2001), 527–30.

31. For details, see the online technical appendix.

wealth and income. Note, however, that the power law applies only to the upper tail of these distributions and that the relation is only approximate and locally valid. It can nevertheless be used to model processes due to multiplicative shocks, like those described earlier.

Note, moreover, that we are speaking not of a single function or curve but of a family of functions: everything depends on the coefficients and parameters that define each individual curve. The data collected in the WTID as well as the data on wealth presented here show that these Pareto coefficients have varied enormously over time. When we say that a distribution of wealth is a Pareto distribution, we have not really said anything at all. It may be a distribution in which the upper decile receives only slightly more than 20 percent of total income (as in Scandinavia in 1970–1980) or one in which the upper decile receives 50 percent (as in the United States in 2000–2010) or one in which the upper decile owns more than 90 percent of total wealth (as in France and Britain in 1900–1910). In each case we are dealing with a Pareto distribution, but the coefficients are quite different. The corresponding social, economic, and political realities are clearly poles apart.[32]

Even today, some people imagine, as Pareto did, that the distribution of wealth is rock stable, as if it were somehow a law of nature.

---

32. The simplest way to think of Pareto coefficients is to use what are sometimes called "inverted coefficients," which in practice vary from 1.5 to 3.5. An inverted coefficient of 1.5 means that average income or wealth above a certain threshold is equal to 1.5 times the threshold level (individuals with more than a million euros of property own on average 1.5 million euros' worth, etc., for any given threshold), which is a relatively low level of inequality (there are few very wealthy individuals). By contrast, an inverted coefficient of 3.5 represents a very high level of inequality. Another way to think about power functions is the following: a coefficient around 1.5 means that the top 0.1 percent are barely twice as rich on average as the top 1 percent (and similarly for the top 0.01 percent within the top 0.1 percent, etc.). By contrast, a coefficient around 3.5 means that they are more than five times as rich. All of this is explained in the online technical appendix. For graphs representing the historical evolution of the Pareto coefficients throughout the twentieth century for the various countries in the WTID, see Anthony B. Atkinson, Thomas Piketty, and Emmanuel Saez, "Top Incomes in the Long Run of History," *Journal of Economic Literature* 49, no. 1 (2011): 3–71.

In fact, nothing could be further from the truth. When we study inequality in historical perspective, the important thing to explain is not the stability of the distribution but the significant changes that occur from time to time. In the case of the wealth distribution, I have identified a way to explain the very large historical variations that occur (whether described in terms of Pareto coefficients or as shares of the top decile and centile) in terms of the difference $r - g$ between the rate of return on capital and the growth rate of the economy.

Why Inequality of Wealth Has Not Returned to the Levels of the Past

I come now to the essential question: Why has the inequality of wealth not returned to the level achieved in the Belle Époque, and can we be sure that this situation is permanent and irreversible?

Let me state at the outset that I have no definitive and totally satisfactory answer to this question. Several factors have played important roles in the past and will continue to do so in the future, and it is quite simply impossible to achieve mathematical certainty on this point.

The very substantial reduction in inequality of wealth following the shocks of 1914–1945 is the easiest part to explain. Capital suffered a series of extremely violent shocks as a result of the wars and the policies to which they gave rise, and the capital / income ratio therefore collapsed. One might of course think that the reduction of wealth would have affected all fortunes proportionately, regardless of their rank in the hierarchy, leaving the distribution of wealth unchanged. But to believe this one would have to forget the fact that wealth has different origins and fulfills different functions. At the very top of the hierarchy, most wealth was accumulated long ago, and it takes much longer to reconstitute such a large fortune than to accumulate a modest one.

Furthermore, the largest fortunes serve to finance a certain lifestyle. The detailed probate records collected from the archives show unambiguously that many rentiers in the interwar years did not reduce expenses sufficiently rapidly to compensate for the shocks to their fortunes and income during the war and in the decade that followed, so that they eventually had to eat into their capital to finance current expenditures. Hence they bequeathed to the next generation fortunes significantly smaller than those they had inherited, and the previous social equilibrium could no longer be sustained. The Parisian data are particularly eloquent on this point. For example, the wealthiest 1 percent of Parisians in the Belle Époque had capital income roughly 80–100 times as great as the average wage of that time, which enabled them to live very well and still reinvest a small portion of their income and thus increase their inherited wealth.[33] From 1872 to 1912, the system appears to have been perfectly balanced: the wealthiest individuals passed on to the next generation enough to finance a lifestyle requiring 80–100 times the average wage or even a bit more, so that wealth became even more concentrated. This equilibrium clearly broke down in the interwar years: the wealthiest 1 percent of Parisians continued to live more or less as they had always done but left the next generation just enough to yield capital income of 30–40 times the average wage; by the late 1930s, this had fallen to just 20 times the average wage. For the rentiers, this was the beginning of the end. This was probably the most important reason for the deconcentration of wealth that we see in all European countries (and to a less extent in the United States) in the wake of the shocks of 1914–1945.

In addition, the composition of the largest fortunes left them (on average) more exposed to losses due to the two world wars. In particular, the probate records show that foreign assets made up as a much as a quarter of the largest fortunes on the eve of World War I, nearly half of which consisted of the sovereign debt of foreign governments (especially Russia, which was on the verge of default). Unfortunately, we do not have comparable data for Britain, but there is no doubt that foreign assets played at least as important a role in the largest British

---

33. That is, they had something like an income of 2–2.5 million euros a year in a society where the average wage was 24,000 euros a year (2,000 a month). See the online technical appendix.

fortunes. In both France and Britain, foreign assets virtually disappeared after the two world wars.

The importance of this factor should not be overstated, however, since the wealthiest individuals were often in a good position to reallocate their portfolios at the most profitable moment. It is also striking to discover that many individuals, and not just the wealthiest, owned significant amounts of foreign assets on the eve of World War I. When we examine the structure of Parisian portfolios in the late nineteenth century and Belle Époque, we find that they were highly diversified and quite "modern" in their composition. On the eve of the war, about a third of assets were in real estate (of which approximately two-thirds was in Paris and one-third in the provinces, including a small amount of agricultural land), while financial assets made up almost two-thirds. The latter consisted of both French and foreign stocks and (public as well as private) bonds, fairly well balanced at all levels of wealth (see Table 10.1).[34] The society of rentiers that flourished in the Belle Époque was not a society of the past based on static landed capital: it embodied a modern attitude toward wealth and investment. But the cumulative inegalitarian logic of $r > g$ made it prodigiously and persistently inegalitarian. In such a society, there is not much chance that freer, more competitive markets or more secure property rights can reduce inequality, since markets were already highly competitive and property rights firmly secured. In fact, the only thing that undermined this equilibrium was the series of shocks to capital and its income that began with World War I.

---

34. Paris real estate (which at the time consisted mainly of wholly owned buildings rather than apartments) was beyond the reach of the modestly wealthy, who were the only ones for whom provincial real estate, including especially farmland, still mattered. César Birotteau, who rejected his wife's advice to invest in some good farms near Chinon on the grounds that this was too staid an investment, saw himself as bold and forward-looking—unfortunately for him. See Table S10.4 (available online) for a more detailed version of Table 10.1 showing the very rapid growth of foreign assets between 1872 and 1912, especially in the largest portfolios.

TABLE 10.1.

The composition of Parisian portfolios, 1872–1912

Year	Real estate assets (buildings, houses, land)	Incl. real estate (Paris)	Incl. real estate (outside Paris)	Financial assets	Incl. equity	Incl. private bonds	Incl. public bonds	Incl. other financial assets (cash, deposits, etc.)	Furniture, jewels, etc.
Composition of total wealth (%)									
1872	42	29	13	56	15	19	13	9	2
1912	36	25	11	62	20	19	14	9	3
Composition of top 1% wealth holders' portfolios (%)									
1872	43	30	13	55	16	16	13	10	2
1912	32	22	10	65	24	19	14	8	2
Composition of next 9% (%)									
1872	42	27	15	56	14	22	13	7	2
1912	41	30	12	55	14	18	15	9	3
Composition of next 40% (%)									
1872	27	1	26	62	13	25	16	9	11
1912	31	7	24	58	12	14	14	18	10

Note: In 1912, real estate assets made up 36% of total wealth in Paris, financial assets made up 62%, and furniture, jewels, etc. 3%.

Sources: See piketty.pse.ens.fr/capital21c.

Finally, the period 1914–1945 ended in a number of European countries, and especially in France, with a redistribution of wealth that affected the largest fortunes disproportionately, especially those consisting largely of stock in large industrial firms. Recall, in particular, the nationalization of certain companies as a sanction after Liberation (the Renault automobile company is the emblematic example), as well as the national solidarity tax, which was also imposed in 1945. This progressive tax was a one-time levy on both capital and acquisitions made during the Occupation, but the rates were extremely high and imposed an additional burden on the individuals affected.[35]

Some Partial Explanations: Time, Taxes, and Growth

In the end, then, it is hardly surprising that the concentration of wealth decreased sharply everywhere between 1910 and 1950. In other words, the descending portion of Figures 10.1–5 is not the most difficult part to explain. The more surprising part at first glance, and in a way the more interesting part, is that the concentration of wealth never recovered from the shocks I have been discussing.

To be sure, it is important to recognize that capital accumulation is a long-term process extending over several generations. The concentration of wealth in Europe during the Belle Époque was the result of

---

35. The national solidarity tax, instituted by the ordinance of August 15, 1945, was an exceptional levy on all wealth, estimated as of June 4, 1945, at rates up to 20 percent for the largest fortunes, together with an exceptional levy on all nominal increases of wealth between 1940 and 1945, at rates up to 100 percent for the largest increases. In practice, in view of the very high inflation rate during the war (prices more than tripled between 1940 and 1945), this levy amounted to a 100 percent tax on anyone who did not sufficiently suffer during the war, as André Philip, a Socialist member of General de Gaulle's provisional government, admitted, explaining that it was inevitable that the tax should weigh equally on "those who did not become wealthier and perhaps even those who, in monetary terms, became poorer, in the sense that their fortunes did not increase to the same degree as the general increase in prices, but who were able to preserve their overall fortunes at a time when so many people in France lost everything." See André Siegfried, *L'Année Politique 1944–1945* (Paris: Editions du Grand Siècle, 1946), 159.

a cumulative process over many decades or even centuries. It was not until 2000–2010 that total private wealth (in both real estate and financial assets), expressed in years of national income, regained roughly the level it had attained on the eve of World War I. This restoration of the capital / income ratio in the rich countries is in all probability a process that is still ongoing.

It is not very realistic to think that the violent shocks of 1914–1945 could have been erased in ten or twenty years, thereby restoring by 1950–1960 a concentration of wealth equal to that seen in 1900–1910. Note, too, that inequality of wealth began to rise again in 1970–1980. It is therefore possible that a catch-up process is still under way today, a process even slower than the revival of the capital / income ratio, and that the concentration of wealth will soon return to past heights.

In other words, the reason why wealth today is not as unequally distributed as in the past is simply that not enough time has passed since 1945. This is no doubt part of the explanation, but by itself it is not enough. When we look at the top decile's share of wealth and even more at the top centile's (which was 60–70 percent across Europe in 1910 and only 20–30 percent in 2010), it seems clear that the shocks of 1914–1945 caused a structural change that is preventing wealth from becoming quite as concentrated as it was previously. The point is not simply quantitative—far from it. In the next chapter, we will see that when we look again at the question raised by Vautrin's lecture on the different standards of living that can be attained by inheritance and labor, the difference between a 60–70 percent share for the top centile and a 20–30 percent share is relatively simple. In the first case, the top centile of the income hierarchy is very clearly dominated by top capital incomes: this is the society of rentiers familiar to nineteenth-century novelists. In the second case, top earned incomes (for a given distribution) roughly balance top capital incomes (we are now in a society of managers, or at any rate a more balanced society). Similarly, the emergence of a "patrimonial middle class" owning between a quarter and a third of national wealth rather than a tenth or a twentieth (scarcely more than the poorest half of society) represents a major social transformation.

What structural changes occurred between 1914 and 1945, and more generally during the twentieth century, that are preventing the concentration of wealth from regaining its previous heights, even though private wealth overall is prospering almost as handsomely today as in the past? The most natural and important explanation is that governments in the twentieth century began taxing capital and its income at significant rates. It is important to notice that the very high concentration of wealth observed in 1900–1910 was the result of a long period without a major war or catastrophe (at least when compared to the extreme violence of twentieth-century conflicts) as well as without, or almost without, taxes. Until World War I there was no tax on capital income or corporate profits. In the rare cases in which such taxes did exist, they were assessed at very low rates. Hence conditions were ideal for the accumulation and transmission of considerable fortunes and for living on the income of those fortunes. In the twentieth century, taxes of various kinds were imposed on dividends, interest, profits, and rents, and this changed things radically.

To simplify matters: assume initially that capital income was taxed at an average rate close to 0 percent (and in any case less than 5 percent) before 1900–1910 and at about 30 percent in the rich countries in 1950–1980 (and to some extent until 2000–2010, although the recent trend has been clearly downward as governments engage in fiscal competition spearheaded by smaller countries). An average tax rate of 30 percent reduces a pretax return of 5 percent to a net return of 3.5 percent after taxes. This in itself is enough to have significant long-term effects, given the multiplicative and cumulative logic of capital accumulation and concentration. Using the theoretical models described above, one can show that an effective tax rate of 30 percent, if applied to all forms of capital, can by itself account for a very significant deconcentration of wealth (roughly equal to the decrease in the top centile's share that we see in the historical data).[36]

---

36. See the online technical appendix.

In this context, it is important to note that the effect of the tax on capital income is not to reduce the total accumulation of wealth but to modify the structure of the wealth distribution over the long run. In terms of the theoretical model, as well as in the historical data, an increase in the tax on capital income from 0 to 30 percent (reducing the net return on capital from 5 to 3.5 percent) may well leave the total stock of capital unchanged over the long run for the simple reason that the decrease in the upper centile's share of wealth is compensated by the rise of the middle class. This is precisely what happened in the twentieth century—although the lesson is sometimes forgotten today.

It is also important to note the rise of progressive taxes in the twentieth century, that is, of taxes that imposed higher rates on top incomes and especially top capital incomes (at least until 1970–1980), along with estate taxes on the largest estates. In the nineteenth century, estate tax rates were extremely low, no more than 1–2 percent on bequests from parents to children. A tax of this sort obviously has no discernible effect on the process of capital accumulation. It is not so much a tax as a registration fee intended to protect property rights. The estate tax became progressive in France in 1901, but the highest rate on direct-line bequests was no more than 5 percent (and applied to at most a few dozen bequests a year). A rate of this magnitude, assessed once a generation, cannot have much effect on the concentration of wealth, no matter what wealthy individuals thought at the time. Quite different in their effect were the rates of 20–30 percent or higher that were imposed in most wealthy countries in the wake of the military, economic, and political shocks of 1914–1945. The upshot of such taxes was that each successive generation had to reduce its expenditures and save more (or else make particularly profitable investments) if the family fortune was to grow as rapidly as average income. Hence it became more and more difficult to maintain one's rank. Conversely, it became easier for those who started at the bottom to make their way, for instance by buying businesses or shares sold when estates went to probate. Simple simulations show that a progressive estate tax can greatly reduce the top centile's share of wealth over the long run.[37] The differences between estate tax regimes in different countries can also help to explain international differences. For example, why have top capital incomes in Germany been more concentrated than in France since World War II, suggesting a higher concentration of wealth? Perhaps because the highest estate tax rate in Germany is no more than 15–20 percent, compared with 30–40 percent in France.[38]

Both theoretical arguments and numerical simulations suggest that taxes suffice to explain most of the observed evolutions, even without invoking structural transformations. It is worth reiterating that the concentration of wealth today, though markedly lower than in 1900–1910, remains extremely high. It does not require a perfect, ideal tax system to achieve such a result or to explain a transformation whose magnitude should not be exaggerated.

The Twenty-First Century: Even More Inegalitarian Than the Nineteenth?

Given the many mechanisms in play and the multiple uncertainties involved in tax simulations, it would nevertheless be going too far to conclude that no other factors played a significant role. My analysis thus far has shown that two factors probably did play an important part, independent of changes in the tax system, and will continue to do so in the future. The first is the probable slight decrease in capital's share of income and in the rate of return on capital over the long run, and the second is that the rate of growth, despite a likely slowing in

---

37. See in particular my *Les hauts revenus en France,* 396–403. See also Piketty, "Income Inequality in France, 1901–1998," *Journal of Political Economy* 111, no. 5 (2003): 1004–42.

38. See the simulations by Fabien Dell, "L'allemagne inégale: Inégalités de revenus et de patrimoine en Allemagne, dynamique d'accumulation du capital et taxation de Bismarck à Schröder 1870–2005," Ph.D. thesis, Paris School of Economics, 2008. See also F. Dell, "Top Incomes in Germany and Switzerland over the Twentieth Century," *Journal of the European Economic Association* 3, no. 2/3 (2005): 412–21.

the twenty-first century, will be greater than the extremely low rate observed throughout most of human history up to the eighteenth century. (Here I am speaking of the purely economic component of growth, that is, growth of productivity, which reflects the growth of knowledge and technological innovation.) Concretely, as Figure 10.11 shows, it is likely that the difference $r > g$ will be smaller in the future than it was before the eighteenth century, both because the return on capital will be lower (4–4.5 percent, say, rather than 4.5–5 percent) and growth will be higher (1–1.5 percent rather than 0.1–0.2 percent), even if competition between states leads to the elimination of all taxes on capital. If theoretical simulations are to be believed, the concentration of wealth, even if taxes on capital are abolished, would not necessarily return to the extreme level of 1900–1910.

There are no grounds for rejoicing, however, in part because inequality of wealth would still increase substantially (halving the middle-class share of national wealth, for example, which voters might well find unacceptable) and in part because there is considerable uncertainty in the simulations, and other forces exist that may well push in the opposite direction, that is, toward an even greater concentration of capital than in 1900–1910. In particular, demographic growth may be negative (which could drive growth rates, especially in the wealthy countries, below those observed in the nineteenth century, and this would in turn give unprecedented importance to inherited wealth). In addition, capital markets may become more and more sophisticated and more and more "perfect" in the sense used by economists (meaning that the return on capital will become increasingly disconnected from the individual characteristics of the owner and therefore cut against meritocratic values, reinforcing the logic of $r > g$). As I will show later, in addition, financial globalization seems to be increasing the correlation between the return on capital and the initial size of the investment portfolio, creating an inequality of returns that acts as an additional—and quite worrisome—force for divergence in the global wealth distribution.

To sum up: the fact that wealth is noticeably less concentrated in Europe today than it was in the Belle Époque is largely a consequence of accidental events (the shocks of 1914–1945) and specific institutions such as taxation of capital and its income. If those institutions were ultimately destroyed, there would be a high risk of seeing inequalities of wealth close to those observed in the past or, under certain conditions, even higher. Nothing is certain: inequality can move in either direction. Hence I must now look more closely at the dynamics of inheritance and then at the global dynamics of wealth. One conclusion is already quite clear, however: it is an illusion to think that something about the nature of modern growth or the laws of the market economy ensures that inequality of wealth will decrease and harmonious stability will be achieved.

ELEVEN

Merit and Inheritance in the Long Run

The overall importance of capital today, as noted, is not very different from what it was in the eighteenth century. Only its form has changed: capital was once mainly land but is now industrial, financial, and real estate. We also know that the concentration of wealth remains high, although it is noticeably less extreme than it was a century ago. The poorest half of the population still owns nothing, but there is now a patrimonial middle class that owns between a quarter and a third of total wealth, and the wealthiest 10 percent now own only two-thirds of what there is to own rather than nine-tenths. We have also learned that the relative movements of the return on capital and the rate of growth of the economy, and therefore of the difference between them, $r - g$, can explain many of the observed changes, including the logic of accumulation that accounts for the very high concentration of wealth that we see throughout much of human history.

In order to understand this cumulative logic better, we must now take a closer look at the long-term evolution of the relative roles of inheritance and saving in capital formation. This is a crucial issue, because a given level of capital concentration can come about in totally different ways. It may be that the global level of capital has remained the same but that its deep structure has changed dramatically, in the sense that capital was once largely inherited but is now accumulated over the course of a lifetime by savings from earned income. One possible explanation for such a change might be increased life expectancy, which might have led to a structural increase in the accumulation of capital in anticipation of retirement. However, this supposed great transformation in the nature of capital was actually less dramatic than is sometimes thought; indeed, in some countries it did not occur at all. In all likelihood, inheritance will again play a significant role in the twenty-first century, comparable to its role in the past.

More precisely, I will come to the following conclusion. Whenever the rate of return on capital is significantly and durably higher than the growth rate of the economy, it is all but inevitable that inheritance (of fortunes accumulated in the past) predominates over saving (wealth accumulated in the present). In strict logic, it could be otherwise, but the forces pushing in this direction are extremely powerful. The inequality $r > g$ in one sense implies that the past tends to devour the future: wealth originating in the past automatically grows more rapidly, even without labor, than wealth stemming from work, which can be saved. Almost inevitably, this tends to give lasting, disproportionate importance to inequalities created in the past, and therefore to inheritance.

If the twenty-first century turns out to be a time of low (demographic and economic) growth and high return on capital (in a context of heightened international competition for capital resources), or at any rate in countries where these conditions hold true, inheritance will therefore probably again be as important as it was in the nineteenth century. An evolution in this direction is already apparent in France and a number of other European countries, where growth has already slowed considerably in recent decades. For the moment it is less prominent in the United States, essentially because demographic growth there is higher than in Europe. But if growth ultimately slows more or less everywhere in the coming century, as the median demographic forecasts by the United Nations (corroborated by other economic forecasts) suggest it will, then inheritance will probably take on increased importance throughout the world.

This does not imply, however, that the structure of inequality in the twenty-first century will be the same as in the nineteenth century, in part because the concentration of wealth is less extreme (there will probably be more small to medium rentiers and fewer extremely wealthy rentiers, at least in the short term), in part because the earned income hierarchy is expanding (with the rise of the supermanager), and finally because wealth and income are more strongly correlated than in the past. In the twenty-first century it is possible to be both a supermanager and a "medium rentier": the new meritocratic order encourages this sort of thing, probably to the detriment of low- and medium-wage workers, especially those who own only a tiny amount of property, if any.

Inheritance Flows over the Long Run

I will begin at the beginning. In all societies, there are two main ways of accumulating wealth: through work or inheritance.[1] How common is each of these in the top centiles and deciles of the wealth hierarchy? This is the key question.

In Vautrin's lecture to Rastignac (discussed in Chapter 7), the answer is clear: study and work cannot possibly lead to a comfortable and elegant life, and the only realistic strategy is to marry Mademoiselle Victorine and her inheritance. One of my primary goals in this work is to find out how closely nineteenth-century French society resembled the society described by Vautrin and above all to learn how and why this type of society evolved over time.

It is useful to begin by examining the evolution of the annual flow of inheritances over the long run, that is, the total value of bequests (and gifts between living individuals) during the course of a year, expressed as a percentage of national income. This figure measures the annual amount of past wealth conveyed each year relative to the total income earned that year. (Recall that earned income accounts for roughly two-thirds of national income each year, while part of capital income goes to remunerate the capital that is passed on to heirs.)

I will examine the French case, which is by far the best known over the long run, and the pattern I find there, it turns out, also applies to a

---

1. I exclude theft and pillage, although these are not totally without historical significance. Private appropriation of natural resources is discussed in the next chapter.

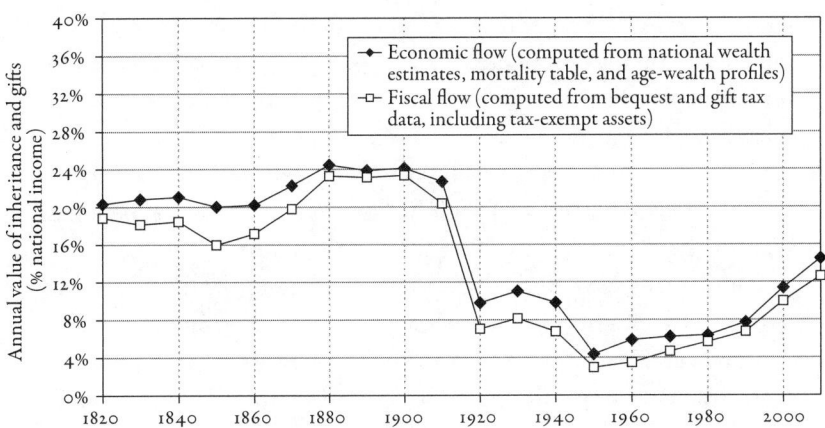

FIGURE 11.1. The annual inheritance flow as a fraction of national income, France, 1820–2010

The annual inheritance flow was about 20–25 percent of national income during the nineteenth century and until 1914; it then fell to less than 5 percent in the 1950s, and returned to about 15 percent in 2010.

Sources and series: see piketty.pse.ens.fr/capital21c.

certain extent to other European countries. Finally, I will explore what it is possible to say at the global level.

Figure 11.1 represents the evolution of the annual inheritance flow in France from 1820 to 2010.[2] Two facts stand out clearly. First, the inheritance flow accounts for 20–25 percent of annual income every year in the nineteenth century, with a slight upward trend toward the end of the century. This is an extremely high flow, as I will show later, and it reflects the fact that nearly all of the capital stock came from inheritance. If inherited wealth is omnipresent in nineteenth-century novels, it was not only because writers, especially the debt-ridden

---

2. In order to focus on long-term evolutions, I use averages by decade here. The annual series are available online. For more detail on techniques and methods, see Thomas Piketty, "On the Long-Run Evolution of Inheritance: France 1820–2050," Paris School of Economics, 2010; a summary version was published in the *Quarterly Journal of Economics* 126, no. 3 (August 2011): 1071–131. These documents are available in the online technical appendix.

Balzac, were obsessed by it. It was above all because inheritance occupied a structurally central place in nineteenth-century society—central as both economic flow and social force. Its importance did not diminish with time, moreover. On the contrary, in 1900–1910, the flow of inheritance was somewhat higher (25 percent of national income compared with barely 20) than it had been in the 1820s, the period of Vautrin, Rastignac, and the Vauquer boardinghouse.

Subsequently, we find a spectacular decrease in the flow of inheritances between 1910 and 1950 followed by a steady rebound thereafter, with an acceleration in the 1980s. There were very large upward and downward variations during the twentieth century. The annual flow of inheritances and gifts was (to a first approximation, and compared with subsequent shocks) relatively stable until World War I but fell by a factor of 5 or 6 between 1910 and 1950 (when the inheritance flow was barely 4 or 5 percent of national income), after which it increased by a factor of 3 or 4 between 1950 and 2010 (at which time the flow accounted for 15 percent of national income).

The evolution visible in Figure 11.1 reflects deep changes in the perception as well as the reality of inheritance, and to a large extent it also reflects changes in the structure of inequality. As we will soon see, the compression of the inheritance flow owing to the shocks of 1914–1945 was nearly twice as great as the decrease in private wealth. The inheritance collapse was therefore not simply the result of a wealth collapse (even if the two developments are obviously closely related). In the public mind, the idea that the age of inheritance was over was certainly even more influential than the idea of an end of capitalism. In 1950–1960, bequests and gifts accounted for just a few points of national income, so it was reasonable to think that inheritances had virtually disappeared and that capital, though less important overall than in the past, was now wealth that an individual accumulated by effort and saving during his or her lifetime. Several generations grew up under these conditions (even if perceptions somewhat exceeded reality), in particular the baby boom generation, born in the late 1940s and early 1950s, many of whom are still alive today, and it was natural for them to assume that this was the "new normal."

Conversely, younger people, in particular those born in the 1970s and 1980s, have already experienced (to a certain extent) the important role that inheritance will once again play in their lives and the lives of their relatives and friends. For this group, for example, whether or not a child receives gifts from parents can have a major impact in deciding who will own property and who will not, at what age, and how extensive that property will be—in any case, to a much greater extent than in the previous generation. Inheritance is playing a larger part in their lives, careers, and individual and family choices than it did with the baby boomers. The rebound of inheritance is still incomplete, however, and the evolution is still under way (the inheritance flow in 2000–2010 stood at a point roughly midway between the nadir of the 1950s and the peak of 1900–1910). To date, it has had a less profound impact on perceptions than the previous change, which still dominates people's thinking. A few decades from now, things may be very different.

Fiscal Flow and Economic Flow

Several points about Figure 11.1 need to be clarified. First, it is essential to include gifts between living individuals (whether shortly before death or earlier in life) in the flow of inheritance, because this form of transmission has always played a very important role in France and elsewhere. The relative magnitude of gifts and bequests has varied greatly over time, so omitting gifts would seriously bias the analysis and distort spatial and temporal comparisons. Fortunately, gifts in France are carefully recorded (though no doubt somewhat underestimated). This is not the case everywhere.

Second, and even more important, the wealth of French historical sources allows us to calculate inheritance flows in two different ways, using data and methods that are totally independent. What we find is that the two evolutions shown in Figure 11.1 (which I have labeled "fiscal flow" and "economic flow") are highly consistent, which is reassuring and demonstrates the robustness of the historical data. This consistency also helps us to decompose and analyze the various forces at work.[3]

Broadly speaking, there are two ways to estimate inheritance flows in a particular country. One can make direct use of observed flows of inheritances and gifts (for example, by using tax data: this is what I call the "fiscal flow"). Or one can look at the private capital stock and calculate the theoretical flow that must have occurred in a given year (which I call the "economic flow"). Each method has its advantages and disadvantages. The first method is more direct, but the tax data in many countries are so incomplete that the results are not always satisfactory. In France, as noted previously, the system for recording bequests and gifts was established exceptionally early (at the time of the Revolution) and is unusually comprehensive (in theory it covers all transmissions, including those on which little or no tax is paid, though there are some exceptions), so the fiscal method can be applied. The tax data must be corrected, however, to take account of small bequests that do not have to be declared (the amounts involved are insignificant) and above all to correct for certain assets that are exempt from the estate tax, such as life insurance contracts, which have become increasingly common since 1970 (and today account for nearly one-sixth of total private wealth in France).

The second method ("economic flow") has the advantage of not relying on tax data and therefore giving a more complete picture of the transmission of wealth, independent of the vagaries of different countries' tax systems. The ideal is to be able to use both methods in the same country. What is more, one can interpret the gap between the two curves in Figure 11.1 (which shows that the economic flow is al-

---

3. The discussion that follows is a little more technical than previous discussions (but necessary to understand what is behind the observed evolutions), and some readers may wish to skip a few pages and go directly to the implications and the discussion of what lies ahead in the twenty-first century, which can be found in the sections on Vautrin's lecture and Rastignac's dilemma.

ways a little greater than the fiscal flow) as an estimate of tax fraud or deficiencies of the probate record-keeping system. There may also be other reasons for the gap, including the many imperfections in the available data sets and the methods used. For certain subperiods, the gap is far from negligible. The long-run evolutions in which I am primarily interested are nevertheless quite consistent, regardless of which method we use.

The Three Forces: The Illusion of an End of Inheritance

In fact, the main advantage of the economic flow approach is that it requires us to take a comprehensive view of the three forces that everywhere determine the flow of inheritance and its historical evolution.

In general, the annual economic flow of inheritances and gifts, expressed as a proportion of national income that we denote b_y, is equal to the product of three forces:

$$b_y = \mu \times m \times \beta,$$

where β is the capital / income ratio (or, more precisely, the ratio of total private wealth, which, unlike public assets, can be passed on by inheritance, to national income), m is the mortality rate, and μ is the ratio of average wealth at time of death to average wealth of living individuals.

This decomposition is a pure accounting identity: by definition, it is always true in all times and places. In particular, this is the formula I used to estimate the economic flow depicted in Figure 11.1. Although this decomposition of the economic flow into three forces is a tautology, I think it is a useful tautology in that it enables us to clarify an issue that has been the source of much confusion in the past, even though the underlying logic is not terribly complex.

Let me examine the three forces one by one. The first is the capital / income ratio β. This force expresses a truism: if the flow of inherited wealth is to be high in a given society, the total stock of private wealth capable of being inherited must also be large.

The second force, the mortality rate m, describes an equally transparent mechanism. All other things being equal, the higher the mortality rate, the higher the inheritance flow. In a society where everyone lives forever, so that the mortality rate is exactly zero, inheritance must vanish. The inheritance flow b_y must also be zero, no matter how large the capital / income ratio β is.

The third force, the ratio μ of average wealth at time of death to average wealth of living individuals, is equally transparent.[4]

Suppose that the average wealth at time of death is the same as the average wealth of the population as a whole. Then $\mu = 1$, and the inheritance flow b_y is simply the product of the mortality rate m and the capital / income ratio β. For example, if the capital / income ratio is 600 percent (that is, the stock of private wealth represents six years of national income) and the mortality rate of the adult population is 2 percent,[5] then the annual inheritance flow will automatically be 12 percent of national income.

If average wealth at time of death is twice the average wealth of the living, so that $\mu = 2$, then the inheritance flow will be 24 percent of national income (assuming $\beta = 6$ and $m = 2$ percent), which is approximately the level observed in the nineteenth and early twentieth centuries.

Clearly, μ depends on the age profile of wealth. The more wealth increases with age, the higher μ will be and therefore the larger the inheritance flow.

Conversely, in a society where the primary purpose of wealth is to finance retirement and elderly individuals consume the capital accumulated during their working lives in their years of retirement (by drawing down savings in a pension fund, for example), in accordance

---

4. The term μ is corrected to take account of gifts (see below).

5. In other words, one of every fifty adults dies each year. Since minors generally own very little capital, it is clearer to write the decomposition in terms of adult mortality (and to define μ in terms of adults alone). A small correction is then necessary to take account of the wealth of minors. See the online technical appendix.

with the "life-cycle theory of wealth" developed by the Italian-American economist Franco Modigliani in the 1950s, then by construction μ will be almost zero, since everyone aims to die with little or no capital. In the extreme case $μ = 0$, inheritance vanishes regardless of the values of β and m. In strictly logical terms, it is perfectly possible to imagine a world in which there is considerable private capital (so β is very high) but most wealth is in pension funds or equivalent forms of wealth that vanish at death ("annuitized wealth"), so that the inheritance flow is zero or close to it. Modigliani's theory offers a tranquil, one-dimensional view of social inequality: inequalities of wealth are nothing more than a translation in time of inequalities with respect to work. (Managers accumulate more retirement savings than workers, but both groups consume all their capital by the time they die.) This theory was quite popular in the decades after World War II, when functionalist American sociology, exemplified by the work of Talcott Parsons, also depicted a middle-class society of managers in which inherited wealth played virtually no role.[6] It is still quite popular today among baby boomers.

Our decomposition of the inheritance flow as the product of three forces ($b_y = μ \times m \times β$) is important for thinking historically about inheritance and its evolution, for each of the three forces embodies a significant set of beliefs and arguments (perfectly plausible a priori) that led many people to imagine, especially during the optimistic decades after World War II, that the end (or at any rate gradual and progressive decrease) of inherited wealth was somehow the logical and natural culmination of history. However, such a gradual end to inherited wealth is by no means inevitable, as the French case clearly illustrates. Indeed, the U-shaped curve we see in France is a consequence of three U-shaped curves describing each of the three forces, μ, m, and β. Furthermore, the three forces acted simultaneously, in part for accidental reasons, and this explains the large amplitude of the overall

---

6. On this subject, see Jens Beckert, trans. Thomas Dunlop, *Inherited Wealth* (Princeton: Princeton University Press, 2008), 291.

change, and in particular the exceptionally low level of inheritance flow in 1950–1960, which led many people to believe that inherited wealth had virtually disappeared.

In Part Two I showed that the capital / income ratio β was indeed described by a U-shaped curve. The optimistic belief associated with this first force is quite clear and at first sight perfectly plausible: inherited wealth has tended over time to lose its importance simply because wealth has lost its importance (or, more precisely, wealth in the sense of nonhuman capital, that is, wealth that can be owned, exchanged on a market, and fully transmitted to heirs under the prevailing laws of property). There is no logical reason why this optimistic belief cannot be correct, and it permeates the whole modern theory of human capital (including the work of Gary Becker), even if it is not always explicitly formulated.[7] However, things did not unfold this way, or at any rate not to the degree that people sometimes imagine: landed capital became financial and industrial capital and real estate but retained its overall importance, as can be seen in the fact that the capital / income ratio seems to be about to regain the record level attained in the Belle Époque and earlier.

For partly technological reasons, capital still plays a central role in production today, and therefore in social life. Before production can begin, funds are needed for equipment and office space, to finance material and immaterial investments of all kinds, and of course

---

7. Becker never explicitly states the idea that the rise of human capital should eclipse the importance of inherited wealth, but it is often implicit in his work. In particular, he notes frequently that society has become "more meritocratic" owing to the increasing importance of education (without further detail). Becker has also proposed theoretical models in which parents can bequeath wealth to less gifted children, less well endowed with human capital, thereby reducing inequality. Given the extreme vertical concentration of inherited wealth (the top decile always owns more than 60 percent of the wealth available for inheritance, while the bottom half of the population owns nothing), this potential horizontal redistribution effect within groups of wealthy siblings (which, moreover, is not evident in the data, of which Becker makes almost no use) is hardly likely to predominate. See the online technical appendix.

to pay for housing. To be sure, the level of human skill and competence has increased over time, but the importance of nonhuman capital has increased proportionately. Hence there is no obvious a priori reason to expect the gradual disappearance of inherited wealth on these grounds.

Mortality over the Long Run

The second force that might explain the natural end of inheritance is increased life expectancy, which lowers the mortality rate m and increases the time to inheritance (which decreases the size of the legacy). Indeed, there is no doubt that the mortality rate has decreased over the long run: the proportion of the population that dies each year is smaller when the life expectancy is eighty than when it is sixty. Other things being equal, for a given β and μ, a society with a lower mortality rate is also a society in which the flow of inheritance is a smaller proportion of national income. In France, the mortality rate has declined inexorably over the course of history, and the same is true of other countries. The French mortality rate was around 2.2 percent (of the adult population) in the nineteenth century but declined steadily throughout the twentieth century,[8] dropping to 1.1–1.2 percent in 2000–2010, a decrease of almost one-half in a century (see Figure 11.2).

It would be a serious mistake, however, to think that changes in the mortality rate lead inevitably to the disappearance of inherited wealth as a major factor in the economy. For one thing, the mortality rate began to rise again in France in 2000–2010, and according to official demographic forecasts this increase is likely to continue until 2040–2050, after which adult mortality should stabilize at around 1.4–1.5 percent. The explanation for this is that the baby boomers, who outnumber previous cohorts (but are about the same size as subsequent ones), will

---

8. Apart from the bloodletting of the two world wars, which is masked in my data by the use of decennial averages. See the online technical appendix for the annual series.

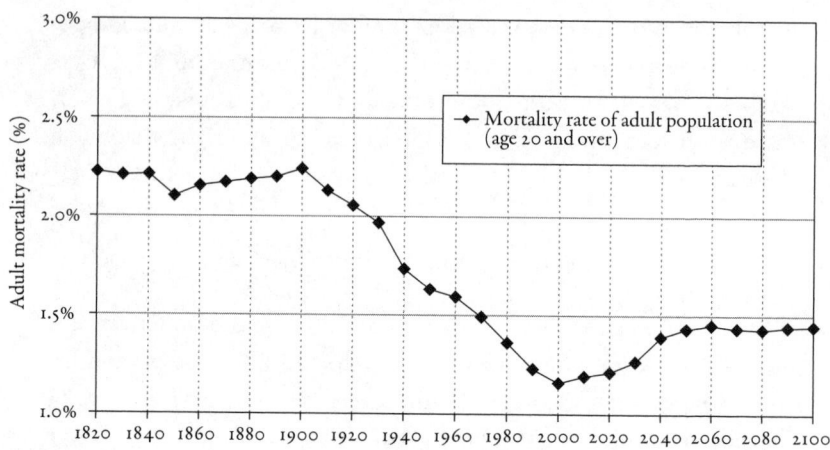

FIGURE 11.2. The mortality rate in France, 1820–2100

The mortality rate fell in France during the twentieth century (rise of life expectancy), and should increase somewhat during the twenty-first century (baby-boom effect). Sources and series: see piketty.pse.ens.fr/capital21c.

reach the end of their life spans in this period.[9] In other words, the baby boom, which led to a structural increase in the size of birth cohorts, temporarily reduced the mortality rate simply because the population grew younger and larger. French demographics are fortunately quite simple, so that it is possible to present the principal effects of demographic change in a clear manner. In the nineteenth century, the population was virtually stationary, and life expectancy was about sixty years, so that the average person enjoyed a little over forty years of adulthood, and the mortality rate was therefore close to 1/40, or actually

---

9. About 800,000 babies were born in France each year (actually between 750,000 and 850,000 with no trend up or down) from the late 1940s until the early 2010s, and according to official forecasts this will continue throughout the twenty-first century. In the nineteenth century there were about a million births per year, but the infant mortality rate was high, so the size of each adult cohort has varied little since the eighteenth century, except for the large losses due to war and the associated decline in births in the interwar years. See the online technical appendix.

about 2.2 percent. In the twenty-first century, the population, according to official forecasts, will likely stabilize again, with a life expectancy of about eighty-five years, or about sixty-five years of adult life, giving a mortality rate of about 1/65 in a static population, which translates into 1.4–1.5 percent when we allow for slight demographic growth. Over the long run, in a developed country with a quasi-stagnant population like France (where population increase is primarily due to aging), the decrease in the adult mortality rate is about one-third.

The anticipated increase in the mortality rate between 2000–2010 and 2040–2050 due to the aging of the baby boom generation is admittedly a purely mathematical effect, but it is nevertheless important. It partly explains the low inheritance flows of the second half of the twentieth century, as well as the expected sharp increase in these flows in the decades to come. This effect will be even stronger elsewhere. In countries where the population has begun to decrease significantly or will soon do so (owing to a decrease in cohort size)— most notably Germany, Italy, Spain, and of course Japan—this phenomenon will lead to a much larger increase in the adult mortality rate in the first half of the twenty-first century and thus automatically increase inheritance flows by a considerable amount. People may live longer, but they still die eventually; only a significant and steady increase in cohort size can permanently reduce the mortality rate and inheritance flow. When an aging population is combined with a stabilization of cohort size as in France, however, or even a reduced cohort size as in a number of rich countries, very high inheritance flows are possible. In the extreme case—a country in which the cohort size is reduced by half (because each couple decides to have only one child), the mortality rate, and therefore the inheritance flow, could rise to unprecedented levels. Conversely, in a country where the size of each age cohort doubles every generation, as happened in many countries in the twentieth century and is still happening in Africa, the mortality rate declines to very low levels, and inherited wealth counts for little (other things equal).

Wealth Ages with Population: The μ × m *Effect*

Let us now forget the effects of variations in cohort size: though important, they are essentially transitory, unless we imagine that in the long run the population of the planet grows infinitely large or infinitely small. Instead, I will adopt the very long-run perspective and assume that cohort size is stable. How does increased life expectancy really affect the importance of inherited wealth? To be sure, a longer life expectancy translates into a structural decrease in the mortality rate. In France, where the average life expectancy in the twenty-first century will be eighty to eighty-five years, the adult mortality rate will stabilize at less than 1.5 percent a year, compared with 2.2 percent in the nineteenth century, when the life expectancy was just over sixty. The increase in the average age of death inevitably gives rise to a similar increase in the average age of heirs at the moment of inheritance. In the nineteenth century, the average age of inheritance was just thirty; in the twenty-first century it will be somewhere around fifty. As Figure 11.3 shows, the difference between the average age of death and the average age of inheritance has always been around thirty years, for the simple reason that the average age of childbirth (often referred to as "generational duration") has been relatively stable at around thirty over the long run (although there has been a slight increase in the early twenty-first century).

But does the fact that people die later and inherit later imply that inherited wealth is losing its importance? Not necessarily, in part because the growing importance of gifts between living individuals has partly compensated for this aging effect, and in part because it may be that people are inheriting later but receiving larger amounts, since wealth tends to age in an aging society. In other words, the downward trend in the mortality rate—ineluctable in the very long run—can be compensated by a similar structural increase in the relative wealth of older people, so that the product μ × *m* remains unchanged or in any case falls much more slowly than some have believed. This is precisely what happened in France: the ratio μ of average wealth at death to average wealth of the living rose sharply after 1950–1960, and this gradual

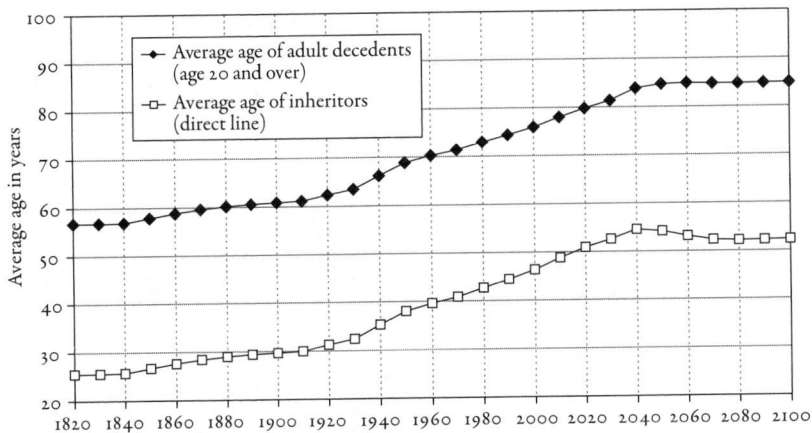

FIGURE 11.3. Average age of decedents and inheritors: France, 1820–2100

The average of (adult) decedents rose from less than 60 years to almost 80 years during the twentieth century, and the average age at the time of inheritance rose from 30 years to 50 years.

Sources and series: see piketty.pse.ens.fr/capital21c.

aging of wealth explains much of the increased importance of inherited wealth in recent decades.

Concretely, one finds that the product $\mu \times m$, which by definition measures the annual rate of transmission by inheritance (or, in other words, the inheritance flow expressed as a percentage of total private wealth), clearly began to rise over the past few decades, despite the continuing decrease in the mortality rate, as Figure 11.4 shows. The annual rate of transmission by inheritance, which nineteenth-century economists called the "rate of estate devolution," was according to my sources relatively stable from the 1820s to the 1910s at around 3.3–3.5 percent, or roughly 1/30. It was also said in those days that a fortune was inherited on average once every thirty years, that is, once a generation, which is a somewhat too static view of things but partially justified by the reality of the time.[10] The transmission rate decreased sharply in

10. The theory of the "rate of estate devolution" was particularly popular in France in the period 1880–1910, thanks to the work of Albert de Foville, Clément Colson,

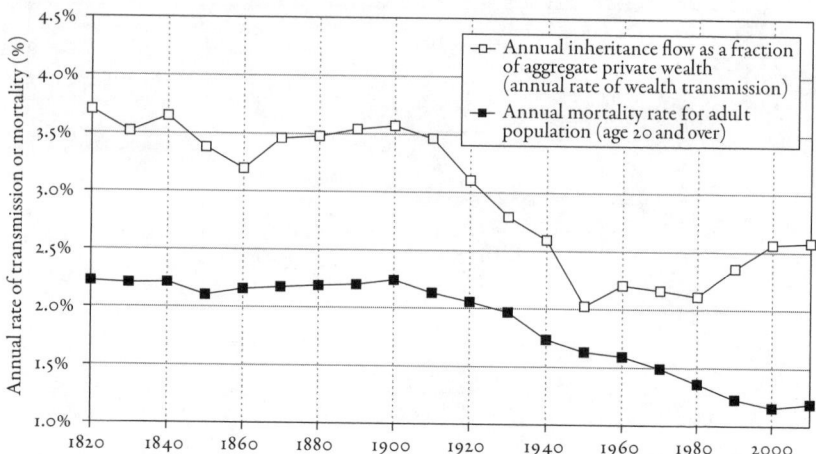

FIGURE 11.4. Inheritance flow versus mortality rate: France, 1820–2010

The annual flow of inheritance (bequests and gifts) is equal to about 2.5 percent of aggregate wealth in 2000–2010 versus 1.2 percent for the mortality rate.

Sources and series: see piketty.pse.ens.fr/capital21c.

the period 1910–1950 and in the 1950s stood at about 2 percent, before rising steadily to above 2.5 percent in 2000–2010.

To sum up: inheritance occurs later in aging societies, but wealth also ages, and the latter tends to compensate the former. In this sense, a society in which people die older is very different from a society in which they don't die at all and inheritance effectively vanishes. Increased life expectancy delays important life events: people study longer, start work later, inherit later, retire later, and die later. But the relative importance of inherited wealth as opposed to earned income does not necessarily change, or at any rate changes much less than people sometimes imagine. To be sure, inheriting later in life may make choosing a

---

and Pierre Emile Levasseur, who were pleased to discover that their estimates of national wealth (obtained through a census of assets) were approximately equal to 30 times the annual inheritance flow. This method, sometimes called the "estate multiplier," was also used in England, particularly by Giffen, even though British economists—who had access to limited estate tax statistics—generally used the capital income flows series coming from the scheduler income tax system.

profession more frequently necessary than in the past. But this is compensated by the inheritance of larger amounts or by the receipt of gifts. In any case, the difference is more one of degree than the dramatic change of civilization that is sometimes imagined.

Wealth of the Dead, Wealth of the Living

It is interesting to take a closer look at the evolution of μ, the ratio between average wealth at death and average wealth of the living, which I have presented in Figure 11.5. Note, first, that over the course of the past two centuries, from 1820 to the present, the dead have always been (on average) wealthier than the living in France: μ has always been greater than 100 percent, except in the period around World War II (1940–1950), when the ratio (without correcting for gifts made prior to death) fell to just below 100 percent. Recall that according to Modigliani's life-cycle theory, the primary reason for amassing wealth, especially in aging societies, is to pay for retirement, so that older individuals should consume most of their savings during old age and should therefore die with little or no wealth. This is the famous "Modigliani triangle," taught to all students of economics, according to which wealth at first increases with age as individuals accumulate savings in anticipation of retirement and then decreases. The ratio μ should therefore be equal to zero or close to it, in any case much less than 100 percent. But this theory of capital and its evolution in advanced societies, which is perfectly plausible a priori, cannot explain the observed facts—to put it mildly. Clearly, saving for retirement is only one of many reasons—and not the most important reason—why people accumulate wealth: the desire to perpetuate the family fortune has always played a central role. In practice, the various forms of annuitized wealth, which cannot be passed on to descendants, account for less than 5 percent of private wealth in France and at most 15–20 percent in the English-speaking countries, where pension funds are more developed. This is not a negligible amount, but it is not enough to alter the fundamental importance of inheritance as a

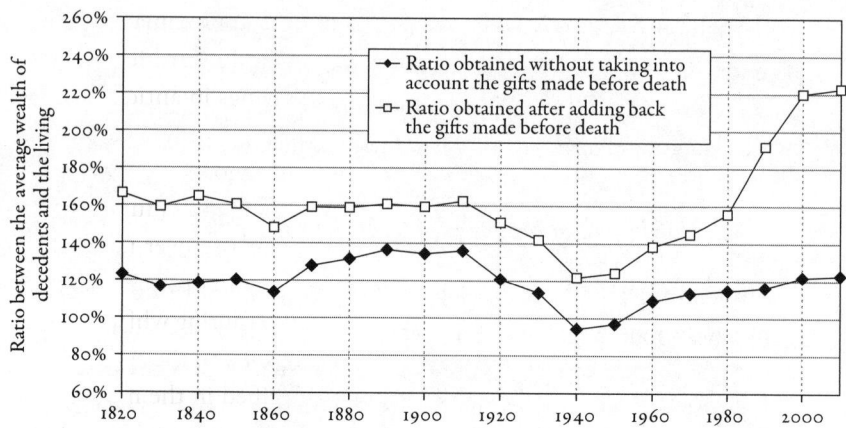

FIGURE 11.5. The ratio between average wealth at death and average wealth of the living: France, 1820–2010

In 2000–2010, the average wealth at death is 20 percent higher than that of the living if one omits the gifts that were made before death, but more than twice as large if one re-integrates gifts.

Sources and series: see piketty.pse.ens.fr/capital21c.

motive for wealth accumulation (especially since life-cycle savings may not be a substitute for but rather a supplement to transmissible wealth).[11] To be sure, it is quite difficult to say how different wealth accumulation would have been in the twentieth century in the absence of pay-as-you-go public pension systems, which guaranteed the vast majority of retirees a decent standard of living in a more reliable and equitable way than investment in financial assets, which plummeted after the war, could have done. It is possible that without such public pension systems, the overall level of wealth accumulation (measured by the capital / income ratio) would have been even greater than it is

---

11. In practice, both types of wealth are often mixed in the same financial products (reflecting the mixed motives of savers). In France, life insurance contracts sometimes include a share of capital that can be passed on to children and another, generally smaller share payable as an annuity (which ends with the death of the policy holder). In Britain and the United States, retirement funds and pension plans increasingly include a transmissible component.

today.[12] In any case, the capital / income ratio is approximately the same today as it was in the Belle Époque (when a shorter life expectancy greatly reduced the need to accumulate savings in anticipation of retirement), and annuitized wealth accounts for only a slightly larger portion of total wealth than it did a century ago.

Note also the importance of gifts between living individuals over the past two centuries, as well as their spectacular rise over the past several decades. The total annual value of gifts was 30–40 percent of the annual value of inheritances from 1820 to 1870 (during which time gifts came mainly in the form of dowries, that is, gifts to the spouse at the time of marriage, often with restrictions specified in the marriage contract). Between 1870 and 1970 the value of gifts decreased slightly, stabilizing at about 20–30 percent of inheritances, before increasing strongly and steadily to 40 percent in the 1980s, 60 percent in the 1990s, and more than 80 percent in 2000–2010. Today, transmission of capital by gift is nearly as important as transmission by inheritance. Gifts account for almost half of total transmission flows (inheritances and gifts), and it is therefore essential to take them into account. Concretely, if gifts prior to death were not included, we would find that average wealth at death in 2000–2010 was just over 20 percent higher than average wealth of the living. But this is simply a reflection of the fact that the dead have already passed on nearly half of their assets. If we include gifts made prior to death, we find that the (corrected) value of μ is actually greater than 220 percent: the corrected wealth of the dead is nearly twice as great as that of the living. We are once again living in a golden age of gift giving, much more so than in the nineteenth century.

It is interesting to note that the vast majority of gifts, today as in the nineteenth century, go to children, often in the context of a real estate investment, and they are given on average about ten years

---

12. To quote the usual proverb, public pensions are "the fortunes of those who have no fortune." I will come back to this in Chapter 13, when I analyze different pension systems.

before the death of the donor (a gap that has remained relatively stable over time). The growing importance of gifts since the 1970s has led to a decrease in the average age of the recipient: in 2000–2010, the average age of an heir is forty-five to fifty, while that of the recipient of a gift is thirty-five to forty, so that the difference between today and the nineteenth or early twentieth centuries is not as great as it seems from Figure 11.3.[13] The most convincing explanation of this gradual and progressive increase of gift giving, which began in the 1970s, well before fiscal incentives were put in place in 1990–2000, is that parents with means gradually became aware that owing to the increase in life expectancy, there might be good reasons to share their wealth with their children at the age of thirty-five to forty rather than forty-five to fifty or even later. In any case, whatever the exact role of each of the various possible explanations, the fact is that the upsurge in gift giving, which we also find in other European countries, including Germany, is an essential ingredient in the revived importance of inherited wealth in contemporary society.

The Fifties and the Eighties: Age and Fortune in the Belle Époque

In order to better understand the dynamics of wealth accumulation and the detailed data used to calculate μ, it is useful to examine the evolution of the average wealth profile as a function of age. Table 11.1 presents wealth-age profiles for a number of years between 1820 and 2010.[14] The most striking fact is no doubt the impressive aging of wealth throughout the nineteenth century, as capital became increasingly concentrated. In 1820, the elderly were barely wealthier on average than people in their fifties (which I have taken as a reference group): sexagenarians were 34 percent wealthier and octogenarians 53

---

13. For detailed data on this subject, see Piketty, "On the Long-Run Evolution of Inheritance."

14. Complete annual data are available online.

TABLE 11.1.

The age-wealth profile in France, 1820–2010: Average wealth of each age group (% of average wealth of 50- to 59-year-olds)

Year	20–29 years	30–39 years	40–49 years	50–59 years	60–69 years	70–79 years	80 years and over
1820	29	37	47	100	134	148	153
1850	28	37	52	100	128	144	142
1880	30	39	61	100	148	166	220
1902	26	57	65	100	172	176	238
1912	23	54	72	100	158	178	257
1931	22	59	77	100	123	137	143
1947	23	52	77	100	99	76	62
1960	28	52	74	100	110	101	87
1984	19	55	83	100	118	113	105
2000	19	46	66	100	122	121	118
2010	25	42	74	100	111	106	134

Note: In 1820, the average wealth of individuals aged 60–69 was 34% higher than that of 50- to 59-year-olds, and the average wealth of those aged 80 and over was 53% higher than that of 50- to 59-year-olds.

Sources: See piketty.pse.ens.fr/capital21c, table 2.

percent wealthier. But the gaps widened steadily thereafter. By 1900–1910, the average wealth of sexagenarians and septuagenarians was on the order of 60–80 percent higher than the reference group, and octogenarians were two and a half times wealthier. Note that these are averages for all of France. If we restrict our attention to Paris, where the largest fortunes were concentrated, the situation is even more extreme. On the eve of World War I, Parisian fortunes swelled with age, with septuagenarians and octogenarians on average three or even four times as wealthy as fifty-year-olds.[15] To be sure, the majority

---

15. To be clear, these estimates include a fairly large correction for differential mortality (that is, for the fact the wealthy individuals on average live longer). This is an important phenomenon, but it is not the explanation for the profile described here. See the online technical appendix.

of people died with no wealth at all, and the absence of any pension system tended to aggravate this "golden-age poverty." But among the minority with some fortune, the aging of wealth is quite impressive. Quite clearly, the spectacular enrichment of octogenarians cannot be explained by income from labor or entrepreneurial activity: it is hard to imagine people in their eighties creating a new startup every morning.

This enrichment of the elderly is striking, in part because it explains the high value of μ, the ratio of average wealth at time of death to average wealth of the living, in the Belle Époque (and therefore the high inheritance flows), and even more because it tells us something quite specific about the underlying economic process. The individual data we have are quite clear on this point: the very rapid increase of wealth among the elderly in the late nineteenth and early twentieth centuries was a straightforward consequence of the inequality $r > g$ and of the cumulative and multiplicative logic it implies. Concretely, elderly people with the largest fortunes often enjoyed capital incomes far in excess of what they needed to live. Suppose, for example, that they obtained a return of 5 percent and consumed two-fifths of their capital income while reinvesting the other three-fifths. Their wealth would then have grown at a rate of 3 percent a year, and by the age of eighty-five they would have been more than twice as rich as they were at age sixty. The mechanism is simple but extremely powerful, and it explains the observed facts very well, except that the people with the largest fortunes could often save more than three-fifths of their capital income (which would have accelerated the divergence process), and the general growth of mean income and wealth was not quite zero (but about 1 percent a year, which would have slowed it down a bit).

The study of the dynamics of accumulation and concentration of wealth in France in 1870–1914, especially in Paris, has many lessons to teach about the world today and in the future. Not only are the data exceptionally detailed and reliable, but this period is also emblematic of the first globalization of trade and finance. As noted, it had modern, diversified capital markets, and individuals held complex portfolios consisting of domestic and foreign, public and private assets paying fixed and variable amounts. To be sure, economic growth was only 1–1.5 percent a year, but such a growth rate, as I showed earlier, is actually quite substantial from a generational standpoint or in the historical perspective of the very long run. It is by no means indicative of a static agricultural society. This was an era of technological and industrial innovation: the automobile, electricity, the cinema, and many other novelties became important in these years, and many of them originated in France, at least in part. Between 1870 and 1914, not all fortunes of fifty- and sixty-year-olds were inherited. Far from it: we find a considerable number of wealthy people who made their money through entrepreneurial activities in industry and finance.

Nevertheless, the dominant dynamic, which explains most of the concentration of wealth, was an inevitable consequence of the inequality $r > g$. Regardless of whether the wealth a person holds at age fifty or sixty is inherited or earned, the fact remains that beyond a certain threshold, capital tends to reproduce itself and accumulates exponentially. The logic of $r > g$ implies that the entrepreneur always tends to turn into a rentier. Even if this happens later in life, the phenomenon becomes important as life expectancy increases. The fact that a person has good ideas at age thirty or forty does not imply that she will still be having them at seventy or eighty, yet her wealth will continue to increase by itself. Or it can be passed on to the next generation and continue to increase there. Nineteenth-century French economic elites were creative and dynamic entrepreneurs, but the crucial fact remains that their efforts ultimately—and largely unwittingly—reinforced and perpetuated a society of rentiers owing to the logic of $r > g$.

The Rejuvenation of Wealth Owing to War

This self-sustaining mechanism collapsed owing to the repeated shocks suffered by capital and its owners in the period 1914–1945. A significant rejuvenation of wealth was one consequence of the two world wars. One sees this clearly in Figure 11.5: for the first time in history—and to this day the only time—average wealth at death in 1940–1950 fell below the average wealth of the living. This fact emerges even more clearly in the detailed profiles by age cohort in Table 11.1. In 1912, on the eve of World War I, octogenarians were more than two and a half times as wealthy as people in their fifties. In 1931, they were only 50 percent wealthier. And in 1947, the fifty-somethings were 40 percent wealthier than the eighty-somethings. To add insult to injury, the octogenarians even fell slightly behind people in their forties in that year. This was a period in which all old certainties were called into question. In the years after World War II, the plot of wealth versus age suddenly took the form of a bell curve with a peak in the fifty to fifty-nine age bracket—a form close to the "Modigliani triangle," except for the fact that wealth did not fall to zero at the most advanced ages. This stands in sharp contrast to the nineteenth century, during which the wealth-age curve was monotonically increasing with age.

There is a simple explanation for this spectacular rejuvenation of wealth. As noted in Part Two, all fortunes suffered multiple shocks in the period 1914–1945—destruction of property, inflation, bankruptcy, expropriation, and so on—so that the capital / income ratio fell sharply. To a first approximation, one might assume that all fortunes suffered to the same degree, leaving the age profile unchanged. In fact, however, the younger generations, which in any case did not have much to lose, recovered more quickly from these wartime shocks than their elders did. A person who was sixty years old in 1940 and lost everything he owned in a bombardment, expropriation, or bankruptcy had little hope of recovering. He would likely have died between 1950 and 1960 at the age of seventy or eighty with nothing to pass on to his heirs. Conversely, a person who was thirty in 1940 and lost everything (which was probably not much) still had plenty of time to accumulate wealth after the war and by the 1950s would have been in his forties and wealthier than that septuagenarian. The war reset all counters to zero, or close to zero, and inevitably resulted in a rejuvenation of wealth. In this respect, it was indeed the two world wars that wiped the slate clean in the twentieth century and created the illusion that capitalism had been overcome.

This is the central explanation for the exceptionally low inheritance flows observed in the decades after World War II: individuals who should have inherited fortunes in 1950–1960 did not inherit much because their parents had not had time to recover from the shocks of the previous decades and died without much wealth to their names.

In particular, this argument enables us to understand why the collapse of inheritance flows was greater than the collapse of wealth itself—nearly twice as large, in fact. As I showed in Part Two, total private wealth fell by more than two-thirds between 1910–1920 and 1950–1960: the private capital stock decreased from seven years of national income to just two to two and a half years (see Figure 3.6). The annual flow of inheritance fell by almost five-sixths, from 25 percent of national income on the eve of World War I to just 4–5 percent in the 1950s (see Figure 11.1).

The crucial fact, however, is that this situation did not last long. "Reconstruction capitalism" was by its nature a transitional phase and not the structural transformation some people imagined. In 1950–1960, as capital was once again accumulated and the capital / income ratio β rose, fortunes began to age once more, so that the ratio μ between average wealth at death and average wealth of the living also increased. Growing wealth went hand in hand with aging wealth, thereby laying the groundwork for an even stronger comeback of inherited wealth. By 1960, the profile observed in 1947 was already a memory: sexagenarians and septuagenarians were slightly wealthier than people in their fifties (see Table 11.1). The octogenarians' turn came in the 1980s. In 1990–2000 the graph of wealth against age was increasing even more steeply. By 2010, the average wealth of people in their eighties was more than 30 percent higher than that of people in their fifties. If one were to include (which Table 11.1 does not) gifts made prior to death in the wealth of different age cohorts, the graph for 2000–2010 would be steeper still, approximately the same as in 1900–1910, with average wealth for people in their seventies and eighties on the order of twice as great as people in their fifties, except that most deaths now occur at a more advanced age, which yields a considerably higher μ (see Figure 11.5).

How Will Inheritance Flows Evolve in the Twenty-First Century?

In view of the rapid increase of inheritance flows in recent decades, it is natural to ask if this increase is likely to continue. Figure 11.6 shows two possible evolutions for the twenty-first century. The central scenario is based on the assumption of an annual growth rate of 1.7 percent for the period 2010–2100 and a net return on capital of 3 percent.[16] The alternative scenario is based on the assumption that growth will be reduced to 1 percent for the period 2010–2100, while the return on capital will rise to 5 percent. This could happen, for instance, if all taxes on capital and capital income, including the corporate income tax, were eliminated, or if such taxes were reduced while capital's share of income increased.

In the central scenario, simulations based on the theoretical model (which successfully accounts for the evolutions of 1820–2010) suggest that the annual inheritance flow would continue to grow until 2030–2040 and then stabilize at around 16–17 percent of national income. According to the alternative scenario, the inheritance flow should increase even more until 2060–2070 and then stabilize at around 24–25 percent of national income, a level similar to that observed in 1870–1910. In the first case, inherited wealth would make only a partial comeback; in the second, its comeback would be complete (as far as the total amount of inheritances and gifts is concerned). In both cases,

---

16. The annual growth rate of 1.7 percent is exactly the same as the average growth rate for 1980–2010. The estimate of net return on capital of 3 percent assumes that capital's share of national income will continue at its average level for 1980–2010 and that the current tax system will remain in place. See the online technical appendix.

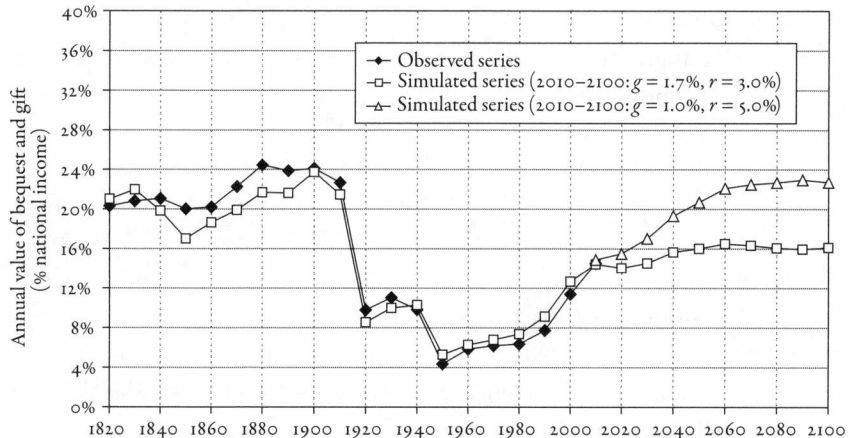

FIGURE 11.6. Observed and simulated inheritance flow: France, 1820–2100

Simulations based upon the theoretical model indicate that the level of the inheritance flow in the twenty-first century will depend upon the growth rate and the net rate of return to capital.

Sources and series: see piketty.pse.ens.fr/capital21c.

the flow of inheritances and gifts in the twenty-first century is expected to be quite high, and in particular much higher than it was during the exceptionally low phase observed in the mid-twentieth century.

Such predictions are obviously highly uncertain and are of interest primarily for their illustrative value. The evolution of inheritance flows in the twenty-first century depends on many economic, demographic, and political factors, and history shows that these are subject to large and highly unpredictable changes. It is easy to imagine other scenarios that would lead to different outcomes: for instance, a spectacular acceleration of demographic or economic growth (which seems rather implausible) or a radical change in public policy in regard to private capital or inheritance (which may be more realistic).[17]

It is also important to note that the evolution of the wealth-age profile depends primarily on savings behavior, that is, on the reasons

---

17. Other variants and scenarios are presented in the online technical appendix.

why different groups of people accumulate wealth. As already discussed at some length, there are many such reasons, and their relative importance varies widely from individual to individual. One may save in anticipation of retirement or job loss (life-cycle or precautionary saving). Or one may save to amass or perpetuate a family fortune. Or, indeed, one may simply have a taste for wealth and the prestige that sometimes goes with it (dynastic saving or pure accumulation). In the abstract, it is perfectly possible to imagine a world in which all people would choose to convert all of their wealth into annuities and die with nothing. If such behavior were suddenly to become predominant in the twenty-first century, inheritance flows would obviously shrink to virtually zero, regardless of the growth rate or return on capital.

Nevertheless, the two scenarios presented in Figure 11.6 are the most plausible in light of currently available information. In particular, I have assumed that savings behavior in 2010–2100 will remain similar to what it has been in the past, which can be characterized as follows. Despite wide variations in individual behavior, we find that savings rates increase with income and initial endowment, but variations by age group are much smaller: to a first approximation, people save on average at a similar rate regardless of age.[18] In particular, the massive dissaving by the elderly predicted by the life-cycle theory of saving does not seem to occur, no matter how much life expectancy increases. The reason for this is no doubt the importance of the family transmission motive (no one really wants to die with nothing, even in aging societies), together with a logic of pure accumulation as well as the sense of security—and not merely prestige or power—that wealth brings.[19] The very high concentration of wealth (with the upper decile always owning at least 50–60 percent of all wealth, even within each age cohort) is the missing link that explains all these facts, which Modigli-

---

18. "Savings rates increase with income and initial endowment": one can save more when one's income is higher or when one does not have to pay rent, and even more when both conditions are true. "Wide variations in individual behavior": some people like wealth, while others prefer automobiles or opera, for example.
19. For example, at a given income level, childless individuals save as much as others.

ani's theory totally overlooks. The gradual return to a dynastic type of wealth inequality since 1950–1960 explains the absence of dissaving by the elderly (most wealth belongs to individuals who have the means to finance their lifestyles without selling assets) and therefore the persistence of high inheritance flows and the perpetuation of the new equilibrium, in which mobility, though positive, is limited.

The essential point is that for a given structure of savings behavior, the cumulative process becomes more rapid and inegalitarian as the return on capital rises and the growth rate falls. The very high growth of the three postwar decades explains the relatively slow increase of μ (the ratio of average wealth at death to average wealth of the living) and therefore of inheritance flows in the period 1950–1970. Conversely, slower growth explains the accelerated aging of wealth and the rebound of inherited wealth that have occurred since the 1980s. Intuitively, when growth is high, for example, when wages increase 5 percent a year, it is easier for younger generations to accumulate wealth and level the playing field with their elders. When the growth of wages drops to 1–2 percent a year, the elderly will inevitably acquire most of the available assets, and their wealth will increase at a rate determined by the return on capital.[20] This simple but important process explains very well the evolution of the ratio μ and the annual inheritance flow. It also explains why the observed and simulated series are so close for the entire period 1820–2010.[21]

Uncertainties notwithstanding, it is therefore natural to think that these simulations provide a useful guide for the future. Theoretically, one can show that for a large class of savings behaviors, when growth is low compared to the return on capital, the increase in μ nearly exactly balances the decrease in the mortality rate m, so that the product $μ \times m$ is virtually independent of life expectancy and is almost entirely

---

20. The growth of wages may drop even lower, if one subtracts the increasing proportion of national income that goes to finance pensions and health care.

21. For a more precise technical description of these simulations, which aim primarily to reproduce the evolution of the wealth profile by age group (on the basis of macroeconomic and demographic data), see the online technical appendix.

determined by the duration of a generation. The central result is that a growth of about 1 percent is in this respect not very different from zero growth: in both cases, the intuition that an aging population will spend down its savings and thus put an end to inherited wealth turns out to be false. In an aging society, heirs come into their inheritances later in life but inherit larger amounts (at least for those who inherit anything), so the overall importance of inherited wealth remains unchanged.[22]

From the Annual Inheritance Flow to the Stock of Inherited Wealth

How does one go from the annual inheritance flow to the stock of inherited wealth? The detailed data assembled on inheritance flows and ages of the deceased, their heirs, and gift givers and recipients enable us to estimate for each year in the period 1820–2010 the share of inherited wealth in the total wealth of individuals alive in that year (the method is essentially to add up bequests and gifts received over the previous thirty years, sometimes more in the case of particularly early inheritances or exceptionally long lives or less in the opposite case) and thus to determine the share of inherited wealth in total private wealth. The principal results are indicated in Figure 11.7, where I also show the results of simulations for the period 2010–2100 based on the two scenarios discussed above.

The orders of magnitude to bear in mind are the following. In the nineteenth and early twentieth centuries, when the annual inheritance flow was 20–25 percent of national income, inherited wealth accounted for nearly all private wealth: somewhere between 80 and 90 percent, with an upward trend. Note, however, that in all societies, at

---

22. More precisely, one can show that $\mu \times m$ approaches $1/H$ when growth decreases, regardless of the life expectancy. With a capital / income ratio β of 600–700 percent, one may see why the inheritance flow b_y tends to return to β/H, that is, about 20–25 percent. Thus the idea of a "rate of estate devolution" developed by nineteenth-century economists is approximately correct in a society where growth is low. See the online technical appendix.

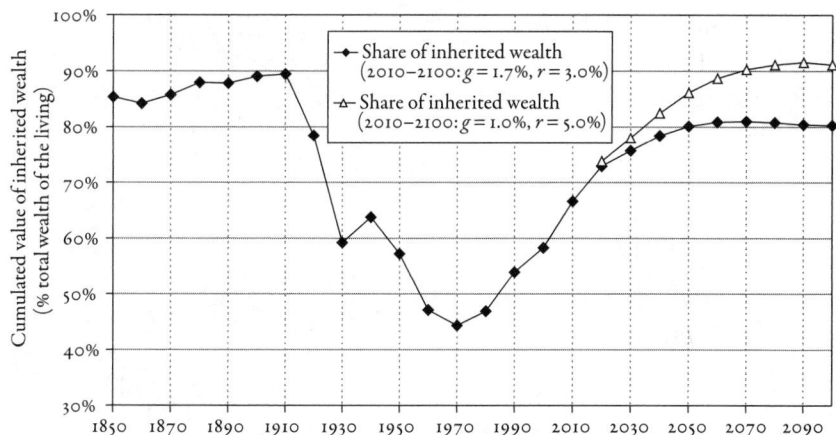

FIGURE 11.7. The share of inherited wealth in total wealth: France, 1850–2100

Inherited wealth represents 80–90 percent of total wealth in France in the nineteenth century; this share fell to 40–50 percent during the twentieth century, and might return to 80–90 percent during the twenty-first century.

Sources and series: see piketty.pse.ens.fr/capital21c.

all levels of wealth, a significant number of wealthy individuals, between 10 and 20 percent, accumulate fortunes during their lifetimes, having started with nothing. Nevertheless, inherited wealth accounts for the vast majority of cases. This should come as no surprise: if one adds up an annual inheritance flow of 20 percent of national income for approximately thirty years, one accumulates a very large sum of legacies and gifts, on the order of six years of national income, which thus accounts for nearly all of private wealth.[23]

Over the course of the twentieth century, following the collapse of inheritance flows, this equilibrium changed dramatically. The low

---

23. In reality, things are somewhat more complex, because we allow for the fact that some heirs consume a part of their inheritance. Conversely, we include in inherited wealth the cumulative income on wealth (within the limits of the heir's wealth: if one fully capitalized all of the bequest, including the income consumed by the inheritor, for example in the form of rent that the inheritor of an apartment does not have to pay, one would obviously exceed 100 percent of total wealth). See the online technical appendix for estimates using different definitions.

point was attained in the 1970s: after several decades of small inheritances and accumulation of new wealth, inherited capital accounted for just over 40 percent of total private capital. For the first time in history (except in new countries), wealth accumulated in the lifetime of the living constituted the majority of all wealth: nearly 60 percent. It is important to realize two things: first, the nature of capital effectively changed in the postwar period, and second, we are just emerging from this exceptional period. Nevertheless, we are now clearly out of it: the share of inherited wealth in total wealth has grown steadily since the 1970s. Inherited wealth once again accounted for the majority of wealth in the 1980s, and according to the latest available figures it represents roughly two-thirds of private capital in France in 2010, compared with barely one-third of capital accumulated from savings. In view of today's very high inheritance flows, it is quite likely, if current trends continue, that the share of inherited wealth will continue to grow in the decades to come, surpassing 70 percent by 2020 and approaching 80 percent in the 2030s. If the scenario of 1 percent growth and 5 percent return on capital is correct, the share of inherited wealth could continue to rise, reaching 90 percent by the 2050s, or approximately the same level as in the Belle Époque.

Thus we see that the U-shaped curve of annual inheritance flows as a proportion of national income in the twentieth century went hand in hand with an equally impressive U-shaped curve of accumulated stock of inherited wealth as a proportion of national wealth. In order to understand the relation between these two curves, it is useful to compare the level of inheritance flows to the savings rate, which as noted in Part Two is generally around 10 percent of national income. When the inheritance flow is 20–25 percent of national income, as it was in the nineteenth century, then the amounts received each year as bequests and gifts are more than twice as large as the flow of new savings. If we add that a part of the new savings comes from the income of inherited capital (indeed, this was the major part of saving in the nineteenth century), it is clearly inevitable that inherited wealth will largely predominate over saved wealth. Conversely, when the inheritance flow

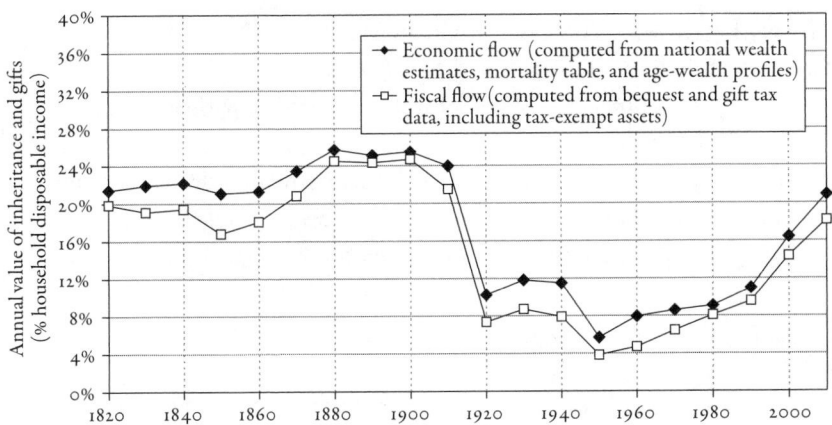

FIGURE 11.8. The annual inheritance flow as a fraction of household disposable income: France, 1820–2010

Expressed as a fraction of household disposable income (rather than national income), the annual inheritance flow is about 20 percent in 2010, in other words, close to its nineteenth-century level.

Sources and series: see piketty.pse.ens.fr/capital21c.

falls to just 5 percent of national income, or half of new savings (again assuming a savings rate of 10 percent), as in the 1950s, it is not surprising that saved capital will dominate inherited capital. The central fact is that the annual inheritance flow surpassed the savings rate again in the 1980s and rose well above it in 2000–2010. Today it is nearly 15 percent of national income (counting both inheritances and gifts).

To get a better idea of the sums involved, it may be useful to recall that household disposable (monetary) income is 70–75 percent of national income in a country like France today (after correcting for transfers in kind, such as health, education, security, public services, etc. not included in disposable income). If we express the inheritance flow not as a proportion of national income, as I have done thus far, but as a proportion of disposable income, we find that the inheritances and gifts received each year by French households amounted to about 20 percent of their disposable income in the early 2010s, so that in this sense inheritance is already as important today as it was in 1820–1910 (see Figure 11.8). As noted in Chapter 5, it is probably better to use national income (rather than disposable income) as the reference denominator for purposes of spatial and temporal comparison. Nevertheless, the comparison with disposable income reflects today's reality in a more concrete way and shows that inherited wealth already accounts for one-fifth of household monetary resources (available for saving, for example) and will soon account for a quarter or more.

Back to Vautrin's Lecture

In order to have a more concrete idea of what inheritance represents in different people's lives, and in particular to respond more precisely to the existential question raised by Vautrin's lecture (what sort of life can one hope to live on earned income alone, compared to the life one can lead with inherited wealth?), the best way to proceed is to consider things from the point of view of successive generations in France since the beginning of the nineteenth century and compare the various resources to which they would have had access in their lifetime. This is the only way to account correctly for the fact that an inheritance is not a resource one receives every year.[24]

Consider first the evolution of the share of inheritance in the total resources available to generations born in France in the period 1790–2030 (see Figure 11.9). I proceeded as follows. Starting with series of annual inheritance flows and detailed data concerning ages of the deceased, heirs, gift givers, and gift recipients, I calculated the share of inherited wealth in total available resources as a function of year of

---

24. In particular, when we say that the inheritance flow represents the equivalent of 20 percent of disposable income, this obviously does not mean that each individual receives 20 percent additional income every year in the form of a regular flow of bequests and gifts. It means rather that at certain points in a person's life (typically on the death of a parent and in some cases on the occasion of receipt of a gift), much larger sums may be transferred, sums equivalent to several years' income, and that all told these bequests and gifts represent the equivalent of 20 percent of the disposable income of all households.

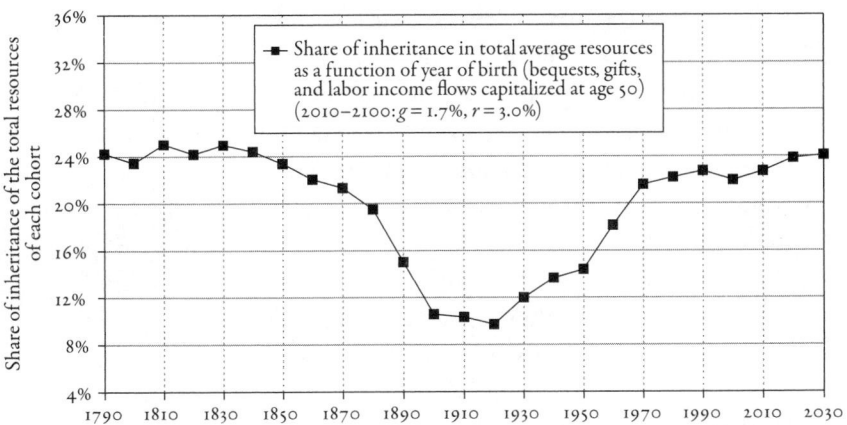

FIGURE 11.9. The share of inheritance in the total resources (inheritance and work) of cohorts born in 1790–2030

Inheritance made about 25 percent of the resources of nineteenth-century cohorts, down to less than 10 percent for cohorts born in 1910–1920 (who should have inherited in 1950–1960).

Sources and series: see piketty.pse.ens.fr/capital21c.

birth. Available resources include both inherited wealth (bequests and gifts) and income from labor, less taxes,[25] capitalized over the individual's lifetime using the average net return on capital in each year. Although this is the most reasonable way to approach the question initially, note that it probably leads to a slight underestimate of the share of inheritance, because heirs (and people with large fortunes more generally) are usually able to obtain a higher return on capital than the interest rate paid on savings from earned income.[26]

The results obtained are the following. If we look at all people born in France in the 1790s, we find that inheritance accounted for about

---

25. Replacement incomes (retirement pensions and unemployment benefits) are included in income from labor, as in Part Two.

26. All resources were capitalized at the age of fifty, but if one uses the same rate of return to capitalize different resources, the choice of a reference age is not important for calculating the shares of inheritance and earned income in the total. The question of unequal returns on capital is examined in the next chapter.

24 percent of the total resources available to them during their lifetimes, so that income from labor accounted for about 76 percent. For individuals born in the 1810s, the share of inheritance was 25 percent, leaving 75 percent for earned income. The same is approximately true for all the cohorts of the nineteenth century and up to World War I. Note that the 25 percent share for inheritance is slightly higher than the inheritance flow expressed as a percentage of national income (20–25 percent in the nineteenth century): this is because income from capital, generally about a third of national income, is de facto reassigned in part to inheritance and in part to earned income.[27]

For cohorts born in the 1870s and after, the share of inheritance in total resources begins to decline gradually. This is because a growing share of these individuals should have inherited after World War I and therefore received less than expected owing to the shocks to their parents' assets. The lowest point was reached by cohorts born in 1910–1920: these individuals should have inherited in the years between the end of World War II and 1960, that is, at a time when the inheritance flow had reached its lowest level, so that inheritance accounted for only 8–10 percent of total resources. The rebound began with cohorts born in 1930–1950, who inherited in 1970–1990, and for whom inheritance accounted for 12–14 percent of total resources. But it is above all for cohorts born in 1970–1980, who began to receive gifts and bequests in 2000–2010, that inheritance regained an importance not seen since the nineteenth century: around 22–24 percent of total resources. These figures show clearly that we have only just emerged from the "end of inheritance" era, and they also show how differently different cohorts born in the twentieth century experienced the relative impor-

---

27. For a complete analysis of the relations between these different ratios, see the online technical appendix. The fact that the inheritance flow (20–25 percent of national income) and capital income (typically 25–35 percent of national income) are sometimes close should be regarded as a coincidence due to specific demographic and technological parameters (the equilibrium inheritance flow $b_y = \beta/H$ depends on the capital/income ratio and the duration of a generation, whereas the equilibrium capital share α depends on the production function).

tance of savings and inheritance: the baby boom cohorts had to make it on their own, almost as much as the interwar and turn-of-the-century cohorts, who were devastated by war. By contrast, the cohorts born in the last third of the century experienced the powerful influence of inherited wealth to almost the same degree as the cohorts of the nineteenth and twenty-first centuries.

Rastignac's Dilemma

Thus far I have examined only averages. One of the principal characteristics of inherited wealth, however, is that it is distributed in a highly inegalitarian fashion. By introducing into the previous estimates inequality of inheritance on the one hand and inequality of earned income on the other, we will at last be able to analyze the degree to which Vautrin's somber lesson was true in different periods. Figure 11.10 shows that the cohorts born in the late eighteenth century and throughout the nineteenth century, including Eugène de Rastignac's cohort (Balzac tells us that he was born in 1798), did indeed face the terrible dilemma described by the ex-convict: those who could somehow lay hands on inherited wealth were able to live far better than those obliged to make their way by study and work.

In order to make it possible to interpret the different levels of resources as concretely and intuitively as possible, I have expressed resources in terms of multiples of the average income of the least well paid 50 percent of workers in each period. We may take this baseline as the standard of living of the "lower class," which generally claimed about half of national income in this period. This is a useful reference point for judging inequality in a society.[28]

---

28. As a general rule, the bottom 50 percent of the income hierarchy collectively received about 30 percent of total earned income (see Table 7.1), and therefore individually received about 60 percent of the average wage (or 40–50 percent of average national income per capita, allowing for the fact that income from labor generally accounts for 65–75 percent of national income). For example, in France today, the least well paid 50 percent have incomes that range between the

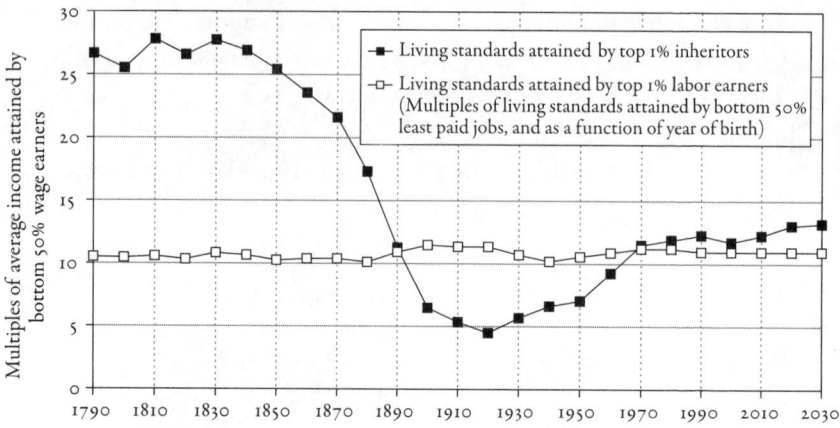

FIGURE 11.10. The dilemma of Rastignac for cohorts born in 1790–2030

In the nineteenth century, the living standards that could be attained by the top 1 percent inheritors were a lot higher than those that could be attained by the top 1 percent labor earners.

Sources and series: see piketty.pse.ens.fr/capital21c.

The principal results obtained are the following. In the nineteenth century, the lifetime resources available to the wealthiest 1 percent of heirs (that is, the individuals inheriting the top 1 percent of legacies in their generation) were 25–30 times greater than the resources of the lower class. In other words, a person who could obtain such an inheritance, either from parents or via a spouse, could afford to pay a staff of 25–30 domestic servants throughout his life. At the same time, the resources afforded by the top 1 percent of earned incomes (in jobs such as judge, prosecutor, or attorney, as in Vautrin's lecture) were about ten times the resources of the lower class. This was not negligible, but it was clearly a much lower standard of living, especially since, as Vautrin observed, such jobs were not easy to obtain. It was not enough to do brilliantly in law school. Often one had to plot and scheme for

---

minimum wage and 1.5 times the minimum wage, and earn on average 15,000 euros a year (1,250 euros a month), compared with 30,000 euros a year (2,500 a month) for average per capita national income.

many long years with no guarantee of success. Under such conditions, if the opportunity to lay hands on an inheritance in the top centile presented itself, it was surely better not to pass it up. At the very least, it was worth a moment's reflection.

If we now do the same calculation for the generations born in 1910–1920, we find that they faced different life choices. The top 1 percent of inheritances afforded resources that were barely 5 times the lower class standard. The best paid 1 percent of jobs still afforded 10–12 times that standard (as a consequence of the fact that the top centile of the wage hierarchy was relatively stable at about 6–7 percent of total wages over a long period).[29] For the first time in history, no doubt, one could live better by obtaining a job in the top centile rather than an inheritance in the top centile: study, work, and talent paid better than inheritance.

The choice was almost as clear for the baby boom cohorts: a Rastignac born in 1940–1950 had every reason to aim for a job in the top centile (which afforded resources 10–12 times greater than the lower class standard) and to ignore the Vautrins of the day (since the top centile of inheritances brought in just 6–7 times the lower class standard). For all these generations, success through work was more profitable and not just more moral.

Concretely, these results also indicate that throughout this period, and for all the cohorts born between 1910 and 1960, the top centile of the income hierarchy consisted largely of people whose primary source of income was work. This was a major change, not only because it was a historical first (in France and most likely in all other European countries) but also because the top centile is an extremely important group in every society.[30] As noted in Chapter 7, the top centile is a relatively broad elite that plays a central role in shaping the economic,

---

29. Recall that 6–7 percent of total wages for the top centile means that each member of that group earned on average 6–7 times the average wage, or 10–12 times the average wage of the least well paid 50 percent. See Chapters 7 and 8.

30. Evolutions similar to those depicted in Figure 11.10 are obtained if one considers the top decile or top thousandth instead of the top centile (which I nevertheless

political, and symbolic structure of society.[31] In all traditional societies (remember that the aristocracy represented 1–2 percent of the population in 1789), and in fact down to the Belle Époque (despite the hopes kindled by the French Revolution), this group was always dominated by inherited capital. The fact that this was not the case for the cohorts born in the first half of the twentieth century was therefore a major event, which fostered unprecedented faith in the irreversibility of social progress and the end of the old social order. To be sure, inequality was not eradicated in the three decades after World War II, but it was viewed primarily from the optimistic angle of wage inequalities. To be sure, there were significant differences between blue-collar workers, white-collar workers, and managers, and these disparities tended to grow wider in France in the 1950s. But there was a fundamental unity to this society, in which everyone participated in the communion of labor and honored the meritocratic ideal. People believed that the arbitrary inequalities of inherited wealth were a thing of the past.

For the cohorts born in the 1970s, and even more for those born later, things are quite different. In particular, life choices have become more complex: the inherited wealth of the top centile counts for about as much as the employment of the top centile (or even slightly more: 12–13 times the lower class standard of living for inheritance versus 10–11 times for earned income). Note, however, that the structure of inequality and of the top centile today is also quite different from what it was in the nineteenth century, because inherited wealth is significantly less concentrated today than in the past.[32] Today's cohorts face a unique set of inequalities and social structures, which are

---

believe is the most significant group to study). See Supplemental Figures S11.9–10, available online.

31. By definition, 500,000 adult individuals in a society of 50 million adults, such as France today.

32. The total value of inherited wealth is not far below its nineteenth-century level, but it has become rarer for individuals to inherit enough wealth to finance, without working, a lifestyle several dozen times the lower-class standard of living.

in a sense somewhere between the world cynically described by Vautrin (in which inheritance predominated over labor) and the enchanted world of the postwar decades (in which labor predominated over inheritance). According to our findings, the top centile of the social hierarchy in France today are likely to derive their income about equally from inherited wealth and their own labor.

The Basic Arithmetic of Rentiers and Managers

To recapitulate: a society in which income from inherited capital predominates over income from labor at the summit of the social hierarchy—that is, a society like those described by Balzac and Austen—two conditions must be satisfied. First, the capital stock and, within it, the share of inherited capital, must be large. Typically, the capital / income ratio must be on the order of 6 or 7, and most of the capital stock must consist of inherited capital. In such a society, inherited wealth can account for about a quarter of the average resources available to each cohort (or even as much as a third if one assumes a high degree of inequality in returns on capital). This was the case in the eighteenth and nineteenth centuries, until 1914. This first condition, which concerns the stock of inherited wealth, is once again close to being satisfied today.

The second condition is that inherited wealth must be extremely concentrated. If inherited wealth were distributed in the same way as income from labor (with identical levels for the top decile, top centile, etc., of the hierarchies of both inheritance and labor income), then Vautrin's world could never exist: income from labor would always far outweigh income from inherited wealth (by a factor of at least three),[33] and the top 1 percent of earned incomes would systematically

---

33. Roughly 3 times larger in the eighteenth and nineteenth centuries as well as the twenty-first century (when income from labor accounted for approximately three-quarters of total resources and income from inherited wealth for roughly one-quarter) and nearly 10 times larger in the twentieth century (when income from

and mechanically outweigh the top 1 percent of incomes from inherited capital.[34]

In order for the concentration effect to dominate the volume effect, the top centile of the inheritance hierarchy must by itself claim the lion's share of inherited wealth. This was indeed the case in the eighteenth and nineteenth centuries, when the top centile owned 50–60 percent of total wealth (or as much as 70 percent in Britain or Belle Époque Paris), which is nearly 10 times greater than the top centile's share of earned income (about 6–7 percent, a figure that remained stable over a very long period of time). This 10:1 ratio between wealth and salary concentrations is enough to counterbalance the 3:1 volume ratio and explains why an inherited fortune in the top centile enabled a person to live practically 3 times better than an employment in the top centile in the patrimonial society of the nineteenth century (see Figure 11.10).

This basic arithmetic of rentiers and managers also helps us to understand why the top centiles of inherited wealth and earned income are almost balanced in France today: the concentration of wealth is about three times greater than the concentration of earned income (the top centile owns 20 percent of total wealth, while the top centile of earners claims 6–7 percent of total wages), so the concentration effect roughly balances the volume effect. We can also see why heirs were so clearly dominated by managers during the Trente Glorieuses (the 3:1 concentration effect was too small to balance the 10:1 mass effect). Apart from these situations, which are the result of extreme shocks and specific public policies (especially tax policies), however, the "natural" structure of inequality seems rather to favor a domination of rentiers over managers. In particular, when growth is low and the return on capital is distinctly greater than the growth rate, it is almost inevitable

---

labor accounted for nine-tenths of resources and income from inherited wealth one-tenth). See Figure 11.9.

34. Roughly 3 times greater in the eighteenth and nineteenth centuries as well as the twenty-first century, and nearly 10 times larger in the twentieth century. The same would be true for the top 10 percent, the top 0.1 percent, etc.

(at least in the most plausible dynamic models) that wealth will become so concentrated that top incomes from capital will predominate over top incomes from labor by a wide margin.[35]

The Classic Patrimonial Society: The World of Balzac and Austen

Nineteenth-century novelists obviously did not use the same categories we do to describe the social structures of their time, but they depicted the same deep structures: those of a society in which a truly comfortable life required the possession of a large fortune. It is striking to see how similar the inegalitarian structures, orders of magnitude, and amounts minutely specified by Balzac and Austen were on both sides of the English Channel, despite the differences in currency, literary style, and plot. As noted in Chapter 2, monetary markers were extremely stable in the inflation-free world described by both novelists, so that they were able to specify precisely how large an income (or fortune) one needed to rise above mediocrity and live with a minimum of elegance. For both writers, the material and psychological threshold was about 30 times the average income of the day. Below that level, a Balzacian or Austenian hero found it difficult to live a dignified life. It was quite possible to cross that threshold if one was among the wealthiest 1 percent (and even better if one approached the top 0.5 or even 0.1 percent) of French or British society in the nineteenth century. This was a well-defined and fairly numerous social group—a minority, to be sure, but a large enough minority to define the structure of society and sustain a novelistic universe.[36] But it was

---

35. See the online technical appendix for an analysis of the mathematical conditions on the various distributions that imply that rentiers dominate managers (and vice versa).

36. The top 1 percent of inherited fortunes enjoyed a standard of living 25–30 times higher than that of the bottom 50 percent in the nineteenth century (see Figure 11.10) or about 12–15 times the average per capita national income. The top 0.1 percent enjoyed a living standard approximately 5 times more opulent (see

totally out of reach for anyone content to practice a profession, no matter how well it paid: the best paid 1 percent of professions did not allow one to come anywhere near this standard of living (nor did the best paid 0.1 percent).[37]

In most of these novels, the financial, social, and psychological setting is established in the first few pages and occasionally alluded to thereafter, so that the reader will not forget everything that sets the characters of the novel apart from the rest of society: the monetary markers that shape their lives, their rivalries, their strategies, and their hopes. In *Père Goriot,* the old man's fall from grace is conveyed at once by the fact that he has been obliged to make do with the filthiest room in the Vauquer boardinghouse and survive on the skimpiest of meals in order to reduce his annual expenditure to 500 francs (or roughly the average annual income at the time—abject poverty for Balzac).[38] The old man sacrificed everything for his daughters, each of whom received a dowry of 500,000 francs, or an annual rent of 25,000 francs, about 50 times the average income: in Balzac's novels, this is the basic unit of fortune, the symbol of true wealth and elegant living. The con-

---

Chapter 10 on Pareto coefficients), or 60–75 times the average income. The threshold chosen by Balzac and Austen, 20–30 times average income, corresponds to the average income of the top 0.5 percent of the inheritance hierarchy (about 100,000 individuals out of an adult population of 20 million in France in 1820–1830, or 50,000 out of a population of 10 million British adults in 1800–1810). Both Balzac and Austen therefore had a vast range of characters to choose from.

37. In the nineteenth century, the best paid 1 percent of jobs offered a standard of living about 10 times greater than that of the lower class (see Figure 11.10), or 5 times the average income. One can estimate that only the best paid 0.01 percent (2,000 people out of 20 million at most) earned on average 20–30 times the average income for the period. Vautrin was probably not far off when he said that there were no more than five lawyers in Paris who earned more than 50,000 francs a year (or 100 times the average income). See the online technical appendix.

38. As in Chapter 2, the average incomes mentioned here are national per capita average incomes. In 1810–1820, the average income in France was 400–500 francs per year and probably a little more than 500 francs in Paris. The wages of domestic servants were one-third to one-half that.

trast between the two extremes of society is thus established at the outset. Nevertheless, Balzac does not forget that between abject poverty and true wealth all sorts of intermediate situations exist—some more mediocre than others. The small Rastignac estate near Angoulême yields barely 3,000 francs a year (or 6 times the average income). For Balzac, this is typical of the moneyless lesser nobility of the provinces. Eugène's family can spare only 1,200 francs a year to pay for his law studies in the capital. In Vautrin's lecture, the annual salary of 5,000 francs (or 10 times average income) that young Rastignac could potentially earn as a royal prosecutor after much effort and with great uncertainty is the very symbol of mediocrity—proof, if proof were needed, that study leads nowhere. Balzac depicts a society in which the minimum objective is to obtain 20–30 times the average income of the day, or even 50 times (as Delphine and Anastasie are able to do thanks to their dowries), or better yet, 100 times, thanks to the 50,000 francs in annual rent that Mademoiselle Victorine's million will earn.

In *César Birotteau,* the audacious perfumer also covets a fortune of a million francs so that he can keep half for himself and his wife while using the other half as a dowry for his daughter, which is what he believes it will take for her to marry well and allow his future son-in-law to purchase the practice of the notary Roguin. His wife, who would prefer to return to the land, tries to convince him that they can retire on an annual rent of 2,000 francs and marry their daughter with only 8,000 francs of rent, but César will not hear of it: he does not want to wind up like his associate, Pillerault, who retired with just 5,000 francs of rent. To live well, he needs 20–30 times the average income. With only 5–10 times the average, one barely survives.

We find precisely the same orders of magnitude on the other side of the Channel. In *Sense and Sensibility,* the kernel of the plot (financial as well as psychological) is established in the first ten pages in the appalling dialogue between John Dashwood and his wife, Fanny. John has just inherited the vast Norland estate, which brings in 4,000 pounds a year, or more than 100 times the average income of the day (which was barely more than 30 pounds a year in 1800–1810).[39] Norland is the quintessential example of a very large landed estate, the pinnacle of wealth in Jane Austen's novels. With 2,000 pounds a year (or more than 60 times the average income), Colonel Brandon and his Delaford estate are well within expectations for a great landowner. In other novels we discover that 1,000 pounds a year is quite sufficient for an Austenian hero. By contrast, 600 pounds a year (20 times average income) is just enough to leave John Willoughby at the lower limit of a comfortable existence, and people wonder how the handsome and impetuous young man can live so large on so little. This is no doubt the reason why he soon abandons Marianne, distraught and inconsolable, for Miss Grey and her dowry of 50,000 pounds (2,500 pounds in annual rent, or 80 times average income), which is almost exactly the same size as Mademoiselle Victorine's dowry of a million francs under prevailing exchange rates. As in Balzac, a dowry half that size, such as Delphine's or Anastasie's, is perfectly satisfactory. For example, Miss Morton, the only daughter of Lord Norton, has a capital of 30,000 pounds (1,500 pounds of rent, or 50 times average income), which makes her the ideal heiress and the quarry of every prospective mother-in-law, starting with Mrs. Ferrars, who has no difficulty imagining the girl married to her son Edward.[40]

From the opening pages, John Dashwood's opulence is contrasted with the comparative poverty of his half-sisters, Elinor, Marianne, and Margaret, who, along with their mother, must get by on 500 pounds a year (or 125 pounds apiece, barely four times the average per capita

---

39. Recall that a pound sterling was worth 25 francs in the nineteenth century and as late as 1914. See Chapter 2.

40. Had not an intimate of George III said to Barry Lyndon thirty years earlier, in the 1770s, that anyone with a capital of 30,000 pounds ought to be knighted? Redmond Barry had come quite a way since enlisting in the British army for barely 15 pounds a year (1 shilling a day), or barely half the average British income in 1750–1760. The fall was inevitable. Note that Stanley Kubrick, who took his inspiration from the celebrated nineteenth-century British novel, is just as precise about amounts as Jane Austen was.

income), which is woefully inadequate for the girls to find suitable husbands. Mrs. Jennings, who revels in the social gossip of the Devonshire countryside, likes to remind them of this during the many balls, courtesy calls, and musical evenings that fill their days and frequently bring them into contact with young and attractive suitors, who unfortunately do not always tarry: "The smallness of your fortune may make him hang back." As in Balzac's novels, so too in Jane Austen's: only a very modest life is possible with just 5 or 10 times the average income. Incomes close to or below the average of 30 pounds a year are not even mentioned, moreover: this, one suspects, is not much above the level of the servants, so there is no point in talking about it. When Edward Ferrars thinks of becoming a pastor and accepting the parish of Deliford with its living of 200 pounds a year (between 6 and 7 times the average), he is nearly taken for a saint. Even though he supplements his living with the income from the small sum left him by his family as punishment for his mésalliance, and with the meager income that Elinor brings, the couple will not go very far, and "they were neither of them quite enough in love to think that three hundred and fifty pounds a year would supply them with the comforts of life."[41] This happy and virtuous outcome should not be allowed to hide the essence of the matter: by accepting the advice of the odious Fanny and refusing to aid his half-sisters or to share one iota of his immense fortune, despite the promises he made to his father on his deathbed, John Dashwood forces Elinor and Marianne to live mediocre and humiliating lives. Their fate is entirely sealed by the appalling dialogue at the beginning of the book.

Toward the end of the nineteenth century, the same type of inegalitarian financial arrangement could also be found in the United States. In *Washington Square,* a novel published by Henry James in 1881 and magnificently translated to the screen in William Wyler's film *The Heiress* (1949), the plot revolves entirely around confusion as to the amount of a dowry. But arithmetic is merciless, and it is best not to

---

41. Jane Austen, *Sense and Sensibility* (Cambridge, MA: Belknap Press, 2013), 405.

make a mistake, as Catherine Sloper discovers when her fiancé flees on learning that her dowry will bring him only $10,000 a year in rent rather than the $30,000 he was counting on (or just 20 times the average US income of the time instead of 60). "You are too ugly," her tyrannical, extremely rich, widower father tells her, in a manner reminiscent of Prince Bolkonsky with Princess Marie in *War and Peace*. Men can also find themselves in very fragile positions: in *The Magnificent Ambersons,* Orson Welles shows us the downfall of an arrogant heir, George, who at one point has enjoyed an annual income of $60,000 (120 times the average) before falling victim in the early 1900s to the automobile revolution and ending up with a job that pays a below-average $350 a year.

Extreme Inequality of Wealth: A Condition of Civilization in a Poor Society?

Interestingly, nineteenth-century novelists were not content simply to describe precisely the income and wealth hierarchies that existed in their time. They often give a very concrete and intimate account of how people lived and what different levels of income meant in terms of the realities of everyday life. Sometimes this went along with a certain justification of extreme inequality of wealth, in the sense that one can read between the lines an argument that without such inequality it would have been impossible for a very small elite to concern themselves with something other than subsistence: extreme inequality is almost a condition of civilization.

In particular, Jane Austen minutely describes daily life in the early nineteenth century: she tells us what it cost to eat, to buy furniture and clothing, and to travel about. And indeed, in the absence of modern technology, everything is very costly and takes time and above all staff. Servants are needed to gather and prepare food (which cannot easily be preserved). Clothing costs money: even the most minimal fancy dress might cost several months' or even years' income. Travel was also expensive. It required horses, carriages, servants to take care of them, feed for the animals, and so on. The reader is made to see that life would have been objectively quite difficult for a person with only 3–5 times the average income, because it would then have been necessary to spend most of one's time attending to the needs of daily life. If you wanted books or musical instruments or jewelry or ball gowns, then there was no choice but to have an income 20–30 times the average of the day.

In Part One I noted that it was difficult and simplistic to compare purchasing power over long periods of time because consumption patterns and prices change radically in so many dimensions that no single index can capture the reality. Nevertheless, according to official indices, the average per capita purchasing power in Britain and France in 1800 was about one-tenth what it was in 2010. In other words, with 20 or 30 times the average income in 1800, a person would probably have lived no better than with 2 or 3 times the average income today. With 5–10 times the average income in 1800, one would have been in a situation somewhere between the minimum and average wage today.

In any case, a Balzacian or Austenian character would have used the services of dozens of servants with no embarrassment. For the most part, we are not even told their names. At times both novelists mocked the pretensions and extravagant needs of their characters, as, for example, when Marianne, who imagines herself in an elegant marriage with Willoughby, explains with a blush that according to her calculations it is difficult to live with less than 2,000 pounds a year (more than 60 times the average income of the time): "I am sure I am not extravagant in my demands. A proper establishment of servants, a carriage, perhaps two, and hunters, cannot be supported on less."[42] Elinor cannot refrain from pointing out to her sister that she *is* being extravagant. Similarly, Vautrin himself observed that it took an income of 25,000 francs (more than 50 times the average) to live with a minimum of dignity. In particular, he insists, with an abundance of detail, on the cost of clothing, servants, and travel. No one tells him that he is exag-

---

42. Austen, *Sense and Sensibility*, 135.

gerating, but Vautrin is so cynical that readers are in no doubt.[43] One finds a similarly unembarrassed recital of needs, with a similar notion of how much it takes to live comfortably, in Arthur Young's account of his travels.[44]

Notwithstanding the extravagance of some of their characters, these nineteenth-century novelists describe a world in which inequality was to a certain extent necessary: if there had not been a sufficiently wealthy minority, no one would have been able to worry about anything other than survival. This view of inequality deserves credit for not describing itself as meritocratic, if nothing else. In a sense, a minority was chosen to live on behalf of everyone else, but no one tried to pretend that this minority was more meritorious or virtuous than the rest. In this world, it was perfectly obvious, moreover, that without a fortune it was impossible to live a dignified life. Having a diploma or skill might allow a person to produce, and therefore to earn, 5 or 10 times more than the average, but not much more than that. Modern meritocratic society, especially in the United States, is much harder on the losers, because it seeks to justify domination on the grounds of justice, virtue,

---

43. His cynicism ultimately persuades Rastignac, who in *La maison de Nucingen* engages in business dealings with Delphine's husband in order to lay hands on a fortune of 400,000 francs.

44. In October 1788, as he is about to leave Normandy, Young notes: "Europe is now so much assimilated, that if one goes to a house where the fortune is 15 or 20,000 livres a year, we shall find in the mode of living much more resemblance than a young traveller will ever be prepared to look for" (Arthur Young, *Travels in 1787, 1788, 1789*, pub. 1792, reprinted as *Arthur Young's Travels in France* [Cambridge: Cambridge University Press, 2012], 145). He is speaking of the livre tournois, equivalent to the franc germinal. This amount was equal to 700–900 pounds sterling, or the equivalent of 30–50 times the average French or British income of the day. Later on he is more specific: with this amount of income, one can afford "six men-servants, five maids, eight horses, a garden, and a regular table." By contrast, with only 6,000–8,000 livres tournois, one can barely afford "2 servants and 3 horses." Note that livestock was an important part of capital and expenses. In November 1789, Young sold his horse in Toulon for 600 livres tournois (or four years of annual wages for an "ordinary servant"). The price was typical for the time. See the online technical appendix.

and merit, to say nothing of the insufficient productivity of those at the bottom.[45]

Meritocratic Extremism in Wealthy Societies

It is interesting, moreover, to note that the most ardent meritocratic beliefs are often invoked to justify very large wage inequalities, which are said to be more justified than inequalities due to inheritance. From the time of Napoleon to World War I, France has had a small number of very well paid and high-ranking civil servants (earning 50–100 times the average income of the day), starting with government ministers. This has always been justified—including by Napoleon himself, a scion of the minor Corsican nobility—by the idea that the most capable and talented individuals ought to be able to live on their salaries with as much dignity and elegance as the wealthiest heirs (a top-down response to Vautrin, as it were). As Adolphe Thiers remarked in the Chamber of Deputies in 1831: "prefects should be able to occupy a rank equal to the notable citizens in the *départements* they live in."[46] In 1881, Paul Leroy-Beaulieu explained that the state went too far by raising only the lowest salaries. He vigorously defended the high civil

---

45. Michael Young expressed this fear in *The Rise of Meritocracy* (London: Thames and Hudson, 1958).

46. The question of the salary scale for civil servants gave rise to many political conflicts in this period. In 1792, revolutionaries had tried to establish a restricted pay scale with a ratio of 8:1 (it was finally adopted in 1948 but was very quickly circumvented by a system of opaque bonuses for the highest civil servants that still exists today). Napoleon created a small number of highly paid posts, so few that Thiers in 1831 saw little reason to reduce their number ("with three million more or less given to or taken from the prefects, generals, magistrates, and ambassadors, we have the luxury of the Empire or American-style simplicity," he added in the same speech). The fact that the highest US civil servants at the time were paid much less than in France was also noted by Tocqueville, who saw it as a sure sign that the democratic spirit prevailed in the United States. Despite many ups and downs, this handful of very high salaries persisted in France until World War I (and thus to the fall of the rentier). On these evolutions, see the online technical appendix.

servants of his day, most of whom received little more than "15,000 to 20,000 francs a year"; these were "figures that might seem enormous to the common man" but actually "make it impossible to live with elegance or amass savings of any size."[47]

The most worrisome aspect of this defense of meritocracy is that one finds the same type of argument in the wealthiest societies, where Jane Austen's points about need and dignity make little sense. In the United States in recent years, one frequently has heard this type of justification for the stratospheric pay of supermanagers (50–100 times average income, if not more). Proponents of such high pay argued that without it, only the heirs of large fortunes would be able to achieve true wealth, which would be unfair. In the end, therefore, the millions or tens of millions of dollars a year paid to supermanagers contribute to greater social justice.[48] This kind of argument could well lay the groundwork for greater and more violent inequality in the future. The world to come may well combine the worst of two past worlds: both very large inequality of inherited wealth and very high wage inequalities justified in terms of merit and productivity (claims with very little factual basis, as noted). Meritocratic extremism can thus lead to a race between supermanagers and rentiers, to the detriment of those who are neither.

It also bears emphasizing that the role of meritocratic beliefs in justifying inequality in modern societies is evident not only at the top of hierarchy but lower down as well, as an explanation for the disparity between the lower and middle classes. In the late 1980s, Michèle Lamont conducted several hundred in-depth interviews with representatives of the "upper middle class" in the United States and France, not only in large cities such as New York and Paris but also in smaller cities such as Indianapolis and Clermont-Ferrand. She asked about their careers,

---

47. See Piketty, *Les hauts revenus en France,* 530.
48. This argument sets aside the logic of need in favor of a logic of disproportion and conspicuous consumption. Thorstein Veblen said much the same thing in *The Theory of the Leisure Class* (New York: Macmillan, 1899): the egalitarian US dream was already a distant memory.

how they saw their social identity and place in society, and what differentiated them from other social groups and categories. One of the main conclusions of her study was that in both countries, the "educated elite" placed primary emphasis on their personal merit and moral qualities, which they described using terms such as rigor, patience, work, effort, and so on (but also tolerance, kindness, etc.).[49] The heroes and heroines in the novels of Austen and Balzac would never have seen the need to compare their personal qualities to those of their servants (who go unmentioned in their texts).

The Society of Petits Rentiers

The time has come to return to today's world, and more precisely to France in the 2010s. According to my estimates, inheritance will represent about one quarter of total lifetime resources (from both inheritance and labor) for cohorts born in the 1970s and after. In terms of total amounts involved, inheritance has thus nearly regained the importance it had for nineteenth-century cohorts (see Figure 11.9). I should add that these predictions are based on the central scenario: if the alternative scenario turns out to be closer to the truth (lower growth, higher net return on capital), inheritance could represent a third or even as much as four-tenths of the resources of twenty-first-century cohorts.[50]

---

49. Michèle Lamont, *Money, Morals and Manners: The Culture of the French and the American Upper-Middle Class* (Chicago: University of Chicago Press, 1992). The individuals Lamont interviewed were no doubt closer to the ninetieth or ninety-fifth percentile of the income hierarchy (or in some cases the ninety-eighth or ninety-ninth percentile) than to the sixtieth or seventieth percentile. See also J. Naudet, *Entrer dans l'élite: Parcours de réussite en France, aux États-Unis et en Inde* (Paris: Presses Universitaires de France, 2012).

50. In order to avoid painting too dark a picture, Figures 11.9–11 show only the results for the central scenario. The results for the alternative scenario are even more worrisome and are available online (Supplemental Figures S11.9–11). The evolution of the tax system explains why the share of inheritance in total resources may exceed its nineteenth-century level even if the inheritance flow as a

The fact that the total volume of inheritance has regained the same level as in the past does not mean that it plays the same social role, however. As noted, the very significant deconcentration of wealth (which has seen the top centile's share decrease by nearly two-thirds in a century from 60 percent in 1910–1920 to just over 20 percent today) and the emergence of a patrimonial middle class imply that there are far fewer very large estates today than there were in the nineteenth century. Concretely, the dowries of 500,000 francs that Père Goriot and César Birotteau sought for their daughters—dowries that yielded an annual rent of 25,000 francs, or 50 times the average annual per capita income of 500 francs at that time—would be equivalent to an estate of 30 million euros today, with a yield in interest, dividends, and rents on the order of 1.5 million euros a year (or 50 times the average per capita income of 30,000 euros).[51] Inheritances of this magnitude do exist, as do considerably larger ones, but there are far fewer of them than in the nineteenth century, even though the total volume of wealth and inheritance has practically regained its previous high level.

Furthermore, no contemporary novelist would fill her plots with estates valued at 30 million euros as Balzac, Austen, and James did. Explicit monetary references vanished from literature after inflation blurred the meaning of the traditional numbers. But more than that, rentiers themselves vanished from literature as well, and the whole social representation of inequality changed as a result. In contemporary fiction, inequalities between social groups appear almost exclusively in the form of disparities with respect to work, wages, and skills. A

---

proportion of national income does not. Labor incomes are taxed today at a substantial level (30 percent on average, excluding retirement and unemployment insurance contributions), whereas the average effective tax rate on inheritances is less than 5 percent (even though inheritance gives rise to the same rights as labor income in regard to access to transfers in kind—education, health, security, etc.—which are financed by taxes). The tax issues are examined in Part Four.

51. The same is true of the landed estates worth 30,000 pounds of which Jane Austen speaks in a world where the average per capita income was around 30 pounds a year.

society structured by the hierarchy of wealth has been replaced by a society whose structure depends almost entirely on the hierarchy of labor and human capital. It is striking, for example, that many recent American TV series feature heroes and heroines laden with degrees and high-level skills, whether to cure serious maladies (*House*), solve mysterious crimes (*Bones*), or even to preside over the United States (*West Wing*). The writers apparently believe that it is best to have several doctorates or even a Nobel Prize. It is not unreasonable to interpret any number of such series as offering a hymn to a just inequality, based on merit, education, and the social utility of elites. Still, certain more recent creations depict a more worrisome inequality, based more clearly on vast wealth. *Damages* depicts unfeeling big businessmen who have stolen hundreds of millions of dollars from their workers and whose even more selfish spouses want to divorce their husbands without giving up the cash or the swimming pool. In season 3, inspired by the Madoff affair, the children of the crooked financier do everything they can to hold on to their father's assets, which are stashed in Antigua, in order to maintain their high standard of living.[52] In *Dirty Sexy Money* we see decadent young heirs and heiresses with little merit or virtue living shamelessly on family money. But these are the exceptions that prove the rule, and any character who lives on wealth accumulated in the past is normally depicted in a negative light, if not frankly denounced, whereas such a life is perfectly natural in Austen and Balzac and necessary if there are to be any true feelings among the characters.

This huge change in the social representation of inequality is in part justified, yet it rests on a number of misunderstandings. First, it is obvious that education plays a more important role today than in the

52. A fortune hidden in the Bahamas also figures in season 4 of *Desperate Housewives* (Carlos Solis has to get back his $10 million, which leads to endless complications with his wife), even though the show is as saccharine as could be and not out to portray social inequalities in a worrisome light, unless, of course, it is a matter of cunning ecological terrorists who threaten the established order or mentally handicapped minorities engaged in a conspiracy.

eighteenth century. (In a world where nearly everyone possesses some kind of degree and certain skills, it is not a good idea to go without: it is in everyone's interest to acquire some skill, even those who stand to inherit substantial wealth, especially since inheritance often comes too late from the standpoint of the heirs.) However, it does not follow that society has become more meritocratic. In particular, it does not follow that the share of national income going to labor has actually increased (as noted, it has not, in any substantial amount), and it certainly does not follow that everyone has access to the same opportunities to acquire skills of every variety. Indeed, inequalities of training have to a large extent simply been translated upward, and there is no evidence that education has really increased intergenerational mobility.[53] Nevertheless, the transmission of human capital is always more complicated than the transmission of financial capital or real estate (the heir must make some effort), and this has given rise to a widespread—and partially justified—faith in the idea that the end of inherited wealth has made for a more just society.

The chief misunderstanding is, I think, the following. First, inheritance did not come to an end: the distribution of inherited capital has changed, which is something else entirely. In France today, there are certainly fewer very large estates—estates of 30 million or even 5 or 10 million euros are less common—than in the nineteenth century. But since the total volume of inherited wealth has almost regained its previous level, it follows that there are many more substantial and even fairly large inheritances: 200,000, 500,000, 1 million, or even 2 million euros. Such bequests, though much too small to allow the beneficiaries to give up all thought of a career and live on the interest, are nevertheless substantial amounts, especially when compared with what much of the population earns over the course of a working lifetime. In other words, we have moved from a society with a small number of very wealthy rentiers to one with a much larger number of less wealthy rentiers: a society of petits rentiers if you will.

---

53. I will come back to this point in Chapter 13.

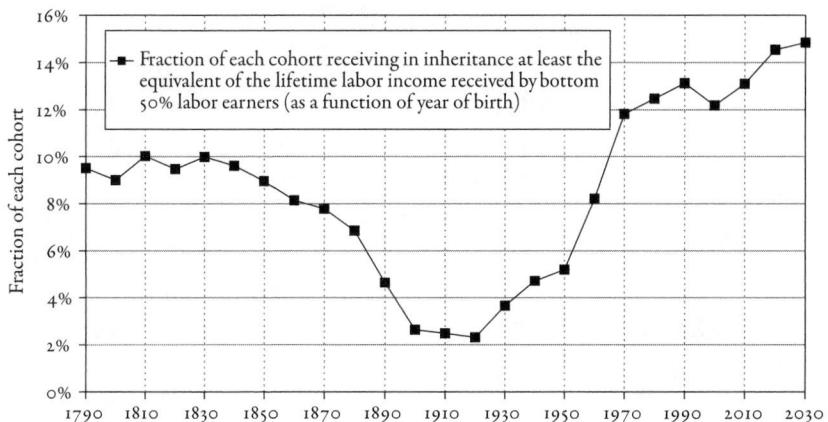

FIGURE II.II. Which fraction of a cohort receives in inheritance the equivalent of a lifetime labor income?

Within the cohorts born around 1970–1980, 12–14 percent of individuals receive in inheritance the equivalent of the lifetime labor income received by the bottom 50 percent less well paid workers.

Sources and series: see piketty.pse.ens.fr/capital21c.

The index that I think is most pertinent for representing this change is presented in Figure II.II. It is the percentage of individuals in each cohort who inherit (as bequest or gift) amounts larger than the least well paid 50 percent of the population earn in a lifetime. This amount changes over time: at present, the average annual wage of the bottom half of the income distribution is around 15,000 euros, or a total of 750,000 euros over the course of a fifty-year career (including retirement). This is more or less what a life at minimum wage brings in. As the figure shows, in the nineteenth century about 10 percent of a cohort inherited amounts greater than this. This proportion fell to barely more than 2 percent for cohorts born in 1910–1920 and 4–5 percent for cohorts born in 1930–1950. According to my estimates, the proportion has already risen to about 12 percent for cohorts born in 1970–1980 and may reach or exceed 15 percent for cohorts born in 2010–2020. In other words, nearly one-sixth of each cohort will receive an inheritance larger than the amount the bottom half of the population earns through labor in a lifetime. (And this group largely coincides with the half of the population that inherits next to nothing.).[54] Of course, there is nothing to prevent the inheriting sixth from acquiring diplomas or working and no doubt earning more through work than the bottom half of the income distribution. This is nevertheless a fairly disturbing form of inequality, which is in the process of attaining historically unprecedented heights. It is also more difficult to represent artistically or to correct politically, because it is a commonplace inequality opposing broad segments of the population rather than pitting a small elite against the rest of society.

The Rentier, Enemy of Democracy

Second, there is no guarantee that the distribution of inherited capital will not ultimately become as inegalitarian in the twenty-first century as it was in the nineteenth. As noted in the previous chapter, there is no ineluctable force standing in the way of a return to extreme concentration of wealth, as extreme as in the Belle Époque, especially if growth slows and the return on capital increases, which could happen, for example, if tax competition between nations heats up. If this were to happen, I believe that it would lead to significant political upheaval. Our democratic societies rest on a meritocratic worldview, or at any rate a meritocratic hope, by which I mean a belief in a society in which inequality is based more on merit and effort than on kinship and rents. This belief and this hope play a very crucial role in modern society, for a simple reason: in a democracy, the professed equality of rights of all citizens contrasts sharply with the very real inequality of living conditions, and in order to overcome this contradiction it is vital to make sure that social inequalities derive from rational and universal principles rather than arbitrary contingencies. Inequalities must therefore be just and useful to all, at least in the realm of discourse and

---

54. If the alternative scenario is correct, this proportion may exceed 25 percent. See Supplemental Figure S11.11, available online.

as far as possible in reality as well. ("Social distinctions can be based only on common utility," according to article 1 of the 1789 Declaration of the Rights of Man and the Citizen.) In 1893, Emile Durkheim predicted that modern democratic society would not put up for long with the existence of inherited wealth and would ultimately see to it that ownership of property ended at death.[55]

It is also significant that the words "rent" and "rentier" took on highly pejorative connotations in the twentieth century. In this book, I use these words in their original descriptive sense, to denote the annual rents produced by a capital asset and the individuals who live on those rents. Today, the rents produced by an asset are nothing other than the income on capital, whether in the form of rent, interest, dividends, profits, royalties, or any other legal category of revenue, provided that such income is simply remuneration for ownership of the asset, independent of any labor. It was in this original sense that the words "rent" and "rentiers" were used in the eighteenth and nineteenth centuries, for example in the novels of Balzac and Austen, at a time when the domination of wealth and its income at the top of the income hierarchy was acknowledged and accepted, at least among the elite. It is striking to observe that this original meaning largely disappeared as democratic and meritocratic values took hold. During the twentieth century, the word "rent" became an insult and a rather abusive one. This linguistic change can be observed everywhere.

It is particularly interesting to note that the word "rent" is often used nowadays in a very different sense: to denote an imperfection in the market (as in "monopoly rent"), or, more generally, to refer to any undue or unjustified income. At times, one almost has the impression that "rent" has become synonymous with "economic ill." Rent is the enemy of modern rationality and must be eliminated root and branch

---

55. Compared with the socioeconomic theories of Modigliani, Becker, and Parsons, Durkheim's theory, formulated in *De la division du travail social* (1893), is primarily a political theory of the end of inheritance. Its prediction has proved no more accurate than those of the other theories, but it may be that the wars of the twentieth century merely postponed the problem to the twenty-first.

by striving for ever purer and more perfect competition. A typical example of this use of the word can be seen in a recent interview that the president of the European Central Bank granted to several major European newspapers a few months after his nomination. When the journalists posed questions about his strategy for resolving Europe's problems, he offered this lapidary response: "We must fight against rents."[56] No further details were offered. What the central banker had in mind, apparently, was lack of competition in the service sector: taxi drivers, hairdressers, and the like were presumably making too much money.[57]

The problem posed by this use of the word "rent" is very simple: the fact that capital yields income, which in accordance with the original meaning of the word we refer to in this book as "annual rent produced by capital," has absolutely nothing to do with the problem of imperfect competition or monopoly. If capital plays a useful role in the process of production, it is natural that it should be paid. When growth is slow, it is almost inevitable that this return on capital is significantly higher than the growth rate, which automatically bestows outsized importance on inequalities of wealth accumulated in the past. This logical contradiction cannot be resolved by a dose of additional competition. Rent is not an imperfection in the market: it is rather the consequence of a "pure and perfect" market for capital, as economists understand it: a capital market in which each owner of capital, including the least capable of heirs, can obtain the highest possible yield on the most diversified portfolio that can be assembled in the national or global economy. To be sure, there is something astonishing about the notion that capital yields rent, or income that the owner of capital obtains without working. There is something in this notion that is an affront to common sense and that has in fact per-

---

56. Mario Draghi, *Le Monde,* July 22, 2012.
57. I do not mean to underestimate the importance of the taxi problem. But I would not venture to suggest that this is the foremost problem faced by Europe or global capitalism in the twenty-first century.

turbed any number of civilizations, which have responded in various ways, not always benign, ranging from the prohibition of usury to Soviet-style communism. Nevertheless, rent is a reality in any market economy where capital is privately owned. The fact that landed capital became industrial and financial capital and real estate left this deeper reality unchanged. Some people think that the logic of economic development has been to undermine the distinction between labor and capital. In fact, it is just the opposite: the growing sophistication of capital markets and financial intermediation tends to separate owners from managers more and more and thus to sharpen the distinction between pure capital income and labor income. Economic and technological rationality at times has nothing to do with democratic rationality. The former stems from the Enlightenment, and people have all too commonly assumed that the latter would somehow naturally derive from it, as if by magic. But real democracy and social justice require specific institutions of their own, not just those of the market, and not just parliaments and other formal democratic institutions.

To recapitulate: the fundamental force for divergence, which I have emphasized throughout this book, can be summed up in the inequality $r > g$, which has nothing to do with market imperfections and will not disappear as markets become freer and more competitive. The idea that unrestricted competition will put an end to inheritance and move toward a more meritocratic world is a dangerous illusion. The advent of universal suffrage and the end of property qualifications for voting (which in the nineteenth century limited the right to vote to people meeting a minimum wealth requirement, typically the wealthiest 1 or 2 percent in France and Britain in 1820–1840, or about the same percentage of the population as was subject to the wealth tax in France in 2000–2010), ended the legal domination of politics by the wealthy.[58] But it did not abolish the economic forces capable of producing a society of rentiers.

---

58. In France, fewer than 1 percent of adult males had the right to vote under the Restoration (90,000 voters out of 10 million); this proportion rose to 2 percent

The Return of Inherited Wealth: A European or Global Phenomenon?

Can our results concerning the return of inherited wealth in France be extended to other countries? In view of the limitations of the available data, it is unfortunately impossible to give a precise answer to this question. There are apparently no other countries with estate records as rich and comprehensive as the French data. Nevertheless, a number of points seem to be well established. First, the imperfect data collected to date for other European countries, especially Germany and Britain, suggest that the U-shaped curve of inheritance flows in France in the twentieth century actually reflects the reality everywhere in Europe (see Figure 11.12).

In Germany, in particular, available estimates—unfortunately based on a limited number of years—suggest that inheritance flows collapsed even further than in France following the shocks of 1914–1945, from about 16 percent of national income in 1910 to just 2 percent in 1960. Since then they have risen sharply and steadily, with an acceleration in 1980–1990, until in 2000–2010 they attained a level of 10–11 percent of national income. This is lower than in France (where the figure for 2010 was about 15 percent of national income), but since Germany started from a lower point in 1950–1960, the rebound of inheritance flows has actually been stronger there. In addition, the current difference between flows in France and Germany is entirely due to the difference in the capital / income ratio (β, presented in Part Two). If total private wealth in Germany were to rise to the same level as in France, the inheritance flows would also equalize (all other things being equal). It is also interesting to note that the strong rebound of inheritance flows in Germany is largely due to a very sharp increase in

---

under the July Monarchy. Property requirements for holding office were even stricter: fewer than 0.2 percent of adult males met them. Universal male suffrage, briefly introduced in 1793, became the norm after 1848. Less than 2 percent of the British population could vote until 1831. Subsequent reforms in 1831 and especially 1867, 1884, and 1918 gradually put an end to property qualifications.

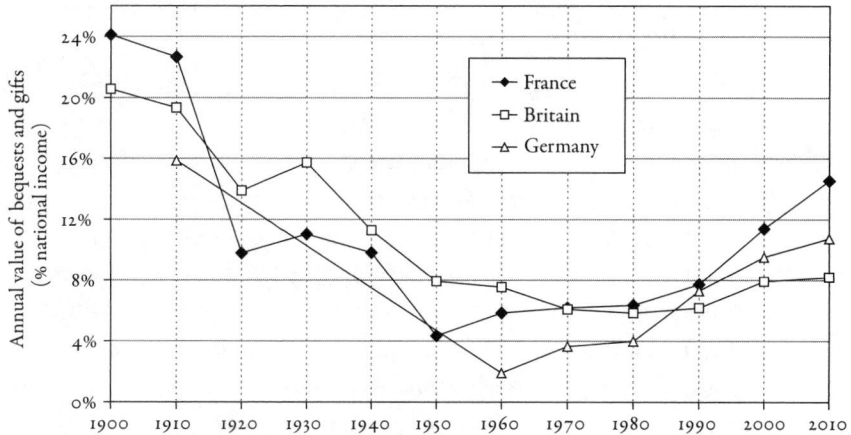

FIGURE 11.12. The inheritance flow in Europe, 1900–2010

The inheritance flow follows a U-shape in curve in France as well as in the United Kingdom and Germany. It is possible that gifts are underestimated in the United Kingdom at the end of the period.

Sources and series: see piketty.pse.ens.fr/capital21c.

gifts, just as in France. The annual volume of gifts recorded by the German authorities represented the equivalent of 10–20 percent of the total amount of inheritances before 1970–1980. Thereafter it rose gradually to about 60 percent in 2000–2010. Finally, the smaller inheritance flow in Germany in 1910 was largely a result of more rapid demographic growth north of the Rhine at that time (the "m effect," as it were). By the same token, because German demographic growth today is stagnant, it is possible that inheritance flows there will exceed those in France in the decades to come.[59] Other European countries affected by demographic decline and a falling birthrate, such as Italy and Spain, should obey a similar logic, although we unfortunately have no reliable historical data on inheritance flows in these two cases.

---

59. The German data presented here were collected by Christoph Schinke, "Inheritance in Germany 1911 to 2009: A Mortality Multiplier Approach," Master's thesis, Paris School of Economics, 2012. See the online technical appendix.

As for Britain, inheritance flows there at the turn of the twentieth century were approximately the same as in France: 20–25 percent of national income.[60] The inheritance flow did not fall as far as in France or Germany after the two world wars, and this seems consistent with the fact that the stock of private wealth was less violently affected (the β effect) and that wealth accumulation was not set back as far (μ effect). The annual inheritance and gift flow fell to about 8 percent of national income in 1950–1960 and to 6 percent in 1970–1980. The rebound since the 1980s has been significant but not as strong as in France or Germany: according to the available data, the inheritance flow in Britain in 2000–2010 was just over 8 percent of national income.

In the abstract, several explanations are possible. The lower British inheritance flow might be due to the fact that a larger share of private wealth is held in pension funds and is therefore not transmissible to descendants. This can only be a small part of the explanation, however, because pension funds account for only 15–20 percent of the British private capital stock. Furthermore, it is by no means certain that life-cycle wealth is supplanting transmissible wealth: logically speaking, the two types of wealth should be added together, so that a country that relies more on pension funds to finance its retirements should be able to accumulate a larger total stock of private wealth and perhaps to invest part of this in other countries.[61]

It is also possible that the lower inheritance flow in Britain is due to different psychological attitudes toward savings and familial gifts and

---

60. The British flows seem to have been slightly smaller (20–21 percent rather than 23–24 percent). Note, however, that this is based on an estimate of the fiscal flow and not the economic flow and is therefore likely to be slightly too low. The British data were collected by Anthony Atkinson, "Wealth and Inheritance in Britain from 1896 to the Present," London School of Economics, 2012.

61. If this were to happen at the global level, the global return on capital might decrease, and greater life-cycle wealth might in part supplant transmissible wealth (because a lower return on capital discourages the second type of accumulation more than the first, which is not certain). I will come back to these questions in Chapter 12.

bequests. Before reaching that conclusion, however, it is important to note that the difference observed in 2000–2010 can be explained entirely by a lower level of gift giving in Britain, where gifts have remained stable at about 10 percent of the total amount of inheritances since 1970–1980, whereas gift giving in France and Germany increased to 60–80 percent of the total. Given the difficulty of recording gifts and correcting for different national practices, the gap seems somewhat suspect, and it cannot be ruled out that it is due, at least in part, to an underestimation of gift giving in Britain. In the current state of the data, it is unfortunately impossible to say with certainty whether the smaller rebound of inheritance flows in Britain reflects an actual difference in behavior (Britons with means consume more of their wealth and pass on less to their children than their French and German counterparts) or a purely statistical bias. (If we applied the same gift / inheritance ratio that we observe in France and Germany, the British inheritance flow in 2000–2010 would be on the order of 15 percent of national income, as in France.)

The available inheritance sources for the United States pose even more difficult problems. The federal estate tax, created in 1916, has never applied to more than a small minority of estates (generally less than 2 percent), and the requirements for declaring gifts are also fairly limited, so that the statistical data derived from this tax leave much to be desired. It is unfortunately impossible to make up for this lack by relying on other sources. In particular, bequests and gifts are notoriously underestimated in surveys conducted by national statistical bureaus. This leaves major gaps in our knowledge, which all too many studies based on such surveys forget. In France, for example, we find that gifts and bequests declared in the surveys represent barely half the flow observed in the fiscal data (which is only a lower bound on the actual flow, since exempt assets such as life insurance contracts are omitted). Clearly, the individuals surveyed tend to forget to declare what they actually received and to present the history of their fortunes in the most favorable light (which is in itself an interesting fact about how inheritance is seen in modern society).[62] In many countries, including the United States, it is unfortunately impossible to compare the survey data with fiscal records. But there is no reason to believe that the underestimation by survey participants is any smaller than in France, especially since the public perception of inherited wealth is at least as negative in the United States.

In any case, the unreliability of the US sources makes it very difficult to study the historical evolution of inheritance flows in the United States with any precision. This partly explains the intensity of the controversy that erupted in the 1980s over two diametrically opposed economic theories: Modigliani's life-cycle theory, and with it the idea that inherited wealth accounts for only 20–30 percent of total US capital, and the Kotlikoff-Summers thesis, according to which inherited wealth accounts for 70–80 percent of total capital. I was a young student when I discovered this work in the 1990s, and the controversy stunned me: how could such a dramatic disagreement exist among serious economists? Note, first of all, that both sides in the dispute relied on rather poor quality data from the late 1960s and early 1970s. If we reexamine their estimates in light of the data available today, it seems that the truth lies somewhere between the two positions but significantly closer to Kotlikoff-Summers than Modigliani: inherited wealth probably accounted for at least 50–60 percent of total private capital in the United States in 1970–1980.[63] More generally, if one tries to estimate for the United States the evolution of the share of inherited wealth over the course of the twentieth century, as we did for France in Figure 11.7 (on the basis of much more complete

---

62. On this subject see the remarkable book by Anne Gotman, *Dilapidation et prodigalité* (Paris: Nathan, 1995), based on interviews with individuals who squandered large fortunes.

63. In particular, Modigliani quite simply failed to include capitalized incomes in inherited wealth. Kotlikoff and Summers, for their part, did take these into account without limit (even if the capitalized inheritance exceeded the wealth of the heir), which is also incorrect. See the online technical appendix for a detailed analysis of these questions.

data), it seems that the U-shaped curve was less pronounced in the United States and that the share of inherited wealth was somewhat smaller than in France at both the turn of the twentieth century and the turn of the twenty-first (and slightly larger in 1950–1970). The main reason for this is the higher rate of demographic growth in the United States, which implies a smaller capital / income ratio (β effect) and a less pronounced aging of wealth (m and μ effects). The difference should not be exaggerated, however: inheritance also plays an important role in the United States. Above all, it once again bears emphasizing that this difference between Europe and the United States has little to do a priori with eternal cultural differences: it seems to be explained mainly by differences in demographic structure and population growth. If population growth in the United States someday decreases, as long-term forecasts suggest it will, then inherited wealth will probably rebound as strongly there as in Europe.

As for the poor and emerging countries, we unfortunately lack reliable historical sources concerning inherited wealth and its evolution. It seems plausible that if demographic and economic growth ultimately decrease, as they are likely to do this century, then inherited wealth will acquire as much importance in most countries as it has had in low-growth countries throughout history. In countries that experience negative demographic growth, inherited wealth could even take on hitherto unprecedented importance. It is important to point out, however, that this will take time. With the rate of growth currently observed in emergent countries such as China, it seems clear that inheritance flows are for the time being quite limited. For working-age Chinese, who are currently experiencing income growth of 5–10 percent a year, wealth in the vast majority of cases comes primarily from savings and not from grandparents, whose income was many times smaller. The global rebound of inherited wealth will no doubt be an important feature of the twenty-first century, but for some decades to come it will affect mainly Europe and to a lesser degree the United States.

TWELVE

Global Inequality of Wealth in the Twenty-First Century

I have thus far adopted a too narrowly national point of view concerning the dynamics of wealth inequality. To be sure, the crucial role of foreign assets owned by citizens of Britain and France in the nineteenth and early twentieth centuries has been mentioned several times, but more needs to be said, because the question of international inequality of wealth concerns the future above all. Hence I turn now to the dynamics of wealth inequality at the global level and to the principal forces at work today. Is there a danger that the forces of financial globalization will lead to an even greater concentration of capital in the future than ever before? Has this not perhaps already happened?

To begin my examination of this question, I will look first at individual fortunes: Will the share of capital owned by the people listed by magazines as "the richest in the world" increase in the twenty-first century? Then I will ask about inequalities between countries: Will today's wealthy countries end up owned by petroleum exporting states or China or perhaps by their own billionaires? But before doing either of these things, I must discuss a hitherto neglected force, which will play an essential role in the analysis: unequal returns on capital.

The Inequality of Returns on Capital

Many economic models assume that the return on capital is the same for all owners, no matter how large or small their fortunes. This is far from certain, however: it is perfectly possible that wealthier people obtain higher average returns than less wealthy people. There are several reasons why this might be the case. The most obvious one is that a person with 10 million euros rather than 100,000, or 1 billion euros rather than 10 million, has greater means to employ wealth management consultants and financial advisors. If such intermediaries make it possible to identify better investments, on average, there may be "economies of scale" in portfolio management that give rise to higher average returns on larger portfolios. A second reason is that it is easier for an investor to take risks, and to be patient, if she has substantial reserves than if she owns next to nothing. For both of these reasons—and all signs are that the first is more important in practice than the second—it is quite plausible to think that if the average return on capital is 4 percent, wealthier people might get as much as 6 or 7 percent, whereas less wealthy individuals might have to make do with as little as 2 or 3 percent. Indeed, I will show in a moment that around the world, the largest fortunes (including inherited ones) have grown at very high rates in recent decades (on the order of 6–7 percent a year)—significantly higher than the average growth rate of wealth.

It is easy to see that such a mechanism can automatically lead to a radical divergence in the distribution of capital. If the fortunes of the top decile or top centile of the global wealth hierarchy grow faster for structural reasons than the fortunes of the lower deciles, then inequality of wealth will of course tend to increase without limit. This inegalitarian process may take on unprecedented proportions in the new global economy. In view of the law of compound interest discussed in Chapter 1, it is also clear that this mechanism can account for very rapid divergence, so that if there is nothing to counteract it, very large fortunes can attain extreme levels within a few decades. Thus unequal returns on capital are a force for divergence that significantly amplifies and aggravates the effects of the inequality $r > g$. Indeed, the difference $r - g$ can be high for large fortunes without necessarily being high for the economy as a whole.

In strict logic, the only "natural" countervailing force (where by "natural" I mean not involving government intervention) is once again growth. If the global growth rate is high, the relative growth rate of very large fortunes will remain moderate—not much higher than the average growth rate of income and wealth. Concretely, if the global growth rate is 3.5 percent a year, as was the case between 1990 and 2012 and may continue to be the case until 2030, the largest fortunes will still grow more rapidly than the rest but less spectacularly so than if the global growth rate were only 1 or 2 percent. Furthermore, today's global growth rate includes a large demographic component, and wealthy people from emerging economies are rapidly joining the ranks of the wealthiest people in the world. This gives the impression that the ranks of the wealthiest are changing rapidly, while leading many people in the wealthy countries to feel an oppressive and growing sense that they are falling behind. The resulting anxiety sometimes outweighs all other concerns. Yet in the long run, if and when the poor countries have caught up with the rich ones and global growth slows, the inequality of returns on capital should be of far greater concern. In the long run, unequal wealth within nations is surely more worrisome than unequal wealth between nations.

I will begin to tackle the question of unequal returns on capital by looking at international wealth rankings. Then I will look at the returns obtained by the endowments of major US universities. This might seem like anecdotal evidence, but it will enable us to analyze in a clear and dispassionate way unequal returns as a function of portfolio size. I will then examine the returns on sovereign wealth funds, in particular those of the petroleum exporting countries and China, and this will bring the discussion back to the question of inequalities of wealth between countries.

The Evolution of Global Wealth Rankings

Economists as a general rule do not have much respect for the wealth rankings published by magazines such as *Forbes* in the United States and other weeklies in many countries around the world. Indeed, such rankings suffer from important biases and serious methodological problems (to put it mildly). But at least they exist, and in their way they respond to a legitimate and pressing social demand for information about a major issue of the day: the global distribution of wealth and its evolution over time. Economists should take note. It is important, moreover, to recognize that we suffer from a serious lack of reliable information about the global dynamics of wealth. National governments and statistical agencies cannot begin to keep up with the globalization of capital, and the tools they use, such as household surveys confined to a single country, are insufficient for analyzing how things are evolving in the twenty-first century. The magazines' wealth rankings can and must be improved by comparison with government statistics, tax records, and bank data, but it would be absurd and counterproductive to ignore the magazine rankings altogether, especially since these supplementary sources are at present very poorly coordinated at the global level. I will therefore examine what useful information can be derived from these league tables of wealth.

The oldest and most systematic ranking of large fortunes is the global list of billionaires that *Forbes* has published since 1987. Every year, the magazine's journalists try to compile from all kinds of sources a complete list of everyone in the world whose net worth exceeds a billion dollars. The list was led by a Japanese billionaire from 1987 to 1995, then an American one from 1995 to 2009, and finally a Mexican since 2010. According to *Forbes,* the planet was home to just over 140 billionaires in 1987 but counts more than 1,400 today (2013), an increase by a factor of 10 (see Figure 12.1). In view of inflation and global economic growth since 1987, however, these spectacular numbers, repeated every year by media around the world, are difficult to interpret. If we look at the numbers in relation to the global population and total private wealth, we obtain the following results, which make somewhat more sense. The planet boasted barely 5 billionaires per 100 million adults in 1987 and 30 in 2013. Billionaires owned just 0.4 percent of global private wealth in 1987 but more than 1.5 percent in 2013, which is above the previous record attained in 2008, on the eve of the global financial crisis and the bankruptcy of Lehman Brothers (see

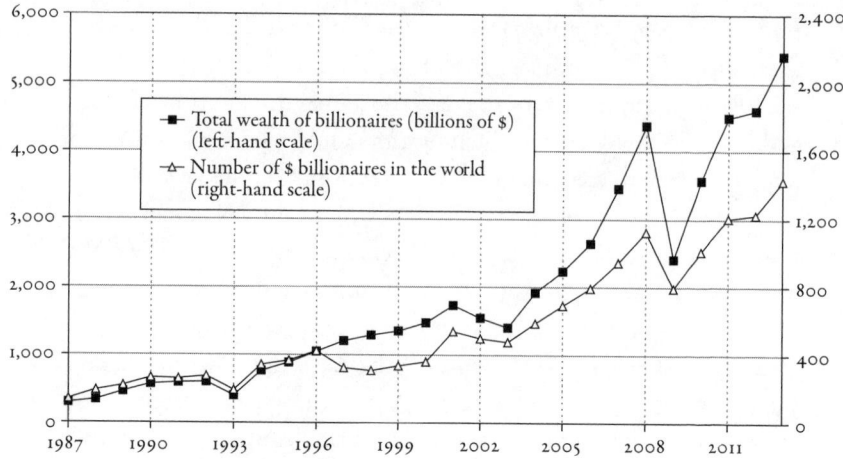

FIGURE 12.1. The world's billionaires according to *Forbes*, 1987–2013

Between 1987 and 2013, the number of $ billionaires rose according to *Forbes* from 140 to 1,400, and their total wealth rose from 300 to 5,400 billion dollars.

Sources and series: see piketty.pse.ens.fr/capital21c.

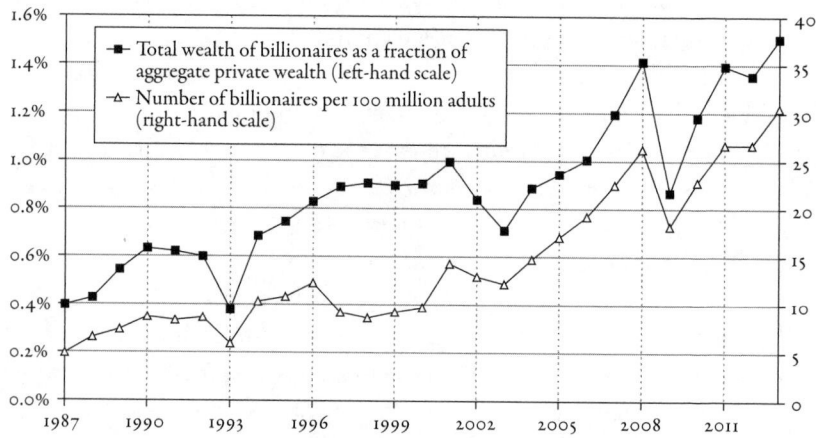

FIGURE 12.2. Billionaires as a fraction of global population and wealth, 1987–2013

Between 1987 and 2013, the number of billionaires per 100 million adults rose from five to thirty, and their share in aggregate private wealth rose from 0.4 percent to 1.5 percent.

Sources and series: see piketty.pse.ens.fr/capital21c.

Figure 12.2).[1] This is an obscure way of presenting the data, however: there is nothing really surprising about the fact that a group containing 6 times as many people as a proportion of the population should own 4 times as great a proportion of the world's wealth.

The only way to make sense of these wealth rankings is to examine the evolution of the amount of wealth owned by a fixed percentage of the world's population, say the richest twenty-millionth of the adult population of the planet: roughly 150 people out of 3 billion adults in the late 1980s and 225 people out of 4.5 billion in the early 2010s. We then find that the average wealth of this group has increased from just over \$1.5 billion in 1987 to nearly \$15 billion in 2013, for an average growth rate of 6.4 percent above inflation.[2] If we now consider the one-hundred-millionth wealthiest part of the world's population, or about 30 people out of 3 billion in the late 1980s and 45 out of 4.5 billion in the early 2010s, we find that their average wealth increased from just over \$3 billion to almost \$35 billion, for an even higher growth rate of 6.8 percent above inflation. For the sake of comparison, average global wealth per capita increased by 2.1 percent a year, and average global income by 1.4 percent a year, as indicated in Table 12.1.[3]

To sum up: since the 1980s, global wealth has increased on average a little faster than income (this is the upward trend in the capital / income ratio examined in Part Two), and the largest fortunes grew much more

---

1. Recall that global GDP, using purchasing power parity, was roughly \$85 trillion (65 trillion euros) in 2012–2013, and according to my estimates total private wealth (real estate, business, and financial assets, net of liabilities) was around four years of global GDP, or about \$340 trillion (250 trillion euros). See Chapters 1 and 6 and the online technical appendix.

2. Inflation in this period averaged 2–2.5 percent a year (and was somewhat lower in euros than in dollars; see Chapter 1). All the detailed series are available in the online technical appendix.

3. If one calculates these averages with respect to the total world population (including children as well as adults), which grew considerably less than the adult population in the period 1987–2013 (1.3 percent a year compared with 1.9 percent), all the growth rates increase, but the differences between them do not change. See Chapter 1 and the online technical appendix.

TABLE 12.1.

The growth rate of top global wealth, 1987–2013

	Average real growth rate per year (after deduction of inflation) (%)
The top 1 / (100 million) highest wealth holders[a]	6.8
The top 1 / (20 million) highest wealth holders[b]	6.4
Average world wealth per adult	2.1
Average world income per adult	1.4
World adult population	1.9
World GDP	3.3

Note: Between 1987 and 2013, the highest global wealth fractiles have grown at 6%–7% per year versus 2.1% for average world wealth and 1.4% for average world income. All growth rates are net of inflation (2.3% per year between 1987 and 2013).

  a. About 30 adults out of 3 billion in the 1980s, and 45 adults out of 4.5 billion in 2010.

  b. About 150 adults out of 3 billion in the 1980s, and 225 adults out of 4.5 billion in the 2010s.

Sources: See piketty.pse.ens.fr/capital21c.

rapidly than average wealth. This is the new fact that the *Forbes* rankings help us bring to light, assuming that they are reliable.

Note that the precise conclusions depend quite heavily on the years chosen for consideration. For example, if we look at the period 1990–2010 instead of 1987–2013, the real rate of growth of the largest fortunes drops to 4 percent a year instead of 6 or 7.[4] This is because 1990 marked a peak in global stock and real estate prices, while 2010 was a fairly low point for both (see Figure 12.2). Nevertheless, no matter what years we choose, the structural rate of growth of the largest fortunes seems always to be greater than the average growth of the average fortune (roughly at least twice as great). If we look at the evolution of the shares of the various millionths of large fortunes in global wealth, we find increases by more than a factor of 3 in less than thirty years (see Figure 12.3). To be

4. See the online technical appendix, Supplemental Table S12.1, available online.

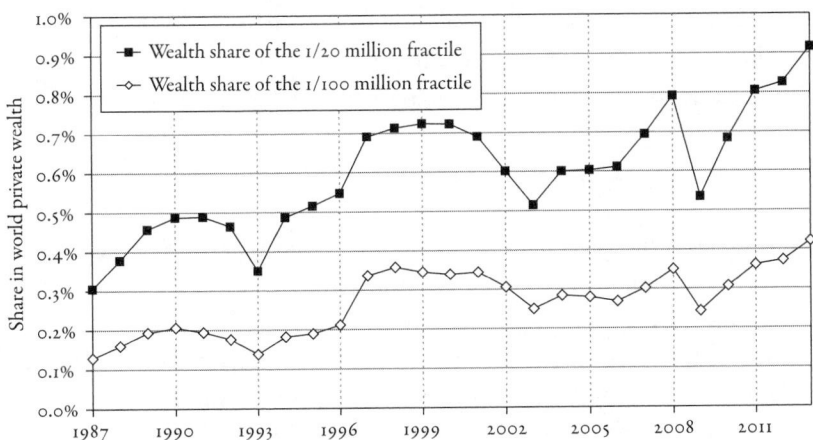

FIGURE 12.3. The share of top wealth fractiles in world wealth, 1987–2013

Between 1987 and 2013, the share of the top 1/20 million fractile rose from 0.3 percent to 0.9 percent of world wealth, and the share of the top 1/100 million fractile rose from 0.1 percent to 0.4 percent.

Sources and series: see piketty.pse.ens.fr/capital21c.

sure, the amounts remain relatively small when expressed as a proportion of global wealth, but the rate of divergence is nevertheless spectacular. If such an evolution were to continue indefinitely, the share of these extremely tiny groups could reach quite substantial levels by the end of the twenty-first century.[5]

Can this conclusion perhaps be extended to broader segments of the global wealth distribution, in which case the divergence would occur much more rapidly? The first problem with the *Forbes* and other magazine rankings is that they list too few people to be truly significant in macroeconomic terms. Regardless of the rapid rates of divergence and the extreme size of certain individual fortunes, the data pertain to only a

---

5. For example, if we assume that the rate of divergence observed between 1987 and 2013 at the level of the top twenty-millionth will continue to apply in the future to the fractile consisting of the 1,400 billionaires included in the 2013 ranking (roughly the top three-millionths), the share of this fractile will increase from 1.5 percent of total global wealth in 2013 to 7.2 percent in 2050 and 59.6 percent in 2100.

few hundred or at most a few thousand individuals, who at the present time represent only a little over 1 percent of global wealth.[6] This leaves out nearly 99 percent of global capital, which is unfortunate.[7]

From Rankings of Billionaires to "Global Wealth Reports"

To proceed further and estimate the shares of the top decile, centile, and thousandth of the global wealth hierarchy, we need to use fiscal and statistical sources of the type I relied on in Chapter 10. There I showed that inequality of wealth has been trending upward in all the rich countries since 1980–1990, so it would not be surprising to discover that the same was true at the global level. Unfortunately, the available sources are marred by numerous approximations. (We may be underestimating the upward trend in the rich countries, and the statistics from many of the emerging countries are so inadequate, in part owing to the absence of any system of progressive taxation worthy of the name, that one hesitates to use them.) Hence it is quite difficult at present to arrive at anything close to a precise estimate of the evolving shares of the top decile, centile, and thousandth in global wealth.

For some years now, a number of international financial institutions have attempted to respond to growing social demand for information on these issues by trying to extend the magazine rankings and publishing "global wealth reports" that include more than just billionaires. In particular, since 2010, Crédit Suisse, one of the leading Swiss banks, has published an ambitious annual report on the global distri-

---

6. The national wealth rankings published by other magazines in the United States, France, Britain, and Germany reach a little lower in the wealth hierarchy than *Forbes's* global ranking, and the share of wealth covered in some cases is as high as 2 or 3 percent of the country's total private wealth. See the online technical appendix.

7. In the media, the wealth of billionaires is sometimes expressed as a proportion of the annual flow of global output (or of the GDP of some country, which gives frightening results). This makes more sense than to express these large fortunes as a proportion of the global capital stock.

bution of wealth covering the entire population of the planet.[8] Other banks, brokerages, and insurance companies (Merrill Lynch, Allianz, etc.) have specialized in the study of the world's millionaires (the famous HNWI, or "high net worth individuals"). Every institution wants its own report, preferably on glossy paper. It is of course ironic to see institutions that make much of their money by managing fortunes filling the role of government statistical agencies by seeking to produce objective information about the global distribution of wealth. It is also important to note that these reports must often rely on heroic hypotheses and approximations, not all of them convincing, in order to arrive at anything like a "global" view of wealth. In any case, they rarely cover anything more than the past few years, a decade at most, and are unfortunately useless for studying long-term evolutions or even reliably detecting trends in global inequality, given the extremely piecemeal nature of the data used.[9]

Like the *Forbes* and similar rankings, these reports have, if nothing else, the merit of existing, and the absence of anything better points up the failure of national and international agencies—and most economists—to play the role they ought to be playing. Democratic transparency requires it: in the absence of reliable information about the global distribution of wealth, it is possible to say anything and everything and to feed fantasies of all kinds. Imperfect as they are, and until better information comes along, these reports can at least impose some discipline on public debate.[10]

---

8. These reports rely in particular on the innovative work of James B. Davies, Susanna Sandström, Anthony Shorrocks, and Edward N. Wolff, "The Level and Distribution of Global Household Wealth," *Economic Journal* 121, no. 551 (March 2011): 223–54, and on data of the type presented in Chapter 10. See the online technical appendix.

9. Generally speaking, the sources used to estimate wealth distributions (separately for each country) pertain to years some distance in the past, updated almost exclusively with aggregate data taken from national accounts and similar sources. See the online technical appendix.

10. For example, the French media, accustomed for years to describing a massive flight of large fortunes from France (without really trying to verify the informa-

If we adopt the same global approach as these reports and compare the various available estimates, we come to the following approximate conclusion: global inequality of wealth in the early 2010s appears to be comparable in magnitude to that observed in Europe in 1900–1910. The top thousandth seems to own nearly 20 percent of total global wealth today, the top centile about 50 percent, and the top decile somewhere between 80 and 90 percent. The bottom half of the global wealth distribution undoubtedly owns less than 5 percent of total global wealth.

Concretely, the wealthiest 0.1 percent of people on the planet, some 4.5 million out of an adult population of 4.5 billion, apparently possess fortunes on the order of 10 million euros on average, or nearly 200 times average global wealth of 60,000 euros per adult, amounting in aggregate to nearly 20 percent of total global wealth. The wealthiest 1 percent—45 million people out of 4.5 billion—have about 3 million euros apiece on average (broadly speaking, this group consists of those individuals whose personal fortunes exceed 1 million euros). This is about 50 times the size of the average global fortune, or 50 percent of total global wealth in aggregate.

Bear in mind that these estimates are highly uncertain (including the figures given for total and average global wealth). Even more than most of the statistics cited in this book, these numbers should be taken simply as orders of magnitude, useful only for focusing one's thoughts.[11]

Note, too, that this very high concentration of wealth, significantly higher than is observed within countries, stems in large part from international inequalities. The average global fortune is barely 60,000

---

tion other than by anecdote), have been astonished to learn every fall since 2010 from the Crédit Suisse reports that France is apparently the European wealth leader: the country is systematically ranked number 3 worldwide (behind the United States and Japan and well ahead of Britain and Germany) in number of millionaire residents. In this case, the information seems to be correct (as far as it is possible to judge from available sources), even if the bank's methods tend to exaggerate the difference between France and Germany. See the online technical appendix.

11. See the online technical appendix.

euros per adult, so that many people in the developed countries, including members of the "patrimonial middle class," seem quite wealthy in terms of the global wealth hierarchy. For the same reason, it is by no means certain that inequalities of wealth are actually increasing at the global level: as the poorer countries catch up with the richer ones, catch-up effects may for the moment outweigh the forces of divergence. The available data do not allow for a clear answer at this point.[12]

The information at our disposal suggests, however, that the forces of divergence at the top of the global wealth hierarchy are already very powerful. This is true not only for the billion-dollar fortunes in the *Forbes* ranking but probably also for smaller fortunes of 10–100 million euros. This is a much larger group of people: the top thousandth (a group of 4.5 million individuals with an average fortune of 10 million euros) owns about 20 percent of global wealth, which is much more than the 1.5 percent owned by the *Forbes* billionaires.[13] It is therefore essential to understand the magnitude of the divergence mechanism acting on this group, which depends in particular on unequal returns to capital in portfolios of this size. This will determine whether divergence at the top is sufficiently powerful to overcome the force of international catch-up. Is the divergence process occurring solely among billionaires, or is it also affecting the groups immediately below?

For example, if the top thousandth enjoy a 6 percent rate of return on their wealth, while average global wealth grows at only 2 percent a year, then after thirty years the top thousandth's share of global capital will have more than tripled. The top thousandth would then own 60

12. In terms of the global income distribution, it seems that the sharp increase in the share of the top centile (which is not happening in all countries) has not prevented a decrease in the global Gini coefficient (although there are large uncertainties in the measurement of inequality in certain countries, especially China). Since the global wealth distribution is much more concentrated at the top of the distribution, it is quite possible that the increase in the share of the top centiles matters more. See the online technical appendix.

13. The average fortune of the top ten-thousandth (450,000 adults out of 4.5 billion) is about 50 million euros, or nearly 1,000 times the global average wealth per adult, and their share of total global wealth is about 10 percent.

percent of global wealth, which is hard to imagine in the framework of existing political institutions unless there is a particularly effective system of repression or an extremely powerful apparatus of persuasion, or perhaps both. Even if the top thousandth's capital returned only 4 percent a year, their share would still practically double in thirty years to nearly 40 percent. Once again, the force for divergence at the top of the wealth hierarchy would win out over the global forces of catch-up and convergence, so that the shares of the top decile and centile would increase significantly, with a large upward redistribution from the middle and upper-middle classes to the very rich. Such an impoverishment of the middle class would very likely trigger a violent political reaction. It is of course impossible at this stage to be certain that such a scenario is about to unfold. But it is important to realize that the inequality $r > g$, amplified by inequality in the returns on capital as a function of initial portfolio size, can potentially give rise to a global dynamic of accumulation and distribution of wealth characterized by explosive trajectories and uncontrolled inegalitarian spirals. As we will see, only a progressive tax on capital can effectively impede such a dynamic.

Heirs and Entrepreneurs in the Wealth Rankings

One of the most striking lessons of the *Forbes* rankings is that, past a certain threshold, all large fortunes, whether inherited or entrepreneurial in origin, grow at extremely high rates, regardless of whether the owner of the fortune works or not. To be sure, one should be careful not to overestimate the precision of the conclusions one can draw from these data, which are based on a small number of observations and collected in a somewhat careless and piecemeal fashion. The fact is nevertheless interesting.

Take a particularly clear example at the very top of the global wealth hierarchy. Between 1990 and 2010, the fortune of Bill Gates—the founder of Microsoft, the world leader in operating systems, and the very incarnation of entrepreneurial wealth and number one in the *Forbes* rankings for more than ten years—increased from $4 billion to $50 billion.[14] At the same time, the fortune of Liliane Bettencourt—the heiress of L'Oréal, the world leader in cosmetics, founded by her father Eugène Schueller, who in 1907 invented a range of hair dyes that were destined to do well in a way reminiscent of César Birotteau's success with perfume a century earlier—increased from \$2 billion to \$25 billion, again according to *Forbes*.[15] Both fortunes thus grew at an annual rate of more than 13 percent from 1990 to 2010, equivalent to a real return on capital of 10 or 11 percent after correcting for inflation.

In other words, Liliane Bettencourt, who never worked a day in her life, saw her fortune grow exactly as fast as that of Bill Gates, the high-tech pioneer, whose wealth has incidentally continued to grow just as rapidly since he stopped working. Once a fortune is established, the capital grows according to a dynamic of its own, and it can continue to grow at a rapid pace for decades simply because of its size. Note, in particular, that once a fortune passes a certain threshold, size effects due to economies of scale in the management of the portfolio and opportunities for risk are reinforced by the fact that nearly all the income on this capital can be plowed back into investment. An individual with this level of wealth can easily live magnificently on an amount equivalent to only a few tenths of percent of his capital each year, and he can therefore reinvest nearly all of his income.[16] This is a basic but important economic mechanism, with dramatic consequences for the long-term

---

14. Bill Gates was number one in the *Forbes* rankings from 1995 to 2007, before losing out to Warren Buffet in 2008–2009 and then to Carlos Slim in 2010–2013.

15. The first dyes invented in 1907 were named "L'Auréale," after a hair style in vogue at the time and reminiscent of an aureole. Their invention led to the creation in 1909 of the French Company for Harmless Hair Dyes, which eventually, after the creation of many other brands (such as Monsavon in 1920) became L'Oréal in 1936. The similarity to the career of César Birotteau, whom Balzac depicts as having made his fortune by inventing "L'Eau Carminative" and "La Pâte des Sultanes" in the early nineteenth century, is striking.

16. With a capital of 10 billion euros, a mere 0.1 percent is enough to finance annual consumption of 10 million euros. If the return on capital is 5 percent, 98 percent of it can be saved. If the return is 10 percent, 99 percent can be saved. In any case, consumption is insignificant.

dynamics of accumulation and distribution of wealth. Money tends to reproduce itself. This stark reality did not escape the notice of Balzac, who describes the irresistible rise of his pasta manufacturer in the following terms: "Citizen Goriot amassed the capital that would later allow him to do business with all the superiority that a great sum of money bestows on the person who possesses it."[17]

Note, too, that Steve Jobs, who even more than Bill Gates is the epitome of the admired and talented entrepreneur who fully deserves his fortune, was worth only about $8 billion in 2011, at the height of his glory and the peak of Apple's stock price. That is just one-sixth as wealthy as Microsoft's founder (even though many observers judge Gates to have been less innovative than Jobs) and one-third as wealthy as Liliane Bettencourt. The *Forbes* rankings list dozens of people with inherited fortunes larger than Jobs's. Obviously wealth is not just a matter of merit. The reason for this is the simple fact that the return on inherited fortunes is often very high solely because of their initial size.

It is unfortunately impossible to proceed further with this type of investigation, because the *Forbes* data are far too limited to allow for systematic and robust analysis (in contrast to the data on university endowments that I will turn to next). In particular, the methods used by *Forbes* and other magazines significantly underestimate the size of inherited fortunes. Journalists do not have access to comprehensive tax or other government records that would allow them to report more accurate figures. They do what they can to collect information from a wide variety of sources. By telephone and e-mail they gather data not available elsewhere, but these data are not always very reliable. There is nothing inherently wrong with such a pragmatic approach, which is inevitable when governments fail to collect this kind of information properly, for example, by requiring annual declarations of wealth, which would serve a genuinely useful public purpose and could be largely automated with the aid of modern technology. But it is important to be aware of the consequences of the magazines' haphazard

---

17. Honoré de Balzac, *Le père Goriot* (Paris: Livre de Poche, 1983), 105–9.

methods. In practice, the journalists begin with data on large publicly traded corporations and compile lists of their stockholders. By its very nature, such an approach makes it far more difficult to measure the size of inherited fortunes (which are often invested in diversified portfolios) as compared with entrepreneurial or other nascent fortunes (which are generally more concentrated in a single firm).

For the largest inherited fortunes, on the order of tens of billions of dollars or euros, one can probably assume that most of the money remains invested in the family firm (as is the case with the Bettencourt family with L'Oréal and the Walton family with Walmart in the United States). If so, then the size of these fortunes is as easy to measure as the wealth of Bill Gates or Steve Jobs. But this is probably not true at all levels: as we move down the list into the $1–10 billion range (and according to *Forbes,* several hundred new fortunes appear in this range somewhere in the world almost every year), or even more into the $10–$100 million range, it is likely that many inherited fortunes are held in diversified portfolios, in which case they are difficult for journalists to detect (especially since the individuals involved are generally far less eager to be known publicly than entrepreneurs are). Because of this straightforward statistical bias, wealth rankings inevitably tend to underestimate the size of inherited fortunes.

Some magazines, such as *Challenges* in France, state openly that their goal is simply to catalog so-called business-related fortunes, that is, fortunes consisting primarily of the stock of a particular company. Diversified portfolios do not interest them. The problem is that it is difficult to find out what their definition of a "business-related fortune" is. How is the ownership threshold defined, that is, when does a portfolio cease being considered diversified and begin to be seen as representing a controlling stake? Does it depend on the size of the company, and if so, how is this decided? In fact, the criteria for inclusion seem thoroughly pragmatic. First, journalists need to have heard of the fortune. Then it has to meet certain criteria: for *Forbes,* to be worth more than a billion dollars; for *Challenges* and magazines in many other countries, to be among the five hundred wealthiest people in the country. Such pragmatism is understandable, but such a haphazard sampling method obviously raises serious problems when it comes to international or intertemporal comparison. Furthermore, the magazine rankings are never very clear about the unit of observation: in principle it is the individual, but sometimes entire family groups are counted as a single fortune, which creates a bias in the other direction, because it tends to exaggerate the size of large fortunes. Clearly, this is not a very robust basis for studying the delicate question of the role of inheritance in capital formation or the evolution of inequalities of wealth.[18]

Furthermore, the magazines often exhibit a rather obvious ideological bias in favor of entrepreneurs and do not bother to hide their wish to celebrate them, even if it means exaggerating their importance. It is no insult to *Forbes* to observe that it can often be read, and even presents itself as, an ode to the entrepreneur and the usefulness of merited wealth. The owner of the magazine, Steve Forbes, himself a billionaire and twice an unsuccessful candidate for the presidential nomination of the Republican Party, is nevertheless an heir: it was his grandfather who founded the magazine in 1917, establishing the Forbes family fortune, which he subsequently increased. The magazine's rankings sometimes break billionaires down into three groups: pure entrepreneurs, pure heirs, and heirs who subsequently "grow their wealth." According to *Forbes's* own data, each of these three groups represents about a third of the total, although the magazine also says that the number of pure heirs is decreasing and that of partial heirs increasing. The problem is that *Forbes* has never given a precise definition of these

---

18. In the case of *Challenges,* there seem to be too few fortunes in the 50–500 million euro range compared with the number of wealth tax declarations in the corresponding brackets (especially since a large part of business capital is not taxable under the wealth tax and therefore does not appear in the statistics). This may be because *Challenges* does not look at diversified fortunes. Indeed, both sources underestimate the actual number of large fortunes for opposite reasons: the *Challenges* source overvalues business capital, while the fiscal source underestimates it, and both rely on vague and shifting definitions. Citizens are left perplexed and made to feel that the subject of wealth is quite opaque. See the online technical appendix.

groups (in particular of the exact boundary between "pure" and "partial"), and the amount of inherited wealth is never specified.[19] Under these conditions, it is quite difficult to reach any precise conclusions about this possible trend.

In view of all these difficulties, what can we say about the respective numbers of heirs and entrepreneurs among the largest fortunes? If we include both the pure and partial heirs in the *Forbes* rankings (and assume that half of the wealth of the latter is inherited), and if we allow for the methodological biases that lead to underestimating the size of inherited fortunes, it seems fairly clear that inherited wealth accounts for more than half of the total amount of the largest fortunes worldwide. An estimate of 60–70 percent seems fairly realistic a priori, and this is a level markedly lower than that observed in France in the Belle Époque (80–90 percent). This might be explained by the currently high global growth rate, which would imply that new fortunes from the emerging countries are rapidly being added to the rankings. But this is a hypothesis, not a certainty.

The Moral Hierarchy of Wealth

In any case, I think there is an urgent need to move beyond the often sterile debate about merit and wealth, which is ill conceived. No one denies that it is important for society to have entrepreneurs, inventions, and innovations. There were many innovations in the Belle Époque, such as the automobile, movies, and electricity, just as there are many today. The problem is simply that the entrepreneurial argument cannot justify all inequalities of wealth, no matter how extreme. The inequality

---

19. Conceptually, moreover, it is no simple matter to define what a normal return on inherited wealth might be. In Chapter 11, I applied the same average return on capital to all fortunes, which no doubt leads to treating Liliane Bettencourt as a very partial heir (in view of the very high return on her capital), more partial than Steve Forbes himself, who nevertheless classifies her as a pure heiress, even though he counts himself among the "nurturers" of inherited wealth. See the online technical appendix.

$r > g$, combined with the inequality of returns on capital as a function of initial wealth, can lead to excessive and lasting concentration of capital: no matter how justified inequalities of wealth may be initially, fortunes can grow and perpetuate themselves beyond all reasonable limits and beyond any possible rational justification in terms of social utility.

Entrepreneurs thus tend to turn into rentiers, not only with the passing of generations but even within a single lifetime, especially as life expectancy increases: a person who has had good ideas at the age of forty will not necessarily still be having them at ninety, nor are his children sure to have any. Yet the wealth remains, in some cases multiplied more than tenfold in twenty years, as in the case of Bill Gates or Liliane Bettencourt.

This is the main justification for a progressive annual tax on the largest fortunes worldwide. Such a tax is the only way of democratically controlling this potentially explosive process while preserving entrepreneurial dynamism and international economic openness. In Part Four we will examine this idea further, as well as its limitations.

The fiscal approach is also a way to move beyond the futile debate about the moral hierarchy of wealth. Every fortune is partially justified yet potentially excessive. Outright theft is rare, as is absolute merit. The advantage of a progressive tax on capital is that it provides a way to treat different situations in a supple, consistent, and predictable manner while exposing large fortunes to democratic control—which is already quite a lot.

All too often, the global debate about great wealth comes down to a few peremptory—and largely arbitrary—assertions about the relative merits of this or that individual. For example, it is rather common to contrast the man who is currently the world's wealthiest, Carlos Slim, a Mexican real estate and telecom tycoon who is of Lebanese extraction and is often described in the Western press as one who owes his great wealth to monopoly rents obtained through (implicitly corrupt) government favors, and Bill Gates, the former number one, who is seen as a model of the meritorious entrepreneur. At times one almost has the impression that Bill Gates himself invented computer science and the microprocessor and that he would be 10 times richer still if he had been paid his full marginal productivity and compensated for his personal contribution to global well-being (and fortunately the good people of the planet have been the beneficiaries of his "positive externalities" since he retired). No doubt the veritable cult of Bill Gates is an outgrowth of the apparently irrepressible need of modern democratic societies to make sense of inequality. To be frank, I know virtually nothing about exactly how Carlos Slim or Bill Gates became rich, and I am quite incapable of assessing their relative merits. Nevertheless, it seems to me that Bill Gates also profited from a virtual monopoly on operating systems (as have many other high-tech entrepreneurs in industries ranging from telecommunications to Facebook, whose fortunes were also built on monopoly rents). Furthermore, I believe that Gates's contributions depended on the work of thousands of engineers and scientists doing basic research in electronics and computer science, without whom none of his innovations would have been possible. These people did not patent their scientific papers. In short, it seems unreasonable to draw such an extreme contrast between Gates and Slim without so much as a glance at the facts.[20]

As for the Japanese billionaires (Yoshiaka Tsutsumi and Taikichiro Mori) who from 1987 to 1994 preceded Bill Gates at the top of the *Forbes* ranking, people in the Western world have all but forgotten their names. Perhaps there is a feeling that these men owe their fortunes

---

20. For some particularly strong assertions about the relative merits of Slim and Gates, unfortunately without any precise factual basis, see, for example, Daron Acemoglu and James A. Robinson, *Why Nations Fail: The Origins of Power, Prosperity, and Poverty* (New York: Crown Publishing, 2012), 34–41. The authors' harsh tone is all the more surprising in that they do not really discuss the ideal distribution of wealth. The book is built around a defense of the role of systems of property rights stemming from the British, American, and French revolutions in the development process (and little is said about more recent social institutions or systems of taxation).

entirely to the real estate and stock market bubbles that existed at the time in the Land of the Rising Sun, or else to some not very savory Asian wheeling and dealing. Yet Japanese growth from 1950 to 1990 was the greatest history had ever seen to that point, much greater than US growth in 1990–2010, and there is reason to believe that entrepreneurs played some role in this.

Rather than indulge in constructing a moral hierarchy of wealth, which in practice often amounts to an exercise in Western ethnocentrism, I think it is more useful to try to understand the general laws that govern the dynamics of wealth—leaving individuals aside and thinking instead about modes of regulation, and in particular taxation, that apply equally to everyone, regardless of nationality. In France, when Arcelor (then the second largest steel company worldwide) was bought by the steel magnate Lakshmi Mittal in 2006, the French media found the actions of the Indian billionaire particularly outrageous. They renewed their outrage in the fall of 2012, when Mittal was accused of failing to invest enough in the firm's factory in Florange. In India, everyone believes that the hostility to Mittal is due, at least in part, to the color of his skin. And who can be sure that this did not play a role? To be sure, Mittal's methods are brutal, and his sumptuous lifestyle is seen as scandalous. The entire French press took umbrage at his luxurious London residences, "worth three times as much as his investment in Florange."[21]

---

21. See, for example, the magazine *Capital,* no. 255, December 3, 2012: "180 million euros . . . a sum that pales in comparison to the value of the real estate that the head of the firm, Lakshmi Mittal, recently acquired in London for three times that amount. Indeed, the businessman recently purchased the former embassy of the Philippines (for 70 million pounds, or 86 million euros), supposedly for his daughter Vanisha. A short while earlier, his son Aditya was the recipient of the generous gift of a home worth 117 million pounds (144 million euros). The two properties are located on Kensington Palace Gardens, known as Billionaires' Row, not far from the paternal palace. Lakshmi Mittal's residence is said to be the 'most expensive private home in the world' and is equipped with a Turkish bath, a jewel-encrusted swimming pool, marble from the same quarry as the Taj Mahal, and servants' quarters. . . . All told, these three homes cost 542 million euros, or 3 times the 180 million invested in Florange."

Somehow, though, the outrage is soft-pedaled when it comes to a certain residence in Neuilly-sur-Seine, a posh suburb of Paris, or a homegrown billionaire like Arnaud Lagardère, a young heir not particularly well known for his merit, virtue, or social utility yet on whom the French government decided at about the same time to bestow the sum of a billion euros in exchange for his share of the European Aeronautic, Defense, and Space Co. (EADS), a world leader in aeronautics.

One final example, even more extreme: in February 2012, a French court ordered the seizure of more than 200 cubic meters of property (luxury cars, old master paintings, etc.) from the Avenue Foch home of Teodorin Obiang, the son of the dictator of Equatorial Guinea. It is an established fact that his share of the company, which was authorized to exploit Guinea's forests (from which he derives most of his income), was acquired in a dubious way and that these forest resources were to a large extent stolen from the people of Equatorial Guinea. The case is instructive in that it shows that private property is not quite as sacred as people sometimes think, and that it was technically possible, when someone really wanted to, to find a way through the maze of dummy corporations by means of which Teodorin Obiang administered his capital. There is little doubt, however, that it would not be very difficult to find in Paris or London other individuals— Russian oligarchs or Quatari billionaires, say—with fortunes ultimately derived from the private appropriation of natural resources. It may be that these appropriations of oil, gas, and aluminum deposits are not as clear-cut cases of theft as Obiang's forests. And perhaps judicial action is more justified when the theft is committed at the expense of a very poor country, as opposed to a less poor one.[22] At the very least, the reader will grant that these various cases are not fundamentally different

---

22. The *Forbes* ranking uses an interesting criterion, but one that is hard to apply in any precise way: it excludes "despots" and indeed anyone whose fortune depends on "their political position" (like the Queen of England). But if an individual acquires his fortune before coming to power, he remains in the ranking: for example, the Georgia oligarch Bidzina Ivanishvili is still in the 2013 list, although he became prime minister in late 2012. He is credited with a fortune of $5 billion,

but belong to a continuum, and that a fortune is often deemed more suspect if its owner is black. In any case, the courts cannot resolve every case of ill-gotten gains or unjustified wealth. A tax on capital would be a less blunt and more systematic instrument for dealing with the question.

Broadly speaking, the central fact is that the return on capital often inextricably combines elements of true entrepreneurial labor (an absolutely indispensable force for economic development), pure luck (one happens at the right moment to buy a promising asset at a good price), and outright theft. The arbitrariness of wealth accumulation is a much broader phenomenon than the arbitrariness of inheritance. The return on capital is by nature volatile and unpredictable and can easily generate capital gains (or losses) equivalent to dozens of years of earned income. At the top of the wealth hierarchy, these effects are even more extreme. It has always been this way. In the novel *Ibiscus* (1926), Alexei Tolstoy depicted the horrors of capitalism. In 1917, in St. Petersburg, the accountant Simon Novzorov bashes in the skull of an antique dealer who has offered him a job and steals a small fortune. The antique dealer had become rich by purchasing, at rock-bottom prices, the possessions of aristocrats fleeing the Revolution. Novzorov manages to multiply his initial capital by 10 in six months, thanks to the gambling den he sets up in Moscow with his new friend Ritechev. Novzorov is a nasty, petty parasite who embodies the idea that wealth and merit are totally unrelated: property sometimes begins with theft, and the arbitrary return on capital can easily perpetuate the initial crime.

The Pure Return on University Endowments

In order to gain a better understanding of unequal returns on capital without being distracted by issues of individual character, it is useful to look at what has happened with the endowments of American univer-

---

or one-quarter of his country's GDP (between 5 percent and 10 percent of Georgia's national wealth).

sities over the past few decades. Indeed, this is one of the few cases where we have very complete data about investments made and returns received over a relatively long period of time, as a function of initial capital.

There are currently more than eight hundred public and private universities in the United States that manage their own endowments. These endowments range from some tens of millions of dollars (for example, North Iowa Community College, ranked 785th in 2012 with an endowment of $11.5 million) to tens of billions. The top-ranked universities are invariably Harvard (with an endowment of some $30 billion in the early 2010s), Yale ($20 billion), and Princeton and Stanford (more than $15 billion). Then come MIT and Columbia, with a little less than $10 billion, then Chicago and Pennsylvania, at around $7 billion, and so on. All told, these eight hundred US universities owned nearly $400 billion worth of assets in 2010 (or a little under $500 million per university on average, with a median slightly less than $100 million). To be sure, this is less than 1 percent of the total private wealth of US households, but it is still a large sum, which annually yields significant income for US universities—or at any rate some of them.[23] Above all—and this is the point that is of interest here—US universities publish regular, reliable, and detailed reports on their endowments, which can be used to study the annual returns each institution obtains. This is not possible with most private fortunes. In particular, these data have been collected since the late 1970s by the National Association of College and University Business Officers, which has published voluminous statistical surveys every year since 1979.

---

23. The total capital endowment of US universities is about 3 percent of GDP, and the annual income on this capital is about 0.2 percent of GDP, which is a little over 10 percent of total US expenditure on higher education. But this share is as high as 30 or 40 percent of the resources of the most richly endowed universities. Furthermore, these capital endowments play a role in the governance of these institutions that often outweighs their monetary importance. See the online technical appendix.

The main results I have been able to derive from these data are shown in Table 12.2.[24] The first conclusion is that the return on US university endowments has been extremely high in recent decades, averaging 8.2 percent a year between 1980 and 2010 (and 7.2 percent for the period 1990–2010).[25] To be sure, there have been ups and downs in each decade, with years of low or even negative returns, such as 2008–2009, and good years in which the average endowment grew by more than 10 percent. But the important point is that if we average over ten, twenty, or thirty years, we find extremely high returns, of the same sort I examined for the billionaires in the *Forbes* rankings.

To be clear, the returns indicated in Table 12.2 are net real returns allowing for capital gains and inflation, prevailing taxes (virtually nonexistent for nonprofit institutions), and management fees. (The latter include the salaries of everyone inside or outside the university who is involved in planning and executing the institution's investment strategy.) Hence these figures reflect the pure return on capital as defined in this book, that is, the return that comes simply from owning capital, apart from any remuneration of the labor required to manage it.

The second conclusion that emerges clearly from Table 12.2 is that the return increases rapidly with size of endowment. For the 500 of 850 universities whose endowment was less than $100 million, the average return was 6.2 percent in 1980–2010 (and 5.1 percent in 1990–2010), which is already fairly high and significantly above the average return on all private wealth in these periods.[26] The greater the endowment, the

---

24. The data used here come mainly from reports published by the National Association of College and University Business Officers, as well as from financial reports published by Harvard University, Yale University, Princeton University, and other institutions. See the online technical appendix.

25. For results by subperiod, see the online technical appendix, Supplemental Table S12.2, available online.

26. Note, however, that the main difference arises from the fact that most owners of private wealth must pay significant taxes: the average real return before taxes was around 5 percent in the United States in 1980–2010. See the online technical appendix.

TABLE 12.2.

The return on the capital endowments of US universities, 1980–2010

	Average real annual rate of return (after deduction of inflation and all administrative costs and financial fees) (%)
All universities (850)	8.2
Harvard, Yale, and Princeton	10.2
Endowments higher than $1 billion (60)	8.8
Endowments between $500 million and 1 billion (66)	7.8
Endowments between $100 and $500 million (226)	7.1
Endowments less than $100 million (498)	6.2

Note: Between 1980 and 2010, US universities earned an average real return of 8.2% on their capital endowments, and all the more so for higher endowments. All returns reported here are net of inflation (2.4% per year between 1980 and 2010) and of all administrative costs and financial fees.

Sources: See piketty.pse.ens.fr/capital21c.

greater the return. For the 60 universities with endowments of more than $1 billion, the average return was 8.8 percent in 1980–2010 (and 7.8 percent in 1990–2010). For the top trio (Harvard, Yale, and Princeton), which has not changed since 1980, the yield was 10.2 percent in 1980–2010 (and 10.0 percent in 1990–2010), twice as much as the less well-endowed institutions.[27]

If we look at the investment strategies of different universities, we find highly diversified portfolios at all levels, with a clear preference for US and foreign stocks and private sector bonds (government bonds,

---

27. The numbers of universities in each category indicated in parentheses in Table 12.2 are based on 2010 endowments, but so as not to bias the results, the returns were calculated by ranking universities according to their endowment at the beginning of each decade. All the detailed results are available in the online technical appendix. See in particular Supplemental Table S12.2, available online.

especially US Treasuries, which do not pay well, account for less than 10 percent of all these portfolios and are almost totally absent from the largest endowments). The higher we go in the endowment hierarchy, the more often we find "alternative investment strategies," that is, very high yield investments such as shares in private equity funds and unlisted foreign stocks (which require great expertise), hedge funds, derivatives, real estate, and raw materials, including energy, natural resources, and related products (these, too, require specialized expertise and offer very high potential yields).[28] If we consider the importance in these various portfolios of "alternative investments," whose only common feature is that they abandon the usual strategies of investing in stocks and bonds accessible to all, we find that they represent only 10 percent of the portfolios of institutions with endowments of less than 50 million euros, 25 percent of those with endowments between 50 and 100 million euros, 35 percent of those between 100 and 500 million euros, 45 percent of those between 500 million and 1 billion euros, and ultimately more than 60 percent of those above 1 billion euros. The available data, which are both public and extremely detailed, show unambiguously that it is these alternative investment strategies that enable the very largest endowments to obtain real returns of close to 10 percent a year, while smaller endowments must make do with 5 percent.

It is interesting to note that the year-to-year volatility of these returns does not seem to be any greater for the largest endowments than for the smaller ones: the returns obtained by Harvard and Yale vary around their mean but not much more so than the returns of smaller institutions, and if one averages over several years, the mean returns of the largest institutions are systematically higher than those of the smaller ones, with a gap that remains fairly constant over time. In other words, the higher returns of the largest endowments are not due

---

28. Real estate can be a very high yield investment if one identifies the right projects around the world. In practice, these include business and commercial as well as residential properties, often on a very large scale.

primarily to greater risk taking but to a more sophisticated investment strategy that consistently produces better results.[29]

How can these facts be explained? By economies of scale in portfolio management. Concretely, Harvard currently spends nearly $100 million a year to manage its endowment. This munificent sum goes to pay a team of top-notch portfolio managers capable of identifying the best investment opportunities around the world. But given the size of Harvard's endowment (around $30 billion), $100 million in management costs is just over 0.3 percent a year. If paying that amount makes it possible to obtain an annual return of 10 percent rather than 5, it is obviously a very good deal. On the other hand, a university with an endowment of only $1 billion (which is nevertheless substantial) could not afford to pay $100 million a year—10 percent of its portfolio—in management costs. In practice, no university pays more than 1 percent for portfolio management, and most pay less than 0.5 percent, so to manage assets worth $1 billion, one would pay $5 million, which is not enough to pay the kind of specialists in alternative investments that one can hire with $100 million. As for North Iowa Community College, with an endowment of $11.5 million, even 1 percent a year would amount to only $115,000, which is just enough to pay a half-time or even quarter-time financial advisor at going market rates. Of course a US citizen at the median of the wealth distribution has only $100,000 to invest, so he must be his own money manager and probably has to rely on the advice of his brother-in-law. To be sure, financial advisors and money managers are not infallible (to say the least), but their ability to identify more profitable investments is the main reason why the largest endowments obtain the highest returns.

These results are striking, because they illustrate in a particularly clear and concrete way how large initial endowments can give rise to

---

29. This is confirmed by the fact that relative rankings do not change much over the thirty-year period 1980–2010. The hierarchy of university endowments remains more or less the same.

better returns and thus to substantial inequalities in returns on capital. These high returns largely account for the prosperity of the most prestigious US universities. It is not alumni gifts, which constitute a much smaller flow: just one-tenth to one-fifth of the annual return on endowment.[30]

These findings should be interpreted cautiously, however. In particular, it would be too much to try to use them to predict how global wealth inequality will evolve over the next few decades. For one thing, the very high returns that we see in the period 1980–2010 in part reflect the long-term rebound of global asset prices (stocks and real estate), which may not continue (in which case the long-term returns discussed above would have to be reduced somewhat in the future).[31] For another, it is possible that economies of scale affect mainly the largest portfolios and are greatly reduced for more "modest" fortunes of 10–50 million euros, which, as noted, account for a much larger share of total global wealth than do the *Forbes* billionaires. Finally, leaving management fees aside, these returns still depend on the institution's ability to choose the right managers. But a family is not an institution: there always comes a time when a prodigal child squanders the family fortune, which the Harvard Corporation is unlikely to do, simply because any number of people would come forward to stand in the way. Because family fortunes are subject to this kind of random "shock," it is unlikely that inequality of wealth will grow in-

---

30. To take Harvard University as an example, annual financial reports show that the endowment yielded an average real return of about 10 percent from 1990 to 2010, whereas new gifts added an average of about 2 percent a year to the endowment. Thus the total real income (from return on the endowment plus gifts) amounted to 12 percent of the endowment; a portion of this, amounting to 5 percent of the endowment, was used to pay current university expenses, while the other 7 percent was added to the endowment. This enabled the endowment to increase from $5 billion in 1990 to nearly $30 billion in 2010 while allowing the university to consume an annual flow of resources 2.5 times as great as it received in gifts.

31. Note, however, that the historic rebound of asset prices appears to add no more than a point of additional annual return, which is fairly small compared with the level of return I have been discussing. See the online technical appendix.

definitely at the individual level; rather, the wealth distribution will converge toward a certain equilibrium.

These arguments are not altogether reassuring, however. It would in any case be rather imprudent to rely solely on the eternal but arbitrary force of family degeneration to limit the future proliferation of billionaires. As noted, a gap $r - g$ of fairly modest size is all that it takes to arrive at an extremely inegalitarian distribution of wealth. The return on capital does not need to rise as high as 10 percent for all large fortunes: a smaller gap would be enough to deliver a major inegalitarian shock.

Another important point is that wealthy people are constantly coming up with new and ever more sophisticated legal structures to house their fortunes. Trust funds, foundations, and the like often serve to avoid taxes, but they also constrain the freedom of future generations to do as they please with the associated assets. In other words, the boundary between fallible individuals and eternal foundations is not as clear-cut as is sometimes thought. Restrictions on the rights of future generations were in theory drastically reduced when entails were abolished more than two centuries ago (see Chapter 10). In practice, however, the rules can be circumvented when the stakes require. In particular, it is often difficult to distinguish purely private family foundations from true charitable foundations. In fact, families often use foundations for both private and charitable purposes and are generally careful to maintain control of their assets even when housed in a primarily charitable foundation.[32] It is often not easy to know what exact rights children and relatives have in these complex structures, because important details are often hidden in legal documents that are not public. In some cases, a family trust whose purpose is primarily to serve as an inheritance vehicle exists alongside a foundation with a

---

32. For example, because Bill Gates maintains effective control over the assets of the Bill and Melinda Gates Foundation, *Forbes* chooses to count those assets as part of Gates's personal fortune. Maintaining control seems incompatible with the idea of a disinterested gift.

more charitable purpose.[33] It is also interesting to note that the amount of gifts declared to the tax authorities always falls drastically when oversight is tightened (for example, when donors are required to submit accurate receipts, or when foundations are required to submit more detailed financial statements to certify that their official purpose is in fact respected and private use of foundation funds does not exceed certain limits), confirming the idea that there is a certain porosity between public and private uses of these legal entities.[34] Ultimately, it is very difficult to say precisely what proportion of foundations fulfill purposes that can truly be characterized as being in the public interest.[35]

What Is the Effect of Inflation on Inequality of Returns to Capital?

The results concerning the returns on university endowments suggest that it may also be useful to say a few words about the pure return on capital and the inegalitarian effects of inflation. As I showed in Chapter 1, the rate of inflation in the wealthy countries has been stable at around 2 percent since the 1980s: this new norm is both much lower than the peak inflation rates seen in the twentieth century and much higher than the zero or virtually zero inflation that prevailed in the nineteenth century and up to World War I. In the emerging coun-

---

33. According to Bernard Arnault, the principal stockholder in LVMH, the world leader in luxury goods, the purpose of the Belgian foundation that holds his assets is neither charitable nor fiscal. Rather, it is primarily an estate vehicle. "Among my five children and two nephews, there is surely one who will prove capable of taking over after I am gone," he remarked. But he is afraid of disputes. By placing his assets in the foundation, he forces his heirs to vote "indissociably," which "ensures the survival of the group if I should die and my heirs should be unable to agree." See *Le Monde,* April 11, 2013.

34. The work of Gabrielle Fack and Camille Landais, which is based on these types of reforms in the United States and France, speaks eloquently to this point. See the online technical appendix.

35. For an incomplete estimate for the United States, see the online technical appendix.

tries, inflation is currently higher than in the rich countries (often above 5 percent). The question, then, is the following: What is the effect on returns to capital of inflation at 2 percent or even 5 percent rather than 0 percent?

Some people think, wrongly, that inflation reduces the average return on capital. This is false, because the average asset price (that is, the average price of real estate and financial securities) tends to rise at the same pace as consumer prices. Take a country with a capital stock equal to six years of national income ($\beta = 6$) and where capital's share of national income equals 30 percent ($\alpha = 30\%$), so that the average return on capital is 5 percent ($r = 5\%$). Imagine that inflation in this country increases from 0 to 2 percent a year. Is it really true that the average return on capital will then decrease from 5 percent to 3? Obviously not. To a first approximation, if consumer prices rise by 2 percent a year, then it is probable that asset prices will also increase by 2 percent a year on average. There will be no capital gains or losses, and the return on capital will still be 5 percent. By contrast, it is likely that inflation changes the distribution of this average return among individual citizens. The problem is that in practice the redistributions induced by inflation are always complex, multidimensional, and largely unpredictable and uncontrollable.

People sometimes believe that inflation is the enemy of the rentier and that this may in part explain why modern societies like inflation. This is partly true, in the sense that inflation forces people to pay some attention to their capital. When inflation exists, anyone who is content to perch on a pile of banknotes will see that pile melt away before his eyes, leaving him with nothing even if wealth is untaxed. In this respect, inflation is indeed a tax on the idle rich, or, more precisely, on wealth that is not invested. But as I have noted a number of times already, it is enough to invest one's wealth in real assets, such as real estate or shares of stock, in order to escape the inflation tax entirely.[36] Our results on university endowments confirm this in the clearest

---

36. See Chapter 5.

possible terms. There can be no doubt that inflation of 2 percent rather than 0 percent in no way prevents large fortunes from obtaining very high real returns.

One can even imagine that inflation tends to improve the relative position of the wealthiest individuals compared to the least wealthy, in that it enhances the importance of financial managers and intermediaries. A person with 10 or 50 million euros cannot afford the money managers that Harvard has but can nevertheless pay financial advisors and stockbrokers to mitigate the effects of inflation. By contrast, a person with only 10 or 50 thousand euros to invest will not be offered the same choices by her broker (if she has one): contacts with financial advisors are briefer, and many people in this category keep most of their savings in checking accounts that pay little or nothing and / or savings accounts that pay little more than the rate of inflation. Furthermore, some assets exhibit size effects of their own, but these are generally unavailable to small investors. It is important to realize that this inequality of access to the most remunerative investments as a reality for everyone (and thus much broader than the extreme case of "alternative investments" available only to the wealthiest individuals and largest endowments). For example, some financial products require very large minimum investments (on the order of hundreds of thousands of euros), so that small investors must make do with less profitable opportunities (allowing intermediaries to charge big investors more for their services).

These size effects are particularly important in regard to real estate. In practice, this is the most important type of capital asset for the vast majority of the population. For most people, the simplest way to invest is to buy a home. This provides protection against inflation (since the price of housing generally rises at least as fast as the price of consumption), and it also allows the owner to avoid paying rent, which is equivalent to a real return on investment of 3–4 percent a year. But for a person with 10 to 50 thousand euros, it is not enough to decide to buy a home: the possibility may not exist. And even for a person with 100 or 200 thousand euros but who works in a big city in a job whose pay is not in the top 2 or 3 centiles of the wage hierarchy, it may be difficult to purchase a home or apartment even if one is willing to go into debt for a long period of time and pay a high rate of interest. As a result, those who start out with a small initial fortune will often remain tenants, who must therefore pay a substantial rent (affording a high return on capital to the landlord) for a long period of time, possibly for life, while their bank savings are just barely protected from inflation.

Conversely, a person who starts out with more wealth thanks to an inheritance or gift, or who earns a sufficiently high salary, or both, will more quickly be in a position to buy a home or apartment and therefore earn a real return of 3–4 percent on their investment while being able to save more thanks to not having to pay rent. This unequal access to real estate as an effect of fortune size has of course always existed.[37] One could conceivably circumvent the barrier by buying a smaller apartment than one needs (in order to rent it) or by investing in other types of assets. But the problem has to some extent been aggravated by modern inflation: in the nineteenth century, when inflation was zero, it was relatively easy for a small saver to obtain a real return of 3 or 4 percent, for example by buying government bonds. Today, many small savers cannot enjoy such returns.

To sum up: the main effect of inflation is not to reduce the average return on capital but to redistribute it. And even though the effects of inflation are complex and multidimensional, the preponderance of the evidence suggests that the redistribution induced by inflation is mainly to the detriment of the least wealthy and to the benefit of the wealthiest, hence in the opposite direction from what is generally desired. To be sure, inflation may slightly reduce the pure return on capital, in that it forces everyone to spend more time doing asset management. One might compare this historic change to the very long-run increase in the rate of depreciation of capital, which requires more frequent investment

---

37. It was even worse in the nineteenth century, at least in the city, and especially in Paris, where before World War I most buildings were not chopped up into apartments. One therefore needed to be wealthy enough to buy an entire building.

decisions and replacement of old assets with new ones.[38] In both cases, one has to work a little harder today to obtain a given return: capital has become more "dynamic." But these are relatively indirect and ineffective ways of combating rent: the evidence suggests that the slight decrease in the pure return on capital due to these causes is much smaller than the increase of inequality of returns on capital; in particular, it poses little threat to the largest fortunes.

Inflation does not do away with rent: on the contrary, it probably helps to make the distribution of capital more unequal.

To avoid any misunderstanding, let me say at once that I am not proposing a return to the gold standard or zero inflation. Under some conditions, inflation may have virtues, though smaller virtues than is sometimes imagined. I will come back to this when I discuss the role of central banks in monetary creation, especially in times of financial crisis and large sovereign debt. There are ways for people of modest means to have access to remunerative saving without zero inflation and government bonds as in the nineteenth century. But it is important to realize that inflation is today an extremely blunt instrument, and often a counterproductive one, if the goal is to avoid a return to a society of rentiers and, more generally, to reduce inequalities of wealth. A progressive tax on capital is a much more appropriate policy in terms of both democratic transparency and real efficacy.

The Return on Sovereign Wealth Funds: Capital and Politics

Consider now the case of sovereign wealth funds, which have grown substantially in recent years, particularly in the petroleum exporting countries. Unfortunately, there is much less publicly available data concerning the investment strategies and returns obtained by sovereign wealth funds than there is for university endowments, and this is all the more unfortunate in that the financial stakes are much, much larger. The Norwegian sovereign wealth fund, which alone was worth

---

38. See Chapter 5.

more than 700 billion euros in 2013 (twice as much as all US university endowments combined), publishes the most detailed financial reports. Its investment strategy, at least at the beginning, seems to have been more standard than that of the university endowments, in part, no doubt, because it was subject to public scrutiny (and the people of Norway may have been less willing than the Harvard Corporation to accept massive investments in hedge funds and unlisted stocks), and the returns obtained were apparently not as good.[39] The fund's officials recently received authorization to place larger amounts in alternative investments (especially international real estate), and returns may be higher in the future. Note, too, that the fund's management costs are less than 0.1 percent of its assets (compared with 0.3 percent for Harvard), but since the Norwegian fund is 20 times larger than Harvard's endowment, this is enough to pay for thorough investment advice. We also learn that during the period 1970–2010, about 60 percent of the money Norway earned from petroleum was invested in the fund, while 40 percent a year went to government expenses. The Norwegian authorities do not tell us what their long-term objective for the fund is or when the country can begin to consume all or part of the returns on its investment. They probably do not know themselves: everything depends on how Norway's petroleum reserves evolve as well as on the price of a barrel of oil and the fund's returns in the decades ahead.

If we look at other sovereign wealth funds, particularly in the Middle East, we unfortunately find that they are much more opaque than the Norwegian fund. Their financial reports are frequently rather scanty. It is generally impossible to know precisely what the investment strategy is, and returns are discussed obliquely at best, with little

---

39. The nominal average return for 1998–2012 was only 5 percent a year. It is difficult to compare these returns with those on university endowments, however, in part because the period 1998–2012 was not as good as 1990–2010 or 1980–2010 (and unfortunately the Norwegian fund's statistics go back only as far as 1998), and because this relatively low return was due in part to appreciation of the Norwegian krone.

consistency from year to year. The most recent reports published by the Abu Dhabi Investment Authority, which manages the world's largest sovereign wealth fund (about the same size as Norway's), speak of a real return greater than 7 percent a year for 1990–2010 and more than 8 percent for 1980–2010. In view of the returns obtained by university endowments, these figures seem entirely plausible, but in the absence of detailed annual information, it is difficult to say more.

It is interesting to note that different funds apparently follow very different investment strategies, which are related, moreover, to very different ways of communicating with the public and very different approaches to global politics. Abu Dhabi is outspoken about its fund's high returns, but Saudi Arabia's sovereign wealth fund, which ranks third after Abu Dhabi and Norway among sovereign wealth funds of petroleum exporting states and ahead of Kuwait, Qatar, and Russia, has chosen to keep a very low profile. The small petroleum states of the Persian Gulf, which have only tiny populations to worry about, are clearly addressing the international financial community as the primary audience for their reports. The Saudi reports are more sober and provide information not only about oil reserves but also about national accounts and the government budget. These are clearly addressed to the people of the Kingdom of Saudi Arabia, whose population was close to 20 million in 2010—still small compared to the large countries in the region (Iran, 80 million; Egypt, 85 million; Iraq, 35 million) but far larger than the microstates of the Gulf.[40] And that is not the only difference: Saudi funds seem to be invested much less aggressively. According to official documents, the average return on the Saudi sovereign wealth fund was no more than 2–3 percent, mainly because much of the money was invested in US Treasury bonds. Saudi

---

40. According to the census of 2010, the United Arab Emirates (of which Abu Dhabi is the largest member state) have a native population of a little over 1 million (plus 7 million foreign workers). The native population of Kuwait is about the same size. Qatar has about 300,000 nationals and 1.5 million foreigners. Saudi Arabia alone employs nearly 10 million foreign workers (in addition to its native population of nearly 20 million).

financial reports do not come close to providing enough information to know how the portfolio has evolved, but the information they do provide is much more detailed than that provided by the Emirates, and on this specific point they seem to be accurate.

Why would Saudi Arabia choose to invest in US Treasury bonds when it is possible to get far better returns elsewhere? The question is worth asking, especially since US university endowments stopped investing in their own government's debt decades ago and roam the world in search of the best return, investing in hedge funds, unlisted shares, and commodities-based derivatives. To be sure, US Treasuries offer an enviable guarantee of stability in an unstable world, and it is possible that the Saudi public has little taste for alternative investments. But the political and military aspects of the choice must also be taken into account: even though it is never stated explicitly, it is not illogical for Saudia Arabia to lend at low interest to the country that protects it militarily. To my knowledge, no one has ever attempted to calculate precisely the return on such an investment, but it seems clear that it is rather high. If the United States, backed by other Western powers, had not driven the Iraqi army out of Kuwait in 1991, Iraq would probably have threatened Saudi Arabia's oil fields next, and it is possible that other countries in the region, such as Iran, would have joined the fray to redistribute the region's petroleum rents. The dynamics of the global distribution of capital are at once economic, political, and military. This was already the case in the colonial era, when the great powers of the day, Britain and France foremost among them, were quick to roll out the cannon to protect their investments. Clearly, the same will be true in the twenty-first century, in a tense new global political configuration whose contours are difficult to predict in advance.

Will Sovereign Wealth Funds Own the World?

How much richer can the sovereign wealth funds become in the decades ahead? According to available (and notoriously imperfect) estimates, sovereign wealth funds in 2013 had total investments worth a little over \$5.3 trillion, of which about \$3.2 trillion belongs to the funds of petroleum exporting states (including, in addition to those mentioned above, the smaller funds of Dubai, Libya, Kazakhstan, Algeria, Iran, Azerbaijan, Brunei, Oman, and many others), and approximately \$2.1 trillion to funds of nonpetroleum states (primarily China, Hong Kong, Singapore, and many smaller funds).[41] For reference, note that this is almost exactly the same total wealth as that represented by the *Forbes* billionaires (around \$5.4 trillion in 2013). In other words, billionaires today own roughly 1.5 percent of the world's total private wealth, and sovereign wealth funds own another 1.5 percent. It is perhaps reassuring to note that this leaves 97 percent of global capital for the rest.[42] One can also do projections for the sovereign wealth funds just as I did for billionaires, from which it follows that they will not achieve decisive importance—10–20 percent of global capital—before the second half of the twenty-first century, and we are still a long way from having to pay our monthly rent to the emir of Qatar (or the taxpayers of Norway). Nevertheless, it would still be a mistake to ignore the issue. In the first place, there is no reason why we should not worry about the rents our children and grandchildren may have to pay, and we need not wait until things come to a head to think about what to do. Second, a substantial part of global capital is in relatively illiquid form (including real estate and business capital that cannot be traded on financial markets), so that the share of truly liquid capital owned by sovereign wealth funds (and to a lesser extent billionaires)— capital that can be used, say, to take over a bankrupt company, buy a football team, or invest in a decaying neighborhood when strapped

---

41. See the online technical appendix.

42. One should also take into account public nonfinancial assets (public buildings, school, hospitals, etc.) as well as financial assets not formally included in sovereign wealth funds, and then subtract public debts. Net public wealth is currently less than 3 percent of private wealth in the rich countries, on average (in some cases net public wealth is negative), so this does not make much difference. See Chapters 3–5 and the online technical appendix.

governments lack the means to do so—is actually much higher.[43] In fact, the issue of investments originating in the petroleum exporting countries has become increasingly salient in the wealthy countries, especially France, and as noted, these are perhaps the countries least psychologically prepared for the comeback of capital.

Last but not least, the key difference between the sovereign wealth funds and the billionaires is that the funds, or at any rate those of the petroleum exporting countries, grow not only by reinvesting their returns but also by investing part of the proceeds of oil sales. Although the future amounts of such proceeds are highly uncertain, owing to uncertainties about the amount of oil still in the ground, the demand for oil, and the price per barrel, it is quite plausible to assume that this income from petroleum sales will largely outweigh the returns on existing investments. The annual rent derived from the exploitation of natural resources, defined as the difference between receipts from sales and the cost of production, has been about 5 percent of global GDP since the mid-2000s (half of which is petroleum rent and the rest rent on other natural resources, mainly gas, coal, minerals, and wood), compared with about 2 percent in the 1990s and less than 1 percent in the early 1970s.[44] According to some forecasting models, the price of petroleum, currently around $100 a barrel (compared with $25 in the early 2000s) could rise as high as $200 a barrel by 2020–2030. If a sufficiently large fraction of the corresponding rent is invested in sovereign wealth funds every year (a fraction that should be considerably larger than it is today), one can imagine a scenario in which the sovereign

---

43. If we exclude real estate and unlisted business assets, financial assets in the narrow sense represented between a quarter and a third of global private wealth in 2010, that is, between a year and a year and a half of global GDP (and not four years). The sovereign wealth funds thus own 5 percent of global financial assets. Here I refer to net financial assets owned by households and governments. In view of the very substantial cross-holdings of financial and nonfinancial corporations within and between countries, gross financial assets amount to much more than three years of global GDP. See the online technical appendix.

44. The rent on natural resources had already exceeded 5 percent of global GDP from the mid-1970s to the mid-1980s. See the online technical appendix.

wealth funds would own 10–20 percent or more of global capital by 2030–2040. No law of economics rules this out. Everything depends on supply and demand, on whether or not new oil deposits and / or sources of energy are discovered, and on how rapidly people learn to live without petroleum. In any event, it is almost inevitable that the sovereign wealth funds of the petroleum exporting countries will continue to grow and that their share of global assets in 2030–2040 will be at least two to three times greater than it is today—a significant increase.

If this happens, it is likely that the Western countries would find it increasingly difficult to accept the idea of being owned in substantial part by the sovereign wealth funds of the oil states, and sooner or later this would trigger political reactions, such as restrictions on the purchase of real estate and industrial and financial assets by sovereign wealth funds or even partial or total expropriations. Such a reaction would neither be terribly smart politically nor especially effective economically, but it is the kind of response that is within the power of national governments, even of smaller states. Note, moreover, that the petroleum exporting countries themselves have already begun to limit their foreign investments and have begun investing heavily in their own countries to build museums, hotels, universities, and even ski slopes, at times on a scale that seems devoid of economic and financial rationality. It may be that this behavior reflects awareness of the fact that it is harder to expropriate an investment made at home than one made abroad. There is no guarantee, however, that the process will always be peaceful: no one knows the precise location of the psychological and political boundaries that must not be crossed when it comes to the ownership of one country by another.

Will China Own the World?

The sovereign wealth funds of nonpetroleum-exporting countries raise a different kind of problem. Why would a country with no particular natural resources to speak of decide to own another country? One possibility is of course neocolonial ambitions, a pure will to power, as in the era of European colonialism. But the difference is that in those days the European countries enjoyed a technological advantage that ensured their domination. China and other emerging nonpetroleum countries are growing very rapidly, to be sure, but the evidence suggests that this rapid growth will end once they catch up with the leaders in terms of productivity and standard of living. The diffusion of knowledge and productive technologies is a fundamentally equalizing process: once the less advanced countries catch up with the more advanced, they cease to grow more rapidly.

In the central scenario for the evolution of the global capital/income ratio that I discussed in Chapter 5, I assumed that the savings rate would stabilize at around 10 percent of national income as this international convergence process neared its end. In that case, the accumulation of capital would attain comparable proportions everywhere. A very large share of the world's capital stock would of course be accumulated in Asia, and especially China, in keeping with the region's future share of global output. But according to the central scenario, the capital/income ratio would be the same on all continents, so that there would be no major imbalance between savings and investment in any region. Africa would be the only exception: in the central scenario depicted in Figures 12.4 and 12.5, the capital/income ratio is expected to be lower in Africa than in other continents throughout the twenty-first century (essentially because Africa is catching up economically much more slowly and its demographic transition is also delayed).[45] If capital can flow freely across borders, one would expect to see a flow of investments in Africa from other countries, especially China and other Asian nations. For the reasons discussed above, this could give rise to serious tensions, signs of which are already visible.

---

45. My hypotheses implicitly include the long-run savings rate in China (and elsewhere), counting both public and private saving. We cannot predict the future relationship between public property (notably in sovereign wealth funds) and private property in China.

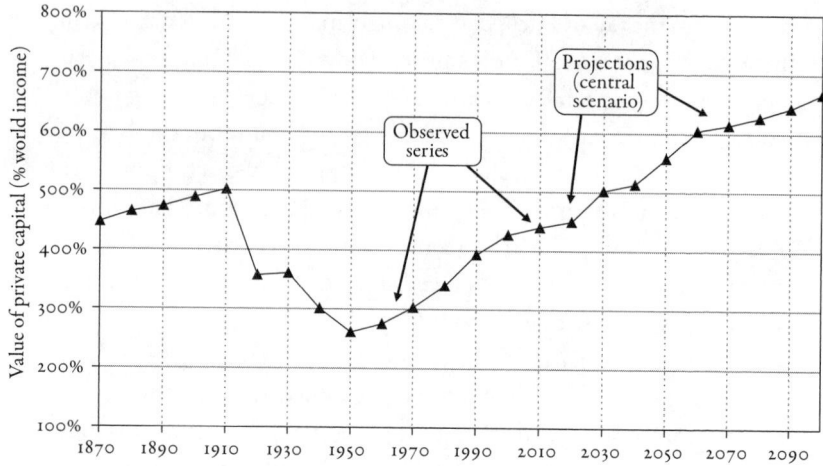

FIGURE 12.4. The world capital / income ratio, 1870–2100

According to the simulations (central scenario), the world capital / income ratio might be near to 700 percent by the end of the twenty-first century.

Sources and series: see piketty.pse.ens.fr/capital21c.

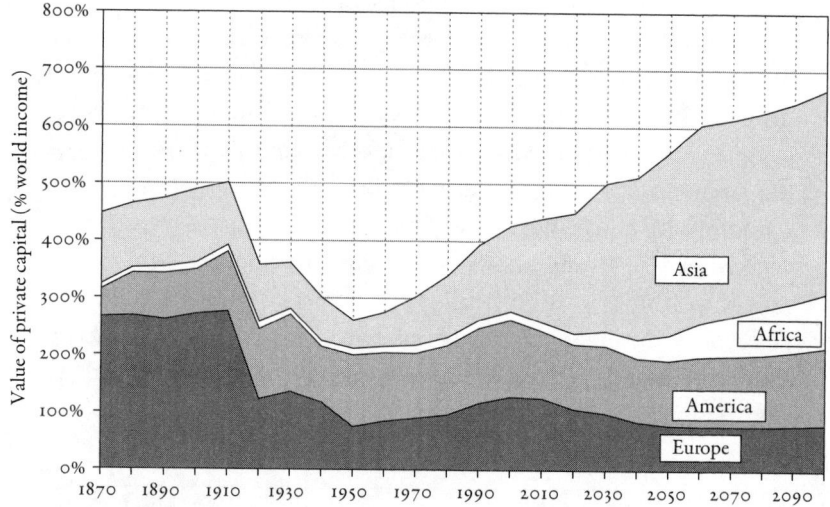

FIGURE 12.5. The distribution of world capital, 1870–2100

According to the central scenatio, Asian countries should own about half of world capital by the end of the twenty-first century.

Sources and series: see piketty.pse.ens.fr/capital21c.

To be sure, one can easily imagine scenarios much more unbalanced than the central scenario. Nevertheless, the forces of divergence are much less obvious than in the case of the sovereign wealth funds, whose growth depends on windfalls totally disproportionate to the needs of the populations benefiting from them (especially where those populations are tiny). This leads to endless accumulation, which the inequality $r > g$ transforms into a permanent divergence in the global capital distribution. To sum up, petroleum rents might well enable the oil states to buy the rest of the planet (or much of it) and to live on the rents of their accumulated capital.[46]

China, India, and other emerging countries are different. These countries have large populations whose needs (for both consumption and investment) remain far from satisfied. One can of course imagine scenarios in which the Chinese savings rate would remain persistently above the savings rate in Europe or North America: for example, China might choose a retirement system funded by investments rather than a pay-as-you-go system—a rather tempting choice in a low-growth environment (and even more tempting if demographic growth is negative).[47] For example, if China saves 20 percent of its national income until 2100, while Europe and the United States save only 10 percent, then by 2100 a large part of the Old and New Worlds will be owned by enormous Chinese pension funds.[48] Although this is logically possible, it is not very plausible, in part because Chinese workers and Chinese society as a whole would no doubt prefer (not without reason) to rely in large part on a public partition system for their retirement (as in

---

46. In any case, this transparent process of rent transformation (from oil rent to a diversified capital rent) illustrates the following point: capital has historically taken a variety of forms (land, oil, financial assets, business capital, real estate, etc.), but its underlying logic has not really changed, or at any rate has changed much less than people sometimes think.

47. In a pay-as-you-go, the contributions to the pension fund by active workers are directly paid out to retirees without being invested. On these issues, see Chapter 13.

48. Between one-quarter and one-half of European and US capital (or even more, depending on various assumptions). See the online technical appendix.

Europe and the United States) and in part because of the political considerations already noted in the case of the petroleum exporting countries and their sovereign wealth funds, which would apply with equal force to Chinese pension funds.

International Divergence, Oligarchic Divergence

In any case, this threat of international divergence owing to a gradual acquisition of the rich countries by China (or by the petroleum exporters' sovereign wealth funds) seems less credible and dangerous than an oligarchic type of divergence, that is, a process in which the rich countries would come to be owned by their own billionaires or, more generally, in which all countries, including China and the petroleum exporters, would come to be owned more and more by the planet's billionaires and multimillionaires. As noted, this process is already well under way. As global growth slows and international competition for capital heats up, there is every reason to believe that r will be much greater than g in the decades ahead. If we add to this the fact that the return on capital increases with the size of the initial endowment, a phenomenon that may well be reinforced by the growing complexity of global financial markets, then clearly all the ingredients are in place for the top centile and thousandth of the global wealth distribution to pull farther and farther ahead of the rest. To be sure, it is quite difficult to foresee how rapidly this oligarchic divergence will occur, but the risk seems much greater than the risk of international divergence.[49]

In particular, it is important to stress that the currently prevalent fears of growing Chinese ownership are a pure fantasy. The wealthy countries are in fact much wealthier than they sometimes think. The total real estate and financial assets net of debt owned by European households today amount to some 70 trillion euros. By comparison,

---

49. The divergence of the petroleum exporters can be seen as an oligarchic divergence, moreover, because petroleum rents go to a small number of individuals, who may be able to sustain a high level of accumulation through sovereign wealth funds.

the total assets of the various Chinese sovereign wealth funds plus the reserves of the Bank of China represent around 3 trillion euros, or less than one-twentieth the former amount.[50] The rich countries are not about to be taken over by the poor countries, which would have to get much richer to do anything of the kind, and that will take many more decades.

What, then, is the source of this fear, this feeling of dispossession, which is partly irrational? Part of the reason is no doubt the universal tendency to look elsewhere for the source of domestic difficulties. For example, many people in France believe that rich foreign buyers are responsible for the skyrocketing price of Paris real estate. When one looks closely at who is buying what type of apartment, however, one finds that the increase in the number of foreign (or foreign-resident) buyers can explain barely 3 percent of the price increase. In other words, 97 percent of today's very high real estate prices are due to the fact that there are enough French buyers residing in France who are prosperous enough to pay such large amounts for property.[51]

To my mind, this feeling of dispossession is due primarily to the fact that wealth is very highly concentrated in the rich countries (so that for much of the population, capital is an abstraction) and the process of the political secession of the largest fortunes is already well under way. For most people living in the wealthy countries, of Europe especially, the idea that European households own 20 times as much capital as China is rather hard to grasp, especially since this wealth is private and cannot be mobilized by governments for public purposes

---

50. The GDP of the European Union was close to 15 trillion euros in 2012–2013, compared with 10 trillion euros for China's GDP at purchasing power parity (or 6 trillion at current exchange rates, which may be better for comparing international financial assets). See Chapter 1. China's net foreign assets are growing rapidly, but not fast enough to overtake the total private wealth of the rich countries. See the online technical appendix.

51. See Aurélie Sotura, "Les étrangers font-ils monter les prix de l'immobilier? Estimation à partir de la base de la chambre des Notaires de Paris, 1993–2008," Paris, Ecoles des Hautes Etudes en Sciences Social and Paris School of Economics, 2011.

such as aiding Greece, as China helpfully proposed not long ago. Yet this private European wealth is very real, and if the governments of the European Union decided to tap it, they could. But the fact is that it is very difficult for any single government to regulate or tax capital and the income it generates. The main reason for the feeling of dispossession that grips the rich countries today is this loss of democratic sovereignty. This is especially true in Europe, whose territory is carved up into small states in competition with one another for capital, which aggravates the whole process. The very substantial increase in gross foreign asset positions (with each country owning a larger and larger stake in its neighbors, as discussed in Chapter 5) is also part of this process, and contributes to the sense of helplessness.

In Part Four I will show how useful a tool a global (or if need be European) tax on capital would be for overcoming these contradictions, and I will also consider what other government responses might be possible. To be clear, oligarchic divergence is not only more probable than international divergence, it is also much more difficult to combat, because it demands a high degree of international coordination among countries that are ordinarily engaged in competition with one another. The secession of wealth tends, moreover, to obscure the very idea of nationality, since the wealthiest individuals can to some extent take their money and change their nationality, cutting all ties to their original community. Only a coordinated response at a relatively broad regional level can overcome this difficulty.

Are the Rich Countries Really Poor?

Another point that needs to be emphasized is that a substantial fraction of global financial assets is already hidden away in various tax havens, thus limiting our ability to analyze the geographic distribution of global wealth. To judge by official statistics alone (relying on national data collated by international organizations such as the IMF), it would seem that the net asset position of the wealthy countries vis-à-vis the rest of the world is negative. As noted in Part Two, Japan and

Germany are in substantial surplus relative to the rest of the world (meaning that their households, firms, and governments own a lot more foreign assets than the rest of the world owns of their assets), which reflects the fact that they have been running large trade surpluses in recent decades. But the net position of the United States is negative, and that of most European countries other than Germany is close to zero, if not in the red.[52] All told, when one adds up the positions of all the wealthy countries, one is left with a slightly negative position, equivalent to about −4 percent of global GDP in 2010, compared with close to zero in the mid-1980s, as Figure 12.6 shows.[53] It is important to recognize, however, that it is a very slightly negative position (amounting to just 1 percent of global wealth). In any case, as I have already discussed at length, we are living in a time when international positions are relatively balanced, at least when compared with the colonial period, when the rich countries enjoyed a much larger positive position with respect to the rest of the world.[54]

Of course this slightly negative official position should in principle be counterbalanced by an equivalent positive position for the rest of the world. In other words, the poor countries should own more assets in the rich countries than vice versa, with a surplus on the order of 4 percent of global GDP (or 1 percent of global wealth) in their favor. In fact, this is not the case: if one adds up the financial statistics for the various countries of the world, one finds that the poor countries also have a negative position and that the world as a whole is in a substantially negative situation. It seems, in other words, that Earth must be owned by Mars. This is a fairly old "statistical anomaly," but according to various international organizations it has gotten worse in recent years. (The global balance of payments is regularly negative: more money leaves countries than enters them, which is theoretically impossible.)

---

52. See in particular Figure 5.7.
53. In Figure 12.6, the "wealthy countries" include Japan, Western Europe, and the United States. Adding Canada and Oceania would change little. See the online technical appendix.
54. See Chapters 3–5.

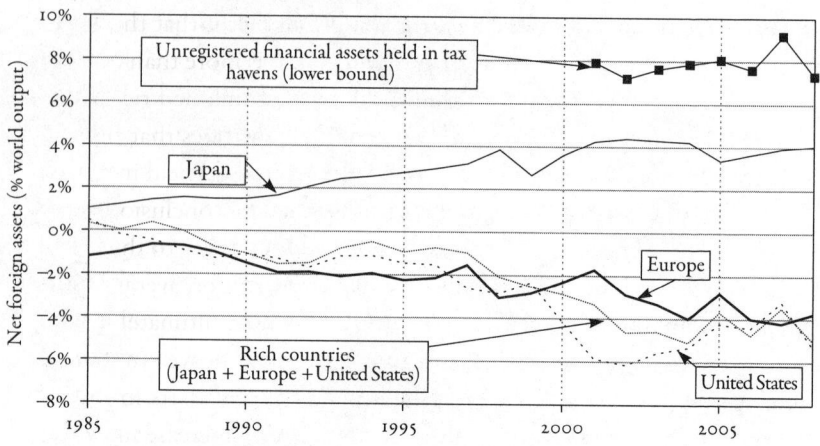

FIGURE 12.6. The net foreign asset position of rich countries

Unregistered financial assets held in tax havens are higher than the official net foreign debt of rich countries.

Sources and series: see piketty.pse.ens.fr/capital21c.

No real explanation of this phenomenon has been forthcoming. Note that these financial statistics and balance-of-payments data in theory cover the entire world. In particular, banks in the tax havens are theoretically required to report their accounts to international institutions. The "anomaly" can presumably be explained by various statistical biases and measurement errors.

By comparing all the available sources and exploiting previously unused Swiss bank data, Gabriel Zucman was able to show that the most plausible reason for the discrepancy is that large amounts of unreported financial assets are held in tax havens. By his cautious estimate, these amount to nearly 10 percent of global GDP.[55] Certain nongovernmental organizations have proposed even larger estimates (up to 2 or 3 times larger). Given the current state of the available sources, I believe that Zucman's estimate is slightly more realistic, but such estimates are by nature uncertain, and it is possible that Zucman's

---

55. Or 7–8 percent of total net financial assets worldwide (see above).

is a lower bound.[56] In any event, the important fact is that this lower bound is already extremely high. In particular, it is more than twice as large as the official negative net position of the combined rich countries (see Figure 12.6).[57] Now, all the evidence indicates that the vast majority (at least three-quarters) of the financial assets held in tax havens belongs to residents of the rich countries. The conclusion is obvious: the net asset position of the rich countries relative to the rest of the world is in fact positive (the rich countries own on average more than the poor countries and not vice versa, which ultimately is not very surprising), but this is masked by the fact that the wealthiest residents of the rich countries are hiding some of their assets in tax havens. In particular, this implies that the very sharp increase in private wealth (relative to national income) in the rich countries in recent decades is actually even larger than we estimated on the basis of official accounts. The same is true of the upward trend of the share of large fortunes in total wealth.[58] Indeed, this shows how difficult it is to track assets in the globalized capitalism of the early twenty-first century, thus blurring our picture of the basic geography of wealth.

56. See the online technical appendix for a discussion of the high estimate made in 2012 by James Henry for the Tax Justice Network, and the intermediate 2010 estimate by Ronen Palan, Richard Murphy, and Christian Chavagneux.

57. The data in Figure 12.6 are from Gabriel Zucman, "The Missing Wealth of Nations: Are Europe and the U.S. Net Debtors or Net Creditors?," *Quarterly Journal of Economics* 128, no. 3 (2013): 1321–64.

58. According to an estimate by Roine and Waldenström, accounting for assets held abroad (estimated from inconsistencies in the Swedish balance of payments) can, under certain assumptions, lead to the conclusion that the top centile in Sweden is close to the same level of wealth as the top centile in the United States (which probably should also be increased). See the online technical appendix.

PART FOUR

REGULATING CAPITAL IN THE TWENTY-FIRST CENTURY

{ THIRTEEN }

A Social State for the Twenty-First Century

In the first three parts of this book, I analyzed the evolution of the distribution of wealth and the structure of inequality since the eighteenth century. From this analysis I must now try to draw lessons for the future. One major lesson is already clear: it was the wars of the twentieth century that, to a large extent, wiped away the past and transformed the structure of inequality. Today, in the second decade of the twenty-first century, inequalities of wealth that had supposedly disappeared are close to regaining or even surpassing their historical highs. The new global economy has brought with it both immense hopes (such as the eradication of poverty) and equally immense inequities (some individuals are now as wealthy as entire countries). Can we imagine a twenty-first century in which capitalism will be transcended in a more peaceful and more lasting way, or must we simply await the next crisis or the next war (this time truly global)? On the basis of the history I have brought to light here, can we imagine political institutions that might regulate today's global patrimonial capitalism justly as well as efficiently?

As I have already noted, the ideal policy for avoiding an endless inegalitarian spiral and regaining control over the dynamics of accumulation would be a progressive global tax on capital. Such a tax would also have another virtue: it would expose wealth to democratic scrutiny, which is a necessary condition for effective regulation of the banking system and international capital flows. A tax on capital would promote the general interest over private interests while preserving economic openness and the forces of competition. The same cannot be said of various forms of retreat into national or other identities, which may well be the alternative to this ideal policy. But a truly global tax on capital is no doubt a utopian ideal. Short of that, a regional or continental tax might be tried, in particular in Europe, starting with countries willing to accept such a tax. Before I come to that, I must first reexamine in a much broader context the question of a tax on capital (which is of course only one component of an ideal social and fiscal system). What is the role of government in the production and distribution of wealth in the twenty-first century, and what kind of social state is most suitable for the age?

The Crisis of 2008 and the Return of the State

The global financial crisis that began in 2007–2008 is generally described as the most serious crisis of capitalism since the crash of 1929. The comparison is in some ways justified, but essential differences remain. The most obvious of these is that the recent crisis has not led to a depression as devastating as the Great Depression of the 1930s. Between 1929 and 1935, production in the developed countries fell by a quarter, unemployment rose by the same amount, and the world did not entirely recover from the Depression until the onset of World War II. Fortunately, the current crisis has been significantly less cataclysmic. That is why it has been given a less alarming name: the Great Recession. To be sure, the leading developed economies in 2013 are not quite back to the level of output they had achieved in 2007, government finances are in pitiful condition, and prospects for growth look gloomy for the foreseeable future, especially in Europe, which is mired in an endless sovereign debt crisis (which is ironic, since Europe is also the continent with the highest capital / income ratio in the world). Yet even in the depths of the recession, in 2009, production did not fall by more than five percentage points in the wealthiest countries. This was enough to make it the most serious global recession since the end of World War II, but it is still a very different thing from the dramatic collapse of output and waves of bankruptcies of the 1930s. Furthermore, growth in the emerging countries quickly bounced back and is buoying global growth today.

The main reason why the crisis of 2008 did not trigger a crash as serious as the Great Depression is that this time the governments and central banks of the wealthy countries did not allow the financial system to collapse and agreed to create the liquidity necessary to avoid the waves of bank failures that led the world to the brink of the abyss in the 1930s. This pragmatic monetary and financial policy, poles apart from the "liquidationist" orthodoxy that reigned nearly everywhere after the 1929 crash, managed to avoid the worst. (Herbert Hoover, the US president in 1929, thought that limping businesses had to be "liquidated," and until Franklin Roosevelt replaced Hoover in 1933, they were.) The pragmatic response to the crisis also reminded the world that central banks do not exist just to twiddle their thumbs and keep down inflation. In situations of total financial panic, they play an indispensable role as lender of last resort—indeed, they are the only public institution capable of averting a total collapse of the economy and society in an emergency. That said, central banks are not designed to solve all the world's problems. The pragmatic policies adopted after the crisis of 2008 no doubt avoided the worst, but they did not really provide a durable response to the structural problems that made the crisis possible, including the crying lack of financial transparency and the rise of inequality. The crisis of 2008 was the first crisis of the globalized patrimonial capitalism of the twenty-first century. It is unlikely to be the last.

Many observers deplore the absence of any real "return of the state" to managing the economy. They point out that the Great Depression, as terrible as it was, at least deserves credit for bringing about radical changes in tax policy and government spending. Indeed, within a few years of his inauguration, Roosevelt increased the top marginal rate of the federal income tax to more than 80 percent on extremely high incomes, whereas the top rate under Hoover had been only 25 percent. By contrast, at the time of this writing, Washington is still wondering whether the Obama administration will be able in its second term to raise the top rate left by Bush (of around 35 percent) above what it was under Clinton in the 1990s (around 40 percent).

In Chapter 14 I will look at the question of confiscatory tax rates on incomes deemed to be indecent (and economically useless), which was in fact an impressive US innovation of the interwar years. To my mind, it deserves to be reconceived and revived, especially in the country that first thought of it.

To be sure, good economic and social policy requires more than just a high marginal tax rate on extremely high incomes. By its very nature, such a tax brings in almost nothing. A progressive tax on capital is a more suitable instrument for responding to the challenges of the twenty-first century than a progressive income tax, which was designed for the twentieth century (although the two tools can play complementary roles in the future). For now, however, it is important to dispel a possible misunderstanding.

The possibility of greater state intervention in the economy raises very different issues today than it did in the 1930s, for a simple reason: the influence of the state is much greater now than it was then, indeed, in many ways greater than it has ever been. That is why today's crisis is both an indictment of the markets and a challenge to the role of government. Of course, the role of government has been constantly challenged since the 1970s, and the challenges will never end: once the government takes on the central role in economic and social life that it acquired in the decades after World War II, it is normal and legitimate for that role to be permanently questioned and debated. To some this may seem unjust, but it is inevitable and natural. Some people are baffled by the new role of government, and vehement if uncomprehending clashes between apparently irreconcilable positions are not uncommon. Some are outspoken in favor of an even greater role for the state, as if it no longer played any role at all, while still others call for the state to be dismantled at once, especially in the country where it is least present, the United States. There, groups affiliated with the Tea Party call for abolishing the Federal Reserve and returning to the gold standard. In Europe, the verbal clashes between "lazy Greeks" and "Nazi Germans" can be even more vitriolic. None of this helps to solve the real problems at hand. Both the antimarket and antistate camps are partly correct:

new instruments are needed to regain control over a financial capitalism that has run amok, and at the same time the tax and transfer systems that are the heart of the modern social state are in constant need of reform and modernization, because they have achieved a level of complexity that makes them difficult to understand and threatens to undermine their social and economic efficacy.

This twofold task may seem insurmountable. It is in fact an enormous challenge, which our democratic societies will have to meet in the years ahead. But it will be impossible to convince a majority of citizens that our governing institutions (especially at the supranational level) need new tools unless the instruments already in place can be shown to be working properly. To clarify all this, I must first take a look backward and briefly discuss how taxation and government spending have evolved in the rich countries since the nineteenth century.

The Growth of the Social State in the Twentieth Century

The simplest way to measure the change in the government's role in the economy and society is to look at the total amount of taxes relative to national income. Figure 13.1 shows the historical trajectory of four countries (the United States, Britain, France, and Sweden) that are fairly representative of what has happened in the rich countries.[1] There are both striking similarities and important differences in the observed evolutions.

---

1. As is customary, I take tax revenues to include all taxes, fees, social contributions, and other payments that citizens must pay under penalty of law. The distinctions between different types of payments, especially taxes and social insurance contributions, are not always very clear and do not mean the same thing in different countries. For the purpose of historical and international comparisons, it is important to consider all sums paid to the government, whether the central government or states or cities or other public agencies (such as social security, etc.). To simplify the discussion, I will sometimes use the word "taxes," but unless otherwise indicated I always include other compulsory charges as well. See the online technical appendix.

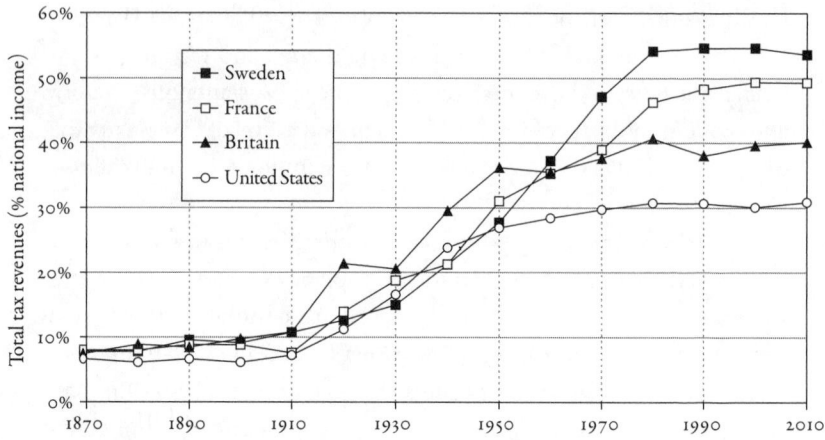

FIGURE 13.1. Tax revenues in rich countries, 1870–2010

Total tax revenues were less than 10 percent of national income in rich countries until 1900–1910; they represent between 30 percent and 55 percent of national income in 2000–2010.

Sources and series: see piketty.pse.ens.fr/capital21c.

The first similarity is that taxes consumed less than 10 percent of national income in all four countries during the nineteenth century and up to World War I. This reflects the fact that the state at that time had very little involvement in economic and social life. With 7–8 percent of national income, it is possible for a government to fulfill its central "regalian" functions (police, courts, army, foreign affairs, general administration, etc.) but not much more. After paying to maintain order, enforce property rights, and sustain the military (which often accounts for more than half of total expenditures), not much remained in the government's coffers.[2] States in this period also paid for some roads and other infrastructure, as well as schools, universi-

---

2. Military expenditures generally amount to at least 2–3 percent of national income and can go much higher in a country that is unusually active militarily (like the United States, which currently devotes more than 4 percent of its national income to the military) or that feels its security and property threatened (Saudi Arabia and the Gulf states spend more than 10 percent of national income on the military).

ties, and hospitals, but most people had access only to fairly rudimentary educational and health services.[3]

Between 1920 and 1980, the share of national income that the wealthy countries chose to devote to social spending increased considerably. In just half a century, the share of taxes in national income increased by a factor of at least 3 or 4 (and in the Nordic countries more than 5). Between 1980 and 2010, however, the tax share stabilized everywhere. This stabilization took place at different levels in each country, however: just over 30 percent of national income in the United States, around 40 percent in Britain, and between 45 and 55 percent on the European continent (45 percent in Germany, 50 percent in France, and nearly 55 percent in Sweden).[4] The differences between countries are significant.[5] Nevertheless, the secular evolutions are closely matched, in particular the almost perfect stability observed in all four countries over the past three decades. Political changes and national peculiarities are also noticeable in Figure 13.1 (between Britain and France, for example).[6] But their

---

3. Health and education budgets were generally below 1–2 percent of national income in the nineteenth century. For a historical view of the slow development of social spending since the eighteenth century and the acceleration in the twentieth century, see P. Lindert, *Growing Public: Social Spending and Economic Growth since the Eighteenth Century* (Cambridge: Cambridge University Press, 2004).

4. Note that the share of compulsory payments is expressed here as a proportion of national income (which is generally around 90 percent of GDP after deduction of about 10 percent for depreciation of capital). This seems to me the right thing to do, in that depreciation is not anyone's income (see Chapter 1). If payments are expressed as a percentage of GDP, then the shares obtained are by definition 10 percent smaller (for example, 45 percent of GDP instead of 50 percent of national income).

5. Gaps of a few points may be due to purely statistical differences, but gaps of 5–10 points are real and substantial indicators of the role played by the government in each country.

6. In Britain, taxes fell by several points in the 1980s, which marked the Thatcherite phase of government disengagement, but then climbed again in 1990–2000, as new governments reinvested in public services. In France, the state share rose somewhat later than elsewhere, continued to rise strongly in 1970–1980, and did not begin to stabilize until 1985–1990. See the online technical appendix.

importance is on the whole rather limited compared with this common stabilization.[7]

In other words, all the rich countries, without exception, went in the twentieth century from an equilibrium in which less than a tenth of their national income was consumed by taxes to a new equilibrium in which the figure rose to between a third and a half.[8] Several important points about this fundamental transformation call for further clarification.

First, it should be clear why the question of whether or not there has been a "return to the state" in the present crisis is misleading: the role of the government is greater than ever. In order to fully appreciate the state's role in economic and social life, other indicators of course need to be considered. The state also intervenes by setting rules, not just by collecting taxes to pay its expenses. For example, the financial markets were much less tightly regulated after 1980 than before. The state also produces and owns capital: privatization of formerly state-owned industrial and financial assets over the past three decades has also reduced the state's role in comparison with the three decades after World War II. Nevertheless, in terms of tax receipts and government outlays, the state has never played as important an economic role as it has in recent decades. No downward trend is evident, contrary to what is sometimes said. To be sure, in the face of an aging population, advances in medical technology, and constantly growing educational needs, the mere fact of having stabilized the tax bill as a percentage of national income is in itself no mean feat: cutting the government budget is always easier to promise in opposition than to achieve once in power. Nevertheless, the fact remains that taxes today claim nearly half of na-

---

7. In order to focus on long-term trends, I have once again used decennial averages. The annual series of tax rates often include all sorts of minor cyclical variations, which are transitory and not very significant. See the online technical appendix.

8. Japan is slightly above the United States (32–33 percent of national income). Canada, Australia, and New Zealand are closer to Britain (35–40 percent).

tional income in most European countries, and no one seriously envisions an increase in the future comparable to that which occurred between 1930 and 1980. In the wake of the Depression, World War II, and postwar reconstruction, it was reasonable to think that the solution to the problems of capitalism was to expand the role of the state and increase social spending as much as necessary. Today's choices are necessarily more complex. The state's great leap forward has already taken place: there will be no second leap—not like the first one, in any event.

To gain a better understanding of what is at stake behind these figures, I want to describe in somewhat greater detail what this historic increase in government tax revenues was used for: the construction of a "social state."[9] In the nineteenth century, governments were content to fulfill their "regalian" missions. Today these same functions command a little less than one-tenth of national income. The growing tax bite enabled governments to take on ever broader social functions, which now consume between a quarter and a third of national income, depending on the country. This can be broken down initially into two roughly equal halves: one half goes to health and education, the other to replacement incomes and transfer payments.[10]

Spending on education and health consumes 10–15 percent of national income in all the developed countries today.[11] There are significant differences between countries, however. Primary and secondary education are almost entirely free for everyone in all the rich countries, but higher education can be quite expensive, especially in the United States and to a lesser extent in Britain. Public health insurance is universal (that is, open to the entire population) in most countries

---

9. The term "social state" captures the nature and variety of the state's missions better than the more restrictive term "welfare state," in my view.

10. See Supplemental Table S13.2, available online, for a complete breakdown of public spending in France, Germany, Britain, and the United States in 2000–2010.

11. Typically 5–6 percent for education and 8–9 percent for health. See the online technical appendix.

in Europe, including Britain.[12] In the United States, however, it is reserved for the poor and elderly (which does not prevent it from being very costly).[13] In all the developed countries, public spending covers much of the cost of education and health services: about three-quarters in Europe and half in the United States. The goal is to give equal access to these basic goods: every child should have access to education, regardless of his or her parents' income, and everyone should have access to health care, even, indeed especially, when circumstances are difficult.

Replacement incomes and transfer payments generally consume 10–15 (or even 20) percent of national income in most of the rich countries today. Unlike public spending on education and health, which may be regarded as transfers in kind, replacement income and transfer payments form part of household disposable income: the government takes in large sums in taxes and social insurance contributions and then pays them out to other households in the form of replacement income (pensions and unemployment compensation) and transfer payments (family allowances, guaranteed income, etc.), so that the total disposable income of all households in the aggregate remains unchanged.[14]

In practice, pensions account for the lion's share (two-thirds to three-quarters) of total replacement income and transfer payments.

---

12. The National Health Service, established in 1948, is such an integral part of British national identity that its creation was dramatized in the opening ceremonies of the 2012 Olympic games, along with the Industrial Revolution and the rock groups of the 1960s.

13. If one adds the cost of private insurance, the US health care system is by far the most expensive in the world (nearly 20 percent of national income, compared with 10–12 percent in Europe), even though a large part of the population is not covered and health indicators are not as good as in Europe. There is no doubt that universal public health insurance systems, in spite of their defects, offer a better cost-benefit ratio than the US system.

14. By contrast, social spending on education and health reduces the (monetary) disposable income of households, which explains why the amount of the latter decreased from 90 percent of national income at the turn of the twentieth century to 70–80 percent today. See Chapter 5.

Here, too, there are significant differences between countries. In continental Europe, pensions alone often consume 12–13 percent of national income (with Italy and France at the top, ahead of Germany and Sweden). In the United States and Britain, the public pension system is much more drastically capped for those at the middle and top of the income hierarchy (the replacement rate, that is, the amount of the pension in proportion to the wage earned prior to retirement, falls rather quickly for those who earned above the average wage), and pensions consume only 6–7 percent of national income.[15] These are very large sums in all cases: in all the rich countries, public pensions are the main source of income for at least two-thirds of retirees (and generally three-quarters). Despite the defects of these public pensions systems and the challenges they now face, the fact is that without them it would have been impossible to eradicate poverty among the elderly, which was endemic as recently as the 1950s. Along with access to education and health, public pensions constitute the third social revolution that the fiscal revolution of the twentieth century made possible.

Compared with pension outlays, payments for unemployment insurance are much smaller (typically 1–2 percent of national income), reflecting the fact that people spend less time in unemployment than in retirement. The replacement income is nevertheless useful when needed. Finally, income support outlays are even smaller (less than 1 percent of national income), almost insignificant when measured against total government spending. Yet this type of spending is often the most vigorously challenged: beneficiaries are suspected of wanting

---

15. Pensions systems with capped payments are usually called, after the architect of Britain's social state, "Beveridgian" (with the extreme case a flat pension amount for everyone, as in Britain), in contrast to "Bismarckian," "Scandinavian," or "Latin" systems, in which pensions are almost proportional to wages for the vast majority of the population (nearly everyone in France, where the ceiling is exceptionally high: eight times the average wage, compared with two to three times in most countries).

to live their lives on the dole, even though the proportion of the population relying on welfare payments is generally far smaller than for other government programs, because the stigma attached to welfare (and in many cases the complexity of the process) dissuades many who are entitled to benefits from asking for them.[16] Welfare benefits are questioned not only in Europe but also in the United States (where the unemployed black single mother is often singled out for criticism by opponents of the US "welfare state").[17] In both cases, the sums involved are in fact only a very small part of state social spending.

All told, if we add up state spending on health and education (10–15 percent of national income) and replacement and transfer payments (another 10–15 or perhaps as high as 20 percent of national income), we come up with total social spending (broadly speaking) of 25–35 percent of national income, which accounts for nearly all of the increase in government revenues in the wealthy countries in the twentieth century. In other words, the growth of the fiscal state over the last century basically reflects the constitution of a social state.

---

16. In France, which stands out for the extreme complexity of its social benefits and the proliferation of rules and agencies, fewer than half of the people who were supposed to benefit from one welfare-to-work program (the so-called active solidarity income, a supplement to very low part-time wages) applied for it.

17. One important difference between Europe and the United States is that income support programs in the United States have always been reserved for people with children. For childless individuals, the carceral state sometimes does the job of the welfare state (especially for young black males). About 1 percent of the adult US population was behind bars in 2013. This is the highest rate of incarceration in the world (slightly ahead of Russia and far ahead of China). The incarceration rate is more than 5 percent for adult black males (of all ages). See the online technical appendix. Another US peculiarity is the use of food stamps (whose purpose is to ensure that welfare recipients spend their benefits on food rather than on drink or other vices), which is inconsistent with the liberal worldview often attributed to US citizens. It is a sign of US prejudices in regard to the poor, which seem to be more extreme than European prejudices, perhaps because they are reinforced by racial prejudices.

Modern Redistribution: A Logic of Rights

To sum up: modern redistribution does not consist in transferring income from the rich to the poor, at least not in so explicit a way. It consists rather in financing public services and replacement incomes that are more or less equal for everyone, especially in the areas of health, education, and pensions. In the latter case, the principle of equality often takes the form of a quasi proportionality between replacement income and lifetime earnings.[18] For education and health, there is real equality of access for everyone regardless of income (or parents' income), at least in principle. Modern redistribution is built around a logic of rights and a principle of equal access to a certain number of goods deemed to be fundamental.

At a relatively abstract level, it is possible to find justifications for this rights-based approach in various national political and philosophical traditions. The US Declaration of Independence (1776) asserts that everyone has an equal right to the pursuit of happiness.[19] In a sense, our modern belief in fundamental rights to education and health can be linked to this assertion, even though it took quite a while to get there. Article 1 of the Declaration of the Rights of Man and the Citizen (1789) also proclaims that "men are born free and remain free and equal in rights." This is followed immediately, however, by the statement that "social distinctions can be based only on common utility." This is an important addition: the second sentence alludes to the existence of very real inequalities, even though the first asserts the principle of absolute equality. Indeed, this is the central tension of any rights-based approach: how far do equal rights extend? Do they simply guarantee the right to enter into free contract—the equality of the market, which at the time

---

18. With variations between countries described above.

19. "We hold these truths to be self-evident, that all men are created equal, that they are endowed by their Creator with certain inalienable Rights, that among these are Life, Liberty and the pursuit of Happiness; that to secure these rights, Governments are instituted among Men, deriving their just powers from the consent of the governed."

of the French Revolution actually seemed quite revolutionary? And if one includes equal rights to an education, to health care, and to a pension, as the twentieth-century social state proposed, should one also include rights to culture, housing, and travel?

The second sentence of article 1 of the Declaration of the Rights of Man of 1789 formulates a kind of answer to this question, since it in a sense reverses the burden of proof: equality is the norm, and inequality is acceptable only if based on "common utility." It remains to define the term "common utility." The drafters of the Declaration were thinking mainly of the abolition of the orders and privileges of the Ancien Régime, which were seen at the time as the very epitome of arbitrary, useless inequality, hence as not contributing to "common utility." One can interpret the phrase more broadly, however. One reasonable interpretation is that social inequalities are acceptable only if they are in the interest of all and in particular of the most disadvantaged social groups.[20] Hence basic rights and material advantages must be extended insofar as possible to everyone, as long as it is in the interest of those who have the fewest rights and opportunities to do so.[21] The "difference principle" in-

---

20. The notion of "common utility" has been the subject of endless debate, and to examine this would go far beyond the framework of this book. What is certain is that the drafters of the 1789 Declaration did not share the utilitarian spirit that has animated any number of economists since John Stuart Mill: a mathematical sum of individual utilities (together with the assumption that the utility function is "concave," meaning that its rate of increase decreases with increasing income, so that redistribution of income from the rich to the poor increases total utility). This mathematical representation of the desirability of redistribution bears little apparent relation to the way most people think about the question. The idea of rights seems more pertinent.

21. It seems reasonable to define "the most disadvantaged" as those individuals who have to cope with the most unfavorable factors beyond their control. To the extent that inequality of conditions is due, at least in part, to factors beyond the control of individuals, such as the existence of unequal family endowments (in terms of inheritances, cultural capital, etc.) or good fortune (special talents, luck, etc.), it is just for government to seek to reduce these inequalities as much as possible. The boundary between equalization of opportunities and conditions is often rather porous (education, health, and income are both opportunities and

troduced by the US philosopher John Rawls in his *Theory of Justice* is similar in intent.[22] And the "capabilities" approach favored by the Indian economist Amartya Sen is not very different in its basic logic.[23]

At a purely theoretical level, there is in fact a certain (partly artificial) consensus concerning the abstract principles of social justice. The disagreements become clearer when one tries to give a little substance to these social rights and inequalities and to anchor them in specific historical and economic contexts. In practice, the conflicts have to do mainly with the means of effecting real improvement in the living conditions of the least advantaged, the precise extent of the rights that can be granted to all (in view of economic and budgetary constraints and the many related uncertainties), and exactly what factors are within and beyond the control of individuals (where does luck end and where do effort and merit begin?). Such questions will never be answered by abstract principles or mathematical formulas. The only way to answer them is through democratic deliberation and political confrontation. The institutions and rules that govern democratic debate and decision-making therefore play a central role, as do the relative power and persuasive capabilities of different social groups. The US and French Revolutions both affirmed equality of rights as an absolute principle—a progressive stance at that time. But in practice, during the nineteenth century, the political systems that grew out of those revolutions concentrated mainly on the protection of property rights.

---

conditions). The Rawlsian notion of fundamental goods is a way of moving beyond this artificial opposition.

22. "Social and economic inequalities . . . are just only if they result in compensating benefits for everyone, and in particular for the least advantaged members of society" (John Rawls, *A Theory of Justice* [Cambridge, MA: Belknap Press, 15]). This 1971 formulation was repeated in *Political Liberalism,* published in 1993.

23. These theoretical approaches have recently been extended by Marc Fleurbaey and John Roemer, with some tentative empirical applications. See the online technical appendix.

Modernizing Rather Than Dismantling the Social State

Modern redistribution, as exemplified by the social states constructed by the wealthy countries in the twentieth century, is based on a set of fundamental social rights: to education, health, and retirement. Whatever limitations and challenges these systems of taxation and social spending face today, they nevertheless marked an immense step forward in historical terms. Partisan conflict aside, a broad consensus has formed around these social systems, particularly in Europe, which remains deeply attached to what is seen as a "European social model." No major movement or important political force seriously envisions a return to a world in which only 10 or 20 percent of national income would go to taxes and government would be pared down to its regalian functions.[24]

On the other hand, there is no significant support for continuing to expand the social state at its 1930–1980 growth rate (which would mean that by 2050–2060, 70–80 percent of national income would go to taxes). In theory, of course, there is no reason why a country cannot decide to devote two-thirds or three-quarters of its national income to taxes, assuming that taxes are collected in a transparent and efficient manner and used for purposes that everyone agrees are of high priority, such as education, health, culture, clean energy, and sustainable development. Taxation is neither good nor bad in itself. Everything depends on how taxes are collected and what they are used for. There are nevertheless two good reasons to believe that such a

---

24. Despite the consensus in Europe there is still considerable variation. The wealthiest and most productive countries have the highest taxes (50–60 percent of the national income in Sweden and Denmark), and the poorest, least developed countries have the lowest taxes (barely 30 percent of national income in Bulgaria and Romania). See the online appendix. In the United States there is less of a consensus. Certain substantial minority factions radically challenge the legitimacy of all federal social programs or indeed of social programs of any kind. Once again, racial prejudice seems to have something to do with this (as exemplified by the debates over the health care reform adopted by the Obama administration).

drastic increase in the size of the social state is neither realistic nor desirable, at least for the foreseeable future.

First, the very rapid expansion of the role of government in the three decades after World War II was greatly facilitated and accelerated by exceptionally rapid economic growth, at least in continental Europe.[25] When incomes are increasing 5 percent a year, it is not too difficult to get people to agree to devote an increasing share of that growth to social spending (which therefore increases more rapidly than the economy), especially when the need for better education, more health care, and more generous pensions is obvious (given the very limited funds allocated for these purposes from 1930 to 1950). The situation has been very different since the 1980s: with per capita income growth of just over 1 percent a year, no one wants large and steady tax increases, which would mean even slower if not negative income growth. Of course it is possible to imagine a redistribution of income via the tax system or more progressive tax rates applied to a more or less stable total income, but it is very difficult to imagine a general and durable increase in the average tax rate. The fact that tax revenues have stabilized in all the rich countries, notwithstanding national differences and changes of government, is no accident (see Figure 13.1). Furthermore, it is by no means certain that social needs justify ongoing tax increases. To be sure, there are objectively growing needs in the educational and health spheres, which may well justify slight tax increases in the future. But the citizens of the wealthy countries also have a legitimate need for enough income to purchase all sorts of goods and services produced by the private sector—for instance, to travel, buy clothing, obtain housing, avail themselves of new cultural services, purchase the latest tablet, and so on. In a world of low productivity growth, on the order of 1–1.5 percent (which is in fact a decent rate of

---

25. In the United States and Britain, the social state also grew rapidly even though economic growth was significantly lower, which may have fostered a powerful sense of loss reinforced by a belief that other countries were catching up, as discussed earlier (see Chapter 2 in particular).

growth over the long term), society has to choose among different types of needs, and there is no obvious reason to think that nearly all needs should by paid for through taxation.

Furthermore, no matter how the proceeds of growth are allocated among different needs, there remains the fact that once the public sector grows beyond a certain size, it must contend with serious problems of organization. Once again, it is hard to foresee what will happen in the very long run. It is perfectly possible to imagine that new decentralized and participatory forms of organization will be developed, along with innovative types of governance, so that a much larger public sector than exists today can be operated efficiently. The very notion of "public sector" is in any case reductive: the fact that a service is publicly financed does not mean that it is produced by people directly employed by the state or other public entities. In education and health, services are provided by many kinds of organizations, including foundations and associations, which are in fact intermediate forms between the state and private enterprise. All told, education and health account for 20 percent of employment and GDP in the developed economies, which is more than all sectors of industry combined. This way of organizing production is durable and universal. For example, no one has proposed transforming private US universities into publicly owned corporations. It is perfectly possible that such intermediary forms will become more common in the future, for example, in the cultural and media sectors, where profit-making corporations already face serious competition and raise concerns about potential conflicts of interest. As I showed earlier when discussing how capitalism is organized in Germany, the notion of private property can vary from country to country, even in the automobile business, one of the most traditional branches of industry. There is no single variety of capitalism or organization of production in the developed world today: we live in a mixed economy, different to be sure from the mixed economy that people envisioned after World War II but nonetheless quite real. This will continue to be true in the future, no doubt more than ever: new forms of organization and ownership remain to be invented.

That said, before we can learn to efficiently organize public financing equivalent to two-thirds to three-quarters of national income, it would be good to improve the organization and operation of the existing public sector, which represents only half of national income (including replacement and transfer payments)—no small affair. In Germany, France, Italy, Britain, and Sweden, debates about the social state in the decades to come will revolve mainly around issues of organization, modernization, and consolidation: if total taxes and social spending remain more or less unchanged in proportion to national income (or perhaps rise slightly in response to growing needs), how can we improve the operation of hospitals and day care centers, adjust doctors' fees and drug costs, reform universities and primary schools, and revise pension and unemployment benefits in response to changing life expectancies and youth unemployment rates? At a time when nearly half of national income goes to public spending, such debates are legitimate and even indispensable. If we do not constantly ask how to adapt our social services to the public's needs, the consensus supporting high levels of taxation and therefore the social state may not last forever.

Obviously, an analysis of the prospects for reform of all aspects of the social state would far exceed the scope of this book. I will therefore confine myself to a few issues of particular importance for the future and directly related to the themes of my work: first, the question of equal access to education, and especially higher education, and second, the future of pay-as-you-go retirement systems in a world of low growth.

Do Educational Institutions Foster Social Mobility?

In all countries, on all continents, one of the main objectives of public spending for education is to promote social mobility. The stated goal is to provide access to education for everyone, regardless of social origin. To what extent do existing institutions fulfill this objective?

In Part Three, I showed that even with the considerable increase in the average level of education over the course of the twentieth century, earned income inequality did not decrease. Qualification levels shifted upward: a high school diploma now represents what a grade school certificate used to mean, a college degree what a high school diploma used to stand for, and so on. As technologies and workplace needs changed, all wage levels increased at similar rates, so that inequality did not change. What about mobility? Did mass education lead to more rapid turnover of winners and losers for a given skill hierarchy? According to the available data, the answer seems to be no: the intergenerational correlation of education and earned incomes, which measures the reproduction of the skill hierarchy over time, shows no trend toward greater mobility over the long run, and in recent years mobility may even have decreased.[26] Note, however, that it is much more difficult to measure mobility across generations than it is to measure inequality at a given point in time, and the sources available for estimating the historical evolution of mobility are highly imperfect.[27] The most firmly established result in this area of research is that intergenerational reproduction is lowest in the Nordic countries and highest in the United States (with a correlation coefficient two-thirds higher than in Sweden).

---

26. According to the work of Anders Bjorklund and Arnaud Lefranc on Sweden and France, respectively, it seems that the intergenerational correlation decreased slightly for cohorts born in 1940–1950 compared with those born in 1920–1930, then increased again for cohorts born in 1960–1970. See the online technical appendix.

27. It is possible to measure mobility for cohorts born in the twentieth century (with uneven precision and imperfect comparability across countries), but it is almost impossible to measure intergenerational mobility in the nineteenth century except in terms of inheritance (see Chapter 11). But this is a different issue from skill and earned income mobility, which is what is of interest here and is the focal point of these measurements of intergenerational mobility. The data used in these works do not allow us to isolate mobility of capital income.

France, Germany, and Britain occupy a middle ground, less mobile than northern Europe but more mobile than the United States.[28]

These findings stand in sharp contrast to the belief in "American exceptionalism" that once dominated US sociology, according to which social mobility in the United States was exceptionally high compared with the class-bound societies of Europe. No doubt the settler society of the early nineteenth century was more mobile. As I have shown, moreover, inherited wealth played a smaller role in the United States than in Europe, and US wealth was for a long time less concentrated, at least up to World War I. Throughout most of the twentieth century, however, and still today, the available data suggest that social mobility has been and remains lower in the United States than in Europe.

One possible explanation for this is the fact that access to the most elite US universities requires the payment of extremely high tuition fees. Furthermore, these fees rose sharply in the period 1990–2010, following fairly closely the increase in top US incomes, which suggests that the reduced social mobility observed in the United States in the past will decline even more in the future.[29] The issue of unequal access to higher education is increasingly a subject of debate in the United States. Research has shown that the proportion of college degrees earned by children whose parents belong to the bottom two quartiles of the income hierarchy stagnated at 10–20 percent in 1970–2010, while it rose from 40 to 80 percent for children with parents in the

---

28. The correlation coefficient ranges from 0.2–0.3 in Sweden and Finland to 0.5–0.6 in the United States. Britain (0.4–0.5) is closer to the United States but not so far from Germany or France (0.4). Concerning international comparisons of intergenerational correlation coefficients of earned income (which are also confirmed by twin studies), see the work of Markus Jantti. See the online technical appendix.

29. The cost of an undergraduate year at Harvard in 2012–2013 was $54,000, including room and board and various other fees (tuition in the strict sense was $38,000). Some other universities are even more expensive than Harvard, which enjoys a high income on its endowment (see Chapter 12).

top quartile.[30] In other words, parents' income has become an almost perfect predictor of university access.

This inequality of access also seems to exist at the top of the economic hierarchy, not only because of the high cost of attending the most prestigious private universities (high even in relation to the income of upper-middle-class parents) but also because admissions decisions clearly depend in significant ways on the parents' financial capacity to make donations to the universities. For example, one study has shown that gifts by graduates to their former universities are strangely concentrated in the period when the children are of college age.[31] By comparing various sources of data, moreover, it is possible to estimate that the average income of the parents of Harvard students is currently about $450,000, which corresponds to the average income of the top 2 percent of the US income hierarchy.[32] Such a finding does not seem entirely compatible with the idea of selection based solely on merit. The contrast between the official meritocratic discourse and the reality seems particularly extreme in this case. The total absence of transparency regarding selection procedures should also be noted.[33]

It would be wrong, however, to imagine that unequal access to higher education is a problem solely in the United States. It is one of the most important problems that social states everywhere must face

---

30. See G. Duncan and R. Murnane, *Whither Opportunity? Rising Inequality, Schools, and Children's Life Chances* (New York: Russell Sage Foundation, 2011), esp. chap. 6. See the online technical appendix.

31. See Jonathan Meer and Harvey S. Rosen, "Altruism and the Child Cycle of Alumni Donations," *American Economic Journal: Economic Policy* 1, no. 1 (2009): 258–86.

32. This does not mean that Harvard recruits its students exclusively from among the wealthiest 2 percent of the nation. It simply means that recruitment below that level is sufficiently rare, and that recruitment among the wealthiest 2 percent is sufficiently frequent, that the average is what it is. See the online technical appendix.

33. Statistics as basic as the average income or wealth of parents of students at various US universities are very difficult to obtain and not much studied.

in the twenty-first century. To date, no country has come up with a truly satisfactory response. To be sure, university tuitions fees are much lower in Europe if one leaves Britain aside.[34] In other countries, including Sweden and other Nordic countries, Germany, France, Italy, and Spain, tuition fees are relatively low (less than 500 euros). Although there are exceptions, such as business schools and Sciences Po in France, and although the situation is changing rapidly, this remains a very striking difference between continental Europe and the United States: in Europe, most people believe that access to higher education should be free or nearly free, just as primary and secondary education are.[35] In Quebec, the decision to raise tuition gradually from $2,000 to nearly $4,000 was interpreted as an attempt to move toward an inegalitarian US-style system, which led to a student strike in the winter of 2012 and ultimately to a change of government and cancellation of the decision.

It would be naïve, however, to think that free higher education would resolve all problems. In 1964, Pierre Bourdieu and Jean-Claude Passeron analyzed, in *Les héritiers,* more subtle mechanisms of social and cultural selection, which often do the same work as financial selection. In practice, the French system of "grandes écoles" leads to spending more public money on students from more advantaged social backgrounds, while less money is spent on university students who come from more modest backgrounds. Again, the contrast between the official discourse of "republican meritocracy" and the reality (in which social spending amplifies inequalities of social origin)

---

34. The highest tuition fee British universities may charge was increased to £1,000 in 1998, £3,000 in 2004, and £9,000 in 2012. The share of tuition fees in total resources of British universities in 2010 is almost as high as in the 1920s and close to the US level. See the interesting series of historical studies by Vincent Carpentier, "Public-Private Substitution in Higher Education," *Higher Education Quarterly* 66, no. 4 (October 2012): 363–90.

35. Bavaria and Lower Saxony decided in early 2013 to eliminate the university tuition of 500 euros per semester and offer free higher education like the rest of Germany. In the Nordic countries, tuition is never more than a few hundred euros, as in France.

is extreme.[36] According to the available data, it seems that the average income of parents of students at Sciences Po is currently around 90,000 euros, which roughly corresponds to the top 10 percent of the French income hierarchy. Recruitment is thus 5 times broader than at Harvard but still relatively limited.[37] We lack the data to do a similar calculation for students at the other grandes écoles, but the results would likely be similar.

Make no mistake: there is no easy way to achieve real equality of opportunity in higher education. This will be a key issue for the social state in the twenty-first century, and the ideal system has yet to be invented. Tuition fees create an unacceptable inequality of access, but they foster the independence, prosperity, and energy that make US universities the envy of the world.[38] In the abstract, it should be possible to combine the advantages of decentralization with those of equal access by providing universities with substantial publicly financed incentives. In some respects this is what public health insurance systems do: producers (doctors and hospitals) are granted a certain independence, but the cost of care is a collective responsibility, thus ensuring

36. One finds the same redistribution from bottom to top in primary and secondary education: students at the most disadvantaged schools and high schools are assigned the least experienced and least trained teachers and therefore receive less public money per child than students at more advantaged schools and high schools. This is all the more regrettable because a better distribution of resources at the primary level would greatly reduce inequalities of educational opportunity. See Thomas Piketty and M. Valdenaire, *L'impact de la taille des classes sur la réussite scolaire dans les écoles, collèges et lycées français* (Paris: Ministère de l'Education Nationale, 2006).

37. As in the case of Harvard, this average income does not mean that Sciences Po recruits solely among the wealthiest 10 percent of families. See the online technical appendix for the complete income distribution of parents of Sciences Po students in 2011–2012.

38. According to the well-known Shanghai rankings, 53 of the 100 best universities in the world in 2012–2013 were in the United States, compared with 31 in Europe (9 of which were in Britain). The order is reversed, however, when we look at the 500 best universities (150 for the United States and 202 for Europe, of which 38 are in Britain). This reflects significant inequalities among the 800 US universities (see Chapter 12).

that patients have equal access to the system. One could do the same thing with universities and students. The Nordic countries have adopted a strategy of this kind in higher education. This of course requires substantial public financing, which is not easy to come by in the current climate of consolidation of the social state.[39] Such a strategy is nevertheless far more satisfactory than other recent attempts, which range from charging tuition fees that vary with parents' income[40] to offering loans that are to be paid back by a surtax added to the recipient's income tax.[41]

If we are to make progress on these issues in the future, it would be good to begin by working toward greater transparency than exists today. In the United States, France, and most other countries, talk about the virtues of the national meritocratic model is seldom based on close examination of the facts. Often the purpose is to justify existing inequalities while ignoring the sometimes patent failures of the current system. In 1872, Emile Boutmy created Sciences Po with a clear mission in mind: "obliged to submit to the rule of the majority, the classes that call themselves the upper classes can preserve their political hegemony only by invoking the rights of the most capable. As

---

39. Note, however, that compared with other expenses (such as pensions), it would be relatively easy to raise spending on higher education from the lowest levels (barely 1 percent of national income in France) to the highest (2–3 percent in Sweden and the United States).

40. For example, tuition at Sciences Po currently ranges from zero for parents with the least income to 10,000 euros a year for parents with incomes above 200,000 euros. This system is useful for producing data on parental income (which unfortunately has been little studied). Compared with Scandinavian-style public financing, however, such a system amounts to a privatization of the progressive income tax: the additional sums paid by wealthy parents go to their own children and not to the children of other people. This is evidently in their own interest, not in the public interest.

41. Australia and Britain offer "income-contingent loans" to students of modest background. These are not repaid until the graduates achieve a certain level of income. This is tantamount to a supplementary income tax on students of modest background, while students from wealthier backgrounds received (usually untaxed) gifts from their parents.

traditional upper-class prerogatives crumble, the wave of democracy will encounter a second rampart, built on eminently useful talents, superiority that commands prestige, and abilities of which society cannot sanely deprive itself."[42] If we take this incredible statement seriously, what it clearly means is that the upper classes instinctively abandoned idleness and invented meritocracy lest universal suffrage deprive them of everything they owned. One can of course chalk this up to the political context: the Paris Commune had just been put down, and universal male suffrage had just been reestablished. Yet Boutmy's statement has the virtue of reminding us of an essential truth: defining the meaning of inequality and justifying the position of the winners is a matter of vital importance, and one can expect to see all sorts of misrepresentations of the facts in service of the cause.

The Future of Retirement: Pay-As-You-Go and Low Growth

Public pension systems are generally pay-as-you-go (PAYGO) systems: contributions deducted from the wages of active workers are directly paid out as benefits to retirees. In contrast to capitalized pension plans, in a PAYGO system nothing is invested, and incoming funds are immediately disbursed to current retirees. In PAYGO schemes, based on the principle of intergenerational solidarity (today's workers pay benefits to today's retirees in the hope that their children will pay their benefits tomorrow), the rate of return is by definition equal to the growth rate of the economy: the contributions available to pay tomorrow's retirees will rise as average wages rise. In theory, this also implies that today's active workers have an interest in ensuring that average wages rise as rapidly as possible. They should therefore invest in schools and universities for their children and promote a higher birth rate. In

---

42. Emile Boutmy, *Quelques idées sur la création d'une Faculté libre d'enseignement supérieur* (Paris, 1871). See also P. Favre, "Les sciences d'Etat entre déterminisme et libéralisme: Emile Boutmy (1835–1906) et la création de l'Ecole libre des sciences politiques," *Revue française de sociologie* 22 (1981).

other words, there exists a bond among generations that in principle makes for a virtuous and harmonious society.[43]

When PAYGO systems were introduced in the middle of the twentieth century, conditions were in fact ideal for such a virtuous series of events to occur. Demographic growth was high and productivity growth higher still. The growth rate was close to 5 percent in the countries of continental Europe, so this was the rate of return on the PAYGO system. Concretely, workers who contributed to state retirement funds between the end of World War II and 1980 were repaid (or are still being repaid) out of much larger wage pools than those from which their contributions were drawn. The situation today is different. The falling growth rate (now around 1.5 percent in the rich countries and perhaps ultimately in all countries) reduces the return on the pool of shared contributions. All signs are that the rate of return on capital in the twenty-first century will be significantly higher than the growth rate of the economy (4–5 percent for the former, barely 1.5 percent for the latter).[44]

Under these conditions, it is tempting to conclude that the PAYGO system should be replaced as quickly as possible by a capitalized system, in which contributions by active workers are invested rather than paid out immediately to retirees. These investments can then grow at 4 percent a year in order to finance the pensions of today's workers when they retire several decades from now. There are several major flaws in this argument, however. First, even if we assume that a capitalized system is indeed preferable to a PAYGO system, the transition from PAYGO to capitalized benefits raises a fundamental problem: an entire generation of retirees is left with nothing. The generation that is about to retire, who paid for the pensions of the previous generation with their contributions, would take a rather dim view of the fact that the contributions of today's workers, which current retirees had

---

43. For an analysis and defense of the "multi-solidarity" model, see André Masson, *Des liens et des transferts entre générations* (Paris: Editions de l'EHESS, 2009).

44. See Figures 10.9–11.

expected to pay their rent and buy their food during the remaining years of their lives, would in fact be invested in assets around the world. There is no simple solution to this transition problem, and this alone makes such a reform totally unthinkable, at least in such an extreme form.

Second, in comparing the merits of the two pension systems, one must bear in mind that the return on capital is in practice extremely volatile. It would be quite risky to invest all retirement contributions in global financial markets. The fact that $r > g$ on average does not mean that it is true for each individual investment. For a person of sufficient means who can wait ten or twenty years before taking her profits, the return on capital is indeed quite attractive. But when it comes to paying for the basic necessities of an entire generation, it would be quite irrational to bet everything on a roll of the dice. The primary justification of the PAYGO system is that it is the best way to guarantee that pension benefits will be paid in a reliable and predictable manner: the rate of wage growth may be less than the rate of return on capital, but the former is 5–10 times less volatile than the latter.[45] This will continue to be true in the twenty-first century, and PAYGO pensions will therefore continue to be part of the ideal social state of the future everywhere.

That said, it remains true that the logic of $r > g$ cannot be entirely ignored, and some things may have to change in the existing pension systems of the developed countries. One challenge is obviously the aging of the population. In a world where people die between eighty and ninety, it is difficult to maintain parameters that were chosen when the life expectancy was between sixty and seventy. Furthermore, increasing the retirement age is not just a way of increasing the re-

---

45. Recall that this volatility is the reason why PAYGO was introduced after World War II: people who had saved for retirement by investing in financial markets in 1920–1930 found themselves ruined, and no one wished to try the experiment again by imposing a compulsory capitalized pension system of the sort that any number of countries had tried before the war (for example, in France under the laws of 1910 and 1928).

sources available to both workers and retirees (which is a good thing in an era of low growth). It is also a response to the need that many people feel for fulfillment through work. For them, to be forced to retire at sixty and to spend more time in retirement in some cases than in a career, is not an appetizing prospect. The problem is that individual situations vary widely. Some people have primarily intellectual occupations, and they may wish to remain on the job until they are seventy (and it is possible that the number of such people as a share of total employment will increase over time). There are many others, however, who began work early and whose work is arduous or not very rewarding and who legitimately aspire to retire relatively early (especially since their life expectancy is often lower than that of more highly qualified workers). Unfortunately, recent reforms in many developed countries fail to distinguish adequately between these different types of individual, and in some cases more is demanded of the latter than of the former, which is why these reforms sometimes provoke strong opposition.

One of the main difficulties of pension reform is that the systems one is trying to reform are extremely complex, with different rules for civil servants, private sector workers, and nonworkers. For a person who has worked in different types of jobs over the course of a lifetime, which is increasingly common in the younger generations, it is sometimes difficult to know which rules apply. That such complexity exists is not surprising: today's pension systems were in many cases built in stages, as existing schemes were extended to new social groups and occupations from the nineteenth century on. But this makes it difficult to obtain everyone's cooperation on reform efforts, because many people feel that they are being treated worse than others. The hodgepodge of existing rules and schemes frequently confuses the issue, and people underestimate the magnitude of the resources already devoted to public pensions and fail to realize that these amounts cannot be increased indefinitely. For example, the French system is so complex that many younger workers do not have a clear understanding of what they are entitled to. Some even think that they will get nothing even though they are paying a substantial amount into the system (something like 25 percent of gross pay). One of the most important reforms the twenty-first-century social state needs to make is to establish a unified retirement scheme based on individual accounts with equal rights for everyone, no matter how complex one's career path.[46] Such a system would allow each person to anticipate exactly what to expect from the PAYGO public plan, thus allowing for more intelligent decisions about private savings, which will inevitably play a more important supplementary role in a low-growth environment. One often hears that "a public pension is the patrimony of those without patrimony." This is true, but it does not mean that it would not be wise to encourage people of more modest means to accumulate nest eggs of their own.[47]

The Social State in Poor and Emerging Countries

Does the kind of social state that emerged in the developed countries in the twentieth century have a universal vocation? Will we see a similar development in the poor and emerging countries? Nothing could be less certain. To begin with, there are important differences among the rich countries: the countries of Western Europe seem to have stabilized government revenues at about 45–50 percent of national income, whereas the United States and Japan seem to be stuck at around the 30–35 percent level. Clearly, different choices are possible at equivalent levels of development.

---

46. This was largely achieved by the Swedish reform of the 1990s. The Swedish system could be improved and adapted to other countries. See for example Antoine Bozio and Thomas Piketty, *Pour un nouveau système de retraite: Des comptes individuels de cotisations financés par répartition* (Paris: Editions rue d'Ulm, 2008).

47. It is also possible to imagine a unified retirement scheme that would offer, in addition to a PAYGO plan, an opportunity to earn a guaranteed return on modest savings. As I showed in the previous chapter, it is often quite difficult for people of modest means to achieve the average return on capital (or even just a positive return). In some respects, this what the Swedish system offers in the (small) part that it devotes to capitalized funding.

If we look at the poorest countries around the world in 1970–1980, we find that governments generally took 10–15 percent of national income, both in Sub-Saharan Africa and in South Asia (especially India). Turning to countries at an intermediate level of development in Latin America, North Africa, and China, we find governments taking 15–20 percent of national income, lower than in the rich countries at comparable levels of development. The most striking fact is that the gap between the rich and the not-so-rich countries has continued to widen in recent years. Tax levels in the rich countries rose (from 30–35 percent of national income in the 1970s to 35–40 percent in the 1980s) before stabilizing at today's levels, whereas tax levels in the poor and intermediate countries decreased significantly. In Sub-Saharan Africa and South Asia, the average tax bite was slightly below 15 percent in the 1970s and early 1980s but fell to a little over 10 percent in the 1990s.

This evolution is a concern in that, in all the developed countries in the world today, building a fiscal and social state has been an essential part of the process of modernization and economic development. The historical evidence suggests that with only 10–15 percent of national income in tax receipts, it is impossible for a state to fulfill much more than its traditional regalian responsibilities: after paying for a proper police force and judicial system, there is not much left to pay for education and health. Another possible choice is to pay everyone—police, judges, teachers, and nurses—poorly, in which case it is unlikely that any of these public services will work well. This can lead to a vicious circle: poorly functioning public services undermine confidence in government, which makes it more difficult to raise taxes significantly. The development of a fiscal and social state is intimately related to the process of state-building as such. Hence the history of economic development is also a matter of political and cultural development, and each country must find its own distinctive path and cope with its own internal divisions.

In the present case, however, it seems that part of the blame lies with the rich countries and international organizations. The initial situation was not very promising. The process of decolonization was marked by a number of chaotic episodes in the period 1950–1970: wars of independence with the former colonial powers, somewhat arbitrary borders, military tensions linked to the Cold War, abortive experiments with socialism, and sometimes a little of all three. After 1980, moreover, the new ultraliberal wave emanating from the developed countries forced the poor countries to cut their public sectors and lower the priority of developing a tax system suitable to fostering economic development. Recent research has shown that the decline in government receipts in the poorest countries in 1980–1990 was due to a large extent to a decrease in customs duties, which had brought in revenues equivalent to about 5 percent of national income in the 1970s. Trade liberalization is not necessarily a bad thing, but only if it is not peremptorily imposed and only if the lost revenue can gradually be replaced by a strong tax authority capable of collecting new taxes and other substitute sources of revenue. Today's developed countries reduced their tariffs over the course of the nineteenth and twentieth centuries at a pace they judged to be reasonable and with clear alternatives in mind. They were fortunate enough not to have anyone tell them what they ought to be doing instead.[48] This illustrates a more general phenomenon: the tendency of the rich countries to use the less developed world as a field of experimentation, without really seeking to capitalize on the lessons of their own historical experience.[49] What we see in

---

48. Here I am summarizing the main results of Julia Cagé and Lucie Gadenne, "The Fiscal Cost of Trade Liberalization," Harvard University and Paris School of Economics Working Paper no. 2012–27 (see esp. figure 1).

49. Some of the problems of health and education the poor countries face today are specific to their situation and cannot really be addressed by drawing on the past experience of today's developed countries (think of the problem of AIDS, for example). Hence new experiments, perhaps in the form of randomized controlled trials, may be justified. See, for example, Abhijit Banerjee and Esther Duflo, *Poor Economics* (New York: Public Affairs, 2012). As a general rule, however, I think that development economics tends to neglect actual historical experience, which, in the context of this discussion, means that too little attention is paid to the difficulty of developing an effective social state with paltry tax reve-

the poor and emerging countries today is a wide range of different tendencies. Some countries, like China, are fairly advanced in the modernization of their tax system: for instance, China has an income tax that is applicable to a large portion of the population and brings in substantial revenues. It is possibly in the process of developing a social state similar to those found in the developed countries of Europe, America, and Asia (albeit with specific Chinese features and of course great uncertainty as to its political and democratic underpinnings). Other countries, such as India, have had greater difficulty moving beyond an equilibrium based on a low level of taxation.[50] In any case, the question of what kind of fiscal and social state will emerge in the developing world is of the utmost importance for the future of the planet.

---

nues. One important difficulty is obviously the colonial past (and therefore randomized controlled trials may offer a more neutral terrain).

50. See Thomas Piketty and Nancy Qian, "Income Inequality and Progressive Income Taxation in China and India: 1986–2015," *American Economic Journal: Applied Economics* 1, no. 2 (April 2009): 53–63. The difference between the two countries is closely related to the greater prevalence of wage labor in China. History shows that the construction of a fiscal and social state and of a wage-earner status often go together.

FOURTEEN

Rethinking the Progressive Income Tax

In the previous chapter I examined the constitution and evolution of the social state, focusing on the nature of social needs and related social spending (education, health, retirement, etc.). I treated the overall level of taxes as a given and described its evolution. In this chapter and the next, I will examine more closely the structure of taxes and other government revenues, without which the social state could never have emerged, and attempt to draw lessons for the future. The major twentieth-century innovation in taxation was the creation and development of the progressive income tax. This institution, which played a key role in the reduction of inequality in the last century, is today seriously threatened by international tax competition. It may also be in jeopardy because its foundations were never clearly thought through, owing to the fact that it was instituted in an emergency that left little time for reflection. The same is true of the progressive tax on inheritances, which was the second major fiscal innovation of the twentieth century and has also been challenged in recent decades. Before I examine these two taxes more closely, however, I must first situate them in the context of progressive taxation in general and its role in modern redistribution.

The Question of Progressive Taxation

Taxation is not a technical matter. It is preeminently a political and philosophical issue, perhaps the most important of all political issues. Without taxes, society has no common destiny, and collective action is impossible. This has always been true. At the heart of every major political upheaval lies a fiscal revolution. The Ancien Régime was swept away when the revolutionary assemblies voted to abolish the fiscal privileges of the nobility and clergy and establish a modern system of universal taxation. The American Revolution was born when subjects of the British colonies decided to take their destiny in hand and set their own taxes. ("No taxation without representation.") Two centuries later the context is different, but the heart of the issue remains the same. How can sovereign citizens democratically decide how much of their resources they wish to devote to common goals such as education, health, retirement, inequality reduction, employment, sustainable development, and so on? Precisely what concrete form taxes take is therefore the crux of political conflict in any society. The goal is to reach agreement on who must pay what in the name of what principles—no mean feat, since people differ in many ways. In particular, they earn different incomes and own different amounts of capital. In every society there are some individuals who earn a lot from work but inherited little, and vice versa. Fortunately, the two sources of wealth are never perfectly correlated. Views about the ideal tax system are equally varied.

One usually distinguishes among taxes on income, taxes on capital, and taxes on consumption. Taxes of each type can be found in varying proportions in nearly all periods. These categories are not exempt from ambiguity, however, and the dividing lines are not always clear. For example, the income tax applies in principle to capital income as well as earned income and is therefore a tax on capital as well. Taxes on capital generally include any levy on the flow of income from capital (such as the corporate income tax), as well as any tax on the value of the capital stock (such as a real estate tax, an estate tax, or a wealth tax). In the modern era, consumption taxes include value-added taxes as well as taxes on imported goods, drink, gasoline, tobacco, and services. Such taxes have always existed and are often the most hated of all, as well as the heaviest burden on the lower class (one thinks of the salt tax under the Ancien Régime). They are often called "indirect" taxes because they do not depend directly on the income or capital of the individual taxpayer: they are paid indirectly, as part of the selling price of a purchased good. In the abstract, one might imagine a direct tax on consumption, which would depend on each taxpayer's total consumption, but no such tax has ever existed.[1]

In the twentieth century, a fourth category of tax appeared: contributions to government-sponsored social insurance programs. These are a special type of tax on income, usually only income from labor (wages and remuneration for nonwage labor). The proceeds go to social insurance funds intended to finance replacement income, whether pensions for retired workers or unemployment benefits for unemployed workers. This mode of collection ensures that the taxpayer will be aware of the purpose for which the tax is to be used. Some countries, such as France, also use social contributions to pay for other social spending such as health insurance and family allowances, so that total social contributions account for nearly half of all government revenue. Rather than clarify the purpose of tax collection, a system of such complexity can actually obscure matters. By contrast, other states, such as Denmark, finance all social spending with an enormous income tax, the revenues from which are allocated to pensions, unemployment and health insurance, and many other purposes. In fact, these distinctions among different legal categories of taxation are partly arbitrary.[2]

Beyond these definitional quibbles, a more pertinent criterion for characterizing different types of tax is the degree to which each type is proportional or progressive. A tax is called "proportional" when its rate is the same for everyone (the term "flat tax" is also used). A tax is progressive when its rate is higher for some than for others, whether it be those who earn more, those who own more, or those who consume

---

1. The British economist Nicholas Kaldor proposed such a tax, and I say more about it later, but for Kaldor it was a complement to progressive income and estate taxes, in order to ensure that they were not circumvented. It was not meant as a substitute for these taxes, as some have argued.

2. For example, in 1990, when some social contributions in France were extended to revenue streams other than employment income (including capital income and retiree income) to create what was called the "generalized social contribution," (*contribution sociale généralisée*, or CSG), the corresponding receipts were reclassified as an income tax under international norms.

more. A tax can also be regressive, when its rate decreases for richer individuals, either because they are partially exempt (either legally, as a result of fiscal optimization, or illegally, through evasion) or because the law imposes a regressive rate, like the famous "poll tax" that cost Margaret Thatcher her post as prime minister in 1990.[3]

In the modern fiscal state, total tax payments are often close to proportional to individual income, especially in countries where the total is large. This is not surprising: it is impossible to tax half of national income to finance an ambitious program of social entitlements without asking everyone to make a substantial contribution. The logic of universal rights that governed the development of the modern fiscal and social state fits rather well, moreover, with the idea of a proportional or slightly progressive tax.

It would be wrong, however, to conclude that progressive taxation plays only a limited role in modern redistribution. First, even if taxation overall is fairly close to proportional for the majority of the population, the fact that the highest incomes and largest fortunes are taxed at significantly higher (or lower) rates can have a strong influence on the structure of inequality. In particular, the evidence suggests that progressive taxation of very high incomes and very large estates partly explains why the concentration of wealth never regained its astronomic Belle Époque levels after the shocks of 1914–1945. Conversely, the spectacular decrease in the progressivity of the income tax in the United States and Britain since 1980, even though both countries had been among the leaders in progressive taxation after World War II, probably explains much of the increase in the very highest earned incomes. At the same time, the recent rise of tax competition in a world of free-flowing capital has led many governments to exempt capital income from the progressive income tax. This is particularly true in Europe, whose relatively small states have thus far proved incapable of

---

3. The poll tax, which was adopted in 1988 and abolished in 1991, was a local tax that required the same payment of every adult no matter what his or her income or wealth might be, so its rate was lower for the rich.

achieving a coordinated tax policy. The result is an endless race to the bottom, leading, for example, to cuts in corporate tax rates and to the exemption of interest, dividends, and other financial revenues from the taxes to which labor incomes are subject.

One consequence of this is that in most countries taxes have (or will soon) become regressive at the top of the income hierarchy. For example, a detailed study of French taxes in 2010, which looked at all forms of taxation, found that the overall rate of taxation (47 percent of national income on average) broke down as follows. The bottom 50 percent of the income distribution pay a rate of 40–45 percent; the next 40 percent pay 45–50 percent; but the top 5 percent and even more the top 1 percent pay lower rates, with the top 0.1 percent paying only 35 percent. The high tax rates on the poor reflect the importance of consumption taxes and social contributions (which together account for three-quarters of French tax revenues). The slight progressivity observed in the middle class is due to the growing importance of the income tax. Conversely, the clear regressivity in the top centiles reflects the importance at this level of capital income, which is largely exempt from progressive taxation. The effect of this outweighs the effect of taxes on the capital stock (which are the most progressive of all).[4] All signs are that taxes elsewhere in Europe (and probably also in the United States) follow a similar bell curve, which is probably even more pronounced than this imperfect estimate indicates.[5]

---

4. See Camille Landais, Thomas Piketty, and Emmanuel Saez, *Pour une révolution fiscale: Un impôt sur le revenu pour le 21e siècle* (Paris: Le Seuil, 2010), 48–53. Also available at www.revolution-fiscale.fr.

5. In particular, the estimate fails to account for income hidden in tax havens (which, as indicated in Chapter 12, is quite a lot) and assumes that "tax shelters" are equally common at all levels of income and wealth (which probably leads to an overestimate of the real rate of taxation at the top of the hierarchy). Note, too, that the French tax system is exceptionally complex, with many special categories and overlapping taxes. (For example, France is the only developed country that does not withhold income tax at the source, even though social contributions have always been withheld at the source.) This complexity makes the system even

If taxation at the top of the social hierarchy were to become more regressive in the future, the impact on the dynamics of wealth inequality would likely be significant, leading to a very high concentration of capital. Clearly, such a fiscal secession of the wealthiest citizens could potentially do great damage to fiscal consent in general. Consensus support for the fiscal and social state, which is already fragile in a period of low growth, would be further reduced, especially among the middle class, who would naturally find it difficult to accept that they should pay more than the upper class. Individualism and selfishness would flourish: since the system as a whole would be unjust, why continue to pay for others? If the modern social state is to continue to exist, it is therefore essential that the underlying tax system retain a minimum of progressivity, or at any rate that it not become overtly regressive at the top.

Furthermore, looking at the progressivity of the tax system by examining how heavily top incomes are taxed obviously fails to weigh inherited wealth, whose importance has been increasing.[6] In practice, estates are much less heavily taxed than income.[7] This exacerbates what I have called "Rastignac's dilemma." If individuals were classified by centile of total resources accrued over a lifetime (including both earned income and capitalized inheritance), which is a more satisfactory criterion for progressive taxation, the bell curve would be even more markedly regressive at the top of the hierarchy than it is when only labor incomes are considered.[8]

One final point bears emphasizing: to the extent that globalization weighs particularly heavily on the least skilled workers in the wealthy

---

more regressive and difficult to understand (just as the pension system is difficult to understand).

6. Only income from inherited capital is taxed under the progressive income tax (along with other capital income) and not inherited capital itself.

7. In France, for example, the average tax on estates and gifts is barely 5 percent; even for the top centile of inheritances, it is just 20 percent. See the online technical appendix.

8. See Figures 11.9–11 and the online technical appendix.

countries, a more progressive tax system might in principle be justified, adding yet another layer of complexity to the overall picture. To be sure, if one wants to maintain total taxes at about 50 percent of national income, it is inevitable that everyone must pay a substantial amount. But instead of a slightly progressive tax system (leaving aside the very top of the hierarchy), one can easily imagine a more steeply progressive one.[9] This would not solve all the problems, but it would be enough to improve the situation of the least skilled significantly.[10] If the tax system is not made more progressive, it should come as no surprise that those who derive the least benefit from free trade may well turn against it. The progressive tax is indispensable for making sure that everyone benefits from globalization, and the increasingly glaring absence of progressive taxation may ultimately undermine support for a globalized economy.

For all of these reasons, a progressive tax is a crucial component of the social state: it played a central role in its development and in the transformation of the structure of inequality in the twentieth century, and it remains important for ensuring the viability of the social state in the future. But progressive taxation is today under serious threat, both intellectually (because its various functions have never been fully debated) and politically (because tax competition is allowing entire categories of income to gain exemption from the common rules).

The Progressive Tax in the Twentieth Century: An Ephemeral Product of Chaos

To gaze backward for a moment: how did we get to this point? First, it is important to realize that progressive taxation was as much a product

---

9. For example, instead of taxing the bottom 50 percent at a rate of 40–45 percent and the next 40 percent at a rate of 45–50 percent, one could tax the bottom group at 30–35 percent and the second group at 50–55 percent.
10. Given the low rate of intergenerational mobility, this would also be more just (in terms of the criteria of justice discussed in Chapter 13). See the online technical appendix.

of two world wars as it was of democracy. It was adopted in a chaotic climate that called for improvisation, which is part of the reason why its various purposes were not sufficiently thought through and why it is being challenged today.

To be sure, a number of countries adopted a progressive income tax before the outbreak of World War I. In France, the law creating a "general tax on income" was passed on July 15, 1914, in direct response to the anticipated financial needs of the impending conflict (after being buried in the Senate for several years); the law would not have passed had a declaration of war not been imminent.[11] Aside from this exception, most countries adopted a progressive income tax after due deliberation in the normal course of parliamentary proceedings. Such a tax was adopted in Britain, for example, in 1909 and in the United States in 1913. Several countries in northern Europe, a number of German states, and Japan adopted a progressive income tax even earlier: Denmark in 1870, Japan in 1887, Prussia in 1891, and Sweden in 1903. Even though not all the developed countries had adopted a progressive tax by 1910, an international consensus was emerging around the principle of progressivity and its application to overall income (that is, to the sum of income from labor, including both wage and nonwage labor, and capital income of all kinds, including rent, interest, dividends, profits, and in some cases capital gains).[12] To many people, such

---

11. The "general tax on income" (impôt général sur le revenu, or IGR) this law created is a progressive tax on total income. It was the forerunner of today's income tax. It was modified by the law of July 31, 1917, creating what was called the *cédulaire* tax (which taxed different categories of income, such as corporate profits and wages, differently). This law was the forerunner of today's corporate income tax. For details of the turbulent history of the income tax in France since the fundamental reforms of 1914–1917, see Thomas Piketty, *Les hauts revenus en France au 20e siècle: Inégalités et redistribution 1901–1998* (Paris: Grasset, 2001), 233–334.

12. The progressive income tax was aimed primarily at top capital incomes (which everyone at the time knew dominated the income hierarchy), and it never would have occurred to anyone in any country to grant special exemptions to capital income.

a system appeared to be both a more just and a more efficient way of apportioning taxes. Overall income measured each person's ability to contribute, and progressive taxation offered a way of limiting the inequalities produced by industrial capitalism while maintaining respect for private property and the forces of competition. Many books and reports published at the time helped popularize the idea and win over some political leaders and liberal economists, although many would remain hostile to the very principle of progressivity, especially in France.[13]

Is the progressive income tax therefore the natural offspring of democracy and universal suffrage? Things are actually more complicated. Indeed, tax rates, even on the most astronomical incomes, remained extremely low prior to World War I. This was true everywhere, without exception. The magnitude of the political shock due to the war is quite clear in Figure 14.1, which shows the evolution of the top rate (that is, the tax rate on the highest income bracket) in the United States, Britain, Germany, and France from 1900 to 2013. The top rate stagnated at insignificant levels until 1914 and then skyrocketed after the war. These curves are typical of those seen in other wealthy countries.[14]

In France, the 1914 income tax law provided for a top rate of just 2 percent, which applied to only a tiny minority of taxpayers. It was only after the war, in a radically different political and financial con-

---

13. For example, the many works the US economist Edwin Seligman published between 1890 and 1910 in praise of the progressive income tax were translated into many languages and stirred passionate debate. On this period and these debates, see Pierre Rosanvallon, *La société des égaux* (Paris: Le Seuil, 2011), 227–33. See also Nicolas Delalande, *Les batailles de l'impôt: Consentement et résistances de 1789 à nos jours* (Paris: Le Seuil, 2011).

14. The top tax rate is generally a "marginal" rate, in the sense that it applies only to the "margin," or portion of income above a certain threshold. The top rate generally applies to less than 1 percent of the population (in some cases less than 0.1 percent). To have a comprehensive view of progressivity, it is better to look at the effective rates paid by different centiles of the income distribution (which can be much lower). The evolution of the top rate is nevertheless interesting, and by definition it gives an upper bound on the effective rate paid by the wealthiest individuals.

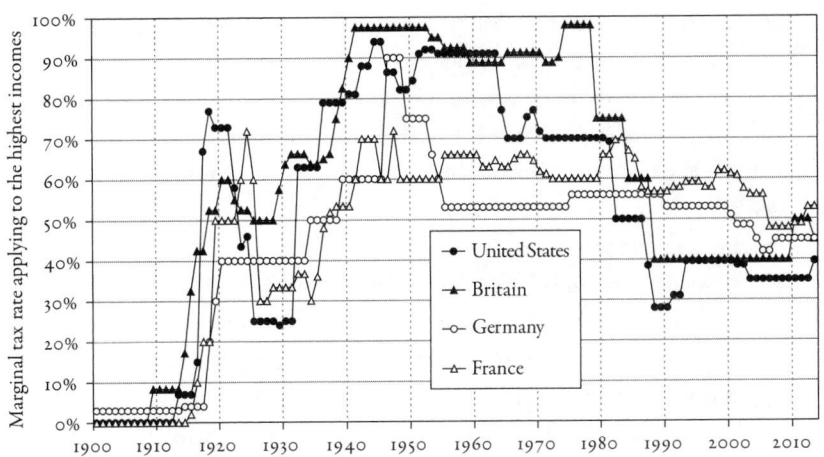

FIGURE 14.1. Top income tax rates, 1900–2013

The top marginal tax rate of the income tax (applying to the highest incomes) in the United States dropped from 70 percent in 1980 to 28 percent in 1988.

Sources and series: see piketty.pse.ens.fr/capital21c.

text, that the top rate was raised to "modern" levels: 50 percent in 1920, then 60 percent in 1924, and even 72 percent in 1925. Particularly striking is the fact that the crucial law of June 25, 1920, which raised the top rate to 50 percent and can actually be seen as a second coming of the income tax, was adopted by the so-called blue-sky Chamber (one of the most right-wing Chambers of Deputies in the history of the French Republic) with its "National Bloc" majority, made up largely of the very delegations who had most vehemently opposed the creation of an income tax with a top rate of 2 percent before the war. This complete reversal of the right-wing position on progressive taxation was of course due to the disastrous financial situation created by the war. During the conflict the government had run up considerable debts, and despite the ritual speeches in which politician after politician declared that "Germany will pay," everyone knew that new fiscal resources would have to be found. Postwar shortages and the recourse to the printing press had driven inflation to previously unknown heights, so that the purchasing power of workers remained below 1914 levels, and several waves of strikes in May and June of 1919 threatened the country with paralysis. In such circumstances, political proclivities hardly mattered: new sources of revenue were essential, and no one believed that those with the highest incomes ought to be spared. The Bolshevik Revolution of 1917 was fresh in everyone's mind. It was in this chaotic and explosive situation that the modern progressive income tax was born.[15]

The German case is particularly interesting, because Germany had had a progressive income tax for more than twenty years before the war. Throughout that period of peace, tax rates were never raised significantly. In Prussia, the top rate remained stable at 3 percent from 1891 to 1914 and then rose to 4 percent from 1915 to 1918, before ultimately shooting up to 40 percent in 1919–1920, in a radically changed political climate. In the United States, which was intellectually and politically more prepared than any other country to accept a steeply progressive income tax and would lead the movement in the interwar period, it was again not until 1918–1919 that the top rate was abruptly increased, first to 67 and then to 77 percent. In Britain, the top rate was set at 8 percent in 1909, a fairly high level for the time, but again it was not until after the war that it was suddenly raised to more than 40 percent.

Of course it is impossible to say what would have happened had it not been for the shock of 1914–1918. A movement had clearly been

---

15. The top tax rates shown in Figure 14.1 do not include the increases of 25 percent introduced in 1920 for unmarried taxpayers without children and married taxpayers "who after two years of marriage still have no child." (If we included them, the top rate would be 62 percent in 1920 and 90 percent in 1925.) This interesting provision of the law, which attests to the French obsession with the birthrate as well as to the limitless imagination of legislators when it comes to expressing a country's hopes and fears through the tax rate, would later be rebaptized, from 1939 to 1944, the "family compensation tax," which was extended from 1945 to 1951 through the family quotient system (under which married couples without a child, normally endowed with 2 shares, were decreased to 1.5 shares if they still had no child "after three years of marriage"). Note that the Constituent Assembly of 1945 increased by one year the grace period set in 1920 by the National Bloc. See *Les hauts revenus en France*, 233–334.

launched. Nevertheless, it seems certain that had that shock not occurred, the move toward a more progressive tax system would at the very least have been much slower, and top rates might never have risen as high as they did. The rates in force before 1914, which were always below 10 percent (and generally below 5), including the top rates, were not very different from tax rates in the eighteenth and nineteenth centuries. Even though the progressive tax on total income was a creation of the late nineteenth and early twentieth centuries, there were much earlier forms of income tax, generally with different rules for different types of income, and usually with flat or nearly flat rates (for example, a flat rate after allowing for a certain fixed deduction). In most cases the rates were 5–10 percent (at most). For example, this was true of the categorical or schedular tax, which applied separate rates to each category (or schedule) of income (land rents, interest, profits, wages, etc.). Britain adopted such a categorical tax in 1842, and it remained the British version of the income tax until the creation in 1909 of a "supertax" (a progressive tax on total income).[16]

In Ancien Régime France, there were also various forms of direct taxation of incomes, such as the *taille,* the *dixième,* and the *vingtième,* with typical rates of 5 or 10 percent (as the names indicate) applied to some but not all sources of income, with numerous exemptions. In 1707, Vauban proposed a "dixième royal," which was intended to be a 10 percent tax on all incomes (including rents paid to aristocratic and ecclesiastical landlords), but it was never fully implemented. Various improvements to the tax system were nevertheless attempted over the course of the eighteenth century.[17] Revolutionary lawmakers, hostile to the inquisitorial methods of the fallen monarchy and probably keen as well to protect the emerging industrial bourgeoisie from bearing too heavy a tax burden, chose to institute an "indicial" tax system: taxes

---

16. A progressive tax on total income had earlier been tried in Britain between the Napoleonic wars, as well as in the United States during the Civil War, but in both cases the taxes were repealed shortly after hostilities ended.

17. See Mirelle Touzery, *L'invention de l'impôt sur le revenu: La taille tarifée 1715–1789* (Paris: Comité pour l'histoire économique et financière, 1994).

were calculated on the basis of indices that were supposed to reflect the taxpayer's ability to pay rather than actual income, which did not have to be declared. For instance, the "door and window tax" was based on the number of doors and windows in the taxpayer's primary residence, which was taken to be an index of wealth. Taxpayers liked this system because the authorities could determine how much tax they owed without having to enter their homes, much less examine their account books. The most important tax under the new system created in 1792, the property tax, was based on the rental value of all real estate owned by the taxpayer.[18] The income tax was based on estimates of average rental value, which were revised once a decade when the tax authorities inventoried all property in France; taxpayers were not required to declare their actual income. Since inflation was slow, this made little difference. In practice, this real estate tax amounted to a flat tax on rents and was not very different from the British categorical tax. (The effective rate varied from time to time and *département* to *département* but never exceeded 10 percent.)

To round out the system, the nascent Third Republic decided in 1872 to impose a tax on income from financial assets. This was a flat tax on interest, dividends, and other financial revenues, which were rapidly proliferating in France at the time but almost totally exempt from taxation, even though similar revenues were taxed in Britain. Once again, however, the tax rate was set quite low (3 percent from 1872 to 1890 and then 4 percent from 1890 to 1914), at any rate in comparison with the rates assessed after 1920. Until World War I, it seems to have been the case in all the developed countries that a tax on income was not considered "reasonable" unless the rate was under 10 percent, no matter how high the taxable income.

---

18. Business inventory and capital were subject to a separate tax, the *patente*. On the system of the *quatre vieilles* (the four direct taxes, which, along with the estate tax, formed the heart of the tax system created in 1791–1792), see *Les hauts revenus en France*, 234–239.

The Progressive Tax in the Third Republic

Interestingly, this was also true of the progressive inheritance or estate tax, which, along with the progressive income tax, was the second important fiscal innovation of the early twentieth century. Estate tax rates also remained quite low until 1914 (see Figure 14.2). Once again, the case of France under the Third Republic is emblematic: here was a country that was supposed to nurse a veritable passion for the ideal of equality, in which universal male suffrage was reestablished in 1871, and which nevertheless stubbornly refused for nearly half a century to fully embrace the principle of progressive taxation. Attitudes did not really change until World War I made change inevitable. To be sure, the estate tax instituted by the French Revolution, which remained strictly proportional from 1791 to 1901, was made progressive by the law of February 25, 1901. In reality, however, not much changed: the highest rate was set at 5 percent from 1902 to 1910 and then at 6.5 percent from 1911 to 1914 and applied to only a few dozen fortunes every year. In the eyes of wealthy taxpayers, such rates seemed exorbitant. Many felt that it was a "sacred duty" to ensure that "a son would succeed his father," thereby perpetuating the family property, and that such straightforward perpetuation should not incur a tax of any kind.[19] In reality, however, the low inheritance tax did not prevent estates from being passed on largely intact from one generation to the next. The effective average rate on the top centile of inheritances was no more than 3 percent after the reform of 1901 (compared to 1 percent under the proportional regime in force in the nineteenth century). In hindsight, it is clear that the reform had scarcely any impact

---

19. One of the many parliamentary committees to consider a progressive estate tax in the nineteenth century had this to say: "When a son succeeds his father, there is strictly speaking no transmission of property but merely continued enjoyment, according to the authors of the Civil Code. If this doctrine is taken to be absolute, then any tax on direct bequests is ruled out. In any case, extreme moderation in setting the rate of taxation is imperative." See ibid., 245.

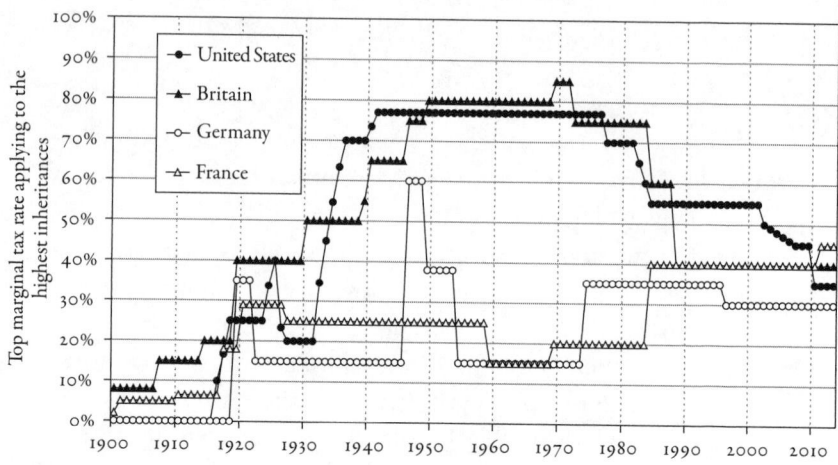

FIGURE 14.2. Top inheritance tax rates, 1900–2013

The top marginal tax rate of the inheritance tax (applying to the highest inheritances) in the United States dropped from 70 percent in 1980 to 35 percent in 2013. Sources and series: see piketty.pse.ens.fr/capital21c.

on the process of accumulation and hyperconcentration of wealth that was under way at the time, regardless of what contemporaries may have believed.

It is striking, moreover, how frequently opponents of progressive taxation, who were clearly in the majority among the economic and financial elite of Belle Époque France, rather hypocritically relied on the argument that France, being a naturally egalitarian country, had no need of progressive taxes. A typical and particularly instructive example is that of Paul Leroy-Beaulieu, one of the most influential economists of the day, who in 1881 published his famous *Essai sur la répartition des richesses et sur la tendance à une moindre inégalité des conditions* (Essay on the Distribution of Wealth and the Tendency toward Reduced Inequality of Conditions), a work that went through numerous editions up to the eve of World War I.[20] Leroy-Beaulieu ac-

20. A professor at the Ecole Libre des Sciences Politiques and the Collège de France from 1880 to 1916 and outspoken champion of colonization among the conserva-

tually had no data of any kind to justify his belief in a "tendency toward a reduced inequality of conditions." But never mind that: he managed to come up with dubious and not very convincing arguments based on totally irrelevant statistics to show that income inequality was decreasing.[21] At times he seemed to notice that his argument was flawed, and he then simply stated that reduced inequality was just around the corner and that in any case nothing of any kind must be done to interfere with the miraculous process of commercial and financial globalization, which allowed French savers to invest in the Panama and Suez canals and would soon extend to czarist Russia. Clearly, Leroy-Beaulieu was fascinated by the globalization of his day and scared stiff by the thought that a sudden revolution might put it all in jeopardy.[22] There is of course nothing inherently reprehensible about such a fascination as long as it does not stand in the way of sober analysis. The great issue in France in 1900–1910 was not the imminence of a Bolshevik revolution (which was no more likely than a revolution is today) but the advent of progressive taxation. For Leroy-Beaulieu and his colleagues of the "center right" (in contrast to the monarchist right), there was one unanswerable argument to progressivity, which right-thinking people should oppose tooth and nail: France, he maintained, became an egalitarian country thanks to the French Revolution,

---

tive economists of the day, Leroy-Beaulieu was also the editor of *L'économiste français,* an influential weekly magazine roughly equivalent to the *Economist* today, especially in its limitless and often undiscerning zeal to defend the powerful interests of its time.

21. For instance, he noted with satisfaction that the number of indigents receiving assistance in France increased by only 40 percent from 1837 to 1860, whereas the number of assistance offices had nearly doubled. Apart from the fact that one would have to be very optimistic to deduce from these figures that the actual number of indigents had decreased (which Leroy-Beaulieu did not hesitate to do), a decrease in the absolute number of the poor in a context of economic growth would obviously tell us nothing about the evolution of income inequality. See ibid., 522–31.

22. At times one has the thought that he might have been responsible for the advertisements that HSBC plastered all over airport walls a few years ago: "We see a world of opportunities. Do you?"

which redistributed the land (up to a point) and above all established equality before the law with the Civil Code, which instituted equal property rights and the right of free contract. Hence there was no need for a progressive and confiscatory tax. Of course, he added, such a tax might well be useful in a class-ridden aristocratic society like that of Britain, across the English Channel, but not in France.[23]

As it happens, if Leroy-Beaulieu had bothered to consult the probate records published by the tax authorities shortly after the reform of 1901, he would have discovered that wealth was nearly as concentrated in republican France during the Belle Époque as it was in monarchical Britain. In parliamentary debate in 1907 and 1908, proponents of the income tax frequently referred to these statistics.[24] This interesting example shows that even a tax with low rates can be a source of knowledge and a force for democratic transparency.

In other countries the estate tax was also transformed after World War I. In Germany, the idea of imposing a small tax on the very largest estates was extensively discussed in parliamentary debate at the end of the nineteenth century and beginning of the twentieth. Leaders of the Social Democratic Party, starting with August Bebel and Eduard Bernstein, pointed out that an estate tax would make it possible to decrease the heavy burden of indirect taxes on workers, who would then be able to improve their lot. But the Reichstag could not agree on a new tax: the reforms of 1906 and 1909 did institute a very small estate tax, but bequests to a spouse or children (that is, the vast ma-

---

23. Another classic argument of the time was that the "inquisitorial" procedure of requiring taxpayers to declare their income might suit an "authoritarian" country like Germany but would immediately be rejected by a "free people" like the French. See *Les hauts revenus en France,* 481.

24. For instance, Joseph Caillaux, minister of finance at the time: "We have been led to believe and to say that France was a country of small fortunes, of infinitely fragmented and dispersed capital. The statistics with which the new estate tax regime provides us force us to retreat from this position. . . . Gentlemen, I cannot hide from you the fact that these figures have altered some of my preconceived ideas. The fact is that a small number of people possess the bulk of this country's wealth." See Joseph Caillaux, *L'impôt sur le revenu* (Paris: Berger, 1910), 530–32.

jority of estates) were entirely exempt, no matter how large. It was not until 1919 that the German estate tax was extended to family bequests, and the top rate (on the largest estates) was abruptly increased from 0 to 35 percent.[25] The role of the war and of the political changes it induced seems to have been absolutely crucial: it is hard to see how the stalemate of 1906–1909 would have been overcome otherwise.[26]

Figure 14.2 shows a slight upward tick in Britain around the turn of the century, somewhat greater for the estate tax than for the income tax. The rate on the largest estates, which had been 8 percent since the reform of 1896, rose to 15 percent in 1908—a fairly substantial amount. In the United States, a federal tax on estates and gifts was not instituted until 1916, but its rate very quickly rose to levels higher than those found in France and Germany.

Confiscatory Taxation of Excessive Incomes: An American Invention

When we look at the history of progressive taxation in the twentieth century, it is striking to see how far out in front Britain and the United States were, especially the latter, which invented the confiscatory tax on "excessive" incomes and fortunes. Figures 14.1 and 14.2 are particularly clear in this regard. This finding stands in such stark contrast to the way most people both inside and outside the United States and Britain have seen those two countries since 1980 that it is worth pausing a moment to consider the point further.

---

25. On the German debates, see Jens Beckert, tr. Thomas Dunlap, *Inherited Wealth*, (Princeton: Princeton University Press, 2008), 220–35. The rates shown in Figure 14.2 concern transmissions in the direct line (from parents to children). The rates on other bequests were always higher in France and Germany. In the United States and Britain, rates generally do not depend on the identity of the heir.

26. On the role of war in changing attitudes toward the estate tax, see Kenneth Scheve and David Stasavage, "Democracy, War, and Wealth: Evidence of Two Centuries of Inheritance Taxation," *American Political Science Review* 106, no. 1 (February 2012): 81–102.

Between the two world wars, all the developed countries began to experiment with very high top rates, frequently in a rather erratic fashion. But it was the United States that was the first country to try rates above 70 percent, first on income in 1919–1922 and then on estates in 1937–1939. When a government taxes a certain level of income or inheritance at a rate of 70 or 80 percent, the primary goal is obviously not to raise additional revenue (because these very high brackets never yield much). It is rather to put an end to such incomes and large estates, which lawmakers have for one reason or another come to regard as socially unacceptable and economically unproductive—or if not to end them, then at least to make it extremely costly to sustain them and strongly discourage their perpetuation. Yet there is no absolute prohibition or expropriation. The progressive tax is thus a relatively liberal method for reducing inequality, in the sense that free competition and private property are respected while private incentives are modified in potentially radical ways, but always according to rules thrashed out in democratic debate. The progressive tax thus represents an ideal compromise between social justice and individual freedom. It is no accident that the United States and Britain, which throughout their histories have shown themselves to value individual liberty highly, adopted more progressive tax systems than many other countries. Note, however, that the countries of continental Europe, especially France and Germany, explored other avenues after World War II, such as taking public ownership of firms and directly setting executive salaries. These measures, which also emerged from democratic deliberation, in some ways served as substitutes for progressive taxes.[27]

---

27. To take an extreme example, the Soviet Union never needed a confiscatory tax on excessive incomes or fortunes because its economic systems imposed direct controls on the distribution of primary incomes and almost totally outlawed private property (admittedly in ways that were much less respectful of the law). The Soviet Union did have an income tax at times, but it was relatively insignificant, with very low top rates. The same is true in China. I come back to this in the next chapter.

Other, more specific factors also mattered. During the Gilded Age, many observers in the United States worried that the country was becoming increasingly inegalitarian and moving farther and farther away from its original pioneering ideal. In Willford King's 1915 book on the distribution of wealth in the United States, he worried that the nation was becoming more like what he saw as the hyperinegalitarian societies of Europe.[28] In 1919, Irving Fisher, then president of the American Economic Association, went even further. He chose to devote his presidential address to the question of US inequality and in no uncertain terms told his colleagues that the increasing concentration of wealth was the nation's foremost economic problem. Fisher found King's estimates alarming. The fact that "2 percent of the population owns more than 50 percent of the wealth" and that "two-thirds of the population owns almost nothing" struck him as "an undemocratic distribution of wealth," which threatened the very foundations of US society. Rather than restrict the share of profits or the return on capital arbitrarily—possibilities Fisher mentioned only to reject them—he argued that the best solution was to impose a heavy tax on the largest estates (he mentioned a tax rate of two-thirds the size of the estate, rising to 100 percent if the estate was more than three generations old).[29] It is striking to see how much more Fisher worried about inequality than Leroy-Beaulieu did, even though Leroy-Beaulieu

28. Paul Leroy-Beaulieu, King put France in the same league as Britain and Prussia, which was substantially correct.

29. See Irving Fisher, "Economists in Public Service: Annual Address of the President," *American Economic Review* 9, no. 1 (March 1919): 5–21. Fisher took his inspiration mainly from the Italian economist Eugenio Rignano. See G. Erreygers and G. Di Bartolomeo, "The Debates on Eugenio Rignano's Inheritance Tax Proposals," *History of Political Economy* 39, no. 4 (Winter 2007): 605–38. The idea of taxing wealth that had been accumulated in the previous generation less heavily than older wealth that had been passed down through several generations is very interesting, in the sense that there is a stronger sense of double taxation in the former than in the latter, even if different generations and therefore different individuals are involved in both cases. It is nevertheless difficult to formalize and implement this idea in practice (because estates often follow complex trajectories), which is probably why it has never been tried.

lived in a far more inegalitarian society. The fear of coming to resemble Old Europe was no doubt part of the reason for the American interest in progressive taxes.

Furthermore, the Great Depression of the 1930s struck the United States with extreme force, and many people blamed the economic and financial elites for having enriched themselves while leading the country to ruin. (Bear in mind that the share of top incomes in US national income peaked in the late 1920s, largely due to enormous capital gains on stocks.) Roosevelt came to power in 1933, when the crisis was already three years old and one-quarter of the country was unemployed. He immediately decided on a sharp increase in the top income tax rate, which had been decreased to 25 percent in the late 1920s and again under Hoover's disastrous presidency. The top rate rose to 63 percent in 1933 and then to 79 percent in 1937, surpassing the previous record of 1919. In 1942 the Victory Tax Act raised the top rate to 88 percent, and in 1944 it went up again to 94 percent, due to various surtaxes. The top rate then stabilized at around 90 percent until the mid-1960s, but then it fell to 70 percent in the early 1980s. All told, over the period 1932–1980, nearly half a century, the top federal income tax rate in the United States averaged 81 percent.[30]

It is important to emphasize that no continental European country has ever imposed such high rates (except in exceptional circumstances, for a few years at most, and never for as long as half a century). In particular, France and Germany had top rates between 50 and 70 percent from the late 1940s until the 1980s, but never as high as 80–90 percent. The only exception was Germany in 1947–1949, when the rate was 90 percent. But this was a time when the tax schedule was fixed by the occupying powers (in practice, the US authorities). As soon as Germany regained fiscal sovereignty in 1950, the country quickly returned to rates more in keeping with its traditions, and the top rate

---

30. To this federal tax one should also add state income tax (which is generally 5–10 percent).

fell within a few years to just over 50 percent (see Figure 14.1). We see exactly the same phenomenon in Japan.[31]

The Anglo-Saxon attraction to progressive taxation becomes even clearer when we look at the estate tax. In the United States, the top estate tax rate remained between 70 and 80 percent from the 1930s to the 1980s, while in France and Germany the top rate never exceeded 30–40 percent except for the years 1946–1949 in Germany (see Figure 14.2).[32]

The only country to match or surpass peak US estate tax rates was Britain. The rates applicable to the highest British incomes as well as estates in the 1940s was 98 percent, a peak attained again in the 1970s—an absolute historical record.[33] Note, too, that both countries distinguished between "earned income," that is, income from labor (including both wages and nonwage compensation) and "unearned income," meaning capital income (rent, interests, dividends, etc.). The top rates indicated in Figure 14.1 for the United States and Britain applied to unearned income. At times, the top rate on earned income was slightly lower, especially in the 1970s.[34] This distinction is interesting,

31. The top Japanese income tax rate rose to 85 percent in 1947–1949, when it was set by the US occupier, and then fell immediately to 55 percent in 1950 after Japan regained its fiscal sovereignty. See the online technical appendix.

32. These rates applied in the direct line of inheritance. The rates applied to brothers, sisters, cousins, and nonrelatives were sometimes higher in France and Germany. In France today, for example, the rate for bequests to nonrelatives is 60 percent. But rates never reached the 70–80 percent levels applied to children in the United States and Britain.

33. The record level of 98 percent was in force in Britain from 1941 to 1952 and again from 1974 to 1978. See the online technical appendix for the complete series. During the 1972 US presidential campaign, George McGovern, the Democratic candidate, went so far as to propose a top rate of 100 percent for the largest inheritances (the rate was then 77 percent) as part of his plan to introduce a guaranteed minimum income. McGovern's crushing defeat by Nixon marked the beginning of the end of the United States' enthusiasm for redistribution. See Beckert, *Inherited Wealth*, 196.

34. For example, when the top rate on capital income in Britain was 98 percent from 1974 to 1978, the top rate on labor income was 83 percent. See Supplemental Figure S14.1, available online.

because it is a translation into fiscal terms of the suspicion that surrounded very high incomes: all excessively high incomes were suspect, but unearned incomes were more suspect than earned incomes. The contrast between attitudes then and now, with capital income treated more favorably today than labor income in many countries, especially in Europe, is striking. Note, too, that although the threshold for application of the top rates has varied over time, it has always been extremely high: expressed in terms of average income in the decade 2000–2010, the threshold has generally ranged between 500,000 and 1 million euros. In terms of today's income distribution, the top rate would therefore apply to less than 1 percent of the population (generally somewhere between 0.1 and 0.5 percent).

The urge to tax unearned income more heavily than earned income reflects an attitude that is also consistent with a steeply progressive inheritance tax. The British case is particularly interesting in a long-run perspective. Britain was the country with the highest concentration of wealth in the nineteenth and early twentieth centuries. The shocks (destruction, expropriation) endured by large fortunes fell less heavily there than on the continent, yet Britain chose to impose its own fiscal shock—less violent than war but nonetheless significant: the top rate ranged from 70 to 80 percent or more throughout the period 1940–1980. No other country devoted more thought to the taxation of inheritances in the twentieth century, especially between the two world wars.[35] In November 1938, Josiah Wedgwood, in the preface to a new edition of his classic 1929 book on inheritance, agreed with his

---

35. British thinkers such as John Stuart Mill were already reflecting on inheritances in the nineteenth century. The reflection intensified in the interwar years as more sophisticated probate data became available. It continued after the war in the work of James Meade and Anthony Atkinson, which I cited previously. It is also worth mentioning that Nicholas Kaldor's interesting proposal of a progressive tax on consumption (actually on luxury consumption) was directly inspired by his desire to require more of idle rentiers, whom he suspected of evading the progressive taxes on both estates and income through the use of trust funds, unlike university professors such as himself, who paid the income tax as required. See Nicholas Kaldor, *An Expenditure Tax* (London: Allen and Unwin, 1955).

compatriot Bertrand Russell that the "plutodemocracies" and their hereditary elites had failed to stem the rise of fascism. He was convinced that "political democracies that do not democratize their economic systems are inherently unstable." In his eyes, a steeply progressive inheritance tax was the main tool for achieving the economic democratization that he believed to be necessary.[36]

The Explosion of Executive Salaries: The Role of Taxation

After experiencing a great passion for equality from the 1930s through the 1970s, the United States and Britain veered off with equal enthusiasm in the opposite direction. Over the past three decades, their top marginal income tax rates, which had been significantly higher than the top rates in France and Germany, fell well below French and German levels. While the latter remained stable at 50–60 percent from 1930 to 2010 (with a slight decrease toward the end of the period), British and US rates fell from 80–90 percent in 1930–1980 to 30–40 percent in 1980–2010 (with a low point of 28 percent after the Reagan tax reform of 1986) (see Figure 14.1).[37] The Anglo-Saxon countries have played yo-yo with the wealthy since the 1930s. By contrast, attitudes toward top incomes in both continental Europe (of which Germany and France are fairly typical) and Japan have held steady. I showed in Part One that part of the explanation for this difference might be that the United States and Britain came to feel that they were being

---

36. See Josiah Wedgwood, *The Economics of Inheritance* (Harmondsworth, England: Pelican Books, 1929; new ed. 1939). Wedgwood meticulously analyzed the various forces at work. For example, he showed that charitable giving was of little consequence. His analysis led him to the conclusion that only a tax could achieve the equalization he desired. He also showed that French estates were nearly as concentrated as British ones in 1910, from which he concluded that egalitarian division of estates, as in France, though desirable, was clearly not enough to bring about social equality.

37. For France, I have included the generalized social contribution or CSG (currently 8 percent) in the income tax, which makes the current top rate 53 percent. See the online technical appendix for the complete series.

overtaken by other countries in the 1970s. This sense that other countries were catching up contributed to the rise of Thatcherism and Reaganism. To be sure, the catch-up that occurred between 1950 and 1980 was largely a mechanical consequence of the shocks endured by continental Europe and Japan between 1914 and 1945. The people of Britain and the United States nevertheless found it hard to accept: for countries as well as individuals, the wealth hierarchy is not just about money; it is also a matter of honor and moral values. What were the consequences of this great shift in attitudes in the United States and Britain?

If we look at all the developed countries, we find that the size of the decrease in the top marginal income tax rate between 1980 and the present is closely related to the size of the increase in the top centile's share of national income over the same period. Concretely, the two phenomena are perfectly correlated: the countries with the largest decreases in their top tax rates are also the countries where the top earners' share of national income has increased the most (especially when it comes to the remuneration of executives of large firms). Conversely, the countries that did not reduce their top tax rates very much saw much more moderate increases in the top earners' share of national income.[38] If one believes the classic economic models based on the theory of marginal productivity and the labor supply, one might try to explain this by arguing that the decrease in top tax rates spurred top executive talent to increase their labor supply and productivity. Since their marginal productivity increased, their salaries increased commensurately and therefore rose well above executive salaries in other countries. This explanation is

---

38. This is true not only of the United States and Britain (in the first group) and Germany, France, and Japan (in the second group) but also for all of the eighteen OECD countries for which we have data in the WTID that allow us to study the question. See Thomas Piketty, Emmanuel Saez, and Stefanie Stantcheva, "Optimal Taxation of Top Labor Incomes: A Tale of Three Elasticities," *American Economic Journal: Economic Policy* 6, no. 1 (2014): 230–271 (see figure 3). See also the online technical appendix.

not very plausible, however. As I showed in Chapter 9, the theory of marginal productivity runs into serious conceptual and economic difficulties (in addition to suffering from a certain naïveté) when it comes to explaining how pay is determined at the top of the income hierarchy.

A more realistic explanation is that lower top income tax rates, especially in the United States and Britain, where top rates fell dramatically, totally transformed the way executive salaries are determined. It is always difficult for an executive to convince other parties involved in the firm (direct subordinates, workers lower down in the hierarchy, stockholders, and members of the compensation committee) that a large pay raise—say of a million dollars—is truly justified. In the 1950s and 1960s, executives in British and US firms had little reason to fight for such raises, and other interested parties were less inclined to accept them, because 80–90 percent of the increase would in any case go directly to the government. After 1980, the game was utterly transformed, however, and the evidence suggests that executives went to considerable lengths to persuade other interested parties to grant them substantial raises. Because it is objectively difficult to measure individual contributions to a firm's output, top managers found it relatively easy to persuade boards and stockholders that they were worth the money, especially since the members of compensation committees were often chosen in a rather incestuous manner.

Furthermore, this "bargaining power" explanation is consistent with the fact that there is no statistically significant relationship between the decrease in top marginal tax rates and the rate of productivity growth in the developed countries since 1980. Concretely, the crucial fact is that the rate of per capita GDP growth has been almost exactly the same in all the rich countries since 1980. In contrast to what many people in Britain and the United States believe, the true figures on growth (as best one can judge from official national accounts data) show that Britain and the United States have not grown any more rapidly since 1980 than Germany, France, Japan, Denmark, or

Sweden.[39] In other words, the reduction of top marginal income tax rates and the rise of top incomes do not seem to have stimulated productivity (contrary to the predictions of supply-side theory) or at any rate did not stimulate productivity enough to be statistically detectable at the macro level.[40]

Considerable confusion exists around these issues because comparisons are often made over periods of just a few years (a procedure that can be used to justify virtually any conclusion).[41] Or one forgets to correct for population growth (which is the primary reason for the structural difference in GDP growth between the United States and Europe). Sometimes the level of per capita output (which has always been about 20 percent higher in the United States, in 1970–1980 as well as 2000–2010) is confused with the growth rate (which has been about the same on both continents over the past three decades).[42] But the principal source of confusion is probably the catch-up phenomenon mentioned above. There can be no doubt that British and US decline ended in the 1970s, in the sense that growth rates in Britain and the United States, which had been lower than growth rates in

---

39. See Piketty et al., "Optimal Taxation of Top Labor Incomes," figs. 3 and A1 and table 2. These results, which cover eighteen countries, are also available in the online technical appendix. This conclusion does not depend on the choice of starting and ending years. In all cases, there is no statistically significant relationship between the decrease in the top marginal tax rate and the rate of growth. In particular, starting in 1980 rather than 1960 or 1970 does not change the results. For growth rates in the wealth countries over the period 1970–2010, see also Table 5.1 here.

40. We can rule out an elasticity of labor supply greater than 0.1–0.2 and justify the optimal marginal income tax rate described below. All the details of the theoretical argument and results are available in Piketty et al., "Optimal Taxation of Top Labor Incomes," and are summarized in the online technical appendix.

41. It is important to average over fairly long periods (of at least ten to twenty years) to have meaningful growth comparisons. Over shorter periods, growth rates vary for all sorts of reasons, and it is impossible to draw any valid conclusions.

42. The difference in per capita GDP stems from the fact that US citizens work more hours than Europeans. According to standard international data, GDP per hour worked is approximately the same in the United States as in the wealthiest countries of the European continent (but significantly lower in Britain: see the online technical appendix).

Germany, France, Scandinavia, and Japan, ceased to be so. But it is also incontestable that the reason for this convergence is quite simple: Europe and Japan had caught up with the United States and Britain. Clearly, this had little to do with the conservative revolution in the latter two countries in the 1980s, at least to a first approximation.[43]

No doubt these issues are too strongly charged with emotion and too closely bound up with national identities and pride to allow for calm examination. Did Maggie Thatcher save Britain? Would Bill Gates's innovations have existed without Ronald Reagan? Will Rhenish capitalism devour the French social model? In the face of such powerful existential anxieties, reason is often at a loss, especially since it is objectively quite difficult to draw perfectly precise and absolutely unassailable conclusions on the basis of growth rate comparisons that reveal differences of a few tenths of a percent. As for Bill Gates and Ronald Reagan, each with his own cult of personality (Did Bill invent the computer or just the mouse? Did Ronnie destroy the USSR singlehandedly or with the help of the pope?), it may be useful to recall that the US economy was much more innovative in 1950–1970 than in 1990–2010, to judge by the fact that productivity growth was nearly twice as high in the former period as in the latter, and since the United States was in both periods at the world technology frontier, this difference must be related to the pace of innovation.[44] A new argument has recently been advanced: it is possible that the US economy has become more innovative in recent years but that this innovation does not show up in the productivity figures because it spilled over into the other wealthy countries, which have thrived on US inventions. It would nevertheless be quite astonishing if the United States, which has not always been hailed for international altruism (Europeans regularly complain about US carbon emissions, while the poor countries

---

43. See in particular Figure 2.3.

44. Per capita GDP in the United States grew at 2.3 percent a year from 1950 to 1970, 2.2 percent between 1970 and 1990, and 1.4 percent from 1990 to 2012. See Figure 2.3.

complain about American stinginess) were proven not to have retained some of this enhanced productivity for itself. In theory, that is the purpose of patents. Clearly, the debate is nowhere close to over.[45]

In an attempt to make some progress on these issues, Emmanuel Saez, Stefanie Stantcheva, and I have tried to go beyond international comparisons and to make use of a new database containing information about executive compensation in listed companies throughout the developed world. Our findings suggest that skyrocketing executive pay is fairly well explained by the bargaining model (lower marginal tax rates encourage executives to negotiate harder for higher pay) and does not have much to do with a hypothetical increase in managerial productivity.[46] We again found that the elasticity of executive pay is greater with respect to "luck" (that is, variations in earnings that cannot have been due to executive talent, because, for instance, other firms in the same sector did equally well) than with respect to "talent" (variations not explained by sector variables). As I explained in Chapter 9, this finding poses serious problems for the view that high executive pay is a reward for good performance. Furthermore, we found that elasticity with respect to luck—broadly speaking, the ability of executives to obtain raises not clearly justified by economic performance—was higher in countries where the top marginal tax rate was lower. Finally, we found that variations in the marginal tax rate can explain why executive pay

---

45. The idea that the United States has innovated for the rest of the world was recently proposed by Daron Acemoglu, James Robinson, and Thierry Verdier, "Can't We All Be More Like Scandinavians? Asymmetric Growth and Institutions in an Interdependent World," (MIT Department of Economics Working Paper no. 12–22, August 20, 2012). This is an essentially theoretical article, whose principal factual basis is that the number of patents per capita is higher in the United States than in Europe. This is interesting, but it seems to be at least partly a consequence of distinct legal practices, and in any case it should allow the innovative country to retain significantly higher productivity (or greater national income).

46. See Piketty et al., "Optimal Taxation of Top Labor Incomes," fig. 5, tables 3–4. The results summarized here are based on detailed data concerning nearly three thousand firms in fourteen countries.

rose sharply in some countries and not in others. In particular, variations in company size and in the importance of the financial sector definitely cannot explain the observed facts.[47] Similarly, the idea that skyrocketing executive pay is due to lack of competition, and that more competitive markets and better corporate governance and control would put an end to it, seems unrealistic.[48] Our findings suggest that only dissuasive taxation of the sort applied in the United States and Britain before 1980 can do the job.[49] In regard to such a complex and comprehensive question (which involves political, social, and cultural as well as economic factors), it is obviously impossible to be totally certain: that is the beauty of the social sciences. It is likely, for instance, that social norms concerning executive pay directly influence the levels of compensation we observe in different countries, independent of the influence of tax rates. Nevertheless, the available evidence suggests that our explanatory model gives the best explanation of the observed facts.

---

47. Xavier Gabaix and Augustin Landier argued that skyrocketing executive pay is a mechanical consequence of increased firm size (which supposedly increases the productivity of the most "talented" managers). See "Why Has CEO Pay Increased So Much?" *Quarterly Journal of Economics* 123, no. 1 (2008): 49–100. The problem is that this theory is based entirely on the marginal productivity model and cannot explain the large international variations observed in the data (company size increased in similar proportions nearly everywhere, but pay did not). The authors rely solely on US data, which unfortunately limits the possibilities for empirical testing.

48. Many economists defend the idea that greater competition can reduce inequality. See, for example, Raghuram G. Rajan and Luigi Zingales, *Saving Capitalism from the Capitalists* (New York: Crown Business, 2003), and L. Zingales, *A Capitalism for the People* (New York: Basic Books, 2012), or Acemoglu, Robinson, and Verdier, "Can't We All Be More Like Scandinavians." Some sociologists also take this line: see David B. Grusky, "Forum: What to Do about Inequality?" *Boston Review,* March 21, 2012.

49. Contrary to an idea that is often taught but rarely verified, there is no evidence that executives in the period 1950–1980 made up for low pay with compensation in kind, such as private planes, sumptuous offices, etc. On the contrary, all the evidence suggests that such benefits in kind have increased since 1980.

Rethinking the Question of the Top Marginal Rate

These findings have important implications for the desirable degree of fiscal progressivity. Indeed, they indicate that levying confiscatory rates on top incomes is not only possible but also the only way to stem the observed increase in very high salaries. According to our estimates, the optimal top tax rate in the developed countries is probably above 80 percent.[50] Do not be misled by the apparent precision of this estimate: no mathematical formula or econometric estimate can tell us exactly what tax rate ought to be applied to what level of income. Only collective deliberation and democratic experimentation can do that. What is certain, however, is that our estimates pertain to extremely high levels of income, those observed in the top 1 percent or 0.5 percent of the income hierarchy. The evidence suggests that a rate on the order of 80 percent on incomes over $500,000 or $1 million a year not only would not reduce the growth of the US economy but would in fact distribute the fruits of growth more widely while imposing reasonable limits on economically useless (or even harmful) behavior. Obviously it would be easier to apply such a policy in a country the size of the United States than in a small European country where close fiscal coordination with neighboring countries is lacking. I say more about international coordination in the next chapter; here I will simply note that the United States is big enough to apply this type of fiscal policy effectively. The idea that all US executives would immediately flee to Canada and Mexico and no one with the competence or motivation to run the economy would remain is not only contradicted by historical experience and by all the firm-level data at our disposal; it is also devoid of common sense. A rate of 80 percent applied to incomes above $500,000 or $1 million a year would not bring the government much in the way of revenue, because it would quickly fulfill its objective: to drastically reduce remuneration at this

---

50. To be precise, 82 percent. See Piketty et al., "Optimal Taxation of Top Labor Incomes," table 5.

level but without reducing the productivity of the US economy, so that pay would rise at lower levels. In order for the government to obtain the revenues it sorely needs to develop the meager US social state and invest more in health and education (while reducing the federal deficit), taxes would also have to be raised on incomes lower in the distribution (for example, by imposing rates of 50 or 60 percent on incomes above $200,000).[51] Such a social and fiscal policy is well within the reach of the United States.

Nevertheless, it seems quite unlikely that any such policy will be adopted anytime soon. It is not even certain that the top marginal income tax rate in the United States will be raised as high as 40 percent in Obama's second term. Has the US political process been captured by the 1 percent? This idea has become increasingly popular among observers of the Washington political scene.[52] For reasons of natural optimism as well as professional predilection, I am inclined to grant more influence to ideas and intellectual debate. Careful examination of various hypotheses and bodies of evidence, and access to better data, can influence political debate and perhaps push the process in a direction more favorable to the general interest. For example, as I noted in Part Three, US economists often underestimate the increase in top incomes because they rely on inadequate data (especially survey data that fails to capture the very highest incomes). As a result, they pay too much attention to wage gaps between workers with different

---

51. Note that the progressive tax plays two very distinct roles in this theoretical model (as well as in the history of progressive taxation): confiscatory rates (on the order of 80–90 percent on the top 0.5 or 1 percent of the distribution) would end indecent and useless compensation, while high but nonconfiscatory rates (of 50–60 percent on the top 5 or 10 percent) would raise revenues to finance the social state above the revenues coming from the bottom 90 percent of the distribution.

52. See Jacob Hacker and Paul Pierson, *Winner-Take-All Politics: How Washington Made the Rich Richer—And Turned Its Back on the Middle Class* (New York: Simon and Schuster, 2010); K. Schlozman, Sidney Verba, and H. Brady, *The Unheavenly Chorus: Unequal Political Voice and the Broken Promise of American Democracy* (Princeton: Princeton University Press, 2012); Timothy Noah, *The Great Divergence* (New York: Bloomsbury Press, 2012).

skill levels (a crucial question for the long run but not very relevant to understanding why the 1 percent have pulled so far ahead—the dominant phenomenon from a macroeconomic point of view).[53] The use of better data (in particular, tax data) may therefore ultimately focus attention on the right questions.

That said, the history of the progressive tax over the course of the twentieth century suggests that the risk of a drift toward oligarchy is real and gives little reason for optimism about where the United States is headed. It was war that gave rise to progressive taxation, not the natural consequences of universal suffrage. The experience of France in the Belle Époque proves, if proof were needed, that no hypocrisy is too great when economic and financial elites are obliged to defend their interests—and that includes economists, who currently occupy an enviable place in the US income hierarchy.[54] Some economists have an unfortunate tendency to defend their private interest while implausibly claiming to champion the general interest.[55] Although data on this are sparse, it also seems that US politicians of both parties are much wealthier than their European counterparts and in a totally different category from the average American, which might explain why they tend to confuse their own private interest with the general interest. Without a radical shock, it seems fairly likely that the current equilibrium will persist for quite some time. The egalitarian pioneer ideal has faded into oblivion, and the New World may be on the verge of becoming the Old Europe of the twenty-first century's globalized economy.

---

53. See Claudia Goldin and Lawrence F. Katz, *The Race between Education and Technology: The Evolution of U.S. Educational Wage Differentials, 1890–2005* (Cambridge, MA: Belknap Press and NBER, 2010), Rebecca M. Blank, *Changing Inequality* (Berkeley: University of California Press, 2011) and Raghuram G. Rajan, *Fault Lines* (Princeton: Princeton University Press, 2010).

54. The pay of academic economists is driven up by the salaries offered in the private sector, especially the financial sector, for similar skills. See Chapter 8.

55. For example, by using abstruse theoretical models designed to prove that the richest people should pay zero taxes or even receive subsidies. For a brief bibliography of such models, see the online technical appendix.

{ FIFTEEN }

A Global Tax on Capital

To regulate the globalized patrimonial capitalism of the twenty-first century, rethinking the twentieth-century fiscal and social model and adapting it to today's world will not be enough. To be sure, appropriate updating of the last century's social-democratic and fiscal-liberal program is essential, as I tried to show in the previous two chapters, which focused on two fundamental institutions that were invented in the twentieth century and must continue to play a central role in the future: the social state and the progressive income tax. But if democracy is to regain control over the globalized financial capitalism of this century, it must also invent new tools, adapted to today's challenges. The ideal tool would be a progressive global tax on capital, coupled with a very high level of international financial transparency. Such a tax would provide a way to avoid an endless inegalitarian spiral and to control the worrisome dynamics of global capital concentration. Whatever tools and regulations are actually decided on need to be measured against this ideal. I will begin by analyzing practical aspects of such a tax and then proceed to more general reflections about the regulation of capitalism from the prohibition of usury to Chinese capital controls.

A Global Tax on Capital: A Useful Utopia

A global tax on capital is a utopian idea. It is hard to imagine the nations of the world agreeing on any such thing anytime soon. To achieve this goal, they would have to establish a tax schedule applicable to all wealth around the world and then decide how to apportion the revenues. But if the idea is utopian, it is nevertheless useful, for several reasons. First, even if nothing resembling this ideal is put into practice in the foreseeable future, it can serve as a worthwhile reference point, a standard against which alternative proposals can be measured. Admittedly, a global tax on capital would require a very high and no doubt unrealistic level of international cooperation. But countries wishing to move in this direction could very well do so incrementally, starting at the regional level (in Europe, for instance). Unless something like this happens, a defensive reaction of a nationalist stripe would very likely occur. For example, one might see a return to various forms of protectionism coupled with imposition of capital controls. Because such policies are seldom effective, however, they would very likely lead to frustration and increase international tensions. Protectionism and capital controls are actually unsatisfactory substitutes for the ideal form of regulation, which is a global tax on capital—a solution that has the merit of preserving economic openness while effectively regulating the global economy and justly distributing the benefits among and within nations. Many people will reject the global tax on capital as a dangerous illusion, just as the income tax was rejected in its time, a little more than a century ago. When looked at closely, however, this solution turns out to be far less dangerous than the alternatives.

To reject the global tax on capital out of hand would be all the more regrettable because it is perfectly possible to move toward this ideal solution step by step, first at the continental or regional level and then by arranging for closer cooperation among regions. One can see a model for this sort of approach in the recent discussions on automatic sharing of bank data between the United States and the European Union. Furthermore, various forms of capital taxation already exist in most countries, especially in North America and Europe, and these could obviously serve as starting points. The capital controls that exist in China and other emerging countries also hold useful lessons for all. There are nevertheless important differences between these existing measures and the ideal tax on capital.

First, the proposals for automatic sharing of banking information currently under discussion are far from comprehensive. Not all asset types are included, and the penalties envisioned are clearly insufficient to achieve the desired results (despite new US banking regulations that are more ambitious than any that exist in Europe). The debate is only beginning, and it is unlikely to produce tangible results unless relatively heavy sanctions are imposed on banks and, even more, on countries that thrive on financial opacity.

The issue of financial transparency and information sharing is closely related to the ideal tax on capital. Without a clear idea of what all the information is to be used for, current data-sharing proposals are unlikely to achieve the desired result. To my mind, the objective ought to be a progressive annual tax on individual wealth—that is, on the net value of assets each person controls. For the wealthiest people on the planet, the tax would thus be based on individual net worth—the kinds of numbers published by *Forbes* and other magazines. (And collecting such a tax would tell us whether the numbers published in the magazines are anywhere near correct.) For the rest of us, taxable wealth would be determined by the market value of all financial assets (including bank deposits, stocks, bonds, partnerships, and other forms of participation in listed and unlisted firms) and nonfinancial assets (especially real estate), net of debt. So much for the basis of the tax. At what rate would it be levied? One might imagine a rate of 0 percent for net assets below 1 million euros, 1 percent between 1 and 5 million, and 2 percent above 5 million. Or one might prefer a much more steeply progressive tax on the largest fortunes (for example, a rate of 5 or 10 percent on assets above 1 billion euros). There might also be advantages to having a minimal rate on modest-to-average wealth (for example, 0.1 percent below 200,000 euros and 0.5 percent between 200,000 and 1 million).

I discuss these issues later on. Here, the important point to keep in mind is that the capital tax I am proposing is a progressive annual tax on global wealth. The largest fortunes are to be taxed more heavily, and all types of assets are to be included: real estate, financial assets, and business assets—no exceptions. This is one clear difference between my proposed capital tax and the taxes on capital that currently exist in one country or another, even though important aspects of those existing taxes should be retained. To begin with, nearly every country taxes real estate: the English-speaking countries have "property taxes," while France has a *taxe foncière*. One drawback of these taxes is that they are based solely on real property. (Financial assets are ignored, and property is taxed at its market value regardless of debt, so that a heavily indebted person is taxed in the same way as a person with no debt.) Furthermore, real estate is generally taxed at a flat rate, or close to it. Still, such taxes exist and generate significant revenue in most developed countries, especially in the English-speaking world (typically 1–2 percent of national income). Furthermore, property taxes in some countries (such as the United States) rely on fairly sophisticated assessment procedures with automatic adjustment to changing market values, procedures that ought to be generalized and extended to other asset classes. In some European countries (including France, Switzerland, Spain, and until recently Germany and Sweden), there are also progressive taxes on total wealth. Superficially, these taxes are closer in spirit to the ideal capital tax I am proposing. In practice, however, they are often riddled with exemptions. Many asset classes are left out, while others are assessed at arbitrary values having nothing to do with their market value. That is why several countries have moved to eliminate such taxes. It is important to heed the lessons of these various experiences in order to design an appropriate capital tax for the century ahead.

Democratic and Financial Transparency

What tax schedule is ideal for my proposed capital tax, and what revenues should we expect such a tax to produce? Before I attempt to answer these questions, note that the proposed tax is in no way intended to replace all existing taxes. It would never be more than a fairly modest supplement to the other revenue streams on which the modern social state depends: a few points of national income (three or four at most—still nothing to sneeze at).[1] The primary purpose of the capital tax is not to finance the social state but to regulate capitalism. The goal is first to stop the indefinite increase of inequality of wealth, and second to impose effective regulation on the financial and banking system in order to avoid crises. To achieve these two ends, the capital tax must first promote democratic and financial transparency: there should be clarity about who owns what assets around the world.

Why is the goal of transparency so important? Imagine a very low global tax on capital, say a flat rate of 0.1 percent a year on all assets. The revenue from such a tax would of course be limited, by design: if the global stock of private capital is about five years of global income, the tax would generate revenue equal to 0.5 percent of global income, with minor variations from country to country according to their capital/income ratio (assuming that the tax is collected in the country where the owner of the asset resides and not where the asset itself is located—an assumption that can by no means be taken for granted). Even so, such a limited tax would already play a very useful role.

First, it would generate information about the distribution of wealth. National governments, international organizations, and statistical offices around the world would at last be able to produce reliable data about the evolution of global wealth. Citizens would no longer be forced to rely on *Forbes,* glossy financial reports from global wealth managers, and other unofficial sources to fill the official statistical void. (Recall that I explored the deficiencies of those unofficial sources in Part Three.) Instead, they would have access to public data based on clearly prescribed methods and information provided under penalty of law. The benefit to democracy would be considerable: it is very difficult to have a rational debate about the great challenges facing the world today—the future of the social state, the cost of the transition

---

1. The additional revenue could be used to reduce existing taxes or to pay for additional services (such as foreign aid or debt reduction; I will have more to say about this later).

to new sources of energy, state-building in the developing world, and so on—because the global distribution of wealth remains so opaque. Some people think that the world's billionaires have so much money that it would be enough to tax them at a low rate to solve all the world's problems. Others believe that there are so few billionaires that nothing much would come of taxing them more heavily. As we saw in Part Three, the truth lies somewhere between these two extremes. In macroeconomic terms, one probably has to descend a bit in the wealth hierarchy (to fortunes of 10–100 million euros rather than 1 billion) to obtain a tax basis large enough to make a difference. I have also discovered some objectively disturbing trends: without a global tax on capital or some similar policy, there is a substantial risk that the top centile's share of global wealth will continue to grow indefinitely—and this should worry everyone. In any case, truly democratic debate cannot proceed without reliable statistics.

The stakes for financial regulation are also considerable. The international organizations currently responsible for overseeing and regulating the global financial system, starting with the IMF, have only a very rough idea of the global distribution of financial assets, and in particular of the amount of assets hidden in tax havens. As I have shown, the planet's financial accounts are not in balance. (Earth seems to be perpetually indebted to Mars.) Navigating our way through a global financial crisis blanketed in such a thick statistical fog is fraught with peril. Take, for example, the Cypriot banking crisis of 2013. Neither the European authorities nor the IMF had much information about who exactly owned the financial assets deposited in Cyprus or what amounts they owned, hence their proposed solutions proved crude and ineffective. As we will see in the next chapter, greater financial transparency would not only lay the groundwork for a permanent annual tax on capital; it would also pave the way to a more just and efficient management of banking crises like the one in Cyprus, possibly by way of carefully calibrated and progressive special levies on capital.

An 0.1 percent tax on capital would be more in the nature of a compulsory reporting law than a true tax. Everyone would be required to report ownership of capital assets to the world's financial authorities in order to be recognized as the legal owner, with all the advantages and disadvantages thereof. As noted, this was what the French Revolution accomplished with its compulsory reporting and cadastral surveys. The capital tax would be a sort of cadastral financial survey of the entire world, and nothing like it currently exists.[2] It is important to understand that a tax is always more than just a tax: it is also a way of defining norms and categories and imposing a legal framework on economic activity. This has always been the case, especially in regard to land ownership.[3] In the modern era, the imposition of new taxes around the time of World War I required precise definitions of income, wages, and profits. This fiscal innovation in turn fostered the development of accounting standards, which had not previously existed. One of the main goals of a tax on capital would thus be to refine the definitions of various asset types and set rules for valuing assets, liabilities, and net wealth. Under the private accounting standards now in force, prescribed procedures are imperfect and often vague. These flaws have contributed to the many financial scandals the world has seen since 2000.[4]

---

2. Every continent has specialized financial institutions that act as central repositories (custodian banks or clearing houses), whose purpose is to record ownership of various types of assets. But the function of these private institutions is to provide a service to the companies issuing the securities in question, not to record all the assets owned by a particular individual. On these institutions, see Gabriel Zucman, "The Missing Wealth of Nations: Are Europe and the U.S. Net Debtors or Net Creditors?" *Quarterly Journal of Economics* 128, no. 3 (2013): 1321–64.

3. For instance, the fall of the Roman Empire ended the imperial tax on land and therefore the land titles and cadastre that went with it. According to Peter Temin, this contributed to economic chaos in the early Middle Ages. See Peter Temin, *The Roman Market Economy* (Princeton: Princeton University Press, 2012), 149–51.

4. For this reason, it would be useful to institute a low-rate tax on net corporate capital together with a higher-rate tax on private wealth. Governments would then be forced to set accounting standards, a task currently left to associations of private accountants. On this subject, see Nicolas Véron, Matthieu Autret, and Alfred Galichon, *L'information financière en crise: Comptabilité et capitalisme* (Paris: Odile Jacob, 2004).

Last but not least, a capital tax would force governments to clarify and broaden international agreements concerning the automatic sharing of banking data. The principle is quite simple: national tax authorities should receive all the information they need to calculate the net wealth of every citizen. Indeed, the capital tax should work in the same way as the income tax currently does in many countries, where data on income are provided to the tax authorities by employers (via the W-2 and 1099 forms in the United States, for example). There should be similar reporting on capital assets (indeed, income and capital reporting could be combined into one form). All taxpayers would receive a form listing their assets and liabilities as reported to the tax authorities. Many US states use this method to administer the property tax: taxpayers receive an annual form indicating the current market value of any real estate they own, as calculated by the government on the basis of observed prices in transactions involving comparable properties. Taxpayers can of course challenge these valuations with appropriate evidence. In practice, corrections are rare, because data on real estate transactions are readily available and hard to contest: nearly everyone is aware of changing real estate values in the local market, and the authorities have comprehensive databases at their disposal.[5] Note, in passing, that this reporting method has two advantages: it makes the taxpayer's life simple and eliminates the inevitable temptation to slightly underestimate the value of one's own property.[6]

---

5. Concretely, the authorities do what is called a "hedonic" regression to calculate the market price as a function of various characteristics of the property. Transactional data are available in all developed countries for this purpose (and are used to calculate real estate price indices).

6. This temptation is a problem in all systems based on self-reporting by taxpayers, such as the wealth tax system in France, where there is always an abnormally large number of reports of wealth just slightly below the taxable threshold. There is clearly a tendency to slightly understate the value of real estate, typically by 10 or 20 percent. A precomputed statement issued by the government would provide an objective figure based on public data and a clear methodology and would thus put an end to such behavior.

It is essential—and perfectly feasible—to extend this reporting system to all types of financial assets (and debts). For assets and liabilities associated with financial institutions within national borders, this could be done immediately, since banks, insurance companies, and other financial intermediaries in most developed countries are already required to inform the tax authorities about bank accounts and other assets they administer. In France, for example, the government knows that Monsieur X owns an apartment worth 400,000 euros and a stock portfolio worth 200,000 euros and has 100,000 euros in outstanding debts. It could thus send him a form indicating these various amounts (along with his net worth of 500,000 euros) with a request for corrections and additions if appropriate. This type of automated system, applied to the entire population, is far better adapted to the twenty-first century than the archaic method of asking all persons to declare honestly how much they own.[7]

A Simple Solution: Automatic Transmission of Banking Information

The first step toward a global tax on capital should be to extend to the international level this type of automatic transmission of banking data in order to include information on assets held in foreign banks in the precomputed asset statements issued to each taxpayer. It is important to recognize that there is no technical obstacle to doing so. Banking data are already automatically shared with the tax authorities in a country with 300 million people like the United States, as well as in countries like France and Germany with populations of 60 and 80 million, respectively, so there is obviously no reason why including the banks in the Cayman Islands and Switzerland would radically increase

---

7. Oddly enough, the French government once again turned to this archaic method in 2013 to obtain information about the assets of its own ministers, officially for the purpose of restoring confidence after one of them was caught in a lie about evading taxes on his wealth.

the volume of data to be processed. Of course the tax havens regularly invoke other excuses for maintaining bank secrecy. One of these is the alleged worry that governments will misuse the information. This is not a very convincing argument: it is hard to see why it would not also apply to information about the bank accounts of those incautious enough to keep their money in the country where they pay taxes. The most plausible reason why tax havens defend bank secrecy is that it allows their clients to evade their fiscal obligations, thereby allowing the tax havens to share in the gains. Obviously this has nothing whatsoever to do with the principles of the market economy. No one has the right to set his own tax rates. It is not right for individuals to grow wealthy from free trade and economic integration only to rake off the profits at the expense of their neighbors. That is outright theft.

To date, the most thoroughgoing attempt to end these practices is the Foreign Account Tax Compliance Act (FATCA) adopted in the United States in 2010 and scheduled to be phased in by stages in 2014 and 2015. It requires all foreign banks to inform the Treasury Department about bank accounts and investments held abroad by US taxpayers, along with any other sources of revenue from which they might benefit. This is a far more ambitious law than the 2003 EU directive on foreign savings, which concerns only interest-bearing deposit accounts (equity portfolios are not covered, which is unfortunate, since large fortunes are held primarily in the form of stocks, which are fully covered by FATCA) and applies only to European banks and not worldwide (again unlike FATCA). Even though the European directive is timid and almost meaningless, it is not enforced, since, despite numerous discussions and proposed amendments since 2008, Luxembourg and Austria managed to win from other EU member states an agreement to extend their exemption from automatic data reporting and retain their right to share information only on formal request. This system, which also applies to Switzerland and other territories outside the European Union,[8] means that a government must already

---

8. For example, the Channel Islands, Liechtenstein, Monaco, etc.

possess something close to proof of fraud in order to obtain information about the foreign bank accounts of one of its citizens. This obviously limits drastically the ability to detect and control fraud. In 2013, after Luxembourg and Switzerland announced their intention to abide by the provisions of FATCA, discussions in Europe resumed with the intention of incorporating some or all of these in a new EU directive. It is impossible to know when these discussions will conclude or whether they will lead to a legally binding agreement.

Note, moreover, that in this realm there is often a chasm between the triumphant declarations of political leaders and the reality of what they accomplish. This is extremely worrisome for the future equilibrium of our democratic societies. It is particularly striking to discover that the countries that are most dependent on substantial tax revenues to pay for their social programs, namely the European countries, are also the ones that have accomplished the least, even though the technical challenges are quite simple. This is a good example of the difficult situation that smaller countries face in dealing with globalization. Nation-states built over centuries find that they are too small to impose and enforce rules on today's globalized patrimonial capitalism. The countries of Europe were able to unite around a single currency (to be discussed more extensively in the next chapter), but they have accomplished almost nothing in the area of taxation. The leaders of the largest countries in the European Union, who naturally bear primary responsibility for this failure and for the gaping chasm between their words and their actions, nevertheless continue to blame other countries and the institutions of the European Union itself. There is no reason to think that things will change anytime soon.

Furthermore, although FATCA is far more ambitious than any EU directive in this realm, it, too, is insufficient. For one thing, its language is not sufficiently precise or comprehensive, so that there is good reason to believe that certain trust funds and foundations can legally avoid any obligation to report their assets. For another, the sanction envisioned by the law (a 30 percent surtax on income that noncompliant banks derive from their US operations) is insufficient. It may be enough to persuade certain banks (such as the big Swiss and Luxembourgian institutions that need to do business in the United States) to abide by the law, but there may well be a resurgence of smaller banks that specialize in managing overseas portfolios and do not operate on US soil. Such institutions, whether located in Switzerland, Luxembourg, London, or more exotic locales, can continue to manage the assets of US (or European) taxpayers without conveying any information to the authorities, with complete impunity.

Very likely the only way to obtain tangible results is to impose automatic sanctions not only on banks but also on countries that refuse to require their financial institutions to provide the required information. One might contemplate, for example, a tariff of 30 percent or more on the exports of offending states. To be clear, the goal is not to impose a general embargo on tax havens or engage in an endless trade war with Switzerland or Luxembourg. Protectionism does not produce wealth, and free trade and economic openness are ultimately in everyone's interest, provided that some countries do not take advantage of their neighbors by siphoning off their tax base. The requirement to provide comprehensive banking data automatically should have been part of the free trade and capital liberalization agreements negotiated since 1980. It was not, but that is not a good reason to stick with the status quo forever. Countries that have thrived on financial opacity may find it difficult to accept reform, especially since a legitimate financial services industry often develops alongside illicit (or questionable) banking activities. The financial services industry responds to genuine needs of the real international economy and will obviously continue to exist no matter what regulations are adopted. Nevertheless, the tax havens will undoubtedly suffer significant losses if financial transparency becomes the norm.[9] Such countries would be unlikely to agree to reform without

---

9. It is difficult to estimate the extent of such losses, but in a country like Luxembourg or Switzerland they might amount to as much as 10–20 percent of national income, which would have a substantial impact on their standard of living. (The same is true of a financial enclave like the City of London.) In the more exotic tax havens and microstates, the loss might be as high as 50 percent or more of

sanctions, especially since other countries, and in particular the largest countries in the European Union, have not for the moment shown much determination to deal with the problem. Note, moreover, that the construction of the European Union has thus far rested on the idea that each country could have a single market and free capital flows without paying any price (or much of one). Reform is necessary, even indispensable, but it would be naïve to think that it will happen without a fight. Because it moves the debate away from the realm of abstractions and high-flown rhetoric and toward concrete sanctions, which are important, especially in Europe, FATCA is useful.

Finally, note that neither FATCA nor the EU directives were intended to support a progressive tax on global wealth. Their purpose was primarily to provide the tax authorities with information about taxpayer assets to be used for internal purposes such as identifying omissions in income tax returns. The information can also be used to identify possible evasion of the estate tax or wealth tax (in countries that have one), but the primary emphasis is on enforcement of the income tax. Clearly, these various issues are closely related, and international financial transparency is a crucial matter for the modern fiscal state across the board.

What Is the Purpose of a Tax on Capital?

Suppose next that the tax authorities are fully informed about the net asset position of each citizen. Should they be content to tax wealth at a very low rate (of, say, 0.1 percent, in keeping with the logic of compulsory reporting), or should a more substantial tax be assessed, and if so, why? The key question can be reformulated as follows. Since a progressive income tax exists and, in most countries, a progressive estate tax as well, what is the purpose of a progressive tax on capital? In fact, these three progressive taxes play distinct and complementary roles.

---

national income, indeed as high as 80–90 percent in territories that function solely as domiciles for fictitious corporations.

Each is an essential pillar of an ideal tax system.[10] There are two distinct justifications of a capital tax: a contributive justification and an incentive justification.

The contributive logic is quite simple: income is often not a well-defined concept for very wealthy individuals, and only a direct tax on capital can correctly gauge the contributive capacity of the wealthy. Concretely, imagine a person with a fortune of 10 billion euros. As we saw in our examination of the *Forbes* rankings, fortunes of this magnitude have increased very rapidly over the past three decades, with real growth rates of 6–7 percent a year or even higher for the wealthiest individuals (such as Liliane Bettencourt and Bill Gates).[11] By definition, this means that income in the economic sense, including dividends, capital gains, and all other new resources capable of financing consumption and increasing the capital stock, amounted to at least 6–7 percent of the individual's capital (assuming that virtually none of this is consumed).[12] To simplify things, imagine that the individual in question enjoys an economic income of 5 percent of her fortune of 10 billion euros, which would be 500 million a year. Now, it is unlikely that such an individual would declare an income of 500 million euros on her income tax return. In France, the United States, and all other countries we have studied, the largest incomes declared on income tax returns are generally no more than a few tens of millions of euros or dollars. Take Liliane Bettencourt, the L'Oréal heiress and the wealthiest person in France. According to information published in the press and revealed by Bettencourt herself, her declared income was never more than 5 million a year, or little more than one ten-thousandth of her wealth (which is currently more than 30 billion

---

10. Social insurance contributions are a type of income tax (and are included in the income tax in some countries; see Chapter 13).

11. See in particular Table 12.1.

12. Recall the classic definition of income in the economic sense, given by the British economist John Hicks: "The income of a person or collectivity is the value of the maximum that could be consumed during the period while remaining as wealthy at the end of the period as at the beginning."

euros). Uncertainties about individual cases aside (they are of little importance), the income declared for tax purposes in a case like this is less than a hundredth of the taxpayer's economic income.[13]

The crucial point here is that no tax evasion or undeclared Swiss bank account is involved (as far as we know). Even a person of the most refined taste and elegance cannot easily spend 500 million euros a year on current expenses. It is generally enough to take a few million a year in dividends (or some other type of payout) while leaving the remainder of the return on one's capital to accumulate in a family trust or other ad hoc legal entity created for the sole purpose of managing a fortune of this magnitude, just as university endowments are managed.

This is perfectly legal and not inherently problematic.[14] Nevertheless, it does present a challenge to the tax system. If some people are taxed on the basis of declared incomes that are only 1 percent of their economic incomes, or even 10 percent, then nothing is accomplished by taxing that income at a rate of 50 percent or even 98 percent. The problem is that this is how the tax system works in practice in the developed countries. Effective tax rates (expressed as a percentage of economic income) are extremely low at the top of the wealth hierarchy, which is problematic, since it accentuates the explosive dynamic of wealth inequality, especially when larger fortunes are able to garner

---

13. Even with a return on capital of 2 percent (much lower than the actual return on the Bettencourt fortune in the period 1987–2013), the economic income on 30 billion euros would amount to 600 million euros, not 5 million.

14. In the case of the Bettencourt fortune, the largest in France, there was an additional problem: the family trust was managed by the wife of the minister of the budget, who was also the treasurer of a political party that had received large donations from Bettencourt. Since the same party had reduced the wealth tax by two-thirds during its time in power, the story naturally stirred up a considerable reaction in France. The United States is not the only country where the wealthy wield considerable political influence, as I showed in the previous chapter. Note, too, that the minister of the budget in question was succeeded by another who had to resign when it was revealed that he had a secret bank account in Switzerland. In France, too, the political influence of the wealthy transcends political boundaries.

larger returns. In fact, the tax system ought to attenuate this dynamic, not accentuate it.

There are several ways to deal with this problem. One would be to tax all of a person's income, including the part that accumulates in trusts, holding companies, and partnerships. A simpler solution is to compute the tax due on the basis of wealth rather than income. One could then assume a flat yield (of, say, 5 percent a year) to estimate the income on the capital and include that amount in the income subject to a progressive income tax. Some countries, such as the Netherlands, have tried this but have run into a number of difficulties having to do with the range of assets covered and the choice of a return on capital.[15] Another solution is to apply a progressive tax directly to an individual's total wealth. The important advantage of this approach is that one can vary the tax rate with the size of the fortune, since we know that in practice larger fortunes earn larger returns.

In view of the finding that fortunes at the top of the wealth hierarchy are earning very high returns, this contributive argument is the most important justification of a progressive tax on capital. According to this reasoning, capital is a better indicator of the contributive capacity of very wealthy individuals than is income, which is often difficult to measure. A tax on capital is thus needed in addition to the income tax for those individuals whose taxable income is clearly too low in light of their wealth.[16]

Nevertheless, another classic argument in favor of a capital tax should not be neglected. It relies on a logic of incentives. The basic idea

---

15. In practice, the Dutch system is not completely satisfactory: many categories of assets are exempt (particularly those held in family trusts), and the assumed return is 4 percent for all assets, which may be too high for some fortunes and too low for others.

16. The most logical approach is to measure this insufficiency on the basis of average rates of return observed for fortunes of each category so as to make the income tax schedule consistent with the capital tax schedule. One might also consider minimum and maximum taxes as a function of capital income. See the online technical appendix.

is that a tax on capital is an incentive to seek the best possible return on one's capital stock. Concretely, a tax of 1 or 2 percent on wealth is relatively light for an entrepreneur who manages to earn 10 percent a year on her capital. By contrast, it is quite heavy for a person who is content to park her wealth in investments returning at most 2 or 3 percent a year. According to this logic, the purpose of the tax on capital is thus to force people who use their wealth inefficiently to sell assets in order to pay their taxes, thus ensuring that those assets wind up in the hands of more dynamic investors.

There is some validity to this argument, but it should not be over-stated.[17] In practice, the return on capital does not depend solely on the talent and effort supplied by the capitalist. For one thing, the average return varies systematically with the size of the initial fortune. For another, individual returns are largely unpredictable and chaotic and are affected by all sorts of economic shocks. For example, there are many reasons why a firm might be losing money at any given point in time. A tax system based solely on the capital stock (and not on realized profits) would put disproportionate pressure on companies in the red, because their taxes would be as high when they were losing money as when they were earning high profits, and this could plunge them into bankruptcy.[18] The ideal tax system is therefore a compromise

---

17. The incentive argument is central to Maurice Allais's tendentious *L'impôt sur le capital et la réforme monétaire* (Paris: Editions Hermann, 1977), in which Allais went so far as to advocate complete elimination of the income tax and all other taxes in favor of a tax on capital. This is an extravagant idea and not very sensible, given the amounts of money involved. On Allais's argument and current extensions of it, see the online technical appendix. Broadly speaking, discussions of a tax on capital often push people into extreme positions (so that they either reject the idea out of hand or embrace it as the one and only tax, destined to replace all others). The same is true of the estate tax (either they shouldn't be taxed at all or should be taxed at 100 percent). In my view, it is urgent to lower the temperature of the debate and give each argument and each type of tax its due. A capital tax is useful, but it cannot replace all other taxes.

18. The same is true of an unemployed worker who has to continue paying a high property tax (especially when mortgage payments are not deductible). The consequences for overindebted households can be dramatic.

between the incentive logic (which favors a tax on the capital stock) and an insurance logic (which favors a tax on the revenue stream stemming from capital).[19] The unpredictability of the return on capital explains, moreover, why it is more efficient to tax heirs not once and for all, at the moment of inheritance (by way of the estate tax), but throughout their lives, via taxes based on both capital income and the value of the capital stock.[20] In other words, all three types of tax—on inheritance, income, and capital—play useful and complementary roles (even if income is perfectly observable for all taxpayers, no matter how wealthy).[21]

A Blueprint for a European Wealth Tax

Taking all these factors into account, what is the ideal schedule for a tax on capital, and how much would such a tax bring in? To be clear, I am speaking here of a permanent annual tax on capital at a rate that must therefore be fairly moderate. A tax collected only once a genera-

---

19. This compromise depends on the respective importance of individual incentives and random shocks in determining the return on capital. In some cases it may be preferable to tax capital income less heavily than labor income (and to rely primarily on a tax on the capital stock), while in others it might make sense to tax capital income more heavily (as was the case in Britain and the United States before 1980, no doubt because capital income was seen as particularly arbitrary). See Thomas Piketty and Emmanuel Saez, *A Theory of Optimal Capital Taxation*, NBER Working Paper 17989 (April 2012); a shorter version is available as "A Theory of Optimal Inheritance Taxation," *Econometrica* 81, no. 5 (September 2013): 1851–86.

20. This is because the capitalized value of the inheritance over the lifetime of the recipient is not known at the moment of transmission. When a Paris apartment worth 100,000 francs in 1972 passed to an heir, no one knew that the property would be worth a million euros in 2013 and afford a saving on rent of more than 40,000 euros a year. Rather than tax the inheritance heavily in 1972, it is more efficient to assess a smaller inheritance tax but to require payment of an annual property tax, a tax on rent, and perhaps a wealth tax as the value of the property and its return increase over time.

21. See Piketty and Saez, "Theory of Optimal Capital Taxation"; see also the online technical appendix.

tion, such as an inheritance tax, can be assessed at a very high rate: a third, a half, or even two-thirds, as was the case for the largest estates in Britain and the United States from 1930 to 1980.[22] The same is true of exceptional one-time taxes on capital levied in unusual circumstances, such as the tax levied on capital in France in 1945 at rates as high as 25 percent, indeed 100 percent for additions to capital during the Occupation (1940–1945). Clearly, such taxes cannot be applied for very long: if the government takes a quarter of the nation's wealth every year, there will be nothing left to tax after a few years. That is why the rates of an annual tax on capital must be much lower, on the order of a few percent. To some this may seem surprising, but it is actually quite a substantial tax, since it is levied every year on the total stock of capital. For example, the property tax rate is frequently just 0.5–1 percent of the value of real estate, or a tenth to a quarter of the rental value of the property (assuming an average rental return of 4 percent a year).[23]

The next point is important, and I want to insist on it: given the very high level of private wealth in Europe today, a progressive annual tax on wealth at modest rates could bring in significant revenue. Take, for example, a wealth tax of 0 percent on fortunes below 1 million euros, 1 percent between 1 and 5 million euros, and 2 percent above 5 million euros. If applied to all member states of the European Union, such a tax would affect about 2.5 percent of the population and bring in revenues equivalent to 2 percent of Europe's GDP.[24] The high return should come as no surprise: it is due simply to the fact that private

---

22. See Figure 14.2

23. For example, on real estate worth 500,000 euros, the annual tax would be between 2,500 and 5,000 euros, and the rental value of the property would be about 20,000 euros a year. By construction, a 4–5 percent annual tax on all capital would consume nearly all of capital's share of national income, which seems neither just nor realistic, particularly since there are already taxes on capital income.

24. About 2.5 percent of the adult population of Europe possessed fortunes above 1 million euros in 2013, and about 0.2 percent above 5 million. The annual revenue from the proposed tax would be about 300 billion euros on a GDP of nearly 15 trillion. See the online technical appendix and Supplemental Table S5.1, available online, for a detailed estimate and a simple simulator with which one can esti-

wealth in Europe today is worth more than five years of GDP, and much of that wealth is concentrated in the upper centiles of the distribution.[25] Although a tax on capital would not by itself bring in enough to finance the social state, the additional revenues it would generate are nevertheless significant.

In principle, each member state of the European Union could generate similar revenues by applying such a tax on its own. But without automatic sharing of bank information both inside and outside EU territory (starting with Switzerland among nonmember states) the risks of evasion would be very high. This partly explains why countries that have adopted a wealth tax (such as France, which employs a tax schedule similar to the one I am proposing) generally allow numerous exemptions, especially for "business assets" and, in practice, for nearly all large stakes in listed and unlisted companies. To do this is to drain much of the content from the progressive tax on capital, and that is why existing taxes have generated revenues so much smaller than the ones described above.[26] An extreme example of the difficulties European

mate the number of taxpayers and the amount of revenue associated with other possible tax schedules.

25. The top centile currently owns about 25 percent of total wealth, or about 125 percent of European GDP. The wealthiest 2.5 percent own nearly 40 percent of total wealth, or about 200 percent of European GDP. Hence it is no surprise that a tax with marginal rates of 1 or 2 percent would bring in about two points of GDP. Revenues would be even higher if these rates applied to all wealth and not just to the fractions over the thresholds.

26. The French wealth tax, called the "solidarity tax on wealth," (impôt de solidarité sur la fortune, or ISF), applies today to taxable wealth above 1.3 million euros (after a deduction of 30 percent on the primary residence), with rates ranging from 0.7 to 1.5 percent on the highest bracket (over 10 million euros). Allowing for deductions and exemptions, the tax generates revenues worth less than 0.5 percent of GDP. In theory, an asset is called a business asset if the owner is active in the associated business. In practice, this condition is rather vague and easily circumvented, especially since additional exemptions have been added over the years (such as "stockholder agreements," which allow for partial or total exemptions if a group of stockholders agrees to maintain its investment for a certain period of time). According to the available data, the wealthiest individuals in France largely avoid paying the wealth tax. The tax authorities publish very few

countries face when they try to impose a capital tax on their own can be seen in Italy. In 2012, the Italian government, faced with one of the largest public debts in Europe and also with an exceptionally high level of private wealth (also one of the highest in Europe, along with Spain),[27] decided to introduce a new tax on wealth. But for fear that financial assets would flee the country in search of refuge in Swiss, Austrian, and French banks, the rate was set at 0.8 percent on real estate and only 0.1 percent on bank deposits and other financial assets (except stocks, which were totally exempt), with no progressivity. Not only is it hard to think of an economic principle that would explain why some assets should be taxed at one-eighth the rate of others; the system also had the unfortunate consequence of imposing a regressive tax on wealth, since the largest fortunes consist mainly of financial assets and especially stocks. This design probably did little to earn social acceptance for the new tax, which became a major issue in the 2013 Italian elections; the candidate who had proposed the tax—with the compliments of European and international authorities—was roundly defeated at the polls. The crux of the problem is this: without automatic sharing of bank information among European countries, which would allow the tax authorities to obtain reliable information about the net assets of all taxpayers, no matter where those assets are located, it is very difficult for a country acting on its own to impose a progressive tax on capital. This is especially unfortunate, because such a tax is a tool particularly well suited to Europe's current economic predicament.

Suppose that bank information is automatically shared and the tax authorities have accurate assessments of who owns what, which may happen some day. What would then be the ideal tax schedule? As usual, there is no mathematical formula for answering this question, which is a matter for democratic deliberation. It would make sense to tax net

---

detailed statistics for each tax bracket (much fewer, for example, than in the case of the inheritance tax from the early twentieth century to the 1950s); this makes the whole operation even more opaque. See the online technical appendix.

27. See esp. Chapter 5, Figures 5.4 and following.

wealth below 200,000 euros at 0.1 percent and net wealth between 200,000 and 1 million euros at 0.5 percent. This would replace the property tax, which in most countries is tantamount to a wealth tax on the propertied middle class. The new system would be both more just and more efficient, because it targets all assets (not only real estate) and relies on transparent data and market values net of mortgage debt.[28] To a large extent a tax of this sort could be readily implemented by individual countries acting alone.

Note that there is no reason why the tax rate on fortunes above 5 million euros should be limited to 2 percent. Since the real returns on the largest fortunes in Europe and around the world are 6 to 7 percent or more, it would not be excessive to tax fortunes above 100 million or 1 billion euros at rates well above 2 percent. The simplest and fairest procedure would be to set rates on the basis of observed returns in each wealth bracket over several prior years. In that way, the degree of progressivity can be adjusted to match the evolution of returns to capital and the desired level of wealth concentration. To avoid divergence of the wealth distribution (that is, a steadily increasing share belonging to the top centiles and thousandths), which on its face seems to be a minimal desirable objective, it would probably be necessary to levy rates of about 5 percent on the largest fortunes. If a more ambitious goal is preferred—say, to reduce wealth inequality to more moderate levels than exist today (and which history shows are not necessary for growth)—one might envision rates of 10 percent or higher on billionaires. This is not the place to resolve the issue. What is certain is that it makes little sense to take the yield on public debt as a reference, as is often done in political debate.[29] The largest fortunes are clearly not invested in government bonds.

---

28. The progressive capital tax would then bring in 3–4 percent of GDP, of which 1 or 2 points would come from the property tax replacement. See the online technical appendix.

29. For example, to justify the recent decrease of the top wealth tax rate in France from 1.8 to 1.5 percent.

Is a European wealth tax realistic? There is no technical reason why not. It is the tool best suited to meet the economic challenges of the twenty-first century, especially in Europe, where private wealth is thriving to a degree not seen since the Belle Époque. But if the countries of the Old Continent are to cooperate more closely, European political institutions will have to change. The only strong European institution at the moment is the ECB, which is important but notoriously insufficient. I come back to this in the next chapter, when I turn to the question of the public debt crisis. Before that, it will be useful to look at the proposed tax on capital in a broader historical perspective.

Capital Taxation in Historical Perspective

In all civilizations, the fact that the owners of capital claim a substantial share of national income without working and that the rate of return on capital is generally 4–5 percent a year has provoked vehement, often indignant, reactions as well as a variety of political responses. One of the most common of the latter has been the prohibition of usury, which we find in one form or another in most religious traditions, including those of Christianity and Islam. The Greek philosophers were of two minds about interest, which, since time never ceases to flow, can in principle increase wealth without limit. It was the danger of limitless wealth that Aristotle singled out when he observed that the word "interest" in Greek (*tocos*) means "child." In his view, money ought not to "give birth" to more money.[30] In a world of low or even near-zero growth, where both population and output remained more or less the same generation after generation, "limitlessness" seemed particularly dangerous.

Unfortunately, the attempts to prohibit interest were often illogical. The effect of outlawing loans at interest was generally to restrict certain types of investment and certain categories of commercial or

---

30. See P. Judet de la Combe, "Le jour où Solon a aboli la dette des Athéniens," *Libération*, May 31, 2010.

financial activity that the political or religious authorities deemed less legitimate or worthy than others. They did not, however, question the legitimacy of returns to capital in general. In the agrarian societies of Europe, the Christian authorities never questioned the legitimacy of land rents, from which they themselves benefited, as did the social groups on which they depended to maintain the social order. The prohibition of usury in the society of that time is best thought of as a form of social control: some types of capital were more difficult to control than others and therefore more worrisome. The general principle according to which capital can provide income for its owner, who need not work to justify it, went unquestioned. The idea was rather to be wary of infinite accumulation. Income from capital was supposed to be used in healthy ways, to pay for good works, for example, and certainly not to launch into commercial or financial adventures that might lead to estrangement from the true faith. Landed capital was in this respect very reassuring, since it could do nothing but reproduce itself year after year and century after century.[31] Consequently, the whole social and spiritual order also seemed immutable. Land rent, before it became the sworn enemy of democracy, was long seen as the wellspring of social harmony, at least by those to whom it accrued.

The solution to the problem of capital suggested by Karl Marx and many other socialist writers in the nineteenth century and put into practice in the Soviet Union and elsewhere in the twentieth century was far more radical and, if nothing else, more logically consistent. By abolishing private ownership of the means of production, including land and buildings as well as industrial, financial, and business capital (other than a few individual plots of land and small cooperatives), the Soviet experiment simultaneously eliminated all private returns on

---

31. In fact, as I have shown, capital in the form of land included improvements to the land, increasingly so over the years, so that in the long run landed capital was not very different from other forms of accumulable capital. Still, accumulation of landed capital was subject to certain natural limits, and its predominance implied that the economy could only grow very slowly.

capital. The prohibition of usury thus became general: the rate of exploitation, which for Marx represented the share of output appropriated by the capitalist, thus fell to zero, and with it the rate of private return. With zero return on capital, man (or the worker) finally threw off his chains along with the yoke of accumulated wealth. The present reasserted its rights over the past. The inequality $r > g$ was nothing but a bad memory, especially since communism vaunted its affection for growth and technological progress. Unfortunately for the people caught up in these totalitarian experiments, the problem was that private property and the market economy do not serve solely to ensure the domination of capital over those who have nothing to sell but their labor power. They also play a useful role in coordinating the actions of millions of individuals, and it is not so easy to do without them. The human disasters caused by Soviet-style centralized planning illustrate this quite clearly.

A tax on capital would be a less violent and more efficient response to the eternal problem of private capital and its return. A progressive levy on individual wealth would reassert control over capitalism in the name of the general interest while relying on the forces of private property and competition. Each type of capital would be taxed in the same way, with no discrimination a priori, in keeping with the principle that investors are generally in a better position than the government to decide what to invest in.[32] If necessary, the tax can be quite steeply progressive on very large fortunes, but this is a matter for democratic debate under a government of laws. A capital tax is the most appropriate response to the inequality $r > g$ as well as to the inequality of returns to capital as a function of the size of the initial stake.[33]

---

32. This does not mean that other "stakeholders" (including workers, collectivities, associations, etc.) should be denied the means to influence investment decisions by granting them appropriate voting rights. Here, financial transparency can play a key role. I come back to this in the next chapter.

33. The optimal rate of the capital tax will of course depend on the gap between the return on capital, r, and the growth rate, g, with an eye to limiting the effect of $r > g$. For example, under certain hypotheses, the optimal inheritance tax rate is

In this form, the tax on capital is a new idea, designed explicitly for the globalized patrimonial capitalism of the twenty-first century. To be sure, capital in the form of land has been taxed since time immemorial. But property is generally taxed at a low flat rate. The main purpose of the property tax is to guarantee property rights by requiring registration of titles; it is certainly not to redistribute wealth. The English, American, and French revolutions all conformed to this logic: the tax systems they put in place were in no way intended to reduce inequalities of wealth. During the French Revolution the idea of progressive taxation was the subject of lively debate, but in the end the principle of progressivity was rejected. What is more, the boldest tax proposals of that time seem quite moderate today in the sense that the proposed tax rates were quite low.[34]

The progressive tax revolution had to await the twentieth century and the period between the two world wars. It occurred in the midst of chaos and came primarily in the form of progressive taxes on income and inheritances. To be sure, some countries (most notably Germany and Sweden) established an annual progressive tax on capital as early as the late nineteenth century or early twentieth. But the United States, Britain, and France (until the 1980s) did not move in this di-

---

given by the formula $t = 1 - G/R$, where G is the generational growth rate and R the generational return on capital (so that the tax approaches 100 percent when growth is extremely small relative to return on capital, and approaches 0 percent when the growth rate is close to the return on capital). In general, however, things are more complex, because the ideal system requires a progressive annual tax on capital. The principal optimal tax formulas are presented and explained in the online technical appendix (but only in order to clarify the terms of debate, not to provide ready-made solutions, since many forces are at work and it is difficult to evaluate the effect of each with any precision).

34. Thomas Paine, in his pamphlet *Agrarian Justice* (1795), proposed a 10 percent inheritance tax (which in his view corresponded to the "unaccumulated" portion of the estate, whereas the "accumulated" portion was not to be taxed at all, even if it dated back several generations). Certain "national heredity tax" proposals during the French Revolution were more radical. After much debate, however, the tax on direct line transmissions was set at no more than 2 percent. On these debates and proposals, see the online technical appendix.

rection.[35] Furthermore, in the countries that did tax capital, the rates were relatively low, no doubt because these taxes were designed in a context very different from that which exists today. These taxes also suffered from a fundamental technical flaw: they were based not on the market value of the assets subject to taxation, to be revised annually, but on infrequently revised assessments of their value by the tax authorities. These assessed valuations eventually lost all connection with market values, which quickly rendered the taxes useless. The same flaw undermined the property tax in France and many other countries subsequent to the inflationary shock of the period 1914–1945.[36] Such a design flaw can be fatal to a progressive tax on capital: the threshold for each tax bracket depends on more or less arbitrary factors such as the date of the last property assessment in a given town or neighborhood. Challenges to such arbitrary taxation became increasingly common after 1960, in a period of rapidly rising real estate and stock prices. Often the courts became involved (to rule on violations of the principle of equal taxation). Germany and Sweden abolished their annual taxes on capital in 1990–2010. This had more to do with the archaic design of these taxes (which went back to the nineteenth century) than with any response to tax competition.[37]

---

35. Despite much discussion and numerous proposals in the United States and Britain, especially in the 1960s and again in the early 2000s. See the online technical appendix.

36. This design flaw stemmed from the fact that these capital taxes originated in the nineteenth century, when inflation was insignificant or nonexistent and it was deemed sufficient to reassess asset values every ten or fifteen years (for real estate) or to base values on actual transactions (which was often done for financial assets). This system of assessment was profoundly disrupted by the inflation of 1914–1945 and was never made to work properly in a world of substantial permanent inflation.

37. On the history of the German capital tax, from its creation in Prussia to its suspension in 1997 (the law was not formally repealed), see Fabien Dell, *L'Allemagne inégale*, PhD diss., Paris School of Economics, 2008. On the Swedish capital tax, created in 1947 (but which actually existed as a supplementary tax on capital income since the 1910s) and abolished in 2007, see the previously cited work of Ohlsson and Waldenström and the references given in the appendix. The rates of

The current wealth tax in France (the impôt de solidarité sur la fortune, or ISF) is in some ways more modern: it is based on the market value of various types of assets, reevaluated annually. This is because the tax was created relatively recently: it was introduced in the 1980s, at a time when inflation, especially in asset prices, could not be ignored. There are perhaps advantages to being at odds with the rest of the developed world in regard to economic policy: in some cases it allows a country to be ahead of its time.[38] Although the French ISF is based on market values, in which respect it resembles the ideal capital tax, it is nevertheless quite different from the ideal in other respects. As noted earlier, it is riddled with exemptions and based on self-declared asset holdings. In 2012, Italy introduced a rather strange wealth tax, which illustrates the limits of what a single country can do on its own in the current climate. The Spanish case is also interesting. The Spanish wealth tax, like the now defunct Swedish and German ones, is based on more or less arbitrary assessments of real estate and other assets. Collection of the tax was suspended in 2008–2010, then restored in 2011–2012 in the midst of an acute budget crisis, but without modifications to its structure.[39] Similar tensions exist almost

---

these taxes generally remained under 1.5–2 percent on the largest fortunes, with a peak in Sweden of 4 percent in 1983 (which applied only to assessed values largely unrelated to market values). Apart from the degeneration of the tax base, which also affected the estate tax in both countries, the perception of fiscal competition also played a role in Sweden, where the estate tax was abolished in 2005. This episode, at odds with Sweden's egalitarian values, is a good example of the growing inability of smaller countries to maintain an independent fiscal policy.

38. The wealth tax (on large fortunes) was introduced in France in 1981, abolished in 1986, and then reintroduced in 1988 as the "solidarity tax on wealth." Market values can change abruptly, and this can seem to introduce an element of arbitrariness into the wealth tax, but they are the only objective and universally acceptable basis for such a tax. Nevertheless, rates and tax brackets must be adjusted regularly, and care must be taken not to allow receipts to rise automatically with real estate prices, for this can provoke tax revolts, as illustrated by the famous Proposition 13 adopted in California in 1978 to limit rising property taxes.

39. The Spanish tax is assessed on fortunes greater than 700,000 euros in taxable assets (with a deduction of 300,000 euros for the principal residence), and the

everywhere: although a capital tax seems logical in view of growing government needs (as large private fortunes increase and incomes stagnate, a government would have to be blind to pass up such a tempting source of revenue, no matter what party is in power), it is difficult to design such a tax properly within a single country.

To sum up: the capital tax is a new idea, which needs to be adapted to the globalized patrimonial capitalism of the twenty-first century. The designers of the tax must consider what tax schedule is appropriate, how the value of taxable assets should be assessed, and how information about asset ownership should be supplied automatically by banks and shared internationally so that the tax authorities need not rely on taxpayers to declare their own asset holdings.

Alternative Forms of Regulation: Protectionism and Capital Controls

Is there no alternative to the capital tax? No: there are other ways to regulate patrimonial capitalism in the twenty-first century, and some of these are already being tried in various parts of the world. Nevertheless, these alternative forms of regulation are less satisfactory than the capital tax and sometimes create more problems than they solve. As noted, the simplest way for a government to reclaim a measure of economic and financial sovereignty is to resort to protectionism and controls on capital. Protectionism is at times a useful way of sheltering relatively undeveloped sectors of a country's economy (until domestic firms are ready to face international competition).[40] It is also a valuable weapon against countries that do not respect the rules (of financial transparency, health norms, human rights, etc.), and it would be

---

highest rate is 2.5 percent (2.75 percent in Catalonia). There is also an annual capital tax in Switzerland, with relatively low rates (less than 1 percent) due to competition among cantons.

40. Or to prevent a foreign competitor from developing (the destruction of the nascent Indian textile industry by the British colonizer in the early nineteenth century is etched into the memory of Indians). This can have lasting consequences.

foolish for a country to rule out its potential use. Nevertheless, protectionism, when deployed on a large scale over a long period of time, is not in itself a source of prosperity or a creator of wealth. Historical experience suggests that a country that chooses this road while promising its people a robust improvement in their standard of living is likely to meet with serious disappointment. Furthermore, protectionism does nothing to counter the inequality $r > g$ or the tendency for wealth to accumulate in fewer and fewer hands.

The question of capital controls is another matter. Since the 1980s, governments in most wealthy countries have advocated complete and absolute liberalization of capital flows, with no controls and no sharing of information about asset ownership among nations. International organizations such as the OECD, the World Bank, and the IMF promoted the same set of measures in the name of the latest in economic science.[41] But the movement was propelled essentially by democratically elected governments, reflecting the dominant ideas of a particular historical moment marked by the fall of the Soviet Union and unlimited faith in capitalism and self-regulating markets. Since the financial crisis of 2008, serious doubts about the wisdom of this approach have arisen, and it is quite likely that the rich countries will have increasing recourse to capital controls in the decades ahead. The emerging world has shown the way, starting in the aftermath of the Asian financial crisis of 1998, which convinced many countries, including Indonesia, Brazil, and Russia, that the policies and "shock therapies" dictated by the international community were not always well advised and the

---

41. This is all the more astonishing given that the rare estimates of the economic gains due to financial integration suggest a rather modest global gain (without even allowing for the negative effects on inequality and instability, which these studies ignore). See Pierre-Olivier Gourinchas and Olivier Jeanne, "The Elusive Gains from International Financial Integration," *Review of Economic Studies* 73, no. 3 (2006): 715–41. Note that the IMF's position on automatic transmission of information has been vague and variable: the principle is approved, the better to torpedo its concrete application on the basis of rather unconvincing technical arguments.

time had come to set their own courses. The crisis also encouraged some countries to amass excessive reserves of foreign exchange. This may not be the optimal response to global economic instability, but it has the virtue of allowing single countries to cope with economic shocks without forfeiting their sovereignty.

The Mystery of Chinese Capital Regulation

It is important to recognize that some countries have always enforced capital controls and remained untouched by the stampede toward complete deregulation of financial flows and current accounts. A notable example of such a country is China, whose currency has never been convertible (though it may be someday, when China is convinced that it has accumulated sufficient reserves to bury any speculator who bets against the renminbi). China has also imposed strict controls on both incoming capital (no one can invest in or purchase a large Chinese firm without authorization from the government, which is generally granted only if the foreign investor is content to take a minority stake) and outgoing capital (no assets can be removed from China without government approval). The issue of outgoing capital is currently quite a sensitive one in China and is at the heart of the Chinese model of capital regulation. This raises a very simple question: Are China's millionaires and billionaires, whose names are increasingly prevalent in global wealth rankings, truly the owners of their wealth? Can they, for example, take their money out of China if they wish? Although the answers to these questions are shrouded in mystery, there is no doubt that the Chinese notion of property rights is different from the European or American notions. It depends on a complex and evolving set of rights and duties. To take one example, a Chinese billionaire who acquired a 20 percent stake in Telecom China and who wished to move to Switzerland with his family while holding on to his shares and collecting millions of euros in dividends would very likely have a much harder time doing so than, say, a Russian oligarch, to judge by the fact that vast sums commonly leave Russia for suspect destinations. One never sees this in China, at least for now. In Russia, to be sure, an oligarch must take care not to tangle with the president, which can land him in prison. But if he can avoid such trouble, he can apparently live quite well on wealth derived from exploitation of Russia's natural resources. In China things seem to be controlled more tightly. That is one of many reasons why the kinds of comparisons that one reads frequently in the Western press between the fortunes of wealthy Chinese political leaders and their US counterparts, who are said to be far less wealthy, probably cannot withstand close scrutiny.[42]

It is not my intention to defend China's system of capital regulation, which is extremely opaque and probably unstable. Nevertheless, capital controls are one way of regulating and containing the dynamics of wealth inequality. Furthermore, China has a more progressive income tax than Russia (which adopted a flat tax in the 1990s, like most countries in the former Soviet bloc), though it is still not progressive enough. The revenues it brings in are invested in education, health, and infrastructure on a far larger scale than in other emerging countries such as India, which China has clearly outdistanced.[43] If China wishes, and above all if its elites agree to allow the kind of democratic transpar-

---

42. The comparison that one sees most often in the press sets the average wealth of the 535 members of the US House of Representatives (based on statements collected by the Center for Responsible Politics) against the average wealth of the seventy richest members of the Chinese People's Assembly. The average net worth of the US House members is "only" $15 million, compared with more than $1 billion for the People's Assembly members (according to the Hurun Report 2012, a *Forbes*-style ranking of Chinese fortunes based on a methodology that is not very clear). Given the relative population of the two countries, it would be more reasonable to compare the average wealth of all three thousand members of the Chinese Assembly (for which no estimate seems to be available). In any case, it appears that being elected to the Chinese Assembly is mainly an honorific post for these billionaires (who do not function as legislators). Perhaps it would be better to compare them to the seventy wealthiest US political donors.

43. See N. Qian and Thomas Piketty, "Income Inequality and Progressive Income Taxation in China and India: 1986–2015," *American Economic Journal: Applied Economics* 1, no. 2 (April 2009): 53–63.

ency and government of laws that go hand in hand with a modern tax system (by no means a certainty), then China is clearly large enough to impose the kind of progressive tax on income and capital that I have been discussing. In some respects, it is better equipped to meet these challenges than Europe is, because Europe must contend with political fragmentation and with a particularly intense form of tax competition, which may be with us for some time to come.[44]

In any case, if the European countries do not join together to regulate capital cooperatively and effectively, individual countries are highly likely to impose their own controls and national preferences. (Indeed, this has already begun, with a sometimes irrational promotion of national champions and domestic stockholders, on the frequently illusory premise that they can be more easily controlled than foreign stockholders.) In this respect, China has a clear advantage and will be difficult to beat. The capital tax is the liberal form of capital control and is better suited to Europe's comparative advantage.

The Redistribution of Petroleum Rents

When it comes to regulating global capitalism and the inequalities it generates, the geographic distribution of natural resources and especially of "petroleum rents" constitutes a special problem. International inequalities of wealth—and national destinies—are determined by the way borders were drawn, in many cases quite arbitrarily. If the world were a single global democratic community, an ideal capital tax would redistribute petroleum rents in an equitable manner. National laws sometimes do this by declaring natural resources to be common property. Such laws of course vary from country to country. It is to be

---

44. For a very long-run perspective, arguing that Europe long derived an advantage from its political fragmentation (because interstate competition spurred innovation, especially in military technology) before it became a handicap with respect to China, see Jean-Laurent Rosenthal and R. Bin Wong, *Before and Beyond Divergence: The Politics of Economic Change in China and Europe* (Cambridge, MA: Harvard University Press, 2011).

hoped that democratic deliberation will point in the right direction. For example, if, tomorrow, someone were to find in her backyard a treasure greater than all of her country's existing wealth combined, it is likely that a way would be found to amend the law to share that wealth in a reasonable manner (or so one hopes).

Since the world is not a single democratic community, however, the redistribution of natural resources is often decided in far less peaceful ways. In 1990–1991, just after the collapse of the Soviet Union, another fateful event took place. Iraq, a country of 35 million people, decided to invade its tiny neighbor, Kuwait, with barely 1 million people but in possession of petroleum reserves virtually equal to those of Iraq. This was in part a geographical accident, of course, but it was also the result of a stroke of the postcolonial pen: Western oil companies and their governments in some cases found it easier to do business with countries without too many people living in them (although the long-term wisdom of such a choice may be doubted). In any case, the Western powers and their allies immediately sent some 900,000 troops to restore the Kuwaitis as the sole legitimate owners of their oilfields (proof, if proof were needed, that governments can mobilize impressive resources to enforce their decisions when they choose to do so). This happened in 1991. The first Gulf war was followed by a second in 2003, in Iraq, with a somewhat sparser coalition of Western powers. The consequences of these events are still with us today.

It is not up to me to calculate the optimal schedule for the tax on petroleum capital that would ideally exist in a global political community based on social justice and utility, or even in a Middle Eastern political community. I observe simply that the unequal distribution of wealth in this region has attained unprecedented levels of injustice, which would surely have ceased to exist long ago were it not for foreign military protection. In 2012, the total budget of the Egyptian ministry of education for all primary, middle, and secondary schools and universities in a country of 85 million was less than $5 billion.[45] A

---

45. See the online technical appendix.

few hundred kilometers to the east, Saudi Arabia and its 20 million citizens enjoyed oil revenues of $300 billion, while Qatar and its 300,000 Qataris take in more than $100 billion annually. Meanwhile, the international community wonders if it ought to extend a loan of a few billion dollars to Egypt or wait until the country increases, as promised, its tax on carbonated drinks and cigarettes. Surely the international norm should be to prevent redistribution of wealth by force of arms insofar as it is possible to do so (particularly when the intention of the invader is to buy more arms, not to build schools, as was the case with the Iraqi invader in 1991). But such a norm should carry with it the obligation to find other ways to achieve a more just distribution of petroleum rents, be it by way of sanctions, taxes, or foreign aid, in order to give countries without oil the opportunity to develop.

Redistribution through Immigration

A seemingly more peaceful form of redistribution and regulation of global wealth inequality is immigration. Rather than move capital, which poses all sorts of difficulties, it is sometimes simpler to allow labor to move to places where wages are higher. This was of course the great contribution of the United States to global redistribution: the country grew from a population of barely 3 million at the time of the Revolutionary War to more than 300 million today, largely thanks to successive waves of immigration. That is why the United States is still a long way from becoming the new Old Europe, as I speculated it might in Chapter 14. Immigration is the mortar that holds the United States together, the stabilizing force that prevents accumulated capital from acquiring the importance it has in Europe; it is also the force that makes the increasingly large inequalities of labor income in the United States politically and socially bearable. For a fair proportion of Americans in the bottom 50 percent of the income distribution, these inequalities are of secondary importance for the very simple reason that they were born in a less wealthy country and see themselves as being on an upward trajectory. Note, moreover, that the mechanism of redistribution through immigration, which enables individuals born in poor countries to improve their lot by moving to a rich country, has lately been an important factor in Europe as well as the United States. In this respect, the distinction between the Old World and the New may be less salient than in the past.[46]

It bears emphasizing, however, that redistribution through immigration, as desirable as it may be, resolves only part of the problem of inequality. Even after average per capita output and income are equalized between countries by way of immigration and, even more, by poor countries catching up with rich ones in terms of productivity, the problem of inequality—and in particular the dynamics of global wealth concentration—remains. Redistribution through immigration postpones the problem but does not dispense with the need for a new type of regulation: a social state with progressive taxes on income and capital. One might hope, moreover, that immigration will be more readily accepted by the less advantaged members of the wealthier societies if such institutions are in place to ensure that the economic benefits of globalization are shared by everyone. If you have free trade and free circulation of capital and people but destroy the social state and all forms of progressive taxation, the temptations of defensive nationalism and identity politics will very likely grow stronger than ever in both Europe and the United States.

Note, finally, that the less developed countries will be among the primary beneficiaries of a more just and transparent international tax system. In Africa, the outflow of capital has always exceeded the in-

---

46. In the period 2000–2010, the rate of permanent integration (expressed as a percentage of the population of the receiving country) attained 0.6–0.7 percent a year in several European countries (Italy, Spain, Sweden, and Britain), compared with 0.4 percent in the United States and 0.2–0.3 percent in France and Germany. See the online technical appendix. Since the crisis, some of these flows have already begun to turn around, especially between southern Europe and Germany. Taken as a whole, permanent immigration in Europe was fairly close to North American levels in 2000–2010. The birthrate remains considerably higher in North America, however.

flow of foreign aid by a wide margin. It is no doubt a good thing that several wealthy countries have launched judicial proceedings against former African leaders who fled their countries with ill-gotten gains. But it would be even more useful to establish international fiscal cooperation and data sharing to enable countries in Africa and elsewhere to root out such pillage in a more systematic and methodical fashion, especially since foreign companies and stockholders of all nationalities are at least as guilty as unscrupulous African elites. Once again, financial transparency and a progressive global tax on capital are the right answers.

SIXTEEN

The Question of the Public Debt

There are two main ways for a government to finance its expenses: taxes and debt. In general, taxation is by far preferable to debt in terms of justice and efficiency. The problem with debt is that it usually has to be repaid, so that debt financing is in the interest of those who have the means to lend to the government. From the standpoint of the general interest, it is normally preferable to tax the wealthy rather than borrow from them. There are nevertheless many reasons, both good and bad, why governments sometimes resort to borrowing and to accumulating debt (if they do not inherit it from previous governments). At the moment, the rich countries of the world are enmeshed in a seemingly interminable debt crisis. To be sure, history offers examples of even higher public debt levels, as we saw in Part Two: in Britain in particular, public debt twice exceeded two years of national income, first at the end of the Napoleonic wars and again after World War II. Still, with public debt in the rich countries now averaging about one year of national income (or 90 percent of GDP), the developed world is currently indebted at a level not seen since 1945. Although the emerging economies are poorer than the rich ones in both income and capital, their public debt is much lower (around 30 percent of GDP on average). This shows that the question of public debt is a question of the distribution of wealth, between public and private actors in particular, and not a question of absolute wealth. The rich world is rich, but the governments of the rich world are poor. Europe is the most extreme case: it has both the highest level of private wealth in the world and the greatest difficulty in resolving its public debt crisis—a strange paradox.

I begin by examining various ways of dealing with high public debt levels. This will lead to an analysis of how central banks regulate and redistribute capital and why European unification, overly focused as it was on the issue of currency while neglecting taxation and debt, has led to an impasse. Finally, I will explore the optimal accumulation of public capital and its relation to private capital in the probable twenty-first-century context of low growth and potential degradation of natural capital.

Reducing Public Debt: Tax on Capital, Inflation, and Austerity

How can a public debt as large as today's European debt be significantly reduced? There are three main methods, which can be combined in various proportions: taxes on capital, inflation, and austerity. An exceptional tax on private capital is the most just and efficient solution. Failing that, inflation can play a useful role: historically, that is how most large public debts have been dealt with. The worst solution in terms of both justice and efficiency is a prolonged dose of austerity—yet that is the course Europe is currently following.

I begin by recalling the structure of national wealth in Europe today. As I showed in Part Two, national wealth in most European countries is close to six years of national income, and most of it is owned by private agents (households). The total value of public assets is approximately equal to the total public debt (about one year of national income), so net public wealth is close to zero.[1] Private wealth (net of debt) can be divided into two roughly equal halves: real estate and financial assets. Europe's average net asset position vis-à-vis the rest of the world is close to equilibrium, which means that European firms and sovereign debt are owned by European households (or, more precisely, what the rest of the world owns of Europe is compensated by

---

1. See in particular Table 3.1.

what Europeans own of the rest of the world). This reality is obscured by the complexity of the system of financial intermediation: people deposit their savings in a bank or invest in a financial product, and the bank then invests the money elsewhere. There is also considerable cross-ownership between countries, which makes things even more opaque. Yet the fact remains that European households (or at any rate those that own anything at all: bear in mind that wealth is still very concentrated, with 60 percent of the total owned by the wealthiest 10 percent) own the equivalent of all that there is to own in Europe, including its public debt.[2]

Under such conditions, how can public debt be reduced to zero? One solution would be to privatize all public assets. According to the national accounts of the various European countries, the proceeds from selling all public buildings, schools, universities, hospitals, police stations, infrastructure, and so on would be roughly sufficient to pay off all outstanding public debt.[3] Instead of holding public debt via their financial investments, the wealthiest European households would become the direct owners of schools, hospitals, police stations, and so on. Everyone else would then have to pay rent to use these assets and continue to produce the associated public services. This solution, which some very serious people actually advocate, should to my mind be dismissed out of hand. If the European social state is to fulfill its mission adequately and durably, especially in the areas of education, health, and security, it must continue to own the related public assets. It is nevertheless important to understand that as things now stand, governments must pay heavy interest (rather than rent) on their outstanding public debt, so the situation is not all that different from

---

2. If we count assets owned by European households in tax havens, then Europe's net asset position vis-à-vis the rest of the world becomes significantly positive: European households own the equivalent of all that there is to own in Europe plus a part of the rest of the world. See Figure 12.6.

3. Together with the proceeds of the sale of public financial assets (which no longer amount to much compared with nonfinancial assets). See Chapters 3–5 and the online technical appendix.

paying rent to use the same assets, since these interest payments weigh just as heavily on the public exchequer.

A much more satisfactory way of reducing the public debt is to levy an exceptional tax on private capital. For example, a flat tax of 15 percent on private wealth would yield nearly a year's worth of national income and thus allow for immediate reimbursement of all outstanding public debt. The state would continue to own its public assets, but its debt would be reduced to zero after five years and it would therefore have no interest to pay.[4] This solution is equivalent to a total repudiation of the public debt, except for two essential differences.[5]

First, it is always very difficult to predict the ultimate incidence of a debt repudiation, even a partial one—that is, it is difficult to know who will actually bear the cost. Complete or partial default on the public debt is sometimes tried in situations of extreme overindebtedness, as in Greece in 2011–2012. Bondholders are forced to accept a "haircut" (as the jargon has it): the value of government bonds held by banks and other creditors is reduced by 10–20 percent or perhaps even more. The problem is that if one applies a measure of this sort on a large scale—for example, all of Europe and not just Greece (which accounts for just 2 percent of European GDP)—it is likely to trigger a banking panic and a wave of bankruptcies. Depending on which banks are holding various types of bonds, as well as on the structure of their balance sheets, the identity of their creditors, the households that have invested their savings in these various institutions, the nature of those investments, and so on, one can end up with quite different final incidences, which cannot be accurately predicted in advance. Furthermore, it is quite possible that the people with the largest portfolios will be able to restructure their investments in time to avoid the

---

4. The elimination of interest payments on the debt would make it possible to reduce taxes and / or finance new investments, especially in education (see below).

5. For the equivalence to be complete, wealth would have to be taxed in a manner consistent with the location of real estate and financial assets (including sovereign bonds issued in Europe) and not simply based on the residence of the owners. I will come back to this point later.

haircut almost entirely. People sometimes think that imposing a haircut is a way of penalizing those investors who have taken the largest risks. Nothing could be further from the truth: financial assets are constantly being traded, and there is no guarantee that the people who would be penalized in the end are the ones who ought to be. The advantage of an exceptional tax on capital, which is similar to a haircut, is precisely that it would arrange things in a more civilized manner. Everyone would be required to contribute, and, equally important, bank failures would be avoided, since it is the ultimate owners of wealth (physical individuals) who would have to pay, not financial institutions. If such a tax were to be levied, however, the tax authorities would of course need to be permanently and automatically apprised of any bank accounts, stocks, bonds, and other financial assets held by the citizens under their jurisdiction. Without such a financial cadaster, every policy choice would be risky.

But the main advantage of a fiscal solution is that the contribution demanded of each individual can be adjusted to the size of his fortune. It would not make much sense to levy an exceptional tax of 15 percent on all private wealth in Europe. It would be better to apply a progressive tax designed to spare the more modest fortunes and require more of the largest ones. In some respects, this is what European banking law already does, since it generally guarantees deposits up to 100,000 euros in case of bank failure. The progressive capital tax is a generalization of this logic, since it allows much finer gradations of required levies. One can imagine a number of different brackets: full deposit guarantee up to 100,000 euros, partial guarantee between 100,000 and 500,000 euros, and so on, with as many brackets as seem useful. The progressive tax would also apply to all assets (including listed and unlisted shares), not just bank deposits. This is essential if one really wants to reach the wealthiest individuals, who rarely keep their money in checking accounts.

In any event, it would no doubt be too much to try to reduce public debt to zero in one fell swoop. To take a more realistic example, assume that we want to reduce European government debt by around

20 percent of GDP, which would bring debt levels down from the current 90 percent of GDP to 70 percent, not far from the maximum of 60 percent set by current European treaties.[6] As noted in the previous chapter, a progressive tax on capital at a rate of 0 percent on fortunes up to 1 million euros, 1 percent on fortunes between 1 and 5 million euros, and 2 percent on fortunes larger than 5 million euros would bring in the equivalent of about 2 percent of European GDP. To obtain one-time receipts of 20 percent of GDP, it would therefore suffice to apply a special levy with rates 10 times as high: 0 percent up to 1 million, 10 percent between 1 and 5 million, and 20 percent above 5 million.[7] It is interesting to note that the exceptional tax on capital that France applied in 1945 in order to substantially reduce its public debt had progressive rates that ranged from 0 to 25 percent.[8]

One could obtain the same result by applying a progressive tax with rates of 0, 1, and 2 percent for a period of ten years and earmarking the receipts for debt reduction. For example, one could set up a "redemption fund" similar to the one proposed in 2011 by a council of economists appointed by the German government. This proposal, which was intended to mutualize all Eurozone public debt above 60 percent of GDP (and especially the debt of Germany, France, Italy, and Spain) and then to reduce the fund gradually to zero, is far from perfect. In particular, it lacks the democratic governance without which the mutualization of European debt is not feasible. But it is a concrete plan that could easily be combined with an exceptional one-time or special ten-year tax on capital.[9]

---

6. I will come back later to the question of the optimal level of long-term public debt, which cannot be resolved independently of the question of the level of public and private capital accumulation.

7. Other tax schedules can be simulated with the aid of Supplemental Table S15.1, available online.

8. See Chapter 10.

9. On the redemption fund, see German Council of Economic Experts, *Annual Report 2011* (November 2011); *The European Redemption Pact: Questions and Answers* (January 2012). Technically, the two ideas can be perfectly complementary. Politically and symbolically, however, it is possible that the notion of

Does Inflation Redistribute Wealth?

To recapitulate the argument thus far: I observed that an exceptional tax on capital is the best way to reduce a large public debt. This is by far the most transparent, just, and efficient method. Inflation is another possible option, however. Concretely, since a government bond is a nominal asset (that is, an asset whose price is set in advance and does not depend on inflation) rather than a real asset (whose price evolves in response to the economic situation, generally increasing at least as fast as inflation, as in the case of real estate and shares of stock), a small increase in the inflation rate is enough to significantly reduce the real value of the public debt. With an inflation rate of 5 percent a year rather than 2 percent, the real value of the public debt, expressed as a percentage of GDP, would be reduced by more than 15 percent (all other things equal)—a considerable amount.

Such a solution is extremely tempting. Historically, this is how most large public debts were reduced, particularly in Europe in the twentieth century. For example, inflation in France and Germany averaged 13 and 17 percent a year, respectively, from 1913 to 1950. It was inflation that allowed both countries to embark on reconstruction efforts in the 1950s with a very small burden of public debt. Germany, in particular, is by far the country that has used inflation most freely (along with outright debt repudiation) to eliminate public debt throughout its history.[10] Apart from the ECB, which is by far the

---

"redemptions" (which connotes long and shared suffering by the entire population) may not sit well with the progressive capital tax, and the word "redemption" may be ill chosen.

10. In addition to debt reduction through inflation, a major part of Germany's debt was simply canceled by the Allies after World War II. (More precisely, repayment was postponed until an eventual German reunification, but it has not been repaid now that reunification has occurred.) According to calculations by the German historian Albrecht Ritschl, the amounts would be quite substantial if recapitalized at a reasonable rate. Some of this debt reflects occupation fees levied on Greece during the German occupation, which has led to endless and largely irreconcilable controversy. This further complicates today's attempts to

most averse to this solution, it is no accident that all the other major central banks—the US Federal Reserve, the Bank of Japan, and the Bank of England—are currently trying to raise their inflation targets more or less explicitly and are also experimenting with various so-called unconventional monetary policies. If they succeed—say, by increasing inflation from 2 to 5 percent a year (which is by no means assured)—these countries will emerge from the debt crisis much more rapidly than the countries of the Eurozone, whose economic prospects are clouded by the absence of any obvious way out, as well as by their lack of clarity concerning the long-term future of budgetary and fiscal union in Europe.

Indeed, it is important to understand that without an exceptional tax on capital and without additional inflation, it may take several decades to get out from under a burden of public debt as large as that which currently exists in Europe. To take an extreme case: suppose that inflation is zero and GDP grows at 2 percent a year (which is by no means assured in Europe today because of the obvious contractionary effect of budgetary rigor, at least in the short term), with a budget deficit limited to 1 percent of GDP (which in practice implies a substantial primary surplus, given the interest on the debt). Then by definition it would take 20 years to reduce the debt-to-GDP ratio by twenty points.[11] If growth were to fall below 2 percent in some years and debt were to rise above 1 percent, it could easily take thirty or forty years. It takes decades to accumulate capital; it can also take a very long time to reduce a debt.

The most interesting historical example of a prolonged austerity cure can be found in nineteenth-century Britain. As noted in Chapter 3,

---

impose a pure logic of austerity and debt repayment. See Albrecht Ritschl, "Does Germany Owe Greece a Debt? The European Debt Crisis in Historical Perspective," paper given at the OeNB 40th Economics Conference, Vienna (London School of Economics, 2012).

11. If GDP grows 2 percent a year and debt 1 percent a year (assuming that one starts with a debt close to GDP), then the debt-to-GDP ratio will decrease by about 1 percent a year.

it would have taken a century of primary surpluses (of 2–3 points of GDP from 1815 to 1914) to rid the country of the enormous public debt left over from the Napoleonic wars. Over the course of this period, British taxpayers spent more on interest on the debt than on education. The choice to do so was no doubt in the interest of government bondholders but unlikely to have been in the general interest of the British people. It may be that the setback to British education was responsible for the country's decline in the decades that followed. To be sure, the debt was then above 200 percent of GDP (and not barely 100 percent, as is the case today), and inflation in the nineteenth century was close to zero (whereas an inflation target of 2 percent is generally accepted nowadays). Hence there is hope that European austerity might last only ten or twenty years (at a minimum) rather than a century. Still, that would be quite a long time. It is reasonable to think that Europe might find better ways to prepare for the economic challenges of the twenty-first century than to spend several points of GDP a year servicing its debt, at a time when most European countries spend less than one point of GDP a year on their universities.[12]

That said, I want to insist on the fact that inflation is at best a very imperfect substitute for a progressive tax on capital and can have some undesirable secondary effects. The first problem is that inflation is hard to control: once it gets started, there is no guarantee that it can be stopped at 5 percent a year. In an inflationary spiral, everyone wants to make sure that the wages he receives and the prices he must pay evolve in a way that suits him. Such a spiral can be hard to stop. In

12. The special one-time or ten-year tax on capital described above might be thought of as a way of applying primary surplus to debt reduction. The difference is that the tax would be a new resource that would not burden the majority of the population and not interfere with the rest of the government's budget. In practice, there is a continuum of points involving various proportions of each solution (capital tax, inflation, austerity): everything depends on the dosage and the way the burdens of adjustment are shared among different social groups. The capital tax puts most of the burden on the very wealthy, whereas austerity policies generally aim to spare them.

France, the inflation rate exceeded 50 percent for four consecutive years, from 1945 to 1948. This reduced the public debt to virtually nothing in a far more radical way than the exceptional tax on capital that was collected in 1945. But millions of small savers were wiped out, and this aggravated the persistent problem of poverty among the elderly in the 1950s.[13] In Germany, prices were multiplied by a factor of 100 million between the beginning of 1923 and the end. Germany's society and economy were permanently traumatized by this episode, which undoubtedly continues to influence German perceptions of inflation. The second difficulty with inflation is that much of the desired effect disappears once it becomes permanent and embedded in expectations (in particular, anyone willing to lend to the government will demand a higher rate of interest).

To be sure, one argument in favor of inflation remains: compared with a capital tax, which, like any other tax, inevitably deprives people of resources they would have spent usefully (for consumption or investment), inflation (at least in its idealized form) primarily penalizes people who do not know what to do with their money, namely, those who have kept too much cash in their bank account or stuffed into their mattress. It spares those who have already spent everything or invested everything in real economic assets (real estate or business capital), and, better still, it spares those who are in debt (inflation reduces nominal debt, which enables the indebted to get back on their feet more quickly and make new investments). In this idealized version, inflation is in a way a tax on idle capital and an encouragement to dynamic capital. There is some truth to this view, and it should not be dismissed out of hand.[14] But as I showed in examining unequal returns on capital as a function of the initial stake, inflation in no way prevents large and well-diversified portfolios from earning a good return

---

13. Savings from the 1920s were essentially wiped out by the stock market crash. Still, the inflation of 1945–1948 was an additional shock. The response was the "old-age minimum" (created in 1956) and the advent of a PAYGO pension system (which was created in 1945 but further developed subsequently).

14. There are theoretical models based on this idea. See the online technical appendix.

simply by virtue of their size (and without any personal effort by the owner).[15]

In the end, the truth is that inflation is a relatively crude and imprecise tool. Sometimes it redistributes wealth in the right direction, sometimes not. To be sure, if the choice is between a little more inflation and a little more austerity, inflation is no doubt preferable. But in France one sometimes hears the view that inflation is a nearly ideal tool for redistributing wealth (a way of taking money from "German rentiers" and forcing the aging population on the other side of the Rhine to show more solidarity with the rest of Europe). This is naïve and preposterous. In practice, a great wave of inflation in Europe would have all sorts of unintended consequences for the redistribution of wealth and would be particularly harmful to people of modest means in France, Germany, and elsewhere. Conversely, those with fortunes in real estate and the stock market would largely be spared on both sides of the Rhine and everywhere else as well.[16] When it comes to decreasing inequalities of wealth for good or reducing unusually high levels of public debt, a progressive tax on capital is generally a better tool than inflation.

What Do Central Banks Do?

In order to gain a better understanding of the role of inflation and, more generally, of central banks in the regulation and redistribution of capital, it is useful to take a step back from the current crisis and to examine these issues in broader historical perspective. Back when the gold standard was the norm everywhere, before World War I, central banks played a much smaller role than they do today. In particular, their power to create money was severely limited by the existing stock

---

15. See in particular the results presented in Chapter 12.

16. The same would be true in case of a breakup of the Eurozone. It is always possible to reduce public debt by printing money and generating inflation, but it is hard to control the distributive consequences of such a crisis, whether with the euro, the franc, the mark, or the lira.

of gold and silver. One obvious problem with the gold standard was that the evolution of the overall price level depended primarily on the hazards of gold and silver discoveries. If the global stock of gold was static but global output increased, the price level had to fall (since the same money stock now had to support a larger volume of commercial exchange). In practice this was a source of considerable difficulty.[17] If large deposits of gold or silver were suddenly discovered, as in Spanish America in the sixteenth and seventeenth centuries or California in the mid-nineteenth century, prices could skyrocket, which created other kinds of problems and brought undeserved windfalls to some.[18] These drawbacks make it highly unlikely that the world will ever return to the gold standard. (Keynes referred to gold as a "barbarous relic.")

Once currency ceases to be convertible into precious metals, however, the power of central banks to create money is potentially unlimited and must therefore be strictly regulated. This is the crux of the debate about central bank independence as well as the source of numerous misunderstandings. Let me quickly retrace the stages of this debate. At the beginning of the Great Depression, the central banks of the industrialized countries adopted an extremely conservative policy: having only recently abandoned the gold standard, they refused to create the liquidity necessary to save troubled banks, which led to a wave of bankruptcies that seriously aggravated the crisis and pushed the world to the brink of the abyss. It is important to understand the trauma occasioned by this tragic historical experience. Since then, everyone agrees that the primary function of central banking is to

---

17. An often-cited historical example is the slight deflation (decrease of prices and wages) seen in the industrialized countries in the late nineteenth century. This deflation was resented by both employers and workers, who seemed to want to wait until other prices and wages fell before accepting decreases in the prices and wages that affected them directly. This resistance to wage and price adjustments is sometimes referred to as "nominal rigidity." The most important argument in favor of low but positive inflation (typically 2 percent) is that it allows for easier adjustment of relative wages and prices than zero or negative inflation.

18. The classic theory of Spanish decline blames gold and silver for a certain laxity of governance.

ensure the stability of the financial system, which requires central banks to assume the role of "lenders of last resort": in case of absolute panic, they must create the liquidity necessary to avoid a broad collapse of the financial system. It is essential to realize that this view has been shared by all observers of the system since the 1930s, regardless of their position on the New Deal or the various forms of social state created in the United States and Europe at the end of World War II. Indeed, faith in the stabilizing role of central banking at times seems inversely proportional to faith in the social and fiscal policies that grew out of the same period.

This is particularly clear in the monumental *Monetary History of the United States* published in 1963 by Milton Friedman and Anna Schwartz. In this fundamental work, the leading figure in monetary economics follows in minute detail the changes in United States monetary policy from 1857 to 1960, based on voluminous archival records.[19] Unsurprisingly, the focal point of the book is the Great Depression. For Friedman, no doubt is possible: it was the unduly restrictive policy of the Federal Reserve that transformed the stock market crash into a credit crisis and plunged the economy into a deflationary spiral and a depression of unprecedented magnitude. The crisis was primarily monetary, and therefore its solution was also monetary. From this analysis, Friedman drew a clear political conclusion: in order to ensure regular, undisrupted growth in a capitalist economy, it is necessary and sufficient to make sure that monetary policy is designed to ensure steady growth of the money supply. Accordingly, monetarist doctrine held that the New Deal, which created a large number of government jobs and social transfer programs, was a costly and useless sham. Saving capitalism did not require a welfare state or a tentacular government: the only thing necessary was a well-run Federal Reserve. In the 1960s–1970s, although many Democrats in the United States still dreamed of completing the New Deal, the US public had begun

---

19. Milton Friedman and Anna J. Schwartz, *A Monetary History of the United States, 1857–1960* (Princeton: Princeton University Press, 1963).

to worry about their country's decline relative to Europe, which was then still in a phase of rapid growth. In this political climate, Friedman's simple but powerful political message had the effect of a bombshell. The work of Friedman and other Chicago School economists fostered suspicion of the ever-expanding state and created the intellectual climate in which the conservative revolution of 1979–1980 became possible.

One can obviously reinterpret these events in a different light: there is no reason why a properly functioning Federal Reserve cannot function as a complement to a properly functioning social state and a well-designed progressive tax policy. These institutions are clearly complements rather than substitutes. Contrary to monetarist doctrine, the fact that the Fed followed an unduly restrictive monetary policy in the early 1930s (as did the central banks of the other rich countries) says nothing about the virtues and limitations of other institutions. That is not the point that interests me here, however. The fact is that all economists— monetarists, Keynesians, and neoclassicals—together with all other observers, regardless of their political stripe, have agreed that central banks ought to act as lenders of last resort and do whatever is necessary to avoid financial collapse and a deflationary spiral.

This broad consensus explains why all of the world's central banks—in Japan and Europe as well as the United States—reacted to the financial crisis of 2007–2008 by taking on the role of lenders of last resort and stabilizers of the financial system. Apart from the collapse of Lehman Brothers in September 2008, bank failures in the crisis have been fairly limited in scope. There is, however, no consensus as to the exact nature of the "unconventional" monetary policies that should be followed in situations like this.

What in fact do central banks do? For present purposes, it is important to realize that central banks do not create wealth as such; they redistribute it. More precisely, when the Fed or the ECB decides to create a billion additional dollars or euros, US or European capital is not augmented by that amount. In fact, national capital does not change by a single dollar or euro, because the operations in which central banks engage are always loans. They therefore result in the creation of financial assets and liabilities, which, at the moment they are created, exactly balance each other. For example, the Fed might lend $1 billion to Lehman Brothers or General Motors (or the US government), and these entities contract an equivalent debt. The net wealth of the Fed and Lehman Brothers (or General Motors) does not change at all, nor, a fortiori, does that of the United States or the planet. Indeed, it would be astonishing if central banks could simply by the stroke of a pen increase the capital of their nation or the world.

What happens next depends on how this monetary policy influences the real economy. If the loan initiated by the central bank enables the recipient to escape from a bad pass and avoid a final collapse (which might decrease the national wealth), then, when the situation has been stabilized and the loan repaid, it makes sense to think that the loan from the Fed increased the national wealth (or at any rate prevented national wealth from decreasing). On the other hand, if the loan from the Fed merely postpones the recipient's inevitable collapse and even prevents the emergence of a viable competitor (which can happen), one can argue that the Fed's policy ultimately decreased the nation's wealth. Both outcomes are possible, and every monetary policy raises both possibilities to one degree or another. To the extent that the world's central banks limited the damage from the recession of 2008–2009, they helped to increase GDP and investment and therefore augmented the capital of the wealthy countries and of the world. Obviously, however, a dynamic evaluation of this kind is always uncertain and open to challenge. What is certain is that when central banks increase the money supply by lending to a financial or nonfinancial corporation or a government, there is no immediate impact on national capital (both public and private).[20]

---

20. Note that there is no such thing as a "money printing press" in the following sense: when a central bank creates money in order to lend it to the government, the loan is recorded on the books of the central bank. This happens even in the most chaotic of times, as in France in 1944–1948. The money is not simply given as a gift. Again, everything depends on what happens next: if the money creation

What "unconventional" monetary policies have been tried since the crisis of 2007–2008? In calm periods, central banks are content to ensure that the money supply grows at the same pace as economic activity in order to guarantee a low inflation rate of 1 or 2 percent a year. Specifically, they create new money by lending to banks for very short periods, often no more than a few days. These loans guarantee the solvency of the entire financial system. Households and firms deposit and withdraw vast sums of money every day, and these deposits and withdrawals are never perfectly balanced for any particular bank. The major innovation since 2008 has been in the duration of loans to private banks. Instead of lending for a few days, the Fed and ECB began lending for three to six months: the volume of loans of these durations increased dramatically in the last quarter of 2008 and the first quarter of 2009. They also began lending at similar durations to nonfinancial corporations. In the United States especially, the Fed also made loans of nine to twelve months to the banking sector and purchased long-dated bonds outright. In 2011–2012, the central banks again expanded the range of their interventions. The Fed, the Bank of Japan, and the Bank of England had been buying sovereign debt since the beginning of the crisis, but as the debt crisis worsened in southern Europe the ECB decided to follow suit.

These policies call for several clarifications. First, the central banks have the power to prevent a bank or nonfinancial corporation from failing by lending it the money needed to pay its workers and suppliers, but they cannot oblige companies to invest or households to consume, and they cannot compel the economy to resume its growth. Nor do they have the power to set the rate of inflation. The liquidity

---

increases inflation, substantial redistribution of wealth can occur (for instance, the real value of the public debt can be reduced dramatically, to the detriment of private nominal assets). The overall effect on national income and capital depends on the impact of policy on the country's overall level of economic activity. It can in theory be either positive or negative, just as loans to private actors can be. Central banks redistribute monetary wealth, but they do not have the ability to create new wealth directly.

created by the central banks probably warded off deflation and depression, but the economic outlook in the wealthy countries remains gloomy, especially in Europe, where the crisis of the euro has undermined confidence. The fact that governments in the wealthiest countries (United States, Japan, Germany, France, and Britain) could borrow at exceptionally low rates (just over 1 percent) in 2012–2013 attests to the importance of central bank stabilization policies, but it also shows that private investors have no clear idea of what to do with the money lent by the monetary authorities at rates close to zero. Hence they prefer to lend their cash back to the governments deemed the most solid at ridiculously low interest rates. The fact that rates are very low in some countries and much higher in others is the sign of an abnormal economic situation.[21]

Central banks are powerful because they can redistribute wealth very quickly and, in theory, as extensively as they wish. If necessary, a central bank can create as many billions as it wants in seconds and credit all that cash to the account of a company or government in need. In an emergency (such as a financial panic, war, or natural disaster), this ability to create money immediately in unlimited amounts is an invaluable attribute. No tax authority can move that quickly to levy a tax: it is necessary first to establish a taxable base, set rates, pass a law, collect the tax, forestall possible challenges, and so on. If this were the only way to resolve a financial crisis, all the banks in the world would already be bankrupt. Rapid execution is the principal strength of the monetary authorities.

The weakness of central banks is clearly their limited ability to decide who should receive loans in what amount and for what duration, as well as the difficulty of managing the resulting financial portfolio. One consequence of this is that the size of a central bank's balance sheet should

---

21. Conversely, the interest rates demanded of countries deemed less solid rose to extremely high levels in 2011–2012 (6–7 percent in Italy and Spain and 15 percent in Greece). This is an indication that investors are skittish and uncertain about the immediate future.

not exceed certain limits. With all the new types of loans and financial market interventions that have been introduced since 2008, central bank balance sheets have roughly doubled in size. The sum of the
Federal Reserve's assets and liabilities has gone from 10 to more than
20 percent of GDP; the same is true of the Bank of England; and the
ECB's balance sheet has expanded from 15 to 30 percent of GDP.
These are striking developments, but these sums are still fairly modest
compared with total net private wealth, which is 500 to 600 percent
of GDP in most of the rich countries.[22]

It is of course possible in the abstract to imagine much larger central bank balance sheets. The central banks could decide to buy up all
of a country's firms and real estate, finance the transition to renewable
energy, invest in universities, and take control of the entire economy.
Clearly, the problem is that central banks are not well suited to such
activities and lack the democratic legitimacy to try them. They can
redistribute wealth quickly and massively, but they can also be very
wrong in their choice of targets (just as the effects of inflation on
inequality can be quite perverse). Hence it is preferable to limit the

---

22. The sum of gross financial assets and liabilities is even higher, since it amounts to
ten to twenty years of GDP in most of the developed countries (see Chapter 5).
The central banks thus hold only a few percent of the total assets and liabilities of
the rich countries. The balance sheets of the various central banks are published
online on a weekly or monthly basis. The amount of each type of asset and liability on the balance sheet is known in aggregate (but is not broken down by recipient of central bank loans). Notes and specie represent only a small part of the
balance sheet (generally about 2 percent of GDP), and most of the rest consists
purely of bookkeeping entries, as is the case for the bank accounts of households,
corporations, and governments. In the past, central bank balance sheets were
sometimes as large as 90–100 percent of GDP (for example, in France in 1944–
1945, after which the balance sheet was reduced to nothing by inflation). In the
summer of 2013, the balance sheet of the Bank of Japan was close to 40 percent of
GDP. For historical series of the balance sheets of the main central banks, see the
online technical appendix. Examination of these balance sheets is instructive and
shows that they are still a long way from the record levels of the past. Furthermore,
inflation depends on many other forces, especially international wage and price
competition, which is currently damping down inflationary tendencies while
driving asset prices higher.

size of central bank balance sheets. That is why they operate under strict mandates focused largely on maintaining the stability of the financial system. In practice, when a government decides to aid a particular branch of industry, as the United States did with General Motors in 2009–2010, it was the federal government and not the Federal Reserve that took charge of making loans, acquiring shares, and setting conditions and performance objectives. The same is true in Europe: industrial and educational policy are matters for states to decide, not central banks. The problem is not one of technical impossibility but of democratic governance. The fact that it takes time to pass tax and spending legislation is not an accident: when significant shares of national wealth are shifted about, it is best not to make mistakes.

Among the many controversies concerning limiting the role of central banks, two issues are of particular interest here. One has to do with the complementary nature of bank regulation and taxation of capital (as the recent crisis in Cyprus made quite clear). The other has to do with the increasingly apparent deficiencies of Europe's current institutional architecture: the European Union is engaged in a historically unprecedented experiment: attempting to create a currency on a very large scale without a state.

The Cyprus Crisis: When the Capital Tax and Banking Regulation Come Together

The primary and indispensable role of central banking is to ensure the stability of the financial system. Central banks are uniquely equipped to evaluate the position of the various banks that make up the system and can refinance them if necessary in order to ensure that the payment system functions normally. They are sometimes assisted by other authorities specifically charged with regulating the banks: for example, by issuing banking licenses and ensuring that certain financial ratios are maintained (in order to make sure that the banks keep sufficient reserves of cash and "safe" assets relative to loans and other assets deemed to be higher risk). In all countries, the central banks and bank regulators (who are often affiliated with the central banks) work together. In current discussions concerning the creation of a European banking union, the ECB is supposed to play the central role. In particularly severe banking crises, central banks also work in concert with international organizations such as the IMF. Since 2009–2010, a "Troika" consisting of the European Commission, the ECB, and the IMF has been working to resolve the financial crisis in Europe, which involves both a public debt crisis and a banking crisis, especially in southern Europe. The recession of 2008–2009 caused a sharp rise in the public debt of many countries that were already heavily indebted before the crisis (especially Greece and Italy) and also led to a rapid deterioration of bank balance sheets, especially in countries affected by a collapsing real estate bubble (most notably Spain). In the end, the two crises are inextricably linked. The banks are holding government bonds whose precise value is unknown. (Greek bonds were subjected to a substantial "haircut," and although the authorities have promised not to repeat this strategy elsewhere, the fact remains that future actions are unpredictable in such circumstances.) State finances can only continue to get worse as long as the economic outlook continues to be bleak, as it probably will as long as the financial and credit system remains largely blocked.

One problem is that neither the Troika nor the various member state governments have automatic access to international banking data or what I have called a "financial cadaster," which would allow them to distribute the burdens of adjustment in an efficient and transparent manner. I have already discussed the difficulties that Italy and Spain faced in attempting to impose a progressive tax on capital on their own in order to restore their public finances to a sound footing. The Greek case is even more extreme. Everyone is insisting that Greece collect more taxes from its wealthier citizens. This is no doubt an excellent idea. The problem is that in the absence of adequate international cooperation, Greece obviously has no way to levy a just and efficient tax on its own, since the wealthiest Greeks can easily move their money abroad, often to other European countries. The European and international authorities have never taken steps to implement the necessary laws and regulations, however.[23] Lacking tax revenues, Greece has therefore been obliged to sell public assets, often at fire-sale prices, to buyers of Greek or other European nationalities, who evidently would rather take advantage of such an opportunity than pay taxes to the Greek government.

The March 2013 crisis in Cyprus is a particularly interesting case to examine. Cyprus is an island with a million inhabitants, which joined the European Union in 2004 and the Eurozone in 2008. It has a hypertrophied banking sector, apparently due to very large foreign deposits, most notably from Russia. This money was drawn to Cyprus by low taxes and indulgent local authorities. According to statements by officials of the Troika, these Russian deposits include a number of very large individual accounts. Many people therefore imagine that the depositors are oligarchs with fortunes in the tens of millions or even billions of euros—people of the sort one reads about in the magazine rankings. The problem is that neither the European authorities nor the IMF have published any statistics, not even the crudest estimate. Very likely they do not have much information themselves, for the simple reason that they have never equipped themselves with the tools they need to move forward on this issue, even though it is absolutely central. Such opacity is not conducive to a considered and rational resolution of this sort of conflict. The problem is that the Cypriot banks no longer have the money that appears on their balance sheets. Apparently, they invested it in Greek bonds that were since written down and in real estate that is now worthless. Naturally, European authorities are hesitant to use the money of European taxpayers to keep the Cypriot banks afloat without some kind of guarantees in return, especially since in the end what they will really be keeping afloat is Russian millionaires.

---

23. As noted in the previous chapter, discussions about possible changes to European rules governing the sharing of bank data have only just begun in 2013 and are a long way from bearing fruit.

After months of deliberation, the members of the Troika came up with the disastrous idea of proposing an exceptional tax on all bank deposits with rates of 6.75 percent on deposits up to 100,000 euros and 9.9 percent above that limit. To the extent that this proposal resembles a progressive tax on capital, it might seem intriguing, but there are two important caveats. First, the very limited progressivity of the tax is illusory: in effect, almost the same tax rate is being imposed on small Cypriot savers with accounts of 10,000 euros and on Russian oligarchs with accounts of 10 million euros. Second, the tax base was never precisely defined by the European and international authorities handling the matter. The tax seems to apply only to bank deposits as such, so that a depositor could escape it by shifting his or her funds to a brokerage account holding stocks or bonds or by investing in real estate or other financial assets. Had this tax been applied, in other words, it would very likely have been extremely regressive, given the composition of the largest portfolios and the opportunities for reallocating investments. After the tax was unanimously approved by the members of the Troika and the seventeen finance ministers of the Eurozone in March 2013, it was vigorously rejected by the people of Cyprus. In the end, a different solution was adopted: deposits under 100,000 euros were exempted from the tax (this being the ceiling of the deposit guarantee envisioned under the terms of the proposed European banking union). The exact terms of the new tax remain relatively obscure, however. A bank-by-bank approach seems to have been adopted, although the precise tax rates and bases have not been spelled out explicitly.

This episode is interesting because it illustrates the limits of the central banks and financial authorities. Their strength is that they can act quickly; their weakness is their limited capacity to correctly target the redistributions they cause to occur. The conclusion is that a progressive tax on capital is not only useful as a permanent tax but can also function well as an exceptional levy (with potentially high rates) in the resolution of major banking crises. In the Cypriot case, it is not necessarily shocking that savers were asked to help resolve the crisis, since the country as a whole bears responsibility for the development strategy chosen by its government. What is deeply shocking, on the other hand, is that the authorities did not even seek to equip themselves with the tools needed to apportion the burden of adjustment in a just, transparent, and progressive manner. The good news is that this episode may lead international authorities to recognize the limits of the tools currently at their disposal. If one asks the officials involved why the tax proposed for Cyprus had such little progressivity built into it and was imposed on such a limited base, their immediate response is that the banking data needed to apply a more steeply progressive schedule were not available.[24] The bad news is that the authorities seem in no great hurry to resolve the problem, even though the technical solution is within reach. It may be that a progressive tax on capital faces purely ideological obstacles that will take some time to overcome.

The Euro: A Stateless Currency for the Twenty-First Century?

The various crises that have afflicted southern European banks since 2009 raise a more general question, which has to do with the overall architecture of the European Union. How did Europe come to create—for the first time in human history on such a vast scale—a currency without a state? Since Europe's GDP accounted for nearly one-quarter of global GDP in 2013, the question is of interest not just to inhabitants of the Eurozone but to the entire world.

The usual answer to this question is that the creation of the euro— agreed on in the 1992 Maastricht Treaty in the wake of the fall of the Berlin Wall and the reunification of Germany and made a reality on January 1, 2002, when automatic teller machines across the Eurozone

---

24. In particular, a steeply progressive tax requires information on all assets held by a single individual in different accounts and at different banks (ideally not just in Cyprus but throughout the European Union). The advantage of a less progressive tax was that it could be applied to each bank individually.

first began to dispense euro notes—is but one step in a lengthy process. Monetary union is supposed to lead naturally to political, fiscal, and budgetary union, to ever closer cooperation among the member states. Patience is essential, and union must proceed step by step. No doubt this is true to some extent. In my view, however, the unwillingness to lay out a precise path to the desired end—the repeated postponement of any discussion of the itinerary to be followed, the stages along the way, or the ultimate endpoint—may well derail the entire process. If Europe created a stateless currency in 1992, it did so for reasons that were not simply pragmatic. It settled on this institutional arrangement in the late 1980s and early 1990s, at a time when many people believed that the only function of central banking was to control inflation. The "stagflation" of the 1970s had convinced governments and people that central banks ought to be independent of political control and target low inflation as their only objective. That is why Europe created a currency without a state and a central bank without a government. The crisis of 2008 shattered this static vision of central banking, as it became apparent that in a serious economic crisis central banks have a crucial role to play and that the existing European institutions were wholly unsuited to the task at hand.

Make no mistake. Given the power of central banks to create money in unlimited amounts, it is perfectly legitimate to subject them to rigid constraints and clear restrictions. No one wants to empower a head of state to replace university presidents and professors at will, much less to define the content of their teaching. By the same token, there is nothing shocking about imposing tight restrictions on the relations between governments and monetary authorities. But the limits of central bank independence should also be precise. In the current crisis, no one, to my knowledge, has proposed that central banks be returned to the private status they enjoyed in many countries prior to World War I (and in some places as recently as 1945).[25] Concretely,

---

25. In France, the two hundred largest shareholders in the Banque de France were statutorily entitled to a central role in the governance of the bank from 1803 to

the fact that central banks are public institutions means that their leaders are appointed by governments (and in some cases by parliaments). In many cases these leaders cannot be removed for the length of their mandate (usually five or six years) but can be replaced at the end of that term if their policies are deemed inadequate, which provides a measure of political control. In practice, the leaders of the Federal Reserve, the Bank of Japan, and the Bank of England are expected to work hand in hand with the legitimate, democratically elected governments of their countries. In each of these countries, the central bank has in the past played an important role in stabilizing interest rates and public debt at low and predictable levels.

The ECB faces a unique set of problems. First, the ECB's statutes are more restrictive than those of other central banks: the objective of keeping inflation low has absolute priority over the objectives of maintaining growth and full employment. This reflects the ideological context in which the ECB was conceived. Furthermore, the ECB is not allowed to purchase newly issued government debt: it must first allow private banks to lend to the member states of the Eurozone (possibly at a higher rate of interest than that which the ECB charges the private banks) and then purchase the bonds on the secondary market, as it did ultimately, after much hesitation, for the sovereign debt of governments in southern Europe.[26] More generally, it is obvious that the ECB's main difficulty is that it must deal with seventeen separate national debts and seventeen separate national governments. It is not easy for the bank to play its stabilizing role in such a context. If the

---

1936 and thus were empowered to determine the monetary policy of France. The Popular Front challenged this status quo by changing the rules to allow the government to name bank governors and subgovernors who were not shareholders. In 1945 the bank was nationalized. Since then, the Banque de France no longer has private shareholders and is a purely public institution, like most other central banks throughout the world.

26. A key moment in the Greek crisis was the ECB's announcement in December 2009 that it would no longer accept Greek bonds as collateral if Greece was downgraded by the bond rating agencies (even though nothing in its statutes obliged it to do so).

Federal Reserve had to choose every morning whether to concentrate on the debt of Wyoming, California, or New York and set its rates and quantities in view of its judgment of the tensions in each particular market and under pressure from each region of the country, it would have a very hard time maintaining a consistent monetary policy.

From the introduction of the euro in 2002 to the onset of the crisis in 2007–2008, interest rates were more or less identical across Europe. No one anticipated the possibility of an exit from the euro, so everything seemed to work well. When the global financial crisis began, however, interest rates began to diverge rapidly. The impact on government budgets was severe. When a government runs a debt close to one year of GDP, a difference of a few points of interest can have considerable consequences. In the face of such uncertainty, it is almost impossible to have a calm democratic debate about the burdens of adjustment or the indispensable reforms of the social state. For the countries of southern Europe, the options were truly impossible. Before joining the euro, they could have devalued their currency, which would at least have restored competitiveness and spurred economic activity. Speculation on national interest rates was in some ways more destabilizing than the previous speculation on exchange rates among European currencies, particularly since crossborder bank lending had meanwhile grown to such proportions that panic on the part of a handful of market actors was enough to trigger capital flows large enough to seriously affect countries such as Greece, Portugal, and Ireland, and even larger countries such as Spain and Italy. Logically, such a loss of monetary sovereignty should have been compensated by guaranteeing that countries could borrow if need be at low and predictable rates.

The Question of European Unification

The only way to overcome these contradictions is for the countries of the Eurozone (or at any rate those who are willing) to pool their public debts. The German proposal to create a "redemption fund," which I touched on earlier, is a good starting point, but it lacks a political component.[27] Concretely, it is impossible to decide twenty years in advance what the exact pace of "redemption" will be—that is, how quickly the stock of pooled debt will be reduced to the target level. Many parameters will affect the outcome, starting with the state of the economy. To decide how quickly to pay down the pooled debt, or, in other words, to decide how much public debt the Eurozone should carry, one would need to empower a European "budgetary parliament" to decide on a European budget. The best way to do this would be to draw the members of this parliament from the ranks of the national parliaments, so that European parliamentary sovereignty would rest on the legitimacy of democratically elected national assemblies.[28] Like any other parliament, this body would decide issues by majority vote after open public debate. Coalitions would form, based partly on political affiliation and partly on national affiliation. The decisions of such a body will never be ideal, but at least we would know what had been decided and why, which is important. It is preferable, I think, to create such a new body rather than rely on the current European Parliament, which is composed of members from twenty-seven states (many of which do not belong to the Eurozone and do not wish to pursue further European integration at this time). To rely on the existing European Parliament would also conflict too overtly with the sovereignty of national parliaments, which would be problematic in regard to decisions affecting national budget deficits. That is probably the reason why transfers of power to the European Parliament have al-

---

27. Another, more technical limitation of the "redemption fund" is that given the magnitude of the "rollover" (much of the outstanding debt comes due within a few years and must be rolled over regularly, especially in Italy), the limit of 60 percent of GDP will be reached within a few years, hence eventually all public debt will have to be mutualized.

28. The budgetary parliament might consist of fifty or so members from each of the large Eurozone countries, prorated by population. Members might be chosen from the financial and social affairs committees of the national parliaments or in some other fashion. The new European treaty adopted in 2012 provides for a "conference of national parliaments," but this is a purely consultative body with no power of its own and a fortiori no common debt.

ways been quite limited in the past and will likely remain so for quite some time. It is time to accept this fact and to create a new parliamentary body to reflect the desire for unification that exists within the Eurozone countries (as indicated most clearly by their agreement to relinquish monetary sovereignty with due regard for the consequences).

Several institutional arrangements are possible. In the spring of 2013, the new Italian government pledged to support a proposal made a few years earlier by German authorities concerning the election by universal suffrage of a president of the European Union—a proposal that logically ought to be accompanied by a broadening of the president's powers. If a budgetary parliament decides what the Eurozone's debt ought to be, then there clearly needs to be a European finance minister responsible to that body and charged with proposing a Eurozone budget and annual deficit. What is certain is that the Eurozone cannot do without a genuine parliamentary chamber in which to set its budgetary strategy in a public, democratic, and sovereign manner, and more generally to discuss ways to overcome the financial and banking crisis in which Europe currently finds itself mired. The existing European councils of heads of state and finance ministers cannot do the work of this budgetary body. They meet in secret, do not engage in open public debate, and regularly end their meetings with triumphal midnight communiqués announcing that Europe has been saved, even though the participants themselves do not always seem to be sure about what they have decided. The decision on the Cypriot tax is typical in this regard: although it was approved unanimously, no one wanted to accept responsibility in public.[29] This type of proceeding is

---

29. The official version is that the virtually flat tax on deposits was adopted at the request of the Cypriot president, who allegedly wanted to tax small depositors heavily in order to prevent large depositors from fleeing. No doubt there is some truth to this: the crisis illustrates the predicament that small countries face in a globalized economy: to carve out a niche for themselves, they may be prepared to engage in ruthless tax competition in order to attract capital, even from the most disreputable sources. The problem is that we will never know the whole truth, since all the negotiations took place behind closed doors.

worthy of the Congress of Vienna (1815) but has no place in the Europe of the twenty-first century. The German and Italian proposals alluded to above show that progress is possible. It is nevertheless striking to note that France has been mostly absent from this debate through two presidencies,[30] even though the country is prompt to lecture others about European solidarity and the need for debt mutualization (at least at the rhetorical level).[31]

Unless things change in the direction I have indicated, it is very difficult to imagine a lasting solution to the crisis of the Eurozone. In addition to pooling debts and deficits, there are of course other fiscal and budgetary tools that no country can use on its own, so that it would make sense to think about using them jointly. The first example that comes to mind is of course the progressive tax on capital.

An even more obvious example is a tax on corporate profits. Tax competition among European states has been fierce in this respect since the early 1990s. In particular, several small countries, with Ireland leading the way, followed by several Eastern European countries, made low corporate taxes a key element of their economic development strategies. In an ideal tax system, based on shared and reliable bank

---

30. The usual explanation is that French leaders remain traumatized by their defeat in the 2005 referendum on the European Constitutional Treaty. The argument is not totally convincing, because that treaty, whose main provisions were later adopted without approval by referendum, contained no important democratic innovation and gave all power to the council of heads of state and ministers, which simply ratifies Europe's current state of impotence. It may be that France's presidential political culture explains why reflection about European political union is less advanced in France than in Germany or Italy.

31. Under François Hollande, the French government has been rhetorically in favor of mutualizing European debts but has made no specific proposal, pretending to believe that every country can continue to decide on its own how much debt it wishes to take on, which is impossible. Mutualization implies that there needs to be a vote on the total size of the debt. Each country could maintain its own debt, but its size would need to be modest, like state and municipal debts in the United States. Logically, the president of the Bundesbank regularly issues statements to the media that a credit card cannot be shared without agreement about how much can be spent in total.

data, the corporate tax would play a limited role. It would simply be a form of withholding on the income tax (or capital tax) due from individual shareholders and bondholders.[32] In practice, the problem is that this "withholding" tax is often the only tax paid, since much of what corporations declare as profit does not figure in the taxable income of individual shareholders, which is why it is important to collect a significant amount of tax at the source through the corporate tax.

The right approach would be to require corporations to make a single declaration of their profits at the European level and then tax that profit in a way that is less subject to manipulation than is the current system of taxing the profits of each subsidiary individually. The problem with the current system is that multinational corporations often end up paying ridiculously small amounts because they can assign all their profits artificially to a subsidiary located in a place where taxes are very low; such a practice is not illegal, and in the minds of many corporate managers it is not even unethical.[33] It makes more sense to give up the idea that profits can be pinned down to a particular state or territory; instead, one can apportion the revenues of the corporate tax on the basis of sales or wages paid within each country.

---

32. Progressive income and capital taxes are more satisfactory than corporate income taxes because they allow adjustment of the tax rate in accordance with the income or capital of each taxpayer, whereas the corporate tax is levied on all corporate profits at the same level, affecting large and small shareholders alike.

33. To believe the statements of the managers of companies like Google, their reasoning is more or less as follows: "We contribute far more wealth to society than our profits and salaries suggest, so it is perfectly reasonable for us to pay low taxes." Indeed, if a company or individual contributes marginal well-being to the rest of the economy greater than the price it charges for its products, then it is perfectly legitimate for it to pay less in tax or even to receive a subsidy (economists refer to this as a positive externality). The problem, obviously, is that it is in everyone's interest to claim that he or she contributes a large positive externality to the rest of the world. Google has not of course offered the slightest evidence to prove that it actually does make such a contribution. In any case, it is obvious that it is not easy to manage a society in which each individual can set his or her own tax rate in this way.

A related problem arises in connection with the tax on individual capital. The general principle on which most tax systems are based is the principle of residence: each country taxes the income and wealth of individuals who reside within its borders for more than six months a year. This principle is increasingly difficult to apply in Europe, especially in border areas (for example, along the Franco-Belgian border). What is more, wealth has always been taxed partly as a function of the location of the asset rather than of its owner. For example, the owner of a Paris apartment must pay property tax to the city of Paris, even if he lives halfway around the world and regardless of his nationality. The same principle applies to the wealth tax, but only in regard to real estate. There is no reason why it could not also be applied to financial assets, based on the location of the corresponding business activity or company. The same is true for government bonds. Extending the principle of "residence of the capital asset" (rather than of its owner) to financial assets would obviously require automatic sharing of bank data to allow the tax authorities to assess complex ownership structures. Such a tax would also raise the issue of multinationality.[34] Adequate answers to all these questions can clearly be found only at the European (or global) level. The right approach is therefore to create a Eurozone budgetary parliament to deal with them.

Are all these proposals utopian? No more so than attempting to create a stateless currency. When countries relinquish monetary sovereignty, it is essential to restore their fiscal sovereignty over matters no longer within the purview of the nation-state, such as the interest rate on public debt, the progressive tax on capital, or the taxation of multinational corporations. For the countries of Europe, the priority now should be to construct a continental political authority capable of reasserting control over patrimonial capitalism and private interests

---

34. There was a recent proposal to pay international organizations the proceeds of a global wealth tax. Such a tax would become independent of nationality and could become a way to protect the right to multinationality. See Patrick Weil, "Let Them Eat Less Cake: An International Tax on the Wealthiest Citizens of the World," *Policy Network,* May 26, 2011.

and of advancing the European social model in the twenty-first century. The minor disparities between national social models are of secondary importance in view of the challenges to the very survival of the common European model.[35]

Another point to bear in mind is that without such a European political union, it is highly likely that tax competition will continue to wreak havoc. The race to the bottom continues in regard to corporate taxes, as recently proposed "allowances for corporate equity" show.[36] It is important to realize that tax competition regularly leads to a reliance on consumption taxes, that is, to the kind of tax system that existed in the nineteenth century, where no progressivity is possible. In practice, this favors individuals who are able to save, to change their country of residence, or both.[37] Note, however, that progress toward

---

35. This conclusion is similar to that of Dani Rodrik, who argues that the nation-state, democracy, and globalization are an unstable trio (one of the three must give way before the other two, at least to a certain extent). See Dani Rodrik, *The Globalization Paradox: Democracy and the Future of the World Economy* (New York: Norton, 2011).

36. The system of "allowance for corporate equity" adopted in Belgium in 2006 authorizes the deduction from taxable corporate profits of an amount equal to the "normal" return on equity. This deduction is said to be the equivalent of the deduction of interest on corporate debt and is supposed to equalize the tax status of debt and equity. But Germany and more recently France have taken a different take: limiting interest deductions. Some participants in this debate, such as the IMF and to a certain extent the European Commission, claim that the two solutions are equivalent, although in fact they are not: if one deducts the "normal" return on both debt and equity, it is highly likely that the corporate tax will simply disappear.

37. In particular, taxing different types of consumption goods at different rates allows for only crude targeting of the consumption tax by income class. The main reason why European governments are currently so fond of value-added taxes is that this type of tax allows for de facto taxation of imported goods and small-scale competitive devaluations. This is of course a zero-sum game: the competitive advantage vanishes if other countries do the same. It is one symptom of a monetary union with a low level of international cooperation. The other standard justification of a consumption tax relies on the idea of encouraging investment, but the conceptual basis of this approach is not clear (especially in periods when the capital / income ratio is relatively high).

some forms of fiscal cooperation has been more rapid than one might imagine at first glance: consider, for example, the proposed financial transactions tax, which could become one of the first truly European taxes. Although such a tax is far less significant than a tax on capital or corporate profits (in terms of both revenues and distributive impact), recent progress on this tax shows that nothing is foreordained.[38] Political and fiscal history always blaze their own trails.

Government and Capital Accumulation in the Twenty-First Century

Let me now take a step back from the immediate issues of European construction and raise the following question: In an ideal society, what level of public debt is desirable? Let me say at once that there is no certainty about the answer, and only democratic deliberation can decide, in keeping with the goals each society sets for itself and the particular challenges each country faces. What is certain is that no sensible answer is possible unless a broader question is also raised: What level of public capital is desirable, and what is the ideal level of total national capital?

In this book, I have looked in considerable detail at the evolution of the capital / income ratio β across space and time. I have also examined how β is determined in the long run by the savings and growth rates of each country, according to the law $\beta = s/g$. But I have not yet asked what β is desirable. In an ideal society, should the capital stock be equal to five years of national income, or ten years, or twenty? How should we think about this question? It is impossible to give a precise answer. Under certain hypotheses, however, one can establish a ceiling

---

38. The purpose of the fiscal transactions tax is to decrease the number of very high-frequency financial transactions, which is no doubt a good thing. By definition, however, the tax will not raise much revenue, because its purpose is to dry up its source. Estimates of potential revenues are often optimistic. They cannot be much more than 0.5 percent of GDP, which is a good thing, because the tax cannot target different levels of individual incomes or wealth. See the online technical appendix.

on the quantity of capital that one can envision accumulating a priori. The maximal level of capital is attained when so much has been accumulated that the return on capital, r, supposed to be equal to its marginal productivity, falls to be equal to the growth rate g. In 1961 Edmund Phelps baptized the equality $r = g$ the "golden rule of capital accumulation." If one takes it literally, the golden rule implies much higher capital/income ratios than have been observed historically, since, as I have shown, the return on capital has always been significantly higher than the growth rate. Indeed, r was much greater than g before the nineteenth century (with a return on capital of 4–5 percent and a growth rate below 1 percent), and it will probably be so again in the twenty-first century (with a return of 4–5 percent once again and long-term growth not much above 1.5 percent).[39] It is very difficult to say what quantity of capital would have to be accumulated for the rate of return to fall to 1 or 1.5 percent. It is surely far more than the six to seven years of national income currently observed in the most capital-intensive countries. Perhaps it would take ten to fifteen years of national income, maybe even more. It is even harder to imagine what it would take for the return on capital to fall to the low growth levels observed before the eighteenth century (less than 0.2 percent). One might need to accumulate capital equivalent to twenty to thirty years of national income: everyone would then own so much real estate, machinery, tools, and so on that an additional unit of capital would add less than 0.2 percent to each year's output.

The truth is that to pose the question in this way is to approach it too abstractly. The answer given by the golden rule is not very useful in practice. It is unlikely that any human society will ever accumulate that much capital. Nevertheless, the logic that underlies the golden rule is not without interest. Let me summarize the argument briefly.[40]

---

39. See Figures 10.9–11. To evaluate the golden rule, one must use the pretax rate of return on capital (supposed to be equal to the marginal productivity of capital).

40. The original article, written with a certain ironic distance in the form of a fable, is worth rereading: Edmund Phelps, "The Golden Rule of Accumulation: A Fable for Growthmen," *American Economic Review* 51, no. 4 (September 1961): 638–43.

If the golden rule is satisfied, so $r=g$, then by definition capital's long-run share of national income is exactly equal to the savings rate: $\alpha=s$. Conversely, as long as $r>g$, capital's long-run share is greater than the savings rate: $\alpha>s$.[41] In other words, in order for the golden rule to be satisfied, one has to have accumulated so much capital that capital no longer yields anything. Or, more precisely, one has to have accumulated so much capital that merely maintaining the capital stock at the same level (in proportion to national income) requires reinvesting all of the return to capital every year. That is what $\alpha=s$ means: all of the return to capital must be saved and added back to the capital stock. Conversely, if $r>g$, than capital returns something in the long run, in the sense that it is no longer necessary to reinvest all of the return on capital to maintain the same capital / income ratio.

Clearly, then, the golden rule is related to a "capital saturation" strategy. So much capital is accumulated that rentiers have nothing left to consume, since they must reinvest all of their return if they want their capital to grow at the same rate as the economy, thereby preserving their social status relative to the average for the society. Conversely, if $r>g$, it suffices to reinvest a fraction of the return on capital equal to the growth rate (g) and to consume the rest $(r-g)$. The inequality $r>g$ is the basis of a society of rentiers. Accumulating enough capital to reduce the return to the growth rate can therefore end the reign of the rentier.

But is it the best way to achieve that end? Why would the owners of capital, or society as a whole, choose to accumulate that much cap-

---

A similar idea, expressed less clearly and without allusion to the golden rule, can be found in Maurice Allais's *Economie et intérêt* (Paris: Librairie des Publications Officielles, 1947) and in articles by Von Neumann (1945) and Malinvaud (1953). Note that all this work (including Phelps's article) is purely theoretical and does not discuss what level of accumulation would be required to make r equal to g. See the online technical appendix.

41. Capital's share is given by $\alpha=r\times\beta$. In the long run, $\beta=s/g$, so $\alpha=s\times r/g$. It follows that $\alpha=s$ if $r=g$, and $\alpha>s$ if and only if $r>g$. See the online technical appendix.

ital? Bear in mind that the argument that leads to the golden rule simply sets an upper limit but in no way justifies reaching it.[42] In practice, there are much simpler and more effective ways to deal with rentiers, namely, by taxing them: no need to accumulate capital worth dozens of years of national income, which might require several generations to forgo consumption.[43] At a purely theoretical level, everything depends in principle on the origins of growth. If there is no productivity growth, so that the only source of growth is demographic, then accumulating capital to the level required by the golden rule might make sense. For example, if one assumes that the population will grow forever at 1 percent a year and that people are infinitely patient and altruistic toward future generations, then the right way to maximize per capita consumption in the long run is to accumulate so much capital that the rate of return falls to 1 percent. But the limits of this argument are obvious. In the first place, it is rather odd to assume that

---

42. The reasons why the golden rule establishes an upper limit are explained more precisely in the online technical appendix. The essential intuition is the following. Beyond the level of capital described by the golden rule, that is, where the return on capital sinks below the growth rate, capital's long-run share is lower than the savings rate. This is absurd in social terms, since it would take more to maintain the capital stock at this level than the capital returns. This type of "dynamic inefficiency" can occur if individuals save without worrying about the return: for example, if they are saving for old age and their life expectancy is sufficiently long. In that case, the efficient policy is for the state to reduce the capital stock, for example, by issuing public debt (potentially in large amounts), thus de facto replacing a capitalized pension system by a PAYGO system. This interesting theoretical policy never seems to occur in practice, however: in all known societies, the average return on capital is always greater than the growth rate.

43. In practice, a tax on capital (or public ownership) can ensure that the portion of national income going to income on private capital (after taxes) is less than the savings rate without needing to accumulate so much. This was the postwar social-democratic ideal: profits should finance investment, not the high life of stockholders. As the German chancellor Helmut Schmidt said, "Today's profits are tomorrow's investments and the day after tomorrow's jobs." Capital and labor work hand in hand. But it is important to understand that this depends on institutions such as taxes and public ownership (unless we imagine unprecedented levels of accumulation).

demographic growth is eternal, since it depends on the reproductive choices of future generations, for which the present generation is not responsible (unless we imagine a world with a particularly underdeveloped contraceptive technology). Furthermore, if demographic growth is also zero, one would have to accumulate an infinite quantity of capital: as long as the return on capital is even slightly positive, it will be in the interest of future generations for the present generation to consume nothing and accumulate as much as possible. According to Marx, who implicitly assumes zero demographic and productivity growth, this is the ultimate consequence of the capitalist's unlimited desire to accumulate more and more capital, and in the end it leads to the downfall of capitalism and the collective appropriation of the means of production. Indeed, in the Soviet Union, the state claimed to serve the common good by accumulating unlimited industrial capital and ever-increasing numbers of machines: no one really knew where the planners thought accumulation should end.[44]

If productivity growth is even slightly positive, the process of capital accumulation is described by the law $\beta = s/g$. The question of the social optimum then becomes more difficult to resolve. If one knows in advance that productivity will increase forever by 1 percent a year, it follows that future generations will be more productive and prosperous than present ones. That being the case, is it reasonable to sacrifice present consumption to the accumulation of vast amounts of capital? Depending on how one chooses to compare and weigh the well-being of different generations, one can reach any desired conclusion: that it is wiser to leave nothing at all for future generations (ex-

---

44. In a sense, the Soviet interpretation of the golden rule simply transferred to the collectivity the unlimited desire for accumulation attributed to the capitalist. In chapters 16 and 24 of *The General Theory of Employment, Interest, and Money* (1936), where Keynes discusses "the euthanasia of the rentier," he develops an idea close to that of "capital saturation": the rentier will be euthanized by accumulating so much capital that his return will disappear. But Keynes is not clear about how much this is (he does not mention $r = g$) and does not explicitly discuss public accumulation.

cept perhaps our pollution), or to abide by the golden rule, or any other split between present and future consumption between those two extremes. Clearly, the golden rule is of limited practical utility.[45]

In truth, simple common sense should have been enough to conclude that no mathematical formula will enable us to resolve the complex issue of deciding how much to leave for future generations. Why, then, did I feel it necessary to present these conceptual debates around the golden rule? Because they have had a certain impact on public debate in recent years in regard first to European deficits and second to controversies around the issue of climate change.

Law and Politics

First, a rather different idea of "the golden rule" has figured in the European debate about public deficits.[46] In 1992, when the Treaty of Maastricht created the euro, it was stipulated that member states should ensure that their budget deficits would be less than 3 percent of GDP and that total public debt would remain below 60 percent of

---

45. The mathematical solution to this problem is presented in the online technical appendix. To summarize, everything depends on what is commonly called the concavity of the utility function (using the formula $r = \theta + \gamma \times g$, previously discussed in Chapter 10 and sometimes called the "modified golden rule"). With infinite concavity, one assumes that future generations will not need a hundredth additional iPhone, and one leaves them no capital. At the opposite extreme, one can go all the way to the golden rule, which may necessitate leaving them several dozen years of national income in capital. Infinite concavity is frequently associated with a Rawlsian social objective and may therefore seem tempting. The difficulty is that if one leaves no capital for the future, it is not at all certain that productivity growth will continue at the same pace. Because of this, the problem is largely undecidable, as perplexing for the economist as for the citizen.

46. In the most general sense, a "golden rule" is a moral imperative that defines people's obligations to one another. It is often used in economics and politics to refer to simple rules defining the current population's obligations to future generations. Unfortunately, there is no simple rule capable of definitively resolving this existential question, which must therefore be asked again and again.

GDP.[47] The precise economic logic behind these choices has never been completely explained.[48] Indeed, if one does not include public assets and total national capital, it is difficult to justify any particular level of public debt on rational grounds. I have already mentioned the real reason for these strict budgetary constraints, which are historically unprecedented. (The United States, Britain, and Japan have never imposed such rules on themselves.) It is an almost inevitable consequence of the decision to create a common currency without a state, and in particular without pooling the debt of member states or coordinating deficits. Presumably, the Maastricht criteria would become unnecessary if the Eurozone were to equip itself with a budgetary parliament empowered to decide and coordinate deficit levels for the various member states. The decision would then be a sovereign and democratic one. There is no convincing reason to impose a priori constraints, much less to enshrine limits on debts and deficits in state constitutions. Since the construction of a budgetary union has only just begun, of course, special rules may be necessary to build confidence: for example, one can imagine requiring a parliamentary supermajority in order to exceed a certain level of debt. But there is no justification for engraving untouchable debt and deficit limits in stone in order to thwart future political majorities.

Make no mistake: I have no particular liking for public debt. As I noted earlier, debt often becomes a backhanded form of redistribution of wealth from the poor to the rich, from people with modest

---

47. These figures were retained in the new treaty signed in 2012, which added a further objective of maintaining a "structural" deficit of less than 0.5 percent of GDP (the structural deficit corrects for effects of the business cycle), along with automatic sanctions if these commitments were not respected. Note that all deficit figures in European treaties refer to the secondary deficit (interest on the debt is included in expenditures).

48. A deficit of 3 percent would allow a stable debt-to-GDP ratio of 60 percent if nominal GDP growth is 5 percent (e.g., 2 percent inflation and 3 percent real growth), in view of the formula $\beta = s/g$ applied to the public debt. But the argument is not very convincing (in particular, there is no real justification for such a nominal growth rate). See the online technical appendix.

savings to those with the means to lend to the government (who as a general rule ought to be paying taxes rather than lending). Since the middle of the twentieth century and the large-scale public debt repudiations (and debt shrinkage through inflation) after World War II, many dangerous illusions have arisen in regard to government debt and its relation to social redistribution. These illusions urgently need to be dispelled.

There are nevertheless a number of reasons why it is not very judicious to enshrine budgetary restrictions in statutory or constitutional stone. For one thing, historical experience suggests that in a serious crisis it is often necessary to make emergency budget decisions on a scale that would have been unimaginable before the crisis. To leave it to a constitutional judge (or committee of experts) to judge such decisions case by case is to take a step back from democracy. In any case, turning the power to decide over to the courts is not without risk. Indeed, history shows that constitutional judges have an unfortunate tendency to interpret fiscal and budgetary laws in very conservative ways.[49] Such judicial conservatism is particularly dangerous in Europe, where there has been a tendency to see the free circulation of people, goods, and capital as fundamental rights with priority over the right of member states to promote the general interest of their people, if need be by levying taxes.

Finally, it is impossible to judge the appropriate level of debts and deficits without taking into account numerous other factors affecting national wealth. When we look at all the available data today, what is

---

49. In the United States, the Supreme Court blocked several attempts to levy a federal income tax in the late nineteenth and early twentieth centuries and then blocked minimum wage legislation in the 1930s, while finding that slavery and, later, racial discrimination were perfectly compatible with basic constitutional rights for nearly two centuries. More recently, the French Constitutional Court has apparently come up with a theory of what maximum income tax rate is compatible with the Constitution: after a period of high-level legal deliberation known only to itself, the Court hesitated between 65 and 67 percent and wondered whether or not it should include the carbon tax.

most striking is that national wealth in Europe has never been so high. To be sure, net public wealth is virtually zero, given the size of the public debt, but net private wealth is so high that the sum of the two is as great as it has been in a century. Hence the idea that we are about to bequeath a shameful burden of debt to our children and grandchildren and that we ought to wear sackcloth and ashes and beg for forgiveness simply makes no sense. The nations of Europe have never been so rich. What is true and shameful, on the other hand, is that this vast national wealth is very unequally distributed. Private wealth rests on public poverty, and one particularly unfortunate consequence of this is that we currently spend far more in interest on the debt than we invest in higher education. This has been true, moreover, for a very long time: because growth has been fairly slow since 1970, we are in a period of history in which debt weighs very heavily on our public finances.[50] This is the main reason why the debt must be reduced as quickly as possible, ideally by means of a progressive one-time tax on private capital or, failing that, by inflation. In any event, the decision should be made by a sovereign parliament after democratic debate.[51]

Climate Change and Public Capital

The second important issue on which these golden rule–related questions have a major impact is climate change and, more generally, the

---

50. The problem is similar to that posed by the return on PAYGO retirement systems. As long as growth is robust and the fiscal base is expanding at a pace equal (or nearly equal) to that of interest on the debt, it is relatively easy to reduce the size of the public debt as a percentage of national income. Things are different when growth is slow: the debt becomes a burden that is difficult to shake. If we average over the period 1970–2010, we find that interest payments on the debt are far larger than the average primary deficit, which is close to zero in many countries, and notably in Italy, where the average interest payment on the debt attained the astronomical level of 7 percent of GDP over this period. See the online technical appendix and Supplemental Table S16.1, available online.

51. If the issue is constitutionalized, however, it is not impossible that a solution such as a progressive tax on capital would be judged unconstitutional.

possibility of deterioration of humanity's natural capital in the century ahead. If we take a global view, then this is clearly the world's principal long-term worry. The Stern Report, published in 2006, calculated that the potential damage to the environment by the end of the century could amount, in some scenarios, to dozens of points of global GDP per year. Among economists, the controversy surrounding the report hinged mainly on the question of the rate at which future damage to the environment should be discounted. Nicholas Stern, who is British, argued for a relatively low discount rate, approximately the same as the growth rate (1–1.5 percent a year). With that assumption, present generations weigh future damage very heavily in their own calculations. William Nordhaus, an American, argued that one ought to choose a discount rate closer to the average return on capital (4–4.5 percent a year), a choice that makes future disasters seem much less worrisome. In other words, even if everyone agrees about the cost of future disasters (despite the obvious uncertainties), they can reach different conclusions. For Stern, the loss of global well-being is so great that it justifies spending at least 5 points of global GDP a year right now to attempt to mitigate climate change in the future. For Nordhaus, such a large expenditure would be entirely unreasonable, because future generations will be richer and more productive than we are. They will find a way to cope, even if it means consuming less, which will in any case be less costly from the standpoint of universal well-being than making the kind of effort Stern envisions. So in the end, all of these expert calculations come down to a stark difference of opinion.

Stern's opinion seems more reasonable to me than Nordhaus's, whose optimism is attractive, to be sure, as well as opportunely consistent with the US strategy of unrestricted carbon emissions, but ultimately not very convincing.[52] In any case, this relatively abstract debate about dis-

---

52. On the way Stern and Nordhaus arrive at their preferred discount rates, see the online technical appendix. It is interesting that both men use the same "modified golden rule" I described earlier but reverse positions entirely when it comes to choosing the concavity of the social utility function. (Nordhaus makes a more Rawlsian choice than Stern in order to justify ascribing little weight to the prefer-

count rates largely sidesteps what seems to me the central issue. Public debate, especially in Europe but also in China and the United States, has taken an increasingly pragmatic turn, with discussion of the need for major investment in the search for new nonpolluting technologies and forms of renewable energy sufficiently abundant to enable the world to do without hydrocarbons. Discussion of "ecological stimulus" is especially prevalent in Europe, where many people see it as a possible way out of today's dismal economic climate. This strategy is particularly tempting because many governments are currently able to borrow at very low interest rates. If private investors are unwilling to spend and invest, then why shouldn't governments invest in the future to avoid a likely degradation of natural capital?[53]

This is a very important debate for the decades ahead. The public debt (which is much smaller than total private wealth and perhaps not really that difficult to eliminate) is not our major worry. The more urgent need is to increase our educational capital and prevent the degradation of our natural capital. This is a far more serious and difficult challenge, because climate change cannot be eliminated at the stroke of a pen (or with a tax on capital, which comes to the same thing). The key practical issue is the following. Suppose that Stern is approximately correct that there is good reason to spend the equivalent of 5 percent of global GDP annually to ward off an environmental catas-

---

ences of future generations.) A logically more satisfactory procedure would introduce the fact that the substitutability of natural capital for other forms of wealth is far from infinite in the long run (as Roger Guesnerie and Thomas Sterner have done). In other words, if natural capital is destroyed, consuming fewer iPhones in the future will not be enough to repair the damage.

53. As noted, the current low interest rates on government debt are no doubt temporary and in any case somewhat misleading: some countries must pay very high rates, and it is unlikely that those that are borrowing today at under 1 percent will continue to enjoy such low rates for decades (analysis of the period 1970–2010 suggests that real interest rates on long-term public debt in the rich countries is around 3 percent; see the online technical appendix). Nevertheless, current low rates are a powerful economic argument in favor of public investment (at least as long as such rates last).

trophe. Do we really know what we ought to invest in and how we should organize our effort? If we are talking about public investments of this magnitude, it is important to realize that this would represent public spending on a vast scale, far vaster than any previous public spending by the rich countries.[54] If we are talking about private investment, we need to be clear about the manner of public financing and who will own the resulting technologies and patents. Should we count on advanced research to make rapid progress in developing renewable energy sources, or should we immediately subject ourselves to strict limits on hydrocarbon consumption? It would probably be wise to choose a balanced strategy that would make use of all available tools.[55] So much for common sense. But the fact remains that no one knows for now how these challenges will be met or what role governments will play in preventing the degradation of our natural capital in the years ahead.

Economic Transparency and Democratic Control of Capital

More generally, it is important, I think, to insist that one of the most important issues in coming years will be the development of new forms of property and democratic control of capital. The dividing line between public capital and private capital is by no means as clear as some have believed since the fall of the Berlin Wall. As noted, there are already many areas, such as education, health, culture, and the media, in which the dominant forms of organization and ownership have little to do with the polar paradigms of purely private capital

---

54. Over the last several decades, annual public investment (net of depreciation of public assets) in most rich countries has been about 1–1.5 percent of GDP. See the online technical appendix and Supplemental Table S16.1, available online.

55. Including tools such as the carbon tax, which increases the cost of energy consumption as a function of the associated emission of carbon dioxide (and not as a function of budget variations, which has generally been the logic of gasoline taxes). There is good reason to believe, however, that the price signal has less of an impact on emissions than public investment and changes to building codes (requiring thermal insulation, for example).

(modeled on the joint-stock company entirely owned by its share-holders) and purely public capital (based on a similar top-down logic in which the sovereign government decides on all investments). There are obviously many intermediate forms of organization capable of mobilizing the talent of different individuals and the information at their disposal. When it comes to organizing collective decisions, the market and the ballot box are merely two polar extremes. New forms of participation and governance remain to be invented.[56]

The essential point is that these various forms of democratic control of capital depend in large part on the availability of economic information to each of the involved parties. Economic and financial transparency are important for tax purposes, to be sure, but also for much more general reasons. They are essential for democratic governance and participation. In this respect, what matters is not transparency regarding individual income and wealth, which is of no intrinsic interest (except perhaps in the case of political officials or in situations where there is no other way to establish trust).[57] For collective action, what would matter most would be the publication of detailed ac-

---

56. The idea that private property and the market allow (under certain conditions) for the coordination and efficient use of the talents and information possessed by millions of individuals is a classic that one finds in the work of Adam Smith, Friedrich Hayek, and Kenneth Arrow and Gérard Debreu. The idea that voting is another efficient way of aggregating information (and more generally ideas, reflections, etc.) is also very old: it goes back to Condorcet. For recent research on this constructivist approach to political institutions and electoral systems, see the online technical appendix.

57. For example, it is important to be able to study where political officials from various countries stand in the wealth and income hierarchies (see previous chapters). Still, statistical summaries might suffice for the purpose; detailed individual data are generally not needed. As for establishing trust when there is no other way to do so: one of the first actions of the revolutionary assemblies of 1789–1790 was to compile a "compendium of pensions" that listed by name and amount the sums paid by the royal government to various individuals (including debt repayments, pensions to former officials, and outright favors). This sixteen-hundred-page book contained 23,000 names and listed detailed amounts (multiple sources of income were combined into a single line for each individual), the ministry involved, the age of the person, the final year of payment, the reasons for the

counts of private corporations (as well as government agencies). The accounting data that companies are currently required to publish are entirely inadequate for allowing workers or ordinary citizens to form an opinion about corporate decisions, much less to intervene in them. For example, to take a concrete case mentioned at the very beginning of this book, the published accounts of Lonmin, Inc., the owner of the Marikana platinum mine where thirty-four strikers were shot dead in August 2012, do not tell us precisely how the wealth produced by the mine is divided between profits and wages. This is generally true of published corporate accounts around the world: the data are grouped in very broad statistical categories that reveal as little as possible about what is actually at stake, while more detailed information is reserved for investors.[58] It is then easy to say that workers and their representatives are insufficiently informed about the economic realities facing the firm to participate in investment decisions. Without real accounting and financial transparency and sharing of information, there can be no economic democracy. Conversely, without a real right to intervene in corporate decision-making (including seats for workers on the company's board of directors), transparency is of little use. Information must support democratic institutions; it is not an end in itself. If democracy is someday to regain control of capitalism, it must start by recognizing that the concrete institutions in which democracy and capitalism are embodied need to be reinvented again and again.[59]

payment, etc. It was published in April 1790. On this interesting document, see the online technical appendix.

58. This is due mainly to the fact that wages are generally aggregated in a single line with other intermediate inputs (that is, with purchases from other firms, which also remunerate both labor and capital). Hence published accounts never reveal the split between profits and wages, nor do they allow us to uncover possible abuses of intermediate consumption (which can be a way of augmenting the income of executives and / or stockholders). For the example of the Lonmin accounts and the Marikana mine, see the online technical appendix.

59. The exigent attitude toward democracy of a philosopher such as Jacques Rancière is indispensable here. See in particular his *La haine de la démocratie* (Paris: La Fabrique, 2005).

Conclusion

I have presented the current state of our historical knowledge concerning the dynamics of the distribution of wealth and income since the eighteenth century, and I have attempted to draw from this knowledge whatever lessons can be drawn for the century ahead.

The sources on which this book draws are more extensive than any previous author has assembled, but they remain imperfect and incomplete. All of my conclusions are by nature tenuous and deserve to be questioned and debated. It is not the purpose of social science research to produce mathematical certainties that can substitute for open, democratic debate in which all shades of opinion are represented.

The Central Contradiction of Capitalism: $r > g$

The overall conclusion of this study is that a market economy based on private property, if left to itself, contains powerful forces of convergence, associated in particular with the diffusion of knowledge and skills; but it also contains powerful forces of divergence, which are potentially threatening to democratic societies and to the values of social justice on which they are based.

The principal destabilizing force has to do with the fact that the private rate of return on capital, r, can be significantly higher for long periods of time than the rate of growth of income and output, g.

The inequality $r > g$ implies that wealth accumulated in the past grows more rapidly than output and wages. This inequality expresses a fundamental logical contradiction. The entrepreneur inevitably tends to become a rentier, more and more dominant over those who own nothing but their labor. Once constituted, capital reproduces itself faster than output increases. The past devours the future.

The consequences for the long-term dynamics of the wealth distribution are potentially terrifying, especially when one adds that the return on capital varies directly with the size of the initial stake and that the divergence in the wealth distribution is occurring on a global scale.

The problem is enormous, and there is no simple solution. Growth can of course be encouraged by investing in education, knowledge, and nonpolluting technologies. But none of these will raise the growth rate to 4 or 5 percent a year. History shows that only countries that are catching up with more advanced economies—such as Europe during the three decades after World War II or China and other emerging countries today—can grow at such rates. For countries at the world technological frontier—and thus ultimately for the planet as a whole—there is ample reason to believe that the growth rate will not exceed 1–1.5 percent in the long run, no matter what economic policies are adopted.[1]

With an average return on capital of 4–5 percent, it is therefore likely that $r > g$ will again become the norm in the twenty-first century, as it had been throughout history until the eve of World War I. In the twentieth century, it took two world wars to wipe away the past and significantly reduce the return on capital, thereby creating the illusion that the fundamental structural contradiction of capitalism $(r > g)$ had been overcome.

To be sure, one could tax capital income heavily enough to reduce the private return on capital to less than the growth rate. But if one did that indiscriminately and heavy-handedly, one would risk killing the motor of accumulation and thus further reducing the growth rate. Entrepreneurs would then no longer have the time to turn into rentiers, since there would be no more entrepreneurs.

The right solution is a progressive annual tax on capital. This will make it possible to avoid an endless inegalitarian spiral while preserving competition and incentives for new instances of primitive accumulation.

---

1. Note, too, that it is perfectly logical to think that an increase in the growth rate g would lead to an increase in the return on capital r and would therefore not necessarily reduce the gap $r - g$. See Chapter 10.

For example, I earlier discussed the possibility of a capital tax schedule with rates of 0.1 or 0.5 percent on fortunes under 1 million euros, 1 percent on fortunes between 1 and 5 million euros, 2 percent between 5 and 10 million euros, and as high as 5 or 10 percent for fortunes of several hundred million or several billion euros. This would contain the unlimited growth of global inequality of wealth, which is currently increasing at a rate that cannot be sustained in the long run and that ought to worry even the most fervent champions of the self-regulated market. Historical experience shows, moreover, that such immense inequalities of wealth have little to do with the entrepreneurial spirit and are of no use in promoting growth. Nor are they of any "common utility," to borrow the nice expression from the 1789 Declaration of the Rights of Man and the Citizen with which I began this book.

The difficulty is that this solution, the progressive tax on capital, requires a high level of international cooperation and regional political integration. It is not within the reach of the nation-states in which earlier social compromises were hammered out. Many people worry that moving toward greater cooperation and political integration within, say, the European Union only undermines existing achievements (starting with the social states that the various countries of Europe constructed in response to the shocks of the twentieth century) without constructing anything new other than a vast market predicated on ever purer and more perfect competition. Yet pure and perfect competition cannot alter the inequality $r > g$, which is not the consequence of any market "imperfection." On the contrary. Although the risk is real, I do not see any genuine alternative: if we are to regain control of capitalism, we must bet everything on democracy—and in Europe, democracy on a European scale. Larger political communities such as the United States and China have a wider range of options, but for the small countries of Europe, which will soon look very small indeed in relation to the global economy, national withdrawal can only lead to even worse frustration and disappointment than currently exists with the European Union. The nation-state is still the right level at which to modernize any number of social and fiscal policies and to develop new forms of governance and shared ownership intermediate between public and private ownership, which is one of the major challenges for the century ahead. But only regional political integration can lead to effective regulation of the globalized patrimonial capitalism of the twenty-first century.

For a Political and Historical Economics

I would like to conclude with a few words about economics and social science. As I made clear in the introduction, I see economics as a subdiscipline of the social sciences, alongside history, sociology, anthropology, and political science. I hope that this book has given the reader an idea of what I mean by that. I dislike the expression "economic science," which strikes me as terribly arrogant because it suggests that economics has attained a higher scientific status than the other social sciences. I much prefer the expression "political economy," which may seem rather old-fashioned but to my mind conveys the only thing that sets economics apart from the other social sciences: its political, normative, and moral purpose.

From the outset, political economy sought to study scientifically, or at any rate rationally, systematically, and methodically, the ideal role of the state in the economic and social organization of a country. The question it asked was: What public policies and institutions bring us closer to an ideal society? This unabashed aspiration to study good and evil, about which every citizen is an expert, may make some readers smile. To be sure, it is an aspiration that often goes unfulfilled. But it is also a necessary, indeed indispensable, goal, because it is all too easy for social scientists to remove themselves from public debate and political confrontation and content themselves with the role of commentators on or demolishers of the views and data of others. Social scientists, like all intellectuals and all citizens, ought to participate in public debate. They cannot be content to invoke grand but abstract principles such as justice, democracy, and world peace. They must make choices and take stands in regard to specific institutions and policies, whether it be the social state, the tax system, or the public debt. Everyone is political in his or her own way. The world is not divided between a political elite on one side and, on the other, an army of commentators and spectators whose only responsibility is to drop a ballot in a ballot box once every four or five years. It is illusory, I believe, to think that the scholar and the citizen live in separate moral universes, the former concerned with means and the latter with ends. Although comprehensible, this view ultimately strikes me as dangerous.

For far too long economists have sought to define themselves in terms of their supposedly scientific methods. In fact, those methods rely on an immoderate use of mathematical models, which are frequently no more than an excuse for occupying the terrain and masking the vacuity of the content. Too much energy has been and still is being wasted on pure theoretical speculation without a clear specification of the economic facts one is trying to explain or the social and political problems one is trying to resolve. Economists today are full of enthusiasm for empirical methods based on controlled experiments. When used with moderation, these methods can be useful, and they deserve credit for turning some economists toward concrete questions and firsthand knowledge of the terrain (a long overdue development). But these new approaches themselves succumb at times to a certain scientistic illusion. It is possible, for instance, to spend a great deal of time proving the existence of a pure and true causal relation while forgetting that the question itself is of limited interest. The new methods often lead to a neglect of history and of the fact that historical experience remains our principal source of knowledge. We cannot replay the history of the twentieth century as if World War I never happened or as if the income tax and PAYGO pensions were never created. To be sure, historical causality is always difficult to prove beyond a shadow of a doubt. Are we really certain that a particular policy had a particular effect, or was the effect perhaps due to some other cause? Nevertheless, the imperfect lessons that we can draw from history, and in particular from the study of the last century, are of inestimable, irreplaceable value, and no controlled experiment will ever be able to equal them. To be useful, economists must above all learn to be more pragmatic in their methodological choices, to make use of whatever tools are available, and thus to work more closely with other social science disciplines.

Conversely, social scientists in other disciplines should not leave the study of economic facts to economists and must not flee in horror the minute a number rears its head, or content themselves with saying that every statistic is a social construct, which of course is true but insufficient. At bottom, both responses are the same, because they abandon the terrain to others.

The Interests of the Least Well-Off

"As long as the incomes of the various classes of contemporary society remain beyond the reach of scientific inquiry, there can be no hope of producing a useful economic and social history." This admirable sentence begins *Le mouvement du profit en France au 19e siècle,* which Jean Bouvier, François Furet, and Marcel Gillet published in 1965. The book is still worth reading, in part because it is a good example of the "serial history" that flourished in France between 1930 and 1980, with its characteristic virtues and flaws, but even more because it reminds us of the intellectual trajectory of François Furet, whose career offers a marvelous illustration of both the good and the bad reasons why this research program eventually died out.

When Furet began his career as a promising young historian, he chose a subject that he believed was at the center of contemporary research: "the incomes of the various classes of contemporary society." The book is rigorous, eschews all prejudgment, and seeks above all to collect data and establish facts. Yet this would be Furet's first and last work in this realm. In the splendid book he published with Jacques Ozouf in 1977, *Lire et écrire,* devoted to "literacy in France from Calvin to Jules Ferry," one finds the same eagerness to compile serial data, no longer about industrial profits but now about literacy rates, numbers of teachers, and educational expenditures. In the main, however, Furet became famous for his work on the political and cultural history of the French Revolution, in which one endeavors in vain to find any trace of the "incomes of the various classes of contemporary society," and in which the great historian, preoccupied as he was in the 1970s with the battle he was waging against the Marxist historians of the French Revolution (who at the time were particularly dogmatic and clearly dominant, notably at the Sorbonne), seems to have turned against economic and social history of any kind. To my mind, this is a pity, since I believe it is possible to reconcile the different approaches. Politics and ideas obviously exist independently of economic and social evolutions. Parliamentary institutions and the government of laws were never merely the bourgeois institutions that Marxist intellectuals used to denounce before the fall of the Berlin Wall. Yet it is also clear that the ups and downs of prices and wages, incomes and fortunes, help to shape political perceptions and attitudes, and in return these representations engender political institutions, rules, and policies that ultimately shape social and economic change. It is possible, and even indispensable, to have an approach that is at once economic and political, social and cultural, and concerned with wages and wealth. The bipolar confrontations of the period 1917–1989 are now clearly behind us. The clash of communism and capitalism sterilized rather than stimulated research on capital and inequality by historians, economists, and even philosophers.[2] It is long since time to move beyond these old controversies and the historical research they engendered, which to my mind still bears their stamp.

As I noted in the introduction, there are also technical reasons for the premature death of serial history. The material difficulty of col-

---

2. When one reads philosophers such as Jean-Paul Sartre, Louis Althusser, and Alain Badiou on their Marxist and / or communist commitments, one sometimes has the impression that questions of capital and class inequality are of only moderate interest to them and serve mainly as a pretext for jousts of a different nature entirely.

lecting and processing large volumes of data in those days probably explains why works in this genre (including *Le mouvement du profit en France au 19e siècle*) had little room for historical interpretation, which makes reading them rather arid. In particular, there is often very little analysis of the relation between observed economic changes and the political and social history of the period under study. Instead, one gets a meticulous description of the sources and raw data, information that is more naturally presented nowadays in spreadsheets and online databases.

I also think that the demise of serial history was connected with the fact that the research program petered out before it reached the twentieth century. In studying the eighteenth or nineteenth centuries it is possible to think that the evolution of prices and wages, or incomes and wealth, obeys an autonomous economic logic having little or nothing to do with the logic of politics or culture. When one studies the twentieth century, however, such an illusion falls apart immediately. A quick glance at the curves describing income and wealth inequality or the capital / income ratio is enough to show that politics is ubiquitous and that economic and political changes are inextricably intertwined and must be studied together. This forces one to study the state, taxes, and debt in concrete ways and to abandon simplistic and abstract notions of the economic infrastructure and political superstructure.

To be sure, the principle of specialization is sound and surely makes it legitimate for some scholars to do research that does not depend on statistical series. There are a thousand and one ways to do social science, and accumulating data is not always indispensable or even (I concede) especially imaginative. Yet it seems to me that all social scientists, all journalists and commentators, all activists in the unions and in politics of whatever stripe, and especially all citizens should take a serious interest in money, its measurement, the facts surrounding it, and its history. Those who have a lot of it never fail to defend their interests. Refusing to deal with numbers rarely serves the interests of the least well-off.

Contents in Detail

Tables and Illustrations

Tables

Illustrations

Index

Abu Dhabi Investment Authority, 580

Access, equality of, 609–611

Accounting: national, 22–23, 70–75, 117, 156, 236n22, 288–289; corporate, 234–235, 236n22, 745

Accounting standards, 669n4

Accumulation of wealth. *See* Wealth accumulation

Accumulation principle, infinite, 8–13, 285–286

Acemoglu, Daron, 563n10, 658n45, 659n48

Africa: population distribution, 77; production in, 77, 80; purchasing power parity and, 84; income in, 87–88, 109n9; growth in, 99, 101, 120; capital / income ratio in, 244, 585; mortality rates, 489; capital outflow to, 585–586; taxes and, 698–699. *See also* North Africa; South Africa; Sub-Saharan Africa

Age-wealth profile, 490–499

Agricultural land: in Britain and France, 145, 146, 148–149n1, 152–153; in Germany, 175; in United States, 187–189, 199; valuing, 246–247; elasticity of substitution and, 279; return on, 451

Albert, Michel, 181n5

Allais, Maurice, 679n17, 734n40

Allen, Robert, 9n5, 255n4, 282

Alternative investments, 570–571, 576, 579, 581

Althusser, Louis, 752n2

Alvaredo, Facundo, 22

America: income in, 72, 87; output, 76, 77, 119; population distribution, 77; birth rate and, 103; growth in, 119–120; capital in, 186–192; structure of

inequality in, 188–189. *See also* United States

"American exceptionalism," 617

American Revolution, 38–39, 631

Ancien Régime: public debt and, 160–161; Catholic Church holdings, 227–228; inequality and, 313, 328, 329–330, 331, 431, 432; taxation and, 630–631, 641–642

Andersen, Gosta Esping, 102n5

Andrieu, Claire, 170n18

"Annuitized wealth," 485, 493–494

The Aristocats (cartoon), 461, 462, 462n29

Arnault, Bernard, 574n33

Arrow, Kenneth, 744n56

Asia: global output and, 77; population distribution, 77; income and, 78, 79; purchasing power parity and, 84; investment in, 87–88; growth in, 99, 120; capital / income ratio in, 244; financial crisis in, 692–693

Assets: financial, 154, 262, 468, 666; public, 154–156; prices of, 228, 233–238, 572n31; real and nominal, 262–265; size effects of, 576–577; taxation of, 642. *See also* Net asset positions; Wealth

Asset structure, twenty-first vs. eighteenth century, 147

Atkinson, Anthony, 22, 23, 24, 27nn21, 35n36, 373n33, 409n26, 434, 464n32, 540n60, 652n35

Austen, Jane, fiction of, 2, 68, 134–135, 141–144, 152, 161, 163, 259–260, 302, 304, 328, 517, 519, 520n36, 521–525, 528, 529, 530, 535; *Sense and Sensibility,* 141–142, 456, 521–523; *Mansfield Park,* 144, 149–150, 201, 259; *Persuasion,* 456

Austerity, public debt and, 363, 701, 707–708

165–167, 171–172, 700; growth in, 217; savings in, 220, 231; capital-labor split in, 250–253; pure rate of return in, 251–252, 257–258; minimum wage in, 390–391; inequality in, 398, 402, 404, 405, 407, 416, 420; taxation and, 427, 637, 640, 644, 647–648, 651–659; wealth distribution in, 434–435, 437; inheritances in, 538, 540–541; voting rights in, 538n57; social state in, 601–608; access to education in, 618–619, 619n34, 621n41; austerity policy in, 707–708

Brown, Frederick, 275–276

Bubbles, 214, 234, 237, 241, 243n30, 369–370; beyond, 216–219

Budgetary parliament, European, 726–727

Buffet, Warren, 557n14

Bush, George W., 317, 389, 599

Cagé, Julia, 628n48

Caillaux, Joseph, 646n24

Cameron, James, 189, 190, 367

Campion, H., 172n19

Canada: US-Canada bloc, 80, 86n31; capital in, 194–196, 212–215; growth rate of, 217; savings in, 220, 231; privatization of wealth and, 229; foreign capital / assets in, 239; inequality in, 398, 404, 405

"Capabilities approach," 611

Capital: human and nonhuman, 28–29, 53, 58–59, 61; depreciation and, 55; defined, 57–59; types of, 58, 59; private vs. public, 59; wealth and, 59–63; economic functions of, 60; residential vs. production, 60; immaterial, 61–62, 149; domestic vs. foreign, 62–63; nature of, 291n36; transformation in nature of, 476–477; production and, 486–487; rents and, 535–537; reproduction of itself, 557–558; government and accumulation of, 732–737; transparency and democratic control of, 743–745.

See also Foreign capital / assets; National wealth / capital; Private wealth / capital; Public wealth / capital; Rate of return on capital

Capital, income from, 23; in twenty-first century, 244–248; reduction in, 341–343; top decile and, 343–345, 350–352, 357, 379; taxation on, 353–355, 651–652. *See also* Inequality of capital ownership

Capital, metamorphoses of: nature of wealth and, 141–144; in Britain and France, 144–149; assess structure (private) and, 147–149; foreign capital and, 149–152; public and private wealth and, 153–159; public debt and, 160–166; Ricardian equivalence and, 166–168; public assets and, 168–173; in Germany, 174–181; twentieth century shocks and, 181–186; in the United States, 186–194; in Canada, 194–196

Capital accumulation, golden rule of, 733–740

Capital controls, 91, 691–693

Capital gains, 399n15; taxes on, 221n11, 355; treatment of, 264n12, 379; United States and, 369–370, 398n13

Capital / income ratio, 63–65, 204–248; global study of, 25–26; in France, Britain, and Germany, 32; U-curve of, 33–34; capital-labor split and, 53–54, 249–253; in Britain and France, 144–149; shocks and, 181–186, 189–190, 191–192; in America, 188; in Europe, 204–205; in United States, 204–205; fundamental laws of capitalism and, 205–212; capital's comeback and, 212–215; beyond bubbles, 216–219; privatization and, 219–232; rebound of asset prices and, 233–238; national capital and net foreign assets and, 238–244; net foreign assets and, 240–241; in twenty-first century, 244–246; world, 245, 585–587; land values and, 246–248; return on capital

rates of, 423, 639, 653–662; Civil Code,
458–462; on earned and unearned
income, 530n50, 631; social insurance
contributions, 601n1, 606, 632, 676n10;
relative to national income, 603–605;
social state and, 612–613; as share of
national income, 627; emerging
countries, 627–629; on wealth, 631,
680–685; on consumption (indirect),
631–632, 652n35, 731n37; progressive vs.
proportional (flat), 632, 633; on
inheritances, 635, 651–653, 687–688n33;
categorical or scheduler, 641; confiscatory tax rates and, 647–653, 661n51;
social justice and, 648, 696; executive
salaries and, 653–659; defining norms
through, 669; residence and,
690–691n39; transparency and,
698–699; debt vs., 700; public debt
and, 700–701; on Eurozone corporate
profits, 728–729; carbon, 739n49,
743n55. *See also* Competition, fiscal;
Estate tax; Global tax on capital;
Income tax; Progressive taxation
Tax havens, 243–244n32, 369, 590,
592–593, 634–635n5, 668, 671–675,
702n2
Tea Party, 600
Technological progress, durable, 12
Technology: return on capital and,
266–267, 271; capital-labor split and,
280–281; caprices of, 293–294; wage
inequality and, 382–387; educational
system and, 384–386
Temin, Peter, 669n3
Thatcher, Margaret, 53, 125, 633, 654, 657
Theil index, 333
Thiers, Adolphe, 527
Third Republic, 429, 432, 435, 639,
642–647
Time preference theory, 451–455
Titanic (film), 189, 367
Tobin's Q, 237, 238
Tocqueville, Alexis de, 188–189, 302,
527n46

Todd, Emmanuel, 102n5, 118n20
Tolstoy, Alexei, *Ibiscus,* 566
Top marginal tax rates, 423, 639,
653–662
Total income, 294, 308, 311–312, 329–332
Touzery, Mirelle, 641n17
Training: investment in, 28, 30, 91, 386,
396; system, state of, 383–386; inequality
and, 531–532
Transfer payments, 605, 606–607
Transfers in kind, 226
Transparency: wealth rankings and, 553;
global tax on capital and, 578, 663,
666–671; lack of, 621; banking
information and, 665; taxation and,
698–699; public debt and, 743–745
Treasury bonds (US), 580–581
Treaty of Maastricht, 737–738
Trente Glorieuses, 13–14, 19, 118n20, 123,
171, 172, 518
Troika, 719–722
Trusts, family, 573–574
Tsutsumi, Yoshiaka, 562–563
Two Cambridges Debate, 289–292
"Two-thirds bankruptcy," 160, 165

U-curve of capital / income ratio, 30–34,
191, 251; capital share of income,
244–245, 271; inheritances, 485–486,
508, 538, 543
Unemployment insurance, 607–608
United Nations, 74n19, 87, 103–104,
477
United States: income hierarchy in
national income, 14–16; income
inequality in, 31–32, 309–311, 312n5, 329,
330, 331, 365–372, 395–397, 398, 399, 402,
404–405, 416–420; growth in, 37–38,
99, 216–217; national income and, 63,
72–73; purchasing power parity and,
84n28; income in, 86–87, 88; employment by sector in, 115; in postwar years,
123–125; inflation in, 136–137; capital in,
186–192, 206, 212–215; public debt in,
189–190; public wealth in, 190, 191;

The epic successor to one of the most important books of the century: at once a retelling of global history, a scathing critique of contemporary politics, and a bold proposal for a new and fairer economic system.

CAPITAL

AND

IDEOLOGY

THOMAS

PIKETTY

TRANSLATED BY ARTHUR GOLDHAMMER

THE BELKNAP PRESS OF HARVARD UNIVERSITY PRESS
ISBN: 978-0-674-98082-2
$39.95 • 1104 pages

THOMAS PIKETTY is Director of Studies at L'École des Hautes Études en Sciences Sociales and Professor at the Paris School of Economics.